Understanding Interpersonal Communication

Making Choices in Changing Times

2nd edition

Richard West
Emerson College

Lynn H. Turner
Marquette University

D1471151

WADSWORTH
CENGAGE Learning™

Australia • Brazil • Japan • Korea • Mexico • Singapore • Spain • United Kingdom • United States

WADSWORTH
CENGAGE Learning™

Understanding Interpersonal Communication: Making Choices in Changing Times, 2nd Edition
Richard West and Lynn H. Turner

Publisher: Lyn Uhl

Executive Editor: Monica Eckman

Senior Development Editor: Greer Lleuad

Assistant Editor: Kimberly Gengler

Editorial Assistant: Kimberly Apfelbaum

Associate Technology Project Manager: Jessica Badiner

Marketing Manager: Erin Mitchell

Marketing Assistant: Mary Anne Payumo

Content Project Manager: Jessica Rasile

Art Director: Linda Helcher

Senior Print Buyer: Betsy Donaghey

Production Service/Compositor: Lachina Publishing Services, Inc.

Text Designer: KeDesign

Cover Illustration: Tim Zeltner/i2i Art

For product information and technology assistance, contact us at
Cengage Learning Academic Resource Center, 1-800-423-0563

For permission to use material from this text or product, submit all requests online at **www.cengage.com/permissions**.
Further permissions questions can be e-mailed to
permissionrequest@cengage.com.

Library of Congress Control Number: 2008923821
ISBN-13: 978-0-495-50246-3
ISBN-10: 0-495-50246-4

Wadsworth Cengage Learning
25 Thomson Place
Boston, MA 02210
USA

Cengage Learning products are represented in Canada by Nelson Education, Ltd.

For your course and learning solutions, visit
academic.cengage.com.

Purchase any of our products at your local college store
or at our preferred online store **www.ichapters.com**.

Printed in the United States of America
1 2 3 4 5 6 7 12 11 10 09 08

Brief Contents

Contents

3   *Communication, Culture, and Identity* 78

4   *Communicating Verbally* 112

8 Sharing Personal Information 252

Preface

The 2nd edition of *Understanding Interpersonal Communication* underscores our ongoing commitment to make research and theory in interpersonal communication more accessible to students. We have been grateful for the many emails and calls we have received from those who used the 1st edition of this text, expressing support for this fundamental belief. We wrote this text because we believe students should have the knowledge, skills, and motivation to communicate in multiple circumstances with a variety of different people. Today, more than ever, students are confronted with choices in communication. For instance, emerging technologies continually expand our choices—whether via email, with a text messenger, through a MySpace page, or writing a blog. To be able to navigate this increasingly complex communication environment effectively, students need a well-developed knowledge base for making informed choices and improving their skills.

We contend that when students enter their interpersonal communication classrooms, they bring with them many habits and beliefs about effective communication that they have acquired from their own experiences observing friends, families, and coworkers. In addition, we cannot ignore the influence that popular culture and the media have played in students' understanding of communication and human relationships. Nonetheless, students lack an understanding of the theory and research that animate and clarify these practices and beliefs. In other words, students simply rely too much on what they have seen and heard, with little understanding of theoretical explanations for communication processes and outcomes. Consequently, students frequently make communication choices from an insufficient knowledge base. Such decisions limit their potential, leaving them frustrated and dissatisfied.

It is our belief that a fundamental approach to learning about an interpersonal communication skill is to ground it in adequate theory and current knowledge about the skill. Although knowledge cannot completely guarantee that students are going to be happy with the outcome of every communication transac-

tion, it does provide them with necessary and important analytical skills. In sum, we believe that theory informs skills and skills refine theory. As such, in *Understanding Interpersonal Communication* we intentionally integrate a theory-skill framework throughout each chapter. In this text, we move toward eliminating the false dichotomy between theory and skills. Additionally, we strive to demystify and clarify the intersection of theory and practice. In doing so, we hope to break down misguided and preconceived negative images of theory. Using a conversational tone, our text integrates research and theory in an inviting and engaging manner.

In addition, our approach to skill development provides a discussion of interpersonal skills and the behavioral choices students can make in order to become more effective communicators. We avoid "telling" students how to apply interpersonal skills to various situations. Instead, we provide a list of skills pertaining to the theory students read about in the chapter so that they will be able to draw upon a sort of toolbox, or set of skills, that are specific and workable.

And finally, we understand that students come to the interpersonal communication course from a variety of life experiences. We worked, therefore, to make our writing clear, to avoid clichés and to use technical terms only when necessary to make a point, explaining their meanings as needed. We also made a conscious effort to use examples that reflect the diversity of interpersonal encounters. Thus, we include examples of interpersonal communication between teacher-student, physician-patient, painter-client, landlord-renter, politician-voter, clergy-layperson, retail clerk-customer, husband-wife, and friend-friend, among others. We have never felt that a book of this nature should be a venue to express unfounded personal value systems. Simultaneously, we do not honor just one way of looking at relationships, but rather embrace an expansive view of human behavior and interpersonal communication.

Understanding Interpersonal Communication appeals to a diverse student population, presents scholarship and skills in a readable manner, and contains pedagogical features that will not only sustain interest, but also make a difference in students' lives. The result of our efforts—this text—reflects our commitment to ensuring that students understand the importance of interpersonal communication in their own lives and in the lives of others.

Features of the Book

Our experience teaching this course over many years has prompted us to offer the following pedagogical approach and features. These features are intended first to appeal to students, then to help them better understand the concepts in each chapter and apply them in their own lives.

A Bridge between Theory and Skills

With a clear, inviting presentation of the intersection of theory and practice, *Understanding Interpersonal Communication* will empower your students with the knowledge they need to be skillful communicators in today's society.

In addition to **chapter goals** that provide students with a basic roadmap of the theory and skills that will be discussed in the chapter, each chapter begins with a **Case in Point** case study pertaining to an issue or topic in interpersonal communication discussed in the chapter. These cases are drawn from real-life situations identified by students in past interpersonal communication courses we have taught. For example, in Chapter 3, "Communication, Culture, and Identity," we begin with an example of a U.S. student who learns more about Mexican culture. In Chapter 6, "Effective Listening," we present a director of volunteers for a local political campaign whose listening skills are called into question by a supervisor. These case studies include people of diverse ages, backgrounds, and educational levels. Videotaped versions of many of these case studies and accompanying critical thinking questions are featured in the book's online resources. Additionally, **Case in Point Revisited** review questions appear throughout each chapter, tying the Case in Point case study to the concepts discussed in that chapter.

So that students can assess their own communication behaviors and attitudes, each chapter features a **Communication Assessment Test (CAT)** inventory. This feature provides students with communication instruments, such as a measure of communication apprehension or a quiz that will help students sharpen their vocabulary. For example, in Chapter 2, "Communication, Perception, and the Self," we include a "self-monitoring scale" quiz that asks students to consider the extent to which they actively think about and control their public behaviors and actions. These types of assessments allow students to evaluate their communication skills and take personal responsibility for skill development. We have found that students are also able to create their own assessments once they have read and understood material. The CATs, then, can be used as an effective way for students to become empowered in their classes.

Each chapter ends with **Questions for Understanding**, review and discussion questions that allow students to check their understanding of the chapter material. At least one question per chapter pertains to the chapter-opening Case in Point feature. This question allows students to reconsider how the concepts in the case study can be approached after learning the material in the chapter. Students can answer these questions by working in small groups or on their own.

A Wealth of Choices

Once students have a strong base in theory and skills, they are then able to make informed choices in their interpersonal communication. Many of the features of this book highlight the types of choices available to students in today's changing and technologically advanced world.

To encourage students to think about the material in a personal way, each chapter includes a prompt to an online **Your Turn** journal activity. With this feature, each student is asked to think about a particular topic and write about it in a journal. For example, in Chapter 1, "Introduction to Interpersonal Communication," we ask students to write about the primary influences shaping their interpersonal communication. Our experiences show that journals are excellent outlets for students to share their perceptions and reactions in a way that is personal, reflective, and informative. The Your Turn activities are also featured in the book's student companion workbook.

The **Ethics & Choice** boxed feature appears in each chapter, raising ethical questions and allowing students to consider ethical implications of the key topics or concepts in each chapter. These boxes include examples of ethical dilemmas and critical-thinking questions that challenge students to apply the ethical systems explained in Chapter 1. For instance, in Chapter 11, "Technology and Interpersonal Communication," students are asked to think about the ethical issues associated with presenting yourself in a false light on the Internet. The Ethics & Choice feature asks students to delve into how their ethical systems have been formed, influenced, and how they relate to communication choices. Online interactive activities about these ethical dilemmas are featured on the book's online resources. These activities allow students to choose possible responses to the dilemma, and then reflect on the consequences their choice brings about.

As appropriate to the content, select chapters feature discussions of the **dark and bright sides of interpersonal communication.** These discussions touch on topics such as domestic abuse, empathy, and forgiveness. For example, Chapter 7, "Communication and Emotion," discusses the notion of *schadenfreude,* or taking pleasure in another's misfortune. These discussions enable students to see that interpersonal communication can be both helpful and harmful.

Additionally, each chapter features a section that discusses interpersonal skills and the behavior choices students can make in order to become more effective communicators.

An Approach that Advocates the Wise Use of Technology

Technology has increased our options and choices in communication. Technology such as email and video-conferencing affects who we speak to and how we speak to them in ways that are continually evolving. *Understanding Interpersonal Communication* shows students how they are influenced by technology and how they can use it to become more effective communicators.

This book includes a full chapter on technology's impact on interpersonal communication, **Chapter 11, "Technology and Interpersonal Communication."** We live in a time of unprecedented technological change. One new technology quickly replaces another, affecting our interactions with others. For example, online relationships are now commonplace among people of various races, ages, and cultures. Chapter 11 addresses this relatively new area of interpersonal communication. The chapter identifies and explains characteristics of communication technology, discusses

the presentation of the self online, discusses the pervasiveness and importance of social networking, explains how relationships function online, and discusses skills that help improve electronic discussions and relationships. We are proud to be among the first to offer students the opportunity to explore the intersection of technology, communication, and human behavior in a chapter that is both interesting and timely.

In addition to emphasizing technology in the text, we also provide **thorough technology integration** and support for users of the text. **InfoTrac® College Edition exercises** found throughout the book make use of the InfoTrac College Edition database, a virtual library that can be accessed from student computers (see Resources for Students on p. xiii for more information). Web-based **Interactive Activities** that enrich and reinforce chapter content are integrated into every chapter, taking learning beyond the printed page. These brief exercises and activities, highlighted by icons, are easily accessed through the book's online resources.

New to This Edition

The 2nd edition of *Understanding Interpersonal Communication* features several new and updated features that enhance its usefulness.

- Chapter 7, "Communication and Emotion," and Chapter 11, "Technology and Interpersonal Communication," feature **new Case in Point case studies and videos.** The Case in Point for Chapter 7 explores how a young woman, Regina, handles telling good news to a friend who finds the news troubling. And the Case in Point for Chapter 11 explores a college student's realization that his online disclosures are influencing his life in ways he had never considered. In addition, the Case in Point for Chapter 8, "Sharing Personal Information," now features a video of Roberta and Philip's interaction.

- **Imagine Yourself** . . . boxed features in each chapter highlight interpersonal communication in various contexts. For example, the Imagine Yourself . . . box in Chapter 6, "Effective Listening," asks students to consider the consequences of their own faulty listening when confronted with a mechanic's bill that is much higher than expected. And in Chapter 3, "Communication, Culture, and Identity," two boxes address situations in which intersections of culture and gender affect interpersonal interactions.

- **IPC in the News** boxes in most chapters provide examples of coverage about interpersonal communication in the popular media. For instance, the IPC in the News box in Chapter 2, "Communication, Perception, and the Self," features an article in *The Oakland Tribune* about the "nocebo effect," which scientists from the Centers for Disease Control and Prevention explain is a form of self-fulfilling prophecy in which illness, and even death, result from a patient's expectation that a drug or illness will be harmful.

- **Interpersonal Explorer** boxes at the conclusion of each chapter provide students with the opportunity to review the theories and skills discussed in the chapter and consider the relationship between theories and skills. Each box also includes a prompt for students to complete an online activity related to the chapter content. Some of these activities are **interactive simulations** that ask students to consider the consequences of their choices in a hypothetical interpersonal situation, and others are critical thinking activities that incorporate **ABC News videos about interpersonal issues**.

- In response to reviewer feedback, the **table of contents has been reorganized** to better correspond to the order in which many instructors teach the chapters. "Chapter 4, Communicating Verbally," and Chapter 5, "Communicating Nonverbally," now precede Chapter 6, "Effective Listening," and Chapter 7, "Communication and Emotion."

- **Chapter 6, "Effective Listening,"** has been updated to include more listening research and more coverage of critical thinking.

- In addition to the coverage of interpersonal relationships in Chapter 10, "Communicating in Close Relationships," **increased discussion** of **relationship choices and contexts** has been integrated throughout the text.

- In addition to the **updated coverage of communication technologies** throughout the book, the **thoroughly revised Chapter 11, "Technology and Interpersonal Communication,"** includes updated coverage and examples of how new technologies influence interpersonal communication in various contexts. New discussions address topics such as the evolution of the World Wide Web from Web 1.0 to Web 2.0, social networking sites such as MySpace and Facebook, and the use of avatars as a means of self-presentation online.

Resources for Students

Understanding Interpersonal Communication features an outstanding array of supplements to assist in making this course as meaningful and effective as possible.

- The *Understanding Interpersonal Communication* **online textbook resources** are designed to meet the demands of today's visual, multimedia learners. These resources are rich with powerful learning resources that will broaden and test your students' critical understanding of each chapter's material. They include the Resource Center for *Understanding Interpersonal Communication*, chapter-by-chapter resources at the book companion website, interactive video activities, and InfoTrac College Edition. References to these resources are integrated throughout the chapters, highlighted with icons, and summarized at the ends of chapters. **Note to faculty:** If you want your students to have access to the online textbook resources, please be sure to order them for your course. The content in these resources can be bundled at no additional charge to your students with every new copy of the text. If you do not order them, your students will not have access to these online resources. *Contact your local Wadsworth Cengage Learning sales representative for more details.*

- The **Resource Center for *Understanding Interpersonal Communication*** offers a variety of rich learning resources designed to enhance the student experience. These resources include self-assessments, images, video, and Web resources such as the interactive simulations described in the Interpersonal Explorer boxes. All resources are mapped to key discipline learning-concepts, and users can browse or search for content in a variety of ways. More than just a collection of ancillary learning materials, the Resource Center also features important content and community tools that extend the education experience beyond a particular class or course semester.

- With the **Book Companion Website**, students have easy access to premium chapter-by-chapter content, including practice chapter quizzes, self-scoring Communication Assessment Test inventories, an interactive glossary that features games and flashcards, interactive Ethics & Choice activities, and InfoTrac College Edition and Internet activities that enrich and reinforce chapter content.

- The **Interactive Video Activities** include the Case in Point scenarios and the ABC News video activities described in the Interpersonal Explorer boxes. All the video activities are accompanied by interactive components that allow students to think critically about the interpersonal situations presented, and then compare their responses to the suggested responses of the authors.

- With **InfoTrac College Edition with Info-Marks**, your students will have access to this virtual library's more than 18 million reliable, full-length articles from 5,000 academic and popular periodicals and retrieve results almost instantly. They also have access to InfoMarks—stable URLs that can be linked to articles, journals, and searches to save valuable time when doing research—and to the InfoWrite online resource center, where students can access grammar help, critical-thinking guide-lines, guides to writing research papers, and much more.

- The **iChapters.com** online store provides students with exactly what they've been asking for: choice, convenience, and savings. A 2005 research study by the National Association of College Stores indicates that as many as 60 percent of students do not purchase all required course material; how-ever, those who do are more likely to succeed. This research also tells us that students want the ability to purchase "a la carte" course material in the format that suits them best. Accordingly, iChapters.com is the only online store that offers eBooks at up to 50 percent off, eChapters for as low as $1.99 each, and new textbooks at up to 25 percent off, plus up to 25 percent off print and digital supple-ments that can help improve student performance.

Resources for Instructors

Understanding Interpersonal Communication also features a full suite of resources for instructors. To evaluate any of these instructor or student resources, please contact your local Wadsworth Cengage Learning representative for an examination copy.

- **Instructor's Resource Manual** This helpful manual includes an overview of the book's features, syllabi and course outlines, chapter outlines, class-tested activities and exercises, transparency masters, and a test bank. The test items are also available electronically via ExamView® (see below).

- The **PowerLecture** CD-ROM contains an electronic version of the Instructor's Resource Manual, ExamView Computerized Testing, predesigned Microsoft® PowerPoint® presenta-tions, and JoinIn™ classroom quizzing. The PowerPoint presentations contain text, images, and cued videos of the case studies and can be used as is or customized to suit your course needs.

- **JoinIn™ on TurningPoint®**. JoinIn content for Response Systems is tailored to *Under-standing Interpersonal Communication*, allowing you to transform your classroom and assess your students' progress with instant in-class quizzes and polls. Turning-Point software lets you pose book-specific questions and display students' answers seamlessly within the Microsoft PowerPoint slides of your own lecture, in conjunction with the "clicker" hardware of your choice. The JoinIn content for each chapter includes two "conditional branching" scenarios that can be used as in-class group activities.

- **Communication Scenarios for Critique and Analysis Videos** Communication concepts previously presented in the abstract come to life in these videos. Each offers a variety of situations that allow students to watch, listen to, and critique model communication scenarios. Video policy is based on adoption size; contact your Wadsworth Cengage Learning representative for more information.

- **InfoTrac College Edition Student Activities Workbook for Interpersonal Communication** by Lori Halverson-Wente. This workbook features extensive individual and groups activities, focusing on specific course topics that make use of InfoTrac College Edition. Also included are guidelines for instructors and students that describe how to maximize the use of this resource.

- With the **TLC (Technology Learning Connects) Technology Training and Support**, you can get trained, get connected, and get the support you need for seamless integration of technology resources into your course. This technology service and training program provides online resources, peer-to-peer instruction, personalized training, and a customizable program. Visit **http://www.academic.cengage.com/tlc/** to sign up for online seminars, first days of class services, technical support, or personalized, face-to-face training. Our online or onsite trainings are frequently led by one of our Lead Teachers, faculty members who are experts in using Wadsworth Cengage Learning technology and can provide best practices and teaching tips.

- With Wadsworth's **Flex-Text Customization Program**, you can create a text as unique as

your course: quickly, simply, and affordably. As part of our flex-text program you can add your personal touch to Understanding Interpersonal Communication with a course-specific cover and up to 32 pages of your own content, at no additional cost.

Acknowledgments

The impetus for writing this book rests primarily with our students. We begin our acknowledgements, therefore, by thanking the thousands of students we have taught over a combined 40-plus years of teaching interpersonal communication. The insights, themes, and examples we've included in this book reflect those students who have provided us inspiration throughout our careers.

This text could not have existed without the generous time and talents afforded to us by the reviewers of the 1st edition and those who class-tested chapters for us. They numbered many, and their thoughts, examples, and critical observations prompted us to write a book that reflects their voices and the voices of their students.

In addition, we'd like to thank the reviewers and survey respondents for this 2nd edition for their insight and suggestions: Emelia Angeli, *Lackawanna College*; Martha Antolik, *Wright State University*; Tonya Blivens, *Tarrant County College*; Allison Carr, *Davidson County Community College*; Harold P. Donle, *Indiana University-Purdue University Indianapolis*; Diane Ferrero-Paluzzi, *Iona College*; Craig Fowler, *California State University, Fresno*; Lisa C. Hebert, *Louisiana State University*; Mark G. Henderson, *Jackson State University*; Mark Higgens, *Cleveland State Community College*; Krista Hoffmann-Longtin, *Indiana University-Purdue University Indianapolis*; Laura Janusik, *Rockhurst University*; Elaine B. Jenks, *West Chester University*; Leslie B. Henderson, *McLennan Community College*; Stan Malm, *Johns Hopkins University*; Tani McBeth, *Portland Community College*; M. Chad McBride, *Creighton University*; Virginia McDermott, *University of New Mexico*; Connie McKee, *West Texas A&M University*; David Moss, *Mt. San Jacinto College*; Keisha C. Paxton, *California State University, Dominguez Hills*; Nancy R. Pearson, *Minot State University*; Narissra Punyanunt-Carter, *Texas Tech University*; Michael Reiter, *Nova Southeastern University*; Curt

VanGeison, *St. Charles Community College*; Don Wallace, *Brewton-Parker College*; Emily Wilkinson Stallings, *Virginia Tech*; Janice Xu, *Western Connecticut State University*; and Christina Yoshimura, *University of Montana*.

We also gratefully acknowledge the excellent team at Wadsworth Cengage Learning, whose skills and thoughtfulness are unmatched. We never realized that writing a book with such a large company would result in lasting friendships. We first thank Holly Allen, former Publisher for Wadsworth's Communication Studies list, for "turning us on" to textbook writing in 1996. We have made many friends and cultivated close colleagues in publishing over these many years, but Holly will always remain a special confidant, and we are forever grateful to her for being the first to have faith in our ideas and writing. For this 2nd edition, the current Cengage Learning team has been nothing short of spectacular! First, we are indebted to Monica Eckman, our Acquisitions Editor, who provided those all-important "friendly nudges" throughout the writing of the book. Her sense of inclusiveness, steadfast support, and overall great persona made writing the 2nd edition a more exciting undertaking. Monica is an integral part of the soul of our writing. Greer Lleuad, our Developmental Editor, is the very *definition* of a perfect Developmental Editor. With Greer, we not only get a colleague with great instincts, but also a kind and generous person. Her sense of humor and persistent words of encouragement served as an important backdrop to the writing of this new edition. We also want to acknowledge the support and enthusiasm of Erin Mitchell, our Marketing Manager. Erin's grasp of our concept and her marketing skills provide a winning combination. Finally, we thank the others on the Cengage Learning team who contributed substantially to our text: Kim Gengler, Assistant Editor; Kim Apfelbaum, Editorial Assistant; Jessica Badiner, Associate Technology Project Manager; Linda Helcher, Art Director; Jessica Rasile, Content Project Manager; Katherine Wilson, Production Service Project Manager; and John Hill and Roberta Broyer, Permissions Account Managers.

We are also grateful to Larry Edmonds of Arizona State University for his expertise in updating the Instructor's Manual. He and Sally Vogl-Bauer, the author of this manual for the 1st edition of *Understanding Interpersonal Communication,* were able to take our text and provide superior teaching aids to supplement it, making it a more useful tool for classroom teachers. We appreciate their hard work. And many thanks to Bill Price of Georgia Perimeter College, Dunwoody Campus, for his dedication and expertise in the development of the InfoTrac College Edition exercises, Interactive Activities, and Ethics & Choice online activities for the book; to Cindy Kistenberg of Johnson C. Smith University, who created the online interpersonal simulations and ABC News video activities; to Christina Yoshimura of the University of Montana, who prepared the JoinIn questions; to Chad McBride of Creighton University, who wrote the quizzes for the companion website; and to Leslie Henderson of McLennan Community College, who prepared the PowerLecture slides and wrote important activities for the book's companion website.

In addition to all those just mentioned, we have a few personal comments. First, Rich thanks his co-author and close friend, Lynn, who, after working with him for more than 25 years, remains one of the most thoughtful and important people in his life. We encounter very few people who have a lasting and profound impact upon our lives. Lynn has been that person, and Rich continues to be honored with her friendship. Rich would also like to thank his mother, Beverly, for her ongoing presence in his life. Her genuineness, care, and sense of ethics are instrumental influences on his life. Rich would also like to thank his partner, Chris, who has helped to frame their relationship with humor, compassion, and ongoing moral support. Finally, Rich thanks his friends and colleagues at Emerson College. There is a wonderful spirit of support on the Emerson campus that has been unmatched in Rich's life. Lynn would also like to thank Rich. His insights, enthusiasm, and enduring friendship are what make writing a joy for her. Lynn also thanks Marquette University, especially Dean Pauly of the College of Communication, who provided enormous support during the writing of this book as well as at other times. Lynn thanks her husband, Ted, for being with her through thick and thin, cooking dinners, bringing coffee, and telling her to shut off the computer every once and a while!

About the Authors

Richard West is Professor and Chairperson of the Department of Communication Studies at Emerson College in Boston. Rich received his B.A. from Illinois State University in Speech Communication Education and his M.A from ISU in Communication Studies. His Ph.D. is from Ohio University in Interpersonal Communication. Rich's research interests span several areas, including family communication, classroom communication, and culture. Rich is the recipient of many teaching awards and has also been recognized with Outstanding Alumni Awards in Communication from both ISU and OU. Rich is co-author of several books and over 30 book chapters and articles with Lynn Turner. He is past President of the Eastern Communication Association (ECA), Director of the Educational Policies Board of the National Communication (NCA), and past Chair of the Instructional Communication Divisions for both ECA and NCA. Although Rich's passion remains in the classroom, he also enjoys gardening and updating his 100-year-old bungalow in Maine.

Lynn H. Turner is Professor in Communication Studies at Marquette University. Lynn received her B.A from University of Illinois, her M.A. from University of Iowa, and her Ph.D. from Northwestern University. At Marquette, she teaches interpersonal communication, among other courses, at both the undergraduate and graduate levels. Her research areas of emphasis include gender and communication, interpersonal and family communication. She is the co-author or co-editor of over ten books, as well as several articles and book chapters. Her articles have appeared in many journals, including *Management Communication Quarterly, Journal of Applied Communication Research, Women and Language,* and *Western Journal of Communication.* Her books include *From the Margins to the Center: Contemporary Women and Political Communication* (co-authored with Patricia Sullivan; recipient of the "Best Book" Award from the Organization for the Study of Communication, Language and Gender [OSCLG]), *Gender in Applied Communication Contexts* (co-edited with Patrice Buzzanell and Helen Sterk), *Introducing Communication Theory* and *Perspectives on Family Communication* (both co-authored with Richard West). In 2007, she was the recipient of the outstanding research award in the Diederich College of Communication. Lynn has served as Director of Graduate Studies for the Diederich College of Communication, President of OSCLG, President of Central States Communication Association, and Chairperson of the Family Communication Division for the National Communication Association.

We dedicate this book to the thousands of students who teach us what interpersonal communication means and to those others—our family, friends, and colleagues—whose interactions with us make these lessons come to life.

Chapter 1

Introduction to Interpersonal Communication

chapter ✚ goals

Explain three prevailing models of human communication

Describe the impersonal–interpersonal communication continuum

Define and interpret interpersonal communication

Understand the principles of interpersonal communication

Demystify stereotypes associated with interpersonal communication

Explain how ethical awareness relates to interpersonal encounters

Jackie Ellis stood in her driveway shoveling snow, she heard her neighbor, Scottie Perona, yell across the yard, "Hey, can't get any hired help for that?!"

Jackie yelled back, "Sure—show me the money! Like we needed to have another storm! Ever wonder why we even live here? I mean, don't you wonder why we're not in Arizona?! Of course, then we'd be complaining about the heat. . .but it's *dry* heat. . .we *have* to remember that!"

They both laughed. As Scottie approached Jackie's driveway, her cat rolled around on the ground. They began a casual conversation about the weather and the town's plows. Soon, however, the topic turned to something that was much more serious: Jackie's sister's death. Jackie told Scottie that it was exactly a year ago that her sister had died of skin cancer.

"I can't believe how fast time goes by, Scottie," Jackie said, sighing.

"Wow," he replied. "Incredible that it's been that long. It seems like we were just telling each other that everything would be fine. I mean where did the time go? I remember that day as if it happened a week ago. You were. . ." Scottie's voice began to trail as he looked at his neighbor's face.

As he spoke, tears welled up in Jackie's eyes. Jackie smiled ruefully and said, "Hey, we got by that one, and we're still here talking about it. And if we can survive that *and* this stupid winter, we'll make it through anything. Right?"

The two laughed awkwardly; both knew that the topic had to change quickly. They began to talk about Scottie's daughters and their holiday concert. As the minutes ticked by, they found themselves talking about everything from Iraq to the *E! Network*. It was almost as if the two were trying to avoid the topic. The snow was now beginning to blow around. After a few minutes, Scottie went back to his house. Jackie finished shoveling her sidewalk and went inside. As she sat in her kitchen thumbing through catalogs, she once again thought about her sister. One year, she thought—it couldn't be possible. She felt lucky to have such a good and caring neighbor as Scottie. He might have been angry when Jackie put up her fence in the back yard, but today, he surely was a friend.

*E*ach day, we perform one of the most ancient of all behaviors: interpersonal communication. We head off to work and greet people on the bus, in the office, in the carpool, or on the street. We talk to our roommates and discuss last night's party over breakfast. Or, we wake up and soon find ourselves in the middle of a heated exchange with a family member about dirty dishes. Although each of these situations differs, they all underscore the pervasiveness of interpersonal communication in our lives.

This chapter's Case in Point scenario between Jackie and Scottie represents one of these interpersonal encounters. In this scenario, Scottie established verbal contact with Jackie. In turn, Jackie moved the conversation from the weather to her sister's death. The entire dialogue lasted only a few minutes, but it carried enormous importance. Scottie and Jackie not only initiated a conversation—their conversation also showed just how close they are to each other. As you can tell from their conversation, they are more than just neighbors; they are also good friends. The content of their brief conversation gives us an idea that they have more than a superficial relationship with each other.

These dialogues take place all the time without our giving them a second thought. And we often feel content about the way we communicate with others. A national poll commissioned by the National Communication Association (*www.natcom.org*), called "Why Americans Communicate," reports that nearly two-thirds of U.S. citizens feel very comfortable communicating with others. Women are more likely than men to feel comfortable, and older respondents (55 years and older) are more comfortable than any other age group. This comfort level pertains to communication in informal settings such as talking to a friend, family member, or partner.

Yet, not everyone is comfortable talking to others. In fact, some people are quite nervous about communicating. The extent to which people exhibit anxiety about speaking to others is called **communication apprehension**. Communication apprehension is a legitimate and real experience that researchers believe usually negatively affects our communication with others (Daly, McCroskey, Ayres, Hopf, & Ayres, 2007; Richmond & McCroskey, 1998). People with communication apprehension can go to great lengths to avoid communication situations because communicating can make them feel shy, embarrassed, and tense. At times, some individuals find themselves fearful or anxious around people from different cultural groups. This **intercultural communication apprehension** (Wrench, Corrigan, McCroskey, & Punyanunt-Carter, 2006) not only impairs quality face-to-face conversations, but also can affect whether or not we wish to communicate with someone *at all*. We will return to culture and communication in Chapter 3.

Even if we don't suffer from communication apprehension, there are many times when we have difficulty getting our message across to others. We may feel unprepared to argue with a supervisor for a raise, to let our

communication apprehension

A fear or an anxiety pertaining to the communication process.

intercultural communication apprehension

A fear or anxiety pertaining to communication with people from different cultural backgrounds.

Communication Assessment Test

Personal Report of Communication Apprehension (PRCA)

Directions:

This instrument is composed of twenty-four statements concerning feelings about communicating with other people. Please indicate the degree to which each statement applies to you using the following five-point scale:

strongly agree = 1   agree = 2   undecided = 3   disagree = 4   strongly disagree = 5

There are no right or wrong answers. Please mark your first impression and answer quickly. You can take this test online. Go to your online Resource Center for *Understanding Interpersonal Communication* and look under the resources for Chapter 1. (To learn how to get started with your online Resource Center, see the inside front cover of this book.)

____ 1. I dislike participating in group discussions.

____ 2. Generally, I am comfortable while participating in group discussions.

____ 3. I am tense and nervous while participating in group discussions.

____ 4. I like to get involved in group discussions.

____ 5. Engaging in a group discussion with new people makes me tense and nervous.

____ 6. I am calm and relaxed while participating in group discussions.

____ 7. Generally, I am nervous when I have to participate in a meeting.

____ 8. Usually, I am calm and relaxed while participating in a meeting.

____ 9. I am calm and relaxed when I am called upon to express an opinion at a meeting.

____ 10. I am afraid to express myself at meetings.

____ 11. Communicating at meetings usually makes me feel uncomfortable.

____ 12. I am relaxed when answering questions at a meeting.

____ 13. While participating in a conversation with a new acquaintance, I feel very nervous.

____ 14. I have no fear of speaking up in conversations.

____ 15. Ordinarily, I am very tense and nervous in conversations.

____ 16. Ordinarily, I am very calm and relaxed in conversations.

____ 17. While conversing with a new acquaintance, I feel very relaxed.

____ 18. I'm afraid to speak up in conversations.

____ 19. I have no fear of giving a speech.

____ 20. Certain parts of my body feel tense and rigid while giving a speech.

____ 21. I feel relaxed while giving a speech.

____ 22. My thoughts become confused and jumbled when I am giving a speech.

____ 23. I face the prospect of giving a speech with confidence.

____ 24. While giving a speech, I get so nervous I forget facts I really know.

Scoring

There are four categories for scoring: **group discussions, meetings, interpersonal conversations, and public speaking.** To compute your scores, add or subtract the numbers you marked for each item as indicated below:

1. Group discussions

   18 + (plus) scores for items 2, 4, and 6 – (minus) scores for items 1, 3, and 5

   = Subtotal _____

(*Continues*)

2. Meetings

   18 + (plus) scores for items 8, 9, and 12 – (minus) scores for items 7, 10, and 11

   = Subtotal _____

3. Interpersonal conversations

   18 + (plus) scores for items 14, 16, and 17 – (minus) scores for items 13, 15, and 18

   = Subtotal _____

4. Public speaking

   18 + (plus) scores for items 19, 21, and 23 – (minus) scores for items 20, 22, and 24

   = Subtotal _____

To obtain your score, add your four subscores together. Your score should range between 24 and 120. If your score is below 24 or above 120, you have made a mistake in computation. Scores can range, in each context, from a low of 6 to a high of 30. Any score above 18 indicates some degree of communication apprehension.

From www.jamescmccroskey.com. Used by permission.

apartment manager know that the hot water is not hot enough, or to tell our partner, "I love you." At times throughout the day, we may struggle with what to say, how to say something, or when to say something. We also may struggle with listening to certain messages because of their content or the manner in which they are presented. In addition, communication may seem difficult when others don't respond as we'd wish or when others don't even seem to pay attention to us.

This book is about improving your ability to interact with other people. Improving your interpersonal communication skills will assist you in becoming more effective in your relationships with a variety of people, including those with whom you are close (e.g., family members, friends, coworkers) and those with whom you interact less frequently (e.g., health care providers, contractors, babysitters).

Throughout this course, you will see how research and theory associated with interpersonal communication informs everyday encounters. You will also be introduced to a number of useful communication skills. We believe that the theoretical and practical applications of interpersonal communication are intertwined to the extent that we cannot ignore the mutual influence of one upon the other—after all, theories inform practice, and practice grows out of theory. At the same time, we agree with Robert Craig (2003), a communication professor and researcher, who maintains that the communication discipline can influence and enhance people's lives only by being practical (p. 18). So, we take a practical approach with this book in the hope that you will be able to use what you learn about the theoretical foundations and practical applications to make effective communication choices in your own interpersonal relationships.

Our first task is to map out a general understanding of interpersonal communication. We begin this journey by providing a brief history of how interpersonal communication came about in the field of communication.

The Study of Interpersonal Communication

Let's explore a brief overview of the communication discipline to give you a sense of its evolution. For a more expansive view of the communication field, we encourage you to look at additional sources that provide a more comprehensive presentation (Craig, 2003; Friedrich & Boileau, 1999, Rogers & Chaffee, 1983; Shepherd, 1993). You can find the full citations for these sources in the References section at the end of this book.

Acknowledging our Past

What we call *communication studies* today has its origins in ancient Greece and Rome, during the formation of what we now know as Western civilization. Being skilled at communication was expected of all Greek and Roman citizens (that is, free land-owning and native-born men). For example, citizens were asked to judge murder and adultery trials, travel as state emissaries, and defend their property against would-be land collectors. This sort of public communication was viewed primarily as a way to persuade other people, and scholars such as Aristotle developed ways to improve a speaker's persuasive powers. His book, the *Rhetoric*, described a way of making speeches that encouraged speakers to incorporate logic, evidence, and emotions and to consider how the audience perceived the speaker's credibility and intelligence.

Aristotelian thinking dominated early approaches to communication for centuries. But as time went on, interest grew in providing speakers with practical ways to improve their communication skills in situations other than public persuasion. And in the modern era, communication scholars began moving beyond the focus on skills to form a more theoretical and philosophical approach to communication. They began trying to answer the question "How do I come to know, to believe, and to act?" in relation to communication. (See Harper, 1979, for more information in this area.)

Contemporary communication courses—like the one you're enrolled in now—were first taught in English departments in the early 1900s. These courses, staying true to early Greek and Roman thinking, emphasized public speaking and were taught by English teachers who had some training in public communication. The English department was considered the appropriate place for communication courses because it was believed that written and spoken communication were synonymous. However, scholars who specialized in the study of public speaking (we call them communication scholars today) were unhappy with this arrangement. They maintained that there were clear differences between the two forms of communication.

In 1913, this debate grew so intense that when the National Council of Teachers of English held its annual convention in Chicago, a group of public speaking teachers proposed that they form their own association, the National Association of Academic Teachers of Public Speaking. This was the beginning of the modern-day National Communication Association (NCA), an organization comprised of more than 8,000 communication teachers, researchers, and practitioners who study over 50 different areas of communication. One of the largest fields of the communication discipline is interpersonal communication, which explores communication within many different relationships, including those between parents and children, teachers and students, supervisors and employees, friends, and spouses, to name just a few.

Understanding the Present

Even though we engage in interpersonal communication daily, it is often difficult to disentangle from everything else we do. To arrive at the definition of interpersonal communication, it helps first to distinguish it from other types of communication. Scholars have identified the following kinds of situations in which human communication exists: intrapersonal, interpersonal, small group, organizational, mass, and public. You may notice that the communication department at your school is organized around some or all of these communication types. Many schools use these categories as an effective way to organize their curriculum and course offerings.

Note that these communication types build on each other because they represent increasing numbers of people included in the process. In addition, keep in mind that although these communication types differ from one another in some significant ways, they aren't mutually exclusive. For example, you may engage in both intrapersonal and interpersonal communication in a single encounter, or interpersonal communication may take place in an organizational context. With these caveats in mind, let's take a closer look at the six types of communication.

- *Intrapersonal communication:* Communication with ourselves. We may find ourselves daydreaming or engaging in internal dialogues even in the presence of another person. These are intrapersonal processes. Intrapersonal communication includes imagining, perceiving, or solving problems in your head. For instance, intrapersonal communication takes place when you debate with yourself, mentally listing the pros and cons of a decision before taking action.

- *Interpersonal communication:* The process of message transaction between people (usually two) who work toward creating and sustaining shared meaning. We will discuss this definition in more detail later in this chapter.

- *Small group communication:* Communication between and among members of a task group who meet for a common purpose or goal. Small group communication occurs in classrooms, the workplace, and in more social environments (for example, sports teams or book clubs).

- *Organizational communication:* Communication with and among large, extended environments with a defined hierarchy. This context also includes communication among members within those environments. Organizational communication may involve other communication types, such as interpersonal communication (for example, supervisor/subordinate relationships), small group communication (for example, a task group preparing a report), and intrapersonal communication (for example, daydreaming at work).

- *Mass communication:* Communication to a large audience via some mediated channel, such as television, radio, the Internet, or newspapers. At times, people seek out others using personal ads either on the Internet or in newspapers or magazines. This is an example of the intersection of mass communication and interpersonal communication.

- *Public communication:* Communication in which one person gives a speech to a large audience in person. Public communication is also often called public speaking. Public speakers have predetermined goals in mind, such as informing, persuading, or entertaining.

Each of these communication types is affected by two pervasive influences: culture and technology. In the twenty-first century especially, acknowledging these two influences is crucial to our understanding of interpersonal communication and human relationships. First, It's nearly impossible to ignore the role that culture plays as we communicate with others. We now live in a country where intercultural contact is commonplace, making effective communication with others even more critical than it would be ordinarily. The ever-increasing presence of intercultural relationships—such as those between exchange students and their host families, and American parents and their children adopted from other countries—has prompted researchers to study the effects of these blended populations on communication effectiveness (e.g., Galvin, 2006). We will delve deeper into the topic of culture, community, and communication in Chapter 3.

Second, as you probably know from your own online experiences, it is now possible to communicate with another person without ever having face-to-face contact. Years ago, interpersonal communication was limited to sending letters or talking with someone personally. But today, relationships are routinely initiated, cultivated, and even terminated via electronic technology. This phenomenon has stimulated much recent research on technology, relationships, and interpersonal communication (e.g., Walther & Bazarova, 2007; Walther, Gay, & Hancock, 2005). Technology has not only made interpersonal communication easier and faster, it has shaped the very nature of our communication and our relationships. Our conversations have become abbreviated, such as when we look at our caller ID and answer the phone with "And when did you get home from vacation?" instead of "Hello?" We develop close relationships with others via online dating services (e.g., Match.com), and our personal web pages (e.g., MySpace.com and Facebook.com) allow us to have tens of millions of "friends." You will get a better sense of the extent of technology's influence on interpersonal relationships in Chapter 11.

Defining Interpersonal Communication

We define **interpersonal communication** as the process of message transaction between people to create and sustain shared meaning. There are three critical components embedded in this definition: process, message exchange, and shared meaning. Let's look at each in turn.

When we state that interpersonal communication is a **process**, we mean that it is an ongoing, unending vibrant activity that is always changing. When we enter into an interpersonal communication exchange, we are entering into an event with no definable beginning or ending, and one that is irreversible. For example, consider the moments when you first meet and begin communicating with classmates during a small group activity in class. Chances are that for the first few minutes everyone in the group feels a little awkward and uncertain. Yet, after you all introduce yourselves to one another, it's highly likely that you all feel more comfortable. This shift from feeling uncertain to feeling comfortable is the ongoing, irreversible interpersonal communication process in action.

The notion of process also suggests that it is not only individuals who change, but also the cultures in which they live. For instance, modern U.S. society is very different today than it was in the 1950s. The climate of the United States in the 1950s can be characterized as a time of postwar euphoria, colored by a concern about communism. The feminist movement of the 1970s had yet to occur, and for many white middle-class families, sex roles were traditional. Women's roles were more rigidly defined as nurturers and primary caretakers for children, whereas men's roles were relegated to emotionless financial providers. These roles influenced decision making in many families (Turner & West, 2006). Nowadays roles are less rigid. Many dads stay at home to care for children, and many moms work outside the home. And more than ever, couples make all kinds of decisions about the family together. Consider a couple communicating in the 1950s about a family issue and another couple discussing the same issue today. In what ways do you think the conversations would be similar or different?

The second element of our definition highlights **message exchange**, by which we mean the transaction of verbal and nonverbal *messages*, or information, being sent simultaneously between people. Messages, both verbal and nonverbal, are the vehicles we use to interact with others. But messages are not enough to establish interpersonal communication. For example, consider an English speaker stating the message, "I need to find the post office. Can you direct me there?" to a Spanish speaker. Although the message was stated clearly in English, no shared meaning results if the Spanish speaker is not bilingual.

Meaning is central to our definition of interpersonal communication because **meaning** is what people extract from a message. As you will learn in Chapter 4, words alone have no meaning; people attribute meaning to words. We create the meaning of a message even as the message unfolds. Perhaps our

interpersonal communication

The process of message transaction between two people to create and sustain shared meaning.

process

When used to describe interpersonal communication, an ongoing, unending, vibrant activity that always changes.

message exchange

The transaction of verbal and nonverbal messages being sent simultaneously between two people.

meaning

What communicators create together through the use of verbal and nonverbal messages.

history with someone helps us interpret the message. Perhaps a message is unclear to us and we ask questions for clarity. Or maybe the message has personal meaning to us, and no one else understands the personal expressions used. Meaning directly affects our relational life. As Steve Duck and Julia Wood (1995) state: "we suspect that 'good' and 'bad' relational experiences are sometimes a matter of personal definition and personal meaning, but always intertwined, sometimes seamlessly, in the broader human enterprise of making sense of experience" (p. 3). In other words, achieving meaning is achieving sense-making in your relationships.

When we say that people work toward creating and sustaining meaning, we are suggesting that there must be some shared meaning for interpersonal communication to take place. Because meaning is affected by culture in more ways than language differences, we have to be careful not to assume that our meaning will automatically be clear to others and result in shared meaning (Martin & Nakayama, 2007). For example, Martin and Nakayama note that in the United States many people tend to dislike Monday, the first day of the work week, and enjoy Friday, which is the end of the workweek. However, many Muslims* dislike Saturday, which is the first day of the week for

*We discuss various cultural groups throughout every chapter of this text. We recognize that although there are many differences within various cultures, some similarities exist. In each chapter, we strive to present conclusions about cultural communities that reflect consistencies in research and honor the integrity of the various populations.

Muslims after Friday, the holy day. Therefore, cultural expressions such as TGIF (Thank God It's Friday) may not communicate the same meaning to all people, even when accurately translated.

To examine the complexity associated with the term *message,* read the article "Where Is the 'Message' in Communication Models?" available through InfoTrac College Edition. Go to your online Resource Center for *Understanding Interpersonal Communication* to access *InfoTrac College Edition Exercise 1.1: Received as Meant to Be Sent?* under your Chapter 1 resources. (To learn how to get started with your online Resource Center, see the inside front cover of this book.)

Models of Communication

To further understand the interpersonal communication process and to provide more information about the evolution of the communication field, we draw upon what theorists call models of communication. **Communication models** are visual, simplified representations of complex relationships in the communication process. They help you see how the communication field has evolved over the years and provide a foundation you can return to throughout the book. The three prevailing models we discuss will give you insight into how we frame our definition of interpersonal communication. Let's start with the oldest model.

Mechanistic Thinking and the Linear Model

More than fifty years ago, Claude E. Shannon, a Bell Telephone scientist, and Warren Weaver, a Sloan Cancer Research Foundation consultant, set out to understand radio and telephone technology by looking at how information passed through various channels (Shannon & Weaver, 1949). They viewed information transmission as a linear process, and their research resulted in the creation of the **linear model of communication.**

This approach frames communication as a one-way process that transmits a message to a destination. You may have seen the commercial for a cell phone in which a man travels to a series of places, at each stop yelling into the phone, "Can you hear me now?" When a message is sent and received, communication takes place. Someone can hear you. That is the essence of the linear model.

Several components comprise the linear model of communication (see Figure 1.1). The **sender** is the source of the **message**, which may be spoken, written, or unspoken. The sender passes the message to the **receiver**, the intended target of the message. The receiver, in turn, assigns meaning to the message. All of this communication takes place in a **channel**, which is a pathway to communication. Typically, channels represent our senses (visual/sight,

communication models

Visual, simplified representations of complex relationships in the communication process.

linear model of communication

A characterization of communication as a one-way process that transmit a message from a sender to a receiver.

sender

The source of a message.

message

Spoken, written, or unspoken information sent from a sender to a receiver.

receiver

The intended target of a message.

Figure 1.1 Linear model of communication

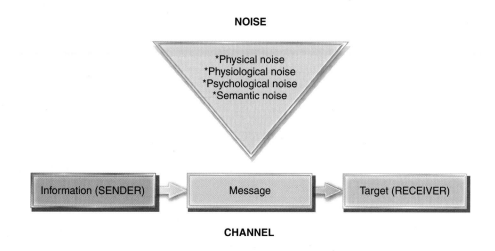

tactile/touch, olfactory/smell, and auditory/hearing). For instance, you use the tactile channel to hug a parent, and you use the auditory channel to listen to your roommate complain about a midterm exam.

In the linear model, communication also involves **noise**, which is anything that interferes with the message. Four types of noise can interrupt a message:

- **Physical noise** (also called *external noise*) involves any stimuli outside of the receiver that makes the message difficult to hear. For example, it would be difficult to hear a message from your professor if someone were mowing the lawn outside the classroom. Physical noise can also take the form of something a person is wearing, such as "loud jewelry" or sunglasses, which may cause a receiver to focus on the object rather than the message.

- **Physiological noise** refers to biological influences on message reception. Examples of this type of noise are articulation problems, hearing or visual impairments, and the physical well-being of a speaker (that is, whether he or she is able to deliver a message).

- **Psychological noise** (or *internal noise*) refers to a communicator's biases, prejudices, and feelings toward a person or a message. For example, you may have heard another person use language that is offensive and derogatory while speaking about a certain cultural group. If you were bothered by this language, you were experiencing psychological noise.

channel

A pathway through which a message is sent.

noise

Anything that interferes with accurate transmission or reception of a message. See also physical noise, physiological noise, psychological noise, and semantic noise.

physical noise

Any stimuli outside of a sender or a receiver that interfere with the transmission or reception of a message. Also called external noise.

physiological noise

Biological influences on a sender or a receiver that interfere with the transmission or reception of a message.

psychological noise

Biases, prejudices, and feelings that interfere with the accurate transmission or reception of a message. Also called internal noise.

"O.K. What part of 'malignant regression and pathogenic reintrojection as a defense against psychic decompensation' don't you understand?"

- **Semantic noise** occurs when senders and receivers apply different meanings to the same message. Semantic noise may take the form of jargon, technical language, and other words and phrases that are familiar to the sender but that are not understood by the receiver. For example, consider Jim, a 40-year-old Franco American living in Maine. Jim's primary language is French, so he frequently uses the English language in ways that are a bit nonsensical. For instance, when asking to look at something, he says "hand me, see me" instead of "may I see that?" Or, at times, he will say "it will go that" in lieu of the phrase "this is the story." These sorts of phrases and their use could be considered conversational semantic noise.

The linear view suggests that communication takes place in a **context**, or the surroundings impacting a message as it's sent. Context is multidimensional and can be physical, cultural, psychological, or historical. The **physical context** is the tangible environment in which communication occurs. Examples of physical contexts are the hotel van on the way to the airport, the dinner table, the apartment, and the church hall. Environmental conditions such as temperature, lighting, and space are also part of the physical context. For example, consider trying to listen to your best friend talk about her financial problems in a crowded coffee shop. The environment does not seem conducive to receiving her message clearly and accurately.

The **cultural context** refers to the rules, roles, norms, and patterns of communication that are unique to particular cultures. Culture always influences the communication taking place between and among people, requiring us to look at the backgrounds of communicators. Immigrants, for instance, may

semantic noise

Occurs when senders and receivers apply different meanings to the same message. Semantic noise may take the form of jargon, technical language, and other words and phrases that are familiar to the sender but that are not understood by the receiver.

context

The environment in which a message is sent.

physical context

The tangible environment in which communication occurs.

cultural context

The cultural environment in which communication occurs.

have difficulties assimilating into U.S. culture, often illustrated by the use of language within the family. Language serves as a primary factor affecting the quality of relationships within the family (Soliz, Lin, Anderson, & Harwood, 2006). So, for example, if grandparents and grandchildren have difficulty communicating with each other because the grandparents speak primarily Spanish and the grandchildren speak primarily English, it's likely that meaning will be jeopardized.

The **social-emotional context** indicates the nature of the relationship that affects a communication encounter. For example, are the communicators in a particular interaction friendly or unfriendly, supportive or unsupportive? Or do they fall somewhere in between? These factors help explain why, for instance, you might feel completely anxious in one employment interview but very comfortable in another. At times, you and an interviewer may hit it off, and at other times you may feel intimidated or awkward. The social-emotional context helps explain the nature of the interaction taking place.

In the **historical context,** messages are understood in relationship to previously sent messages. Thus, when Billy tells Tina that he missed her while they were separated over Spring Break, Tina hears that as a turning point in their relationship. Billy has never said that before and, in fact, he has often mentioned that he rarely misses anyone when he is apart from him or her. Therefore, his comment is colored by their history together. If Billy regularly told Tina he missed her, she would interpret the message differently.

We will return to the notion of context often in this book. For now, keep in mind that context has a significant influence on our relationships with others. Further, context involves people and their conversations and relationships. If we don't consider context in our interactions with others, we have no way to judge our interpersonal effectiveness.

Although the linear model was highly regarded when it was first conceptualized, it has been criticized because it presumes that communication has a definable beginning and ending (Anderson & Ross, 2002). In fact, Shannon and Weaver (1999) later emphasized this aspect of their model by claiming people receive information in organized and discrete ways. Yet, we know that communication can be messy. We have all interrupted someone or had someone interrupt us. The linear model also presumes that listeners are passive and that communication occurs only when speaking. But we know that listeners often affect speakers and are not simply passive receivers of a speaker's message. With these criticisms in mind, researchers developed another way to represent the human communication process: the interactional model.

Feedback and the Interactional Model

To emphasize the two-way nature of communication between people, Wilbur Schramm (1954) conceptualized the **interactional model of communication.** Schramm's model shows that communication goes in two directions: from sender to receiver and from receiver to sender. This circular, or interactional,

social-emotional context

The relational and emotional environment in which communication occurs.

historical context

A type of context in which messages are understood in relationship to previously sent messages.

interactional model of communication

A characterization of communication as a two-way process in which a message is sent from sender to receiver and from receiver to sender.

Figure 1.2   Interactional model of communication

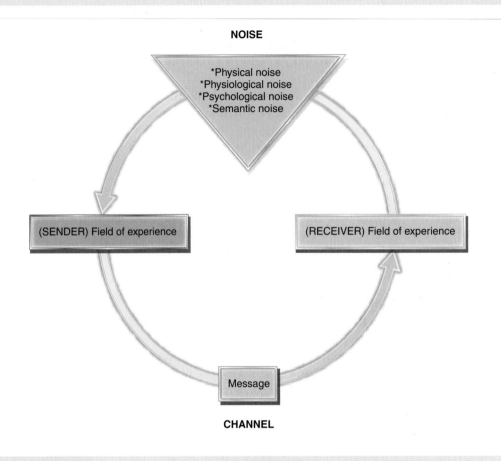

process suggests that communication is ongoing rather than linear. In the interactional model, individuals in a conversation can be both sender and receiver, but not both simultaneously (see Figure 1.2).

The interactional approach is characterized primarily by **feedback**, which can be defined as responses to people, their messages, or both. Feedback may be verbal (meaning we respond in words) or nonverbal (meaning we respond in facial expressions, body posture, and so forth). Feedback may also be internal or external. **Internal feedback** occurs when you assess your own communication (for example, by thinking "I never should have said that"). **External feedback** is the feedback you receive from other people (for example, "Why did you say that? That was dumb!").

A person can provide external feedback that results in important internal feedback for himself or herself. For example, let's say that Alexandra gives Dan the following advice about dealing with the death of his partner: "You feel sad as long as you need to. Don't worry about what other people think. I'm sick of

feedback

A verbal or nonverbal response to a message. See also internal feedback and external feedback.

internal feedback

The feedback we give ourselves when we assess our own communication.

external feedback

The feedback we receive from other people.

people telling others how they should feel about something. These are your feelings." While giving Dan this external feedback, Alexandra may realize that her advice can also be applied to her own recent breakup. Although she may intend to send Dan a comforting message, she may also provide herself internal feedback as she deals with her relational circumstances.

Like the linear model, the interactional model has been criticized primarily for its view of senders and receivers—that is, one person sends a message to another person. Neither model takes into consideration what happens when nonverbal messages are sent at the same time as verbal messages. For example, when a father disciplines his child and finds the child either looking the other way or staring directly into his eyes, the father will "read" the meaning of the child's nonverbal communication as inattentive or disobedient. What happens if the child doesn't say anything during the reprimand? The father will still make some meaning out of the child's silence. The interactional view acknowledges that human communication involves both speaking and listening, but it asserts that speaking and listening are separate events and thus does not address the effect of nonverbal communication as the message is sent. This criticism led to the development of a third model of communication, the transactional model.

Shared Meaning and the Transactional Model

Whereas the linear model of communication assumes that communication is an action that moves from sender to receiver, and the interactional model suggests that the presence of feedback makes communication an interaction between people, the **transactional model of communication** (Barnlund, 1970; Watzlawick, Beavin, & Jackson, 1967) underscores the fact that giving and receiving messages is simultaneous and mutual. In fact, the word *transactional* indicates that the communication process is cooperative. In other words, communicators (senders and receivers) are both responsible for the effect and effectiveness of communication. In a transactional encounter, people do not simply send meaning from one to the other and then back again; rather, they build shared meaning.

A unique feature of the transactional model is its recognition that messages build upon each other. Further, both verbal and nonverbal behaviors are necessarily part of the transactional process. For example, consider Alan's conversation with his coworker Pauline. During a break, Pauline asks Alan about his family in Los Angeles. He begins to tell Pauline that his three siblings all live in Los Angeles and that he has no idea when they will be able to "escape the prison" there. When he mentions "prison," Pauline looks confused. Seeing Pauline's puzzled facial expression, Alan clarifies that he hated Los Angeles because it was so hot, people lived too close to each other, and he felt that he was being watched all the time. In sum, he felt like he was in a prison. This example shows how much both Alan and Pauline are actively involved in this communication interaction. Pauline's nonverbal response to Alan prompted him to clarify his original message. As this interaction shows,

transactional model of communication

A characterization of communication as the reciprocal sending and receiving of messages. In a transactional encounter, the sender and receiver do not simply send meaning from one to the other and then back again; rather, they build shared meaning through simultaneous sending and receiving.

Figure 1.3 Transactional model of communication

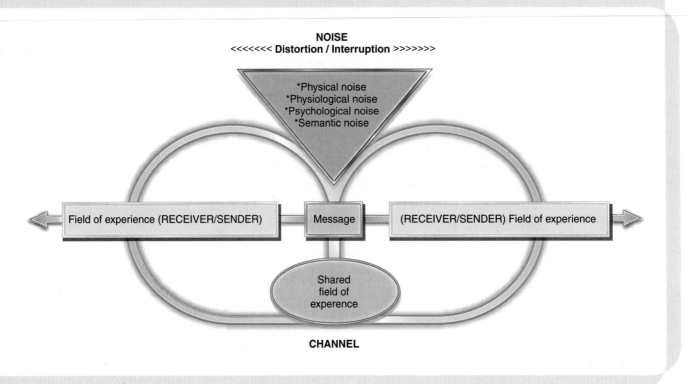

the nonverbal message works in conjunction with the verbal message, and the transactional process requires ongoing negotiation of meaning.

Note that the transactional model in Figure 1.3 is characterized by a common field of experience between communicator A and communicator B. The **field of experience** refers to a person's culture, past experiences, personal history, and heredity, and how these elements influence the communication process.

People's fields of experience overlap at times, meaning that people share things in common. Where two people's fields of experience overlap, they can communicate effectively. And as they communicate, they create more overlap in their experiences. This process explains why initial encounters often consist of questions and answers between communicators, such as "Where are you from?", "What's your major?", "Do you ski?" The answers to these questions help establish the overlap in the communicators' experiences: "Oh, I was in Chicago over the holidays last year," "Really, that's my major, too," "Yeah, I don't ski either." Further, fields of experience may change over time.

For instance, in class, Rhonda and Marcy have little in common and have little overlap in their fields of experience. They just met this term, have never taken a course together before, and Rhonda is eighteen years older than

field of experience

The influence of a person's culture, past experiences, personal history, and heredity on the communication process.

Marcy. It would appear, then, that their fields of experience would be limited to being women enrolled in the same course together. However, consider the difference if we discover that both Rhonda and Marcy are single parents, have difficulty finding quality child care, and have both received academic scholarships. The overlap in their fields of experience would be significantly greater. In addition, as the two continue in the class together, they will develop new common experiences, which, in turn, will increase the overlap in their fields of experience. This increased overlap may affect their interactions with each other in the future.

Interpersonal communication scholars have embraced the transactional process in their research, believing that human communication "is always tied to what came before and always anticipates what may come later" (Wood, 1998, p. 6). Wood believes that many misunderstandings occur in relationships because people are either unaware of or don't attend to the transactional communication process. Consider her words:

> The dynamic quality of communication keeps it open to revision. If someone misunderstands our words or nonverbal behavior, we can say or do something to clarify our meaning. If we don't understand another person's communication, we can look puzzled to show our confusion or ask questions to discover what the other person meant. (p. 6)

REVISITING CASEINPOINT

1. *How does the conversation between Jackie and Scottie depict a transactional process?*

2. *One feature of the transactional model is that messages build on each other. Apply this feature to Jackie and Scottie's interaction.*

You can answer these questions online under the resources for Chapter 1 at your online Resource Center for Understanding Interpersonal Communication. *(To learn how to get started with your online Resource Center, see the inside front cover of this book.)*

In summary, early communication models showed that communication is linear and that senders and receivers have separate roles and functions. The interactional approach expanded that thinking and suggested less linearity and more involvement of feedback between communicators. The transactional model refined our understanding by noting the importance of a communicator's background, by demonstrating the simultaneous sending and receiving of messages, and by focusing on the communicators' mutual involvement in creating meaning. To check out interactive versions of these models, go to your online Resource Center for *Understanding Interpersonal Communication* and access *Interactive Activity 1.1: Interactive Models of Communication* under the resources for Chapter 1. (To learn how to get started with your online Resource Center, see the inside front cover of this book.)

Before we move on to the next discussion, consider that our notion of communication models is continually evolving. The transactional model may soon become outdated as technology shapes how we view, and enact, the communication process. Communication scholars may reconsider the communication model to take into account email, keyboard symbols that indicate emotions, and geographically dispersed people. In addition, we recognize that the communication roles described by the models are not absolute and can vary depending on the situation.

With this foundation, let's now discuss the nature of interpersonal communication.

The Interpersonal Communication Continuum

Before we continue this journey toward understanding interpersonal communication, let's pause a moment. By now, we hope you are starting to realize that the interpersonal communication process is a complex one. Although it shares some overlap with other types of communication, it also differs from them in important ways. It is marked by two people who simultaneously send and receive messages, attempting to create meaning. We explained interpersonal communication by elaborating on three models that describe its components. Another way to understand interpersonal communication is by examining its nature through the interpersonal communication continuum.

More than three decades ago, Gerald Miller and Mark Steinberg (1975) proposed looking at communication along a continuum. It was a unique view at the time and remains significant today. Like many interpersonal communication researchers, Miller and Steinberg believed that not all human communication is interpersonal. Our interactions with others can be placed on a continuum from impersonal to interpersonal (see Figure 1.4).

Think about the various interactions you have that could be considered impersonal or closer to the impersonal end of the continuum. You sit next to a person in the waiting room of your dentist and ask whether she watched *American Idol* the night before. You tell a man hawking tickets to a sold-out Spurs game that you're not interested. You tell the woman sitting next to you at a wedding that you're a friend of the groom. Typically, these episodes remain on the impersonal end of the continuum because the conversations remain superficial. You do not acknowledge the people in these examples as unique individuals who are important in your life.

Now, consider the many times you talk to people on a much deeper level. You share confidences with a close friend with whom you have tea. You laugh with your grandfather about a treasured family story. You commiserate with a classmate who is disappointed about a grade. In these cases, your communi-

Figure 1.4 The continuum of interpersonal communication

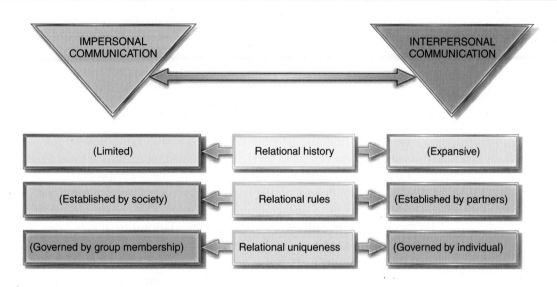

cation is not superficial. You share yourself and respond to the other person as a unique individual.

These two ends of the continuum—impersonal and interpersonal—are the extremes. But, most of our communication encounters with others aren't either impersonal or interpersonal. Rather, most fall in between or along various points on the continuum. Your talks with a physician, professor, coworker, or car mechanic may not be particularly emotionally fulfilling but probably have a personal dimension to them. You have to share your health status with your doctor. Your professor sometimes delicately asks what personal problems might have caused a failing grade on an exam. A coworker may share family stories. And a car mechanic may ask if you have enough money for a new transmission. Each of these interactions entails some degree of closeness but not a lot of emotional depth.

What will determine the extent to which an encounter is impersonal, interpersonal, or in between? Three issues seem most important: relational history, relational rules, and relational uniqueness.

First, **relational history** pertains to the prior relationship experiences two people share. For example, Rolanda and Maria have worked as servers in a restaurant for several years. Their relational history is apparent when you consider the amount of time they have spent together. This history may include working the same hours, sharing with each other their personal feelings about their boss, or having social times with each other's friends. Their relational history, then, spans both their professional and personal lives. This

relational history

The prior relationship experiences two people share.

relational rules

Negotiable rules that indicate what two relational partners expect and allow when they talk to each other.

relational uniqueness

The ways in which the particular relationship of two relational partners stands apart from other relationships they experience.

Although most of us interact with people all day, the nature of our relationships is what determines whether our interactions are interpersonal.

© Gabe Palmer/Corbis

rich history enables their conversations to be interpersonal rather than impersonal.

Relational rules indicate what the people in a relationship expect and allow when they talk to each other. Relational rules, often unstated, differ from social rules in that the two relational partners negotiate them themselves as opposed to having them set by an outside source. Rules help relational partners negotiate how information is managed and stored (Petronio, 2002; Serewicz & Petronio, 2007). For example, one relational rule that Rolanda and Maria may share is the belief that all restaurant gossip should remain private. Another one of their relational rules may communicate the need to be professional while on the job and to avoid "inside" jokes. If the restaurant manager had set these rules, then when Rolanda and Maria followed them, their communication would be more impersonal.

A final influence on the relationship continuum is **relational uniqueness**, which pertains to how communicators frame their relationship and compare it to others. In other words, how is their relationship unique from others? In the relationship between Rolanda and Maria, they know and treat each other as unique individuals, not as generic coworkers. Thus, Rolanda asks Maria for help in making a financial decision because she knows that Maria has a good head for business. And Maria refrains from teasing Rolanda when she drops a tray (even though many other servers engage in that kind of banter) because she knows Rolanda is sensitive about being clumsy. Their relational history and rules help develop their sense of relational uniqueness.

Again, much of our communication isn't purely impersonal or interpersonal; rather, it falls somewhere between the two ends of the continuum. Further, the relationship you have with someone doesn't always indicate whether your communication is personal or not. At times, personal communication occurs in our impersonal relationships. For example, consider telling your dry cleaner about your divorce or confiding to a fellow passenger that you are deathly afraid of flying. At other times, we may have impersonal communication in our close relationships. For instance, a couple with five children may be too exhausted to worry about being sensitive, loving, and compassionate with each other. Feeding the kids, bathing them, preparing their lunches, and getting them to the bus present enough challenges. In fact, for the sake of communication efficiency, many couples have developed abbreviated communication systems (Pearson, 1992) that fit the description of impersonal encounters.

Now that you are getting a clearer picture of what interpersonal communication is, let's turn to a discussion of the value of interpersonal communication in our lives.

The Value of Interpersonal Communication

Most of you are seeking a college degree in order to secure an excellent job. Along the way, do not ignore the importance of interpersonal communication. In job interviews, interpersonal communication skills are essential. Understanding how to employ these skills effectively relates directly to getting a job (DuBrin, 2007). Further, the National Association of Colleges and Employers (2005) reports that interpersonal skills rank in the top three skills employers look for in new hires in virtually all professions. In his book *10 Things Employers Want You to Learn in College*, William Coplin (2004) writes that communication skills are paramount. Without effective communication skills, Coplin writes, employees will not be productive. Clearly, without some knowledge and skill in interpersonal communication, you may have a difficult time finding a job in today's marketplace. To take a look at the communication model applied to today's business environment, access *InfoTrac College Edition Exercise 1.2: The Communication Model at Work* to read the article "Avoiding Breakdowns in the Communication Process," available through InfoTrac College Edition. (To learn how to get started with your online Resource Center, see the inside front cover of this book.)

There are other reasons, in addition to job success, why we need to learn about interpersonal communication. Most of us desire long-term, satisfying relationships, and effective interpersonal communication can help us establish such relationships. Learning about interpersonal communication can improve our lives physically, emotionally, and psychologically, as well as improve our relationships with others. A number of recent conclusions by both the academic and medical communities (for example, American Cancer Society, 2001; Fleishman, Sherbourne, & Crystal, 2000; Iezzoni & O'Day, 2006; Jeffrey, 2005; Support4Hope, 2004) show the value of communication and relationships:

- Older people with the ability to communicate in extended interpersonal networks improve their physical and emotional well-being.

- All aspects of health care quality are directly related to the quality of communication between patient and clinician.

- The American Cancer Society encourages cancer patients to establish an interpersonal relationship with their physicians. This relationship involves taking the time to ask questions, making concerns known, sharing information, and making choices.

self-actualization

The process of gaining information about ourselves in an effort to tap our full potential, our spontaneity, and our talents, and to cultivate our strengths and eliminate our shortcomings.

- Patient perceptions of quality end-of-life care are directly related to the communication between doctor and patient.

- A chat room for those with depression indicates that limited or no interpersonal contact may lead to permanent changes in brain function that increase one's chances of becoming clinically depressed.

- Patients have a preference for physicians who show a "patient-centered" approach that includes quality communication skills and a desire to establish a partnership between patient and physician.

To read an article that offers an interesting look at how our interactions with others affect our health, read "Nuances of Interpersonal Relationships Influence Blood Pressure," available through InfoTrac College Edition. Go to your online Resource Center for *Understanding Interpersonal Communication* to access **InfoTrac College Edition Exercise 1.3: Interpersonal Communication and Health** under the resources for Chapter 1. (To learn how to get started with your online Resource Center, see the inside front cover of this book.)

An additional benefit of studying interpersonal communication is that it can improve relationships with family and friends. Communicating in close relationships can be tough. Yet, think about the advantages, for instance, of (1) improving your listening skills with a roommate, (2) using more sensitive language with a sibling, (3) employing nondefensive reactions in your conflicts with parents, and (4) accepting responsibility for your feelings in your interactions. These are a few areas that we explore in this book.

Effective interpersonal communication can help us feel better physically, psychologically, and emotionally. Think of how good it feels to have someone take the time to talk with you when you're feeling lonely, sick, or depressed.

Another value associated with learning about interpersonal communication pertains to the classroom. Research has shown that using your communication skills in the classroom may improve your academic performance. For instance, students who are considered to have high degrees of interaction involvement in class are more likely to increase their learning, motivation, and satisfaction with the course (Myers & Bryant, 2002). Learning to listen, to participate, and to be involved in class, then, has lasting positive effects on your learning and grades.

A final way that learning about interpersonal communication can improve your life is that it can help you gain information about yourself. Psychologist Abraham Maslow (1954/1970) calls this the process of **self-actualization**. When we are self-actualized, we become the best person we can be. We are tapping our full potential in terms of our creativity, our spontaneity, and our talents. When we self-actualize, we try to cultivate

© Karen Preuss/The Image Works

our strengths and eliminate our shortcomings. At times, others help us to self-actualize. For instance, in the movie *As Good As It Gets*, Jack Nicholson's character, Melvin, suffers from an obsessive-compulsive disorder. His date, Carol, portrayed by Helen Hunt, has her own family problems but tries to help Melvin overcome some of his idiosyncrasies. In a poignant exchange that occurs during their first date, Carol becomes distressed and tells Melvin that she will leave the restaurant unless he gives her a compliment. Carol pleads: "Pay me a compliment, Melvin. I need one quick." Melvin responds by saying, "You make me want to be a better man." Although Melvin clearly frames the compliment from his vantage point, he still, nonetheless, manages to help Carol see her value through his eyes.

Overall, then, we can reap a number of benefits from practicing effective interpersonal skills. Aside from the fact that it allows us to function every day, becoming adept at interpersonal communication helps us in the workplace, improves our health, and aids us in our relationships with family and friends. We have now set the stage for examining some principles and misconceptions about interpersonal communication.

Principles of Interpersonal Communication

To better understand interpersonal communication, let's explore some major principles that shape it. Interpersonal communication is unavoidable, irreversible, symbolic, rule-governed, learned, and has both content and relationship levels.

IPC $\overset{in}{the}$ News

If you want to learn to pick up cues so that you can communicate with different types of people more accurately, says an article in the *Boston Globe*, then check out a company called SpeedReading People. Founded by a former jury consultant who helped attorneys evaluate potential jurors for trials, the core mission of the company is to help people rapidly identify another's personality traits, "tailoring your communication to match theirs" (p. E6). One participant in the program stated that this behavior-training program "is about being aware of behavior that will be counter-productive in an interaction with the other person. You just modify your behavior in the name of better interpersonal interaction" (p. E4). Participants and SpeedReading's personnel contend that the program "teaches not only how to categorize other people's temperaments, but how to communicate more effectively with them" (p. E4). There are many behavioral cues that are indicative of an individual's communication patterns, including energy level, body language, pace of speech, sentence structure, and word choices. According to the article, these cues "are best picked up in face-to-face interaction, which isn't always practical in this Internet era" (p. E4). Nonetheless, you can gain some insights into a person's communication behaviors by the way they email (detailed or terse?) or speak on the phone (hurried or leisurely?), and these insights can help you determine which communication behaviors *you'll* use to get your message across.

Pfeiffer, S. (2007, July 23). You can't read minds, but. . . *Boston Globe*, pp. E1, E4.

Interpersonal Communication Is Unavoidable

Researchers have stated that "you cannot *not* communicate" (Watzlawick, Beavin, & Jackson, 1967). Read that phrase again. This means that as hard as we try, we cannot prevent someone else from making meaning out of our behavior—it is inevitable and unavoidable. No matter what poker face we try to establish, we are still sending a message to others. Even our silence and avoidance of eye contact are communicative. It is this quality that makes interpersonal communication transactional. For instance, imagine that Maresha and her partner, Chloe, are talking about the balance in their checking account. In this scenario, the two engage in a rather heated discussion because Maresha has discovered that $300 cannot be accounted for in the balance. As Maresha speaks, Chloe simply sits and listens to her. Yet, Maresha can't help but notice that Chloe is unable to look her in the eye. Maresha begins to think that Chloe's shifting eyes and constant throat clearing must signify something deceptive. Although Chloe hasn't spoken a word, she is communicating. Her nonverbal communication is being perceived as highly communicative. We return to the impact that nonverbal communication has on creating meaning in Chapter 5.

Interpersonal Communication Is Irreversible

There are times when we wish that we hadn't said something. Wouldn't it be great if we could take back a comment and pretend that it hadn't been spoken? Think about the times you told a parent, a partner, a roommate, or your child something that you later felt was a terrible thing to say. Or what about the times you told a good friend that you couldn't stand his new hair color ("It's too bleached out. You look like an idiot") or her new car ("For *that you paid how much? You got way ripped off!*"). Although we might later wish to eat our words, the principle of **irreversibility** means that what we say to others cannot be reversed.

In fact, the principle of irreversibility affects even mediated interpersonal communication such as email. Think about sending an email that was written in haste. It may have been filled with personal attacks against someone because you were upset and venting. Now imagine that email getting into the hands of the person you were slamming. An apology may help, but saying you're sorry does nothing to erase the original message. The irreversibility of your message becomes apparent.

Interpersonal Communication Is Symbolic

The study of the use of symbols is part of the theory of **semiotics** (Barthes, 1988). Semiotics refers to signs and symbols, their form and content. One important reason interpersonal communication occurs is because symbols are mutually agreed upon by the participants in the process. **Symbols** are arbitrary

irreversibility
The fact that our communication with others cannot be "unsaid" or reversed.

semiotics
The study of signs and symbols in relation to their form and content.

symbols
Arbitrary labels or representations (such as words) for feelings, concepts, objects, or events.

labels or representations for feelings, concepts, objects, or events. Words are symbols. For instance, the word *table* represents something we sit at. Similarly, the word *hate* represents the idea of hate, which means strong feelings for someone or something.

Words like *fear* suggest that symbols may be somewhat abstract, and with this abstraction comes the potential for miscommunication. For instance, consider how hard it would be for someone who has never attended college to understand the following:

> I have no idea what the *prereqs* are. I know that the *midterm* is pretty much *objective*. And the prof doesn't like to follow the *syllabus* too much. I wish that stuff was in the *undergrad* catalog. I'm sure I'd rather do an *independent study* than take that class.

Because the verbal symbols used in this message are not understood by everyone, the message would be lost to someone who had never encountered words such as those italicized. This example underscores the importance of developing a transactional viewpoint because communication requires mutual understanding. In Chapter 4, we look in more detail at the importance of language in interpersonal relationships.

Interpersonal Communication Is Rule-Governed

Consider the following examples of communication rules:

- As long as you live under my roof, you'll do what I say.
- Always tell the truth.
- Don't talk back.
- Always say "thank you" when someone gives you a present.
- Don't interrupt while anyone is talking.

You probably heard at least one of these while growing up. We noted earlier that rules are important ingredients in our relationships. They help guide and structure our interpersonal communication. Rules essentially say that individuals in a relationship agree that there are appropriate ways to interact in their relationship. Like the rules in our childhood, most of the rules in our relationships today tell us what we can or can't do. Susan Shimanoff (1980) has defined a **rule** as "a followable prescription that indicates what behavior is obligated, preferred, or prohibited in certain contexts" (p. 57). In other words, Shimanoff, like many other communication researchers, thinks that we can choose whether or not we wish to follow a rule. Ultimately, we must decide whether the rule must be adhered to or can be ignored in our interpersonal exchanges.

To understand this principle, consider the Chandler family, a family of three that finds itself homeless. The Chandlers live day to day in homeless shelters in a large city in the South. The family members agree on a communication rule explicitly stating that they will not discuss their economic situation in public. This rule requires all family members to refrain from talking

rule

A prescribed guide that indicates what behavior is obligated, preferred, or prohibited in certain contexts.

From birth, we are taught how to communicate interpersonally, most significantly by our family. As we grow older, we refine our skills as we interact with a wider and wider group of people, such as our teachers, friends, coworkers, and partners.

about what led to their homelessness. Each member of the family is obligated to keep this information private, an intrafamily secret of sorts. Whether or not people outside the Chandler family agree on the usefulness of such a rule is not important. Yet, one test of the rule's effectiveness is whether or not family members can refrain from discussing their circumstances with others. Further, if the rule is not followed, what will the consequences be? Rules, therefore, imply choice, and participants in a relationship may choose to ignore a particular rule.

Interpersonal Communication Is Learned

People obviously believe that interpersonal communication is a learned process. Otherwise, why would we be writing this book, and why would you be taking this course? Yet, as we mentioned at the beginning of this chapter, we often take for granted our ability to communicate. Still, we all need to refine and cultivate our skills to communicate with a wide assortment of people. As our book's theme underscores, you must be able to make informed communication choices in changing times.

You're in this course to learn more about interpersonal communication. But you've also been acquiring this information throughout your life. We learn how to communicate with one another from television, our peer group, and our partners. Early in our lives, most of us learn from our family. Consider this dialogue between Laura Reid and her 7-year-old son, Tucker:

Tucker: Mom, I saw Holly's dad driving a motorcycle today.

Laura: Really? That must've been cool to see. Holly's dad's name is Mr. Willows.

Tucker: What's his name?

Laura: Mr. Willows.

Tucker: No, Mom—what's his real name?

Laura: Honey, I told you. Mr. Willows.

Tucker: Doesn't he have a name like I do?

Laura: Little kids call him Mr. Willows. Grownups call him Kenny.

Tucker: Why can't I call him Kenny?

Laura: Because you're not a grownup and because he is older than you, you should call him Mr. Willows.

Clearly, Laura Reid is teaching her child a communication rule she believes leads to interpersonal effectiveness. She tells her son that he should use titles for adults. Implied in this teaching is that kids do not have the same conversational privileges as adults. Interestingly, this learned interpersonal skill evolves with age. For example, at age 24, what do you think Tucker will call Kenny Willows? This awkwardness about names is frequently felt by newlyweds as they become members of their spouse's family. Does a husband call his wife's mother "Mom," or does he call her by her first name? Of course, his mother-in-law may ask to be called "Mom," and yet her son-in-law may be uncomfortable with accommodating her request, especially if his own biological mother is still alive.

Interpersonal Communication Has Both Content and Relationship Levels

Each message that you communicate to another contains information on two levels. The **content level** refers to the information contained in the message. The words you speak to another person and how you say those words consti-tute the content of the message. Content, then, includes both verbal and nonverbal components. A message also contains a **relationship level**, which can be defined as how you want the receiver of a message to interpret your mes-sage. The relational dimension of a message gives us some idea how the speaker and the listener feel about each other. Content and relationship lev-els work simultaneously in a message, and it is difficult to think about send-ing a message that doesn't, in some way, comment on the relationship between the sender and receiver (Knapp & Vangelisti, 2005). In other words, we can't really sepa-rate the two. We always express an idea or thought (content), but that thought is always presented within a relational framework. Consider the following example.

Father Paul is a Catholic priest who is the pastor of a large parish in the Rocky Mountains. Corrine Murphy is the parish administrative assistant. Both have been at the parish for more than ten years and have been good friends throughout that time. One of the most stressful times in the church is during the Christmas season. The pastor is busy visiting homebound parish-ioners, while Corrine is busy overseeing the annual holiday pageant. With this stress comes a

content level

The verbal and nonverbal information contained in a message that indicates the topic of the message.

relationship level

The information contained in a message that indicates how the sender wants the receiver to interpret the message.

REVISITING CASEINPOINT

1. *Apply any of the principles of interper-sonal communication to Jackie and Scottie's conversation.*

2. *Indicate the content and relational dimensions associated with Jackie and Scottie's interaction.*

You can answer these questions online under the resources for Chapter 1 at your online Resource Center for Understanding Interper-sonal Communication. (To learn how to get started with your online Resource Center, see the inside front cover of this book.)

lot of shouting between the two. On one occasion, several parishioners hear Father Paul yell, "Corrine, you forgot to tell me about the Lopez family! When do they need me to visit? Where is your mind these days?" Corrine shoots back: "I've got it under control. Just quit your nagging!" The parishioners listening to the two were a bit taken aback by the way they yelled at each other.

In this example, the parishioners who heard the conversation were simply attuned to the content dimension and failed to understand that the ten-year relationship between Father Paul and Corrine was unique to the two of them. Such direct interpersonal exchanges during stressful times were not out of the ordinary. Father Paul and Corrine frequently raised their voices to each other, and neither gave it a second thought. In a case like this, the content should be understood with the relationship in mind.

In this chapter so far, we have explored the definition of interpersonal communication in some detail and have described several principles associated with interpersonal communication. Now that you know what interpersonal communication is, let's focus on some of the misconceptions about interpersonal communication.

Myths about Interpersonal Communication

Maybe it's the media. Maybe it's Hollywood. Maybe it's Dr. Phil or Oprah. Whatever the source, for one reason or another, people operate under several misconceptions about interpersonal communication. These myths impede our understanding and enactment of effective interpersonal communication.

Interpersonal Communication Solves All Problems

We cannot stress enough that simply being skilled in interpersonal communication does not mean that you are prepared to work out all of your relational problems. When you learn to communicate well, you may communicate clearly about a problem but not necessarily be able to solve it. Also, keep in mind that communication involves both talking and listening. Many students have told us during their advising appointments that sometimes when they try to "talk out a problem," they achieve no satisfaction. It seems, then, that with the emphasis the media place on talking, many students forget about the role of listening. We hope you leave this course with an understanding of how to communicate effectively with others in a variety of relationships. We also hope you realize that simply because you are talking does not mean that you will solve all of your relationship problems.

Interpersonal Communication Is Always a Good Thing

National best-selling self-help books and famous self-improvement gurus have made huge amounts of money promoting the idea that communication is the magic potion for all of life's ailments. Most often, communication is a good thing in our relationships with others. We wouldn't be writing this book if we didn't think that! Yet, there are times when communication results in less-than-satisfying relationship experiences. A relatively new area of research in interpersonal communication is called "the dark side" (Cupach & Spitzberg, 1994, 2004; Spitzberg & Cupach, 1998).

The **dark side of interpersonal communication** generally refers to negative communication exchanges between people. People can communicate in ways that are manipulative, deceitful, exploitive, homophobic, racist, and emotionally abusive (Cupach & Spitzberg, 1994). In other words, we need to be aware that communication can be downright nasty at times and that interpersonal communication is not always satisfying and rewarding. Although most people approach interpersonal communication thoughtfully and with an open mind, others are less sincere. To contrast the dark side, we also discuss the **bright side of interpersonal communication**, which focuses on the altruistic, supportive, and affirming reasons that people communicate with others. Look for discussions of the dark and bright sides of interpersonal communication throughout the chapters of this book.

Interpersonal Communication Is Common Sense

Consider the following question: If interpersonal communication is just a matter of common sense, why do we have so many problems communicating with others? We need to abandon the idea that communication is simply common sense.

It is true that we should be sure to use whatever common sense we have in our personal interactions, but this strategy will get us only so far. In some cases, a skilled interpersonal communicator may effectively rely on his or her common sense, but we usually also need to make use of an extensive repertoire of skills to make informed choices in our relationships. One problem with believing that interpersonal communication is merely common sense relates to the diversity of our population. As we discuss in Chapter 3, cultural variation continues to characterize U.S. society. Making the assumption that all people intuitively know how to communicate with everyone ignores the significant cultural differences in communication norms. Even males and females tend to look at the same event differently (e.g., Dow & Wood, 2006).

dark side of interpersonal communication

Negative communication exchanges between people, such as manipulation, deceit, and verbal aggression.

bright side of interpersonal communication

Altruistic, supportive, and affirming communication exchanges between people.

To rid ourselves of the myth of common sense, we simply need to take culture and gender into consideration.

Interpersonal Communication Is Synonymous with Interpersonal Relationships

We don't automatically have an interpersonal relationship with someone merely because we are exchanging interpersonal communication with him or her. Interpersonal communication *can* lead *to* interpersonal relationships, but an accumulation of interpersonal messages does not *automatically* result in an interpersonal relationship. Sharing a pleasant conversation about your family with a stranger riding on the bus with you doesn't mean you have a relationship with that person.

Relationships do not just appear. William Wilmot (1995) remarked that relationships "emerge from recurring episodic enactments" (p. 25). That is, for you and another person to develop an interpersonal relationship, a pattern of intimate exchanges must take place over time. Relationships usually will not happen unless two people demonstrate a sense of caring and respect, and have significant periods of time to work on their relational issues.

Explore the similarities and differences in the way you communicate with your neighbors, family, friends, and coworkers. If you like, you can use your student workbook or your **Understanding Interpersonal Communication** Online Resources to complete this activity.

Interpersonal Communication Is Always Face to Face

Throughout this chapter, most of our discussion has centered on face-to-face encounters between people. Indeed, this is the primary way that people meet and cultivate their interpersonal skills with each other. It is also the focus of most of the research in interpersonal communication. Yet, large numbers of people are beginning to utilize the Internet in their communication with others. This mediated interpersonal communication requires us to expand our discussion of interpersonal communication beyond personal encounters. In the spirit of inclusiveness, we incorporate technological relations into our interpretation of interpersonal communication and devote Chapter 11 to this important topic.

Thus far, this chapter has given you a fundamental framework for examining interpersonal communication. We close the chapter by examining a feature of the interpersonal communication process that is not easily taught and is often difficult to comprehend: ethics.

Interpersonal Communication Ethics

Communication ethicist Richard Johanneson (2002) concluded that "ethical issues may arise in human behavior whenever that behavior could have significant impact on other persons, when the behavior involves conscious choice of means and ends, and when the behavior can be judged by standards of right and wrong" (p. 1). In other words, ethics is the cornerstone of interpersonal communication.

Ethics is the perceived rightness or wrongness of an action or behavior. Researchers have identified ethics as a type of moral decision making, determined in large part by society (Pfeiffer & Forsberg, 2005). A primary goal of ethics is to "establish appropriate constraints on ourselves" (Englehardt, 2001, p. 1). Ethical decisions involve value judgments, and not everyone will agree with those values. For instance, do you tell racist jokes in front of others and think that they are harmless ways to make people laugh? What sort of value judgment is part of the decision to tell or not to tell a joke? In interpersonal communication, acting ethically is critical. As Raymond Pfeiffer and Ralph Forsberg (2005) concluded, "To act ethically is, at the very least, to strive to act in ways that do not hurt other people, that respect their dignity, individuality, and unique moral value, and that treat others as equally important to oneself " (p. 7). If we're not prepared to act in this way, one can conclude that we do not consider ethics important. Overall, being ethical means having respect for others, shouldering responsibility, acting thoughtfully with others, and being honest. The following section fleshes out these ethical behaviors more thoroughly.

Ethics is necessarily part of not only our personal relationships, but our work relationships as well. To get a sense of the interplay between ethics and various jobs, consider Table 1.1 on page 34, which shows what the U.S. public views as being the most and least ethical occupations. See if you agree with how the country views ethical occupations and if your career choice is found among the top 23 listed. What do you think the rankings look like today?

ethics

The perceived rightness or wrongness of an action or behavior, determined in large part by society.

"Miss Dugan, will you send someone in here who can distinguish right from wrong?"

Five Ethical Systems of Communication

There are many ways to make value judgments in interpersonal communication. Researchers have discussed a number of different ethical systems of communication relevant to our interpersonal encounters (e.g., Andersen, 1996; Englehardt, 2001; Jensen, 1997). We will discuss five of them here. As we briefly overview each system, keep in mind that these systems attempt to let us know what it means to act morally.

Table 1.1   Ethics on the job: Views of the most ethical occupations

Occupation	1999 Rating*	2006 Rating*
Nurses	73%	84%
Druggists/pharmacists	69%	73%
Veterinarians	63%	71%
Medical doctors	58%	69%
Dentists	52%	62%
Engineers	50%	61%
Clergy	56%	58%
College teachers	52%	58%
Police officers	52%	54%
Psychiatrists	N/A	38%
Bankers	30%	37%
Chiropractors	26%	36%
Journalists	24%	26%
State governors	24%	22%
Business executives	23%	18%
Lawyers	13%	18%
Stockbrokers	16%	17%
Senators	17%	15%
Members of Congress	11%	14%
Insurance salespeople	10%	13%
HMO managers	10%	12%
Advertising personnel	9%	11%
Car salespeople	8%	7%

*Based on those who responded "very high" or "high" in ethics.

From *USA Today*, December 12, 2006, p. 8A.

categorical imperative

An ethical system, based on the work of philosopher Immanuel Kant, that advances the notion that individuals follow moral absolutes. The underlying tenet in this ethical system suggests that we should act as an example to others.

Categorical Imperative

The first ethical system, the **categorical imperative**, is based on the work of philosopher Immanuel Kant (Kuehn, 2001). Kant's categorical imperative refers to individuals following moral absolutes. This ethical system suggests that we should act as though we are an example to others. According to this system, the key question when making a moral decision is: What would happen if everyone did this? Thus, you should not do something that you wouldn't feel is fine for everyone to do all the time. Further, Kant believed that the consequences of actions are not important; what matters is the ethical principle behind those actions.

For example, let's say that Mark confides to Karla, a coworker, that he has leukemia. Karla tells no one else because Mark fears his health insurance will be threatened if management finds out. Elizabeth, the supervisor, asks Karla if she knows what's happening with Mark because he misses work and is always tired. The categorical imperative dictates that Karla tell her boss the truth, despite the fact that telling the truth may affect Mark's job, his future with the company, and his relationship with Karla. The categorical imperative requires us to tell the truth because Kant believed that enforcing the principle of truth telling is more important than worrying about the short-term consequences of telling the truth.

Utilitarianism

The second ethical system, **utilitarianism**, was developed in 1861 by John Stuart Mill (Capaldi, 2004). According to this system, what is ethical is what will bring the greatest good for the greatest number of people. Unlike Kant, Mill believed the consequences of moral actions are important. Maximizing satisfaction and happiness is essential. For example, suppose you're over at a friend's house and her younger sister is crying incessantly. You notice your friend grabbing her sister, shaking her, and yelling for her to be quiet. Afterward, you observe red marks on the child's arms. Do you report your friend to the authorities? Do you remain quiet? Do you talk to your friend?

Making a decision based on utilitarianism or what is best for the greater good means that you will speak out or take some action. Although it would be easier on you and your friend if you remained silent, doing so would not serve the greater good. According to utilitarianism, you should either talk to your friend or report your friend's actions to an appropriate individual.

The Golden Mean

The **golden mean**, a third ethical system, proposes that we should aim for harmony and balance in our lives. This principle, articulated more than 2,500 years ago by Aristotle (Metzger, 1995), suggests that a person's moral virtue stands between two vices, with the middle, or the mean, being the foundation for a rational society.

Let's say that Cora, Jackie, and Lester are three employees who work for a large insurance company. During a break one afternoon, someone asks what kind of childhood each had. Cora goes into specific detail, talking about her abusive father: "He really let me have it, and it all started when I was 5," she begins before launching into a long description. On the other hand, Jackie tells the group only, "My childhood was okay." Lester tells the group that his was a pretty rough childhood: "It was tough financially. We didn't have a lot of money. But we really all got along well." In this example, Cora was on one extreme, revealing too much information. Jackie was at the other extreme, revealing very little, if anything. Lester's decision to reveal a reasonable amount of information about his childhood was an ethical one; he practiced

utilitarianism

An ethical system, developed by John Stuart Mill, that suggests that what is ethical will bring the greatest good for the greatest number of people. In this system, consequences of moral actions, especially maximizing satisfaction and happiness, are important.

golden mean

An ethical system, articulated by Aristotle, that proposes a person's moral virtue stands between two vices, with the middle, or the mean, being the foundation for a rational society.

the golden mean by providing a sufficient amount of information but not too much. In other words, he presented a rational and balanced perspective. In this case, note that revealing too much and revealing too little may make another awkward or uncomfortable. Finding the "balance" in self-disclosure is especially difficult, a topic we discuss in greater detail in Chapter 8.

Ethic of Care

An **ethic of care**, the fourth ethical system, means being concerned with connection. Carol Gilligan first conceptualized an ethic of care by looking at women's ways of moral decision making. She felt that because men have been the dominant voices in society, women's commitment toward connection has gone unnoticed. Gilligan (1982) initially felt that an ethic of care was a result of how women were raised. Although her ethical principles pertain primarily to women, Gilligan's research applies to men as well. Some men adopt the ethic, and some women do not adopt the ethic. In contrast to the categorical imperative, for instance, the ethic of care is concerned with consequences of decisions.

For instance, suppose that Ben and Paul are having a conversation about whether it's right to go behind a person's back and disclose that he or she is gay (called *outing* a person). Ben makes an argument that it's a shame that people won't own up to being gay; they are who they are. If someone hides his or her sexuality, Ben believes that it's fine to "out" that person. Paul, expressing an ethic of care, tells his friend that no one should reveal another person's sexual identity. That information should remain private unless an individual wishes to reveal it. Paul explains that outing someone would have serious negative repercussions for the relationships of the person being outed and thus shouldn't be done. In this example, Paul exemplifies a symbolic connection to those who don't want to discuss their sexual identity with others.

Significant Choice

The fifth ethical system, **significant choice**, is an ethical orientation conceptualized by Thomas Nilsen (Nilsen, 1966). Nilsen argued that communication is ethical to the extent that it maximizes people's ability to exercise free choice. Information should be given to others in a noncoercive way so that they can make free and informed decisions. For example, if you place a personal ad on the Internet and fail to disclose that you are married, you are not ethical in your communication with others. However, if you give information regarding your relationship status and other details, you are practicing the ethical system of significant choice.

Understanding Ethics and Our Own Values

Ethics permeates interpersonal communication. We make ongoing ethical decisions in all our interpersonal encounters. Should someone's sexual past

ethic of care

An ethical system, based on the concepts of Carol Gilligan, that is concerned with the connections among people and the moral consequences of decisions.

significant choice

An ethical system, conceptualized by Thomas Nilsen, underscoring the belief that communication is ethical to the extent that it maximizes our ability to exercise free choice. In this system, information should be given to others in a noncoercive way so that people can make free and informed decisions.

Table 1.2 Ethical systems of interpersonal communication

Ethical System	Responsibility	Action
Categorical imperative	To adhere to a moral absolute	Tell the truth
Utilitarianism	To ensure the greatest good for the greatest number of people	Produce favorable consequences
Golden mean	To achieve rationality and balance	Create harmony and balance for the community and the individual
Ethic of care	To establish connection	Establish caring relationships
Significant choice	To enable free choice	Maximize individual choice

Adapted from Englehardt, 2001.

be completely revealed to a partner? How do you treat an ex-friend or ex-partner in future encounters? Is it ever okay to lie to protect your friend? These kinds of questions challenge millions of interpersonal relationships.

Raymond Pfeiffer and Ralph Forsberg (2005) conclude that when we are confronted with ethical decisions, "we should not ignore our society's cultural, religious, literary, and moral traditions.

Our values have emerged from and are deeply enmeshed in these traditions. They often teach important lessons concerning the difficult decisions we face in life" (p. 8).

The five ethical systems, summarized in Table 1.2, can give you strategies for making ethical decisions. However, making sense of the world and of our interpersonal relationships requires us to understand our own values. And, these values are apparent not only in our face-to-face conversations, but our online conversations as well. Ethical behavior is essential when we communicate with people whom we don't see or with whom we have no shared physical space. We return to this topic later in the book.

We need to understand that because ethical choices can have lasting physical, emotional, financial, and psychological consequences, a sense of ethics should guide us on a daily basis. Being aware of and sensitive to your decisions and their consequences will help you make the right choices in these changing times.

"On the Internet, nobody knows you're a dog."

Choices for Changing Times: Competency and Civility

Ethics & Choice

We close Chapter 1 by reiterating two themes that guide this book: choice and changing times. Throughout this text, you will explore many topics associated with interpersonal communication. We encourage you to consider the importance of choice and change as you read the material.

Lenora Watkins was clearly in a bind. She had dated Luke for about a month. She didn't have any serious complaints about him but felt that Luke was sending her mixed messages. One day, he'd come over to her dorm room, and they'd sit together studying on the bed. The next time they were together, Luke would act distant, not wanting to even hold her hand. This back-and-forth intimacy was driving Lenora nuts, and she was quite frustrated with the situation.

Lenora thought nothing could be much worse than her current experiences with Luke, so she let her friend Carmen set her up with a coworker. On a coffee date, Lenora met Rodney, a professional who had divorced about three months ago. Lenora and Rodney got along great, and she felt less frustration with him than with Luke. They started dating regularly, and Lenora enjoyed his company a lot.

Lenora wasn't sure what she should do in this situation. Although neither Luke nor Rodney had said they expected an exclusive relationship with her, she knew they probably assumed she wasn't dating anyone else. Plus, she just felt funny trying to juggle the two relationships. She felt her silence to each of the men about the other was a lie of omission, but she wasn't sure what would happen if she told them the truth.

Lenora faces an ethical dilemma. Discuss the ethical problems pertaining to her relationships with Luke and Rodney. How should she handle the question of whether to tell them about each other? Justify your answers by using one or more of the ethical systems of communication (categorical imperative, utilitarianism, golden mean, ethic of care, or significant choice).

Go to your online Resource Center for *Understanding Interpersonal Communication* to access an interactive version of this scenario under the resources for Chapter 1. The interactive version of this scenario allows you to choose an appropriate response to this dilemma and then see what consequences your choice brings about. You can also compare your answers to the questions at the end of the scenario to those provided by the authors and, if requested, email your response to your instructor. (To learn how to get started with your online Resource Center, see the inside front cover of this book.)

communication competency

The ability to communicate with knowledge, skills, and thoughtfulness.

First, we believe that you have an abundance of choices available to you in your communication with others, and we hope that you will always choose to become a more effective communicator. Yet, we know that our communication with others is sometimes filled with anxiety, confusion, unpleasantness, excitement, and angst. Having a toolbox of ways to adapt and respond appropriately to all sorts of communication situations will help you achieve the meanings you intend to convey.

At the core of communication effectiveness are two behaviors: competency and civility. **Communication competency**, or the ability to communicate with knowledge, skills, and thoughtfulness, should be foremost when trying to meet a communication challenge. When we are competent, our communication is both appropriate and effective. We use communication appropriately when we accommodate the cultural expectations for communicating, including using the rules, understanding the roles, and being "other-centered." When we are effective, we have acquired meaning and each communicator has achieved his or her goals in a conversation or a relationship.

As you read the following chapters, you will acquire a lot of knowledge about interpersonal communication. You will also be asked to apply that knowledge as you consider several interpersonal skills that we discuss at the end of each chapter. Developing a large repertoire

of skills and applying them appropriately is a hallmark of a competent communicator.

A second ingredient of being
an effective communicator is civility. **Civil communication** is the acceptance of another person as an equal
partner in achieving meaning during communication. Civility
requires sensitivity to the experiences of the other communicator.
When we are civil communicators,
we avoid sending hateful emails to
others, accept that not all communication encounters will go our
way, acknowledge multiple viewpoints, and avoid harming others.
And, although most people would
state that being civil is critical in
society, "we do not yet know
enough about what makes people
more civil to one another" (Poole &
Walther, 2002, p. 11). Therefore, learning about interpersonal communication will assist you in being part of a "civil"ization.

These days, civil communication seems to be lacking. We have witnessed
profanity in Congress, name-calling on talk radio, family members openly
attacking each other on television talk shows, and people belittling of individuals who lack English language skills. On a more personal level, you may
have been the recipient of incivility by classmates and even close friends. As
interpersonal communicators, we should remain intolerant of such uncivil
interactions. Throughout this book, we will offer ways to enhance civil
communication.

As we have already noted, we live in changing times. Communication
skills that were once effective may have to be revisited. Adapting to the cultures and individuals around us is paramount in a country where race, ethnicity, gender, sexual identity, religion, and belief systems pervade contemporary conversations. As you learned earlier in this chapter, interacting with
others is often challenging because of their various fields of experience. Varying backgrounds can affect how a message is sent and received.

Assess your current communication skills by going to your online
Resource Center for *Understanding Interpersonal Communication* to access
Interactive Activity 1.2: Communication Skills Test. (To learn how to get started
with your online Resource Center, see the inside front cover of this book.)

interpersonal explorer

Before you finish reading this chapter, take
a moment to review the theory discussed.
How do you think this theory can help
you better understand interpersonal
communication?

Theory
• **Semiotics**
The study of symbols, their meaning, and
their use

Explore your interpersonal choices
Are you ready to explore your choices regarding interpersonal communication?
Use your online Resource Center for *Understanding Interpersonal Communication* to access an interactive simulation that allows you to view the beginning
of an interpersonal scenario between roommates, make a choice

about how the people in the scenario should proceed with their
interaction, consider the consequences of your choice, and
then see three possible outcomes to the interaction.

civil communication

*The acceptance of another
person as an equal partner in
achieving meaning during
communication.*

Summary

We often take our ability to communicate for granted, and the majority of people living in the United States believe they communicate well. However, some people experience communication apprehension in uncomfortable situations, and all of us can improve our interpersonal communication skills in some way.

Interpersonal communication is a complex process that is unique from other forms of communication, such as intrapersonal, small group, organizational, mass, and public. The definition of interpersonal communication has evolved over the years as several models of communication have been advanced. The earliest, the linear model, says that communication is a one-way process in which a sender transmits a message to a receiver. In this model, several types of noise—physiological, physical, psychological, or semantic—can interfere with a message while it's being transmitted. The linear view also specifies that context—be it physical, cultural, or social-emotional—affects communication. The drawback of this model is that it fails to account for the receiver as an active participant in conversations.

According to the interactional model, communication goes from sender to receiver and from receiver to sender. This approach focuses on feedback, which can consist of words (verbal) or body language (nonverbal). Feedback can be internal, meaning you assess your own communication, or external, meaning you receive feedback from others. The drawback of this model is that it assumes that nonverbal and verbal messages cannot be sent concurrently.

The transactional model views communication as a cooperative process in which the sender and receiver are both responsible for the effectiveness of communication. In this model, messages build upon each other as people negotiate shared meaning. This model also takes into account people's fields of experience, which are their culture, heredity, and personal history. The more people's fields of experience overlap, the more they have in common, which can lead to more and deeper personal communication. The transactional model may soon become a bit outdated because technological communication, such as email, may affect scholars' view of the communication process.

Another way to understand the nature of interpersonal communication is to look at the interpersonal communication continuum. Interactions come in all degrees of closeness, not just the extremes of impersonal and interpersonal, which are at either end of the continuum. Where an interaction falls on the continuum depends on the relational history, relational rules, and relational uniqueness of the people involved.

After you understand the definition, evolution, and nature of interpersonal communication, you can appreciate its value. Employers look for strong interpersonal skills in their employees, and good communication skills can reap personal benefits as well. To make the most of interpersonal communication, you need to understand that it is unavoidable, is irreversible, involves symbol exchange, is rule-governed, is learned, and involves both content and relationship dimensions. Also, you need to avoid the common myths of interpersonal communication, such as that it will solve all your problems, is always a good thing, is common sense, is synonymous with interpersonal relationships, and is always face to face.

Finally, you have to understand the ethics—that is, the perceived rightness or wrongness of an action or behavior—involved in interpersonal communication. Five systems—categorical imperative, utilitarianism, ethic of care, golden mean, and significant choice—can guide you, but ultimately you need to understand your own values as well as the consequences of your actions. This book is geared to improve your communication competency and civility in the changing times in which we live.

Understanding Interpersonal Communication Online

Now that you've read Chapter 1, use your online Resource Center for *Understanding Interpersonal Communication* for quick access to the electronic study resources that accompany this text. Your online Resource Center gives you access to the video of Jackie and Scottie's interaction on page 3, the Communication Assessment Test on page 5, the Your Turn journal activity on page 32, the Ethics & Choice interactive activity on page 38, the Interpersonal Explorer activity on page 39, InfoTrac College Edition, and study aids including a digital glossary, review quizzes, and the chapter activities.

Terms for Review

bright side of interpersonal
    communication 31
categorical imperative 34
channel 13
civil communication 39
communication
    apprehension 4
communication
    competency 38
communication models 12
content level 29
context 14
cultural context 14
dark side of interpersonal
    communication 31
ethic of care 36
ethics 33
external feedback 16
feedback 16

field of experience 18
golden mean 35
historical context 15
interactional model of
    communication 15
intercultural communication
    apprehension 4
internal feedback 16
interpersonal
    communication 10
irreversibility 26
linear model of
    communication 12
meaning 10
message 12
message exchange 10
noise 13
physical context 14
physical noise 13

physiological noise 13
process 10
psychological noise 13
receiver 12
relational history 21
relational rules 22
relational uniqueness 22
relationship level 29
rule 27
self-actualization 24
semantic noise 13
semiotics 26
sender 12
significant choice 36
social-emotional context 15
symbols 26
transactional model of
    communication 17
utilitarianism 35

Questions for Understanding

Comprehension Focus

1. Distinguish between interpersonal communication and the other types of human communication.

2. Compare and contrast the primary models of communication.

3. Identify several principles associated with interpersonal communication.

4. Explain the myths pertaining to interpersonal communication.

5. Why should we consider ethical systems of communication while relating to others?

Application Focus

1. CASE IN POINT Our chapter opening story represents the sort of interpersonal exchanges we all often experience. Do you believe that Scottie and Jackie's dialogue is realistic? Discuss the various types of conversations that start out quite simply and then proceed to a more complex level.

2. Discuss how you developed your interpersonal communication skills before enrolling in this course. What strategies did you undertake—if any—to make sure that meaning was achieved in your exchanges? Include examples in your response.

3. Indicate times when physiological, physical, psychological, or semantic noise affected how you received a message. Recount the specifics of the situation and explain how you managed the noise.

4. What do you hope to gain from enrolling in this course? What practical results do you expect to gain from studying interpersonal communication?

5. Discuss your career choice and how you think interpersonal communication skills will be needed in your future occupation.

Interactive Activities and InfoTrac College Edition Exercises

Interactive Activities

InfoTrac College Edition Exercises

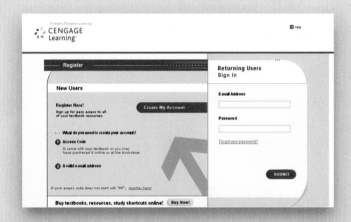

Chapter 2

Communication, Perception, and the Self

chapter ✚ goals

Explain the influences on the perception process

Discuss the dimensions of self-concept

Identify the relationship between identity management and facework

Describe the strategies for identity management

Select skills for perception checking

CASEᴵɴPOINT

As he approached the third-floor waiting room late in the evening, Dr. Gomez felt butterflies in his stomach. He was used to giving bad news to families, but he was especially troubled about telling Elise and Barry Camara that their baby girl was going to die soon. All he could think about was what it would be like to be told similar news about his 4-year-old daughter, Isabella. Entering the waiting room, he saw a fragile mother and father sitting on the arms of overstuffed chairs. He could tell by looking at their red eyes that the two had been crying. Dreading the inevitable communication, the doctor took a deep breath and asked the parents to enter the private conference room. This was a scene that the physician had been through before with other families. Yet, talking to Elise and Barry seemed to be particularly difficult. In the room, holding the mother's hand, he related the terrible news. He listened as the parents talked together. He watched them hold each other and cry in each other's arms. As Barry Camara turned to shake Dr. Gomez hand, the doctor returned the tender shake. He immediately sensed the couple needed time alone.

Dr. Gomez left the conference room and looked down at his hands; they were trembling. He thought about his Isabella. He also thought about his other patients who were near death and how he handled giving this type of news to their families. As he walked into the physicians' lounge, Roberto Gomez kept hoping that the couple could see how terrible he felt. He didn't want to be viewed as a cold-hearted medical professional. He wished that the Camaras could see him as a compassionate person who was trying to overcome some of his own personal grief about the situation. Doctors are usually viewed, he thought, simply as messengers. They communicate something good or bad to a patient and then go along their way. He lay down, closed his eyes, and thought about his precious daughter and how lucky he was to have a healthy toddler.

Go to your online Resource Center for *Understanding Interpersonal Communication* to watch a video clip of Dr. Gomez's interaction with the Camaras about their daughter.

> Access the resources for Chapter 2 and select "Dr. Gomez" to watch the video (it takes a minute for the video to load). As you watch Dr. Gomez talk with the Camaras and think about his own daughter, consider his self-concept dilemma. > Do you believe he handled the situation appropriately? You can respond to this and other analysis questions, and then click "Done" to compare your answers to those provided by the authors.

L ook around you right now—at your apartment, office, or dorm room. Are people milling around? Is music playing? Is the television on? Is your computer turned on and logged on to a particular website? Is your cell phone ringing? What are you wearing? Do you hear noises outside? Are you sick or healthy? Are you fully awake?

Now think about how you felt the last time you had a heated argument with another person. What did you find particularly aggravating about the argument? How did you feel about yourself as you engaged in the conflict? What reactions did you receive from the person you were arguing with during the exchange? Did anyone "win" the argument? If so, how did that happen? How do you think you will handle the next conflict with this person?

You answered these questions based on two important topics in interpersonal communication: perception and the self. As you stopped to consider what was around you, you perceived your immediate surroundings. Some things you may have noticed before we prompted you to do so. However, you may not have thought about other things until we mentioned them. In both cases, you were engaged in the perception process.

As you thought about the last argument you had, you inevitably had to look at another critical part of interpersonal communication: the self. We asked you to think about your personal reactions to the conflict and how the conflict affected you. You probably thought about the effect of the conflict on your relationship with the other person. You also likely considered how your identity influenced the type of conflict and the way the conflict developed. These considerations are part of your "self."

We discuss the perception process and an understanding of the self together in this chapter for a few reasons. First, we perceive the world around us with a personal lens (Stone, Patton, & Heen, 2002). That lens is necessarily part of our perceptions. Second, we can't talk about perception unless we talk about how those perceptions influence and affect all aspects of our self. Finally, we believe that perceiving requires an understanding of the self. In other words, we can't begin to unravel why we recognize some things and ignore others without simultaneously figuring out how our individual identity functions (sometimes unconsciously) within those realizations. Our focus in this chapter is on face-to-face communication between people. Although there are perceptual issues associated with mediated interpersonal relationships, research in interpersonal communication, perception, and technology is still in its infancy.

Our opening story of Dr. Gomez shows the interrelationship between perception and identity. We saw that the physician perceived the couple as grieving. He also sensed that the two needed some private time, so he left them alone. Dr. Gomez's realization that his hands were trembling shows that the physician was aware of his own physiological reactions to his news. Finally, think about Dr. Gomez's concern about how the Camaras perceived him. It seems clear that their perception affects how Dr. Gomez views himself.

As Joseph Forgas (2002) states, perception and individual identity go hand in hand. This intersection is the focus of our chapter. We begin by explaining the perception process.

Understanding Perception: A Seesaw Experience

In most of our interpersonal encounters, we form an impression of the other person. These impressions, or perceptions, are critical to achieving meaning. The process of looking at people, things, activities, and events can involve many factors. For instance, in a face-to-face meeting with a teacher to challenge a low grade on a paper, you would probably notice not only your instructor's facial reactions and body position but also your own. You might also be attentive to the general feeling you get when going into the instructor's office. And you would probably prepare for the encounter by asking other students what their experiences with the instructor had been with respect to grade challenges.

Perceiving an interpersonal encounter, then, involves much more than hearing the words of another person. Perception is an active and challenging process that involves all five senses: touch, sight, taste, smell, and hearing. Through perception, we gain important information about the interpersonal communication skills of others and of ourselves. For our purposes, then, we define **perception** as a process of using our senses to respond to stimuli. The perception process occurs in four stages: attending and selecting, organizing, interpreting, and retrieving. Because perception is the foundation of all of our interpersonal communication, we will describe each stage (see Table 2.1 on page 48).

Attending and Selecting

The first stage, **attending and selecting**, requires us to use our visual, auditory, tactile, and olfactory senses to respond to stimuli in our interpersonal environment. When we are attentive and selective, we are **mindful**. Ellen Langer (1989) believes that mindful communicators pay close attention to detail. Being mindful means being observant and aware of your surroundings. In the case of interpersonal communication, this includes engaging your senses. For example, take Dr. Gomez's mindfulness as he attended to the parents' grief, his own personal reaction to the news, and his perceptions of how the couple might perceive him as a medical professional. Further, he is attentive and focused. He saw the couple's sorrowful expressions (sight), held the mother's hand (touch), and listened as they talked about their situation (hearing).

Dr. Gomez was in a situation that called for mindfulness, but not every situation requires complete mindfulness. We are constantly bombarded with stimuli that make it almost impossible to focus on every detail of an encounter.

perception

The process of using our senses to understand and respond to stimuli. The perception process occurs in four stages: attending and selecting, organizing, interpreting, and retrieving.

attending and selecting

The first stage of the perception process, requiring us to use our visual, auditory, tactile, and olfactory senses to respond to stimuli in our interpersonal environment.

mindful

Having the ability to engage our senses so that we are observant and aware of our surroundings.

Table 2.1   Stages of the interpersonal perception process

Stage	Description	Example
Attending and selecting	First stage in the perception process. It involves sorting out stimuli. We choose to attend to some stimuli and to ignore others.	At the campus library, Kendrick notices his friend talking to a woman in one of his classes he had wanted to meet and date.
Organizing	Second stage in the perception process. It involves categorizing stimuli to make sense of them.	Kendrick creates the belief that his friend and the woman are close.
Interpreting	Third stage in the perception process. It involves assigning meaning to stimuli.	Kendrick decides not to ask his classmate out for a date because she is already dating his friend.
Retrieving	Fourth stage in the perception process. It involves recalling information we have stored in our memories.	Kendrick remembers that the two were together at a concert on campus a few weeks earlier.

As a result, we use **selective perception**. When we selectively perceive, we decide to attend to things that fulfill our own needs, capture our own interests, or meet our own expectations. We pay attention to some things while ignoring others. You can explore this idea further in an article that discusses how we attend to and select what is important to us from the sometimes overwhelming number of messages we receive each day. Go to your online Resource Center for *Understanding Interpersonal Communication* to access *InfoTrac College Edition Exercise 2.1: Attending to What Is Important* under the resources for Chapter 2. Read "Bet You Can't Remember How to Tie the Bows on Your Life Jackets," available through InfoTrac College Edition.

In our relationships with others, we use selective perception all the time. For example, let's say that Luke has decided to end his relationship with Melissa. He explains that he thinks it is in her best interest as well as his for them to break up. However, he says that he has learned a lot while in the relationship. Luke continues talking, telling Melissa several of the things he feels he learned from being with her, and explains that he is grateful to have spent time with her.

As Melissa selectively perceives this unexpected conversation, she probably attends to the reason why Luke is breaking up with her. Regardless of everything else Luke says, Melissa listens for a particular piece of information. As a result, she filters and ignores other information, such as what Luke learned while being in the relationship. As would most people in such a situation, Melissa wants to know what motivated Luke's decision to break up. In addition to selectively perceiving his words, Melissa also selectively attends to

selective perception

Directing our attention to certain stimuli while ignoring other stimuli.

some of Luke's nonverbal signals while ignoring others. His eye contact and tone of voice, for instance, are especially important to her.

In this example, Melissa could consider a number of different stimuli—Luke's behaviors, the time of day, the noises in the room, and so on. But, she remains focused on fulfilling her need to hear why the relationship no longer works for Luke.

Organizing

After we are done selecting and attending to stimuli in our environment, we need to organize them in such a way that we can make sense of them. The **organizing** stage in the perception process requires us to place what are often a number of confusing pieces of information into an understandable, accessible, and orderly fashion. We frequently categorize when we organize. For example, patients organize information they receive from physicians to reduce their uncertainty about their illness. Because doctors tend to use language that is highly abstract and usually technical, patients must organize the doctor's confusing information into specific and understandable bits of information. Researchers have found that patients' organizing reduces their uncertainty and results in a clearer understanding of their illness (Babrow, Hines, & Kasch, 2000).

When we organize, we usually use a **relational schema** (Baldwin, Keelan, Fehr, Enns, & Koh-Rangarajoo, 2006), which is a mental framework or memory structure that people rely on to understand experience and to guide their future behavior. We need a recognized way of understanding something or someone. Therefore, we use schema to help sort out the perception process. Each time we communicate, we use a relational schema to facilitate that communication. For example, you may classify your boss according to *leadership style* (autocratic, diplomatic, yielding, and so forth), *work ethic* (hard-working, lazy, and so forth), or *personality characteristic* (rude, compassionate, insincere, and so forth). These schemas help you recognize aspects of your boss's communication effectiveness without having to do a lot of thinking. Workers frequently use these types of classifications to help them organize the numerous messages given by a supervisor. For example, if the only types of messages

organizing

The second stage of the perception process, in which we place what are often a number of confusing pieces of information into an understandable, accessible, and orderly arrangement.

relational schema

A mental framework or memory structure that we rely on to understand experience and to guide our future behavior in relationships.

that Jenny gets from her boss are insensitive and rude, she will inevitably categorize all of her boss's comments in that manner, regardless of whether the messages are framed that way.

When organizing, we look for consistencies rather than inconsistencies. Most of us would have a difficult time trying to communicate with each person we meet in the subway, in the elevator, on the street, and in the grocery store in an individual manner. We, therefore, seek out familiar patterns of classifications: seniors, children, men, women, and so forth. Your decision of which classification to use is a selective process because when you choose to include one category, you necessarily ignore or eliminate another.

Organizing is essential because it expedites the perception process. However, the impulse to lump people into recognizable categories can be problematic. Using broad generalizations to describe groups of people is considered stereotyping. **Stereotyping** means having fixed mental images of a particular group and communicating with an individual as if he/she is a member of that group. Not all stereotypes are negative—for instance, many professors stereotype students as wanting to learn or willing to make sacrifices, and many of us view police officers as concerned for our safety. However, in many cases, stereotypes get in the way of effective interpersonal communication. When we stereotype others, we use schema without being concerned with individual differences, and such categorization is problematic when we begin to adopt a fixed impression of a group of people. Consider the following dialogue between Jackson and Ryan, two students who happen to be on the school baseball team, as they talk about their first day of class:

stereotyping

Categorizing individuals according to a fixed impression, whether positive or negative, of an entire group to which they belong.

Jackson:	What's with all these older students in class?
Ryan:	What do you mean?
Jackson:	I mean I need to get an A in this class! It's not fair. They have more time to study because they take only one or two classes. And they keep to themselves.
Ryan:	You're nuts! My fiction class last semester had some nontraditional students in there, and I loved it. They helped a lot in study groups come test time.
Jackson:	And they ruined the curve, right?
Ryan:	Get rid of these issues, man. You certainly don't want other people to think that all baseball players are dumb jocks, right? Think about what you're saying.

In this scene, Jackson obviously uses a unique schema to communicate about nontraditional-aged learners in his class. He stereotypes this group of people as having free time, not wanting to help other students, and being uninvolved in campus activities. Ryan attempts to dispel Jackson's perceptions by focusing on the value of nontraditional students in class and reminding Jackson that he wouldn't want to be treated like a stereotype.

We encounter problems when we act upon our stereotypes in the perception process. When we perceive people to possess a particular characteristic because they belong to a particular group, we risk communication problems. Perceiving men as lacking emotion, immigrants as recipients of public assistance, or car dealers as slick and dishonest makes honest and ethical communication difficult. People who stereotype in this way oversimplify the complex process of perception. It's a delicate balance—we need some shortcuts so all the stimuli bombarding us doesn't overwhelm us, but not so many shortcuts that we treat people unfairly.

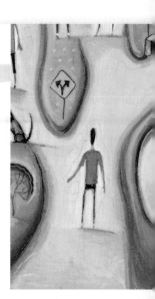

REVISITING CASEINPOINT

1. Discuss how Dr. Gomez used the process of organizing in his conversation with the Camara family.

2. Discuss how Dr. Gomez used the process of interpreting in his conversation with the Camara family.

You can answer these questions online under the resources for Chapter 2 at your online Resource Center for Understanding Interpersonal Communication.

Interpreting

Consider the following two sets of words and phrases:

A. *beer, lake, student ID, cell phone*, The Price is Right

B. *Canada, cheddar cheese, Mercedes-Benz, wheelchair*, Grey's Anatomy

As you looked at both sets of words and phrases, chances are you tried to find some commonality or difference among them. And, despite the fact that the lists were simply random words we chose with no intention, you may have begun to find some ways in which the words are related. This process is at the core of interpretation.

After attention /selection and organization are complete, we are then ready to interpret. When we **interpret**, we assign meaning to what we perceive. Interpreting is required in every interpersonal encounter. And, despite our best efforts, we often fail to bring everything we know about something to the interpretation stage, resulting in a bias or a misinterpretation (Wyer & Adaval, 2003). We need to understand the source's objective(s) in communicating with us, something that requires us to be transactional.

As we established when we discussed the transactional nature of communication in Chapter 1, we need to achieve meaning for interpersonal communication to occur. What should you think of the friend who tells you to "get lost" after an argument? Do you take him literally? Or, what about the neighbor who decides to build a fence and then proceeds to tell you that she loves being your neighbor? How do you assign meaning to the comment

interpreting

The third stage of the perception process, in which we assign meaning to what we perceive.

made by your sibling who says, "So, do you want a closer relationship with me or not?"

The process of interpreting something is not simple; it is influenced by relational history, personal expectations, and knowledge of the self and other. First, your relational history, a concept we addressed in Chapter 1, affects your perception. Consider how you would perceive a statement by a close friend with whom you have had a relationship for more than 11 years versus a coworker with whom you have had a professional relationship for about a year. Because of your previous relationship experiences, perhaps your friend can get away with being sarcastic or pushy. However, your past experiences with the coworker are limited, and you may not be so open to sarcasm or pushiness. This example reflects the impersonal-interpersonal continuum we addressed in Chapter 1.

Second, your personal expectations of an individual or situation can also affect how you interpret behavior. Let's say that you work in an office in which the department supervisor, Jonathan, is grouchy and intimidating. Consequently, whenever department meetings are held, workers avoid expressing their views openly, fearing verbal backlash. At one of these meetings, how would you talk about ways to improve efficiency in the office, fearing that Jonathan would react harshly?

In addition to relational history and personal expectations, your knowledge of yourself and others can greatly affect your interpretation of behavior. For instance, are you aware of your personal insecurities and uncertainties? Do they influence how you receive off-the-cuff or insensitive comments? What do you know about your own communication with others? Do you recognize your strengths and shortcomings in an interpersonal encounter? Finally, what do you know about the other person? What shared fields of experience can be identified in your encounter? What assumptions about human behavior do you and others bring into a communication exchange? Such questions can help you assess how much knowledge you have about yourself and about the other communicator.

Retrieving

So far, we have attended to and selected stimuli, organized them, and interpreted them to achieve meaning in the encounter. The final stage of perception, **retrieving**, asks us to recall information stored in our memories. At first glance, retrieving appears to be pretty straightforward. Yet, as you think about it further, you'll see that the retrieval process involves selection as well. At times, we use **selective retention**, a behavior that recalls information that agrees with our perceptions and selectively forgets information that does not. Here is an example that highlights the retrieval process and some potential conflict associated with it.

Crystal sits with her friends as they talk about Professor Wendall. She doesn't really like what she hears. They talk about how boring the professor is and that his tests are too hard. They also make fun of his Southern drawl as they imitate his teaching. Crystal remembers that she had Professor Wendall for a class more than two years ago, but doesn't recall him being such a bad professor. In fact, she remembers the biology course she took from him as challenging and interesting. It doesn't make sense that her friends don't like Professor Wendall.

So, why do Crystal's friends and Crystal perceive Professor Wendall differently? Crystal has retrieved information about her professor differently. He may have ridiculed students, but Crystal doesn't recall that. She remembers his accent, but she does not remember it causing any problems. She also recollects Wendall's exams to be fair; she never received anything below a grade of B. Crystal's retrieval process, then, has influenced her perception of Professor Wendall in the classroom. When we exercise selective retention in the perception process, then, it affects our communication with others.

So far, we have examined the perception process and its components. As we know, interpersonal communication can be difficult at times. Understanding how perception functions in those encounters helps clarify potential problems. We now turn our attention to several influences on our perception process. As you will learn, a number of factors affect the accuracy of our perceptions.

Influences on Perception

When we perceive activities, events, or other people, our perceptions are a result of many variables. In other words, we don't all perceive our environment in the same way because individual perceptions are shaped by individual differences. We now discuss five factors that shape our perceptions: culture, sex and gender, physical factors, technology, and our sense of self.

Culture

Culture is an important teacher of perception (Martin & Nakayama, 2007) and provides the meaning we give to our perceptions (Chen & Starosta, 2006). In Chapter 3, you will learn how culture pervades our lives and affects communication. With regard to perception, culture dictates how something should be organized and interpreted. For instance, Bantu refugees from Somalia perceive time differently after they arrive in the United States. In Somalia,

retrieving
The fourth and final stage of the perception process, in which we recall information stored in our memories.

selective retention
Recalling information that agrees with our perceptions and selectively forgetting information that does not.

they do not have wall clocks or watches, but in the United States, they learn to be punctual and watch the clock. In addition, William Hamilton (2004) notes:

> Bantu parents learn that hitting their children is discouraged, though that was how they were disciplined in Africa. . . . they learn that Fourth of July fireworks are exploded to entertain not kill, and that being hit by a water balloon, as Bantu children were in one incident at school, is a game and not a hateful fight. (p. A14)

As another example, in the United States, most people expect others to maintain direct eye contact during conversation. This conversational expectation is influenced by a European American cultural value. However, traditional Japanese culture does not dictate direct eye contact during conversation (McDaniel, 2005), so we may feel a classmate from Japan is not listening to us during conversation when he or she doesn't maintain eye contact. As a final illustration, the teachings of Islam and Christianity guide many Lebanese American families in virtually every decision of life, including birth, death, education, courtship, marriage, divorce, and contraception (Hashem, 1997). This adherence to religious principles may be difficult for someone without any religious connection to understand. Recall that each time you communicate with another person, you're drawing upon relational schema, a topic we discussed earlier. It may be difficult for two people with differing cultural backgrounds to sustain meaning if they are using two different schemata. We highlight ways to improve competency in this area at the end of the chapter.

To better understand how perceptions stemming from cultural beliefs affect people in important aspects of their lives, read the article "Asian-

Our culture influences how we perceive ourselves and others. By the same token, when we immerse ourselves in another culture, our perception of ourselves and others can evolve and change.

Americans Face Great Wall; Perceptions, Cultural Traditions Hinder Advancement to Top Corporate Ranks," available through InfoTrac College Edition. Go to your online Resource Center for *Understanding Interpersonal Communication* to access **InfoTrac College Edition Exercise 2.2: Cultural Perceptions and the Glass Ceiling** under the resources for Chapter 2.

You can see, then, that cultural heritage affects how people perceive the world. In turn, that same cultural heritage affects how people communicate with and receive communication from others. Cultural variation is sometimes the reason we can't understand why someone does something or the reason why others question our behavior. Although it's natural to believe that others look at things the same way you do, remember that cultures can vary tremendously in their practices, and these differences affect perception.

Sex and Gender

Sex refers to the biological make-up of an individual (male or female). **Gender** refers to the learned behaviors a culture associates with being a male or female. For example, we have a masculine or feminine gender. If we possess both masculine and feminine traits in equally large amounts, we are called *androgynous*. Possessing relatively low amounts of masculinity and femininity is termed *undifferentiated* (see Figure 2.1). It is possible to be a masculine female or a feminine male.

Researchers have investigated the relationship between perception and sex. Looking at perceptions of body type, researchers found that boys and

sex

The biological make-up of an individual (male or female).

gender

The learned behaviors a culture associates with being a male or female, known as masculinity or femininity.

Figure 2.1   Gender roles in communication

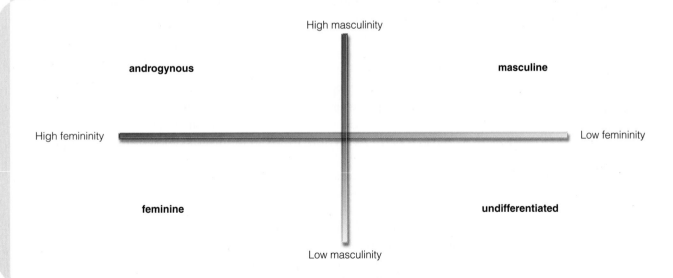

girls in kindergarten and second grade differed in preferences for body types. Girls preferred a thinner figure than boys, and girls perceived thinness as both attractive and feminine. Boys preferred more athletic builds by kindergarten and were indirectly communicating "preferences for being smart, moderately strong, and somewhat prone to fighting" (Miller, Plant, & Hanke, 1993, p. 56). Other researchers have noted that when asked to compare themselves with others, college-aged women—more than men—were inclined to compare themselves with professional models when evaluating their sexual attractiveness and weight (Franzoi & Klaber, 2007).

Many of these differences are a result of the way men and women have been raised. **Gender role socialization** is the process by which women and men learn the gender roles appropriate to their sex (for example, being masculine if you are biologically a male). This socialization affects the way the sexes perceive the world. Messages about masculinity and femininity are communicated to children early in life, and these messages stick with us into adulthood. Sandra Bem (1993) notes that when we understand and organize our world around masculinity and femininity, we are using a **gender schema**. Specifically, she believes that through a schema, we process and categorize beliefs, ideas, and events as either masculine or feminine. If new information doesn't fit our gender schema, Bem maintains that we simply discard it.

Think about your perceptions of the following situations:

- A 5-year-old boy playing house with a 6-year-old neighbor girl
- A retired elderly male dancing with another male at a New Year's Eve party
- A newborn girl wearing a pink dress with flowers
- An adolescent female helping her father change the oil in his car

gender role socialization

The process by which women and men learn the gender roles appropriate to their sex. This process affects the way the sexes perceive the world.

gender schema

A mental framework we use to process and categorize beliefs, ideas, and events as either masculine or feminine in order to understand and organize our world.

Do any of these situations contradict how you normally view male and female behavior? Does the age of the person make a difference? If so, why? What contributes to these perceptions? Parents? Teachers? Peers? Games? In all likelihood, each of these—in some way—has helped shape your current perceptions.

Men and women frequently look at things differently (Ivy & Backlund, 2003), depending on what gender schema they bring to a circumstance. As people sort out the various stimuli in their environment, gender cannot be ignored or devalued. Certainly, men and women can reject gender prescriptions and help society expand its perceptual expectations. However, most people continue to look at their worlds with rigid interpretations of the sexes, resulting in perceptions that may be distorted or inaccurate. To further explore the power of perception in relation to gender and communication, read the article "Exploring the Impact of Gender Role Self-Perception on Communication Style," available through InfoTrac College Edition. Go to your online Resource Center for *Understanding Interpersonal Communication* to access *InfoTrac College Edition Exercise 2.3: Sex, Gender, and Perception about Communication* under the resources for Chapter 2.

Physical Factors

Our physical make-up is another element that contributes to variations in perceptions. *Age* is one example. We seem to perceive things differently as we age because of our life experiences. Being single and in debt at age 19 is different than being in debt as a single parent of three young children at age 45. No one is relying on a single teenager for sustenance, whereas a parent needs to consider his or her three children at home. The aging process allows us to frame our life experiences. Our *health*, too, helps shape perceptions. We broadly define health to include such things as fatigue, stress, biorhythms, and physical ability. For instance, women with HIV/AIDS (Cline & McKenzie, 1996), individuals who are terminally ill (Thompson, 1996), and alcoholics (Thomas & Seibold, 1996) have all been found to have limitations in their perceptual abilities. Additionally, some people simply do not have the physical *ability* to see another person's behaviors or to listen attentively to his or her words. Others need some accommodation to be able to attend to stimuli in their surroundings. Our senses vary, often according to our physical limitations. Imagine the difficulty a wheelchair-reliant individual has trying to navigate nonaccessible curbs compared with someone who does not use a wheelchair. If you don't use a wheelchair, you won't perceive the curbs as potential obstacles.

For dramatic—and fun—examples of how our visual capabilities affect our perceptions, go to your online Resource Center for *Understanding Interpersonal Communication* to access **Interactive Activity 2.1: Optical Illusions and Perception** under the resources for Chapter 2.

Technology

Now more than ever, technology affects our perceptions. The Internet in particular—which has little oversight and no accountability—requires us to be critical in our perceptions. We need to remember that websites have been created by a variety of people with different backgrounds (for example, psychiatrists, talk-show hosts, video store owners, and so on). Keep in mind that the trustworthiness of websites varies. We revisit this topic in Chapter 11.

Technology makes possible the cultivation of online relationships. If, for instance, you visit a dating website and find a match, you need to remember that you are relying on text written onscreen and a downloaded picture. The picture may be inauthentic or out-of-date, or you might be the victim of someone who gives false information. Further, you are unable to read the facial expressions, listen to the vocal characteristics, look at the clothing, watch the body movement, and observe the eye contact of the other person, all critical parts of the perception process outlined above. In sum, the Internet can leave us relationally shortchanged because we can't perceive the whole picture—we are receiving only what the other person wants us to receive. Likewise, we communicate only what we wish to communicate to the other person. As Sue Barnes (2003) observes, "screen names, signature lines, personal profiles, and personal Web pages can be carefully designed to present an image of self" (p. 133).

The Internet is not the only technological development that affects our perceptions. For example, consider how our perceptions are altered when we observe various people with cell phones, pagers, iPhones, or palm organizers. For instance, what do you think when you see a teenager talking on a cell phone? Now, consider your reaction to an older man in a suit talking on a cell phone while walking down the street. Do you experience any difference in perception? Now, change the context. A teenager is sitting with her mother at the bus stop and the older man is driving in his Saab. Does the context make a difference in your perceptions?

We can't escape the influence that technology has on our perceptions. This influence occurs in both overt and covert ways. We may be conscious of how our perceptions change, or be unaware of technology's influence. Nowadays, the reaction we have to electronic technology ranges from indifference to awe. At times, we expect everyone we meet to own some technology; other times, we are impressed by the latest technology, privately vowing to own it once we have enough money! As you continue to understand your own perceptual behaviors, keep in mind that technology plays a significant role in how those perceptions are developed and sustained.

self-concept

A relatively stable set of perceptions we hold of ourselves.

Our Sense of Self

A final factor that shapes our perceptions is self-concept, which we discuss later in this chapter. For now, it's important to point out that our perceptions of ourselves are influential in the perception process. We define **self-concept** as a relatively stable set of perceptions a person holds of himself or herself. Our self-concept is rather consistent from one situation to another. For instance, our core beliefs and values about our intellectual curiosity or charitable ways stay fairly constant. Self-concept is flexible, though; for example, our beliefs about our ability to climb a mountain may differ at age 30 and age 65.

Self-concept affects our perceptions of others' feelings about us. Generally, statements from people we trust and respect carry more weight than statements from those we don't. Consider, then, the way you would perceive the same words depending on whether they came from a close friend or from a classmate. Suppose, for instance, you perceive yourself to be an excellent listener. If a classmate tells you that she thinks you don't listen well, you might not be as willing to consider changing your behavior as you would if a close friend made the same observation. To further explore the factors that influence our perceptions, such as our needs, values, and education, go to your online Resource Center for *Understanding Interpersonal Communication* to access *Interactive Activity 2.2: Perception Filters* under the resources for Chapter 2. To read an article that examines the link between perception and the self, particularly regarding our positive and negative impressions of others, access *InfoTrac College Edition Exercise 2.4: Positive and Negative First Impressions* to read the article "Quality Interpersonal Communication—Perception and Reality," available through InfoTrac College Edition.

Thus far, we have given you a sense of what perception is, noted why it's important in interpersonal communication, and identified some significant influences on the perception process. Throughout our discussion, you have seen that it's virtually impossible to separate our sense of self from our perceptions. Now, we delve further into the self and explain the importance of the self in interpersonal communication. We start by explaining the self and its dimensions.

Understanding the Self: The "I's" Have It

How do you see yourself? This is the key question guiding our discussion of the self. Answering this question is not easy. Certainly, we realize that you can't answer this question in a word or two. Previously, we noted that self-concept is both fixed and flexible. It makes sense, then, that you would inevitably begin your answer to this question with "well, it depends."

This chapter will help you formulate and clarify a response to this question. If you think "it depends," you're partially correct. However, there are ways to articulate a more complete response. We hope you that you will think about this question as you read this section. We are guided by the following principle as we introduce this information: To have a relationship with someone else, you must first have a relationship with your self. In other words, communication begins and ends with you. Let's explore self-concept and what it entails.

Ethics & Choice

After living in an abusive home environment nearly all her life, Karena Paulsen was looking forward to her upcoming marriage to Nick Corsetti. The two had dated for over two years and felt comfortable with each other and each other's values. Yet, Karena's feelings of self-worth became compromised one day as she and Nick discussed having a family. Karena wanted to wait a few years and try to get her footing at her new job. Nick wanted to have children immediately.

As the two discussed the issue, it became apparent that Karena's past would come into play. Nick told her that the real reason that she wanted to postpone a family had everything to do with her childhood. He reasoned that she had never worked out her "childhood demons," which she feared would prevent her from really loving children of her own. Karena denied such an allegation, trying to explain to Nick her anxiety about discussing her past with him again.

The low-key conversation eventually turned into a shouting match. Karena accused Nick of resurrecting an old issue, and Nick responded by telling Karena that as long as she avoided going to counseling, she couldn't really move on with the subject. He felt that she needed to get in touch with who she was, and that her relationship with her father was significant in how Karena perceived herself.

Karena's and Nick's conflict underscores how important perceptions of the self are in interpersonal relationships. First, comment on whether or not Nick should push Karena to talk about her background with him again. Second, what ethical system of communication should be followed in this example (categorical imperative, utilitarianism, ethic of care, golden mean, significant choice)?

Go to your online Resource Center for *Understanding Interpersonal Communication* to access an interactive version of this scenario under the resources for Chapter 2. The interactive version of this scenario allows you to choose an appropriate response to this dilemma and then see what consequences your choice brings about. You can also compare your answers to the questions at the end of the scenario to those provided by the authors and, if requested, email your response to your instructor.

Self-Concept

Earlier, we defined self-concept as a relatively fixed set of perceptions we hold of ourselves. The self-concept is everything we believe about ourselves. This collection of perceptions is more stable than fleeting, but that does not mean that our self-concept is permanent. One reason self-concept changes is because it emerges from our various interpersonal encounters with others. George Herbert Mead (1934), more than 70 years ago, posited that communication with others shapes personal identity. This theory is called **symbolic interactionism**.

To begin our discussion, consider two versions of the following story regarding Terrence Washington. As a self-employed painter, Terrence relies on small projects to make a living. His recent surgery to correct tendonitis has caused him to be laid up at home, unable to continue to paint homes. His inability to take on jobs has not only caused him some financial problems but has also affected his psychological well-being. Terrence feels useless and can't seem to shake a sense of self-doubt.

Now consider Terrence's situation again. This time, though, Terrence's friends visit him, assuring him that this circumstance is only temporary. One friend suggests that Terrence help her figure out a color scheme for her living room. Another friend gets Terrence a temporary job advising customers in a local paint store. Although he is unable to paint homes, Terrence finds himself as busy as ever. His self-doubt begins to dissipate, and his feelings about himself take on a positive cast.

The two examples result in different self-concepts for Terrence. In the first example, we see a man who is beginning to doubt his own abilities, and whose self-concept will likely proceed into a negative spiral: He wants to get better, but to get better, he needs to feel good about himself. Because he doesn't feel good about himself, he won't get better. The second scenario underscores the importance of others in our self-concept. Terrence's friends positively affect his career prospects, and, in turn, his self-concept.

Figure 2.2 Components of self-concept

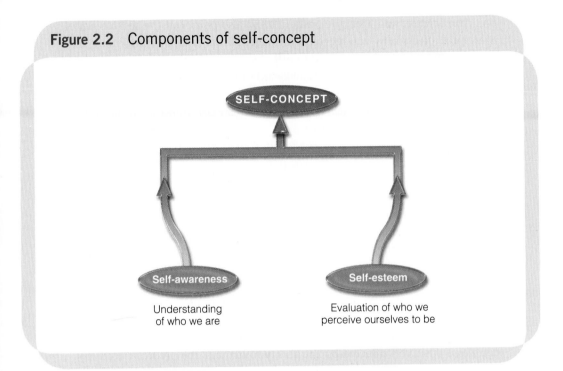

Terrence's self-concept is influenced by both an awareness of himself and an assessment of his potential. These influences, self-awareness and self-esteem, are the two primary components of self-concept (Figure 2.2).

Self-Awareness

Self-awareness is our understanding of who we are. According to symbolic interaction theorists, we begin our lives as blank slates—that is, we are born with no consciousness of who we are. We rely on our parents, guardians, or family members to help us recognize our selves. When we hear our parents cooing to us, for instance, we realize we exist. The adults around us soon start speaking to us in baby talk. This talk may not sound all that important, but it initiates the process of self-awareness that continues throughout our lifetimes.

In Terrence Washington's case, his self-awareness as an adult stems from the belief that he is a painter who has successfully made a living painting other people's homes. Understanding self-awareness serves as the first step toward understanding our self-esteem.

Self-Esteem

Self-esteem is a bit more complicated than self-awareness. Our **self-esteem** is an evaluation of who we perceive ourselves to be. In a sense, our self-esteem is our self-worth, or how we feel about our talents, abilities, knowledge, expertise, and appearance. Our self-esteem comprises the images we hold— that is, our social roles (for example, father, receptionist, electrician, and so on), the words we use to describe these social roles (for example, doting grandparent, courteous police officer, skilled nurse, and so on), and how others see us in those roles (for example, competent, negligible, thorough, and so

symbolic interactionism theory

The theory that our understanding of ourselves and of the world is shaped by our interactions with those around us.

self-awareness

Our understanding of who we are.

self-esteem

An evaluation of who we perceive ourselves to be.

on). Ann Frymier and Marjorie Nadler (2007) also point out the self-esteem of the source affects how you receive a message. This is especially important in situations where you are required to offer feedback. In an interview situation, for example, if your interviewer is awkward or uncomfortable and fumbling through the interview, you, as the potential employee, may have a difficult time achieving meaning. Clearly, the interviewer's communication skills do not elicit an opportunity for clarity.

We develop our self-esteem as a result of overcoming setbacks, achieving our goals, and helping others in their pursuits (Sternberg & Whitney, 2002). Even when we fail, our feelings of self-worth may not be jeopardized if we think we have beaten obstacles along the way. Think, for instance, about the difficulties of divorce. For many married couples, divorce is an acrimonious process pitting one spouse against the other. Yet, some ex-spouses survive these break-ups as friends. Elizabeth Graham (1997; 2003) found that ex-spouses following a divorce do not remain angry forever. What appears to be an insurmountable relational episode, then, can actually result in some couples being able to talk to one another on intimate terms. Some couples, overcoming obstacles, report being able to retain some of the original feelings of affirmation they once held for each other. Clearly, the self-esteem of such couples is positively affected by the ability to manage the divorce effectively.

Other people do not always enhance our feelings of self-worth. Regardless of how many family or friends surround us during difficult times, it might be the case that nothing helps us feel better about ourselves. At times, others may unwittingly contribute to our negative self-perceptions. For example, if you try to encourage someone after the loss of a relational partner by showering him with platitudes or cliché phrases (for example, "I'm sure you'll make it" or "Hey, not all relationships were meant to be"), you may unknowingly cause your friend to feel worse.

Like our self-concept, self-esteem may fluctuate. One day we consider ourselves to be excellent, and the next day we are down on ourselves. This variation in self-esteem is often due to our interactions with others in our lives. We usually listen more carefully to those we admire or whose previous advice was worthwhile. We generally reject the opinions of those we don't know. Most of us are able to understand that one situation shouldn't necessarily affect our feelings of self-worth.

Explore a time when your self-concept was affected by your communication with another person. If you like, you can use your student workbook or your **Understanding Interpersonal Communication** Online Resources to complete this activity.

Self-Fulfilling Prophecy

The self is also formed, in part, by the predictions you make about yourself. When predictions about a future interaction lead you to behave in ways that make certain that the interaction occurs as you imagined, you have created a **self-fulfilling prophecy**. Our self-concepts frequently lead to self-fulfilling prophecies. These prophecies may either be *self-imposed*, which occurs when your own expectations influence your behavior, or *other-imposed*, which occurs when the expectations of another person influence your behavior. Self-fulfilling prophecies can take place within a number of interpersonal situations, from the family to the workplace. Consider the following:

- Mario is nervous about talking to someone he respects and admires, thinking that he probably is going to blunder when he speaks with that person. When he meets the person, he trips over his words.

- Hank approaches a job interview thinking that his job expertise and communication skills will get him the job and he prepares thoroughly for the interview. The job is offered to him.

Although each of these prophecies is different, self-fulfilling prophecies usually follow a pattern. First, we form expectations of ourselves, others, or particular events. Next, we communicate those expectations to others. Third, others respond to our behaviors. Fourth, our expectations become reality, and our expectations confirm our original thinking about ourselves. However, each stage returns to the first stage, because the original perception prompted the prophecy itself (Figure 2.3). Here is an example of how self-fulfilling prophecies function in a person's life.

As a young child, Jennifer felt that she was ugly and awkward. As a result, she wasn't particularly social and avoided talking to people face to face, especially in social settings (Step 1: Form expectation of event). While attending a

self-fulfilling prophecy

A prediction or expectation about our future behavior that is likely to come true because we believe it and thus act in ways that make it come true.

Figure 2.3 Stages of self-fulfilling prophecies

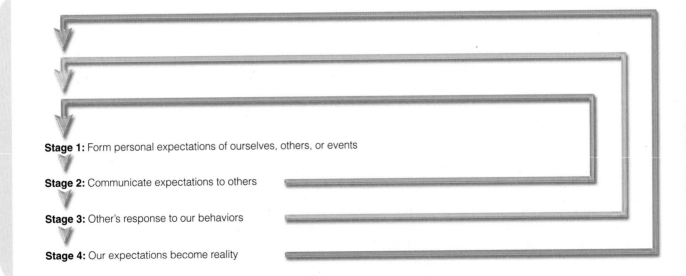

Stage 1: Form personal expectations of ourselves, others, or events

Stage 2: Communicate expectations to others

Stage 3: Other's response to our behaviors

Stage 4: Our expectations become reality

wedding reception, Rodney, one of the guests at her table, asked Jennifer to dance. She told him that she was not a good dancer, was not interested in making a fool of herself on the dance floor, and did not want to dance with Rodney (Step 2: Communicate expectation to other). When Rodney returned to his seat, he thought to himself: "Wow, she is shy! And talk about not wanting to hang out with people" (Step 3: Others respond to behavior). On the other hand, Jennifer thought that Rodney did not want to talk to her because she was not as pretty or outgoing as the other women at the reception (Step 4: Confirmation of original perception).

To read about a famous and interesting study that tested the power of self-fulfilling prophecies in an elementary school class, go to your online Resource Center for *Understanding Interpersonal Communication* to access *Interactive Activity 2.3: Pygmalion in the Classroom* under the resources for Chapter 2. In addition, further explore how the ideas of self-concept and self-fulfilling prophecy can apply to the workplace by accessing *InfoTrac College Edition Exercise 2.5: The Self and the Workplace* to read the article "Quality Interpersonal Communication—Managing Self-Concept," available through InfoTrac College Edition.

As you can tell, the self doesn't simply develop without being influenced in some way. After you gain an understanding of your self, you can begin to address how you present your self to others. Researchers refer to this as identity management, which is the topic we explore in the next section.

Identity Management: Let's Face It

At the heart of our discussion of the self is **identity management theory** (Cupach & Imahori, 1993), which refers to the ways we handle the various situations in which we find ourselves. In a general sense, one's identity is viewed as "what is attached to an individual due to his or her membership in a particular category," such as sex, age, occupation, and so on (Heisterkamp & Alberts, 2000). This theory suggests that people behave according to their goals and that a person's competency and identity all work together in our interactions with others (Imahori, 2006). When we manage our identities, we decide upon a particular communication behavior to influence how others perceive us. Another important reason to communicate our identities is to be active citizens. As Nikolas Coupland and Jon Nussbaum (1993) state, "to be our social selves, to be individuals functioning within social and political communities, we need to *voice* our identities and so participate in the reproduction of these communities" (p. 1).

identity management theory
The theory that explains the manner in which you handle your "self" in various circumstances; includes competency, identity, and face.

One of the first people to discuss identity management was sociologist Erving Goffman (1959). Goffman believed that identity is best explained using an analogy to theatrical performances. He believed that "when an individual appears before others, he [or she] will have many motives for trying to control the impression they receive of the situation" (p. 15). Goffman goes on to say that we play characters in a performance and are concerned about "coherence among setting, appearance, and manner" (p. 25). In other words, we are actors who "perform" for the audiences around us. And, subsequently, "the performer requests that the audience takes his or her performance seriously" (Dillard, Browning, Sitkin, & Sutcliffe, 2000, p. 405).

This image of a theatrical production may seem a bit odd to you. After all, who wants to admit to "acting" in an interpersonal encounter? We're not like the monarchy who "hold court" with the public or the Pope who is often associated with "having an audience." Still, Goffman believes that we all take on particular social roles and manage these roles to achieve meaning in our relationships with others.

Identity management does not happen without some risk and consequence. For instance, suppose that Victor is a 25-year-old who decides to move back in with his parents for financial reasons, one of a group of people that the Population Reference Bureau calls "boomerang kids" (http://www .prb.org/Articles/2006/TheUnitedStatesat300 Million.aspx). The rules that were once part of the household (for example, "No profanity" or "Clean up your room") may now seem out of date to Victor. As he figures out how to act at home and in turn, formulate his "new identity," he may reject the household rules because he feels that he is too old to have to abide by them. Yet, what happens if his mom or dad requires adherence to the rules? Aren't they also managing their identity as Victor manages his? How Victor handles these different identities will affect the quality of the interpersonal communication he has with his parents.

Because identity management requires some risk, we may find ourselves in situations that compromise our sense of self. We become preoccupied with protecting the image we decide to present to others. In doing so, we are engaged in facework, a topic we now explore in more detail.

© Creatas Images/Jupiter Images

IPC $^{in}_{the}$ News

Communication may not always be a matter of life and death, but according to an article in *The Oakland Tribune* there are times when communication may be just that influential. This article focused on the "nocebo effect," which scientists from the Centers for Disease Control and Prevention explain is a form of self-fulfilling prophecy in which illness and even death result from a patient's expectation that a drug or illness will be harmful. The article reports on deaths that occur when patients are simply told that they have a fatal diagnosis, like cancer, even when the illness has not yet progressed to a terminal stage. Also explored is the finding that deaths from heart disease are 27 percent higher on the fourth day of the month for people of Asian descent, but not for Caucasians. The word *four* is pronounced similarly to the word *death* in Cantonese, Mandarin, and Japanese. Could it be that the similarity of the words for *four* and *death* induce a self-fulfilling prophecy for death? Although scholars cannot be sure, the idea of death as a self-fulfilling prophecy induced by communication is too consequential to simply ignore.

Holder, D. (2007, November 12). Does the fear of dying become a self-fulfilling prophecy for people? *The Oakland Tribune.*

Identity Management and Facework

In interpersonal interactions, people shape their identities to display a particular sense of self. When we get into conversations with others, we offer our

identity and hope that others will accept it. This is essential to our self-concept overall and to our self-esteem in particular. The image of the self—the public identity—that we present to others in our interpersonal encounters is called **face**. Generally, face is somewhat automatic (Cupach & Metts, 1994). The metaphor of face pervades U.S. society. We talk about "saving face," "in your face," and especially in this book, "face-to-face" communication all the time. Face is how you want to be perceived by others, how you want others to treat you, and how you end up treating others. The essence of face, some scholars contend (Domenici & Littlejohn, 2006), is dignity, honor, and respect.

We take it for granted that there is a give and take in maintaining face. In other words, following the transactional nature of communication that we identified in Chapter 1, both communicators in an interaction are responsible for facework, the set of coordinated behaviors that help us either to reinforce or threaten our competence. Facework is usually a two-person event in an interpersonal relationship. As Cupach and Metts (1994) conclude, "face is not merely what one individual dictates. Rather, partners negotiate (usually subtly) who each other 'is' with respect to one another" (p. 96).

We present two types of face in our conversations with others: positive face and negative face. **Positive face** pertains to our desire to be liked by significant people in our lives. It is the favorable image that people present to others, hoping that others validate that image. We have positive face when others confirm our beliefs, respect our abilities, and value what we value. That's not to say that individuals have to agree with everything we have to say or with everything we believe—that would be impossible! Most of us simply want to relate to people who make efforts to understand, to appreciate, and to respect our perceptions and competencies.

Negative face refers to our desire for others to refrain from imposing their will on us. Negative face is maintained when people respect our individuality and avoid interfering with our actions or beliefs. Again, this is not to say that people will simply become dutiful and obedient in our conversations without challenging us. Rather, we're suggesting that people periodically need to feel autonomous and want others to be flexible enough to respect this need in interpersonal encounters.

face

The image of the self we choose to present to others in our interpersonal encounters.

positive face

Our desire to be liked by significant others in our lives and have them confirm our beliefs, respect our abilities, and value what we value.

negative face

Our desire that others refrain from imposing their will on us, respect our individuality and our uniqueness, and avoid interfering with our actions or beliefs.

When we receive messages that do not support either our positive or negative face, our identities become threatened. Face threats can jeopardize meaning in an interpersonal encounter. As Joseph Forgas (2002) concluded, "to fail in a performance leads to loss of face, which upsets the pattern of social intercourse" (p. 29). If our positive face is threatened—such as when another person challenges our skills—we have to figure out how to deal with the threat to our identity. For instance, let's say that Pat is a hairstylist and that Nola, a client of 19 years, threatens Pat's positive face by asking Pat, "Where *did* you find this horrid color? In your attic?" Because Pat takes pride in her abilities, this insult may be difficult to overcome. Pat will have to figure out a way to preserve her positive face with Nola. Indeed, this process happens frequently in our lives, and we have to learn how to handle these face threats. In the United States, we are normally not conditioned to help others "save" their face (Pan, 2000) although people in other cultures (for example, Asian cultures) are attuned to maintaining everyone's face in an interaction.

As we discuss the topic of identity management, recognize that managing our identities is important because so much of our interpersonal meaning is based upon our competency, identity, and face. One way to work on your identity management is to pay attention to timing. For example, although you might perceive yourself as the sort of person who is not interested in "meaningless jobs," expressing that perception during an interview would be foolish. A second way is to stop worrying about the future; instead committing to conversations as they are happening and concentrating on the message. For instance, if you meet a person to whom you're attracted, be less concerned with what impression you're making on the other person and more focused on the content of the message in your exchange. A third way is to practice self-monitoring. People vary in their abilities to pay attention to their own actions and the actions of others (Snyder, 1979). The term **self-monitoring** refers to the extent to which people actively think about and control their public behaviors and actions. Self-monitoring is important in identity management because people who are aware of their behaviors and the effects of their behaviors in a conversation are viewed as more competent communicators. Be careful, however. Practicing self-monitoring too much will result in being preoccupied with details that may

self-monitoring

Actively thinking about and controlling our public behaviors and actions.

REVISITING
CASEINPOINT

1. *Discuss how identity management functioned in the interaction between Dr. Gomez and the Camara family.*

2. *How does "face" relate to the interaction between Dr. Gomez and Elise and Barry Camara?*

Y*ou can answer these questions online under the resources for Chapter 2 at your online Resource Center for Understanding Interpersonal Communication.*

...with a doctor in the emergency room

After driving a family member to the emergency room, you ask the attending physician whether the illness is serious. She states that you have to wait and see. "Some tests take a long time," she says, "and we still don't have definitive results." As the doctor leaves your side, she comments that "family members are usually quite impatient for test results." First, how does your interpretation of the doctor's message affect your willingness to accept the message as accurate? Second, to what extent is your sense of self influenced by her comments?

person showed up late? What were your thoughts while waiting? If the person was someone you liked, you probably attributed the lateness to something out of his or her control, such as car trouble, congested traffic, disobedient children, and so forth. If the person was someone you didn't know well or didn't like, you probably attributed the delay to something within the person's control. Perhaps you viewed the person's behavior as intentional. Yet, the person might have been late for unforeseen circumstances. We may be "naive," then, to the number of different influences on behavior. In Chapter 7, we look further into how feelings and emotions affect our relationships with others.

Third, the self undergoes a continual process of modification. Our sense of who we are changes as our relationships change. In other words, our identity is a process, not a constant. This conclusion implies that we and our relationships are changing. Consequently, our interpersonal communication should reflect these changes. Think about the way you were as a sophomore in high school. Now look at who you are now. Your perceptions of your own strengths and shortcomings have inevitably changed over the years. Imagine what it would be like if you didn't change or if others didn't change.

Finally, the self responds to a variety of stimuli. To understand this conclusion, consider the fact that we respond to people (e.g., father or mother), surroundings (e.g., noise level or lighting), and technology (e.g., an Internet site or a television program). Each has the capacity to affect the self.

Choices for Checking Perceptions and Improving Self-Concept

You should be developing a clear idea about the importance of perception and the self in our communication with others. How can you work toward checking your perceptions so that you don't make erroneous assumptions about others or their behavior? What can you do to improve your self-concept? How do our perceptions and self-concepts function in our interpersonal communication? Let's look at a number of skills to consider as you respond to these questions.

Improving Perception Checking

When we check our perceptions, we attempt to rid ourselves of our predisposed biases and images of people. Checking our perceptions also helps build meaning in our relationships. Let's examine the five skills of perception checking.

Understand Your Personal Worldview

Each of us enters a communication situation with a unique **worldview**, a personal frame for viewing life and life's events. Your worldview is different from your classmate's. You may believe that humans are basically good creatures; your classmate may have a more cynical view of humanity, citing war, famine, and greed. We all enter interpersonal encounters with various worldviews, and we need to recognize the influence that these views have on our communication.

Realize the Incompleteness of Perception

There is no possible way for us to perceive our environment completely. By its nature, perception is an incomplete process. When we attend to certain aspects of our surroundings, as you learned earlier, we necessarily fail to attend to something else. If you are working on a group project and think a group member is lazy, you should check your perception further. Perhaps there is some other issue, such as working a late-night job or caring for a sick relative, which is contributing to the group member's behavior. And don't forget that people, objects, and situations change, thereby making it important to update your perceptions periodically.

Seek Explanation and Clarification

We need to double-check with others to make sure that we are accurately perceiving a person, situation, or event. Seeking explanation and clarification requires us to foster a dialogue with others. Trying to understand whether or not your perceptions are accurate communicates to others that you are eager to gain an accurate understanding, which will help you achieve meaning in interpersonal exchanges.

Consider the following encounter between Wes and Lee. The two have been happily dating for one month, but their fifteen-year age difference has prompted Wes to reconsider his future with Lee. Wes calls Lee at 10 p.m. to let her know that they had better stop dating. Lee is puzzled by the call because the last time the two were together, three nights earlier, Wes talked about how much he enjoyed being with her. Lee wonders how things could have changed so quickly. Immediately, Lee feels defensive and thinks that Wes is breaking up with her because he is critical of her manner of communicating. She knows she talks a lot, and some of her previous boyfriends didn't

worldview

A unique personal frame for viewing life and life's events.

There are social, collegial, and legal implications to confusing facts with inferences. For instance, if you see Tad staring at a coworker, you may make the inference that Tad is attracted to that coworker. You may subsequently communicate your perception to a colleague, who may then tell another coworker. Soon, despite the fact that Tad was not attracted to the coworker at whom he was staring, a workplace rumor has started. This rumor may affect the work environment, the level of trust among coworkers, and also influence how workplace policies are written, such as those relating to sexual harassment and workplace relationships. Can you identify other consequences of confusing facts and inferences in the workplace?

like that. She doesn't realize that Wes's being 15 years older than her is really what is troubling him.

Most likely, Lee could have avoided her feelings of confusion, frustration, and anger if she had sought out clarification and explanation of Wes's perceptions. If she had, they could have arrived at a more amicable end to their relationship or perhaps even reconciled.

Distinguish Facts from Inferences

One way to explain and to clarify is to distinguish facts from inferences. **Facts** are statements based on observations; **inferences** are personal interpretations of facts. Looking at the tense lips and angry look on a woman at the baggage claim at an airport may prompt you to draw the conclusion that she is unhappy that the airline lost her luggage. But this is your inference, not a fact.

During the perception process, we need to be careful not to confuse facts and inferences. Remember implicit personality theory, which we explained earlier? Take extra care and avoid filling in the blanks or extending a perception beyond the facts. At the very least, recognize when you are using an inference.

Be Patient and Tolerant

We cannot overemphasize the importance of being patient and tolerant in your perceptions. Because we live in an "instant society," we expect things to happen quickly. However, you can't expect to develop quality communication skills overnight; they take time and practice to learn. The effort is worth it, because without patience and tolerance, you won't be able to check the accuracy of your perceptions.

fact

A piece of information that is verifiable by direct observation.

inference

A conclusion derived from a fact, but it does not reflect direct observation or experience.

Improving Self-Concept

When you improve your sense of self, you are on your way toward increasing your self-awareness and self-esteem. In turn, your relationships improve. In this section, we explore five skills necessary to improve your self-concept.

© Brad Wrobleski/Masterfile

Our self-concept often changes as we grow older. Sometimes we want to change the way we see ourselves but we're not sure we can. By taking a calculated risk, you may find that the way you see yourself—and, in turn, the way you see others—can change dramatically.

Have the Desire and Will to Change

As we mentioned earlier in the chapter, our self-concept changes as we grow. Therefore, we should be willing to change our self-concepts throughout our lifetimes. If you want to be more sensitive to others, make that commitment. If you'd like to be more assertive, take the initiative to change. Having the desire or will to change your self-concept is not always easy. We grow comfortable with ourselves, even when we recognize ways we'd like to change. We need to realize that a changing self-concept can help us grow just as much as it can help our relationships grow.

Decide What You Would Like to Change

After you establish a will to change, describe what it is specifically about yourself that needs to change. Further, describe why you feel a change may be needed. Are others telling you to change? If so, what significance do these individuals have in your life? Are their concerns legitimate, or are you uncritically accepting their judgments?

Set Reasonable Personal Goals

Always strive to have reasonable goals. Don't set goals that are impossible to meet. Otherwise, you may feel a sense of failure. A reasonable goal for a college student might be to do all the assigned reading in each class for a semester. Studying hard, reading and rereading the classroom readings and textbook, participating in class when appropriate, and being a good listener seem like reasonable and attainable goals. Setting a goal of getting a perfect grade point average, writing error-free papers, and understanding the course content without asking questions seems unreasonable. And don't expect to be

interpersonal explorer

Before you finish reading this chapter, take a moment to review the theories and skills discussed. How do you think the theories discussed in this chapter can help you better understand interpersonal communication and the self? In what ways can the skills discussed help you interact more effectively with other people in your life?

Theories that relate to perception and the self

- **Symbolic interactionism**
  Our understanding of ourselves and the world is shaped by our interactions with others
- **Identity management theory**
  The manner in which you handle your "self" in various circumstances; includes competency, identity, and face
- **Implicit personality theory**
  Drawing inferences about another's characteristics and communicating with another person based upon those inferences
- **Attribution theory**
  Attaching meaning to another person's behaviors or our own

Practical skills for improving perception checking
- Understand your personal worldview
- Realize the incompleteness of perception
- Seek explanation and clarification
- Distinguish facts from inferences
- Be patient and tolerant

Practical skills for improving self-concept
- Have the desire and will to change
- Decide what you'd like to change
- Set reasonable personal goals
- Review and revise
- Surround yourself with "relational uppers"

Explore your interpersonal choices

Are you ready to explore your interpersonal choices regarding perception and the self? Use your online Resource Center for *Understanding Interpersonal Communication* to access an interactive simulation that allows you to view the beginning of an interpersonal scenario regarding perception, make a choice about how the people in the scenario should proceed with their interaction, consider the consequences of your choice, and then see three possible outcomes to the interaction.

someone that you are not. Avoid societal expectations of perfection. Look beyond the superficial expectations that we find in the media.

Review and Revise

At times, you may make changes to your self-concept that are not entirely beneficial. Think about the implication of these changes and consider revising them if necessary. For instance, you may have tried to be more accommodating to your family members, but the result was that your integrity was trampled. Perhaps you made some changes at work, trying to engage people who annoy you daily, and now you're having trouble getting your work finished on time because these people stop to talk for long periods of time during the day. Perhaps some of your past behaviors now need to be refreshed.

Consider Hillary, who, at age 18, described herself as a "really boring person." To bolster her self-esteem and to assert her independence, Hillary decided to get a tattoo, much to the surprise and shock of her parents. As an 18-year-old, she felt that she was an adult and did not have to abide by her parents' rules. Now, as a 30-year-old, Hillary is rethinking her image-boosting behavior. She thinks that the tattoo, located on her right forearm, communicates an image that is contrary to the one she wants to convey as a middle school teacher. Now, it seems, demonstrating independence is not as important to her self-concept as it used to be.

Occasions in which you revise past changes may force you to think about whether changes to your self-concept were justified in the first place or whether they are appropriate for you now. For Hillary, her reflections on whether or not the tattoo was important at age 18 no doubt occupy her mind from time to time. At age 30, she probably regrets being so impulsive in her behavior without thinking about the consequences.

Surround Yourself with "Relational Uppers"

Think, for a moment, about the amount of stress in your life right now. You may be working full time, raising children, taking a full course load, coping with a health issue, or having a hard time with a particular course. Now, think about hanging around people who do nothing but tell you that you need to change. Or, consider interpersonal relationships with people who constantly tell you that you are deficient in one way or another. We believe that you need to avoid these types of people in favor of **relational uppers**, those people who support and trust you as you improve your self-concept. Take care to surround yourself with relational uppers because these individuals will be instrumental for you to achieve your potential.

relational uppers
People who support and trust us as we improve our self-concept.

Summary

A significant part of our interpersonal communication effectiveness is based upon our perceptions and on our self-concepts. Our perceptions are influenced by our self-identity, and our self-identity is influenced by our perceptions. The two are inseparable in our communication with others.

Perception is the process of using our physical senses to respond to the world around us. The perception process occurs in four stages: attending and selecting, organizing, interpreting, and retrieving. In the attending and selecting stage, we use our senses to respond to our interpersonal environment, then decide which stimuli we will attend to. In the organizing stage, we order the information we have selected so that it is understandable and accessible. In the interpreting stage, we assign meaning to what we perceive, based on our relational history, personal expectations, and knowledge of ourselves and others. In the retrieving stage, we recall information we have stored in our memories, which affects how we communicate with others. Perception is influenced by many factors, including culture, sex and gender, physical factors, technology, and self-concept.

A person's self-concept is the relatively stable set of perceptions a person holds of himself or herself. Our self-concept is shaped by self-awareness, an understanding of who we are; by self-esteem, an evaluation of who we perceive ourselves to be; and by self-fulfilling prophecy, predictions we make about ourselves.

An important component of the self is identity management, or the ways we handle various interpersonal situations to influence how others perceive us. When we present our identity to others, we are presenting a particular sense of self. The image of the self we present to others is called face, and we typically present two types of face in our interactions with others: positive face and negative face. Positive face is our desire to be liked, understood, and respected by others. Negative face is our desire for others to respect our individuality and to refrain from imposing their will on us.

After ridding yourself of your predisposed biases, you can employ several skills to improve your perceptual abilities. First, understand your personal worldview, or personal frame for viewing life and life's events. Second, be aware of why you choose to select and attend to particular stimuli in your interpersonal environment over others, and check your perceptions as needed. Third, check in with others to make sure you are accurately perceiving a person, situation, or event. Fourth, distinguish facts from inferences. And fifth, practice being patient and tolerant.

In addition, you can implement five strategies to improve your self-concept. First, have the desire and will to work at changing your self-concept. Second, make the decision to change and be specific about what you will change. Third, set reasonable personal goals for changing so that you experience success and avoid a sense of failure. Fourth, review and revise your changing self-concept as needed, retaining those changes that are beneficial. And fifth, surround yourself with "relational uppers," people who support and trust you as you work to improve your self-concept.

Understanding Interpersonal Communication Online

Now that you've read Chapter 2, use your online Resource Center for *Understanding Interpersonal Communication* for quick access to the electronic study resources that accompany this text. Your online Resource Center gives you access to the video of Dr. Gomez's interaction with the Camaras on page 45,

the Ethics & Choice interactive activity on page 60, the Your Turn journal activity on page 62, the Communication Assessment Test on page 68, the Interpersonal Explorer activity on page 74, InfoTrac College Edition, and study aids including a digital glossary, review quizzes, and the chapter activities.

Terms for Review

Questions for Understanding

Comprehension Focus

1. What are the stages in the perception process?
2. Define relational schema.
3. Differentiate between positive and negative face.
4. What is a self-fulfilling prophecy?
5. What are the two primary components of self-concept?

Application Focus

1. CASE IN POINT Look again at our chapter opening. Discuss your reaction to the perceptual and self-concept dilemma presented to Dr. Gomez. Do you believe the physician spoke to the family appropriately? Why or why not?

2. How might your personal insecurities or anxieties affect your perception of a college classroom?

3. Explain the perception process by examining how a child and parent may differ on the issue of curfew. Use all the stages of perception in your discussion.

4. Use implicit personality theory to explain how the dating process may function. In your discussion, be sure to include the halo effect and its relationship to dating.

5. Discuss how facework might function in a job interview. Look at face from both the perspective of the interviewer and the interviewee.

Interactive Activities and InfoTrac College Edition Exercises

Interactive Activities

InfoTrac College Edition Exercises

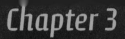

Chapter 3
Communication, Culture, and Identity

chapter ✚ goals

Recognize and understand the complexity of culture

Identify reasons for the importance of intercultural communication

Explain the obstacles to achieving intercultural effectiveness

Employ strategies to improve intercultural communication

CASE IN POINT

Brad Atchison wanted to get away. He had just graduated from college and, although he was in debt, he figured that he could afford a one-week vacation. He heard that it didn't cost that much to travel to Mexico, and the dollar was doing particularly well there. He figured that he would spend most of his time in the bars and on the beach, which shouldn't be too expensive. And he thought this was a once-in-a-lifetime opportunity to get away before job responsibilities set in.

As he waited at the airport for his plane to Mexico City, Brad sat next to Miguel, a 22-year-old Mexican who was going to college in the United States. As guys who were around the same age, Miguel and Brad hit it off immediately. They talked about college life, women, tattoos, and their mutual interest in cycling. But the following comment by Brad caused Miguel to think twice about his new-found acquaintance: "Man, you Mexicans know how to relax. I'd love to take a *siesta* every day!"

At first, Miguel did not know quite what to say, but he knew he had to say something. He didn't want to antagonize Brad, but he also felt that he shouldn't ignore the comment. So, Miguel spoke up: "Look, man, what you don't know about Mexico is obvious. That *siesta* stuff is so old. Don't you know anything about the country you're going to?" Brad replied, "Look, I'm sorry . . . just trying to have some fun here. Heck, I don't know a lot about Mexico, but, let's face it. I'm not on this trip to get a lecture. I'm going to have fun."

A bit of awkwardness developed between the two men. But, Miguel, a newly certified public school teacher, wanted to take this chance to educate Brad. He didn't want to push the issue, but he thought that Brad could handle a little lecture, and, well, he deserved one at this point. As a first-generation college student studying in the United States, Miguel was used to dispelling myths about his country. He decided to take this opportunity to explain to Brad some cultural facts about Mexico. He described dating rituals, the roles of women and men, and the importance of the family in Mexico. Brad listened attentively, interested in what Miguel had to say about his culture. He also felt embarrassed. Brad realized that he should have informed himself about Mexican culture before leaving on the trip. He was grateful to Miguel and hoped he hadn't offended him too much by his ignorance.

Go to your online Resource Center for *Understanding Interpersonal Communication* to watch a video clip of Brad's interaction with Miguel.

> Access the resources for Chapter 3 and select "Brad" to watch the video (it takes a minute for the video to load). As you watch Brad and Miguel talk, consider Miguel's decision to educate Brad about Mexican culture. > Do you think he handled the situation appropriately? > You can respond to this and other analysis questions, and then click "Done" to compare your answers with those provided by the authors.

*M*ost people communicate with the belief that others will understand them. For instance, in the United States, most people don't think twice about using the English language to make their point, despite the fact that many people who live in the United States speak different languages and are members of various cultural groups. Also, most English speakers use their own nonverbal codes without thinking about how nonverbal communication differs across cultures. For example, looking someone directly in the eyes during a conversation is the norm in the United States, but is viewed as disrespectful or a sign of aggression in many parts of the world. In addition, many people in the United States value emotional expressiveness, yet research shows that some cultural groups, such as Chinese Americans, do not freely express their feelings (Gao & Ting-Toomey, 1998). Today more than ever, much of the meaning in our interactions with others depends on the cultural backgrounds of the communicators.

In our opening Case in Point, Brad's understanding of Mexico appeared to be based on outdated images of the country. Fortunately for Brad, Miguel shared with him his firsthand knowledge of Mexican culture. Miguel's information provided Brad with insight that made his subsequent encounters in Mexico much more pleasing than they would have been.

In the first two chapters, we noted that communication is a process influenced by many factors such as gender and identity. In this chapter, we look at the role culture plays in interpersonal communication. Culture pervades virtually every component of interpersonal communication and cultural diversity is a fact of life. By understanding culture, we can learn a lot about the ways we and others communicate.

The focus of this chapter is intercultural communication. For our purposes, **intercultural communication** refers to communication between and among individuals and groups whose cultural backgrounds differ. Some researchers distinguish between communication across national cultures (for example, between people from Japan and from the United States) and communication between groups within one national culture (for example, African Americans and European Americans). In this text, we refer to all such encounters as intercultural encounters. In many U.S. communities, these intercultural encounters were once very rare because most communities were comprised primarily of Caucasians who were fully assimilated into the dominant U.S. culture. But today, according to the 2006 U.S. Census (http://www.census .gov/Press-Release/www/releases/archives/population/010482.html), non-white people of various cultural backgrounds now make up a majority in nearly one-third of the most populous counties in the country and in nearly 1 of every 10 of all 3,100 counties.

intercultural communication

Communication between and among individuals and groups from different cultural backgrounds.

As you read and review the material, keep in mind two of the words in this book's title: "changing times." We live in a society that is more culturally diverse than ever. We describe this cultural complexity in this chapter and look at the significant issues associated with culture and communication. The words of Larry Samovar and Richard Porter (2004) underscore our rationale for this chapter: "What members of a particular culture value and how they perceive the universe are usually far more important than whether they eat with chopsticks, their hands, or metal utensils" (p. 24). Knowledge of others' cultural values and practices enhances intercultural communication.

For intercultural communication to occur, individuals don't have to be from different countries. In a diverse society such as the United States, we can experience intercultural communication within one state, one town, or even one neighborhood. You may live in an urban center where it's likely people from various cultural backgrounds live together. In the South End of Boston, for instance, it is common to see people with Caribbean, Cambodian, and Latino backgrounds all living on the same street. In Milwaukee, one would be able to find both Polish and Mexican communities on the south side of the city.

Trying to understand people who may think, talk, look, and act differently from us can be challenging at times. Just think about the words people use to describe those who may be culturally different from them: odd, weird, strange, unusual, and unpredictable. These associations have existed over centuries. Consider the words of fifth century Greek playwright Aeschylus: "Everyone is quick to blame the alien." As we discuss in this chapter, today, the "alien" takes many troubling shapes and forms, especially with anti-immigration perceptions permeating society.

Intercultural communication theorists (for example, Jackson, 2002) argue that humans cannot exist without culture. Our individuality is constructed around culture. As we learned in Chapter 2, our identities are shaped by our conversations and relationships with others and vice versa. Our cultural background enters into this mix by shaping our identity, our communication practices, and our responses to others. We tend to use other people as "guideposts for normative behavior" (Jackson, p. 360). In doing so, we can focus on how others from diverse cultures differ from us. For instance, when Jean from the United States meets Lee from China in her philosophy class, she might notice how Lee smiles more frequently than her U.S. counterparts. Jean might also observe that Lee is much more deferential to the professor than she and her U.S. friends are. Yet, this comparison is incomplete. Intercultural scholars believe that despite their cultural differences, people continue to have a great deal in common. This chapter explores both what factors culturally bind us as well as what elements divide us.

Defining Culture

Culture is a difficult concept to define, in part because it is complex, multidimensional, and abstract. Some researchers (e.g., Kroeber & Kluckhohn, 1993) have discovered over 300 different definitions for the word! For our purposes, we define **culture** as the shared, personal, and learned life experiences of a group of individuals who have a common set of values, norms, and traditions. The values of a culture are its standards and what it emphasizes most. Norms are patterns of communication. Traditions are the customs of a culture. These values, norms, and traditions affect our interpersonal relationships within a culture. It's almost impossible to separate values, norms, and traditions from any conversation pertaining to intercultural communication.

As we define the term culture, keep in mind that we are embracing a "global" interpretation. That is, we acknowledge culture to include commonly-held components such as race, ethnicity, physical ability, age, gender, and sex. Yet, we also believe that a person's religious identity, career path, sexual identity, and family background are all necessarily part of our discussions of culture. Our examples in this book reflect this expansive view of culture. We now look at three underlying principles associated with our definition of culture: culture is learned, culture creates community, and culture is multileveled.

Culture Is Learned

We aren't born with knowledge of the practices and behaviors of our culture. People learn the values, norms, and traditions of their culture through the communication of symbols for meaning. We learn about culture both consciously and unconsciously. We can learn about culture directly, such as when someone actually teaches us, and indirectly, such as when we observe cultural practices. In the United States, our family, friends, and the media are the primary teachers of our culture.

Let's look at an example of a learned ritual that varies depending on culture. Bradford Hall (2005) observes some differences in dating in New Zealand and the United States. In New Zealand, it is uncommon for someone to exclusively date another unless he or she has gone out with that person in a group of friends first. Even television shows in New Zealand suggest that romantic relationships begin in groups. Further, exclusive dating in New Zealand occurs only after the couple makes long-term relationship plans. As Hall observes (and as most of you already know), in the United States, exclusive dating does not have to be preceded by group interactions, and many people in exclusive dating relationships in the United States haven't made long-term plans.

When you have acquired the knowledge, skills, attitudes, and values that allow you to become fully functioning in your culture, you are said to be enculturated. **Enculturation** occurs when a person—either consciously or unconsciously—learns to identify with a particular culture and a culture's thinking, way of relating, and worldview. Enculturation allows for successful participation in a particular society and makes a person more accepted by that society. Learning about a society usually takes place within a family or

culture

The shared, personal, and learned life experiences of a group of individuals who have a common set of values, norms, and traditions.

enculturation

Occurs when a person—either consciously or unconsciously—learns to identify with a particular culture and a culture's thinking, way of relating, and worldview.

close relationships. Isa becomes enculturated, for instance, when as a little girl she learns the rules about not using profanity, dressing "like a girl," and going to church each Sunday. Although she is young, she is slowly being enculturated into the United States, and this process will continue throughout her lifetime.

Whereas enculturation occurs when you are immersed in your own culture, **acculturation** exists when you learn, adapt to, and adopt the appropriate behaviors and rules of a host culture. Acculturated individuals have effectively absorbed themselves into another society. However, you don't have to sacrifice your personal set of principles simply because you've found yourself in another culture. For example, some immigrants to the United States may attend school in a large city such as Phoenix or Miami. These individuals may adapt to the city by using its services, understanding the laws of the city, or participating in social gatherings on campus. Yet, they may return to many of their cultural practices while in their homes, such as participating in spiritual healings.

To sum up, enculturation is first-culture learning and acculturation is second-culture learning.

*E*xplore how the media contribute to stereotypes of various cultures and influences what we learn about our own culture. If you like, you can use your student workbook or your **Understanding Interpersonal Communication** Online Resources to complete this activity.

Culture Creates Community

Central to our definition of culture is the assumption that it helps to create a sense of community. We view **community** as the common understandings among people who are committed to coexisting together. Cultures create their own sets of values, norms, rules, and customs, which help them to communicate.

In the United States, communities are filled with a number of cultures within cultures, sometimes referred to as **co-cultures** (Orbe, 1998). For example, a Cuban American community, a Chinese American community, and a community of people with disabilities are all co-cultures within one larger culture (the United States). Each community has unique communication behaviors and practices, but each also subscribes to behaviors and practices embraced by the larger United States culture. Many times, the two cultures mesh effortlessly; however, sometimes a **culture clash**, or a conflict over cultural expectations, occurs. For instance, imagine how three European American students using slang while working on a group project might alienate a Mexican American group member who is still learning English. Or, consider the reaction a recently immigrated Islamic woman, who is accustomed to

acculturation

Occurs when a person learns, adapts to, and adopts the appropriate behaviors and rules of a host culture.

community

The common understandings among people who are committed to coexisting.

co-culture

A culture within a culture.

culture clash

A conflict over cultural expectations and experiences.

© J. Emilio Flores/Getty Images

For the most part, the United States embraces the notion of co-cultures. Although U.S. co-cultures often clash, most co-culture members balance their own cultural practices with those of the larger culture and sometimes even invite people outside their co-culture to participate in their traditions.

wearing hijab (traditional Muslim head and body covering), might have to more revealing Western dress. Culture clashes are not necessarily bad; in fact, having the opportunity to view a situation from a different cultural point-of-view can be productive. Michael Jonas of the *Boston Globe* (August 5, 2007) observes that "culture clashes can produce a dynamic give-and-take, generating a solution that may have eluded a group of people with more similar backgrounds and approaches" (p. D2).

Culture Is Multileveled

On the national level of culture, we assume that people of the same national background share many things that bind them in a common culture: language, values, norms, and traditions. Thus, we expect Germans to differ from Hmong based on differing national cultures. However, as discussed in the previous section, cultures can be formed on other levels, such as generation, sexual identity, gender, race, and region, among others. For example, in many parts of the country, regionalisms exist. People who live in the middle of the United States (in states such as Kansas, Illinois, Iowa, Nebraska, Indiana, and Wisconsin) are often referred to as "Midwesterners." People who live in Vermont, New Hampshire, Maine, Massachusetts, Rhode Island, and Connecticut are called "New Englanders." Both Midwesterners and New Englanders have their own unique way of looking at things, but the two regions also share a great deal in common—namely, pragmatic thinking and an independent spirit.

Another example of a co-culture that is not based on nationality is a culture that develops around a certain age cohort. People who grew up in different time frames grew up in different cultural eras, as the labels we attach to various generations suggest—for example, Depression Babies of the 1930s or Flower Children of the 1960s. The culture of the Great Depression in the 1930s reflected the efforts of people trying to survive during troubling financial times. Thus, values of frugality and family unity dominated. In contrast, the 1960s was a prosperous era in which individualism and protest against the government flourished. As people age, they find it difficult to abandon many of the values they learned during childhood.

Furthermore, our interpersonal relationships can constitute "minicultures" (Wilmot, 2006). A "relational culture" (Galvin & Wilkinson, 2006) develops when an interpersonal relationship is characterized by a unique system of communication, including "nicknames, joint storytelling, inside jokes, and code words" (p. 10). Like the members of a particular generation described above, two people with their own relational culture share a common worldview, but it is one they have constructed themselves. We have given you a general framework for understanding culture. We continue by addressing the diversity that exists within the United States.

REVISITING CASEINPOINT

1. Embedded in Brad and Miguel's conversation are some assumptions of culture. Identify how at least one assumption relates to their dialogue in the airport.

2. One of the assumptions to consider when defining culture relates to culture creating community. Within that assumption is the notion of a culture clash. Discuss the presence of elements associated with a culture clash in Brad's discussion with Miguel.

You can answer these questions online under the resources for Chapter 3 at your online Resource Center for Understanding Interpersonal Communication.

Diversity in the United States: A Nation of Newcomers

Intercultural contact is pervasive in the United States. This diversity affects family structure, corporations, religious institutions, schools, and the media. With more than 300 million citizens, our nation is a heterogeneous mix of various cultures. See Figure 3.1 for a look at how ancestral groups, and their root cultures, are distributed across the United States. The increase in diversity over the past several years is not without consequence. Rubin Martinez (2000) observes that our diversity can be challenging: "All across the country, people of different races, ethnicities, and nationalities, are being thrown together and torn apart . . . it is a terrifying experience, this coming together, one for which we have of yet only the most awkward vocabulary" (pp. 11–12).

Figure 3.1 Diversity in the United States

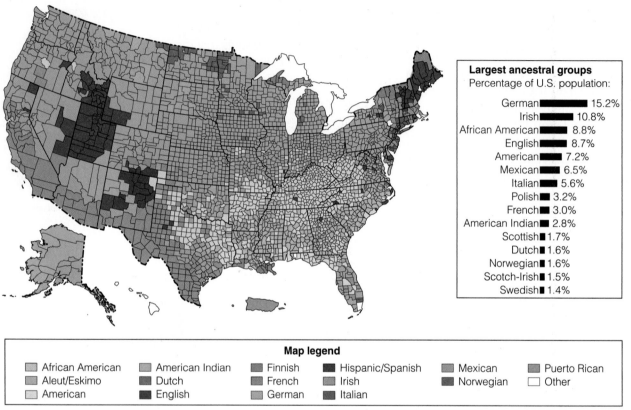

Largest ancestral groups
Percentage of U.S. population:

German	15.2%
Irish	10.8%
African American	8.8%
English	8.7%
American	7.2%
Mexican	6.5%
Italian	5.6%
Polish	3.2%
French	3.0%
American Indian	2.8%
Scottish	1.7%
Dutch	1.6%
Norwegian	1.6%
Scotch-Irish	1.5%
Swedish	1.4%

Map legend

African American	American Indian	Finnish	Hispanic/Spanish	Mexican	Puerto Rican
Aleut/Eskimo	Dutch	French	Irish	Norwegian	Other
American	English	German	Italian		

From *USA Today* July 1, 2004, p. 7A.

With the exception of Native peoples, who were the first cultural group in the United States, we live in a nation that experiences almost constant immigration. For example, Fred Jandt (2006) notes that Latinos, many from Mexico, are the fastest growing cultural group in the United States, growing considerably over the past decade in particular. The United States traditionally supports cultural newcomers. However, a backlash of sorts is increasing. For example, an "English only" movement has gained momentum across the country. Politicians and activists, feeling that the arrival of new cultural groups in the United States risks dividing the country along language and cultural lines, continue to try to make English the official language of the country. In 1996, the United States House of Representatives passed the English Language Empowerment Act, which would have made English the official language of the United States. It never became law, but it highlighted feelings by some that multiple cultures with multiple languages can cost the United States economically (Hayakawa, 1990).

Over the past several years, immigration has caused increased anxiety. The Migration Policy Institute (2007) notes that the September 11, 2001 terrorist attacks in the United States prompted security concerns about "illegal" immigration. Some of the more drastic reforms that have been advocated include building a large fence on the Mexican-American border, denying immigrant families access to health care, and deporting all undocumented immigrants to their native countries (http://blog.lib.umn.edu/ihrc/immigration/immigration _and_the_law). With over 700,000 legal immigrants and nearly 500,000 undocumented immigrants entering the country (Migration Policy Institute, 2007), this topic will continue to resonate within families and across society in general.

Almost 50 years ago, anthropologist Edward T. Hall (1959) noted that "culture is communication and communication is culture" (p.169). In other words, we learn how, where, why, when, and to whom we communicate through cultural teachings. Conversely, when we communicate, we reproduce and reinforce our cultural practices. Hall's words still apply today. The United States is more diverse than ever, and almost everyone has been exposed to this growing diversity in some way. The nation's growing diversity has been hotly debated, with some cultural critics believing that the increase in diversity results in honoring only those voices that support it (for example, McGowan, 2001). However, other writers (for example, Knott, 2006) contend that diversity allows for informed perspectives from many cultural backgrounds. Regardless of the divergent opinions on this matter, we cannot ignore that we now live in a country with expanding cultural variability.

Learning how to communicate effectively with members of different cultures is a hallmark of a thoughtful and effective communicator. Let's explore this issue further by examining the importance of intercultural communication.

Why Study Intercultural Communication?

Intercultural communication scholars Judith Martin and Thomas Nakayama (2008) note several reasons to study intercultural communication. We identify

add that citizens of the United States can't be expected to learn about others through osmosis, either.

Peace Imperative

The Lakota Indians have a saying: "With all beings and all things we shall be as relatives." Yet, as Judith Martin and Thomas Nakayama (2008) ask, is it really possible for cultures to work together and get along on one planet? Our current state of world affairs makes it difficult to answer this question. On one hand, the Berlin Wall has been torn down, but on the other hand, other types of walls have been put up. For instance, violence in the Middle East, Africa, and Russia, coupled with tensions between China and Taiwan, make this a challenging time for cultural understanding. We're not suggesting that if cultures understood each other, cultural warfare would end; rather, we believe that learning about other cultures aids in understanding conflicting points of view, perhaps resulting in a more peaceful world. Looking at an issue from another's perspective, as we will learn in Chapter 8, is critical to interpersonal relationships and communication.

Self-Awareness Imperative

As we mentioned in Chapter 2, each of us has a worldview, which is a unique way of seeing the world through our own lens of understanding. Worldviews can help you understand your "place and space" (e.g., privilege, comfortability, etc.) in society. Although these perspectives are often unconscious, they are directly derived from our cultural identity. When we have a clear understanding of who we are and what forces brought us to our current state, we can begin to understand others' worldviews. For example, remember what it was like when you first discovered your sexual identity. Some of you may have experienced a physical attraction to a member of the opposite sex, while others may have been attracted to a person of the same sex. A same-sex attraction would affect you differently if you practice a religion that considers homosexuality immoral than if you come from a background that is more accepting of gay men and lesbians. Becoming personally aware of your own worldview and the worldviews of others will inevitably help you manage the cultural variation in your relationships.

Ethical Imperative

Recall from Chapter 1 that ethics pertains to what is perceived as right and wrong. Culturally speaking, ethics can vary tremendously (Buber, 1970). That is, different fields of cultural experience dictate different opinions of what constitutes ethical behavior. For example, let's consider behavior associated with the family that may be viewed differently in the United States versus in China. In the Chinese culture, boys are valued more than girls (Galvin,

Table 3.1 Reasons for studying intercultural communication

Imperative Type	Example
Technological imperative	*Email* is facilitating communication between and among cultures. The Internet facilitates cross-cultural understanding of societies around the world.
Demographic imperative	The *influx of immigrants* from Mexico, Russia, and Vietnam has changed the workforce in the United States.
Economic imperative	The *global market* has prompted overseas expansion of U.S. companies. Business transactions and negotiation practices require intercultural understanding.
Peace imperative	*Resolution of world conflicts,* such as those in the Middle East, requires cultural understanding.
Self-awareness imperative	*Self-reflection* of cultural biases aids in cultural sensitivity. Understanding personal *worldviews* promotes cultural awareness.
Ethical imperative	*Cultural values* are frequently difficult to understand and accept. We have an ethical obligation to appreciate the cultural variations in dating, marriage, and intimacy.

2004), and parents are required by Chinese policy to have only one child. As a result, when a mother gives birth to a girl in China, the child may be abandoned or given up for adoption to allow the parents to try again to have a boy.

You may agree or disagree with this practice based upon your ethical perspective(s). Regardless of our personal opinions, each of us has an ethical obligation to ensure that cultural behaviors are depicted in the context of cultural values. We also have an ethical obligation to ensure that we fully understand cultural practices before deciding whether to impose our own cultural will upon others.

We summarize the six imperatives in Table 3.1. Each imperative is accompanied by examples of how that imperative applies to the study of intercultural communication.

Dimensions of Culture

Dutch management scholar Geert Hofstede (1980; 1984; 1991; 2001; 2003) examined work attitudes across 40 cultures. His work showed that four dimensions of cultural values were held by more than 100,000 corporate managers and employees in multinational corporations: uncertainty avoidance, distribution of power, masculinity-femininity, and individualism-collectivism. These four areas comprise **cultural variability theory**. We describe each dimension below.

cultural variability theory

A theory that describes the four value dimensions (individualism/collectivism, uncertainty avoidance, power distance, masculinity/ femininity) that offer information regarding the value differences in a particular culture.

Uncertainty Avoidance

Uncertainty avoidance can be tricky to understand. Overall, the concept refers to how tolerant (or intolerant) you are of uncertainty. Those cultures that resist change and have high levels of anxiety associated with change are said to have a high degree of uncertainty avoidance. Because cultures with a *high* degree of uncertainty avoidance desire predictability, they need specific laws to guide behavior and personal conduct. The cultures of Greece, Chile, Portugal, Japan, and France are among those that tolerate little uncertainty. Risky decisions are discouraged in these cultures because they increase uncertainty.

Those cultures that are unthreatened by change have a *low* degree of uncertainty avoidance. The cultures of the United States, Sweden, Britain, Denmark, and Ireland tend to accept uncertainty. They are comfortable taking risks and are less aggressive and less emotional than cultures with a high degree of uncertainty avoidance.

Intercultural communication problems can surface when a person raised in a culture that tolerates ambiguity encounters another who has little tolerance. For instance, if a student from a culture with high uncertainty avoidance is invited to a party in the United States, he or she will probably ask many questions about how to dress, what to bring, exactly what time to arrive, and so forth. These questions might perplex a U.S. host, who would typically have a high tolerance for uncertainty, including a laid-back attitude toward the party—"Just get here whenever." Recall that cultures with high uncertainty avoidance prefer to have rules and clear protocol more than cultures with low uncertainty avoidance.

Distribution of Power

How a culture deals with power is called **power distance**. Citizens of nations that are *high* in power distance (for example, Philippines, Mexico, India, Singapore, and Brazil) tend to show respect to people with higher status. They revere authoritarianism, and the difference between the powerful and the powerless is clear. Differences in age, sex, and income are exaggerated in these cultures and people accept these differences.

India is an example of a culture that is high in power distance, exemplified by the caste system of the Hindu people. The caste system is a social classification which organizes people into four castes or categories: *Brahmins* (priests), *Kashtryas* (administrators/rulers), *Vaisyas* (businesspeople or farmers), and *Sudras* (laborers) (Hayavadana, 1996). Each caste has various duties and rights. This caste hierarchy inhibits communication among caste groups. In fact, only one group (the priests, who historically have been afforded full respect) has the prerogative to communicate with all other social groups.

The cultures that are *low* in power distance include the United States, Austria, Israel, Denmark, and Ireland. People in these cultures believe that power should be equally distributed regardless of a person's age, sex, or status. Cultures with low degrees of power distance minimize differences among the

uncertainty avoidance

A cultural mindset that indicates how tolerant (or intolerant) a culture is of uncertainty and change.

power distance

How a culture perceives and distributes power.

classes and accept challenges to power in interpersonal relationships. Although included on the list of cultures low in power distance, the United States is becoming higher in power distance because of the growing disparity between rich and poor (Jandt, 2006).

Intercultural encounters between people from high and low power distance cultures can be challenging. For instance, a supervisor from a high power distance culture may have difficulty communicating with employees who come from lower power distance cultures. Although the supervisor may be expecting complete respect and follow-through on directives, the employees may be questioning the legitimacy of such directives.

Masculinity-Femininity

Hofstede (2001) identifies the dimension of masculinity-femininity as the extent to which cultures represent masculine and feminine traits in their society. Remember from our discussion of masculinity and femininity in Chapter 2 that masculinity is not the same as "male," and femininity is not the same as "female," although use of these terms still reinforces stereotypical notions of how men and women should behave. **Masculine cultures** focus on achievement, competitiveness, strength, and material success—that is, characteristics stereotypically associated with masculine people. Money is important in masculine cultures. Further, masculine cultures are those where the division of labor is based on sex. **Feminine cultures** emphasize sexual equality, nurturance, quality of life, supportiveness, and affection—that is, characteristics stereotypically associated with feminine people. Compassion for the less fortunate also characterizes feminine cultures.

Hofstede's (2001) research showed that countries such as Mexico, Italy, Venezuela, Japan, and Austria are masculine-centered cultures, where the division of labor is based on sex. Countries such as Thailand, Norway, the Netherlands, Denmark, and Finland are feminine-centered cultures, where a promotion of sexual equality exists. The United States falls closer to masculinity.

What happens when a person from a culture that honors such masculine traits as power and competition intersects with a person from a culture that honors such feminine traits as interdependence and quality of life? For example, suppose that a woman is asked to lead a group of men. In Scandinavian countries, such as Denmark and Finland, such a task would not be problematic. Many political leaders in these countries are feminine (and female), and gender roles are more flexible. Yet, in a masculine culture, a female leader might be viewed with skepticism and her leadership might be challenged.

Individualism-Collectivism

When a culture values **individualism**, it prefers competition over cooperation, the individual over the group, and the private over the public. Individualistic cultures have an "I" communication orientation, emphasizing self-concept

masculine culture

A culture that emphasizes characteristics stereotypically associated with masculine people, such as achievement, competitiveness, strength, and material success.

feminine culture

A culture that emphasizes characteristics stereotypically associated with feminine people, such as sexual equality, nurturance, quality of life, supportiveness, affection, and a compassion for the less fortunate.

individualism

A cultural mindset that emphasizes self-concept and personal achievement and that prefers competition over cooperation, the individual over the group, and the private over the public.

and personal achievement. Individualistic cultures, including the United States, Canada, Britain, Australia, and Italy, tend to reject authoritarianism (think, for instance, how many rallies have occurred in the United States denouncing U.S. Presidents and their policies), and typically support the belief that people should "pull themselves up by their own bootstraps."

Collectivism suggests that the self is secondary to the group and its norms, values, and beliefs. Group orientation takes priority over self-orientation. Collectivistic cultures tend to value duty, tradition, and hierarchy. A "we" communication orientation prevails. Collectivistic cultures such as Columbia, Peru, Pakistan, Chile, and Singapore lean toward working together in groups to achieve goals. Families are particularly important, and people have higher expectations of loyalty to family, including taking care of extended family members.

Interestingly, the collectivistic and individualistic orientations intersect at times. For instance, in the Puerto Rican community, a collectivistic sense of family coexists with the individualistic need for community members to become personally successful. Hector Carrasquillo (1997) observed that "a Puerto Rican is only fully a person insofar as he or she is a member of a family" (p. 159). Still, Carrasquillo points out that younger Puerto Ricans have adopted more independence and have accepted and adapted to the individualistic ways of the United States culture. We see, therefore, that even within one culture, the individualism-collectivism dimension is not static.

Hofstede's work regarding dimensions of culture is often applied to business settings. To read an article that discusses how Hofstede's dimensions of culture can be applied specifically to business negotiation, go to your online Resource Center for *Understanding Interpersonal Communication* and access *InfoTrac College Edition Exercise 3.1: Culture and Negotiation* under the resources for Chapter 3 and read "Next for Communicators: Global Negotiation."

collectivism

A cultural mindset that emphasizes the group and its norms, values, and beliefs over the self.

In many Asian countries, doing things together underscores the collectivistic nature of society. In the United States, people sometimes have trouble identifying with the collectivistic value of placing the group before the individual. At the same time, they often embrace collectivistic values, such as the importance of family and tradition.

Consider the summary of Hofstede's four dimensions of culture provided in Table 3.2. As we did in the previous sections, we provide representative cultures as identified by Hofstede. Keep in mind that because his results are based on averages, you will most likely be able to think of individuals you know who are exceptions to the categorization of nations. For another summary of these concepts and an even more extensive list of representative countries, use your online Resource Center for Understanding Interpersonal Communication to access *Interactive Activity 3.2: Hofstede's Dimensions of Culture* under the resources for Chapter 3.

One additional cultural dimension merits consideration: context. Recall from Chapter 1 that context is the surrounding in which communication takes place. Intercultural communication theorists find that people of different cultures use context to varying degrees to determine the meaning of a message. Scholars have referred to this as context orientation theory (Hall & Hall, 1990). **Context orientation theory** answers the following question: Is meaning derived from cues outside of the message or from the words in the message?

The cultures of the world differ in the extent to which they rely on context. Researchers have divided context into two areas: high-context and low-context (Victor, 1992). In **high-context cultures**, the meaning of a message is primarily drawn from the surroundings. People in high-context cultures do

context orientation theory:
The theory that meaning is derived from either the setting of the message or the words of a message and that cultures can vary in the extent to which message meaning is made explicit or implicit.

high-context culture
A culture in which there is a high degree of similarity among members and in which the meaning of a message is drawn primarily from its context, such as one's surroundings, rather than from words.

Table 3.2 Hofstede's cultural dimensions

Dimension	Description
Uncertainty avoidance	• Cultures high in uncertainty avoidance desire predictability (for example, Greece, Japan). • Cultures low in uncertainty avoidance are unthreatened by change (for example, United States, Great Britain).
Distribution of power	• Cultures high in power distance show respect for status (for example, Mexico, India). • Cultures low in power distance believe power should be equally distributed (for example, United States, Israel).
Masculinity-femininity	• Masculine cultures value competitiveness, material success, and assertiveness (for example, Italy, Austria). • Feminine cultures value quality of life, affection, and caring for the less fortunate (for example, Sweden, Denmark).
Individualism-collectivism	• Individualistic cultures value individual accomplishments (for example, Australia, United States). • Collectivistic cultures value group collaboration (for example, Chile, Columbia).

not need to say much when communicating because there is a high degree of similarity among members of such cultures. Further, people read nonverbal cues with a high degree of accuracy because people share the same structure of meaning. Native American, Latin American, Japanese, Chinese, and Korean cultures are all high-context cultures. On a more fundamental level, high-context communities are less formal and decisions take into consideration the relationships between and among people.

In **low-context cultures**, communicators find meaning primarily in the words in messages, not the surroundings. In low-context cultures, meanings are communicated explicitly; very little of the conversation is left open to interpretation. As a result, nonverbal communication is not easily comprehended. Examples of low-context cultures include Germany, Switzerland, the United States, Canada, and France.

Think about how cultural differences in context might affect interaction during conflict episodes, job interviews, or dating. If one person relies mainly on the spoken word and the other communicates largely through nonverbal messages, what might be the result?

So far in this chapter, we have discussed why you need to understand intercultural communication. We're confident that you are beginning to appreciate the cultural diversity in your lives and that you are prepared to work on improving your intercultural communication skills. A critical step toward understanding your culture and the cultures of others is to understand the problems inherent in intercultural communication. We examine five such challenges now.

Challenges of Intercultural Communication

Although intercultural communication is important and pervasive, becoming an effective intercultural communicator is easier said than done. In this section, we explain five obstacles to intercultural understanding: ethnocentrism, stereotyping, anxiety and uncertainty, misinterpretation of nonverbal and verbal behaviors, and the assumption of similarity.

Ethnocentrism

Ethnocentrism is the process of judging another culture using the standards of your own culture. Ethnocentrism is derived from two Greek words, *ethno*, or nation, and *kentron*, or center. When combined, the meaning becomes clear: nation at the center. Ethnocentrism is a belief in the superiority of your own culture. Myron Lustig and Jolene Koester (1999b) claim that cultures "train their members to use the categories of their own cultural experiences when judging the experiences of people from other cultures" (p. 146). Normally,

low-context culture

A culture in which there is a high degree of difference among members and in which the meaning of a message must be explicitly related, usually in words.

ethnocentrism

The process of judging another culture using the standards of our own culture.

"Excuse me. We're Americans. Would you give us your table?"

ethnocentric tendencies exaggerate differences and usually prevent intercultural understanding.

At first glance, being ethnocentric may appear harmless. Few people even realize the extent to which they prioritize their culture over another. For instance, you will note that throughout this book, we avoid the use of the term *American*. Like many researchers and practitioners, we believe that *American* can refer to people in North America, Central America, and South America. To suggest that the word pertains only to those in the United States is ethnocentric.

We tend to notice when people from other cultures prioritize their cultural customs. For example, although many people in the United States value open communication, not all cultures do. Many Asian cultures (for example, China and Japan) revere silence. In fact, the Chinese philosopher Confucius said that "Silence is a friend who will never betray." Now, consider what happens in conversations when the Western and Eastern worlds meet. Let's say that Ed, a business executive from the United States, travels to China to offer Yao, another executive, a business deal. Ed is taken aback when, after he makes the offer, Yao remains silent for a few minutes. Ed repeats the specifics of the offer, and Yao acknowledges his understanding. This standstill in their discussion leads Ed to believe that Yao is going to reject the offer. However, if Ed had studied Chinese culture before his trip, he would know that to the Chinese, silence means agreement. One speaks only if he or she has something of value to add. Ed's cultural ignorance may cost the company both money and respect. Ed's inability to look beyond his own Western view of

Communication Assessment Test
Revised Ethnocentrism Scale

Directions:
Below are items that relate to the cultures of different parts of the world. Work quickly and record your first reaction to each item. There are no right or wrong answers. Please indicate the degree to which you agree or disagree with each item using the following five-point scale:

strongly agree = 1   agree = 2   undecided = 3   disagree = 4   strongly disagree = 5

You can take this test online. Go to your online Resource Center for *Understanding Interpersonal Communication* and look under the resources for Chapter 3.

_____ 1. Most other cultures are backward compared to my culture.

_____ 2. My culture should be the role model for other cultures.

_____ 3. People from other cultures act strangely when they come to my culture.

_____ 4. Lifestyles in other cultures are just as valid as those in my culture.

_____ 5. Other cultures should try to be more like my culture.

_____ 6. I am not interested in the values and customs of other cultures.

_____ 7. People in my culture could learn a lot from people in other cultures.

_____ 8. Most people from other cultures just don't know what's good for them.

_____ 9. I respect the values and customs of other cultures.

_____ 10. Other cultures are smart to look up to our culture.

_____ 11. Most people would be happier if they lived like people in my culture.

_____ 12. I have many friends from different cultures.

_____ 13. People in my culture have just about the best lifestyles of those in any culture.

_____ 14. Lifestyles in other cultures are not as valid as those in my culture.

_____ 15. I am very interested in the values and customs of other cultures.

_____ 16. I apply my values when judging people who are different.

_____ 17. I see people who are similar to me as virtuous.

_____ 18. I do not cooperate with people who are different.

_____ 19. Most people in my culture just don't know what is good for them.

_____ 20. I do not trust people who are different.

_____ 21. I dislike interacting with people from different cultures.

_____ 22. I have little respect for the values and customs of other cultures.

Scoring
1. Recode questions 4, 7, and 9 with the following format:

    1 = 5   2 = 4   3 = 3   4 = 2   5 = 1

2. Drop questions 3, 6, 12, 15, 16, 17, and 19.
3. Add up the numbers you marked for the remaining responses. This is your composite ethnocentrism score. The higher the score, the more you are ethnocentric. The lower the score, the less you are ethnocentric.

Accessed at www.jamesmccroskey.com. From J. W. Neuliep, "Assessing the reliability and validity of the Generalized Ethnocentrism Scale," *Journal of Intercultural Communication Research*, 31, 2002, p. 201–215. Reprinted by permission of Taylor & Francis Group.

silence represents ethnocentrism. To read an interesting article that discusses international competition and how some non-Western athletes feel pressure to adjust their cultural style to win higher marks with a Western-style performance, check out "Putting Patriotism on Ice: Top Figure Skating Duo Shen and Zhao Crave Gold—with Chinese Characteristics," available through Info-Trac College Edition. Use your online Resource Center for *Understanding Interpersonal Communication* to access **InfoTrac College Edition Exercise 3.2: Putting Patriotism on Ice** under the resources for Chapter 3.

Stereotyping

Consider the following statements:

- Old people are crabby and like to complain.
- Italians love to use their hands while speaking.
- African Americans are loud.
- Boys don't cry.

These statements are stereotypes, the "pictures in our heads" (Lippman, 1922, p. 3) that we discussed in Chapter 2. We have all stereotyped at one point or another in our lives. Stereotypes are everywhere in U.S. society, including politics ("All politicians are crooked"), medicine ("Doctors know best"), entertainment ("Hollywood stars live perfect lives and have no problems"), journalism ("The media are so liberal"), and sports ("They're just dumb jocks"). Such statements generalize the qualities of some members of a group to the group as a whole.

As we learned in Chapter 2, stereotypes can be good or bad. Think about the positive stereotypes of firefighters, police officers, emergency personnel, and other rescue workers after the terrorist attacks on the United

© Frank Micelotta/Getty Images

IPC *in the* News

A celebrity roast of African American rap star Flavor Flav, a former member of the celebrated rap group Public Enemy, has evoked images of unsavory cultural stereotypes, according to the *Los Angeles Times* website. The success of Flavor Flav's *Flavor of Love* on the Comedy Central television network provoked the outpouring of the "crudest insults" from other celebrities who were present at the roast. Throughout it all, Flavor Flav jumped up and down, "clapping with childish delight, his smile a veritable prospector's pan of gold chunks." The article laments the sad state of cultural affairs in television programming and the various responses that Flavor Flav elicits: "To some, he's a lovable parody of the crazy ghetto denizens feared by white bigots. To others, including a pastor who referred to him as a 'coon act,' he's the living embodiment of offensive stereotypes." Underscoring the tenor of the article, a comedian noted that Flavor Flav has gone from "Public Enemy to Public Embarrassment."

Collins, S. (2007, July 30). Channel island: A weak roast for Flavor Flav. Retrieved July 31, 2007, from http://www.latimes.com.

States on 9/11. Words like "heroic," "compassionate," "daring," and "fearless" have all been attributed to these groups of individuals, regardless of the cultural identification of the members of these groups. However, right after the attacks, many Arabs living in the United States were accused of being terrorists simply because of their ethnicity. People used hurtful and hateful speech while interacting with Arab Americans. The point is that we must be willing to look beyond the generalizations about a particular group and communicate with people as individuals.

...in a group project for a communication class

As the only male in a group of six for your communication class, you begin to realize that you are a minority voice for the first time. The words you normally use have now been replaced by Spanish phrases used by a few of the women who are Latina. While accustomed to having little side conversations about sports and *Celebrity Poker* with your male buddies in a group, you now are ridiculed by the women who want you to stay on task while preparing for the presentation. Finally, when your time to present arrives, the people in your group who went before you took up too much time, and instead of having 10 minutes, you are only allocated 3 minutes. Your frustration and anger levels are now palpable. Given your understanding of culture, cultural empathy, community, and co-cultures, how do you communicate your feelings to the rest of the group? Do you see any obstacles to intercultural communication present? What if the other group members had a chance to grade you on your final performance? Would that grade influence how you communicate your views on being a "cultural minority?"

Anxiety and Uncertainty

You may feel anxiety and uncertainty when you are introduced to people who speak, look, and act differently from you (Gudykunst & Kim, 1997). Our society has few guidelines to help us through some of the early awkward moments between people from different cultures. People commonly question what words or phrases to use while discussing various cultural groups. Most of us want to be culturally aware and use language that doesn't offend, yet we frequently don't know what words might be offensive to members of cultures other than our own. For example, you might wonder whether you should refer to someone as Indian or Native American.

In Chapter 2, we observed that our family and friends usually influence our perceptions. Their observations and reactions to cultural differences are often passed on to us. And they can prompt us to either feel that we are members of an in-group or an out-group. **In-groups** are groups to which a person feels he or she belongs, and **out-groups** are those groups to which a person feels he or she does not belong.

Perceptions of belonging are directly proportional to the level of connection an individual feels toward a group. Let's say that Rob and Nate, a gay couple, meet Nate's best friend, Rose. Although Rose is not a lesbian, she feels that she has in-group affiliation with the gay men. Now suppose that Rob and Nate meet Rose's mom, Sandra, who is not accepting of homosexuality. Sandra will view Rob and Nate as an out-group because she does not feel a sense of belong-

in-group

A group to which a person feels he or she belongs.

out-group

A group to which a person feels he or she does not belong.

ing with gay men. Being a member of either an in-group or an out-group influences our degree of comfort in intercultural communication.

Misinterpretation of Nonverbal and Verbal Behaviors

Speakers expect to receive nonverbal cues that are familiar. However, nonverbal behaviors differ dramatically across and within cultures. For example, let's say that Lena, from New York City, is meeting a member of the Western Apache nation in Arizona or an immigrant from India. She will probably introduce herself and initiate some small talk. However, she may run into problems, because these cultures typically value silence in conversations. The Apache use silence when they meet strangers (Basso, 1990). For many Asian Indians, silence means agreement, is used as a sign of conversational respect, or is a way to show sensitivity to the speaker (Pais, 1997).

An Asian proverb states that "those who know, do not speak; those who speak, do not know." In this example, if Lena is a person who believes that communication must be constant to be effective, she may struggle with interpersonal exchanges with the Western Apache or the Asian Indian. However, as is true of other facets of culture, nonverbal communication varies within cultures as well as between cultures. For instance, although Italians might gesture more than people from the United States in general, not all Italians use expansive gestures. We could certainly find someone from Italy who gestures less than someone we pick from the United States. We return to the topic of culture and nonverbal communication in Chapter 5.

In addition to nonverbal differences, verbal communication differences exist between and among cultures and co-cultures. Aside from the obvious language differences that separate cultures, verbal communication styles can differ. For example, words used from one generation to the next vary in meaning. Words such as *smooching* and *necking* once referred to an act most people today refer to as *kissing*. We cover the use of language extensively in Chapter 4. We must understand nonverbal and verbal differences between cultures if we are to achieve meaning in our intercultural relationships.

The Assumption of Similarity or Difference

This assumption suggests that intercultural communication is possible because it simply requires homing in on people's inherent similarities. At the other end of the continuum is the belief that people from different cultures are vastly different from one another, and, therefore, communication between them is difficult if not impossible. Assuming similarity fails to appreciate difference, and assuming difference fails to appreciate cultural commonalities.

In the United States, we need to be careful when we place a premium on the "American way." We are ethnocentric if we believe that other cultures should do things the way that we do things here or if we think that cultures that do things the way we do them here are imitating U.S. culture. For instance, consider the following conversation between Jasmine and Renny, two friends talking about an anthropology class:

Jasmine:	So, I don't get it. You think that women should be forced to wear those veils over their heads. I don't. They want to be free to show their faces. Men don't have to do it, so why should women?
Renny:	You need to read more, Jasmine. I read that the veils are called *hijab* and they are part of the dress that women have worn for years. Some women wear them so that they can be treated as human beings instead of targets of beauty or objects of affection.
Jasmine:	Okay, but don't they know that it can be seen as oppressive?
Renny:	Says who? You? Me? We live in the United States, a country where most women don't wear the hijab, but that doesn't mean that it's an oppressive thing. Look at our country. What about women in other countries who don't understand why married women here take their husband's name? What about women in other countries who laugh at how much women in the United States spend on cosmetics for their faces? What about . . .
Jasmine:	Okay, okay, I get the point.

REVISITING
CASEɪɴPOINT

1. *Discuss how stereotyping is part of Brad's and Miguel's conversation.*

2. *Explain how cultural uncertainty and anxiety may have affected Brad's conversation with Miguel.*

Y*ou can answer these questions online under the resources for Chapter 3 at your online Resource Center for* Under-standing Interpersonal Communication.

This conversation reflects the fact that simply because something is practiced or revered in the United States does not mean that it is similarly practiced or revered in other cultures. Renny helps us see through the problems of assuming similarity across cultures.

We have given you a number of issues to consider in this chapter so far. First, we defined culture and co-culture and discussed the dimensions of culture. We then proceeded to outline several reasons for studying intercultural communication. Next, we addressed some of the most common challenges to intercultural communication. We now offer you some suggestions for improving your intercultural effectiveness in relationships.

Choices for Intercultural Understanding

In this section, we present several ways to improve your communication with people from different cultures. Because most cultures and co-cultures have unique ways of communicating, our suggestions are necessarily broad. As we have emphasized in this chapter, communicating with friends, classmates, coworkers, and others from different cultural backgrounds is both exciting and challenging.

Know Your Biases and Stereotypes

Despite our best efforts, we enter conversations with biases and stereotypes. How do we know we have biases and stereotypes? Listening carefully to others' responses to our ideas, words, and phrases is an excellent first step. Have you ever told a story about a cultural group that resulted in a friend saying, "I can't believe you just said that!" That friend may be pointing out that you should rethink some culturally offensive language or risk facing challenges from others during conversations.

We need to avoid imposing our predispositions and prejudices on others. Perceptions of different cultural groups are frequently outdated or otherwise inaccurate and require a constant personal assessment. Facing your biases and even your fears or anxieties is an essential first step toward intercultural effectiveness.

Recall that ethnocentrism is seeing the world through your own culture's lens. We may like to think that our particular culture is best, but as you have seen through our many examples, no culture can claim superiority. We first need to admit that we all are biased and ethnocentric to some extent. Next, we need to honestly assess how we react to other cultures. As we previously mentioned, you can listen to others for their reactions. Looking inward is also helpful; ask yourself the following questions:

- What have I done to prepare myself for intercultural conversations?

- Do I use language that is biased or potentially offensive to people from different cultures?

- What is my reaction to people who use offensive words or phrases while

...at work

Suppose you and your colleague James are chatting at the office during a break. He mentions that he thinks women get a "free ride" at work because they can go home early if their children are sick or if there is a family emergency. He goes on to say that women usually can curry favor with their bosses, whether the boss is a man or woman. According to James, most male supervisors don't want to get into trouble denying women "family time," and most female supervisors can identify with mothers who have family needs. How would you respond to James and his prejudices, regardless of your sex? What intercultural challenges are you and James facing in your conversation?

describing cultural groups—am I
silent? If so, do I consider my silence problematic?

- How have my perceptions and biases been shaped? By the media? By school? By talking to others?

These are among the questions you should consider as you begin to know yourself, your perceptions, and how you may act upon those perceptions. We all need to understand our outdated and misguided views of others that have falsely shaped our impressions of other cultures.

Tolerate the Unknown

Earlier in the chapter, we noted that some cultures tolerate uncertainty more easily than others. Although we noted that the United States is one such culture, tolerating things of which you are unaware does not always come naturally. We may wish to *think* we are tolerant, but the truth is that differences can bother us at times.

You may be unfamiliar with various cultural practices of coworkers, craftspeople you hire for home repair, and others whose backgrounds and fields of experience differ from yours. For instance, consider the Romanian who is accustomed to greeting people by kissing the sides of both cheeks. Think about the colleague who is Japanese and who may not shake your hand upon meeting. Or, perhaps as a Christian, you find people who don't believe in God uninformed and unworthy of your conversational time. Some cultural behaviors are simply different from yours. It will take time to understand the differences. Be patient with yourself and with others. If you encounter a cultural unknown, think about asking questions about a particular custom, practice, or behavior.

Practice Cultural Respect

Various traditions, customs, and practices allow cultures and co-cultures to function effectively. Skilled intercultural communicators respect those cultural conventions. No one culture can claim superiority over others in terms of knowing "the right way" to solve work problems, raise children, and manage interpersonal relationships. **Cultural imperialism** is a process whereby individuals, companies, and/or the media impose their way of thinking and behaving upon another culture. With cultural imperialism, a belittling of another culture occurs. We can avoid this nasty practice by using cultural respect; this requires us to show that we accept another culture's way of thinking and relating, even though

© Ethel Wolvovitz/The Image Works

cultural imperialism

The process whereby individuals, companies, and/or the media impose their way of thinking and behaving upon another culture.

cultural empathy

The learned ability to accurately understand the experiences of people from diverse cultures and to convey that understanding responsively.

When we learn to respect and appreciate our differences and discover what we have in common, we increase our ability to communicate with one another in an effective and mutually beneficial way.

we may disagree with or disapprove of it. Different societies have different moral codes, and judging a culture using only one moral yardstick can be considered both arrogant and self-serving.

When you practice cultural respect, you empathize with another culture. **Cultural empathy** refers to the learned ability to accurately understand the experiences of people from diverse cultures and to convey that understanding responsively (Ting-Toomey & Chung, 2005). When you are empathic, you are able to develop an emotional and psychological bond with another person or social group. In other words, you try to reach beyond the words to the feelings that the communicator is trying to show. You become other-oriented and engage in the sort of civil communication we referred to in Chapter 1.

Developing cultural respect involves trying to look at a culture from the inside. As difficult as it sounds, we all must try to understand what it is like to be a member of another culture. Avoid reading verbal and nonverbal communication solely from your own cultural point of view. Refrain from becoming easily insulted if another person is not using your language or is having a hard time communicating.

Practicing cultural respect does not require us to practice complete cultural relativity, however. **Cultural relativity** means that an observer can never condemn any practice in which any culture engages. In other words, cultural relativity doesn't ever allow us to judge another culture, even when its practices are inhumane. Cultural respect requires us to be aware that our own ways are not the only ways, but it allows us to judge other cultures when warranted.

Educate Yourself

Aside from taking this course in interpersonal communication, you can take advantage of numerous opportunities to educate yourself about other cultures. First, simply reading about other cultures will give you a backdrop for future reference and will allow you to discover more about your own culture as well. Second, educating yourself requires that you learn about cultures through others. Listen to community lectures and discussions about cultural groups. Talk to people who represent another race, religion, nationality, or other cultural group. Be interested in their experiences, both good and bad, but avoid patronizing them.

In addition to reading about cultures and talking to others, visit Internet sites dedicated to co-cultural issues. For instance, the home site for Education World allows you to electronically visit a different culture. WorldBiz.com and Intercultural-Relations.com (click on the link "The Edge: The E-Journal of Intercultural Relations") provide links to information about cultures all over the world. For an international understanding of culture, check out the Society for Intercultural Education, Training and Research—Europe (click on the link "Doc Centre" at the top of the home page, then on the link "Newsletters & Journals Online"). To better understand religious diversity, visit www.

cultural relativity

The ability to avoid judging or condemning any practice in which any other culture engages.

adherents.com. For information on tribal nations, www.nativeculture. com is helpful. These are just a few of the active websites students have chosen as important intercultural resources. (You can find links to all these sites under the resources for Chapter 3 at your online Resource Center for *Understanding Interpersonal Communication*.) Don't accept everything written about culture and communication as truth. Be rigorous in your reading and tentative in your acceptance. Be willing to seek out all available information that is based on both research and personal experience.

Ethics & Choice

Roberto, a Guatemalan exchange student, wasn't sure what to do about his living situation. He had been thrilled to be assigned to one of the best dorms on campus, and had been excited about the roommate the computer had paired him with—a student from India. On move-in day, Roberto met his roommate, Eddy, for the first time. Roberto had limited experience with speaking to anyone outside of his hometown in Guatemala, so his enthusiasm about his new living arrangement was tempered by a little bit of nervousness.

Despite the cordial overtures in Roberto's and Eddy's relationship, after several weeks Roberto's initial excitement gave way to uncertainty. First, Roberto was bothered by the fact that Eddy constantly talked about Hinduism. He knew that Eddy was a devout Hindu, but he hadn't realized the extent to which Eddy's religion influenced his life. And although they sometimes met for lunch, Roberto didn't want to spend much additional time with Eddy because he didn't care for the kind of music he listened to and didn't like his friends.

Eddy, too, was having second thoughts about the living arrangement. He felt upset about Roberto's broken promise to study together. He also was irritated by the lingering smell of the spicy meals that Roberto often cooked in the room, and with Roberto's family's numerous late-night phone calls. Eddy was at his wits' end and wanted to figure out what to do next.

The roommates are clearly conflicted over what, if anything, to say to each other. This intercultural dilemma raises a few important points. Would you advise Roberto or Eddy to say anything to the other? Are their concerns related to their different cultures or to the fact that they are roommates? What ethical system of communication that we discussed in Chapter 1 (categorical imperative, utilitarianism, golden mean, ethic of care, significant choice) do you believe is appropriate to consider in this scenario?

Go to your online Resource Center for *Understanding Interpersonal Communication* to access an interactive version of this scenario under the resources for Chapter 3. The interactive version of this scenario allows you to choose an appropriate response to this dilemma and then see what consequences your choice brings about. You can also compare your answers to the questions at the end of the scenario to those provided by the authors and, if requested, email your response to your instructor.

Be Prepared for Consequences

Although we may make a serious effort to be thoughtful and considerate, having a conversation with an individual from a different culture can be challenging. So many issues operate simultaneously in a conversation—verbal differences (word choice, dialect, syntax, and so forth), nonverbal differences (clothing, eye contact, conversation space, and so forth), nervousness, cultural customs, rules, symbols, and norms. We may try to attend to all these aspects of our conversation, but things still may go awry. There is no way to completely control all the things that can go astray in our cultural dialogues. What we can work toward, however, is preempting potential problems.

Relate to the Individual, Not the Culture

Although we know that we have drawn upon some generalizations to make some of the points in this chapter, we remain concerned about painting broad cultural strokes to define individuals. Identifying with the person and not the cultural group is paramount in intercultural communication.

Accepting individual cultural uniqueness is important. First, as we learned earlier, there are variations within cultures and co-cultures. For instance, not all Christians have the same beliefs, nor do all elderly people sit around play-ing Scrabble. Second, people's com-munication behaviors and skills can vary tremendously within cultures. Some people use a lot of personal space in conversations, whereas oth-ers use little. Some people are direct and forthright in their dialogues, but others are more reserved and timid. Some individuals may be reluctant to share personal tragedies; however, others may have no qualms with such disclosure. Constantly remind-ing yourself that not all members of a certain cultural group think alike, act alike, and talk alike allows you to focus on the person instead of the group to which he or she belongs.

Reevaluate and Eliminate Your Prejudices

As we noted previously, knowing your biases is a good way to begin to improve your intercultural commu-nication effectiveness. We expand this suggestion to encourage you, while reevaluating your prejudices, to rid yourself of some that you may have had for years. Recognizing that your family, friends, coworkers, school, and the media influence your prejudices is critical. Getting rid of the unwanted or misguided preju-dices is essential if we are to begin to forge intercultural relationships with others.

We cannot understate the impor-tance of actively eliminating harmful biases. Working toward eliminating those prejudices should be a priority. For example, because the media saturate

---

interpersonal explorer

Before you finish reading this chapter, take a moment to review the theories and skills discussed. How do you think the theories discussed in this chapter can help you better understand interpersonal communi-cation, culture, and identity? In what ways can the skills discussed help you interact more effectively with other people in your life?

Theories that relate to culture and identity

- **Cultural variability theory**
  Four value dimensions (individualism/collectivism, uncertainty avoidance, power distance, masculinity/femininity) offer information pertaining to the value differences in a particular culture

- **Context orientation theory**
  Meaning is derived from either the setting of the message or the words of a message and cultures can vary in the extent to which message meaning is made explicit or implicit

Practical skills for intercultural understanding

- Know your biases and stereotypes
- Tolerate the unknown
- Practice cultural respect
- Educate yourself
- Be prepared for consequences
- Relate to the individual, not the culture
- Reevaluate and eliminate your prejudices

Explore your interpersonal choices

Are you ready to explore your interpersonal choices regarding culture and identity? Use your online Resource Center for *Understanding Interpersonal Communication* to access an ABC News video, "How Kids See Black and White," about the fact that today's African American girls still overwhelmingly prefer white dolls to black ones, years after the civil rights and black pride movements. Compare your answers to the questions at the end of the video with those provided by the authors.

our lives, they frequently influence our prejudices. We encourage you to be an engaged consumer of the media instead of consciously and unconsciously accepting as truth what the media present. Think about the thousands of websites that post hate-filled language and pictures. Newspapers frequently focus on cultural issues, but be on the alert for stereotypical and uninformed perspectives. Television, too, may communicate images that are less than authentic. Let the media know when they present faulty or inaccurate representations of cultural groups. At this point in your life, you have some foundation from which to argue your points.

Summary

Our cultural background shapes our identity, our communication practices, and our responses to others. Intercultural communication refers to communication between and among individuals and groups whose cultural backgrounds differ. As the populations of countries become more diverse, communicators today need to have knowledge of others' cultural values and practices to inform their communication.

The United States is a heterogeneous mix of various cultures, with 2.4 percent of the population identifying with more than one race. We can experience intercultural communication at the national level or at the small scale of a neighborhood. The United States generally supports cultural newcomers, including Latinos, the fastest growing cultural group.

Family, friends, and the media teach us culture. The national culture is made up of numerous co-cultures, or cultures within cultures, membership in which is determined by factors such as sexual identity, gender, and race. Cultures and co-cultures create a sense of community for members.

Culture has four dimensions. Cultures vary in the degree that they desire predictability (the uncertainty avoidance dimension) and how much they show respect for status (the distribution of power dimension). They also differ on what they value, such as competitiveness or quality of life (the masculinity-femininity dimension) and individual or group accomplishments (the individualism-collectivism dimension). Another important ingredient in culture is context; members of high-context cultures draw the meaning of the message from the surroundings, whereas people in low-context cultures derive the meaning from the message itself.

In today's world, there are six reasons, or imperatives, to study intercultural communication. The technology imperative shows that technology makes communication with those in other countries easier than ever before. The demographic imperative recognizes that the United States is a symphony of cultures that should accommodate and appreciate each other. The economic imperative states that all societies—and their businesses— are interconnected in a global village. The peace imperative says that looking at world affairs from other countries' perspectives is a step in the right direction, especially if you have taken advantage of the self-awareness imperative, which encourages us to have a clear understanding of our own worldview. Finally, according to the ethical imperative, we have an obligation to ensure that cultural behaviors are depicted in the context of cultural values.

The chapter discusses five obstacles to intercultural communication. Ethnocentrism makes us judge other cultures using the standards of our own culture. As we learned in Chapter 2, stereotyping is an often misguided process that associates certain traits with individuals just because they are part of a group. Anxiety influences our communication; feeling like a member of an in-group or out-group can affect our relationships. Nonverbal behaviors differ across cultures. Finally, if we assume we are similar to those in other cultures, we don't appreciate the differences between us, and the reverse is also true.

You can make positive choices to improve your intercultural understanding, including knowing and eliminating your biases, tolerating the unknown, practicing cultural respect, educating yourself, being prepared for consequences, and relating to the individual instead of the culture. Intercultural communication requires patience, knowledge, sensitivity, and respect. We hope that you work toward establishing and maintaining intercultural relationships with the information we outline in this chapter.

Understanding Interpersonal Communication Online

Now that you've read Chapter 3, use your online Resource Center for *Understanding Interpersonal Communication* for quick access to the electronic study resources that accompany this text. Your online Resource Center gives you access to the video of Brad's interaction with Miguel on page 79, the Your Turn journal activity on page 83, the Communication Assessment Test on page 98, the Ethics & Choice interactive activity on page 106, the Interpersonal Explorer activity on page 107, InfoTrac College Edition, and study aids including a digital glossary, review quizzes, and the chapter activities.

Terms for Review

acculturation 83	cultural variability theory 91	in-group 100
co-culture 83	culture 82	intercultural
collectivism 94	culture clash 83	communication 80
community 83	enculturation 82	low-context culture 96
context orientation	ethnocentrism 96	masculine culture 93
theory 95	feminine culture 93	out-group 100
cultural empathy 104	global village 89	outsourcing 89
cultural imperialism 104	high-context culture 95	power distance 92
cultural relativity 105	individualism 93	uncertainty avoidance 92

Questions for Understanding

Comprehension Focus

1. What is culture?
2. What are the dimensions of culture?
3. Differentiate between high-context and low-context cultures.
4. Define and explain cultural imperialism.
5. Define and explain ethnocentrism.

Application Focus

1. CASE IN POINT Examine our opening story of Brad Atchison. What advice would you offer to Brad when he returns to the United States after his visit to Mexico? Who would you suggest he speak to, and where could you direct him for additional information on cultural relationships?

2. Discuss the notion of cultural relativity and its relationship to the workplace, the classroom, or family life. Use examples from your personal and professional lives to support your views.

3. What would you say to someone who told you that too many cultural voices are being heard in society?

4. Explain how the media influence our perceptions, beliefs, and values associated with intercultural communication. Use examples from both print and nonprint media.

5. If you had a chance to talk to an intercultural communication researcher about some of the rules and laws in society pertaining to intercultural relationships, what would you talk about? What would guide your discussion?

Interactive Activities and InfoTrac College Edition Exercises

Interactive Activities

InfoTrac College Edition Exercises

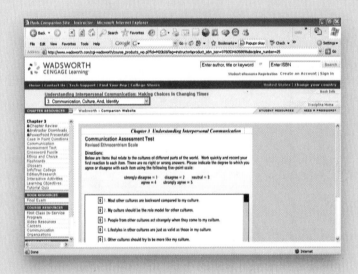

Chapter 4
Communicating Verbally

chapter ✚ goals

Understand the nature of verbal symbols and their relationship to language and meaning

Identify how factors such as culture, gender, generation, and context affect verbal symbols

Explain the ways in which verbal symbols may be used both positively and negatively

Demonstrate skill and sensitivity in using verbal communication

CASEinPOINT

CARLOS PADILLA AND LIZ CARSON

Carlos Padilla saw Liz Carson every Tuesday and Thursday while walking to his part-time job after class at Midtown University. He liked the way she smiled and waved at him as they passed. Carlos wanted to talk to her, but he wasn't sure exactly what to say. He was afraid Liz was just being polite when she smiled at him; in fact, he was pretty sure she didn't know his name. But, he hoped that if they had a chance to talk he'd win her over. Carlos decided that next Tuesday he'd talk to her.

When Tuesday came, he walked up to Liz, smiling broadly. She smiled back and slowed her pace. Soon they were facing each other and looking at one another a little awkwardly. "Hi," Carlos finally managed. "Buenos días," Liz replied. Carlos was taken aback. Was Liz mocking him? Did she think he couldn't speak English? He turned away slightly. Liz sensed his discomfort but she wasn't sure what had happened. She frowned and leaned forward. Then she asked, "Is something wrong, Carlos?" Carlos smiled; she did know his name. "No,

nothing's wrong, Liz. I was wondering if we could grab a cup of coffee later. I hope you don't think it's untoward of me to ask." Liz looked at Carlos for a moment, trying not to laugh. "Untoward?" she repeated. "Have you been reading the dictionary?" she giggled. Carlos shook his head, cleared his throat, and decided to make a joke of it. "Yeah, I'm trying out new vocabulary words, but I'd really like to get together," he said, laughing. "Well, Carlos, I'd like that but I can't make it today. I'm working in the library after class and then I have a ton of work—I have a huge paper due tomorrow. But I'd love to another time." Liz looked away from Carlos at the cars on the street. Carlos backed away one step, saying, "Uh, okay, Liz, maybe another time then." He turned and walked away thinking that the encounter had been a failure. Liz left hoping they'd have a chance to get together another time.

Go to your online Resource Center for *Understanding Interpersonal Communication* to watch a video clip of Carlos's and Liz's interaction.

> Access the resources for Chapter 4 and select "Carlos" to watch the video (it takes a minute for the video to load). As you watch the video, ask yourself what Carlos could have said to Liz before he left her so that he would have walked away feeling better about their encounter. > You can respond to this and other analysis questions, and then click "Done" to compare your answers with those provided by the authors.

Verbal symbols are important in interpersonal communication for many reasons. First, language cements social relationships. Words connect people to one another and interpersonal relationships are constructed in everyday conversation (Duck, 2007). For example, the use of profanity illustrates one way that language and relationships intertwine. Some research indicates that people who swear around each other may do so to reinforce that their relationship is special and not bound by normal conventions (Winters & Duck, 2001).

Further, language developed as a means to differentiate members of an in-group from those of an out-group (Dunbar, 1998). Recalling information from Chapter 3 on in-groups and out-groups, consider the following example from a Dell computer instruction manual:

> The only two valid memory configurations are: a pair of matched memory modules installed in connectors RIMM1 and RIMM2 with continuity modules installed in connectors RIMM3 and RIMM4 or a pair of matched memory modules installed in connectors RIMM1 and RIMM2 and another matched pair installed in connectors RIMM3 and RIMM4.

People who are familiar with computer technology will be defined as part of an in-group when they use and understand statements like this one. Those who are puzzled by such jargon will be assigned out-group status.

In the case in point scenario above, Carlos and Liz experienced some of the problems we all encounter when we communicate. The verbal and non-verbal symbols systems we use to interact with others are imprecise. Misunderstandings, misinterpretations, and inaccuracies often result from our necessary dependence on these symbol systems. For example, Liz didn't realize that Carlos was offended by her response to his use of the word *untoward,* and Carlos believed that Liz's laughter meant she was ridiculing him.

Verbal messages can have dramatic (even if unintended) effects. When Liz greeted Carlos using the Spanish phrase "Buenos días" he was upset. He felt she was belittling his Mexican American heritage and insulting him by indicating she thought he couldn't speak English. The simple use of the Spanish words prompted powerful emotions in Carlos and almost ended the conversation altogether.

In this chapter, we will discuss verbal symbols and describe their unique attributes. Although we have separated our presentation of verbal and non-verbal message systems into two chapters, it's important to remember that they are inextricably intertwined, and it's really the interplay between them that makes meaning. For example, Carlos's disappointment when interacting with Liz resulted from how he "heard" both her verbal messages (using a

Young people are masters of language that assigns in-group and out-group status, particularly slang. Slang is most often used within the in-group by speakers to distinguish themselves from an out-group (such as parents or other authority figures), to fit in with the in-group, and to express common social and emotional experiences in efficient shorthand.

Spanish phrase and saying she's too busy for coffee) and her nonverbal messages (laughing at him for using an uncommon word and looking away from him).

Understanding Verbal Symbols

To begin our discussion, we need to distinguish among the related terms language, verbal symbols, and grammar. **Language** is a system consisting of verbal symbols and grammar that enables us to engage in meaning making with others. **Verbal symbols** are the words or the vocabulary that make up a language. **Grammar** refers to a set of rules dictating how words can be combined to make a meaningful message.

Verbal symbols are important to a language system, but they must be accompanied by grammatical rules telling us how to use them. If a man walked up to you and said, "Look on sky balloon is hanging," you would assume he was not a native English speaker or that something was wrong. The words in the sentence are all recognizable as part of the English vocabulary, but their arrangement does not follow any rules for a sentence in English. The processes of **encoding**, or putting our thoughts into meaningful language, and **decoding**, or developing a thought based on hearing language, require an adequate vocabulary and a grasp of the rules of grammar.

Discussion of the rules of grammar is beyond the scope of our book. However, we do want to turn our attention to verbal symbols, which form the building blocks of interpersonal communication. Let's consider some specific attributes of verbal symbols.

language

A system comprised of vocabulary and rules of grammar that allows us to engage in verbal communication.

verbal symbols

Words, or the vocabulary that make up a language.

grammar

The rules that dictate the structure of language.

encoding

The process of putting thoughts and feelings into verbal symbols, nonverbal messages, or both.

decoding

The process of developing a thought based on hearing verbal symbols, observing nonverbal messages, or both.

Attributes of Verbal Symbols

In this section, we outline five attributes of words: they are symbolic, their meanings evolve, they are powerful, their meanings are denotative and connotative, and they vary in levels of abstraction. These five attributes help us understand how verbal symbols are used in interpersonal communication.

Words Are Symbolic

As we discussed in Chapter 1, symbols are arbitrary, mutually agreed upon labels or representations for feelings, concepts, objects, or events. Because words are arbitrary symbols, there is not a direct relationship between the word and the thing. For instance, the letters *c-a-t* form an agreed upon symbol for the actual furry animal English speakers call a cat. The Spanish word *gato* and the German word *katze* are equally arbitrary symbols used to represent the same animal. Figure 4.1 illustrates this concept by graphically representing the thought, the thing, and the word that stands for the thing on the three points of the triangle of meaning (Ogden & Richards, 1923). This illustration shows that the word is *not* the thing but merely a symbol we have agreed to use to stand for it. By agreeing on symbols, we can engage in communication with one another about things.

Usually, a group of speakers (or a culture) records their agreement about the meaning of words in a dictionary. However, a dictionary is not static because language and the verbal symbols that constitute it keep evolving.

Figure 4.1 The triangle of meaning

thing

thought
(furry feline house pet)

word
(cat)

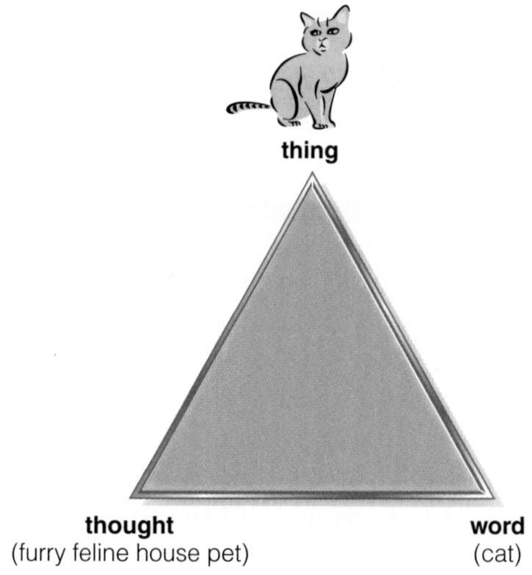

Language Evolves

As time passes, some words become out of date and aren't used any longer. For example, the words *petticoat, girdle, dowry,* and even *typewriter* are becoming obsolete and disappearing from our vocabulary. Some expressions that were popular in earlier times simply aren't used now, illustrating that language is susceptible to fads and fashion. If you are younger than 80 years old, you probably have never used the phrase *the bees' knees,* 1920s slang that meant something was wonderful or "hot." In the 1950s and 1960s, it was common for people to say "tootle-loo" instead of "goodbye," and when couples wanted to go find a romantic spot, they'd tell others that they were "going to the submarine races," although there was no evidence of any water nearby! Some researchers talk of words and phrases as having "careers," in the course of which their meaning may undergo dramatic changes (Bowdle & Gentner, 2005).

Sometimes words experience a revival after they had been popular during an earlier era. For example, the word *groovy* was popular in the 1960s, fell out of favor for a while, and then became trendy again in the late 1990s with the release of the popular Austin Powers movies. *Groovy's* revival didn't last long among the larger population, but smaller segments of society still use the word frequently. Sometimes our vocabulary changes as a result of social changes. For example, we don't use the word *Negro* anymore, but instead favor *African American.* These sorts of language changes might be ridiculed as political correctness and thought of as over-concern for how things are said. But confusing political correctness with important language reform is a mistake. Changing language to give people respect and to be accurate is a goal that shouldn't be trivialized. Further, using language that is appropriate to a culture's evolution strengthens a person's credibility.

Because verbal symbols are so powerful, they can symbolize prejudicial attitudes that we should eliminate (Mills, 1981). For instance, the words *colored, Negro, Afro-American, African American,* and *person of color* reflect changes in the position of black people in the United States. The words are not synonyms but actually have different meanings (McGlone, Beck, & Pfiester, 2006). *African American* communicates an emphasis on ethnicity rather than race, and *person of color* attempts to be more positive than *nonwhite.*

Similarly, the language used to describe people with disabilities has evolved. For example, when Dale tells his parents about his friend Abby, who uses a wheelchair because she has muscular dystrophy, he calls her a *person with a disability.* He doesn't use the word *handicapped* or *crippled* because language reform has helped him see people in wheelchairs as people first, not as their disabilities. He knows Abby as a great friend with a biting sense of humor who uses a wheelchair to get around. To further explore language reform, use your online Resource Center for *Understanding Interpersonal Communication* to access *Interactive Activity 4.1: Politically Correct Language* under the resources for Chapter 4.

Some college campuses are making efforts to accommodate transgender students, including using pronouns that those in the transgender community favor: *ze* in place of *he* or *she* and *hir* instead of *him* or *her* (Bernstein, 2004). This accommodation is important for ease and accuracy of communication. For example, when Natalie wants to refer to a friend, Noel, who identifies as transgender, she can simply say, "ze is a friend of mine" instead of "he or she is a friend of mine."

Verbal symbols continue to evolve and their meanings change. For instance, the words *calling card* used to mean an engraved card that you left at the home of someone whom you had just visited. Today, we still use the term *calling card,* but now it refers to prepaid cards for making phone calls. Similarly, the word *gay* used to refer to being happy and lighthearted, as in "we'll have a gay old time." Today, *gay* is a sexual identity. Incidentally, the term *gay* was chosen intentionally by people in gay communities because of the positive associations it carried from its former meaning.

People have coined new words such as *Googling, metrosexual, hyperlink, Crackberry* (referring to the addictive qualities of Blackberries and other electronic devices), and *blog* to name a few. These new words give labels to recent innovations. As Paul McFedries (2004) observes, "when there's a new invention, service, trend or idea, we need a new way to describe these things. The emerging vocabulary becomes a mirror to the culture" (p. 12).

"I'm hearing a lot of buzzwords from you, but I'm not getting a buzz."

Finally, vocabularies tend to reflect the current times. The second edition of the *Oxford Dictionary of English* (2003) contained 3,000 new words and the themes they expressed centered on terrorism, technology, and television ("Are you suffering from data smog?" 2003). The new words included *24/7* (all the time), *counterterrorism* (military or political activities designed to thwart or prevent terrorism), *dirty bomb* (a conventional bomb containing material that is radioactive), *egosurfing* (searching the Internet for references to oneself), and *bada bing* (a term from *The Sopranos* used to emphasize that something will happen effortlessly and predictably).

Words Are Powerful

Certain words have the power to affect people dramatically. As we've said previously, words are arbitrary symbols, so their power is not intrinsic; it derives from our having agreed to give them power. As we mentioned above, these agreements change over time. For example, in the 17th century, the word "blackguard" was a potent insult but that's no longer the case. But other words (like "ass") have taken on power they didn't have in the 17th century (Duck, 2007).

People have made many words powerful. For instance, in 2004, CNN reported that the state of Georgia was considering banning the word *evolution* in the science curriculum in the public schools ("Georgia considers banning 'evolution'," 2004). The school superintendent said that the *concept* of evolution would still be taught but that the *word* would no longer be used. This case points to the power that Georgians gave the term *evolution*, although in the end, the word was not banned.

In 2002, in one of his more famous speeches, President Bush labeled North Korea, Iraq, and Iran an "axis of evil." Some critics thought Bush began a war of words with that phrase. On its editorial page, *USA Today* said that Bush's rhetoric was inflammatory as well as inaccurate because the three countries' political positions differed from one another. The editorial concluded by stating that "treating Iran, Iraq and North Korea as a unified, monolithic axis—vulnerable to the same rhetoric and tactics—is a formula for failure, not to mention an invitation to a multifront war" ("'Axis of evil' remark sparks damaging backlash," 2002, p. 16A). Others might argue that Bush's phrase was an example of strong, motivational rhetoric. Either way, it's a dramatic example of the power of words. To read an interesting student editorial about the media's use of the terms *terrorist* and *suicide bomber,* use your online Resource Center for *Understanding Interpersonal Communication* to access *Interactive Activity 4.2: The Power of Words* under the resources for Chapter 4.

The power of words in the English language is illustrated by a study looking at how the phrase *think positive* affected breast cancer patients (Kitzinger, 2000). The study found that in general, the phrase *think positive* sent a message that if you don't get better it's because you're not being positive enough. This phrase, then, had a great deal of power, often making patients feel inadequate or responsible for their own illness.

These definitions form the denotative meaning of the word *gun*. Denotative meanings can be confusing; because the dictionary provides more than one meaning for *gun*, your listener must decide if you are using definition 1a, 1b, 1c, 2a, or 2b.

The **connotative meaning** of a term varies from person to person. Connotative meanings derive from people's personal and subjective experience with a verbal symbol. For example, someone who had a close friend or relative shot to death would have a different emotional or connotative meaning for *gun* than would a hunter or a member of the National Rifle Association. Although both of these people would be aware of the denotative meanings of *gun*, their definition of the word would be colored by their personal connotative meanings.

Words Vary in Level of Abstraction

You can place a word on a continuum from concrete to abstract. If a word is **concrete**, you are able to detect its **referent** (the thing the word represents) with one of your senses. Stated another way, concrete words are those that you can see, smell, taste, touch, or hear. The more a word restricts the number of possible referents, the more concrete the word is. For instance, if Sara has 15 relatives but only 3 brothers, brother is a more specific, concrete term than *relative*, and *Scott* (the name of one of Sara's brothers) is more specific than either of the two other terms. The word *relative* is the term with the fewest restrictions, so it is the most **abstract**. We can envision a ladder of abstraction (see Figure 4.2) that begins with the most concrete symbol for a referent and moves to the most abstract.

connotative meaning

The meaning of a verbal symbol that is derived from our personal and subjective experience with that symbol.

concrete

Able to be seen, smelled, tasted, touched, or heard.

referent

The thing a verbal symbol represents.

abstract

Not able to be seen, smelled, tasted, touched, or heard.

framing theory

A theory that argues that when we compare two unlike things in a figure of speech, we are unconsciously influenced by this decision.

Figure 4.2   The ladder of abstraction

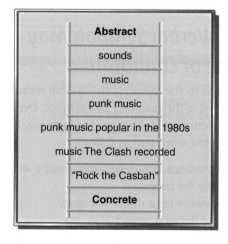

Abstract

sounds

music

punk music

punk music popular in the 1980s

music The Clash recorded

"Rock the Casbah"

Concrete

Some referents are naturally somewhat abstract. Ideas like love and democracy do not have terms that correspond to the lower rungs of the ladder of abstraction. Language skills allow us to talk about the concepts involved in abstract terms. For example, when we speak about *justice,* we use other abstract terms, such as *fairness,* to get our message across. To make our ideas more concrete so others can better understand our meaning, we often use figures of speech such as metaphors and similes. Metaphors equate two terms—for example, *"Love* is a *roller-coaster ride."* Similes make comparisons using the word *like* or *as*—for example, *"Justice* is like *redistributing portions of a pie."*

Although they do not provide perfect descriptions, figures of speech can be beautiful, allowing language to soar to poetic heights and enabling us to see something in a new way. Yet, it is also true that some metaphors are used so often that they become "frozen" or "conventional" and we don't even recognize that they are metaphoric ("my mood is down") (Sopory, 2006). Sometimes the comparisons provided by metaphors and similes don't help us understand meaning better, but rather mislead us. One theory about how figures of speech affect us is **framing theory** (Lakoff, 2003). Framing theory argues that when we compare two unlike things in a figure of speech, we are unconsciously influenced by the comparison. For example, comparing differences between men and women to war (i.e. the battle of the sexes) focuses our thinking on oppositions and a basic animosity between the sexes. We don't consciously reflect on this—the metaphor just causes us to make this association. Imagine how our thinking might differ if we instead used the metaphor "gender union" (DeFrancisco & Palczewski, 2007) to talk about the sexes.

When referents are not right in front of us, we can visualize them through the **process of abstraction** (the ability to move up and down the ladder of abstraction from specific to general and vice versa). For instance, let's say

The NewsHour with Jim Lehrer/
© MacNeil-Lehrer Productions

FORMER CAPT. PHILLIP CARTER
U.S. ARMY

IPC $_{the}^{in}$ News

The power of metaphor to bring two separate ideas together is illustrated in a *USA Today* article that discusses how military officials and government spokespeople talk about the war in Iraq. The article observes that sports metaphors are no longer used to talk about the war: "No one will ever characterize anything again as a 'slam dunk'." Instead, comments like those of retired Army captain Phillip Carter on PBS's *NewsHour* compare the war to liquids: "You squeeze the bad guys out of Baghdad, and they pop like a water balloon up into the Diyala province." The article speculates that liquid metaphors may be useful because of the "amorphous nature of the enemy" as well as the fact that everyone can relate to them— who hasn't played with a water balloon? The article also cautions against throwing around all such metaphors casually: "The military should tell it like it is, not dress up the war in cutesy language."

Beehner, L. (2007, June 4) A squirt or a surge? Both are miscast war metaphors. *USA Today,* p. 11A.

process of abstraction

The ability to move up and down the ladder of abstraction from specific to general and vice versa.

that Jay wants to tell his friends about his fabulous new red and white Mini Cooper. As he uses descriptors to talk about his car in its absence, his friends are able to imagine it pretty clearly. Later Jay sees a friend, Lois, who just totaled her car. Jay decides to tell Lois about his new car, but he uses words that are less concrete, leaving out the brand name and color so that Lois won't be too envious. To read an interesting article that examines how journalists tend to move up and down the ladder of abstraction, check out "The Ladder of Abstraction" by using your online Resource Center for *Understanding Interpersonal Communication* to access *InfoTrac College Edition Exercise 4.1: Moving Up and Down the Ladder of Abstraction.*

Because words vary in their level of abstraction, meaning is often ambiguous. This ambiguity may be unintentional or strategic. For instance, if Jane lacks the verbal skills of clarity and audience analysis, her communication may seem vague, even though she doesn't intend it to be. However, sometimes it may serve a purpose to be ambiguous. Researchers have described this phenomenon in two ways: strategic ambiguity and equivocation.

Your turn

*R*eflect on ambiguity in verbal symbols by tracking language you hear in conversation and in the media, particularly in political speeches and advertising. If you like, you can use your student workbook or your **Understanding Interpersonal Communication** Online Resources to complete this activity.

Strategic ambiguity refers to how people talk when they do not want others to completely understand their intentions (Eisenberg, 1984). In organizations people (especially at the management level) may leave out cues on purpose to encourage multiple interpretations by others. It is possible that ambiguity moderates tensions in an organization. To promote harmony, leaders of organizations may have to be ambiguous enough to allow for many interpretations while simultaneously encouraging agreement (Eisenberg). This strategy can also be used by a person in a conflict. Saying something like "I am not sure about that" allows several interpretations and may achieve the end of the argument.

Equivocation is a type of ambiguity that involves choosing your words carefully to give a listener a false impression without actually lying. For instance, if your grandmother sends you a birthday gift that you don't like, but you value your relationship with your grandmother and don't want to hurt her feelings, you might equivocate in your thank-you. You might say: "Thanks so much for the sweater. It was so thoughtful of you to think about keeping me warm in the cold winters!" You have not said the sweater was attractive, nor have you said you liked it, so you haven't lied overtly. However, if you are a good equivocator, you have given your grandmother the impression that you are really pleased with a sweater that you, in fact, dislike. Keep in mind that such a tactic could have long-term consequences. In this case, you could receive similar unwanted sweaters for several birthdays to come.

strategic ambiguity

Leaving out cues in a message on purpose to encourage multiple interpretations by others.

equivocation

A type of ambiguity that involves choosing our words carefully to give a listener a false impression without actually lying.

Equivocating involves saying things that are true but misleading. It should be no surprise that the language of advertising makes use of equivocation. When an ad says that a car's seats "have the look and feel of fine leather" that means that they are *not* made of fine leather, but the use of the words *fine leather* leads an unsuspecting listener to think that they are. In addition, the word *virtually* is a good equivocal word. The phrase *virtually spotless* means that the described item may have some spots on it, but the phrase leads you to believe otherwise.

Sometimes *euphemisms* are a kind of equivocal speech. **Euphemisms** are milder or less direct words substituted for other words that are more blunt or negative. They are used to reduce the discomfort related to an unpleasant or sensitive subject. For example, we say we're going to the *restroom* even though we're not planning to rest, we refer to a person's *passing* rather than their death, or we talk about *adult entertainment* rather than pornography.

Factors Affecting Verbal Symbols

...at work

In the workplace, we need to pay particular attention to the words we choose to express our thoughts because word choice can have job advancement implications. For instance, if you approach your boss, Martha, about changing your vacation dates, it is important how you phrase your request. If you say, "Martha, I need to take my vacation from February 10th to the 21st instead of in March," Martha might find your directness too terse. She might expect you to show deference in your request ("Is it all right with you if I change when I take my vacation?") or include an explanation ("I have had an unexpected event in my family").

Word choice affects both outcome and process. That is, you might be able to change your vacation time (outcome) but at the expense of annoying your boss (process), or your request might be denied altogether because Martha feels you are being too direct (outcome and process). Of course, words don't determine all outcomes in the workplace, but choosing your words carefully is a good start to getting what you want. Can you identify other consequences of word choice in the workplace?

We understand and use words differently depending on a variety of factors. In this section, we discuss the relationships between verbal symbols and each of the following: culture and ethnicity, gender, generation, and context. Although we discuss these factors in isolation, they can form many combinations. For example, an elderly African American man living in the United States talking to his granddaughter at home uses verbal symbols quite differently than a young Asian woman living in Korea speaking to a group of business associates at an annual meeting.

Culture and Ethnicity

On the most basic level, culture affects language (and vice versa) because most cultures develop their own language. Thus, people of Kenya tend to speak Swahili, and those living in Poland usually speak Polish. This section addresses some of the many other ways culture and ethnicity relate to language.

Let's first look at idioms. An **idiom** is a word or a phrase that has an understood meaning within a culture, but that meaning doesn't come from exact

euphemism

A milder or less direct word substituted for another word that is more blunt or negative.

idiom

A word or a phrase that has an understood meaning within a culture but whose meaning is not derived by exact translation.

REVISITING CASE IN POINT

1. How does the conversation between Carlos and Liz illustrate the idea that the meaning for words is both connotative and denotative?

2. When Carlos says, "I was wondering if we could grab a cup of coffee later," how is he using the levels of abstraction of language strategically?

You can answer these questions online under the resources for Chapter 4 at your online Resource Center for Understanding Interpersonal Communication.

translation. Thus, people who are learning a language have to learn the meaning of each idiom as a complete unit; they cannot simply translate each of the words and put their meanings together. For example, in English we say "it was a breeze" when we mean that something was easy. If someone tried to translate "it was a breeze" without knowing it functions as an idiom, they would mistake the statement's meaning. However, a listener also has to pay attention to context. If "it was a breeze" is the response to the question "What messed up all the papers I had laid out under the window?" English speakers know not to access the statement's idiomatic meaning but rather to rely on the meaning of each word.

Let's look at another example. Madeline works for the International Student Center at Western State University, and some of the international students tell her that U.S. students are unfriendly. When they parted company with a group of U.S. students, they said, those students said "see you later," but the U.S. students made no attempt to do so. The international students believed that the U.S. students failed to keep their promise for future social interactions. Madeline explained to the international students that "see you later" is an example of a particular type of idiom called phatic communication. **Phatic communication** consists of words and phrases that are used for interpersonal contact only and are not meant to be translated directly word for word. This type of communication can be thought of as content-free because listeners are not supposed to think about the meaning of the statement; rather, they are expected to respond to the polite contact the speaker is making. When you see someone and say "Hi, how are you doing?" you probably don't really want to know how the details about how the other person is doing—you're just making contact. "How's it going?" or "How are you doing?" should elicit a response such as "Okay—how about you?" If you said "how's it going?" to your acquaintance Katy, and she started to tell you about her recent breakup or the big fight she had with her brother, you would likely be surprised and might think that Katy was odd.

Now we'll discuss some verbal behaviors thought to characterize two specific groups, African Americans and Mexican Americans. There are many

phatic communication

Communication consisting of words and phrases that are used for interpersonal contact only and are not meant to be translated verbatim.

other groups we could examine, but these two are the most studied in terms of the effects of ethnicity on language. Although the findings do not apply to every member of these two groups, African Americans and Mexican Americans are often considered distinct language groups. African Americans and Mexican Americans spend a great deal of time with one another in social and neighborhood settings, and most people in both groups identify with race as a way of establishing identity (Johnson, 2000). Let's look at the way language and ethnicity interact within each of these groups.

Some research suggests that African American speech is more assertive than European American speech (Ribeau, Baldwin, & Hecht, 2000). According to this research, in a conversation between Tisha, an African American, and Lee, a European American, Lee might say "Is everything okay between us?" and Tisha might respond "You know something is wrong—just say it out aloud." African Americans and European Americans may truly differ in how assertive their speech is, or this finding may be complicated by perceptions. One study found that African American women think European American women are highly conflict avoidant. European American women reported their belief that African American women are assertive and confrontational. However, neither group of women characterized themselves as highly avoidant or confrontational (Shuter & Turner, 1997).

Black speech is also seen as vibrant and enduring (Smitherman, 2000). Black speech has had a long evolution and many of its words and phrases have found their way into the vocabulary of white speakers as well. For example, when white speakers say, "She can talk the talk, but can she walk the walk?" or use words like hip, phat, or testify, they owe a debt to African American speakers. In addition to being rooted in tradition, black speech is often humorous, witty, and wise (Smitherman, 2000).

The Linguistic Society of America issued a resolution making this same assertion. They passed this resolution in support of the Oakland School Board's decision to recognize black English (variously known as African American Vernacular English [AAVE] or Ebonics). The Linguistic Society stated,

> The systematic and expressive nature of the grammar and pronunciation patterns of the African American vernacular has been established by numerous scientific studies over the past thirty years. Characterizations of Ebonics as "slang," "mutant," "lazy," "defective," "ungrammatical," or "broken English" are incorrect and demeaning (Linguistics Society of America, 1997).

© Mike Blake/Reuters/Corbis

With clever, ironic references to societal traditions and pop culture, such as "gimme some suga", I am your neighbor" and "shake it like a Polaroid picture," Outkast lyrics are examples of the black speech that is a staple in rap and hip hop songs.

To further explore views in support and in opposition to the use of Ebonics, read the article "Q: Would Ebonics Programs in Public Schools Be a Good Idea?" available through InfoTrac College Edition. Go to your online Resource Center for *Understanding Interpersonal Communication* to access **InfoTrac College Edition Exercise 4.2: Ebonics: Opposing Viewpoints.**

Chicano English, spoken by Mexican Americans, is also frequently studied by researchers. Mexican Americans form only a part of the Latino/Latina culture, sometimes known as Hispanic culture. This culture includes Cubans, Puerto Ricans, Chileans, Peruvians, Columbians, and many more. It is difficult to generalize about all Hispanics, but national, ancestral, and language ties seem to be important to all Latinos and Latinas, and "the Spanish language also functions to create and cement cultural unity" (Johnson, 2000, p. 167).

Mexican Americans, like other Hispanics, exhibit great variety in terms of their bilingualism. Some Mexican Americans speak English or Spanish exclusively, others speak Spanish in private and English in public, whereas still others engage in **code-switching**, or shifting back and forth between languages in the same conversation. When Luís says to José, "Yo no le creí, you know" ("I didn't believe him, you know") (Silva-Corvalán, 1994), he demonstrates code-switching by saying the statement in Spanish and ending with the slang English phrase "you know," just as a native English speaker would.

On a broader level, remember that culture pertains to more than just national origin. Cultures or co-cultures can form around people who share certain things in common, such as religious beliefs or professional experiences. People become **speech communities** when they share norms about how to speak, what words to use, and when, where, and why to speak (Labov, 1972). In this way a speech community resembles a national or ethnic culture. One example of a unique speech community is people who are incarcerated. Prison vocabulary is rich and quite different from the English spoken by those outside of prison walls. In fact, a San Diego consulting firm that prepares convicts to serve their sentences has compiled a dictionary to acculturate future prisoners to prison culture (Rough Guide, August, 2007). See Table 4.1 for examples of prison vocabulary.

A theory that explains how words relate to culture is **symbolic interactionism** (Blumer, 1969; Mead, 1934). Symbolic interactionism says that cultures are held together by their common use of symbols and that things do not exist in an objective form; they exist based on cultural agreement about them. In short, "all the 'things' which make up our world, including ourselves, are products of symbolic actions, constituted and created through the communication process" (Trenholm, 1986, p. 37). Symbolic interactionism, then, points us to an understanding of how culture or society is tied to words. To read an article that examines the connection between a particular culture in Vermont and its language, check out "Vermont Area Struggles to Keep Welsh Culture Alive," available through InfoTrac College Edition. Go to your online Resource Center for Understanding Interpersonal Communication to access **InfoTrac College Edition Exercise 4.3: The Ties between Language and Culture.**

Another framework that links culture and verbal symbols is linguistic determinism, a theory put forth simultaneously by anthropologists Benjamin

code-switching

Shifting back and forth between languages in the same conversation.

speech community

A group of people who share norms about how to speak, what words to use, and when, where, and why to speak.

symbolic interactionism theory

The theory that our understanding of ourselves and of the world is shaped by our interactions with those around us.

Table 4.1   The language of a particular speech community: prison vocabulary

Birds on the line	A warning that someone is listening to the conversation
Bling bling	A warning that officers are coming
Bonaroo	A prisoner's best clothes
Buck Rogers time	A parole date so far in the future that the prisoner can't imagine being released
Cat nap	A short sentence
Escape dust	Fog
T-Jones	A prisoner's mother

Whorf and Edward Sapir (Hoijer, 1994; Whorf, 1956). **Linguistic determinism** argues that words determine our ability to perceive and think. Both Whorf and Sapir believed that culture affects our thinking through the vehicle of language. Researchers have suggested that without a word for something in the environment, a person has difficulty perceiving that thing or thinking that it is important. For example, Pacific Islanders' languages in the past had hundreds of names for the fish that were so crucial to their livelihood. However, some of these languages are disappearing and, as a result, the knowledge of the diversity of fish is also lost (Nettle & Romaine, 2000). As Nettle and Romaine state,

> Much of what is culturally distinctive in language—for example vocabulary for flora, fauna—is lost when language shift takes place. The typical youngster today in Koror, Palau's capital, cannot identify most of Palau's native fish; nor can his father. (p. 16)

The principle that language determines what you perceive and think about is apparent in the comments of Elizabeth Seay (2004) who studied Native American languages in Oklahoma. As she observes,

> Learning new languages can bring unnoticed ideas into focus. The Comanches have a word for the bump on the back of the neck which is thought to be a place where the body is centered. The Muscogee-Creeks single out the particular kind of love that children and their parents and grandparents feel for each other, using a word that also means "to be stingy." (p. 17)

These examples, along with many others (such as the fact that the Chinese have no word for *privacy*) support the idea that language determines how we think and that speakers of different languages perceive the world in different ways.

However, not all researchers agree with linguistic determinism. Even Benjamin Whorf wondered if linguistic determinism might be overstating the

linguistic determinism

A theory that argues that our language determines our ability to perceive and think about things. If we don't have a word for something in our language, this theory predicts we won't think about it or notice it.

case. He devised another theory, **linguistic relativity** (Whorf, 1956), which states that language influences our thinking but doesn't determine it. Both linguistic determinism and linguistic relativity point to the connections among culture, language, and thought, and they are sometimes referred to together as the strong and weak forms of the **Sapir-Whorf hypothesis**, a statement referring to the relationship between language and perception.

Further, even though compelling examples illustrate both theories, empirical evidence hasn't completely supported the theories' assertions. One of the most famous examples illustrating the Sapir-Whorf hypothesis has been called into question. Whorf (1956) said that linguistic relativity was supported by the fact that the Inuit have many words for *snow* because it is so crucial to their everyday lives. In addition, the Inuit actually see snow differently from others whose lives are not as dependent on snow. Whereas English speakers simply see monolithic white "stuff," due to having only one word, *snow,* the Inuit see all the varieties their language allows. Whorf didn't specify how many Inuit words for *snow* exist; some say about two dozen, but the numbers vary, and the *New York Times* once mentioned that there were 100 (Pullum, 1991). This example has been shown to be inaccurate, however (Pullum). Although the Inuit do use many different terms for snow, other languages allow their speakers to perceive the same variety through phrases and modifiers (fluffy, slushy, good-packing, and so forth).

The Arabic language doesn't have a single word for *compromise,* which some have said is the reason that Arabs seem to be unable to reach a compromise. Yet, the Arabic language does provide several ways to articulate the concept of compromise, the most common being an expression that translates in English to "we reached a middle ground" (Nunberg, 2003). This example illustrates **codability**, which refers to the ease with which a language can express a thought. When a language has a convenient word for a concept, that concept is said to have high codability. Thus, the existence of the word *compromise* gives that idea high codability in English. When a concept requires more than a single word for its expression, it possesses lower codability. It is accurate, then, to say that the idea of compromise has lower codability in Arabic than in English. However, having a phrase rather than a single word to express an idea does not mean that the idea is nonexistent in a given culture, only that it is less easily put into the language code (Nunberg).

Cultures dictate attitudes toward language and certain language practices. For example, in the United States, speech functions primarily as a vehicle for expressing one's ideas clearly and forcefully. On the other hand, the Chinese have the attitude that actions are more powerful than words, exemplified in proverbs such as "Talk does not cook rice." Other language traditions include the following:

- In the Lakota tradition, it is sacrilegious to say the name of a dead person in public.
- Jewish people believe that children should not be named for any living person.

linguistic relativity

A theory that states that language influences our thinking but doesn't determine it. Thus, if we don't have a word for something in our language, this theory predicts it will be difficult, but not impossible, to think about it or notice it.

Sapir-Whorf hypothesis

A theory that points to connections among culture, language, and thought. In its strong form, this theory is known as linguistic determinism, and in its weak form, it is known as linguistic relativity.

codability

The ease with which a language can express a thought.

- The Japanese avoid saying words in wedding toasts that refer to home or going back home.

- In traditional Native American communities, silence is an important way to communicate respect.

Sex and Gender

Sex and gender, especially with regard to language and verbal symbols, have been studied extensively. However, despite decades of research examining and comparing men and women's communication behaviors, we still don't have definitive information. Early research held that women and men spoke differently. Women were seen as using a different vocabulary from men that included, among other things, more words for colors (for example, *mauve*), more polite words and phrases (for example, "would you please open the door" rather than "open the door"), and more modifiers (for example, *very* and *so*) (Lakoff, 1975).

Some researchers theorized that children played in sex-segregated groups, and that the different ways of interacting within the groups resulted in different speech behaviors (Maltz & Borker, 1982). Little girls tended to play in small groups where it was difficult to gain entry; however, after a girl was accepted in the group, it was easy for her to speak up and be heard. Further, the preferred play activities for girls were creative interactions like house and school, which involve the players in setting the rules. In contrast, little boys played in large groups where it was easy to gain access but difficult to be heard. These boys played baseball, war, and soccer, which have set rules. Thus, whereas girls learned negotiation and cooperation, boys learned assertive communication behaviors and that little talk is necessary for play.

Ethics & Choice

When Andrea Madison entered Oklahoma City University, she was proud to follow in the footsteps of both her parents and her paternal grandparents. She loved everything about OCU—her classes, the parties, and the close relationships she was able to develop with faculty and friends.

One thing she especially enjoyed was going to the basketball games and cheering the outstanding OCU team—the Warriors—to victory. Andrea's grandfather had played on the OCU basketball team that went to the Sweet Sixteen, and her father's basketball team had been NCAA champions. Andrea and her best friends, Molly Byer and Sam Goodwin, spent a lot of time talking about the basketball team and organizing their schedules around basketball games. They hoped that the team would make it to the Final Four in March, and they were already planning how they could make the trip to the tournament to root for their team. Andrea had heard about March Madness all her life, and she was really excited that she might have her own stories to tell after this season. Andrea didn't know too much about Indian history, but she loved the traditions associated with being a fan, including doing war chants along with the team's Indian brave mascot during the exciting parts of the games.

As Andrea enjoyed a basketball game one evening, elsewhere on campus, OCU students Michael Whitefeather and Todd Olden attended a meeting of the First Peoples Association, a group for the Native American students on campus. The students at the meeting appreciated the opportunity to talk about the situations they faced as members of the smallest minority group on campus. The discussion at the meeting centered on the fact that OCU still used symbols of Native culture in a disrespectful way by having a brave as a mascot and screaming a war chant during games. The speaker at the meeting, Paula Redfern, said that she cried each time she saw the mascot. She said that her feelings at OCU games were similar to how Catholic students would feel if the team mascot were dressed like the Pope and people bought toy crucifixes to wave whenever the team scored. The students at the meeting decided that they would stage a demonstration at the next basketball game. They wanted to peacefully, but firmly, get across their message that it was wrong to appropriate another culture's symbols and use them for sport. Michael and Todd, who were moved by the speaker, agreed to be at the demonstration.

As the team's successful season continued, Andrea got more and more excited, so she was surprised when she saw Molly and Sam at the student union looking depressed. Molly told Andrea that a group of Native American students was planning to demonstrate at the next game to protest the team's name,

(Continues)

This belief that sex operated in the same way as culture in establishing different rules, norms, and language patterns for men and women came to be known as the **two-culture theory.** (Maltz & Borker, 1982). This theory was grounded in the notion that "differences in men's and women's language use reflects different experiences, different worlds . . ." (Mulac, Bradac, & Gibbons, 2001, p. 121). Much of Deborah Tannen's (for example, 1995) writing comparing women and men's language use stems from the two-culture theory. For instance, she argues that women prefer "rapport" talk, or talking for pleasure, while men prefer "report" talk, or talk that accomplishes a task.

mascot, and the use of the war chants, which the students said were disrespectful of their traditions. Andrea's jaw dropped. She had never thought that anyone could feel that way. She started forming arguments in her mind against the demonstration. She wondered if changing this tradition would mean that other revered OCU traditions would crumble, too.

What would you advise Andrea to do? What are the ethical implications in this scenario and in the choices Andrea has to make? Is it possible to respect the traditions of both Oklahoma City University and the Native Americans? Why is a name so important to Andrea and her friends and to the Native American students? What are the ethical issues for Michael and the other Native American students? In answering these questions, think about the five ethical systems we described in Chapter 1 (categorical imperative, utilitarianism, ethic of care, golden mean, significant choice). Explain how your answers relate to these systems. Do you prefer one of these ethical systems over the others for resolving this dilemma? Explain.

Go to your online Resource Center for *Understanding Interpersonal Communication* to access an interactive version of this scenario under the resources for Chapter 4. The interactive version of this scenario allows you to choose an appropriate response to this dilemma and then see what consequences your choice brings about. You can also compare your answers to the questions at the end of the scenario to those provided by the authors and, if requested, email your response to your instructor.

Although some research in the last two decades has supported the idea that men and women speak differently in the ways described above (for example, Coates & Cameron, 1989; Mulac, et al., 2001; Treichler & Kramarae, 1983; Wood, 1998), other studies (for example, Canary & Hause, 1993; Goldsmith & Fulfs, 1999; Turner, Dindia, & Pearson, 1995) question whether women and men actually differ much in their speech. For example, in an analysis of more than 1,200 research studies, researchers found that the differences in communication behavior attributable to sex totaled only around one percent (Canary & Hause, 1993).

Do women and men really communicate differently? That question is difficult to answer. However, keep in mind that sex makes a big difference in U.S. society. People in the United States consistently remark on sex even when sex distinctions aren't important to the situation. For example, a grade school teacher commands, "Quiet, boys and girls!" rather than "Quiet, students!" or "Quiet, children!" Similarly, a performer's usual greeting to the audience is "Good evening, ladies and gentlemen." Given this interest in dividing people based on sex, the fact that some sense of language community based on sex arises in the United States is not surprising. Perhaps more tellingly, men and women's language use is perceived differently even when it's essentially the same (Mulac, Incontro, & James, 1985). Sex continues to be a factor that affects language as it's spoken, heard, or both.

two-culture theory

A theory that asserts that sex operates in the same way as culture in establishing different rules, norms, and language patterns for men and women.

Generation

As we discussed earlier in this chapter, one of the functions of language is differentiating in-group members from those on the outside. One of the tasks of each generation is to distinguish itself from the generation that came before it. Generational differences form age cohorts that, to some extent, share experiences and beliefs. The members of any age cohort—for example, GenX, the Baby Boomers, or the Greatest Generation—share a popular culture, which leads to a common language. Slang such as *cheaters* (eyeglasses), *gams* (a woman's legs), *none of your beeswax* (none of your business), *the cat's meow* (something wonderful), and *hitting on all sixes* (giving 100% effort) peppered the talk of youth in the 1920s but is rarely, if ever, heard today. Explore how new words and phrases like these are coined by reading the article "How New Words Come to Be," available through InfoTrac College Edition. Go to your online Resource Center for *Understanding Interpersonal Communication* to access **InfoTrac College Edition Exercise 4.4: How Words Come to Be**.

REVISITING CASEinPOINT

1. *Do you think that the conversation between Carlos and Liz was more complicated by language issues relating to culture or to sex? Why?*

2. *Give an example of a U.S. idiom in the conversation between Liz and Carlos.*

You can answer these questions online under the resources for Chapter 4 at your online Resource Center for Understanding Interpersonal Communication.

Technological changes may affect language across generations as well. A story on Yahoo news ("British girl baffles teacher," 2003) noted how text messaging shorthand caused a communication dilemma between a 13-year-old girl and her teacher in Britain. The teacher commented that she could not translate an essay the student had turned in describing her summer holidays. The teenager had written, in part:

> My smmr hols wr CWOT. B4, we used 2go2 NY 2C my bro, his GF & thr 3 : kids FTF. ILNY, it's a gr8 plc.

In translation, the above reads:

> My summer holidays were a complete waste of time. Before, we used to go to New York to see my brother, his girlfriend and their three screaming kids face to face. I love New York. It's a great place.

E-mail addresses may also indicate age differences. Many young people opt for creative e-mail names that are sometimes outrageous, like Venuschick, Juliaiscoolia, and so forth. However, what seems cool to a 16-year-old can seem embarrassing a few years later, especially because colleges often take

© George Pickow/Hulton Archive/Getty Images

Language use varies from generation to generation, as do the systems used to record and transmit language. For example, if your grandmother was a secretary in the 1940s or 1950s, she probably learned shorthand, a system of handwritten symbols used to transcribe the spoken word. You probably never had to learn shorthand and don't know how to decipher it. But if you use your cell phone to send text messages, you use a newer form of shorthand that consists of numbers, abbreviations, and acronyms that are easy to type from a tiny keypad.

e-mailed applications. One young woman, whose email name is "artzyfartzygirl" said she plans to change the name when she sends emails for college applications so admission committees don't get the wrong idea about her (Sweeney, 2004). A recent study reported by Jeanna Bryner (2007) on MSNBC.com (http://www.msnbc.msn.com/id/18057158) showed that even young people recognized that some email names were unprofessional. Two hundred college students rated actual email names on various criteria including professionalism. Names deemed unprofessional included gigglez217, bacardigirl, bighotdaddy, and drunkensquirl. We return to the topic of identity and technology later in Chapter 11.

The *Chicago Tribune* (Warren, 2004) featured an article discussing what Baby Boomers who are becoming grandparents wish to be called by their grandchildren. The consensus of the grandparents interviewed for the article was that "Grandma" or "Grandpa" sounded too old. They were opting for younger sounding names such as Zsa Zsa, Moogie, Muna, Mima, Gigi, Boo-Boo, and LaLa. Baby Boomers becoming grandparents are "launching a small semantic revolution to avoid the traditional label of senior citizen status" (Warren, Section 5, p.1). Baby Boomers generally don't think of themselves as old, so they invent new names to avoid the connotations of the "blue-haired old granny stereotype" that come with the name "Grandma."

Context

Contextual cues subsume all the other elements we have discussed because the culture, ethnicity, gender, and generation of the people who are interacting factor into the context. Generally, in communication research, the context involves the setting or situation in which the encounter takes place. Thus, as we discussed in Chapter 1, context means all of the elements surrounding the people who are interacting. Here, we briefly address the following contextual cues: situation, time, relationship, and nonverbal cues.

You can understand the impact of situation if you think of the same statement, "You have good legs," being said in each of the following situations:

- By construction workers to a woman walking by a construction site
- By a coach to an athlete running on a track
- By a doctor to a child in the doctor's office

Although the words remain the same, each of these situations would create a different sense of the meaning of the statement. As we discussed previously in this chapter, the meanings of words can change over time. In the 1940s and 1950s, females over the age of 18 referred to themselves as *girls* without a negative connotation. In the 1970s, some feminists rejected the word *girl* as demeaning when applied to adult females. In the 1990s and more recently, some feminists have reclaimed that word and use the term *girl power* with positive connotations. However, many women in their 40s and 50s still reject the term *girl* and do not use it or like to hear it, retaining negative connotations for it.

Relationships between speakers also contribute to the contextual cues that affect meaning. People who are close to you can say things that would be considered impolite if said by mere acquaintances. Teasing, joking, and various forms of humor such as "loving abuse" depend on a strong prior relationship between the speakers. If the relationship isn't positive, these types of interactions would probably be judged as insulting rather than friendly. Of course, even among good friends or family members, people can go too far, and a comment that was intended to be humorous can be interpreted as insulting.

Rhunette Diggs and Kathleen Clark (2002) discuss how racial considerations can complicate a comment meant to be a joke between friends. Diggs and Clark write an account of their own interracial friendship, begun in graduate school and sustained over several years after graduation. At a birthday party for Diggs, Clark, who was the only white person present, made a joke about Diggs being obedient. Although Clark meant it as a humorous jibe between friends, Diggs framed the comment as problematic, in large part because of the interracial context. Diggs saw the comment as giving her outsider status, being labeled by a white person.

As we discuss in Chapter 5, people depend on nonverbal cues to interpret verbal codes. If someone comments that you look nice, you probably check their tone and facial expressions to confirm that their verbal comment is sincere. If the speaker sounds sarcastic in tone, you will undoubtedly believe that you don't look good in their eyes. The nonverbal part of the context is powerful and persuasive in helping people make sense of verbal codes.

Although we don't know exactly when speech began, we can cautiously speculate that gestures preceded vocalizations. One explanation for the fact that humans are the only primates that lack pigment on their palms is that this coloration may have helped early humans communicate (Shlain, 1998). As Shlain states, "before the full development of spoken language, our ancestors sat around the fire speaking and gesturing to each other. It would have been a distinct advantage for the palms to be pale and thus more visible in dim light" (p. 41). In this example, we can see some evolutionary evidence of the importance of nonverbal behaviors in contextualizing verbal symbols.

In sum, when we communicate, we are doing much more than exchanging words. The verbal symbols we use are powerful, ever-evolving abstractions that have both denotative and connotative meanings. They are affected by culture, gender, generation, and context. You have seen that the meaning of a statement often goes beyond the simple definitions of each word. We will now address how verbal symbols may be problematic in interpersonal communication.

The Dark Side of Verbal Symbols

Verbal symbols are not inherently positive or negative. Rather, the value of verbal symbols is determined by how people use them. Verbal symbols in the English language may be easily used for negative ends; they may be exclusionary and derisive, provide inaccurate impressions, mislead listeners, and promote stereotypes. As you remember from Chapter 2, stereotypes are fixed mental pictures of groups that are applied to each member of the group. As we discussed in that chapter, some stereotypes may be positive, but in this section we focus on negative images conveyed by language. The first four categories below illustrate ways that language can be inaccurate, misleading, and unhelpful to its speakers. We then discuss sexist, racist, and homophobic language, all of which reveal a very dark side to language use.

Static Evaluation

Language reflects **static evaluation** when it obscures change. When we speak and respond to people today the same way we did ten years ago, we engage in static evaluation. To a degree, we need to think that people and things are stable. If we recognized that everything is in a constant state of flux, it would be difficult to talk or think because we would be paralyzed by the notion of how little control we have. However, if we ignore change, we cause problems, too. Language contributes to these problems because labels aren't always updated to indicate the changes that take place over time.

For instance, *Mom* is what you call your female parent when you are 4, 18, and 40. However, your relationship with your mother, as well as you and your mother herself, all change greatly over time. When parents say to their children, "No matter how old you get, you will always be my little baby," they are naming the very problem that exists with static evaluation.

Polarization

Polarization occurs when people utilize the either-or aspect of the English language and speak of the world in extremes. When we refer to people as *smart* or *dumb*, *nice* or *mean*, *right* or *wrong*, we are polarizing. Polarization is troubling because most people, things, and events fall somewhere between the extremes named by polar opposites. Most people are good some of the time and bad some of the time. Labeling them as one or the other fails to recognize their totality. For example, when Kayla tells her friend Marsha about her Professor, Dr. Lee, she focuses on how much she dislikes Lee. Kayla says, "He is such a sarcastic jerk! I cannot stand his class. All he ever does is make fun of students. He doesn't even realize how many stupid things he says!"

static evaluation

The tendency to speak and respond to someone today the same way we did in the past, not recognizing that people and relationships change over time.

polarization

The tendency to use "either-or" language and speak of the world in extremes.

Although Kayla is entitled to her opinion of Dr. Lee as a poor teacher, her use of such words as *jerk* and *stupid* is polarizing.

Polarization is also problematic because of static evaluation. If we settle on an extreme label for someone at one time and then encounter the same person later, we will probably not take into account the possibility that the person may have changed over time. For example, let's say that Christie briefly dated Rick in high school when they were both juniors, but she broke it off because she thought he was too immature. Two years later, they meet at a party in college. Christie remembers Rick from high school and immediately thinks of the polarizing term *immature*. Keeping this word in her mind will hinder Christie's ability to see Rick's changes and interact appropriately. Polarization also causes communication problems because of reification, which we address next.

Reification

Reification is the tendency to respond to words, or labels for things, rather than the things themselves. Thus, if we call someone by an extreme label, reification suggests that is how we will respond to them, regardless of what they might do. Reification is often referred to as confusing the symbol and the thing. When people have a strong reaction to a symbol such as a national flag or a school mascot, they are fusing the symbol (flag or mascot) with the thing itself (their country or their school). Although symbols are potent, they are not the same as the things they represent. People who cut up the U.S. flag or burn it may be as patriotic as those who fly the flag in front of their home each day.

Muting

Language fails its users by letting some experiences and ideas go unnamed, creating what theorists call **lexical gaps**. Lexical gaps indicate that language does not serve all its users equally. The **muted group theory** (Kramarae, 1981) explains what happens to people whose experiences are not well represented in verbal symbols. This theory posits that when people suffer with many lexical gaps they have trouble articulating their thoughts and feelings because language doesn't give them an adequate vocabulary for their unique experiences.

Additionally, the theory suggests that groups are muted when language draws more on others' experiences than their own. For instance, some researchers say that expressions from sports ("hit it out of the park") and war ("he attacked all his opponents' ideas") show that English is shaped more by the experiences of men than women (Johnson, 2000). Also, if language doesn't supply a specific verbal symbol to label experiences common to women, they may struggle to express them. For example, Mary wants to talk about how her partner, Jed, uses flattery to manipulate her into doing more of the housework than he does. She is troubled when he says things like, "Oh, you're so much better at cooking, cleaning, and so forth than I am,

reification
The tendency to respond to words or labels for things as though they were the things themselves.

lexical gaps
Experiences that are not named.

muted group theory
Theory that explains what happens to people whose experiences are not well represented in verbal symbols and who have trouble articulating their thoughts and feelings verbally because their language doesn't give them an adequate vocabulary.

Working Title/Havoc/The Kobal Connection/Todd Demmie

We often see static evaluation, polarization, and reification at work in language used to describe crime. Criminals are seen as "scumbags" or "monsters," and people affected by crime are called "victims." Yet, not all people who commit crimes are inherently bad, and not all people affected by crime are inherent victims. Through mediation and counseling, sometimes criminals and victims can come to see themselves and each other as complete human beings rather than simply "monster" or "victim." This process was illustrated in the film **Dead Man Walking,** *which told the story of Sister Helen Prejean's work counseling a convicted murderer before he was executed.*

can't you just do it?" Yet, when Mary tries to describe this experience, she has to tell a long story because she can't find a single word that pinpoints exactly what Jed is doing (Kramarae, 1981).

Other researchers suggest that African Americans (Orbe, 1998) and fathers (Chopra, 2001) are also muted by the English language. For instance, African Americans can be muted when language labels their experiences and behaviors in pejorative ways. When black speakers are said to be "aggressive" or "confrontational," they are being judged by white standards. Further, when Black English is marginalized and considered substandard, black speakers are muted. When parenting is assumed to be mainly a woman's experience and the words "parent" and "mother" are used interchangeably, fathers are muted.

Language is flexible, and people can come up with new words that fill lexical gaps. As we've discussed, people invent words all the time. However, gaining acceptance of new words isn't always easy. For example, feminists point to the trouble they have had getting people to use "Ms." instead of "Miss" and "Mrs."

Sexist Language

Sexist language refers to language that is demeaning to one sex. Most of the research has examined how language can be detrimental to women. For instance, some researchers assert that the fact that English uses the generic *he* is an example of sexism in language. The **generic *he*** refers to the rule in English grammar, dating from 1553, that requires the masculine pronoun *he* to function generically when the subject of the sentence is of unknown gender. For instance, in the following sentence, *his* would be the correct word to fill in the blanks using the generic *he* rule: "A person should do _____ homework to succeed in _____ classes." Researchers have argued that this rule excludes women because *he* isn't truly generic; rather, it conjures up images of male people (Gastil, 1990; Ivy, Bullis-Moore, Norvell, Backlund, & Javidi, 1995; Martyna, 1978).

Another example of language that some people think is sexist is **man-linked words**. These words—such as *chairman, salesman, repairman, mailman,* and *mankind*—include *man* but are supposed to operate generically to include women as well. Man-linked expressions such as *manning the phones* and *manned space flight* are also problematic. In addition, the practice of referring to a group of people as *guys,* as in "hey, you guys, let's go to the movies," reinforces sexism in language. Relatively easy alternatives to these exclusionary verbal symbols are becoming more commonplace (see Table 4.2). Test your skills at replacing man-linked words with gender-neutral terms by taking

sexist language

Language that is demeaning to one sex.

generic *he*

The use of the masculine pronoun he *to function generically when the subject of the sentence is of unknown gender or includes both men and women.*

man-linked words

Words that include the word man *but that are supposed to operate generically to include women as well, such as* mankind.

Table 4.2 Eliminating sexism in language

Sexist Language	Nonsexist Alternative
The scholar opened his book.	The scholar opened a book.
The pioneers headed West with their women and children.	The pioneer families headed West.
You're needed to man the table.	You're needed to staff the table.
Beth was salesman of the month.	Beth was the top seller this month.
Playing computer games cost the company a lot of man hours.	Playing computer games cost the company a lot of productive time.
Manhole cover	Sewer access cover
Freshman	First-year student
Postman	Letter carrier
A person needs his sleep.	People need their sleep.
Mankind	Humankind, humanity

Although sexist language is often used to exclude women, it can also be used to attack men. Insults directed toward men and boys often equate them with women or girls, such as when a father reprimands his son by saying, "Look at you, crying like a little girl!" or a coach criticizes his team by telling them they're playing like women. What does language like this communicate to men and boys about how they should perceive the women and girls in their lives?

the Gender-Free Language Quiz. Go to your online Resource Center for *Understanding Interpersonal Communication* to access **Interactive Activity 4.3: Gender-Free Language**.

Other examples of sexism in language include the practice of renaming a woman after marriage, the wealth of negative terms for women, and the lack of parallel terms for the sexes. When a woman marries she attains the honorific *Mrs.* Yet, *Mrs.* has no male counterpart; men remain *Mr.* regardless of marital status. In addition, referring to a married woman by her formal married name (for example, Mrs. John Jones) obscures her identity under her husband's. Some researchers have pointed to the fact that there are more derogatory terms for women than there are for men. See how many negative terms you can think of that label women (i.e. slut, bitch, etc.) and do the same for men. Your first list is probably longer. Researchers have also noted that parallel terms for men and women are not, in actuality, parallel (Pearson, West, & Turner, 1995). As Table 4.3 illustrates, many of the feminine words exist only to mark the person as a female.

Language offers opportunities to "gender-tag human referents more or less automatically, that is, without stopping to consider how such usages reinforce the importance of gender-categorization" (Stringer & Hopper, 1998, p. 218). We have a network of grammatical "resources" that allow us to sort the subjects we speak of by sex and that most of these resources "effortlessly emphasize men over women" (Stringer & Hopper, p. 218). To read an article that focuses on sexist language commonly—and often unconsciously—used in the workplace, read the article "Benefiting from Nonsexist Language in the Workplace," available through InfoTrac College Edition. Go to your online Resource Center for *Understanding Interpersonal Communication* to access **InfoTrac College Edition Exercise 4.5: Sexist Language in the Workplace**.

Table 4.3   "Parallel" terms for women and men

Female	Male	Female	Male
mistress	master	majorette	major
stewardess	steward	waitress	waiter
governess	governor	comedienne	comedian
actress	actor	hostess	host
spinster	bachelor	songstress	singer
slut	stud	sculptress	sculptor

Racist Language

The feminist movement has sensitized us to sexism in language, but we have to remain alert to language that systematically offends one group, including racist language (language that demeans those of a particular ethnicity). In the 21st century, most people avoid overt racial slurs, but language can be racist in other, more subtle, ways. The practice of associating negativity with black ("Black Monday," the bad guys wear black hats," "you're the black sheep of the family") perpetuates racial stereotypes on a subtle level. When Miranda, a white woman, met Lyle, a black man, she hadn't known too many black people before. She tried to speak in a way that wouldn't offend him. It didn't even occur to her that Lyle would find her use of the terms *blackmail* and *blackball* troubling. Some researchers argue that racism comes from being taught language that reflects a thought system that values one race over another. For example, when whites are taught from a Eurocentric perspective and don't learn anything about African or Asian history or accomplishments, racism flourishes (Asante, 1998).

Homophobic Language

When the actor Isaiah Washington from *Grey's Anatomy* referred to his cast mate, T. R. Knight as a "f****t" in 2006, national attention was focused on the issue of homophobic language. Washington's repeated use of the hot button word resulted in his eventual firing from the cast of the show. Washington's language is not at all an isolated incident. A 2003 national study of ninth- to twelve-grade students across the Unites States (reported in Snorton, 2004) found that 66 percent of students report using homophobic language, such as "that's so gay" to describe something that is wrong, bad or stupid; 81 percent report hearing homophobic language in their schools frequently or often. The survey found that four out of five lesbian, gay, bisexual, and transgender students reported hearing homophobic remarks often in their school. Further, over 80 percent of the time faculty or staff did not intervene when such language was used.

The Bright Side of Verbal Codes

Although verbal symbols can cause the problems we just discussed, it (coupled with nonverbal communication) is our only means to connect with others. Through language, we can express **confirmation**, or the acknowledgment, validation, and support of another person (Schrodt, Ledbetter, & Ohrt, 2007). Through the use of confirmation, we can build supportive relationships with others. Confirming messages help another person understand that you are paying attention to him or her and that you recognize that person as an equal. You don't have to agree with someone to confirm him or her—you simply have to express that you are hearing that person and paying attention.

confirmation

A response that acknowledges and supports another.

Table 4.4   Confirming and disconfirming communication

Disconfirming	Confirming
Ignoring	Attending
Silence	Appropriate talk
"You don't matter to me."	"You matter to me."
"You're on your own."	"We're in this together."
"You shouldn't feel that way."	"I hear how you feel."

For example, when Maddy listens intently to her sister, Charlene, complain about their mother, she confirms that she cares enough about Charlene to pay attention. Even though Maddy doesn't agree with Charlene (Maddy has a positive relationship with their mother), Charlene feels confirmed. There's some evidence that when parents confirm their children it improves the children's mental health outcomes (Schrodt, Ledbetter, & Ohrt).

In contrast, **disconfirmation** occurs when someone feels ignored and disregarded. Disconfirmation makes people feel that you don't see them—that they are unimportant. See Table 4.4 for examples of confirming and disconfirming responses to others.

We can also use language to develop inclusion rather than exclusion. Using the language of inclusion means that you are thoughtful and attentive to when others seem to be offended and that you ask what in your language might have given offense. Although we might accidentally exclude someone from time to time, through careful language use, we can build supportive relationships. In addition, as we discuss in Chapter 6, we can use empathic language to connect with others. When we try to understand another's feelings, we show we care enough about that person to spend time and energy listening, and we can establish genuine relationships.

Further, verbal codes help us solve problems. When we use open-ended questions (for example, "What do you think is the problem?" or "How would you like me to respond to you?"), we can work toward problem solving in our interpersonal relationships. Language helps us explain our position while conveying that we're also interested in the other person's position.

Choices for Improving Verbal Communication

To improve your verbal communication skills, we suggest cultivating an attitude of respect for others. To do so, you need to engage in **perspective-taking**,

disconfirmation

A response that fails to acknowledge and support another, leaving the person feeling ignored and disregarded.

perspective-taking

Acknowledging the viewpoints of those with whom we interact.

which means acknowledging the viewpoints of those with whom you interact. For example, if you talk frequently with a friend who is a different ethnicity than you, perspective-taking requires you to understand that ethnicity matters and that your friend will have somewhat different experiences from yours as a result.

Marsha Houston (2004), a communication studies scholar who is African American, writes that she doesn't like it when white women friends try to empathize with her by saying that they know exactly how she feels about racism because they have experienced sexism (or some other "ism"). Houston says that it erases her experience to state that your experience is just like it. Listening to others before assuming that you already know exactly what their experience is will help you in perspective-taking.

In addition to developing respect for others and working on perspective-taking, you can practice four skills to help you be more effective in using verbal symbols: owning and using I-messages, understanding the ladder of abstraction, indexing, and probing the middle ground.

Owning and Using I-Messages

Each of us must take responsibility for our own behaviors and feelings in communication with others. Owning, which refers to our ability to take responsibility for our own thoughts and feelings, is often accomplished through I-messages. I-messages acknowledge our own positions, whereas you-messages direct responsibility onto others, often in a blaming fashion. For example, if you are bored during a lecture, you could communicate your thought to the professor with a you-message ("Your lecture is boring") or an I-message ("I'm having trouble getting interested in this material"). See Table 4.5 for more examples of how to change you-messages to I-messages.

Table 4.5 You-messages and I-messages

You-Messages	I-Messages
You are insensitive.	I need you to pay attention to me.
You make me mad.	I get angry when you ignore me.
You don't understand anything.	I don't feel understood when you interrupt me.
You never listen to me.	I want you to put down the paper when I talk to you.
You are so rude.	I was hurt when you said you thought my hair looked bad.
You're a liar.	I need to be able to trust you, and I feel betrayed because you didn't tell me the truth about the car accident.

Understanding the Ladder of Abstraction

Earlier in the chapter, we mentioned that you can engage in the process of abstraction by using words at different levels on the ladder of abstraction—for example, vehicle, car, red 1960 Chevy convertible. The first term allows the listener to imagine a wide range of vehicles, the second term narrows the field somewhat, and the third restricts the referent much more. The more abstract you are, the more you allow a listener to interpret what you mean. The more concrete you are, the more you direct the listener to your precise meaning.

Being skillful in this area requires you to diagnose when a situation needs specificity and when general information might suffice. A simple guideline suggests that the better you know someone, the less concrete you have to be. For example, when two people have a developed relationship, they may understand each other without providing a concrete description. For example, when Tom tells Martha that he wants to spend some time relaxing, she knows from her five years' experience with him that he means he wants to go into his workshop and would appreciate not being disturbed. Tom doesn't need to tell Martha concretely what the abstract term *relaxing* means to him at this point in their relationship. However, when Tom is at work and tells a new coworker that they need to get a project finished as soon as possible, he probably should specify that *as soon as possible,* in this case, means by the end of the week. Otherwise, the coworker could spend eight hours working to finish the project, only to discover that Tom didn't need the project finished that soon.

Imagine yourself...

...with your family at the dinner table

You have recently graduated from college and are looking for your first job. While you are job hunting, you have moved back in with your parents. You have been getting along fine with them, but you have been picking up some cues that they are getting impatient for you to move out on your own. Last night at dinner your mom asked, "How do you think you can improve your job search techniques?" You are somewhat hurt, and wonder exactly what she means by "improve." What are the consequences of how you interpret that word?

Indexing

A way to avoid static evaluation, one of the problems we mentioned earlier, involves dating your statements to indicate you are aware something may have changed (Korzybski, 1958). **Indexing** requires that you acknowledge the time frame of your judgments of others and yourself. For example, if Alex notes that Rucha is self-centered, he would index that by saying, "Yesterday, when she wouldn't stop talking about herself, Rucha was self-centered." Indexing reminds us that the way people act at one given time may not be the way they are for all time.

indexing

Avoiding generalizations by acknowledging the time frame in which we judge others and ourselves.

Probing the Middle Ground

Probing the middle ground is a skill that helps you avoid polarization in your verbal communication. When you are tempted to label something with an extreme judgment, try to explore the shades of gray that might be more descriptive of the behavior. For instance, if you think someone is against you, try to discover the places where you agree so you can see that the person disagrees with you on some things, but not on all things. If you are tempted to label someone as irresponsible, try to discover the areas where the person has acted responsibly so you can see that they are not completely at one extreme on the responsibility scale. Thinking about the middle ground will help restrain you from polarizing or using extreme labels that can easily become inflammatory.

Probing the middle ground might involve more than simply one middle choice. For example, one study (Loftus & Palmer, 1974) showed that people responded to an accident report differently depending on what word was used to describe it. When people were told that there had been an accident involving two cars and then asked what speed the cars were traveling, their answers varied depending on whether the word used to describe the crash was *contacted, collided, bumped, hit,* or *smashed.* Those that were told that the cars "contacted each other" thought the cars were traveling the slowest, and the speed increased with each word listed. This study illustrates how powerful words can be, reminding us to choose them carefully.

interpersonal explorer

Before you finish reading this chapter, take a moment to review the theories and skills discussed. How do you think the theories discussed in this chapter can help you better understand interpersonal communication and verbal communication? In what ways can the skills discussed help you interact more effectively with other people in your life?

Theories that relate to verbal communication
- **Framing theory**
  Metaphors influence how people think at an unconscious level
- **Muted group theory**
  People are silenced by the limits of their language
- **Symbolic interactionism**
  People develop a sense of themselves through the verbal interactions they have with others
- **Linguistic determinism and linguistic relativity**
  Determinism says our language determines our perceptions and relativity says our language influences our perceptions
- **Two-culture theory**
  Little girls and little boys grow up socializing mainly with their own sex and in doing so learn different ways to communicate

Practical skills for improving verbal communication
- Use I-messages to own your thoughts and feelings
- Understand how the ladder of abstraction applies to your messages
- Index to acknowledge the time frame of your judgments
- Probe the middle ground to avoid polarization

Explore your interpersonal choices
Are you ready to explore your interpersonal choices regarding verbal communication? Use your online Resource Center for *Understanding Interpersonal Communication* to access an interactive simulation that allows you to view the beginning of an interpersonal scenario regarding verbal communica- tion, make a choice about how the people in the scenario should proceed with their interaction, consider the consequences of your choice, and then see three possible outcomes to the interaction.

Summary

We use words, or verbal symbols, to achieve our ultimate goal: sharing meaning with others. Verbal symbols are only symbolic representations, but they still can be quite powerful and flexible. As we use language, we are both expressing our thoughts and creating our thoughts, even deciding what is worth thinking about.

The lexicon is ever-changing; new words are coined as new technology emerges. Other words are discarded because the things they refer to are obsolete or because the words of one generation are ignored by the next, replaced by language that characterizes a generational in-group. In addition, the meanings of existing words evolve. For example, although a word's denotative meaning (its dictionary definition) might stay the same, its connotative meaning (the ideas or feelings people associate with a term) might change.

Words are affected by factors such as culture and ethnicity. Idioms (words or phrases that have an understood meaning in a culture) such as phatic communication (words not meant to be literally translated) complicate communication between people of different cultures. Some people who navigate two cultures engage in code-switching, or shifting between languages in the same conversation. Other variables, such as gender, generation, and context, also influence our use of verbal symbols.

Our use of verbal symbols or language can be explained in many ways. Symbolic interactionism holds that the meanings of words are determined by cultural agreement, not by anything inherent in the words themselves. Linguistic determinism states that words determine our ability to perceive and think, and linguistic relativity proposes that language influences, but doesn't determine, our thinking.

Words can be inflammatory. Language can be perceived as sexist, such as use of the generic *he* (using the pronoun *he* for all people, male and female) and the prevalence of man-linked words (such as *salesman*). Other words, such as *blackmail*, can be considered racist. We can also use phrases such as "that's so gay," which communicate homophobia. Language can be problematic when it encourages speakers to ignore change (static evaluation), to characterize another person as either good or bad (polarization), and to respond to the symbol rather than the thing itself (reification).

On the other hand, language can be restorative. We can use it to express confirmation and to develop inclusion. When we practice perspective-taking, we acknowledge the viewpoints of those with whom we interact. We can also use I-messages to own our behaviors and feelings. We can choose to communicate using concrete or abstract terms, depending on the circumstances. In addition, we can index the time frame of our judgments to avoid static evaluation. Lastly, we can probe the middle ground to avoid polarization.

Understanding Interpersonal Communication Online

Now that you've read Chapter 4, use your online Resource Center for *Understanding Interpersonal Communication* for quick access to the electronic study resources that accompany this text. Your online Resource Center gives you access to the video of Carlos and Liz's encounter on page 113, the Communication Assessment Test on page 120, the Your Turn journal activity on page 124, the Ethics & Choice interactive activity on page 131, the Interpersonal Explorer activity on page 145, InfoTrac College Edition, and study aids including a digital glossary, review quizzes, and the chapter activities.

Terms for Review

abstract 122
codability 130
code-switching 128
concrete 122
confirmation 141
connotative meaning 122
decoding 115
denotative meaning 121
disconfirmation 142
encoding 115
equivocation 124
euphemism 125
framing theory 123

generic *he* 139
grammar 115
idiom 125
indexing 144
language 115
lexical gaps 137
linguistic determinism 129
linguistic relativity 130
man-linked words 139
muted group theory 137
perspective-taking 142
phatic communication 126
polarization 136

process of abstraction 123
referent 122
reification 137
Sapir-Whorf hypothesis 130
sexist language 139
speech community 128
static evaluation 136
strategic ambiguity 124
symbolic interactionism
    theory 128
two-culture theory 132
verbal symbols 115

Questions for Understanding

Comprehension Focus

1. Distinguish between language and verbal symbols.

2. Define each of the five attributes of verbal symbols.

3. Define idioms and provide an example.

4. Explain how context affects verbal messages.

5. Compare and contrast the dark and bright sides of verbal messages.

Application Focus

1. CASE IN POINT What verbal skills could Carlos and Liz practice that might make their encounter more satisfactory? Where do you think Liz got the idea that Carlos would call her? Where do you think Carlos got the idea that they didn't have much of a chance for a relationship? What verbal symbols played a role in each of their conclusions?

2. Is it ethical to be equivocal or to use strategic ambiguity? Explain your answer. Think about the ethical systems we introduced in Chapter 1 as you formulate your answer.

3. Explain the theories of linguistic determinism and linguistic relativity. What are the differences between them? Which one do you think is more accurate in describing the relationship between language/culture and thought/perception? Explain your answer.

4. How do gender, ethnicity, and age affect language use and understanding? Is it fair to say that people of different genders, ethnicities, and ages speak different languages? Why or why not?

5. How can a speaker avoid the dark side of verbal codes? Is there any way to speak to others who are different from you are and not offend them at one time or another? Is the effort given to speaking in inclusionary terms misplaced? Explain your answer.

Interactive Activities and InfoTrac College Edition Exercises

Interactive Activities

InfoTrac College Edition Exercises

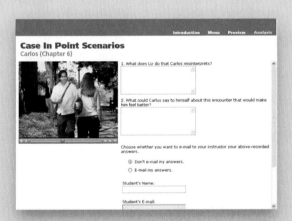

Chapter 5

Communicating Nonverbally

chapter ➕ goals

Understand nonverbal communication and its importance in human interaction

Identify the primary principles of nonverbal communication

Explain and exemplify the types of nonverbal communication

Articulate the relationship between nonverbal communication and culture

Apply a variety of strategies to improve skills in nonverbal communication

CASEinPOINT

MARK MATTSON

Watching his mother, Julia, get up from a chair in her kitchen, Mark Mattson knew her days of living independently were numbered. Today, in particular, Mark thought his mom looked every one of her 75 years. As she rose from the chair, she staggered and held onto its back. And she appeared more disheveled than ever; her hair wasn't brushed, she had on her bathrobe (which looked dirty), and she was muttering to herself even more than she had in past weeks. The two had never spoken about an alternative living arrangement for Julia, but Mark knew the time may now have arrived.

Each day since his father's death three years ago, Mark picked up two cups of coffee and the *Los Angeles Times* and drove fifteen minutes to his mom's house. There, he and his mother would sit, frequently in silence.

The two didn't often feel the need to say anything to each other; they both enjoyed just being together. Julia had never spoken to Mark about her husband's death, a fact that saddened and sometimes even angered Mark.

This morning, Mark's dominant emotion was definitely sadness. As he and his mother each read a section of the paper, Mark snuck glances at his mother. He tried to ignore her unkempt look and think about what a great mother she had been. Memories of her soft voice and hugs came rushing back to Mark. He wanted to make things like they used to be, but he knew that no hug could change the difficult days that were ahead for him and his mother.

Go to your online Resource Center for *Understanding Interpersonal Communication* to watch a video clip of Mark and his mother.

> Access the resources for Chapter 5 and select "Mark" to watch the video (it takes a minute for the video to load). As you watch the video, can you identify the nonverbal signals Julia sends that trigger sadness in Mark? > You can respond to this and other analysis questions, and then click "Done" to compare your answers with those provided by the authors.

We all communicate without saying a word and we all "speak" without talking. Nonverbal communication has been called the "unspoken dialogue" (Burgoon, Buller, & Woodall, 1996), and scholars have noted its importance in conversations. Some researchers report that around 65 percent of overall message meaning is conveyed nonverbally (Hickson, Stacks, & Moore, 2004) (see Figure 5.1). Other researchers assert that nearly 93 percent of emotional meaning is conveyed nonverbally (Mehrabian & Ferris, 1967).

When we attend to nonverbal behaviors, we draw conclusions about others, and others simultaneously draw conclusions about us. This process is part of the transactional nature of communication we discussed in Chapter 1. For instance, consider our opening story of Mark Mattson and his mother, Julia, who clearly have a close relationship. Instead of speaking aloud to Julia, Mark notes her nonverbal cues and makes various judgments. When deciding whether or not Julia should consider leaving her home, he observes her difficulty getting out of a chair and her dirty bathrobe. As he sits and reads the paper with her, he recalls an earlier time, and he remembers her voice and hugs.

The influence of nonverbal behavior on our perceptions, conversations, and relationships cannot be overstated. Although we are frequently unaware of our use of nonverbal communication, it is always present in our interac-

Figure 5.1   Communication of interpersonal meaning

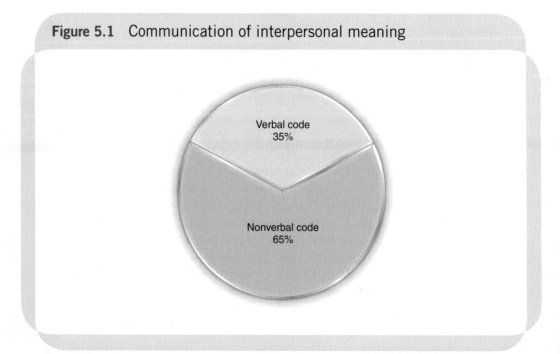

Verbal code
35%

Nonverbal code
65%

tions. Nonverbal communication is an integral part of the communication process and always a part of our relationships with others.

This chapter explores nonverbal communication and its importance in our lives. We focus our discussion on how nonverbal behavior functions, both directly and indirectly, in our daily activities. Before we move on in our discussion about nonverbal communication, let's spend a few moments defining it. **Nonverbal communication** encompasses all behaviors—other than spoken words—that communicate messages and have shared meaning between people. This definition has three associated parameters. First, electronic communication (a subject we return to in Chapter 11) is not included in our definition. Second, when we note that there is "shared meaning," we are saying that a national culture agrees on how to construe a behavior. For example, in many co-cultures in the United States, when a parent sees a child do something unsafe, the parent might wag his or her index finger. The child must know the meaning behind this nonverbal shaming technique to respond to the parent's reprimand. Third, as we mentioned in Chapter 4, verbal and nonverbal communication usually work together to create meaning.

Nonverbal communication is central to our relational lives. Howard Giles and Beth Le Poire (2006) thoughtfully illustrate that the way people communicate nonverbally influences 1) how relationships are established, maintained, and dissolved, 2) the diagnosis of health-related problems such as autism, 3) the number of sexual partners a person has, 4) how babies show emotional distress, 5) marital satisfaction and stability, and 6) perceptions of beauty. These reasons are just a snapshot of why the area of nonverbal communication is valued and essential to discuss in a book on interpersonal communication.

nonverbal communication

All behaviors other than spoken words that communicate messages and create shared meaning between people.

"Say what's on your mind, Harris—the language of dance has always eluded me."

Nonverbal communication competence requires us to be able to encode and decode nonverbal messages (Burgoon & Hoobler, 2002). We also have to use nonverbal communication ourselves to get across our meaning. Being able to adapt to people around you is a hallmark of a competent nonverbal communicator. **Interaction adaptation theory** suggests that individuals simultaneously adapt their communication behavior to the communication behavior of others (Burgoon, Stern, & Dillman, 1995). Thus, the better we are able to adapt, the better we are able to understand the meaning of a message. Suppose, for example, that Rosa and her roommate, Nadine, are in a noisy place talking about a conflict they've had pertaining to their apartment's cleanliness. Nadine is practicing interaction adaptation if, when Rosa leans forward to talk about the topic, Nadine simultaneously leans forward to listen to the story. This "postural echo" suggests that Nadine is not only mirroring Rosa's behavior but that she is also trying to understand Rosa's meaning.

With our definition of nonverbal communication established, we're now ready to explore some of the principles of nonverbal communication before moving on to discuss nonverbal communication codes and cultural variations in nonverbal communication.

Principles of Nonverbal Communication

Although it is often overlooked, nonverbal communication is a vital aspect of interpersonal communication. Consider times when we don't say a word but manage to "say" so much. Imagine, for example, hugging a close friend at her father's funeral. In this situation, nonverbal communication is probably more comforting than any words you could say. This apparent inconsistency of efficient communication without words is what makes nonverbal communication so important in our conversations with others. We now explore four principles of this type of communication.

Nonverbal Communication Is Often Ambiguous

One reason nonverbal communication is so challenging in our relationships is that our nonverbal messages often mean different things to different people, which can lead to misunderstandings. Compared to verbal messages, nonverbal messages are usually more ambiguous. For example, suppose that Lena prolongs her eye contact with Todd and, in turn, Todd refocuses on Lena. While Lena may be showing some attraction to Todd, he may be returning the eye contact because he believes that something is wrong. Clearly, the same nonverbal behavior (eye contact) can elicit two different meanings.

Mark Hickson, Don Stacks, and Nina-Jo Moore (2004) capture the challenge of nonverbal communication by noting that it is more difficult to understand because it is intangible and more abstract. A major reason for this ambiguity is that many factors influence the meaning of nonverbal behav-

interaction adaptation theory

A theory that suggests individuals simultaneously adapt their communication behavior to the communication behavior of others.

iors, including shared fields of experience, current surroundings, and culture. Consider the following conversation between a father and son as they talk about the son's staying out past his curfew:

Father: Look, I told you to be home by 11! It's past midnight now. And get that smirk off your face!

Son: First, dad, you might have told me 11, but you also didn't say anything when I asked if I could stay out till 12. You didn't say anything for sure. I mean, like, you were changing the oil on the truck when I asked you. You didn't even look at me. I couldn't hear you that much while you were under the car. And, how am I . . .

Father: You heard what you wanted to hear. I told you . . .

Son: I swear, Dad. I thought my curfew was midnight. And I've stayed out till midnight before.

This scenario suggests a few things about the ambiguous nature of nonverbal communication. First, the father seems to be annoyed by his son's smirk. Is he truly smirking, or is the father misinterpreting his son's facial expression because he is angry? Second, the son took his dad's verbal message about the 11 p.m. deadline less seriously because his father neglected to make eye contact when delivering it. In addition, the son thought that his dad hesitated when he asked about a later curfew, and also claimed that he couldn't clearly hear his father's response from under the car, further eroding the power of the father's verbal communication. In this example, ambiguity results from the interaction of the verbal and nonverbal behaviors of both the father and son.

© Ryan McVay/The Image Bank/Getty Images

The ambiguity of nonverbal gestures can lead to misunderstandings. For example, if someone winks at you, is he flirting with you, letting you in on a joke, showing affection, or does he simply have something in his eye?

Nonverbal Communication Regulates Conversation

People use nonverbal communication to manage the ebb and flow of conversations. Nonverbal regulators allow speakers to enter, exit, or maintain the conversation. Who talks when and to whom, referred to as **turn-taking**, is based primarily on nonverbal communication. For instance, if we want a chance to speak, we usually lean forward, toward the speaker. When we don't want to be interrupted in a conversation, we may avoid eye contact and keep our vocal pattern consistent so that others don't have an opportunity to begin talking until we are finished. When we are ready to yield the conversation to another, we typically stop talking, look at the other person, and perhaps make a motion with our hands to indicate that it is now okay for the other person to respond.

We can also yield the conversation floor by raising or lowering our pitch level to stress our last word or syllable. As we mentioned earlier, we are often unconscious of such behaviors. For example, let's say that Bruce, a student in Professor Brownstone's biology class, decides to challenge a grade. When Bruce arrives at Professor Brownstone's office, the straight-A student launches into a rehearsed, detailed story about not having enough time to study because he was sick with the flu. He avoids making eye contact with Professor Brownstone and doesn't pause to allow the professor to react until he has finished his entire memorized speech. As he finishes his last sentence, "I know that you have a policy on make-ups, but I think I have an extenuating situation," he looks up to meet the professor's eyes and raises the pitch level of his voice so that his statement almost becomes a question. Whether or not he realizes it, Bruce uses nonverbal communication to regulate the conversation with his professor. At first he prevents his professor from entering the exchange, and then he uses the pitch of his voice to yield the floor.

Nonverbal Communication Is More Believable than Verbal Communication

Although, as we noted earlier, nonverbal communication is often ambiguous, people believe nonverbal messages over verbal messages. You've no doubt heard the expression "actions speak louder than words." This statement suggests that someone's nonverbal behavior can influence a conversational partner more than what is said. For instance, a job candidate being interviewed may verbally state her commitment to being professional, yet if she wears jeans and arrives late to the interview, these nonverbal cues will cause the interviewer to regard her statement with skepticism.

Consider how Esther reacts to the nonverbal communication of the customers at a local gas station where she is an attendant. She makes judgments about people based on their appearance. For example, Esther is more inclined to give the store's restroom key to someone who appears calm than to some-

turn-taking

In a conversation, nonverbal regulators that indicate who talks when and to whom.

one who looks rushed, nervous, and sweaty. However, as we learned in Chapter 2, her perception may be inaccurate or incomplete.

Nonverbal Communication May Conflict with Verbal Communication

Although nonverbal and verbal communication frequently operate interdependently, sometimes our nonverbal messages are not congruent with our verbal messages. We term this incompatibility a **mixed message**. When a friend asks you, "What's wrong?" after observing you with tears in your eyes, and you reply "Nothing," the contradiction between your nonverbal and verbal behavior is evident. When a physician frowns as she reveals to her patient that the prognosis "looks good," she gives a mixed message. Or, consider a wife, who after being asked by her husband if she loves him, shouts, "Of course I love you!" Most of us would agree that angrily shouting to express our affection sends a mixed message.

mixed message

The incompatibility that occurs when our nonverbal messages are not congruent with our verbal messages.

When confronted with a mixed message, people have to choose whether to believe the nonverbal or the verbal behaviors. Because children are generally not sophisticated enough to understand the many meanings that accompany nonverbal communication, they rely on the words of a message more than the nonverbal behaviors (Morton & Trehub, 2001). However, most children understand nonverbal messages such as shaking the head for "no" and a finger to the lips for "keep quiet." In contrast, adults who encounter mixed messages pay the most attention to nonverbal messages and neglect much of what is being stated. The multiple messages that originate from the eyes, voice, body movement, facial expressions, and touch usually overpower the verbal message.

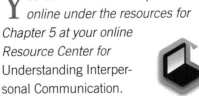

REVISITING CASE IN POINT

1. Identify one principle of nonverbal communication and apply it to Mark Mattson's perception of his mother.

2. How has Julia Mattson's appearance regulated any conversation between Mark and her?

You can answer these questions online under the resources for Chapter 5 at your online Resource Center for Understanding Interpersonal Communication.

To further explore how our nonverbal behaviors often conflict with our verbal messages, check out "Your Body Speaks Volumes, but Do You Know What It Is Saying?" available through InfoTrac College Edition. Use your online Resource Center for *Understanding Interpersonal Communication* to access *InfoTrac College Edition Exercise 5.1: What Is Your Body Language Saying?* To read about mixed messages in a specific context, business negotiations, access *Interactive Activity 5.1: Mixed Messages in Negotiations.*

Nonverbal Communication Codes

Extensive study of nonverbal communication indicates that we employ several different forms of nonverbal codes in our conversations with others. Later in the chapter, we will look at a number of these codes and discuss their cultural implications. In this section, we examine a classifying system articulated by Burgoon et al. (1996), which is set out in Table 5.1. This system includes visual-auditory codes, contact codes, and place and time codes.

Visual-Auditory Codes

As their name reflects, visual-auditory codes include categories of nonverbal communication that you can see and hear. These categories are kinesics (body movement), physical appearance (such as attractiveness), facial communication (such as eye contact), and paralanguage (such as pitch and whining).

Kinesics (Body Movement)

Body communication is also called **kinesics**, a Greek word meaning "movement." Kinesics refers to the study of body motions and how people use them to communicate. Kinesic behavior is wide-ranging; it can include anything from staying put at a party after being asked to leave, to gesturing during a speech.

The primary components of kinesics are gestures and body posture/orientation. Gestures have been analyzed for almost 2,500 years. For example, writings by the Greek philosopher Aristotle explained that gestures are impor-

kinesics

The study of a person's body movement and its effect on the communication process.

Table 5.1   Categories of nonverbal communication

Code	Nonverbal Category
Visual-auditory	Kinesics (*body movement*)
	Physical appearance (*body size, body artifacts, attractiveness*)
	Facial communication (*eye contact, smiling*)
	Paralanguage (*pitch, rate, volume, speed, silence*)
Contact	Haptics (*touch*)
	Space (*personal space, territoriality*)
Place and time	The environment (*color, lighting, room design*)
	Chronemics (*time*)

tant when delivering a public speech. Further, Michael Corballis (2002) notes that gestures preceded verbal communication by tens of thousands of years.

What can we learn from gestures? First, we need to consider the context of gestures to understand them. Think about the gestures that the following individuals would use: parking lot attendant, nurse, radio disc jockey, landscaper, and auctioneer. What gestures would they have in common? What gestures are unique to these occupations? In the classroom setting, gestures such as raising a hand, writing on a chalkboard, pointing, and waving at a student to come sit in a particular seat are common. Janet Bavelas (1994) describes the following gesture types:

Many people use gestures to communicate nonverbally on the job, particularly when they work in a noisy environment or need to communicate with one another silently. Do you commonly use gestures in your workplace? What do they communicate?

- **Delivery gestures** signal shared understanding between communicators. Clifton, for example, nods his head to let his friend, Kaitlin, know that he understands what she is talking about.

- **Citing gestures** acknowledge another's feedback. For instance, in a conversation with her employee, Ms. Rasmussen uses a citing gesture when she disagrees with what her employee is saying; she raises her hand, palm flat to the receiver, her index finger extended upward.

- **Seeking gestures** request agreement or clarification from the speaker. For instance, we may extend both our arms out, keep our palms flat, and shrug. This gesture is used when someone is communicating "I don't know what you mean."

- **Turn gestures** indicate that another person can speak or are used to request the conversation floor. We referenced this nonverbal communication earlier in the chapter when we discussed the regulating function of nonverbal messages. Turn gestures include pointing at another to indicate it is his or her turn, or extending your hand outward and rotating your wrist in a clockwise motion to show that the other person should continue speaking.

In addition to gestures, our body posture and orientation reveal important information. Posture is generally a result of how tense or relaxed we are. For example, your body posture would differ depending on whether you were reading this chapter while you were alone in your room or in the campus library. **Body orientation** is the extent to which we turn our legs, shoulders, and head toward (or away) from a communicator. Albert Mehrabian (1981) found that body orientation affects conversations. For example, when people communicate with those of higher status, they tend to stand directly facing him or her. Conversely, those with higher status tend to use a leaning posture when speaking to subordinates.

To further explore how we use our bodies to convey interpersonal feelings and attitudes, use your online Resource Center for *Understanding Interpersonal Communication* to access *Interactive Activity 5.2: Feelings, Attitudes, and Kinesics.*

delivery gestures

Gestures that signal shared understanding between communicators in a conversation.

citing gestures

Gestures that acknowledge another's feedback in a conversation.

seeking gestures

Gestures that request agreement or clarification from a sender during a conversation.

turn gestures

Gestures that indicate that another person can speak or that are used to request to speak in a conversation.

body orientation

The extent to which we turn our legs, shoulders, and head toward (or away) from a communicator.

REVISITING
CASEINPOINT

1. *Identify several areas of nonverbal communication pertaining to Mark and Julia Mattson.*

2. *Looking at physical appearance specifi- cally, how does Mark make a decision associated with his mother's mental and physical competency? Do you believe his impending decision is appropriate?*

Y*ou can answer these questions online under the resources for Chapter 5 at your online Resource Center for* Under- standing Interpersonal Communication.

Physical Appearance

In interpersonal exchanges, physical appearance plays a role in our evaluations of others ("How could he have done that?! He is such a good-looking guy"). Physical appearance encom- passes all of the **physical charac- teristics** of an individual, includ- ing body size, skin color, hair color and style, facial hair, and facial features (for example, nose size, skin texture, and so on).

How does physical appear- ance influence our interper- sonal communication? Although we are unable to dis- cuss every aspect of physical appearance, a few thoughts merit attention. Certainly, skin color has affected the commu- nication process. Even today— decades after civil rights legislation took effect—some people won't commu- nicate with people who are of a particular race or ethnicity. Body size, too, can influence our interpersonal relationships. Do you find yourself making judgments about people who appear overweight or too thin? What is your first assessment of a person who is more than six feet tall? What is your ini- tial impression of a bodybuilder? Do you evaluate women who shave their body hair differently from women who choose not to shave?

Body artifacts refer to our possessions and how we decorate ourselves and our surroundings. Clothing, for example, can convey social status or group identification. In the corporate world, tailored clothing bolsters one's status among many peers. During Kwanzaa, a holiday celebration in African Ameri- can communities, participants frequently wear traditional African clothing, which serves as a nonverbal connection among African Americans. People who wear religious symbols, such as a crucifix or the Star of David, may be exhibiting religious commitments. Military clothing is usually accompanied by medals or stripes to depict rank, which suggests military accomplishment. Body piercings and tattoos can communicate many different messages; those who have them are often viewed as nonconformists, and may be rated poorly by employers. Walking down the street with your iPod, talking on your cell phone while standing in a line at Burger King, or wearing Ray-Ban sunglasses and a Red Sox (or Yankees!) hat backwards are all examples of bodily artifacts.

Physical appearance also includes the level of attractiveness of the inter- personal communicators. Research (e.g., Floyd, 2006) exists on interpersonal attractiveness. Mark Knapp and Judith Hall (2005) have compiled a number

physical characteristics

Aspects of physical appear- ance, such as body size, skin color, hair color and style, facial hair, and facial features.

body artifacts

Items we wear that are part of our physical appearance and that have the potential to communicate, such as clothing, religious symbols, military medals, body piercings, and tattoos.

of conclusions based on their review of the research findings. Two seem particularly pertinent to our discussion. First, generally speaking, people seek out others who are similar to themselves in attractiveness, just as they seek out others who are similar to themselves in other characteristics. If you are a nonsmoker, are you likely to be compatible with a smoker? If you are vegetarian, will you be attracted to a carnivore? Although people are not so narrow and simplistic that they use only one behavior to determine attractiveness, it is true that we are interested in being around those people who are similar to us.

Second, Knapp and Hall (2005) note that physically attractive people are often judged to be more intelligent and friendly than those not deemed attractive. This conclusion resonates in a number of different environments, including the classroom. For example, researchers note that physically attractive students are viewed as more intelligent and friendly than less attractive students (Ritts, Patterson, & Tubbs, 1992). However, in the business setting, "more attractive women in executive roles are often the victims of prejudice, taken less seriously and often resented, thus feeling the pressure to come up with glasses and hairstyles that project a more severe aura" (Jones, 2004, p. 3B). We should make an effort not to allow our judgments of other people to be based on their level of physical attractiveness.

...at work

You are J.T.'s supervisor at a data-processing company. J.T. has been a conscientious employee for over seven years, but in the past month, you have noticed that his appearance has changed. His shirts are always wrinkled, his hair is continually messy, and other employees have privately complained to you about his body odor. Although J. T. is a productive worker and has been cited as "Employee as the Month" several times over the years, you feel you need to approach him, both because you fear something might be wrong and you worry about the effect his disheveled appearance could have on his relationships with his colleagues. Knowing what you do about the importance of physical appearance to interpersonal communication, how do you go about talking to J. T. about his appearance?

Facial Communication

More than any other part of the body, the face gives others insight into how someone is feeling. Our facial expressions cover the gamut of emotional meaning, from eagerness to exhaustion. We often have difficulty shielding authentic feelings from others because we usually don't have much control over our facial communication. This fact further explains the point we made earlier in this chapter, that people tend to believe our nonverbal codes over our verbal codes—it's tough to hide our feelings. While looking at an infant or toddler, try suppressing a smile. When talking to a parent who has lost a child in a war, repressing a sad look on your face is probably impossible. It's simply too challenging to control a region of our body that is so intimately connected to our emotions.

The part of the face with the most potential for communication is the eye. Eye contact is a complex part of human behavior. For most of us, a single eye movement communicates on multiple levels. If we hold a glance for a split second, in a certain context that glance may be interpreted in an intimate way

(Bates & Cleese, 2001), even if we don't intend to send such a message. We can look directly into someone's eyes to communicate interest, power, or anger. We roll our eyes to signal disbelief or disapproval. We avoid eye contact when we are uninterested, nervous, or shy. Our eyes also facilitate our interactions. We look at others while they speak to get a sense of their facial and body communication. Simultaneously, others often look at us while we speak. We also make judgments about others simply by looking at their eyes, deciding if they are truthful, uninterested, tired, involved, or credible. Although our conclusions may be erroneous, most people rely on eye contact in their conversations.

Finally, smiling is one of the most recognizable nonverbal behaviors worldwide. Although in some contexts a smile can have a negative effect, it usually has a positive effect on an encounter. In an experiment testing the effects of smiling on helping behavior, Nicolas Gueguen and Marie-Agnes De Gail (2003) report that smiling at others encourages them to assist in tasks. Studying 800 passersby, the research team had eight research assistants ask others for help. One group of assistants smiled at some of the people exiting a grocery store. A few seconds later, passersby had an opportunity to help an assistant who dropped a computer diskette on the ground. Results showed that the previous smile of a stranger enhanced later helping behavior. That is, those who were smiled at earlier were more likely to help the stranger with the computer disk.

Smiling at another nearly always results in a more pleasant encounter. However, smiling at ill-conceived times may prompt others to react unfavorably. In conflict, for instance, smiling is often perceived as an inappropriate behavior. Smiling during a heated exchange can aggravate an already difficult situation, unless the smile is well timed to ease tensions. Smiling has multiple meanings (for example, a smirk and a sneer communicate two different things), so context is definitely important when we interpret another's smile.

For an interactive look at how our eyes, mouth, and tilt of the head provide clues about our emotions, use your online Resource Center for *Understanding Interpersonal Communication* to access *Interactive Activity 5.3: Eyes, Mouth, and Tilt of Head*. And to read an interesting article about emotions that are recognized across cultures, access *InfoTrac College Edition Exercise 5.2: Universal Facial Expressions* to check out "Emotions Revealed: Recognizing Facial Expressions."

Paralanguage (Voice)

To introduce the concept of paralanguage, let's examine the story of Charles. A few years ago, Charles contracted HIV, the virus that can lead to AIDS. Charles is frequently an upbeat man, and everyone around him enjoys his company. However, sometimes his best friend, Melissa, can hear a "voice" that is different from the one Charles normally uses. For example, sometimes when Charles says that he feels fine and that no one should be concerned about his health, Melissa hears a different message. During such conversations, Charles frequently lapses into silence. He pauses awkwardly as he talks

about his doctor's appointments. He laughs at odd times, convincing Melissa that he is nervous, anxious, and afraid of what the future holds.

This story underscores a vocal characteristic called **paralanguage**, or vocalics, which is the study of a person's voice. Paralanguage refers not to *what* a person says but to *how* a person says it. Paralanguage covers a vast array of nonverbal behaviors such as pitch, rate, volume, inflection, tempo, and pronunciation, which we call **vocal qualities.** We also consider **vocal distractors** (the "ums" and "ers" of conversation) and the use of silence as vocal qualities. Paralanguage also encompasses such nonverbal behaviors as crying, laughing, groaning, muttering, whispering, and whining; we call these **vocal characterizers**. Don't underestimate the usefulness of studying these paralinguistic behaviors. They give us our uniqueness as communicators, help us differentiate among people, and influence people's perceptions of us and our perceptions of them.

Our vocal qualities include the rate (speed), volume (loudness/softness), inflection (vocal emphasis), pitch (highness/lowness), intensity (volume), tempo (rhythm), and pronunciation associated with voices. Vocal qualities lead listeners to form impressions about a speaker's socioeconomic status, personality type, persuasiveness, and work ethic (Griffin, 2009). One way to tap into these vocal nuances is to practice saying the same sentence with various rates, volume, inflection, sighs, and tempo. For example, try saying the following statement to show *praise,* then *blame,* and then *exasperation:*

You really did it this time.

The next time you want to borrow a friend's car, tell your mother a secret, ask your professor a question, or engage in a debate with your roommate about religion or politics, you will probably utilize a number of different vocal qualities.

The "uhs," "ers," and "ums" in our conversations may seem unimportant, but these vocal distractors compose an increasingly researched area of vocal qualities because they can predict whether a conversation will continue and the fluency of that conversation. Further, how do you react when you hear a speaker use these disfluencies? You may find them appropriate for many social situations, but what happens in more professional settings, such as formal presentations at work, job interviews, or class oral reports? When vocal distractors are used excessively, people view them as bad habits that can jeopardize credibility.

paralanguage

The study of a person's voice. Also called vocalics.

vocal qualities

Nonverbal behaviors that include pitch, rate, volume, inflection, tempo, and pronunciation, as well as the use of vocal distractors and silence.

vocal distractors

The "ums" and "ers" used in conversation.

vocal characterizers

Nonverbal behaviors such as crying, laughing, groaning, muttering, whispering, and whining.

We include silence in our discussion of the vocal qualities of paralanguage because a person's use of his or her voice includes the decision not to use it. Strange as it may sound, in our relationships, we should all exercise our right to remain silent. However, how many of us do? Society seems to have a love affair with talking. Self-help books exclaim that communication is the way to relational bliss and long-lasting happiness. Therapists tell their patients to open up and communicate. And what adolescent doesn't hear from a parent: "Talk to me!" We live in a culture that places a premium on the spoken word.

Yet, at times, as we touched on in Chapters 3, honoring silence may be the most powerful way to communicate to another person. Silence communicates and informs the communication process in a number of ways. First, silence indicates that we need some time for reflection. Silence gives us a chance to think about the circumstances or events surrounding an interpersonal relationship. For instance, if you have been battling with your sibling, taking some time to withdraw from the conversation can help you refocus on the original issue and how you want to go about resolving it.

Silence can also be part of the dark side of communication between people. At times, silence serves as an interpersonal weapon. Suppose that Andrew and Jessica, who have been married for six months, are having a fight about whether or not they can afford to have a child. Because Andrew is not comfortable talking about this topic so early in their marriage, he remains silent on the issue. On the other hand, Jessica wants to talk about it because she feels that having children is an important part of being married. Each time Jessica tries to bring up the subject, Andrew simply says he doesn't want to talk about it and leaves the room.

You may have been the target of this "silent treatment" or may have decided yourself that giving this sort of punishment in a relationship was necessary. Silence can be a frustrating nonverbal behavior to respond to, as Jessica probably knows all too well. What does a person say or do when another person is not saying or doing anything? A sort of communication spiral ensues: Someone wants to jump-start the conversation to get the issues clarified and resolved, but after the issues are clarified, the fighting continues, resulting in one or both people shutting down. Unfortunately, using silence to hurt or undermine another person is commonplace. Understanding when silence is effective and when it sabotages the interpersonal communication process takes time and experience.

... with a political candidate before his public speech

As the campaign adviser to mayoral candidate Tom Ryder, you are frequently asked for your opinion on the words that candidate Ryder uses in his speeches. However, you are finding more and more that *how* Mr. Ryder delivers his words can be as important as the words themselves. Further, you have received comments that Mr. Ryder should be concerned with how he looks and think twice before wearing a suit *every* time he speaks in public. Considering the multifaceted nature of nonverbal communication, what would you advise Mr. Ryder in terms of paralanguage, appearance, body movement, and facial communication? What prescriptions for "political success" would you offer?

Vocal characterizers such as laughing, moaning, or whining also communicate a great deal about how to interpret verbal messages. For example, if Rhonda tells José, "I'm so over you," but does so with laughter, José probably can infer that the comment should not be taken seriously. Or, suppose Ron is a member of a task group at work. Each time the group meets, his coworker Linda complains about the time it takes to get the group together, the assignment, and the time constraints. Linda's moaning about the task will certainly affect Ron's conversations with her.

To read an interesting article about one culture's use of paralanguage, check out the article "A Whistle a Day Keeps Globalization Away," available through InfoTrac College Edition. Use your online Resource Center for *Understanding Interpersonal Communication* to access *InfoTrac College Edition Exercise 5.3: A Whistle a Day*. You can also test your accuracy in interpreting another's paralanguage by accessing *Interactive Activity 5.4: Test Your Paralanguage Skills*.

Contact Codes

Contact codes include touch (haptics) and space (such as personal space).

Touch (Haptics)

Touch communication, or **haptics**, is the most primitive form of human communication. Research has concluded that touch has lasting value. Ben Benjamin and Ruth Werner (2004) support this claim:

> Human touch can completely change the way the body functions. From your heart rate to your blood pressure to the efficiency of your digestive system, welcomed touch can make your body work better. Humans need touch. We crave it, we hunger for it, and we get sick and can even die from the lack of it. (pp. 30, 31)

Touch behavior is the ultimate in privileged access to people. That is, when you touch another person, you have decided—whether intentionally or unintentionally—to invade another's personal space (a subject we return to later in this chapter). When forced into circumstances where everyone is close—for example, standing in a crowded elevator, sitting next to someone on the train or bus, or standing in a line—we normally offer an apology or an excuse if we accidentally touch someone. Interestingly, at public celebrations like Mardi Gras and New Year's Eve parties, touching another person doesn't seem as intrusive. In fact, some people enjoy it!

haptics

The study of how we communicate through touch.

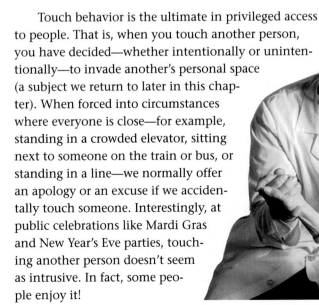

Doctors often use different forms of touch to communicate in different contexts. They routinely touch patients to examine or treat them. They may greet a patient or a patient's family with handshakes or pats on the back. And sometimes they touch patients to comfort them.

© Bob Mahoney/The Image Works

Touch behavior is an ambiguous form of communication because touching has various meanings depending on the context. Touching another person takes different forms and signals multiple messages. Shaking hands upon meeting someone, making love, slapping an old friend on the back, physically abusing a partner, and tickling a small child are all examples of touch behavior.

Touch has several functions (Jones & Yarbrough, 1985):

- Touch is used for *positive affect*, which includes support, appreciation, inclusion, and affection. The mother who hugs her child after he falls off his bike exemplifies positive affect through touch.

- Touch has a *playful* function; it serves to lighten an interaction. This type of touch is apparent when two kids wrestle each other or when baseball players slap each other on the butt after a home run.

- Touch is used to *control* or to direct behavior in an encounter. Touching another person while saying "move aside" is an example of touching to control.

- *Ritualistic* touch refers to the touches we use on an everyday basis, such as a handshake to say hello or goodbye.

- The *task* function pertains to touch that serves a professional or functional purpose. For instance, hairstylists and dentists are allowed to touch you to accomplish their tasks.

- A *hybrid touch* is a touch that greets a person and simultaneously demonstrates affection for that person. For instance, kissing a family member hello is an example of a hybrid touch.

- Touch that is *accidental* is done without apparent intent. This type of touching includes touching in close spaces, such as intimate restaurants, in elevators, at graduation ceremonies, or at a religious service.

Touch is only part of a larger nonverbal (and verbal) system of behaviors. For example, when talking to an ailing relative, many people not only hold the other's hand but also speak softly and use calming language.

Space

Spatial communication is important in conversation. **Proxemics**, the study of how communication is influenced by space and distance, is historically related to how people use, manipulate, and identify their space. **Personal space** is the distance we put between ourselves and others. We carry informal personal space from one encounter to another; think of this personal space as a sort of invisible bubble that encircles us wherever we go. Our personal space provides some insight into ourselves and how we feel about other people. For instance, some research shows that happily married couples stand closer to one another (11.4 inches) than those who are maritally distressed (14.8 inches) (Crane, 1987).

Anthropologist Edward T. Hall (1959) was the first to devise categories of personal space. His system suggests that in most co-cultures in the United States, people communicate with others at a specific distance, depending on

proxemics

The study of how people use, manipulate, and identify their personal space.

personal space

The distance we put between ourselves and others.

Figure 5.2 Edward T. Hall's four types of personal distance

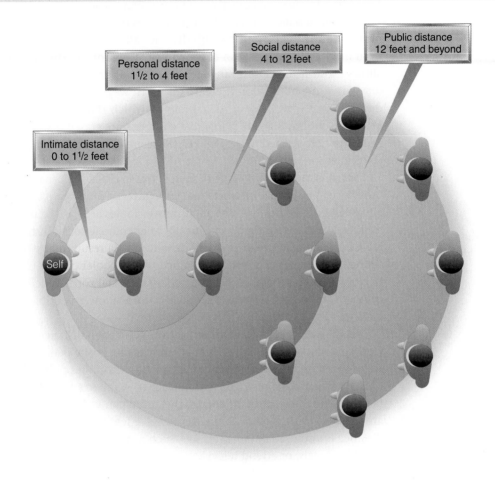

Personal distance
1½ to 4 feet

Social distance
4 to 12 feet

Public distance
12 feet and beyond

Intimate distance
0 to 1½ feet

Self

the nature of the conversation. Starting with the closest contact and the least amount of personal space, and moving to the greatest distance between communicators, the four categories of personal space are intimate distance, personal distance, social distance, and public distance (Figure 5.2). Examine Hall's categories and think about your own interpersonal encounters.

Intimate distance covers the distance that extends from you to around 18 inches. This spatial zone is normally reserved for those people with whom you are close—for example, close friends, romantic partners, and family members. Of course, in some situations, you have little choice but to allow others within an intimate distance (for example, attending a movie or theater production, sitting on a train, watching a rock concert, and so forth). If you let someone be a part of your intimate distance zone, you are implying that

intimate distance

The distance that extends about eighteen inches around each of us that is normally reserved for people with whom we are close, such as close friends, romantic partners, and family members.

this person is meaningful to you. In fact, zero personal space—in other words, touch—suggests a very close relationship with someone because you are willing to give someone part of your private space.

Personal distance, ranging from 18 inches to 4 feet, is the space most people use during conversations. This distance allows you to feel some protection from others who might wish to touch you. The range in this distance type allows those at the closest range to pick up your physical nuances (such as dry skin, acne, body odor or breath odor). However, we are still able to conduct business with those at the far range—which Hall (1959) calls "arm's length"—but any signs of nonverbal closeness are erased. Examples of relationships accustomed to personal distance are casual friends or business colleagues.

Social distance, which is 4–12 feet, is the spatial zone usually reserved for professional or formal interpersonal encounters. Some office environments are arranged specifically for social distance. Tables are aligned in a particular way, and cubicles are set up specifically to encourage social distance (rather than intimate distance or personal distance). As a result, many business transactions take place within social distance. Water-cooler chat or conversations in a break room at work also characterize the social zone. Whereas in the intimate and personal spatial zones we can use a lower vocal volume, social distance typically requires increased volume.

At the **public distance**, communication occurs at a distance of 12 or more feet. This spatial zone allows listeners to scan the entire person while he or she is speaking. The classroom environment exemplifies public distance. Most classrooms are arranged with a teacher in the front and rows of desks or tables facing the teacher. Of course, this setup can vary, but many classrooms are arranged with students more than twelve feet from their professor. Public distance is also used in large settings, such as when we listen to speakers, watch musicals, or attend television show tapings.

A theoretical model can help us understand the differences in distance between people. The **expectancy violations theory** (Burgoon, 1978) states that we expect people to maintain a certain distance in their conversations with us. If a person violates our expectations (if, for instance, a work colleague stands in our intimate space while talking with us), our response to the violation will be based on how much we like that person. That is, if we like a person, we're probably going to allow a distance violation. We may even reciprocate that conversational distance. If we dislike the person, we will likely be irritated by the violation and perhaps move away from the person. According to this theory, the degree to which we like someone can be based on factors that include our assessment of their credibility and physical attractiveness. Personal space violations, therefore, have consequences on our interactions.

Before moving on, we'd like to address one final point about space. Whereas personal space is that invisible bubble we carry from one interaction to another, **territoriality** is our sense of ownership of space that remains fixed. Humans mark their territories in various ways, usually with items or objects that are called **territorial markers**. For example, perhaps you go to a coffee shop

personal distance

Ranging from eighteen inches to four feet, the space most people use during conversations.

social distance

Ranging from four to twelve feet, the spatial zone usually reserved for professional or formal interpersonal encounters.

public distance

Communication that occurs at a distance of twelve or more feet, allowing listeners to see a person while he or she is speaking.

expectancy violations theory

A theory that maintains that we expect other people to maintain a certain distance from us in their conversations with us.

territoriality

Our sense of ownership of space that remains fixed.

territorial markers

Items or objects that humans use to mark their territories, such as a table in a coffee shop.

each morning and stake out your table with a newspaper. Or, maybe you live near a house where a fence separates one house from the next. Although one doesn't always own a particular territory, we nonetheless presume "owner-ship" by the sheer frequency with which we occupy a space or by the markers we use to communicate that the territory is "ours." In a sense, we believe we have proprietary rights over some particular location. If, for example, you take the train each morning to work and sit in the same seat, you have claimed your territory. If someone were to occupy your seat one day, the only thing you could do about it besides merely experience displeasure would be to ask the person to leave.

Place and Time Codes

We do not often think of place and time codes when we think of nonverbal communication, but they affect us deeply. The categories of nonverbal com-munication included in place and time codes are environment (such as color and smell) and chronemics (time).

The Environment

Where you sit, sleep, dance, climb, jog, write, sing, play, sew, or worship are all parts of your **physical environment.** How we utilize the parts of the environ-ment, how we manage them, and their influence upon us are all part of non-verbal communication. Or, as Burgoon and her research team (1996) con-cluded, "Humans have always altered the environment for their purposes, interpreted meaning from it, and relied on environmental cues for guides to behavior" (pp. 109–110). Our physical environment includes a number of features, including the smell (for example, restaurant), clutter (for example, attic, garage, basement, closet), and sounds (for example, music, chatter) of our surroundings. But what do we do to the environment, and what does it "do" to us? Let's explore three prominent environmental factors that affect communication between people: color, lighting, and room design.

Color is one of the most subtle environmental influences. Most research-ers conclude that color affects our moods and perceptions. In other words, color has symbolic meaning in the environment and in our society (Sadka, 2004). Red, for instance, embodies an interesting contradiction: It both facili-tates togetherness and incites anger. Couples share their (red) hearts of candy on Valentine's Day; later, this same couple may see red in each other's eyes when they get into a fight. The color blue also has several meanings. Many people associate blue with calmness (think about lakes and oceans), whereas others feel "blue" when they are sad or depressed. Yellow (joy), black (sad-ness), and purple (wisdom) are less paradoxical.

Our perceptions of color, which can be based on cultural interpretations, can affect our perception of the physical environment. Do you feel that a certain color is most conducive to learning? Now, notice what color your communication classroom is. At work, do you believe that the color of your work environment affects yours or others' productivity? Regarding your living

physical environment
The setting in which our behavior takes place.

Beachfront tourist areas, such as those in Miami, often feature brightly colored buildings to convey a sense of fun and relaxation. Tourists wear brightly colored bathing suits or Hawaiian shirts, which indicate freedom from the more conservative colors and expectations of the workplace. Bright neon signs attract crowds at night with the promise of excitement and abandon.

© Alan Schein Photography/Corbis

environment, do you like bold and bright colors, or are you more of an earth tone person? One reason that so many educational and work environments remain neutral in coloring is because we cannot universally agree upon what color is best.

In addition to color, the *lighting* of the environment can modify behavior (Meer, 1985). The effect of lighting on worker productivity has been investigated for many decades (Roethlisberger & Dickson, 1939). Lighting levels also seem to affect behavior within interpersonal interactions. Next time you're in a department store, look at how the lighting level varies in the different departments. Some departments, such as cosmetics, have soft lighting because it makes the customer look good and thus more inclined to buy the store's beauty products. Or, think about how lighting in dimly lit restaurants affects our behavior; it may prompt us to feel relaxed, causing us to prolong our evening (and increase our dinner tab). Brightly lit restaurants, such as McDonald's or Wendy's, may increase people's rate of eating (thus, the term *fast food*).

Room design, including room size, also affects communication. For example, many retirement villages are now being designed to allow for both independence and interaction. Individual living units similar to small condominiums are built to promote privacy, but the units converge to form a meeting room where activities, events, and group functions take place. To further explore room design and how one company is changing its space to be more consistent with its mission and goals, read the article "Lessons from Frank Lloyd Wright," available through InfoTrac College Edition. Use your online Resource Center for *Understanding Interpersonal Communication* to access *InfoTrac College Edition Exercise 5.4: What Does Office Space Communicate?*

Time (Chronemics)

Chronemics, the study of a person's use of time, helps us to understand how people perceive and structure time in their dialogues and relationships with others. Time is an abstract concept that we describe using figures of speech (which we discussed in Chapter 4)—for example, "time is on your side," "time well spent," "time to kill," "time on your hands," "don't waste time," "on time," and "quality time." Dawna Ballard and David Seibold (2000) observed the reciprocal relationship between time and communication. They believe that communication creates a person's understanding of time and yet, our sense of time restricts our communication.

Edward T. Hall (1959) noted three time systems. *Technical time* is the scientific measurement of time. This system is associated with the precision of keeping time. *Formal time* is the time that society formally teaches. For example, in the United States, the clock and the calendar are our units of formal time. We know that when it is 1 a.m., it is usually time to sleep, and at 1 p.m. we find ourselves at work or school. Further, in the United States, our arrangement of time is fixed and rather methodical. We learn to tell time based on the hour, and children are usually taught how to tell time by using the "big hand" and the "little hand" as references. *Informal time* is time that includes three concepts: duration, punctuality, and activity:

- Duration pertains to how long we allocate for a particular event. In our schedules, we may earmark forty minutes for grocery shopping or an hour for a religious service. Some of our estimates are less precise. For instance, what does it mean when we respond "be there right away"? Does that mean we will be there in ten minutes, one hour, or as long as it takes you? And, despite its vague and odd-sounding nature, the statement "I want it done yesterday" is clear to many.

- Punctuality is the promptness associated with keeping time. We're said to be punctual when we arrive for an appointment at the designated time. Despite the value placed on punctuality in the United States, friends may arrive late to lunch, professors late to class, physicians late to appointments, and politicians late to rallies. (In fact, with the tendency of some people to always be tardy, we may question why we even make appointments in the first place.)

- Activity is a somewhat chronemic value. People in Western cultures are encouraged to "use their time wisely"—in other words, they should make sure their time is used to accomplish something, whether it's a task or a social function. Simultaneously, they should avoid being so time-occupied that others view them as focused and obsessive. Our use and management of time is associated with status and power. For example, the old adage "time is money," which equates an intangible (time) with a tangible (money), suggests

chronemics

The study of a person's use of time.

Ethics & Choice

As Kyle Wood navigated the icy streets in his car, he glanced at the dashboard clock. 9:50 a.m. He couldn't imagine arriving on time for his 10 a.m. job interview. Kyle, a newly minted graduate, really wanted this job, which seemed like a perfect match for him. The company was highly recommended by Kyle's best friend, Lou, who had worked there for almost three years.

As he continued driving, Kyle thought about calling Ms. Littleton, the human resources director, on his cell phone to inform her that he would be late. He hesitated, recalling his friend's warning that Ms. Littleton was a stickler about punctuality who didn't believe in excuses for being late. However, he knew that he would never get to her office in ten minutes, so he decided to call her.

As he waited to be connected to human resources, Kyle began to wonder whether he should tell the truth about the slippery roads or simply make up an entirely different excuse, such as a sick sister or mother. He even considered saying that his mother had just been rushed to the hospital, so he needed to reschedule the appointment. Then, as quickly as he thought about that scenario, Kyle thought about how hard it was for him to lie to another person. He just couldn't do it. In fact, when his best friend, Bud, had cheated on a midterm exam last year, Kyle had been angry at him for a week. Kyle had chastised Bud about how low his friend's ethics had sunk. Kyle remembered Bud's shaky voice and fidgety body movements when Kyle confronted him. Would Kyle have the same reaction as he lied to Ms. Littleton over the phone? Would she be able to tell he was lying by his voice? What would be his physical reaction during his rescheduled interview, if he was ever given another chance? Would he be able to finish the deceptive story when he was face to face with the human resources director? Ms. Littleton was now on the phone, and Kyle had to make a decision.

As you reflect on Kyle Wood's situation, consider the dilemma he faces. He wants to be interviewed for the job so badly that he is considering lying. What is your reaction to Kyle's ethical challenge? Should he tell the truth to Ms. Littleton, who has a reputation as a punctuality czar? If not, what would you advise him to do? What ethical system of communication should be followed in this example (categorical imperative, utilitarianism, ethic of care, golden mean, significant choice)?

Go to your online Resource Center for *Understanding Interpersonal Communication* to access an interactive version of this scenario under the resources for Chapter 5. The interactive version of this scenario allows you to choose an appropriate response to this dilemma and then see what consequences your choice brings about. You can also compare your answers to the questions at the end of the scenario to those provided by the authors and, if requested, email your response to your instructor.

that we place a value on our use of time. And as a country with individualistic values (see Chapter 3), the United States is a society that supports the belief that time is intimately linked to status and power.

Suppose, for instance, that Joan arrives at an interview five minutes late. Joan probably won't get the job because punctuality is an important value to communicate to a future boss. However, let's say that the interviewer, Mr. Johansen, is five minutes late for the interview. Of course, he would not lose his job. Similarly, John's optometrist could be late for his appointment with no consequence, but if John is late for his own appointment, he might have to pay a "no show" fee.

Let's look at a few more examples. Some professors are regularly late for class, but these same professors have policies about student punctuality. And many of you have waited in long lines for a school loan, concert tickets, or a driver's license. If you truly had power, you wouldn't have to spend time waiting in line. Time is clearly related to status and power differences between individuals (Hickson et al. 2004).

We have spent a great deal of time identifying the primary types of nonverbal communication so you can better understand their comprehensive nature. We close this chapter by considering how culture affects nonverbal messages. As we learned in Chapter 3, culture influences virtually every aspect of interpersonal communication. Understanding various cultural influences on nonverbal behavior helps you realize that not everyone shares your beliefs, values, and meanings. Particularly in the area of nonverbal communication—which, as we noted earlier in the chapter, is often ambiguous and open to interpretation—remembering cultural variations helps us become more competent communicators.

Cultural Variations in Nonverbal Communication

We could write an entire text about the influence of culture on nonverbal behavior. In fact, several books examine this topic in detail (for example, Martin & Nakayama, 2008; Samovar & Porter, 2004). Nonverbal behaviors convey different meanings among (co)cultures. We learn how to interpret nonverbal behaviors as children. Yet, as we noted in Chapter 3, our population is so culturally diverse that we can't always rely on these interpretations; the meaning of nonverbal communication between and among cultures can vary. Unless you are sensitive to this variation, you may have a tough time communicating with someone with a different cultural background from you. To provide you with a sense of how culture affects nonverbal behavior, we'll give you a glimpse into this area. Let's explore a few conclusions related to body movement, facial expressions, personal space, and touch.

Body Movement

Kinesic behavior is one area where nonverbal communication and culture intersect. For example, research has shown that greetings vary from one culture to another. For instance, most Westerners are accustomed to shaking hands upon meeting. In other cultures, however, the handshake is not common. In Japan, for instance, individuals bow when they meet (Morrison, Conaway, & Borden, 1994). The person with the lower status initiates bowing and is expected to bow deeper than the individual with higher status. The person with elevated status decides when the bowing ends.

Gesturing has also been studied across cultures. For instance, while speaking, Mexicans, Greeks, and people from many South American countries are dramatic and animated. Mexicans use lots of hand gestures in their conversations, and Morrison et al. (1994) note that Italians "talk with their hands" in expressive gestures. However, people in a number of Asian cultures consider such overt body movements rude, and Germans consider bold hand gestures too flashy. In addition, the A-okay sign used in the U.S. has sexual meaning in some European communities.

Another cultural difference in nonverbal communication is the way the concept of "two" is communicated. For example, in the United States, people use the forefinger and the middle finger, whereas Filipinos hold up the ring finger and the little finger.

Facial Expressions

Since the eye is the foundation of the face, it's logical that this area has been studied extensively. The extent to which a person looks at another during a conversation is culturally based. Members of most co-cultures in the United States are socialized to look at a listener while speaking (Burgoon et al., 1996).

It's common for two people from the United States to look at each other's eyes while communicating. In this country, frequent eye aversion may communicate a lack of trust. However, in other cultures, such as Japan and Jamaica, direct eye contact is perceived as communicating disrespect.

While we tend to focus on cultural differences, research has also uncovered similarities across cultures. Collectively, research conducted as far back as the early 1970s (Ekman, 1972, 1973; Ekman & Friesen, 1971) has shown that facial expressions are universal. That is, six expressions have been shown to be judged consistently across cultures: anger, disgust, fear, happiness, sadness, and surprise. Today, there may be some variation because of the co-cultural backgrounds of communicators, but essentially, this universality remains (Matsumoto, 2006).

Personal Space

Spacial distances have been the focus of research in intercultural communication. In the United States, as previously discussed, we tend to clearly demarcate our territory. Edward Hall and Mildred Reed Hall (1990) discuss the territoriality of Germans and the French:

> Germans . . . barricade themselves behind heavy doors and sound-proof walls to try to seal themselves from others in order to concentrate on their work. The French have a close personal distance and are not as territorial. They are tied to people and thrive on constant interaction. (p. 180)

In addition, interpretations of personal space vary from culture to culture. People in many South American countries, such as Brazil, require little personal space in an interaction. Arabs, Hungarians, and Africans similarly

The reduced conversational distance expected by people in collectivistic cultures can be disconcerting to people who require greater distance. How much conversational distance do you require when you're talking to someone? Does the amount of distance you require depend on the situation, with whom you're talking, or the information you're trying to convey?

© Richard Bickel/Corbis

reduce conversational distance (Lewis, 1999). Generally speaking, people from individualistic cultures (for example, United States, Germany, Canada) require more space than do those from collectivistic cultures (Costa Rica, Venezuela, Ecuador). The personal space requirements of people from collectivistic cultures can be partially explained by the fact that people from those cultures tend to work, sleep, and have fun in close proximity to one another (Andersen, 2003).

Touch

Researchers have also investigated touch behavior within a cultural context. For example, Tiffany Field (1999) found that adolescents from the United States touched each other less than adolescents from France did. Field observed friends at McDonald's restaurants in Miami and Paris and found that the U.S. teenagers did less hugging, kissing, and caressing than their French counterparts. However, the U.S. adolescents engaged in more self-touching, such as primping, than the French adolescents.

Some cultures accept more same-sex touching than others. For example, men frequently hold hands in Indonesia, and men frequently walk down the street with their arms around each other in Malaysia. Such overt touching, however, would be frowned upon in Japan or in Scandinavia.

In the United States, touching is usually avoided. To get a sense of the extent to which you avoid touch, complete the Touch Avoidance Inventory.

As you can see from the variety of cultural differences in nonverbal behavior discussed in this section and summarized in Table 5.2, nonverbal behaviors should always be understood within a cultural context. We cannot assume that others automatically understand our nonverbal displays because

Table 5.2 Culture and nonverbal communication

Nonverbal Type	Nonverbal Behavior	Cultural Difference
Kinesics	Greeting another	*United States*:* Varies; generally,shaking hands
		Japan: Bowing
Facial expression	Eye contact during conversation	*United States*:* Varies; generally, conversation direct
		Cambodia: Indirect
Proxemics	Personal space during conversation	*United States*:* Varies; generally, large
		Costa Rica: Small
Haptics	Same-sex touching during conversation	*United States:* Taboo
		Malaysia: Same-sex hand-holding is common

*Due to the co-cultural differences in the United States, broad cultural generalizations about the behavior are difficult.

their meanings can differ significantly within and across cultures. Further, as we pointed out in Chapter 3, the U.S. population continues to grow more diverse. Being sensitive to cultural communication differences and seeking clarification will help you in your interpersonal relationships. If you'd like to explore how your nonverbal behaviors compare with those used by people in another country, use your online Resource Center for *Understanding Interpersonal Communication* to access *Interactive Activity 5.5: Nonverbal Behavior in Japan*.

Choices for Increasing Nonverbal Communication Effectiveness

As we have previously stated, nonverbal behavior is difficult to pin down with precision. We may think we understand what a person's hand gesture or eye behavior means, but there are often multiple ways to interpret a particular nonverbal behavior. Therefore, we must be cautious when we interpret messages. We now turn our attention to identifying six skills for improving nonverbal communication effectiveness. As you practice these skills, keep in mind that you may have to alter your verbal communication (a topic we examine in Chapter 4) since nonverbal communication is closely aligned with what we say.

Recall the Nonverbal-Verbal Relationship

Throughout this chapter, we have reminded you that nonverbal communication is often best understood with verbal communication. That is, we need to pay attention to what is said in addition to the nonverbal behavior. Most of us blend nonverbal and verbal messages. We raise our voice to underscore something we've said. We frown when we tell a sad story. We motion with our hands when we tell others to get going. And, when young toddlers are angry, we see them jump up and down on the floor while they scream "No." These examples illustrate the integration of nonverbal and verbal messages. We need to remain aware of this relationship to achieve meaning in our conversations. In addition, we need to be aware that our nonverbal and verbal message should match. Imagine Lucas, for instance, telling an interviewer, "My biggest strength as an employee is that I'm a great listener" only to follow up that statement by reading the sign on the wall behind the interviewer while she provides salary information.

Be Tentative When Interpreting Nonverbal Behavior

In this chapter, we have reiterated the ambiguous nature of nonverbal communication, including cultural differences in nonverbal expressions. Because

Communication Assessment Test
Touch Avoidance Inventory

Use the following scale to respond to the statements. Try to record your first reaction, and don't go back and change your responses. You can take this test online. Go to your online Resource Center for *Understanding Interpersonal Communication* and look under the resources for Chapter 5.

strongly agree = 1   agree = 2   undecided = 3   disagree = 4   strongly disagree = 5

_____ 1. A hug from a same sex friend is a true sign of friendship.

_____ 2. Opposite sex friends enjoy it when I touch them.

_____ 3. I often put my arm around friends of the same sex.

_____ 4. When I see two people of the same sex hugging, it revolts me.

_____ 5. I like it when members of the opposite sex touch me.

_____ 6. People shouldn't be so uptight about touching persons of the same sex.

_____ 7. I think it's vulgar when members of the opposite sex touch me.

_____ 8. When a member of the opposite sex touches me, I find it unpleasant.

_____ 9. I wish I were free to show emotions by touching members of the same sex.

_____ 10. I'd enjoy giving a massage to an opposite sex friend.

_____ 11. I enjoy kissing persons of the same sex.

_____ 12. I like to touch friends that are of the same sex as I am.

_____ 13. Touching friends of the same sex does not make me feel uncomfortable.

_____ 14. I find it enjoyable when I and a close friend of the opposite sex embrace.

_____ 15. I enjoy getting a back rub from members of the opposite sex.

_____ 16. I dislike kissing relatives of the same sex.

_____ 17. Intimate touching with members of the opposite sex is pleasurable.

_____ 18. I find it difficult to be touched by members of my own sex.

_____ 19. Touching between people of the opposite sex bothers me.

_____ 20. I am comfortable around members of the same sex who are touching.

There is no particular touch avoidance score in this inventory. Rather, look at those items where you responded with a "5" and those items where you responded with a "1." Do you see consistencies in your responses? For instance, questions 13 and 20 ask about your comfort level with same sex touching. Did you respond similarly to these questions? Also, does it make a difference whether you (or others) are touching relatives, friends, or intimate partners? Looking at the personal, social, and legal implications of touch, what sorts of conclusions can you draw from these questions and your responses?

From student website to accompany *Strategic Communication in Business and the Professions*, 5th ed., Dan O'Hair et al. Reprinted by permission of Pearson Education.

of individual differences, we can never be sure what a specific nonverbal behavior means. For example, when Gene walks into Professor Hereford's office, he may be confident in thinking that she is busy. After all, there are books everywhere, the phone is ringing, and the professor is seated behind a desk with many papers on it. However, these environmental artifacts and conditions may not be accurately communicating the professor's availability. Gene needs to clarify his interpretation of this nonverbal communication by asking the professor if she has time to talk to him. Finally, consider the cultural background of communicators. We identified how nonverbal communication varies between and among (co)cultures; this is an important foundation to draw upon as you interpret the meaning of a nonverbal message.

Monitor Your Nonverbal Behavior

Being a self-monitor is crucial in conversations (Snyder, 1979). Becoming aware of how you say something, your proximity to the other person, the extent to which you use touch, or your use of silence is just as important as the words used. This self-monitoring is not easy. For example, let's say that Maria is in a heated exchange with her roommate, Sue, who refused to clean the apartment. When Maria tries to make her point, it's not easy for her to think about how she is saying something or whether or not she is screaming or standing too close. Like most people, Maria simply wants to make her point. However, Maria's nonverbal communication can carry significance, particularly if Sue is focusing on it and Maria is ignoring it. You need to look for meaning in both your behavior and the behavior of others.

Reflect on how a specific type of nonverbal communication functions in all the close relationships you have. If you like, you can use your student workbook or your **Understanding Interpersonal Communication** Online Resources to complete this activity.

Ask Others for Their Impressions

When applying for a job, we ask others for their interview strategies. When going out on a date, we ask friends how we look or smell. When choosing a class, we may ask our friends about their experiences with a particular professor. Yet, when we try to improve our communication with others, we generally neglect to ask others about our nonverbal effectiveness. Whom should we consult to ensure accuracy and clarity in our nonverbal communication?

The easy answer is that we should ask someone with whom we are close. Our close relationships can provide us valuable information, such as that our silent reactions to others' disclosures make them uncomfortable or that our constant eye rolling during a conflict is irritating. Perhaps others can let us know that our verbal and nonverbal behaviors are inconsistent, such as when a spouse yells to another, "Of course I love you!" Those who are close to us are more likely to be up-front with us about problems in our nonverbal communication.

Avoid Nonverbal Distractions

The old saying, "Get out of your own way!" has meaning when we communicate nonverbally. At times, our nonverbal communication can serve as noise in an interpersonal exchange. Consider, for example, playing with your hair, shifting your eyes, using vocal distractors, or fiddling with a piece of jewelry while talking to someone. The person is likely to focus more on your nonverbal displays than on what you are saying. In turn, it's likely that meaning would be obscured or little meaning would be exchanged in the interaction.

Place Nonverbal Communication in Context

Earlier in this chapter, we discussed the fact that we live in a society that embraces simplistic notions associated with nonverbal communication. For instance, in the 1970s and 1980s, John Molloy (1978) made millions of dollars from his book *Dress for Success*. This simplistic source told business professionals how to dress to look "professional"

interpersonal explorer

Before you finish reading this chapter, take a moment to review the theories and skills discussed. How do you think the theories discussed in this chapter can help you better understand interpersonal communication and nonverbal communication? In what ways can the skills discussed help you interact more effectively with other people in your life?

Theories that relate to nonverbal communication
- **Interaction adaptation theory**
  Individuals concurrently adapt their communication behaviors to the communication behavior of others
- **Expectancy violations theory**
  People have expectations for others to maintain a particular conversation distance

Practical skills for improving nonverbal effectiveness
- Keep in mind the relationship between verbal and nonverbal messages
- Be tentative when interpreting nonverbal behavior
- Monitor your own nonverbal behavior
- Check in with others about their impressions of your nonverbal behavior
- Avoid nonverbal distractions
- Place nonverbal communication in context

Explore your interpersonal choices
Are you ready to explore your interpersonal choices regarding nonverbal communication? Use your online Resource Center for *Understanding Interpersonal Communication* to access ABC News video, "Personal Best," about the

importance of nonverbal communication, such as eye contact and clothing, in professional and business interactions. Compare your answers to the questions at the end of the video with those provided by the authors.

and to be taken seriously in the workplace. Scores of companies embraced the basic suggestions of the book and used its conclusions to mandate changes to corporate attire.

However, when discussing human behavior, we need to avoid such superficial ideas about our nonverbal communication. We should pay attention to nonverbal cues, but we should place them in appropriate context. Be careful of assigning too much meaning to a wink, a handshake, a pair of dangling earrings, or a voice that sounds uptight. These may carry no significant meaning in a conversation. To acquire meaning, you must consider the entire communication process, not just one element of it.

Summary

Nonverbal communication plays a significant role in our interpersonal relationships. It is often ambiguous, meaning different things to people of different cultures and co-cultures. People use nonverbal cues to regulate conversation, such as using body language to facilitate turn-taking. Nonverbal communication is more credible than verbal communication because it is harder to mask. Sometimes, nonverbal and verbal communication are at odds, resulting in mixed messages.

Nonverbal communication manifests itself in many forms. Kinesics includes gestures and body posture/orientation. Physical appearance encompasses the physical characteristics of an individual (including attractiveness) and body artifacts such as clothing, jewelry, and tattoos. Facial expressions, especially the eyes and smiling, are the nonverbal cues that give the most insight into how someone is feeling.

Paralanguage, or vocalics, involves vocal qualities such as vocal distractors (the "ums" and "ers" of conversation), the use of silence, and pitch, rate, volume, inflection, tempo, and pronunciation. Paralanguage also encompasses vocal characterizers such as crying, laughing, whining, and so on. Touch communication, or haptics, the most primitive form of communication, represents the ultimate in privileged access to people, and can perform diverse functions.

Proxemics, the study of distance, involves people's personal space (which can vary by circumstance and culture) as well as their territoriality, or their need to "own" certain spaces. Aspects of the physical environment, such as color, lighting, and room design, can affect our nonverbal communication. And chronemics, or the study of a person's use of time, explains how people perceive and structure time, including how the management of time is associated with status and power.

Culture affects nonverbal behavior and interpretation of nonverbal behavior. People of different cultures vary in their mode of greeting and gesturing, how much they engage in eye contact, the personal space they require, and their acceptance of touching.

To improve our nonverbal communication, we must remember that verbal and nonverbal communication work together. We also need to avoid jumping to conclusions about what certain nonverbal cues mean. Furthermore, we need to monitor our nonverbal behavior and ask others for their impressions of our nonverbal cues. Finally, we must not only avoid nonverbal distractions during our conversations, but also ensure that we interpret nonverbal communication within its context.

Understanding Interpersonal Communication Online

Now that you've read Chapter 5, use your online Resource Center for *Understanding Interpersonal Communication* for quick access to the electronic study resources that accompany this text. Your online Resource Center gives you access to the video of Mark's interaction with his mother on page 151, the Ethics & Choice interactive activity on page 172, the Communication Assessment Test on page 177, the Your Turn journal activity on page 178, the Interpersonal Explorer activity on page 179, InfoTrac College Edition, and study aids including a digital glossary, review quizzes, and the chapter activities.

Terms for Review

body artifacts 160
body orientation 159
chronemics 171
citing gestures 159
delivery gestures 159
expectancy violations
    theory 168
haptics 165
interaction adaptation
    theory 154
intimate distance 167

kinesics 158
mixed message 157
nonverbal
    communication 153
paralanguage 163
personal distance 168
personal space 166
physical characteristics 160
physical environment 169
proxemics 166

public distance 168
seeking gestures 159
social distance 168
territoriality 168
territorial markers 168
turn gestures 159
turn-taking 156
vocal characterizers 163
vocal distractors 163
vocal qualities 163

Questions for Understanding

Comprehension Focus

1. Explain how nonverbal communication is a part of every personal message a communicator delivers.

2. Identify at least three principles of nonverbal communication.

3. Define paralanguage and explain its importance in conversations.

4. What are the consequences of touch in our society?

5. Describe the influence of culture on at least two types of nonverbal communication.

Application Focus

1. CASE IN POINT Reread the opening story of Mark Mattson and his mother, Julia. If you found yourself in Mark's situation, what do you think you would discuss with your mother (or father)? Discuss the importance of "reading" someone's nonverbal communication and its affect on a relationship similar to that of Mark and Julia.

2. Identify several nonverbal behaviors during the dating (courtship) stage of an interpersonal relationship.

3. Spend some time during the day interacting without using any gestures or touch behavior. Was it possible? If not, why not? If so, what did it feel like?

4. Defend or criticize the following statement: Touch is a double-edged sword in close relationships. Use examples as you explain your view.

5. Write a brief dialogue between a married couple in a conflict and insert appropriate nonverbal codes that you believe would be part of that conflict. (Assume the couple has been together for 10 years.) What patterns do you see with respect to conflict and nonverbal communication? What sorts of nonverbal behaviors accompany the conflict? Explain.

Interactive Activities and InfoTrac College Edition Exercises

Interactive Activities

InfoTrac College Edition Exercises

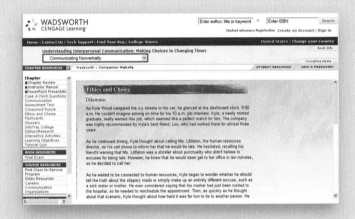

Chapter 6
Effective Listening

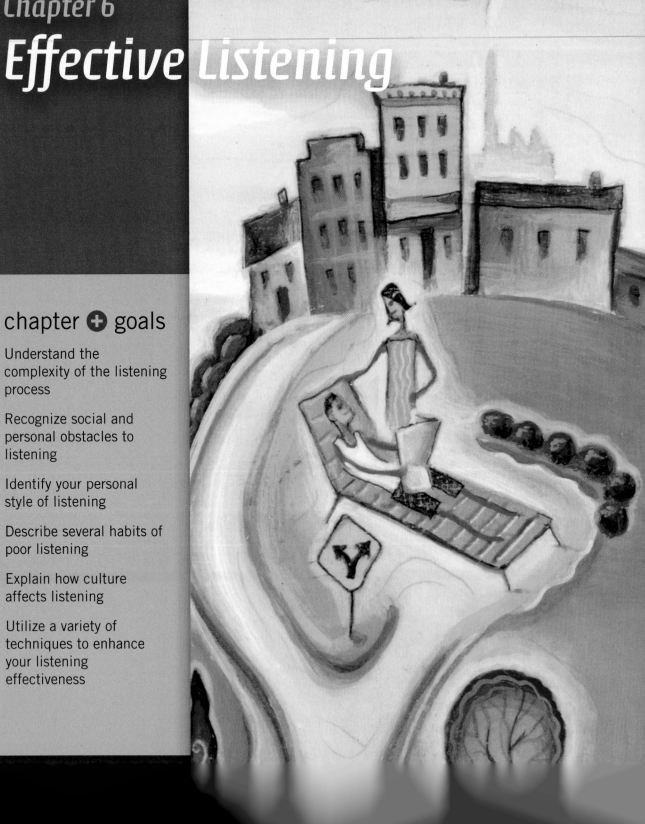

chapter ➕ goals

Understand the complexity of the listening process

Recognize social and personal obstacles to listening

Identify your personal style of listening

Describe several habits of poor listening

Explain how culture affects listening

Utilize a variety of techniques to enhance your listening effectiveness

CASEinPOINT

Jacqueline Mitchell, age 25, had been the director of volunteers for a local political campaign for almost a month. She knew that she was perceived as an important gatekeeper because both political and community leaders considered the campaign to be a critical one.

Jacqueline's responsibilities consisted primarily of coordinating the schedules of the candidate's nearly 20 campaign volunteers. She also answered about 50 phone calls a day for the campaign. With a degree in communication and public policy, Jacqueline thought this was the ideal job. She wasn't paid a lot, but she thought she would gain beneficial experience. At one point, the campaign director, Mara, asked Jacqueline to do some quick research to prepare the candidate for an upcoming interview. Although Jacqueline felt unqualified for this task, she listened to Mara's directions and did her best. Successfully completing this assignment made Jacqueline feel even more confident about her job performance, but she soon learned that even the most self-assured can make mistakes.

Jacqueline scheduled a few important appointments for her candidate at the precise time that the candidate would be attending a rally. In addition, Jacqueline told a campaign secret to one of her volunteers, who then told a member of the media. When the campaign director verbally reprimanded Jacqueline for scheduling appointments when the candidate would be busy at a rally, Jacqueline was confused because she thought she remembered hearing that there were no rallies scheduled for several weeks. Mara also admonished Jacqueline for not keeping campaign secrets. Mara told Jacqueline that she might not be cut out for the fast pace of politics. Jacqueline, too, wondered whether she was suited to the job or whether her listening skills needed a major overhaul. Mara told Jacqueline that she would be given one more chance because she was new to the job.

Go to your online Resource Center for *Understanding Interpersonal Communication* to watch a video clip of Jacqueline's situation.

> Access the resources for Chapter 6 and select "Jacqueline" to watch the video (it takes a minute for the video to load). As you watch Mara scold Jacqueline, consider some strategies Jacqueline might have used to help her listen better. > You can respond to this and other analysis questions, and then click "Done" to compare your answers with those provided by the authors.

*A*t times, it's not all that devastating if we fail to listen. In the course of an average day most of us don't listen with complete attention to the barrage of messages from the media, our friends, family, and coworkers. Some of these messages are useless or meaningless to us ("And let me tell you about my niece's new boyfriend"), others we've heard over and over again ("When I was a teenager. . ."), others don't make sense to us ("When I cook, I usually think of Gayle's bridal dress"), and still other messages we tune out ("And now let me talk about New Zealand's foreign policy").

Many times, however, failing to listen can have serious consequences. Sometimes a relationship we have may suffer or a partner decides to leave us. Other times, valuable medical information may be missed. Still other times, as in Jacqueline's case, a job can be on the line.

Think of scenarios in which listening is crucial. For example, how would you feel if your physician didn't listen to your health problems? Or, how would you feel if your counselor didn't listen to some of your psychological troubles? What effects would poor listening skills have on the construction of new bridges or airport runways? Consider the implications of a supervisor not listening to a colleague who knows of unethical practices in the company. What would happen if your best friend failed to listen when you were recounting an important problem? This chapter discusses the importance of listening, explores reasons why we don't always listen, and suggests ways we can overcome our bad listening habits.

Listening is a communication behavior we may assume we all understand, but some further explanation will ensure that we share a common understanding of it. We continue our discussion by first differentiating listening from hearing. Although the two terms are often used interchangeably, hearing and listening are different processes and mean different things.

Distinguishing the Difference: Hearing and Listening

hearing

The physical process of letting in audible stimuli without focusing on the stimuli.

working memory theory

A theory that states that we can pay attention to several stimuli and simultaneously store stimuli for future reference.

You may have "heard" this before, but listening and hearing are not the same thing. Hearing occurs when a sound wave hits an eardrum. The resulting vibrations or stimuli are sent to the brain. For our purposes, we define **hearing** as the physical process of letting in auditory stimuli, but without trying to understand that stimuli. **Working memory theory** (Baddeley & Hitch, 1974) states that we can pay attention to several stimuli and simultaneously store stimuli for future reference. When we try to organize the stimuli, we have to retrieve previous experiences and information to match it to the current stimuli. Again, all of this "processing and storage" is done simultaneously and all of it is conducted at the point in the communication process that we call hearing.

We introduced you to the issue of stimuli in Chapter 2. With respect to its relationship to working memory theory, consider the following. When Polly sits at The Coffee Bean drinking coffee and reading the morning paper, she hears all types of noises, including people ordering coffee, couples laughing, the door squeaking as it opens and closes, and even the hum of the fluorescent lights. However, she is not paying attention to these background noises. Instead, she is hearing the stimuli without thinking about them. Polly must be able to tune out these stimuli because otherwise she wouldn't be able to concentrate on reading the paper. For instance, Polly's tuning out the stimuli around her might cause her not to register a fight occurring outside the coffee shop, and so she may not immediately do anything about it (e.g., tell one of the shop employees). However, she may unconsciously store "the fight scene," and retrieve it in the future (say, if she engages in a conversation about street crime).

Like Polly, we find ourselves hearing a lot of stimuli throughout our day, whether it's the buzz of lights, music in a restaurant, or the sounds of cars passing on the street. Most of us are able to continue our conversations without attending to these noises.

Being a good listener is much more than letting in audible stimuli. Listening is a communication activity that requires us to be thoughtful. The choices we make when we listen affect our interpersonal encounters. People often take listening for granted as a communication skill in interpersonal relationships. As Harvey Mackay (2001) of the International Communication Association concluded, "listening is the hardest of the 'easy' tasks." Unlike hearing, listening is a learned communication skill. People often have a difficult time describing what being an effective listener is, but seem to know when another person is not listening. Within this framework, we define **listening** as the dynamic, transactional process of receiving, responding to, recalling, and rating, stimuli and/or messages from another. When we listen, we are making sense of the message of another communicator.

Listening is dynamic because it is an active and ongoing way of demonstrating that you are involved in an interpersonal encounter. Further, listening is transactional because both the sender and the receiver are active agents in the process, as we discussed in Chapter 1. In other words, listening is a two-way street. Merely showing that we are listening is a necessary but insufficient way to maintain relationships. We need others to show us they know we are listening.

The remaining four concepts of the definition require a more detailed discussion. We already know that hearing is the starting point in the listening process. Stimuli have to be present, but much more, is required. The **four "Rs" of listening** —receiving, responding, recalling, and rating—make up the listening process (see Figure 6.1 on page 188). Each of the following sections discusses a component of the listening process and the specific skill it requires, including a few recommendations for improving that skill.

Take a moment to notice all the auditory stimuli around you. On an average day, how much stimuli do you think you ignore so that you can concentrate on a task or on another person's message?

listening

The dynamic, transactional process of receiving, recalling, rating, and responding to stimuli, messages, or both.

four "Rs" of listening

The four components of the listening process: receiving, responding, recalling, and rating.

Figure 6.1   The listening process

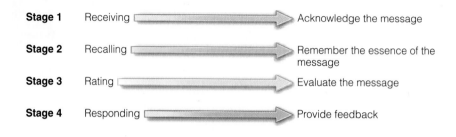

Stage 1	Receiving	→	Acknowledge the message
Stage 2	Recalling	→	Remember the essence of the message
Stage 3	Rating	→	Evaluate the message
Stage 4	Responding	→	Provide feedback

Receiving

When we receive a message, we hear and attend to it. **Receiving** involves the verbal and nonverbal acknowledgment of communication. We are selective in our reception and usually screen out those messages that are least relevant to us. Perhaps one reason we don't receive every message is that our attention spans are rather short, lasting from around two to twenty seconds (Wolvin & Coakley, 1996). Our short-term memory, then, affects the receiving process.

When we are receiving, we are being mindful, a concept we discussed in Chapter 2. Mindfulness, you may recall, means we are paying close attention to the stimuli around us. Mindful listening requires us to be engaged with another person as he or she communicates. We can also become **mindless**, which means we aren't paying attention to the stimuli around us. Imagine what your life would be like if you were always mindful—you would be over-whelmed in your communication activities. Being mindless at times is neces-sary, but keep in mind that some stimuli that are perceived as unimportant can be beneficial (think about listening to the rain falling as a way to reduce stress).

The following two suggestions should improve your ability to receive messages effectively. First, eliminate unnecessary noises and physical barriers to listening. If possible, try to create surroundings that allow you to receive a message fully and accurately. Talking on a cell phone, watching MTV, or cleaning house while receiving a personal message are poor listening habits. Second, try not to interrupt the reception of a message. Although you may be tempted to cut off a speaker when he or she communicates a message about which you have a strong opinion, yield the conversational floor so you can receive the entire message and not simply a part of it.

Responding

Responding means giving feedback to another communicator in an interper-sonal exchange. Responding suggests the transactional nature of the interper-sonal communication process. That is, although we are not speaking to

receiving

The verbal and nonverbal acknowledgment of a message.

mindless

Being unaware of the stimuli around us.

responding

Providing observable feedback to a sender's message.

Our nonverbal behaviors can provide important feedback to others about whether or not we're really listening to what they're saying. Compare the nonverbal behavior of the man in the photo on the left and the man in the photo on the right. Which person do you think is listening effectively?

another person, we are engaged in communicating by listening. This suggests that responding is critical to achieve interpersonal meaning.

Responding, which lets a speaker know that the message was received, happens during and after a conversation. We provide both nonverbal and verbal feedback to someone as he or she talks and, at times, our feedback continues even though the conversation has ended.

Feedback, as you learned in Chapter 1, can be nonverbal, verbal, or both. Margaret Imhof (2003) differentiated between good and bad listeners in a pool of U.S. and German communicators. Good listeners provided feedback while maintaining frequent eye contact, displaying an open body position (e.g., body position angled toward speaker), and paraphrasing or restating relevant statements. Poor listeners jumped to conclusions, talked only about themselves, displayed a closed body position (e.g., arms closed, body positioned away from speaker), and interrupted.

You can enhance the way you respond in several ways. Adopting the other's point of view is important. This skill (which we talk about later in this chapter) is particularly significant when communicating with people with cultural backgrounds different from your own. Also, take ownership of your words and ideas. Don't confuse what you say with what the other person says. Finally, don't assume that your thoughts are universal; not everyone will agree with your position on a topic.

Recalling

Recalling involves understanding a message, storing it for future encounters, and remembering it later. We have sloppy recall if we understand a message when it is first communicated but forget it later. When we do recall a conversation, we don't recall it word-for-word; rather, we remember a personal version

recalling

Understanding a message, storing it for future encounters, and remembering it later.

(or essence) of what occurred (Bostrom, 1990). Recall is immediate, short-term, or long-term (Bostrom & Waldhart, 1988), and people's recall abilities vary.

Suppose another person criticizes you for recalling a conversation incorrectly. You might simply tell the other person that he or she is wrong. This is what happens in the following conversation between Matt and Dale. The two have been good friends for years. Matt is a homeowner who needed some painting done, and Dale verbally agreed to do it. Now that Dale has given Matt the bill, the two remember differently their conversation about how the bill was to be paid:

Dale: Matt, I remember you said you'd pay the bill in two installments. We didn't write it down, but I remember your words: "I can pay half the bill when you give it to me and then the other half two weeks later." Now you're telling me you didn't say that. What's up with that?

Matt: That's not it at all. I recall telling you that I would pay the bill in two installments *only* after I was satisfied that the work was finished. Look, I know this is not what you want to hear, but the hallway wall is scratched and needs to be repainted. I see gouges on the hardwood floors by the living room, and look at the paint drips on the molding in the dining room.

Dale: I told you that I would come in later to do those small repairs, and you said you'd pay me.

Matt: I don't remember the story that way.

Matt and Dale clearly have different recollections of their conversation. Their situation is even more challenging because both money and friendship are involved.

A number of strategies can help you improve your ability to later recall a message. First, repeating information helps to clarify terms and provide you an immediate confirmation of whether the intended message was received accurately. Second, using *mnemonic* (pronounced "ni-MON-ik") devices as memory-aiding guides will likely help you recall things more easily. Abbreviations such as MADD (for Mothers Against Drunk Driving) and PETA (People for the Ethical Treatment of Animals) use acronyms as mnemonic devices. Finally, chunking can assist you in recalling. **Chunking** means placing pieces of information into manageable and retrievable sets. For example, if Matt and Dale discussed several issues and sub-issues—such as a payment schedule, materials, furniture protection, paint color, timetables, worker load, and so on—chunking those issues into fewer, more manageable topics (for example, finances, paint, and labor) may have helped reduce their conflict.

chunking

Placing pieces of information into manageable and retrievable sets.

rating

Evaluating or assessing a message.

Rating

Rating means evaluating or assessing a message. When we listen critically, we rate messages on three levels: We decide whether or not we agree with the message, we place the message in context, and we evaluate whether the message has value to us.

You don't always agree with messages you receive from others. However, when you disagree with another person, you should try to do so from the other's viewpoint. Rating a message from another's field of experience allows us to distinguish among facts, inferences, and opinions (Brownell, 2002) and these three are critical in evaluating a message. Although we briefly explored facts and inferences in Chapter 2, let's refresh you on the subject. Facts are verifiable and can be made only after direct observation. Inferences fill in a conversation's "missing pieces" and require listeners to go beyond what was observed. **Opinions** can undergo changes over time and are based on a communicator's beliefs or values.

When we evaluate a message, we need to understand the differences among facts, inferences, and opinions. Let's say, for example, that Maggie knows the following:

- Her best friend, Oliver, hasn't spoken to her in three weeks.

- Oliver is healthy and calling other people.

- Maggie has called Oliver several times and has left messages on his answering machine.

These are the facts. If Maggie claims that Oliver is angry at her, doesn't care about her well-being, or has redefined the relationship without her knowledge, she is not acting on facts. Rather, she is using inferences and expressing opinions. Maggie's conclusions may not be accurate at all.

Here are two recommendations that will help you improve your ability to rate messages. First, detect speaker bias, if possible. At times, you may find it difficult to listen to a message and to evaluate its content. The cause of this problem may be the speaker's bias; information in a message may be distorted because a speaker may be prejudiced in some way. Second, listeners should be prepared to change their position. After you have rated a message, you may want to modify your opinions or beliefs on a subject. Avoid being the know-it-all and try to become more flexible in your thinking.

So far, we have distinguished hearing from listening and introduced you to the components of

opinion

A view, judgment, or appraisal based on our beliefs or values.

REVISITING
CASEINPOINT

1. *Explain how hearing a message, rather than listening to a message, in a campaign office can have lasting effects.*

2. *How might Jacqueline have been a more effective listener by practicing the "four Rs" of listening?*

Y*ou can answer these questions online under the resources for Chapter 6 at your online Resource Center for Understanding Interpersonal Communication.*

the listening process. To read about another listening model (prepare, receive, process, store, and respond), read the article "Power Up Your Listening Skills," available through InfoTrac College Edition. Go to your online Resource Center for *Understanding Interpersonal Communication* to access *InfoTrac College Edition Exercise 6.1: Listening Model* under the resources for Chapter 6.

The Importance of Listening

Although we like to think that we are good listeners, the truth is that we all need help in this area. Listening is an ongoing interpersonal activity that requires lifelong training. Active listening, a behavior we discuss in more detail later in the chapter, is particularly crucial. Because we listen for a variety of important reasons (see Figure 6.2), listening needs to be a high priority in our lives. Let's offer a few more reasons why studying this topic has lasting value.

Listening is essential to our relationships with others, whether they are coworkers, family members, friends, or other important people in our lives. Listening is used at least three times as much as speaking and at least four times as much as reading and writing (Grognet & Van Duzer, 2002).

Employers rank listening as the most important skill on the job (Career Solutions Training Group, 2000). Listening expert Michael Purdy suggests that hourly employees spend 30 percent of their time listening, managers 60 percent, and executives 75 percent or more (Purdy, 2004). Liz Simpson (2003), a writer for the *Harvard Management Communication Letter,* offers the

Figure 6.2   Why we listen

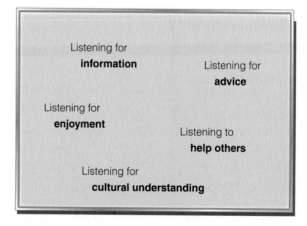

following advice to those in the workplace: "To see things from another's point of view and to build trust with her [him], you have to listen closely to what she [he] says" (p. 4).

Listening has been called a twenty-first century skill (Bentley, 2000; Grau & Grau, 2003) because it is now more important than ever. Sheila Bentley (2000) remarked that "new technology and changes in current business practices have changed whom we listen to, what we are listening for, when we listen to them, and how we listen to them" (p. 130). Listening errors can influence worker productivity (Barker & Watson, 2001) and good listening is considered to be the "doorway to leadership, for every executive, manager, and supervisor" (Simonton, 2005, p. 22). Writing from a corporate vantage point, Jennifer Grau and Carole Grau (2003) note that "expanding listening capability and well-developed conflict management skills are not dispensable management tools" (p. 3). To read an article about the importance of listening in the workplace and to check out listening skill training offered to business managers, go to your online Resource Center for *Understanding Interpersonal Communication* to access *Interactive Activity 6.1: Listening in the Workplace* under the resources for Chapter 6.

Good listening skills are valuable in other types of interpersonal relationships as well. For example, successful medical students must develop effective listening skills because, on average, a medical practitioner conducts approximately 150,000 medical interviews with patients during a 40-year career (Watson, Lazarus, & Thomas, 1999). More recent research reported by Donaghue (2007) shows that doctor-patient communication, of which listening is identified as paramount, is especially pivotal in health care. Many hospitals, responding to national surveys on patient satisfaction, are now requiring assessments of a physician's listening skills for fear of malpractice suits. Answers to questions such as "During this hospital stay, how often did doctors listen carefully to you?" will now be collated and provided to patients to use to make health care choices.

Other contexts require skill in listening. In the educational context, researchers have found that effective listening is associated with more positive teacher-student relationships (Wolvin & Coakley, 2000). On the home front, many family conflicts can be resolved by listening more effectively (Greenhaus & Friedman, 2000; Turner & West, 2006). And, in our friendships, some research has shown that the intimacy level between two friends is directly related to the listening skills brought into the relationship (Karbo, 2006).

Although it dates to the 1940s (Nichols, 1948), the topic of listening is clearly relevant today. You would have trouble thinking of any interpersonal relationship in your life that doesn't require you to listen. Improving your listening skills will help improve your relational standing with others. To read an interesting article that reinforces the importance of listening and that offers steps to effective listening, go to your online Resource Center for *Understanding Interpersonal Communication* to access *Interactive Activity 6.2: The Importance of Listening.*

Before we discuss the listening process further, we should point out that not everyone has the physical ability to hear. Although our discussion in this chapter focuses on those who are able to hear physiologically, we are aware that many individuals rely on another communication system to create and share symbols: **American Sign Language (ASL)**. ASL is the third most popular language in the United States after English and Spanish. A visual rather than auditory form of communication, ASL is composed of precise hand shapes and movements. According to the "About ASL" page of a website dedicated to American Sign Language (www.aslinfo.com), approximately half a million people communicate in this manner in the United States and Canada alone. In fact, ASL is seen as a natural communication method for visual learners who aren't hearing-impaired, making it commonplace in many schools across the country (Toppo, 2002). The hard-of-hearing and deaf community has embraced ASL, and it is used to create and to sustain communication within the community.

At this point, you can see how important the skill of listening is in our interpersonal communication with others. Yet, for a number of reasons, people don't listen well. We now present several reasons why we don't always listen effectively in our relationships with others.

Your turn

Think about how being a good listener affects your family relationships. If you like, you can use your student workbook or your **Understanding Interpersonal Communication** Online Resources to complete this activity.

The Barriers: Why We Don't Listen

People don't want to acknowledge that they are often poor listeners. As we present the following context and personal barriers to listening, try to recall times when you have faced these obstacles during interpersonal encounters. We hope that making you aware of these issues will enable you to avoid them or deal with them effectively. Table 6.1 presents examples of these obstacles in action.

Noise

As we mentioned earlier in Chapter 1, the physical environment and all of its distractions can prevent quality listening. Noise, you will remember, is anything that interferes with the message. Suppose, for instance, that a deaf student is trying to understand challenging subject matter in a classroom. Attempting to communicate the professor's words, the signer begins to sign words that are incorrect because she does not understand the content. Or, the signs are slurred or incoherent because the signing is too fast. These dis-

American Sign Language (ASL)

A visual rather than auditory form of communication that is composed of precise hand shapes and movements.

Table 6.1 Barriers to listening

Barrier type	In action
Noise (physical, semantic, psychological)	Marcy tries to listen to Nick's comments, but his racist words cause her to stop listening.
Message overload	As a receptionist for a church, Carmen's daily tasks include reading about 20 emails, listening to approximately 10 voice mails, opening nearly 50 pieces of mail, and answering about 40 phone calls. When the minister approaches her with advice on how to organize the church picnic, Carmen's message overload interferes with receiving the minister's words accurately.
Message complexity	Dr. Jackson tells her patient Mark that his "systemic diagnosis has prevented any follow-up"; Mark tunes out because he doesn't understand what she means.
Lack of training	Jamie is asked to supervise a task force at work. He has never taken a course on communication, and he does not have any formal training in listening. He struggles with wanting to listen to the group and wishes he better understood how to listen.
Preoccupation	As Sara talks with Kevin, a coworker, she tries to listen to him talk about his job, but she is thinking about what time she will need to leave work to get to her little brother's graduation that evening. Sara also continues to search the Web to find her last-minute graduation gift.
Listening gap	As Loretta tells her grandkids how she and her husband met, the 6- and 7-year-olds grow impatient and tell their grandma to hurry up.

tractions would certainly influence the reception of the message by the deaf student.

Distractions can include physical, semantic, and psychological noise that prevent a listener from receiving the sender's message. Let's clarify each type of noise a bit further. Physical noise can take place anywhere. We may have difficulty listening to our boss at work because a printer is running. Maybe a friend is not able to listen to you at a bar because the music is too loud. Perhaps the noisy dishwasher at home interferes with a parent-child conversation. Or, a signer may be signing too quickly for hearing-impaired communicators. We run into physical distractions on a daily basis. Semantic noise occurs when the receiver fails to grasp the intended meaning of the sender. Semantic noise may take the form of antiquated words or phrases, or language that is confusing or filled with jargon. If you are listening to your grandfather talk about retirement planning, 401K plans, and stock percentages, you may "check out" of the conversation because his language may be too technical or irrelevant to you. Finally, psychological noise occurs when the sender and/or receiver have biases and prejudices that distort the message meaning. We may enter a conversation with preconceptions or stereotypes that affect our understanding of what the other person is going to say, and, our assumptions may get in the way of effective listening. For example, if your sister is a practicing Catholic, you may avoid any conversation with her about the right to an abortion since Catholicism condemns abortion.

Message Overload

Senders frequently receive more messages than they can process, which is called **message overload**. With the advent of more and more media and advanced media technology, **multitasking**, or the simultaneous performance of two or more tasks, is now commonplace both at work and home. The average worker in the United States handles about 200 messages in one day (http://news.bbc.co.uk/hi/english/sci/tech/newsid_357000/357993.stm) and spends nearly 50 minutes a day managing email alone (http://www.gartner.com). We used to visit a coworker's desk just a few feet away, but now we email her. Before, we'd visit a neighbor to borrow something; now we call him instead. Telecommuting is now commonplace with 40 million corporate employees spending at least one day a week away from the office working from their homes (Deloitte, 2006). We now find ourselves talking on the phone while downloading a document, sending an email while chatting with a roommate, and text messaging while driving (Please don't do this!). With all of this technological maneuvering, who wouldn't be tired of listening at some point during the day?

Message Complexity

Messages we receive that are filled with details, unfamiliar language, and challenging arguments are often hard to understand. For example, at the "closing" of a property sale, many homebuyers are overwhelmed by the number of documents they have to sign, the complex federal, state, and local laws they are told about, and the stress of signing financial papers that will put them in debt for 20 years or more. This is a great deal to manage and listen to, and it's likely that the unfamiliar and cumbersome language will negatively affect their listening skills. This can be a serious problem, because important information is communicated at the "closing." Many people in technical professions (for example, computing, engineering, biological sciences, and so on) are changing their behaviors. For example, because others don't understand the technical language of the engineering profession, engineers have begun to change their explanations to respond to different types of people (Darling & Dannels, 2003).

Lack of Training

Both the academic and corporate environments include opportunities to learn about listening, but more could be done. Although listening is a learned activity, only a few schools—such as the University of Northern Iowa, Nassau Community College (New York), Penn State University, and the University of

message overload

The result when senders receive more messages than they can process.

multitasking

The simultaneous performance of two or more tasks.

Maryland—offer courses on the topic. Most students' preparation in listening is limited to a chapter such as the one you are reading now. Very few companies offer their employees training in listening (Brownell, 2002).

Preoccupation

Even the most effective listeners become preoccupied at times. When we are preoccupied, we are thinking about our own life experiences and everyday troubles. Those who are preoccupied may be prone to what Anita Vangelisti, Mark Knapp, and John Daly (1990) call **conversational narcissism**, or engaging in an extreme amount of self-focusing to the exclusion of another person. Those who are narcissistic are caught up in their own thoughts and are inclined to interrupt others. Most of us have been narcissistic at one time or another; think of the many times you've had a conversation with someone while you were thinking about your rent, your upcoming test, or your vacation plans. Although such personal thoughts are important, they can obstruct our listening.

Preoccupation can also result from focusing on the technology in front of us. How many times have you been on the phone and typing at your computer at the same time? How often have you been told to "listen up" by a friend, only to simultaneously text message another friend. This preoccupation with technology while others are communicating with us can undercut effective and engaged listening.

conversational narcissism

Engaging in an extreme amount of self-focusing during a conversation, to the exclusion of another person.

"I'm sorry, I didn't hear what you said. I was listening to my body."

Listening Gap

We generally think faster than we speak. In fact, research shows that we speak an average rate of 150 to 200 words per minute, yet we can understand up to 800 words per minute (Wolvin & Coakley, 1996). That is, we can think about three or four times faster than we can talk. The **listening gap** is the time difference between your mental ability to interpret words and the speed at which they arrive to your brain. When we have a large listening gap, we may daydream, doodle on paper, or allow our minds to wander. This drifting off may cause us to miss the essence of a message from a sender. It takes a lot of effort to listen to someone. Closing the listening gap can be challenging for even the most attentive listeners.

Poor Listening Habits

The six behaviors set out in Table 6.2 and described in this section are poor listening habits that we may have picked up over the years. Although some of these occur more frequently than others in conversations, each is serious enough to affect the reception and meaning of a message.

Selective Listening

You engage in **selective listening**, or spot listening, if you attend to some parts of a message and ignore others. Typically, you selectively listen to those parts of the message that interest you. For an example of how spot listening can be problematic, consider what happens when jurors listen to a witness's testimony. One juror may listen to only the information pertaining to *where* a witness was during a crime to assess the witness's credibility. Another juror may selectively listen to *why* a witness was near the crime scene. Their spot listening prevents them from receiving all relevant information about the crime. Controlling for selective listening first requires us to glean the entire

listening gap

The time difference between our mental ability to interpret words and the speed at which they arrive at our brain.

selective listening

Responding to some parts of a message and rejecting others.

Table 6.2   How to overcome poor listening habits

Poor listening habit	Strategy for overcoming habit
Selective listening	Embrace entire message
Talkaholism	Become other-oriented
Pseudolistening	Center attention on speaker
Gap filling	Fill gap by mentally summarizing message
Defensive listening	Keep self-concept in check
Ambushing	Play fair in conversations

message. Attending to only those message parts that interest you or tuning out because you believe that you know the rest of a message may prompt others to question your listening skills.

Talkaholism

Some people become consumed with their own communication (McCroskey & Richmond, 1995). These individuals are **talkaholics**, defined as compulsive talkers who hog the conversational stage and monopolize encounters. When talkaholics take hold of a conversation, they interrupt, directing the conversational flow. And, of course if you're talking all the time, you don't take the time to listen. For instance, consider Uncle Randy, the talkaholic in the Norella family. The nearly thirty members of the Norella clan who gather each Thanksgiving dread engaging Uncle Randy in conversation because all he does is talk. And talk. Some family members privately wonder whether Randy understands that many of his more than two dozen relatives would like to speak. But without fail, Uncle Randy comes to dinner with story after story to tell, all the while interrupting those who'd like to share their stories, too.

Not all families have an Uncle Randy, but you may know someone who is a talkaholic—that is, someone who won't let you get a word in edgewise. If you are a talkaholic and have the urge to interrupt others, take a deep breath and remain silent while the other person finishes speaking. If you find yourself talking in a stream of consciousness without much concern for the other person, you are susceptible to becoming a talkaholic. Remember that other people like to talk, too.

Pseudolistening

We are all pretty good at faking attention. Many of us have been indirectly trained to **pseudolisten**, or to pretend to listen by nodding our heads, by looking at the speaker, by smiling at the appropriate times, or by practicing other kinds of attention feigning. The classroom is a classic location for faking attention. Professors have become adept at spotting students who pseudolisten; they usually laugh a bit later than others in the class and have a glazed

talkaholic

A compulsive talker who hogs the conversational stage and monopolizes encounters.

pseudolisten

To pretend to listen by nodding our heads, looking at the speaker, smiling at the appropriate times, or practicing other kinds of attention feigning.

look. You can correct this poor listening habit by making every effort to center your attention on the speaker.

Gap Filling

Listeners who think that they can correctly guess the rest of the story a speaker is telling and who don't need the speaker to continue are called **gap fillers**. Gap fillers often assume they know how a narrative or interpersonal encounter will unfold. Further, gap fillers also frequently interrupt; when this happens, the listener alters the message, and its meaning may be lost. Although an issue may be familiar to listeners, they should give speakers the chance to finish their thoughts.

Defensive Listening

Defensive listening occurs when people view innocent comments as personal attacks or hostile criticisms. Consider Jeannie's experiences. As the owner of a small jewelry shop in the mall, she is accustomed to giving directions to her small staff. Recently, one of her employees commented: "Look, Jeannie, I think you could get more young girls in here if you brought in some rainbow beads. The young ones love them." Jeannie's response was immediate: "Well. . . .here's what I recommend: Why don't you find a lot of money, get your own store, and then you can have all of the rainbow beads you want! I've been in this business for almost ten years, and I think I know what to buy! Why is it that everyone thinks they know how to run a business?"

Jeannie's response fits the definition of defensive listening. Those who are defensive listeners often perceive threats in messages and may be defensive because of personal issues. In the preceding example, Jeannie may not have any animosity toward her employee; she simply may have misinterpreted the comment. To ensure that you are not a defensive listener, keep your self-concept in check. Don't be afraid to ask yourself the following question: Am I too quick to defend my thoughts?

Ambushing

People who listen carefully to a message and then use the information later to attack the individual are **ambushing**. Ambushers want to retrieve information to discredit or manipulate another person. Gathering information and using it to undercut an opponent is now considered routine in politics. Divorce attorneys frequently uncover information to discredit their client's spouse. Ambushing in this manner should be avoided; words should never be viewed as ammunition for a verbal battle.

What are some of your poor listening habits? To help you identify areas in which you can improve your listening, go to your online Resource Center for *Understanding Interpersonal Communication* to access *Interactive Activity 6.3: Identify Your Listening Problems* under the resources for Chapter 6. To read about

---

gap fillers

Listeners who think they can correctly guess the rest of the story a speaker is telling and don't need the speaker to continue.

defensive listening

Viewing innocent comments as personal attacks or hostile criticisms.

ambushing

Listening carefully to a message and then using the information later to attack the sender.

listening style

A predominant and preferred approach to listening to the messages we hear.

people-centered listening style

A listening style associated with concern for other people's feelings or emotions.

strategies you can use to become a better listener, access *Interactive Activity 6.4: Overcome Bad Listening Habits*.

By now, it should be obvious that your listening skills affect your personal and professional relationships with others. Next, we focus on the styles of listening and then on the influence of culture on the listening process.

Styles of Listening

Typically, we adopt a style of listening in our interpersonal interactions. A **listening style** is a predominant and preferred approach to the messages we hear. We adopt a listening style to understand the sender's message. Researchers have identified four listening styles (Johnston, Weaver, Watson, & Barker, 2000): people-centered, action-centered, content-centered, and time-centered. We call this a P-A-C-T between communicators (see Figure 6.3).

People-Centered Listening Style

The style associated with being concerned with other people's feelings or emotions is called the **people-centered listening style**. People-oriented listeners try to compromise and find common areas of interest. Research shows that people-centered listeners are less apprehensive in groups, meetings, and interpersonal situations than other types of listeners (Sargent, Weaver, & Kiewitz, 1997; Watson & Barker, 1995). People-centered listeners quickly notice others' moods and provide clear verbal and nonverbal feedback.

Imagine yourself...

...with a mechanic at the garage

Driving to a friend's house, you hear an odd rattle coming from the front of your car and a squeak in the dash. You stop the vehicle and look under the hood, but can't seem to find anything wrong. That evening you make an appointment with a local garage to find out what the problem is. After placing the car on the lift and searching underneath it, the mechanic approaches you in the waiting area. He tells you that the noises are being caused by a problem with your steering shaft and that fixing it won't cost more than $50. You are so relieved to hear this good news that you tune out the rest of the mechanic's report. You fail to listen to him tell you that he has found a host of other problems unrelated to the noises you were hearing. Unfortunately, you agree to have the mechanic "get it all fixed," which he interprets to mean that he'll fix *all* the problems discovered, not just the steering shaft. As you wait beyond an hour, you check into the status of the repair, only to find out that "getting it all fixed" will cost about $250. You now have to confront the mechanic. How do you explain your faulty listening skills to him? In this situation, which barriers to listening might you have encountered? Which poor listening habits might you have exhibited?

Action-Centered Listening Style

The **action-centered listening style** pertains to listeners who want messages to be highly organized, concise, and error-free. These people help speakers focus on what is important in the message. Action-centered listeners want speakers to get to the point; they grow impatient when people tell stories in a disorganized or random fashion. They also **second-guess** speakers—that is, they question the assumptions underlying a message (Kirtley & Honeycutt, 1996). If a

action-centered listening style

A listening style associated with listeners who want messages to be highly organized, concise, and error-free.

second-guess

To question the assumptions underlying a message.

Figure 6.3   Styles of listening

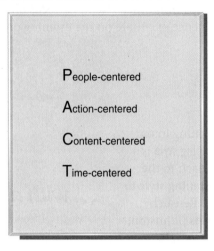

Ppeople-centered

Aaction-centered

Ccontent-centered

Ttime-centered

second-guesser believes a message is false, he or she develops an alternative explanation which they view as more realistic.

Action-centered listeners also clearly tell others that they want unambiguous feedback. For instance, as an action-centered listener, a professor may tell her students that if they wish to challenge a grade, they should simply delineate specific reasons why they deserve a grade change and what grade they feel is appropriate.

Content-Centered Listening Style

Individuals who engage in the **content-centered listening style** focus on the facts and details of a message. Content-centered listeners consider all sides of an issue and welcome complex and challenging information from a sender. However, they may intimidate others by asking pointed questions or by discounting information from those the listener deems to be non-experts. Content-centered listeners are likely to play devil's advocate in conversations. Therefore, attorneys and others in the legal profession are likely to favor this style of listening in their jobs.

content-centered listening style

A listening style associated with listeners who focus on the facts and details of a message.

time-centered listening style

A listening style associated with listeners who want messages to be presented succinctly.

Time-Centered Listening Style

When listeners adopt a **time-centered listening style**, they let others know that messages should be presented succinctly. Time-oriented listeners discourage wordy explanations from speakers and set time guidelines for conversations, such as prefacing a conversation with "I have only five minutes to talk."

Some time-centered listeners constantly check their watches or abruptly end encounters with others.

Which listening style is the best? It depends on the situation and the purpose of the interpersonal encounter. You may have to change your listening style to meet the other person's needs. For example, you might need to be a time-centered listener for the coworker who needs information quickly, but you might need to be person-centered while speaking to your best friend about his divorce. However, remember that just because you adjusted your style of listening does not mean that the other person adjusted his or her style. You will both have to be aware of each other's style. Know your preferred style of listening, but be flexible in your style depending on the communication situation.

Our listening style is often based on our cultural background. We now turn our attention to the role of culture in listening. When speakers and listeners come from various cultural backgrounds, message meaning can be affected.

Culture and the Listening Process

As we learned in Chapter 3, we are all members of a culture and various co-cultures. We understand that cultural differences influence our communication with others. Because all our interactions are culturally based, cultural differences affect the listening process (Brownell, 2002). Much of the research in this area pertains solely to race, ethnicity, and ancestry.

Recall from Chapter 3 our discussion of individualistic and collectivistic cultures. We noted that the United States is an individualistic country, meaning that it focuses on an "I" orientation rather than a "we" orientation. Individualistic cultures value direct communication, or speaking one's mind. Some collectivistic cultures, such as Japan, respect others' words, desire harmony, and believe in conversational politeness

Ethics & Choice

*F*our fraternity brothers were sitting in the lounge of their fraternity house on a cold winter day. Gabe Walther listened to his friends talk about their roommates, and wondered who was telling the truth. First, Patrick related a story about how his roommate had tried to commit suicide but couldn't work up the guts to swallow all of the sleeping pills. Gabe then listened to Victor's tale about his roommate stealing a copy of the biology final exam. And then Chris told the group about his roommate's financial problems.

Finally, Patrick spoke directly to the group: "Listen, guys, I've got to tell you something that I don't want repeated to anyone. This story is something I heard about a week ago, and it's about Professor Weinberg." Gabe knew that he was about to hear another story based on gossip. He was fed up with all of the stories and what he felt were violations of trust among the guys in the house.

Gabe Walther was obviously struggling with an ethical dilemma: Should he continue to sit through the gossip and listen to the stories, or should he excuse himself and leave? He didn't want his friends to think he was a prude, but he also didn't want to hear all these malicious rumors. He thought to himself: "Man, these guys have got to get a life. I just can't sit here and listen to this stuff."

What would you advise Gabe to do? Should he politely leave the lounge? Or, should he tell his housemates that he disliked their gossip? What ethical system of communication should be followed in this example (categorical imperative, utilitarianism, ethic of care, golden mean, significant choice)?

Go to your online Resource Center for *Understanding Interpersonal Communication* to access an interactive version of this scenario under the resources for Chapter 6. The interactive version of this scenario allows you to choose an appropriate response to this dilemma and then see what consequences your choice brings about. You can also compare your answers to the questions at the end of the scenario to those provided by the authors and, if requested, email your response to your instructor.

(Lewis, 1999). While listening to others, communicators need to remember that differences in feedback (direct or indirect) may affect message meaning.

Richard Lewis (1999) suggests that listening variations across cultures affect the ability to be an effective salesperson. For example, Lewis points out that for the French, listening for information is the main concern. For citizens of several Arab countries, however, listening is done for know-how or for gain. And Lewis indicates that people in some cultures, such as Germany, do not ask for clarification; asking a presenter to repeat himself or herself is seen as a sign of impoliteness and disrespect. As a practical application of this information, consider how a salesperson's recognition of these cultural differences might positively affect his or her company's bottom line.

Donal Carbaugh (1999) offers additional information on ways that culture and listening work together. Looking at listening as a personal opportunity to interrelate with the environment, Carbaugh cites an example of the Blackfeet Indians:

> Blackfeet listening is a highly reflective and revelatory mode of communication that can open one to the mysteries of unity between the physical and spiritual, to the relationships between natural and human forms, and to the intimate links between places and persons. (p. 265)

In fact, Native American communities have come together to form an "Intertribal Monitoring Association on Indian Trust Funds" (www.imaitrustfunds .org) with the sole purpose of having "listening conferences." Representatives from various tribal nations gather to listen to how the Federal Government is adhering to Trust Fund Standards, to provide tribal forums, to keep up-to-date on policies and regulations on federal initiatives, among others. These listening conferences have been taking place for over 15 years.

The common thread in these examples is the notion that cultures vary in their value systems and yet, listening remains a critical part of the various cultural communities. Staying culturally aware of these variations as you consider the message of another person is important.

What strategies can you use to become a better listener with individuals from various cultures? First, don't expect every-

REVISITING
CASEINPOINT

1. *Choose one style of listening and apply it to Jacqueline and her volunteer work in a political campaign.*

2. *Consider the listening styles and discuss whether one style is more useful than another for Jacqueline, who serves as a director of volunteers.*

Y*ou can answer these questions online under the resources for Chapter 6 at your online Resource Center for* Understanding Interpersonal Communication.

one else to adapt to your way of communicating. Second, accept new ways of receiving messages. Third, wait as long as possible before merging another's words into your words—don't define the world on your terms. Finally, seek clarification when possible. Asking questions in intercultural conversations reduces our processing load, and we are better equipped to translate difficult concepts as they emerge (Hall, 2005).

We spend the rest of the chapter reviewing effective listening skills you should practice. Improving your listening habits is a difficult, often lifelong, process, so you shouldn't expect changes to your listening behaviors to happen overnight.

Choices for Effective Listening

This section outlines six primary skills for improving listening. Whether we communicate with a partner, boss, friend, family member, coworker, or others, we all must choose whether we will develop good or bad listening habits. Let's explore the following guidelines for effective listening.

Evaluate Your Current Skills

The first step toward becoming a better listener is assessing and understanding your personal listening strengths and weaknesses. First, think about the poor listening habits you have seen others practice. Do you use any of them while communicating? Which listening behaviors do you exhibit consistently, and which do you use sporadically? Also, which of your biases, prejudices, beliefs, and opinions may interfere with receipt of a message?

In addition, we have stresses and personal problems that may affect our listening skills. For example, if you were told that your company was laying off workers, how would this affect your communication with people on a daily basis? Could you be an effective listener even though you would find yourself preoccupied with the financial and emotional toll you would experience if you were downsized? In such a situation, it would be nearly impossible to dismiss your feelings, so you should just try to accept them and be aware that they will probably affect your communication with others. To take a listening quiz that was developed for insurance agents but that is applicable to everyone, read the article "Are You a Good Listener? Take the Skills Quiz," available through InfoTrac College Edition. Go to your online Resource Center for *Understanding Interpersonal Communication* to access *InfoTrac College Edition Exercise 6.2: Are You a Good Listener?* under the resources for Chapter 6.

Prepare to Listen

After you assess your listening abilities, the next step is to prepare yourself to listen. Preparation requires both physical and mental activities. You may have to locate yourself closer to the source of the message (of course, depending on who the speaker is, your physical proximity will vary). If you have problems concentrating on a message, try to reduce or remove as many distractions as possible, such as the TV or stereo. Place yourself in a situation where you will not be distracted by looking out a window or watching other people interact.

To prepare yourself mentally, do your homework beforehand if you are going to need information to listen effectively. For example, if you want to ask your boss for a raise, you would want to have ready a mental list of the reasons why you deserve a raise and possible responses to reasons why you do not. If you are a student, reading the material before class will make the lecture or discussion much more meaningful because you will have the background knowledge to be able to offer your thoughts on issues as they arise. In your personal relationships, you should be mentally prepared to consider other points of view as well as your own.

empathy

The process of identifying with or attempting to experience the thoughts, beliefs, and actions of another.

Empathy is an important component of listening. By providing empathic responses, we show that we value another person's thoughts and feelings. In the process, we may even help alleviate that person's anxiety, which is a useful emotional support skill.

Provide Empathic Responses

When we use empathy, we tell other people that we value their thoughts. **Empathy** is the process of identifying with or attempting to experience the thoughts, beliefs, and actions of another. Empathy tells people that although we can't feel their exact feelings or precisely identify with a current situation, we are trying to co-create experiences with them. As Judi Brownell (2002) observed: "you do not *reproduce* the other person's experiences. Rather, you and your partner work together to *produce,* or co-create, meanings" (p. 185). We show we're responsive and empathic by giving well-timed verbal feedback throughout a conversation, not simply when it is our turn to speak. Doing so suggests a genuine interest in the sender's message and has the side benefit of keeping us attentive to the message. To show empathy, we must also demonstrate that we're engaged nonverbally in the message. This can be accomplished through sustained facial involvement (avoiding a blank look that communicates boredom), frequent eye contact (maintaining some focus on the speaker's face), and body positioning that communicates interest.

Learning to listen with empathy is sometimes difficult. We have to show support for another while making sure that we are not unnecessarily exacerbating negative feelings. For instance, consider the following dialogue between two friends, Camilla and Tony. Camilla is angry that her boss did not positively review her work plan:

© Richard Lord/The Image Works

Dilbert © Scott Adams/Dist. by
United Features Syndicate, Inc.

Camilla: He's self-righteous, that's all there is to it. He didn't even tell me that my idea made sense. I think he's just jealous because he didn't come up with it first.

Tony: Yeah, I bet you're right. He really didn't show you any respect. And because he's the boss, I'm sure he wanted to take credit.

Although Tony meant to show empathy, he may have unintentionally perpetuated the idea that Camilla's boss was a "bad" man. Because Tony seems to be supporting her thoughts, Camilla will have a difficult time changing her perception of her boss. This negative view won't help Camilla in future conversations with her boss. Now, consider an alternative response from Tony that doesn't reinforce Camilla's negative perception:

Camilla: He's self-righteous, that's all there is to it. He didn't even tell me that my idea made sense. I think he's just jealous because he didn't come up with it first.

Tony: I know you're pretty frustrated and angry at him. You sound like you want to quit. I know that it has to be pretty rough for you, but hang in there.

In this example, Tony not only demonstrated some empathic listening skills but helped Camilla redirect her thinking about her boss. When Tony changed the direction of the conversation in this way, Camilla could consider less resentful impressions of the situation. Helping others alleviate their anxiety is a necessary emotional support skill for many interactions (Burleson, 2003). To read an article that reinforces the notion that empathy is key to effective listening, check out "Leaders Know How to Listen," available through InfoTrac College Edition. Go to your *Understanding Interpersonal Communication* to access *InfoTrac College Edition Exercise 6.3: Empathy and Listening* under the resources for Chapter 6.

Use Nonjudgmental Feedback

Most of us provide feedback without any concern for how the receiver will interpret it. When we give **nonjudgmental feedback**, we describe another's

nonjudgmental feedback

Feedback that describes another's behavior and then explains how that behavior made us feel.

behavior and then explain how that behavior made us feel. As we discussed in Chapter 4, centering a message on your own emotions without engaging in accusatory finger-wagging can help reduce interpersonal conflict.

Consider the difference between the following statements:

- "You are so rude to come in late. You made me a nervous wreck! You're pretty inconsiderate to make me feel this way!"

- "When you come home so late, I really worry. I thought something had gone wrong."

In heated moments especially, taking ownership of your feelings and perceptions, as in the second statement, is difficult. Owning your feelings rather than blaming others for your feelings results in more effective interpersonal communication.

Practice Active Listening

We define active listening as a transactional process in which a listener communicates reinforcing messages to a speaker. When we actively listen, we show support for another person and his or her message. Active listeners *want to* listen rather than feel *obligated to* listen. Particularly in close relationships with others, demonstrating that you are actively involved in the conversation will help both your credibility as a communicator and your relationship standing with others. Additional elements of active listening are paraphrasing, dialogue enhancers, questions, and silence. We briefly discuss each of these in the following subsections.

paraphrasing

Restating the essence of a sender's message in our own words.

dialogue enhancers

Supporting statements, such as "I see" or "I'm listening," that indicate we are involved in a message.

Paraphrasing

Active listening requires **paraphrasing**, or restating the essence of another's message in our own words. Paraphrasing is a perception check in an interpersonal encounter; it allows us to clarify our interpretation of a message. When paraphrasing, try to be concise and simple in your response. For instance, you can use language such as "In other words, what you're saying is . . ." or "I think what I heard is that you . . ." or "Let me see if I get this right." Such phrases show others that you care about understanding the intended meaning of a message. To read an article that reinforces the benefits of paraphrasing, check out "Practice Listening Skills as a Leader," available through Info-Trac College Edition. Go to your *Understanding Interpersonal Communication* to access *InfoTrac College Edition Exercise 6.4: Paraphrasing and Listening* under the resources for Chapter 6.

Dialogue Enhancers

Active listening requires us to show the speaker that even though we may disagree with his or her thoughts, we accept and are open to them. As we noted earlier, speakers need support in their conversations. **Dialogue enhancers** take the form of supporting expressions such as "I see" or "I'm listening." Dialogue enhancers should not interrupt a message. They should be used as indications that you are involved in the message. In other words, these statements enhance the discussion taking place.

Questions

Asking well-timed and appropriate questions in an interpersonal interaction can be a hallmark of an engaged active listener. Asking questions is not a sign of ignorance or stupidity. What questions demonstrate is a willingness to make sure you receive the intended meaning of the speaker's message. If you ask questions, you may receive information that is contrary to your instincts or assumptions, thereby avoiding gap filling, a problem we identified earlier. Don't be afraid to respectfully ask questions in your relationships with others. Your input will likely be met with gratitude as the other communicator realizes your desire to seek information.

Silence

Author Robert Fulghum (1989) comments in *All I Really Need to Know I Learned in Kindergarten* that silence is a big part of a satisfying life. It may seem strange to talk about the importance of being silent in interpersonal communication. In fact, in the self-help book sections in U.S. book stores, we

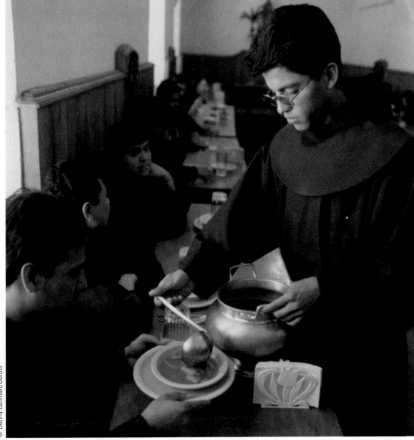

© Danny Lehman/Corbis

The value of silence is not lost on monks who take a vow of silence as part of their spiritual practice. In such a tradition, practicing silence is not meant as a way to reject others but as a means to clear away noise so the monks are better able to listen.

interpersonal explorer

Before you finish reading this chapter, take a moment to review the theories and skills discussed. How do you think the theories discussed in this chapter can help you better understand listening? In what ways can the skills discussed help you interact more effectively with other people in your life?

Theories that relate to listening

- **Working memory theory**
  We have the ability to simultaneously attend to multiple stimuli, to store other stimuli, and/or to retrieve information from long-term memory storage

Practical skills for improving listening

- Evaluate current personal listening skills
- Prepare to listen
- Provide empathy
- Use critical and nonjudgmental feedback
- Practice active listening techniques

Explore your interpersonal choices

Are you ready to explore your interpersonal choices regarding listening? Use your online Resource Center for *Understanding Interpersonal Communication* to access an interactive simulation that allows you to view the beginning of an interpersonal scenario regarding listening, make a choice about how the people in the scenario should proceed with their interaction, consider the consequences of your choice, and then see three possible outcomes to the interaction.

rarely find books on the importance of keeping quiet because the culture rewards talkativeness. Silence is a complicated concept in conversations. As communication ethicist J. Vernon Jensen (1997) stated, "silence can warmly bind friends together, but can chillingly separate individuals" (p. 151). We live in a society in which overt communication is embraced—just look at television talk shows for proof.

As the old saying goes, silence is golden. We should honor silence when another person is struggling with what to say. We need to allow the entire message to be revealed before jumping in. We also need to be silent because, at times, words are not needed. For example, after a conflict has been resolved and two people are looking at each other and holding each other's hands, they don't need to speak to communicate. Silence in this context may be more effective than words in making the people in the relationship feel closer.

However, silence is not always positive. It can also be used to manipulate or coerce another person in an interpersonal exchange. This is an example of the dark side of communication that we discussed in Chapter 1. For instance, giving someone "the silent treatment"—that is, refusing to talk to someone—may provoke unnecessary tension. Also, imposing your own code of silence in an encounter may damage a relationship. For example, if you chose to remain silent in an interpersonal conflict, you would most likely exacerbate the problem.

Listening is one of the keys to success in all areas of your life. In addition to reading the advice given in this chapter, check out seven strategies to better listening by using your *Understanding Interpersonal Communication* online Resource Center to access *Interactive Activity 6.5: Keys to Better Listening* under the resources for Chapter 6. And for more techniques for better listening, including active listening, read the article "Improving Your Listening Skills," available through InfoTrac College Edition. Access *InfoTrac College Edition Exercise 6.5: Guidelines for Better Listening.*

Communication Assessment Test
The Listening Inventory

To get a general understanding of your beliefs about listening, complete the following assessment. Be sure to consider your general response to a question rather than a specific episode. Complete each sentence as honestly as possible. You can take this test online. Go to your online Resource Center for *Understanding Interpersonal Communication* and look under the resources for Chapter 6.

1. Listening is not taught in our society because . . .
2. One job that does not require you to be a good listener is . . .
3. One big reason why I'm not the best listener is . . .
4. My family members listen . . .
5. Listening is as important as speaking because . . .
6. I would like to improve my listening skills because . . .
7. The ways in which listening will help me at school include . . .
8. The ways in which listening will help me at work include . . .
9. One person whom I consider a great listener is . . .
10. I can overcome many listening obstacles by . . .

Now review your responses. Which responses surprised you? Based on what you learned in this chapter, what would you change about your listening behaviors?

Summary

Listening is called a twenty-first century skill because it is essential in all arenas, including home, school, and work. Indeed, employers rank listening as the most important skill on the job, and listening is important in our friendships and other personal relationships. When we listen effectively we are communicating to senders that their messages are important to us.

Whereas hearing is the process of letting in, but not attending to, audible stimuli, listening is the dynamic, transactional process of the four Rs: receiving, responding to, recalling, and rating stimuli and/or messages. When we receive messages, we are being mindful and acknowledging the speaker verbally and nonverbally. When we respond, we provide nonverbal and verbal feedback to the speaker. When we recall the message, we understand it and store it for later retrieval using the following strategies: repetition, use of mnemonic devices, and chunking. When we rate messages, we have to be sure we don't confuse facts with inferences and opinions. There are many barriers to listening. Physical distractions such as semantic, psychological, or physiological noise interfere. Modern phenomena such as multitasking, telecommuting, and being bombarded by many messages from numerous media can lead to message overload. Messages that are too complex—such as those filled with unfamiliar jargon or challenging arguments—can be difficult to listen to and to understand. Businesses and schools seldom offer listening training or courses. Preoccupation with personal issues, including extreme self-focusing (conversational narcissism), can inhibit the processing of messages. Lastly, the time difference between the mental ability to interpret words and the speed at which they arrive at the brain (the listening gap) can cause the mind to wander.

Our poor listening habits also interfere with listening. When we selectively listen, we don't attend to those parts of the message that are uninteresting to us. Talkaholics hog the conversational stage, resulting in one-sided conversations. We may or may not fool others when we pseudolisten, or pretend to listen, to a message. Gap fillers interrupt because they believe they know the rest of the message. When we defensively listen, we perceive innocent comments as hostile in intent. Ambushers retrieve information so they can later use it to discredit or manipulate another person.

Researchers have identified four listening styles. Your listening style may vary depending on the situation and the purpose of the personal encounter. People-centered listeners are concerned with other people's feelings or emotions. Action-centered listeners are listeners who want messages to be highly organized and who sometimes second-guess, or question, the assumptions underlying the message. Content-centered listeners focus on the facts and details of a message and are likely to play devil's advocate. Time-centered listeners discourage wordy explanations from speakers and set time guidelines for conversations. In addition to noting a communicator's listening style, keep in mind that people from different cultures give different types of feedback (direct or indirect), which may affect message meaning.

To improve your listening skills, you need to evaluate your current skills, prepare to listen, provide empathic responses, use nonjudgmental feedback, and practice active listening. When we actively listen, we communicate reinforcing messages to the speaker through paraphrasing (restatements), dialogue enhancers (supporting expressions), questioning, and the use of silence. When you work on your listening skills, you are striving to become a more engaged and competent communicator.

Understanding Interpersonal Communication Online

Now that you've read Chapter 6, use your online Resource Center for *Understanding Interpersonal Communication* for quick access to the electronic study resources that accompany this text. Your online Resource Center gives you access to the video of Jacqueline's situation on page 185, the Your Turn journal activity on page 194, the Ethics & Choice interactive activity on page 203, the Communication Assessment Test on page 211, the Interpersonal Explorer activity on page 210, InfoTrac College Edition, and study aids including a digital glossary, review quizzes, and the chapter activities.

Terms for Review

action-centered listening
    style 201
ambushing 200
American Sign Language
    (ASL) 192
chunking 190
content-centered listening
    style 202
conversational narcissism
    197

defensive listening 200
dialogue enhancers 208
empathy 206
four "Rs" of listening 187
gap fillers 200
hearing 186
listening 187
listening gap 198
listening style 201
message overload 196

mindless 188
multitasking 196
nonjudgmental
    feedback 207
opinions 191
paraphrasing 208
people-centered listening
    style 201
pseudolisten 199
rating 190

Questions for Understanding

Comprehension Focus

1. Differentiate between hearing and listening.

2. What are the four components of the listening process?

3. What are the barriers that prevent us from listening well?

4. Explain the styles of listening and provide an example of each.

5. Identify at least one way that culture relates to the listening process.

Application Focus

1. CASE IN POINT Look at our opening story of Jacqueline Mitchell. If you were Jacqueline, how would you rate your personal listening skills? Do you believe that she should be penalized for her blunders? Why or why not?

2. Are there any times in a relationship when you would be justified practicing any of the six poor listening habits (selective listening, talkaholism, pseudolistening, gap filling, defensive listening, and ambushing)? Indicate why or why not with examples to support your view.

3. Describe times when you felt that your best friend wasn't listening to you. What were the circumstances surrounding the event, and what types of behaviors did your friend engage in? How did you respond?

4. During a job interview, what would you say to a prospective employer about your listening skills? Be specific and use examples.

5. Defend or criticize the following statement: Listening should be taught in grade schools alongside writing, speaking, and reading. Provide examples to defend your position.

Interactive Activities and InfoTrac College Edition Exercises

Interactive Activities

InfoTrac College Edition Exercises

Chapter 7
Communication and Emotion

chapter ✚ goals

Understand the intricacies of emotion

Identify the relationships among emotion, reason, and the body

Distinguish between two theories of emotion

Explain how emotion is communicated

Recognize the negative and positive aspects associated with emotional communication

Employ skills for emotional communication to increase satisfaction in interpersonal interactions

CASEINPOINT

Each Saturday morning, graduate students Regina Chen and Allison Yang met for coffee, something they've done ever since they were undergraduate sophomores. This Saturday, however, was not a day just for chit chat. Although both women certainly had enough to talk about—including their courses, printer problems, and men—today would involve a different sort of conversation. Regina had something very important to tell her friend Allison.

As soon as Regina got her coffee, she darted over to Allison with an enormous grin. "Guess you can't imagine what *I'm* so happy about today," she said to her friend.

"Well," Allison said, "if you got another gorgeous guy to ask you out, I'm gonna leave this table now!"

"No, it's much, much better than that!," Regina responded, sitting down and leaning toward Allison. Although she was a bit nervous to tell Allison about the news, somehow she found a way: "I forgot to pick up my mail yesterday, and when I went downstairs this morning to the mailbox, I found a letter from the Stern Foundation. You know what's next, don't you?"

Allison shook her head quickly. "Tell me already!" she begged Regina.

"Well, I opened the letter and saw that I got the Federation Prize. Do you know what this means?! I am now the proud recipient of a $20,000 scholarship! *I can't believe this!* I never imagined that this last year of grad school I wouldn't have to worry about money issues. And now I can finish my thesis—without getting a job! This has to be the best day of grad school so far! Oh, listen, Ali—I know we both applied for this, and I'm sorry you didn't get it, but you *have* to be excited for me! Please tell me that you are!"

As soon as she finished talking, Regina pulled the letter out of her purse and put it on the table. Suddenly, however, she saw that Allison was not smiling. Regina's friend obviously didn't share in the excitement. "Wow," Allison said, calmly, looking out the window. "Look, I'm very happy for you. But I have to tell you, this is tougher than I thought. I really want my best friend to get good things, but this is a hard way to find out that I didn't get the money. Of course, like I said, I'm really happy. But you'll have to excuse me here. I'm not really all that into coffee talk today." Allison

Use your online Resource Center for *Understanding Interpersonal Communication* to watch a video clip of Regina and Allison's interaction.

> Access the resources for Chapter 7 and select "Regina" to watch the video (it takes a minute for the video to load). As you watch the video, consider the way in which Regina broke her news to Allison. Could she have done it in a way that better took into account Allison's potential emotional response? > You can respond to this and other analysis questions, and then click "Done" to compare your answers with those provided by the authors.

got up to leave. She felt ashamed of herself for not being able to really share in Regina's happiness. But she was so disappointed for herself that she had trouble not crying.

As Allison hugged her friend and left the café, Regina sat in a daze. She thought that maybe this hadn't been the most sensitive way of handling her good news with her friend. She thought that Allison would have been more excited about the award, but now she couldn't help but think that her best friend was now either envious, very sad, or both.

*E*veryone experiences the powerful impact of emotion: the joy of falling in love, the grief of losing a loved one, the pride in an accomplishment, the embarrassment of a public mistake, or the anger that boils up when we think someone is standing in the way of a cherished goal. In our opening Case in Point, Allison struggles with emotion when Regina gets an award that Allison wanted. Emotion affects our daily lives in powerful ways.

Experiencing emotion shapes our lives and our relationships. Emotion is often what we remember about interpersonal encounters. Jay barely remembers any of his high school teachers now that he's 32. But his ninth grade English teacher, Ms. Laurent, is someone he'll never forget. He often thinks of how she helped him feel proud of his work and optimistic about the future. Emotion often influences how we judge interpersonal interactions. For exam-

Emotion and interpersonal communication often go hand in hand. Not only does emotion influence how, when, and why we communicate with others, but our displays of emotion communicate messages themselves. For example, this family doesn't have to say a word to communicate their joy, gratitude, and relief when they receive a new house from Habitat for Humanity—their expressions say it all.

ple, when Andy thinks back to her friendship with Roz, she's glad it's over because of all the arguments between them, which left Andy feeling angry most of the time.

In this chapter, we investigate emotion and its powerful relationship to the interpersonal communication process. We all know intuitively how important emotion is, but often we don't have enough information about emotion—it isn't a subject discussed much in school. But when we don't pay attention to emotion, we can't be competent communicators. For instance, both Allison and Regina might have been helped in the opening Case In Point if they had information about emotion and became more emotionally competent. As with so many aspects of interpersonal communication, we need to gain adequate knowledge before we can develop our skills. Let's begin by defining emotion.

Defining Emotion: More than Just a Feeling

Defining the term *emotion* is complicated. Some researchers (for example, Fehr & Russell, 1984; Ortony, Clore, & Foss, 1987) argue that emotion involves only one person's feelings (like anger, fear, anxiety, happiness, and so forth). Other researchers include in their definition those emotions we feel in relationship with others like envy and love (Planalp & Fitness, 1999). Still other scholars (Buzzanell & Turner, 2003; Tracy, 2005) differentiate between *real* feelings and *manufactured* feelings that are produced because some outside norm dictates that they are appropriate. For instance, if you are a server in a restaurant, your job requires you to smile and act happy around your customers even if you've had a horrible day and don't feel like smiling at all. Manufacturing a feeling that you're not actually experiencing is called *emotion labor*.

In this book, we take an inclusive position and define **emotion** as the critical internal structure that orients us to, and engages us with, what matters in our lives: our feelings about ourselves and others. Thus, the term *emotion* encompasses both the internal feelings of one person (for instance, when Joe feels anxious before he meets Ana's parents) as well as feelings that can be experienced only in a relationship (for instance, when Joyce feels competitiveness when she hears how well Barb did on the chemistry exam). Emotion labor falls outside the definition we're using here.

The definition of emotion also rests on the notion of process; although we have names for discrete emotions such as fear, sadness, depression, ecstasy, and so forth, emotion is often experienced as a blend of several emotions (Oatley & Duncan, 1992). Think again of Allison from our opening Case In Point scenario. When she learns that Regina got the scholarship and she didn't, she feels disappointed, ashamed, envious, and happy for her friend all at once.

emotion

The critical internal structure that orients us to and engages us with what matters in our lives: our feelings about ourselves and others. Emotion encompasses both the internal feelings of one person (for instance, anxiety or happiness) as well as feelings that can be experienced only in a relationship (for instance, jealousy or competitiveness).

Strategic embarrassment is another example of an emotional blend. Although embarrassment is an unpleasant emotional state, people often plan embarrassing situations for others, and planning an embarrassing moment for someone else is often socially acceptable (Bradford & Petronio, 1998). For example, it is a common practice among adolescents to use strategic embarrassment in the following way (Bradford, 1993). Tom knows his friend, Jesús, is interested in Amy. He also knows that Jesús is shy and won't introduce himself to her. As Amy and Jesús pass in the school hallway, Tom purposely pushes Jesús into Amy. Jesús is embarrassed but recognizes that Tom actually helped him connect with Amy.

In a study illustrating how common emotional blends are, college students were asked to describe emotions they observed others communicating (Planalp, DeFrancisco, & Rutherford, 1996). The participants usually picked more than one emotion, even though the question was phrased to elicit a single emotion ("What emotion did you observe, e.g. anger, happiness, fear, etc.?"). Forty-five percent of the respondents chose two emotions for their answer, and 22 percent used three or more emotions. To explicate our definition of emotion more completely, we'll now discuss two category systems for emotion and explore the relationships among emotion, reason, and physicality (the body).

Two Category Systems for Emotion

To capture the complexity of emotion, some researchers have created category systems classifying common emotions in the U.S. These systems focus on attributes of emotion, such as **valence** (whether it reflects a positive or negative feeling), **activity** (whether it implies action or passivity), or **intensity** (how strongly felt it is).

One system (Russell, 1978, 1980, 1983) categorizes emotion along two dimensions at once: valence and activity. This system allows us to see how specific emotions cluster together depending on whether they are active-negative, active-positive, passive-negative, or passive-positive (see Figure 7.1). For example, when Luis feels an emotion such as excitement we can see on Figure 7.1 that it is positive and implies some action. When he feels an emotion like contentment, the figure shows that it's less positive and less active than excitement.

Another system for classifying individual emotion is based on its intensity. Robert Plutchik's (1984) emotion cone provides a graduated image of emotional range (see Figure 7.2). The lowest level of each vertical slice represents the mildest version of the emotion, and each successive level represents a more intense state. This system points to the impact of labeling an emotion with a particularly intense name. For example, if Jenna says she is bored in French class, that carries a much different meaning, and is far less intense, than if she says she loathes French. For another look at Plutchik's emotion cone and the various dimensions of emotion, go to your online Resource

valence

An attribute of emotion that refers to whether the emotion reflects a positive or negative feeling.

activity

An attribute of emotion that refers to whether the emotion implies action or passivity.

intensity

An attribute of emotion that refers to how strongly an emotion is felt.

Figure 7.1 Category system for emotions: positive-negative and active-passive

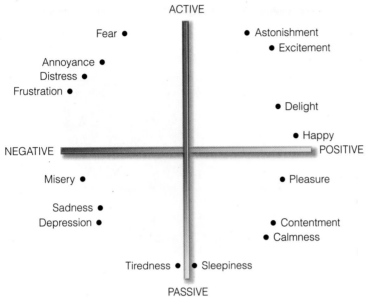

ACTIVE

Fear •   • Astonishment
                                       • Excitement
Annoyance •
Distress •
Frustration •
                                           • Delight

                                             • Happy
NEGATIVE ————————————————————————— POSITIVE

Misery •   • Pleasure

Sadness •
Depression •   • Contentment
                                      • Calmness

Tiredness • | • Sleepiness
PASSIVE

From Guerrero, Anderson, Trost, eds. *Handbook of Communication and Emotion*, 1998, p. 14. Reprinted by permission of Elsevier.

Center for *Understanding Interpersonal Communication* to access **Interactive Activity 7.1: Emotion Cone** under the resources for Chapter 7.

Emotion, Reason, and the Body

From the preceding discussion, you can see that *emotion* is more than just feelings. It's more complicated than that. One of the complexities of emotion is that it's linked with the dualism that characterizes Western thought. **Dualism**, which originated in the 18th century with philosophers Immanuel Kant, and Rene Descartes, is a way of thinking that constructs polar opposite categories to encompass the totality of a thing, prompting us to think about it in an "either/or" fashion. For example, dualism encourages us to think about all of temperature as either hot or cold; all of gender as either feminine or masculine; all of a person as either good or bad. See Table 7.1 on page 221 for a listing of common dualisms that pervade our language and thinking.

When we phrase things as either/or choices we can't see a third (or fourth) possibility. Recall President George W. Bush's frequent comment after

dualism

A way of thinking that constructs polar opposite categories to encompass the totality of a thing. Dualism prompts us to think about things in an "either-or" fashion.

Figure 7.2   Emotion cone

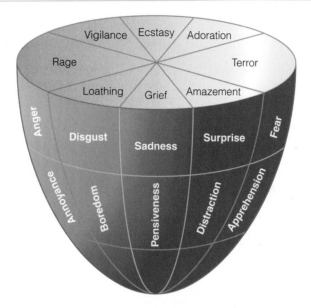

R. Plutchik, R. "Emotions: A general psychoevolutionary theory." In K. R. Scherer & P. Ekman, eds., *Approaches to Emotion*, 1984, pp. 197–219. Reprinted by permission.

September 11, 2001, that countries had to decide: They were *either* allied with the United States against terrorism, *or* they were against the United States and implicitly terrorists themselves. There is no room for a middle position in Bush's statement.

Dualism also encourages us to consider a person to be split into two parts—mind and body—that operate completely independently. The historic division between mind and body is further split when the mind is seen, in another dualism, as either reason or emotion.

Thinking about emotion as separate from reason and the body is reflected in medical school curricula. Many courses teach students to treat physical symptoms, but relatively few address the thoughts and feelings of patients and their families. And dualism is illustrated whenever someone says to another in a conflict: "Stop being hysterical about this! You have to be reasonable."

However, on some level we also understand that emotion, the body, and reason are inextricably linked. Our language can help us see the connections. Think about words we use to describe emotion: *heartache, heartsick, heartened, bighearted, heartless, heartfelt, light-hearted*. All these words indicate our instinctive knowledge of the connection among the mind, emotion, and the body.

Table 7.1 Common dualisms in western thought

hot ↔ cold	strong ↔ weak
male ↔ female	right ↔ wrong
good ↔ bad	public ↔ private
mind ↔ body	black ↔ white
reason ↔ emotion	thinking ↔ feeling
liberals ↔ conservatives	active ↔ passive

Further, experiencing emotion seems to affect people's physical functioning in ways that are not simply physical manifestations of the emotion. Journalist Bill Moyers (1993) interviewed Margaret Kemeny, a psychologist with training in immunology (the study of the immune system). She told him that evidence suggests that experiencing emotion has an effect on health. Based on her studies, she theorizes that prolonged depression makes people vulnerable to heart attacks and other debilitating diseases.

Psychiatrist Ana Fels agrees. A cardiologist referred a patient to her after a heart attack because the doctor hoped that treating the patient's depression would help stabilize the heart disease. Fels observed the relationship between body and emotion by stating, "Not only had his heart attack set off his depression, but his depression could worsen his heart disease" (Fels, 2002, p. D5). To read an interesting article about how the brain and body changes when recalling emotional experiences, go to your online Resource Center for *Understanding Interpersonal Communication* to access *Interactive Activity 7.2: Feeling Emotion*. For more about the links among emotion, the body, feeling, and the mind, access *Interactive Activity 7.3: Emotions, the Body, and the Mind*.

The reverse is also true: reason is dependent on emotion. Hunches and gut reactions show emotion in service of reason. Emotion helps us to decide between competing alternatives when all else is equal. How do you choose between a brown scarf and a black scarf when both look equally good with your coat? How do you choose whether to visit your friend Mark or your friend Sam, when you like them each the same? We would be paralyzed by indecision if we didn't have emotional responses to help us make decisions.

As we learned in Chapter 2, when we perceive something, we first attend to stimuli. So, let's say that stimuli is coming to you and you feel threatened in some way and that your safety is at risk. That is, you feel the emotion of fear. This insight involves reason. You must notice that something dangerous is happening (for example, someone approaches you looking threatening). In this step, you compare your knowledge of a non-dangerous event to what is actually happening, and you see the discrepancy (for example, you say to

© Ellen B. Senisi/The Image Works

IPC $^{in}_{the}$ News

The relationship between reason and emotion is illustrated in a *USA Today* article discussing brain research that examined the role of emotion in decision making. The article reports on a study by neuroscientists showing that people use emotional biases in making so-called rational decisions. The lead researcher for this study says that to make healthy decisions, emotion and reason must be intertwined. He observes that what makes people rational isn't the suppression of emotion, but rather the tempering of emotion so that emotion and reason can work hand-in-hand. He also notes that one of the biggest insights from the study should be directed to educators, commenting that "our education system ignores the role of emotion in learning and decision making" (p. 6D). The results of the study show that we ought to be teaching about emotion in schools.

Vergano, D. (2006, August 7). Study: Ask with care. *USA Today.* p. 6D.

yourself, "I could have no one bothering me, but that's not happening"). You also have to determine the importance of this behavior and evaluate the context (for example, you and this person are friends playing football, or you are walking down a dark street and the person is a stranger). All these judgments are part of the cognitive element of emotion. Emotion also has a physiological component. For example, if someone approaches you with a scowl on his or her face, you are likely to experience physiological reactions such as accelerated heart rate, breathing changes, a lump in your throat, and tense muscles. Table 7.2 presents a listing of common emotions with their accompanying cognitive and physical elements.

Explaining Emotion: Biology and Social Interaction

Many theories help us understand emotion. We will now review two theories that explain how emotions originate: the biological and social (Hochschild, 1983). These theories help us understand emotion more comprehensively.

The Biological Theory of Emotion

Proponents of the biological theory agree with Charles Darwin and others (Hochschild, 1983) that emotion is mainly biological, related to instinct and energy. Because advocates of this view believe that emotions are similar across many types of people, they propose that people from a variety of cultures should experience feelings in the same manner.

Further, this theory assumes that emotion exists separately from thought and that we need thought only to bring a preexisting emotion to our conscious awareness. For example, let's say that Maura is arguing with her friend, Barbara, about how to plan a campus event. While they talk, Maura is thinking about advancing her ideas in the argument and is not paying any attention to the emotion she is experiencing. However, as she walks away from Barbara, she notices that she's slightly irritated because Barbara disagrees with her about the best way to advertise the event. Although Maura had been

Table 7.2 Emotions, physical reactions, and cognitions

Emotions	Physical Reactions	Cognitions
Joy	Warm temperature Fast heartbeat	"I am so happy, and this feels different"
Anger	Fast heartbeat Tense muscles	"I feel anger, and I want to do something"
Sadness	Lump in throat Tense muscles	"I am feeling sadness wash over me"
Shame	Hot flushes Fast heartbeat	"I am ashamed. What can I do?"

experiencing emotion during the argument, she needed introspection, or thought, to bring it to her attention.

Darwin placed importance on observable emotional expressions, not the meaning associated with them. Darwin argued that these "gestures" of emotion were remnants of prehistoric behaviors that served important functions. For instance, when we bare our teeth in rage, our behavior is a remnant of the action of biting. When we hug someone in an expression of love, our action is a remnant of the act of copulation. And when our mouths form an expression of disgust, our action is a remnant of the need to regurgitate a poisonous substance or spoiled food. Thus, in the biological theory, "emotion . . . is our experience of the body ready for an imaginary action" (Hochschild, 1983, p. 220). Furthermore, Darwin argued that people enact these gestures as a result of experiencing emotion. However, he also asserted that the opposite is true—that is, when people enact a certain gesture, they experience the related emotion. Darwin also believed that these emotive gestures (with a few exceptions, such as weeping and kissing) are universal, meaning that they cross all cultures.

The Social Interaction Theory of Emotion

The social interaction theory (Gerth & Mills, 1964) acknowledges that biology affects emotion and emotional communication. However, proponents of this theory are also interested in how people interact with their social situation before, during, and after the experience of emotion. In this way, the theory adds social factors, like interactions with others, to the biological basis for explaining emotion.

Our biology has a tremendous effect on our emotional expression. Smiling is a good example of an inherent human behavior—we don't have to be taught to smile to express happiness, pleasure, and many other emotions.

© Reuters/Corbis

For example, let's say that Catherine finds out on Tuesday that her best friend, Lola, is having a party on Friday. Lola hasn't invited Catherine. The social theory is interested in the following questions: What elements in Catherine's cultural milieu contribute to how she perceives being left off the guest list? That is, do any contextual elements affect her experience of emotion? For example, if Catherine's birthday is coming up, she might think Lola is giving her a surprise party. The biological theory of emotion considers these questions unimportant, but they are central to the social theory.

Like the biological theory, the social theory talks about gesture. However, the social theory focuses on how the reactions of others to our gestures help us define what we are feeling. For example, let's say that Catherine tells another friend, Allen, about not being invited to the party, and she starts to cry because she feels hurt. Allen interprets Catherine's tears as a manifestation of anger, saying to Catherine, "You must be really mad!" Catherine hears this and agrees, "Yes, I can't believe that jerk didn't invite me after all the times she's been to my parties!" Catherine's sense of her own emotional experience may have been confused before she talked to Allen, but his interpretation swayed her and influenced how she labeled her emotion.

See Table 7.3 for a comparison of the biological and social theories. To take a look at several other theories of emotion, including the "common sense" theory, use your online Resource Center for *Understanding Interpersonal Communication* to access *Interactive Activity 7.4: Theories of Emotion.*

Now that we have defined emotion and discussed some theories that help us understand it, we are ready to address our primary concern in this chapter: how emotion relates to interpersonal communication.

Table 7.3 The biological and social theories of emotion

	The biological theory	The social theory
Definition of emotion	Biological processes	Feeling states resulting from social interaction
Relationship of emotions to cognitions	Separate	Interrelated
Assumption of universality	Yes	No
Concern with subjective meaning	No	Yes

Emotion and Communication

Emotion clearly affects interpersonal communication. It influences how we talk to others, how others hear what we say and how our communication affects our relational outcomes (Theiss & Solomon, 2007). For example, people who feel betrayed by a relational partner have many communication choices to express their feelings. Research shows that if they use explicit strategies to forgive their partner, their relationships improve (Waldron & Kelley, 2005). Emotion permeates communication from birth to death. One study showed that the emotion embodied in the final conversation with a loved one before death makes a big difference in the survivor's ability to cope with the loss (Keeley, 2007).

Interpersonal communication can be influenced by the feelings of those around us through **emotional contagion**, or the process of transferring emotions from one person to another. Emotional contagion occurs when one person's feelings "infect" those around him or her. You have probably experienced emotional contagion yourself. Think of a time when you were with a friend who communicated in a nervous manner. Didn't you find yourself becoming nervous, too, just watching her fidget? Or you may have become depressed yourself after spending time with a friend who expressed that he was down in the dumps. Conversely, if you are around someone who expresses positive feelings, you usually find your own mood brightening and your communication becoming more upbeat. Daniel Goleman (2006) calls this *emotional afterglow*.

In examining the relationship between interpersonal communication and emotion, we need to clarify several terms: emotional experience, emotional communication, communicating emotionally, and emotional effects. **Emotional experience** refers to feeling emotion and thus is intrapersonal in nature (Belle felt nervous before her interview). **Emotional communication** means actually talking about the experience of emotion to someone else (Essie told Patrick how she was feeling about the possibility of adopting a child as a single mom). **Communicating emotionally** suggests that the emotion itself is not the

emotional contagion

The process of transferring emotions from one person to another.

emotional experience

The feeling of emotion.

emotional communication

Talking about an emotional experience.

communicating emotionally

Communicating such that the emotion is not the content of the message but rather a property of it.

content of the message but rather a property of it (Roberto yells at his wife Tessa, telling her that she is making them late for their dinner reservations). **Emotional effects** relate to how emotional experience impacts communication behavior (Burleson & Planalp, 2000). (When Sophie ran into her friend Alexa at the mall and accidentally called her Deanna, the name of another friend, Sophie was so embarrassed and flustered that she was unable to conduct the rest of the conversation with Alexa without stammering and stuttering).

The first part of this section focuses on the language used in the United States to portray emotion—that is, the metaphors we employ that center on emotion. The second part of this section discusses how we communicate emotion through a variety of verbal and nonverbal cues.

Metaphors for Emotion

As we discussed in Chapter 4, people often employ figurative language, especially metaphors, to talk about abstract ideas like emotion. Further, people use metaphoric language to distinguish among various emotions as well as "the subtle variations in a speaker's emotional state (e.g., *get hot under the collar* refers to . . . [a] less intense state of anger than does *blow your stack*" [Leggitt & Gibbs, 2000, p. 3]). Table 7.4 lists some common metaphors for emotion.

Our figurative language may imply that emotion has a presence independent of the person experiencing it—as in the phrase "she succumbed to depression." Emotions are frequently framed as opponents ("he struggled with his feelings") or as wild animals ("she felt unbridled passion") (Kovecses, 2000). We speak of guilt as something that "haunts" us, fear as something that "grips" us, and anger as something that "overtakes" us (Hochschild, 1983).

Although these phrases are evocative of the feelings that various emotions engender, they leave the impression that people are not responsible for their emotion—that is, that people are acted upon by emotional forces beyond their control. This way of talking about emotion fits in with our earlier discussion of the division between emotion and reason. Such language depicts emotion as something that can make us lose our minds completely as we are overwhelmed by forces beyond our rational control.

How Emotion Is Communicated

As we discussed in Chapters 4 and 5, the tools we have for communicating are verbal and nonverbal cues. In this section, we'll briefly discuss verbal and nonverbal cues that communicate emotion. We'll also discuss how people use combinations of these cues.

Nonverbal Cues

Facial expressions are obviously one of the most important means for communicating emotion. When people view photos of facial expressions for a variety of emotions, they are accurate in their ability to discern one emotion

emotional effects

The ways in which an emotional experience impacts communication behavior.

Table 7.4 Common metaphors and emotions

Anger	
A hot fluid in a container	She is boiling with anger.
A fire	He is doing a slow burn.
Insanity	George was insane with rage.
A burden	Tamara carries her anger around with her.
A natural force	It was a stormy relationship.
A physical annoyance	He's a pain in the neck.
Fear	
A hidden enemy	Fear crept up on him.
A tormentor	My mother was tortured by fears.
A natural force	Mia was engulfed by fear.
An illness	Jeff was sick with fright.
Happiness	
Up	We had to cheer him up.
Being in heaven	That was heaven on earth.
Light	Miguel brightened up at the news.
Warm	Your thoughtfulness warmed my spirits.
An animal that lives well	Tess looks like the cat that ate the canary.
A pleasurable physical sensation	I was tickled pink.
Sadness	
Down	He brought me down with what he said.
Dark	Phil is in a dark mood.
A natural force	Waves of depression swept over Todd.
An illness	Lora was heartsick.
A physical force	The realization was a terrible blow.

Adapted from Koveçses, 2000.

from another (Gosselin, Kirouac, & Dore, 1995). The most researched facial expression is the smile. Smiles usually indicate warmth and friendliness, but, as we mentioned in Chapter 5, smiles can be interpreted to mean something other than positive emotion. For example, Donna's boss, Melanie, often uses a smile as a mocking gesture. Therefore, when Melanie approaches Donna's office with a smile on her face, Donna feels frustration and braces herself for some type of unpleasant interaction.

Although it is not as well researched as the face, the voice is probably equally important in conveying emotion. How loudly people talk, how high-pitched their tone, how fast they talk, how many pauses they take, and so forth give clues to emotion. In addition, "the voice also carries information about whether emotions are positive and negative because, based on vocal cues alone, pride is more likely to be confused with elation, happiness, and interest than it is with the negative emotions" (Planalp, 1999, p. 46). For example, when Jack calls his coworker Theo one morning before work, Theo can tell right away by the way Jack says "hello" that something is wrong. Before Jack explains his problem verbally, Theo is cued by the tone in Jack's voice.

Emotion is "embodied." This means that "people scratch their heads, clench their fists, shake, gesture wildly, hug themselves, pace the floor, lean forward, fidget in their seats, walk heavily, jump up and down, slump, or freeze in their tracks" (Planalp, 1999, pp. 46–47) when they're communicating emotion. However, there isn't a great deal of research on gestures and body movement. Some research has indicated that depressed people gesture less than those who are not depressed (Segrin, 1998).

Some research (Miller, 2007) suggests that caregivers can communicate compassion nonverbally through place and time codes. For example, caregivers stated that they tried to show compassion to patients by being on time to see them and by structuring the environment so that the temperature is comfortable and so forth. One obstetrician in this study said that an environmental concern was organizing appointments so that pregnant women weren't coming to the office at the same time as women struggling with fertility issues.

Verbal Cues

People often fail to state a specific emotion directly (Shimanoff, 1985, 1987). Instead, they use indirect cues. For example, Max infers that Russ is angry with him when Russ calls Max an idiot and tells him that he wants to be alone. Russ doesn't tell Max any direct information about his emotion, but calling him a name and saying that he wants to be by himself are indirect verbal indicators of Russ's emotional state.

We often infer people's emotional states when they use sarcasm or rhetorical questions (Leggitt & Gibbs, 2000). For instance, let's say that Isabella invites Ruth over for dinner, and Ruth shows up an hour late. When Isabella greets Ruth by saying, "Nice of you to show up on time," Ruth gets the idea that Isabella is angry. Ruth would also probably get the same message about Isabella's emotional state if she asked Ruth rhetorically, "Do you ever look at your watch?" In neither case did Isabella say she was angry directly, but her comments were indirect indicators of anger. Later in this chapter, we show you how to use I-messages to verbalize your emotions, which can prevent the confusion that might result from indirect communication.

Combinations of Cues

Although we have discussed these cues separately, people usually communicate emotion through a mixture of cues. People often use verbal and vocal cues while gesturing and smiling. For example, when Dwight surprises Pat with a vacation to Acapulco, Pat tells him that she's happy in a high-pitched voice while grinning and giving him a hug. Sometimes cues are conflicting or incongruent. For example, when Sandy tells her son, Jake, that she is angry that he hasn't put away all his toys, she laughs indulgently. Especially in cases of conflicting cues, people rely on other information to try to discern the meaning. We discuss some of these other influences in the following section.

Influences on Emotional Communication

In this section, we explain a few areas that will help you understand that emotional communication is not a fixed behavior in our conversations with others. Emotional communication is influenced by several factors, including meta-emotions, culture, gender and sex, and context. We briefly discuss each below.

Meta-emotion

How people communicate about emotion is influenced by a related topic: meta-emotion. **Meta-emotion** means emotion about emotion. People who study emotion tend to focus on the process of emotion and specific emotions, but they have not paid much attention to how people feel about expressing certain emotions. For example, in the case of anger, "some people are ashamed or upset about becoming angry, others feel good about their capacity to express anger, and still others think of anger as natural, neither good nor bad" (Gottman, Katz, & Hooven, 1997, p. 7).

Differences in the effects of communicating emotion may result in part because of meta-emotion. For example, compare the emotions of two couples who have been dating for a year: Andrea and José, and Marla and Leo.

meta-emotion
Emotion felt about experiencing another emotion.

REVISITING CASE IN POINT

1. *How does Allison's response to Regina illustrate the concept of meta-emotion?*

2. *How do you think Allison's meta-emotion will affect how she'll communicate with Regina in the future?*

Y*ou can answer these questions online under the resources for Chapter 7 at your online Resource Center for* Understanding Interpersonal Communication.

Andrea's expression of love for José is accompanied by the meta-emotion pride about her ability to engage in a committed relationship. José feels the same way. On the other hand, when Marla expresses love to Leo, she experiences the meta-emotion shame for becoming so vulnerable in a relationship. Communication transactions between Andrea and José will likely differ significantly from those between Marla and Leo because one couple is proud of their commitment whereas one part of the other couple (that is, Marla) feels shame.

Culture

Remember from our discussion of the biological theory of emotion that Darwin asserted that emotions are primarily universal—that is, people of all cultures respond to the same emotions in the same way. Few people agree with that assertion today. Although some emotional states and expressions—such as joy, anger, and fear—are thought to be universal, the current focus of research is on differences in emotional communication across cultures. As you remember from our discussion in Chapter 3, culture is an important influence on most communication behaviors. The brief review in this section gives you an overview of how different cultures think about emotion and how emotion is communicated in various cultures.

Cultures and Thinking about Emotion

Cultures differ in how much they think and talk about emotion (Planalp & Fitness, 1999). For example, 95 percent of Chinese parents report that their children understand the meaning of shame by age 3, whereas only 10 percent of U.S. parents say their children do. Because of this dif-

Ethics & Choice

M*arco Petrillo felt conflicted, and wasn't sure where to turn for help. He had studied hard during his first three years of college to keep his grades up and to make connections so that he could land a choice internship for his senior year. His hard work had paid off; he'd recently begun working for Jones and Markum, one of the best advertising agencies in the city. He was initially overjoyed about the position and had been patting himself on the back for landing it. He thought his advertising classes had prepared him well for this, and he wanted to be successful so he had a chance of being offered a job with the agency after graduation.*

Everything seemed to be going well until he was assigned to a group working on a campaign for a video game targeted at kids ages 9 to 13. The game was offensive to Marco because it seemed to glorify violence and was disrespectful of women. In the game, the player received points for beating up people encountered in the street, including a prostitute. The player got double points for picking her up and then throwing her out of the car. Marco had grown up in a pretty rough neighborhood, and he had never found violence fun—he'd seen too much at close range.

(Continues)

ference, it seems that shame plays a more important role in Chinese culture than it does in U.S. culture. Yet, a recent study (Seiter & Bruschke, 2007) found that Chinese respondents suffered less from shame after engaging in deception than did U.S. respondents. This is possibly because deception is more acceptable in a culture like China than it is in the U.S. Thus, it is important to consider not just the emotion but also what triggers the emotion.

Some research (Planalp & Fitness, 1999) notes that the Chinese think less about love than do those in the United States. Further, when the Chinese do think of love, they have a cluster of words to describe "sad-love," or love that does not succeed; such words are absent in U.S. culture. Other research (Lazarus, 1991) points to a similar dynamic in Japanese culture. In Japanese stories, when a conflict exists between a couple and the families of the couple, it is resolved in favor of the families, even when that means the couple has to give each other up. In Japan, stories that end with the lovers separating because of family objections are celebrated as showing the triumph of right. In contrast, in the United States and other Western European cultures, many of the stories in books, magazines, and movies end with the couple staying together against the wishes of their families. In these cultures, listeners cheer the lovers on, enjoying the triumph of romantic love.

When Marco reported for the group's first meeting, he was surprised to discover that none of the other group members had a problem with the game. In fact, two of them had come up with what they thought were some great emotional appeals to sell it. They argued that the game should be surrounded with bright colors that kids in the target age group liked, to achieve an immediate nonverbal response. They then proceeded to present a clever series of print ads and television commercials that played on kids' desires and fears. Marco had to give them credit; the ads were good. They pushed a lot of emotional buttons and implied that owning this game would resolve the emotional confusion that the ads themselves created.

What would you advise Marco to do? Should he talk to his advisor at the college? Should he raise his concerns in his work group or with his bosses at the ad agency? Should he quit? Should he stick with it but try to get the group to tone down the emotional appeals? Or should he just keep quiet and go along with the group? What would be the consequences of each of these decisions?

In answering these questions, think about the five ethical systems described in Chapter 1 (categorical imperative, utilitarianism, ethic of care, golden mean, significant choice). Explain how your answers relate to these systems. Do you prefer one course of action over another? Explain.

Go to your online Resource Center for *Understanding Interpersonal Communication* to access an interactive version of this scenario under the resources for Chapter 7. The interactive version of this scenario allows you to choose an appropriate response to this dilemma and then see what consequences your choice brings about. You can also compare your answers to the questions at the end of the scenario to those provided by the authors and, if requested, email your response to your instructor.

How Emotion Is Communicated across Cultures

People of different cultures express emotion differently (Aune & Aune, 1996). For instance, people from warmer climates have been found to be more emotionally expressive than those from colder climates. In addition, people from collectivistic cultures (like Korea, China, and Japan), which we discussed in Chapter 3, are discouraged from expressing negative feelings for fear of their effect on the overall harmony of the community. Thus, people from these cultures are less inclined to express negative feelings. This does not mean that people from collectivistic cultures do not have negative feelings; it simply means that emotional restraint in communication is a shared cultural value (Nakayama & Martin, 2007). People from individualistic cultures like the

United States have no such cultural value—in fact, emotional openness is valued—so they are more expressive of negative emotions.

Gender and Sex

Gender and sex differences in emotional communication are widely researched. The U.S. culture, which divides many activities according to sex, is interested in the ways in which men and women are presumed to differ. For example, although gender roles are in flux in the United States, parenting is still seen as primarily the responsibility of women, whereas men are expected to work to pay the bills. The two sexes are expected to do different things and have different strengths in the workplace and at home (Buzzanell, Sterk, & Turner, 2004). In this section, we review research that examines emotion and gender stereotypes and then explore research on the expression of emotion and gender.

Emotion and Gender Stereotypes

Of course, the stereotypical view holds that women are more emotional, more emotionally expressive, and more attuned to the emotions of others than are men. Agneta Fischer (2000) wonders why women are thought to be the emotional sex while men are perceived to be unemotional. She asserts:

> As far back as I can remember I have encountered emotional men; indeed, I have met more emotional men than emotional women. My father could not control his nerves while watching our national sports heroes on television (which made watching hardly bearable); my uncle immediately got damp eyes on hearing the first note of the Dutch national anthem; a friend would lock himself in his room for days when angry; a teacher at school once got so furious that he dragged a pupil out of the class room and hung him up by his clothes on a coat-hook; one of the male managers at our institute was only able to prevent having a nervous breakdown by rigidly trying to exercise total control over his environment; and a male colleague's constant embarrassment in public situations forced him to avoid such settings altogether. (p. ix)

Fischer's point is not that men are *more* emotional than women. Rather, she observes that all these examples of men expressing emotion go unnoticed because they do not support the stereotype we have of men as unemotional.

Stephanie Shields (2000) makes a similar point when she argues that emotional expression (or lack of it) defines the essence of femininity and masculinity. She notes that people even use gender stereotypes to make judgments about their own emotions. Shields reports on an earlier study she and her colleagues conducted (Robinson, Johnson, & Shields, 1998, as cited in Shields, 2000), in which participants played a competitive word game. In the study, participants were asked about their emotional experience both immediately after playing and then a week later. The researchers found that the reports about the emotions matched gender stereotypes more closely the longer after the event the reports were recorded. The researchers concluded that when the participants forgot exactly how they felt, they used stereotypes (that is, men are stereotyped as more stoic and women as more emotional) to provide an answer.

Another study also showed the power of gender stereotypes on emotion. This study (Shields & Crowley, 1996) asked college students to read an emotion-provoking scenario and then to answer open-ended questions about the scenario. The scenario was identical for all participants except that in some cases the protagonist was male and in others female. The scenario stated one of the following:

"Karen was emotional when she found out that her car had been stolen."

"Brian was emotional when he found out that his car had been stolen."

The researchers found that the respondents judged the word *emotional* in the scenario differently depending on whether they read the Karen version or the Brian version. If participants thought the protagonist was Karen, they attributed the cause of her emotions more to her personality than to her situation, and they imagined her reaction was extreme and hysterical. Respondents who thought Brian's car was stolen downplayed the word *emotional* in the story and described his emotion as what any rational person

© Michelle D. Bridwell/PhotoEdit

How do gender stereotypes influence your perception of how men and women should communicate emotion and how you yourself should communicate emotion? What have been the main social or cultural influences that led you to accept or reject gender stereotypes in regard to emotion: your family, your friends, school, the workplace, the media?

might feel who had worked hard making money to buy the car. The researchers concluded that the respondents used gender stereotypes to answer the questions.

To read more about stereotypes concerning gender and emotion, read the article "Speaking from the Heart: Gender and the Social Meaning of Emotion," available through College Edition. Go to your online Resource Center for *Understanding Interpersonal Communication* to access *InfoTrac College Edition Exercise 7.1: Gender, Emotions, and Stereotypes.*

Emotional Expression and Sex and Gender

Researchers are interested in the differences between men and women in nonverbal expressions of emotion, such as smiling. Four differences are well documented and may be caused by men and women conforming to stereotyped gender roles (Hall, Carter, & Horgan, 2000). Women smile more than men in social situations (Hall et al.). Men and women also differ in nonverbal expressiveness, or facial animation and the liveliness of gestures. Again, women tend to demonstrate their emotional states by using more nonverbal cues than men do (Hall et al.; Jones & Wirtz, 2007). Women are also more accurate than men in figuring out what others' emotional states are based on nonverbal cues (Hall et al.).

Scholars have also investigated sex differences in the verbal expression of emotional support to others. In general men are less likely to give emotional support to a person in distress and when they do provide it, they are less focused on emotion and less person-centered than women (Burleson, Holmstrom, & Gilstrap, 2005). The results of one study (Burleson et al.) suggest that men provide poorer emotional support than women because they see good emotional support as not fitting a masculine gender identity.

"Federal Bureau of Feelings, sir. It seems that last night you neglected to ask your wife how her day was. You have the right to remain silent."

As people age, these gender stereotypes seem to exert less influence on their behaviors. Men tend to become more emotionally expressive, and women become more instrumental or task oriented. A study of 20 married couples over the age of 60 who had been married on average for 42 years shows this change. The researchers interviewing the couples found the men to be expressive about their emotions (saying things like they fell in love with their wives at first sight and reporting how nervous they'd been to meet her parents), whereas wives were more matter-of-fact in their accounts (Dickson & Walker, 2001).

To further explore gender and emotion and how they relate to context, read the article "Gender-Emotion Stereotypes Are Context Specific," available through InfoTrac College Edition. Use your online Resource Center for *Understanding Interpersonal Communication* to access *InfoTrac College Edition Exercise 7.2: Gender, Emotion, and Context.*

REVISITING CASEinPOINT

1. Do you think the fact that Allison and Regina are both female influenced their interaction and their communication of emotion? Explain your answer.

2. Do you think the fact that Allison and Regina are Chinese American affected their interaction? Do you think it played any role in their communication of emotion? Explain.

You can answer these questions online under the resources for Chapter 7 at your online Resource Center for Understanding Interpersonal Communication.

Context

The contexts in which we express emotion are infinite: We express emotion at work, with friends, in our families, at school, over the phone, in person, and so on. We discuss two specific contexts here: historical period and online communication.

Historical Period

The book *American Cool* (Stearns,1994) traces the changes in emotional communication in the United States from the Victorian period (beginning approximately in the 1830s) to the 1960s. The main thesis is that the Victorians were much more emotionally expressive than U.S. citizens of the 1960s. A North American in the 1960s favored "cool" over the emotional excesses of the Victorians. This is the case because culture is governed by **feeling rules**, or "the recommended norms by which people are supposed to shape their emotional expressions and react to the expressions of others" (p. 2) and the feeling rules of U.S. culture changed considerably from the Victorian period to the 1960s.

feeling rules

The cultural norms used to create and react to emotional expressions.

In the 1890s, men in the United States were instructed to express their anger. However, 70 years later, child-rearing experts warned parents not to encourage boys to express anger, arguing that an angry man is possessed by the devil. In the area of romantic love, Victorian men were also encouraged to be expressive, in contrast to the 1960s vision of male love as primarily sexual and silent. A love letter written by a man of the Victorian era illustrates the flowery emotional expression that was the norm:

> "I don't love you and marry you to promote my happiness. To love you, to marry you is a mighty END in itself. . . . I marry you because my own inmost being mingles with your being and is already married to it, both joined in one by God's own voice." (Sterns, 1994, p. 3)

Obviously, a man in Victorian times would be influenced by the feeling rules of his time and would express himself much differently than a man of the 1960s, who would be equally influenced by a very different set of feeling rules. Today, we have different feeling rules as well, although the influence of "cool" is still strong in contemporary U.S. society.

Online Communication

As we discussed in Chapter 1, the channel for a communication transaction influences the communication. Because more and more of our communication time is spent in electronic communication or computer-mediated communication (CMC), online emotional communication is a worthwhile subject of study. You might wonder how email users and frequenters of chat rooms can express emotion without nonverbal cues. As you probably know, the answer to that question is the emoticon. **Emoticons** are icons that can be typed on the keyboard to express emotions. They are used to compensate for the lack of nonverbal cues in CMC.

Emotional communication is obviously vital to online interactions; a preliminary online search yielded more than 100,000 sites in at least five languages that deal with emoticons. Most emoticons look like a face (eyes, nose, and mouth) when rotated 90 degrees clockwise. See Table 7.5 for examples of commonly used emoticons and their translations.

Some research (Rourke, Anderson, Garrison, & Archer, 2001) argues that when people become experienced users of CMC, it is just as rich a communication process as any other, including face to face. Further, CMC doesn't necessarily inhibit emotional expression; one study found that 27 percent of the total message content consisted of emotional communication (Rourke et al., 2001). Yet a *New York Times* article (Williams, 2007), while stating that emoticons are widely used and important to help avoid misunderstandings, also notes that some people are offended when they see the "smileys" or "frownys" appear in a message. One realtor quoted in the article commented that it didn't make her feel any better to see a :(on an email saying she'd lost a deal worth hundreds of thousands of dollars. In fact, she found it highly annoying!

One study investigated emoticon use by males and females (Wolf, 2000). The study showed that when people moved from a same-sex newsgroup to a

emoticon

An icon that can be typed on a keyboard to express emotions; used to compensate for the lack of nonverbal cues in computer-mediated communication.

Table 7.5   Emoticons

:) or :-)	Happiness, sarcasm, or a joke
: (or :-(	Unhappiness
:] or :-]	Jovial happiness
: [or :-[	Despondent unhappiness
:D or :-D	Jovial happiness
: I or :-I	Indifference
:-/ or :-\	Indecision, confusion, or skepticism
:Q or :-Q	Confusion
:S or :-S	Incoherence or loss of words
:@ or :-@	Shock or a scream
:O or :-O	Surprise, a yell, or realization of an error ("uh-oh!")

Common emoticons (n.d.)

mixed-sex newsgroup, men adopted the female standard and began express-ing more emotion as evidenced by a greater use of emoticons. We explore the topic of technology and interpersonal communication further in Chapter 11.

The Dark Side of Emotional Communication

As we discussed earlier in this chapter, some classification systems of specific emotions use positive and negative (that is, valence) as a primary dimension for typing those emotions. We are all familiar with the emotions that fall on the dark side: embarrassment, guilt, hurt, jealousy, anger, depression, and loneliness, to name a few. When we discussed the dark side of communica-tion in Chapter 1, we mentioned that hurtful messages are part of the dark side. Indeed, hurtful messages have received recent attention from researchers exploring how this type of emotional communication operates in relation-ships (for example, Vangelisti & Young, 2000; Young & Bippus, 2001). One study found that if hurtful messages were phrased humorously, they were perceived as less intentionally hurtful and thus caused fewer wounded feel-ings (Young & Bippus, 2001).

Some dark side emotions are the polar opposites of bright side emotions. For example, empathy, a bright side emotion, is the opposite of the dark side emotion *schadenfreude*. Later in this chapter, we suggest empathy (a skill we discussed in Chapter 6) as a recommended practice for becoming an effective communicator. On the other hand, *schadenfreude* is a German word that, loosely translated, means to take pleasure in another's misfortune. The term is derived from the words *damage* and *joy*. In 2002, some reporters used *schadenfreude* to describe how many people felt when they saw Martha Stewart's image tarnished by her suspected involvement with insider trading (St. John, 2002). Some people might think that the public's fascination with the problems of young stars like Lindsay Lohan and Britney Spears stems from *schadenfreude*.

The fact that *schadenfreude* blends two emotions should come as no surprise. As we mentioned earlier in this chapter, emotions are often experienced in blends, and bright and dark, love and hate, are entangled with one another. Another way that negative emotional communication can have a bright side is that negative expressions of anger can be functional in certain contexts, including the following example (Tavris, 2001):

> A 42-year-old businessman, Jay S., described how his eyes were opened when he overheard his usually even-tempered boss on the phone one afternoon: "I've never heard him so angry. He was enraged. His face was red and the veins were bulging on his neck. I tried to get his attention to calm him down, but he waved me away impatiently. As soon as the call was over, he turned to me and smiled. "There," he said. "That ought to do it." If I were the guy he'd been shouting at, let me tell you, it would have done it, too. (p. 251)

The boss's yelling and showing anger accomplished a goal. There are no simple guidelines specifying when talking is better than yelling because the context, the receiver, the sender, and the social goal all make a difference. It may even be that the categorization of an emotion or even a mode of emotional communication as either dark or bright is problematic because it all depends on whether the context called for the emotion, the sender and the receiver expected the emotion, and the social goals of the situation were accomplished through the emotional communication (Tavris, 2001).

As Tavris (2001) states, "the calm, nonaggressive reporting of your anger (those "I messages" that so many psychologists recommend) is the kindest, most civilized and usually most effective way to express anger, but even this mature method depends on its context" (p. 250).

The Bright Side of Emotional Communication

Communication that offers comfort, social support, warmth, affection, forgiveness, or desire falls on the positive end of the emotional spectrum. However, like the dark side, the bright side of emotional communication does not present a simplistic picture. Some of the research on social support provides a glimpse at the mixture of bright and dark that is expressed simultaneously.

David Spiegel and Rachel Kimerling (2001) introduce an example from a support group for family members of breast cancer patients by saying, "the expression of positive feelings often brackets the expression of painful sadness" (p. 101). Following is the vignette they quote:

> A 20-year-old daughter was tearfully coming to terms with the sudden downhill pre-terminal course of her mother's breast cancer: "I see this black hole opening up in my life. I don't think I will want to live without my Mom. She would stay up at 2 A.M. and talk me through my misery for two hours. She won't be there, but I don't want to make her feel guilty for dying." Her father, also at the family group meeting, held her hand and tried to comfort her, but he clearly was overwhelmed by his own sadness and his lifelong fear of strong emotion and dependency on him by others. The husband of another woman whose breast cancer was progressing rapidly started to comfort her but found his voice choked with emotion: "I am sure you will get through this—there's so much love in your family." "Why are you crying?" the father asked. "I don't know," he replied, and everyone, tearful daughter included, found themselves laughing. (p. 101)

The mix of bright and dark shows a complex tapestry of emotion. Another instance that shows a mixture of bright and dark was reported in the *Annals of Behavioral Medicine* (Ullrich & Lutgendorf, 2002). When college students were asked to write their feelings about a traumatic event as well as their efforts to understand and make sense of it, they became more aware of the benefits of the trauma, such as improved relationships, greater personal strength, spiritual growth, and a greater appreciation of life. The authors concluded that the process of communicating their thoughts and emotion made a negative event seem brighter.

Yet another example of the complexity involved in classifying emotional communication as dark or bright can be seen in the emotional communication of forgiveness. Forgiveness, which is based in numerous religious teachings, represents the bright side because it allows for peace and reconciliation.

Archbishop Desmond Tutu (1999), who wrote a book about reconciliation in South Africa titled *No Future Without Forgiveness,* places a high priority on forgiveness. To stress the importance of reconciliation, he invokes the African concept of *ubuntu,* which means that a person is only a person through other people. Archbishop Tutu chaired South Africa's Truth and Reconciliation Commission, which advocated forgiveness as an alternative to racial hatred. The commission presided over hundreds of hearings in which blacks and whites spoke of past grievances and asked forgiveness for those they had harmed. Archbishop Tutu claims in his book that the commission and the process of forgiveness it supervised spared South Africa from the violence and civil unrest that many expected after years of white-minority rule.

Dean Murphy (2002) writes in the *New York Times* about the power and problematic nature of forgiveness. He cites Roger W. Wilkins, a civil rights

Ethan Miller/Getty Images

When we experience traumatic events as a community, such as the hurricane that hit New Orleans in 2005 or the terrorist attacks of September 11, 2001, we express emotions not only on the negative side of the emotional spectrum but often on the positive side as well. In helping others, receiving assistance, and talking about the experience, we may express gratitude at our ability to stay strong in a crisis, we may experience a greater sense of closeness to our families and friends, and we may feel a heightened appreciation for those things in life that matter to us most.

activist and history professor at George Mason University, who notes that people need to forgive for their own sense of self-preservation. Mr. Wilkins observes,

> After a while you figure it out for yourself: you can't be consumed by this stuff because then your oppressors have won. . . . If you are consumed by rage, even at a terrible wrong, you have been reduced. (Murphy, 2002)

However, Mr. Wilkins recognizes the limits of forgiveness when he reflects on the bombing of the 16th Street Baptist Church in Birmingham, Alabama, in 1963, which killed four young black girls. In 2002, Bobby Frank Cherry was convicted of the bombing deaths and sentenced to life imprisonment. He has not asked for forgiveness and continues to deny his guilt. This makes things complicated because forgiveness requires participation from both sides. In this case, Mr. Wilkins suggests that people can purge hatred from their hearts without actually forgiving.

Murphy (2002) relates another difficult case: Amy Biehl, a Fulbright scholar and California native was stoned and stabbed to death in South Africa

Figure 7.3 The interdependence of the bright and dark sides of emotion

in 1993 and her parents managed to forgive. They quit their jobs to work for racial reconciliation, they testified in favor of political amnesty for the killers, and offered two of them jobs. They said that they found forgiveness liberating.

Forgiveness highlights the bright and dark sides in tandem. To experience the liberation of forgiveness, the Biehls had to suffer the torment of grief. Figure 7.3 illustrates the interdependence of the bright and dark sides of emotional communication.

Reflect on your experiences with the dark and bright sides of emotional communication. If you like, you can use your student workbook or your **Understanding Interpersonal Communication** Online Resources to complete this activity.

Your turn

Choices for Developing Emotional Communication Skills

Competence in expressing emotion and in listening and responding to the emotional communication of others is critical to your success as an interpersonal communicator. Some have called this competence *emotional intelligence*. This concept has received a great deal of attention since the 1995 publication of Daniel Goleman's best-selling book by that title. Goleman notes that communicative skills are central to emotional intelligence (E-IQ) and that E-IQ is required to be successful in contemporary society. To help you develop emotional communication competence, we provide several skills for you to consider: knowing your feelings, analyzing the situation, owning, reframing, and empathizing.

Know Your Feelings

Competence in emotional communication begins with your ability to identify the emotion or mix of emotions you are experiencing at a particular time. This skill requires you to do several things:

1. Recognize the emotion you're feeling.

2. Establish that you are stating an emotion.

3. Create a statement that identifies why you are experiencing the emotion. (You may or may not choose to share this statement with anyone else; it is sufficient that you make the statement to yourself.)

Recognizing Your Emotion

This step requires you to stop for a moment and ask yourself what your emotional state is at the present. In other words, you are to take a time out from the ongoing process and take your emotional temperature. It is important not to skip this step, because it involves making a link between yourself and outer reality. To name your feelings signals how you perceive them and alerts you to what your expectations are. For instance, when you recognize that you are irritable, that cues you that you have less patience than usual, and you may expect others to make allowances for you. The opposite process occurs as well. When you give a feeling a name, you respond to that label, which triggers perceptions and expectations.

This step is difficult for several reasons. First, in the heat of an emotional encounter, you may not be prepared to stop and take a time out. Second, we are often so detached from our feelings that it is difficult to name them. And third, some people are simply less aware than others of their emotional states. If you are "low affective-oriented" (Booth-Butterfield & Booth-Butterfield, 1998), you will be relatively unaware of your own emotional experiences.

You need to practice this skill and work on methods to overcome these obstacles. For example, in a highly charged emotional interaction, you can

Communication Assessment Test
Emotional Intelligence (E-IQ)

Although there is no current, valid pencil-and-paper test for your E-IQ that works as reliably as the IQ test, the following test was devised by Daniel Goleman, author of the best-selling 1995 book *Emotional Intelligence*. Answering these questions will give you a rough idea of what your E-IQ might be. You can take this test online. Go to your online Resource Center for *Understanding Interpersonal Communication* and look under the resources for Chapter 7.

_____ 1. You're on an airplane that suddenly hits extremely bad turbulence and begins rocking from side to side. What do you do?
  A. Continue to read your book or magazine, or watch the movie, paying little attention to the turbulence.
  B. Become vigilant for an emergency, carefully monitoring the flight attendant reading the emergency instructions card.
  C. A little of both A and B.
  D. Not sure—never noticed.

_____ 2. You've taken a group of 4-year-olds to the park, and one of them starts crying because the others won't play with her. What do you do?
  A. Stay out of it—let the kids deal with it on their own.
  B. Talk to her and help her figure out ways to get the other kids to play with her.
  C. Tell her in a kind voice not to cry.
  D. Try to distract the crying girl by showing her some other things she could play with.

_____ 3. Assume you're a college student who had hoped to get an A in a course, but you have just found out you got a C– on the midterm. What do you do?
  A. Sketch out a specific plan for ways to improve your grade and resolve to follow through on your plans.
  B. Resolve to do better in the future.
  C. Tell yourself it really doesn't matter how you do in the course, and concentrate instead on other classes where your grades are higher.
  D. Go to see the professor and try to talk her into giving you a better grade.

_____ 4. Imagine you're an insurance salesperson calling prospective clients. Fifteen people in a row have hung up on you, and you're getting discouraged. What do you do?
  A. Call it a day and hope you have better luck tomorrow.
  B. Assess qualities in yourself that may be undermining your ability to make a sale.
  C. Try something new in the next call, and keep plugging away.
  D. Consider another line of work.

_____ 5. You're a manager in an organization that is trying to encourage respect for racial and ethnic diversity. You overhear someone telling a racist joke. What do you do?
  A. Ignore it—it's only a joke.
  B. Call the person into your office for a reprimand.
  C. Speak up on the spot, saying that such jokes are inappropriate and will not be tolerated in your organization.
  D. Suggest to the person telling the joke that they go through a diversity training program.

_____ 6. You're trying to calm down a friend who has worked himself up into a fury at a driver in another car who has cut dangerously close in front of him. What do you do?
  A. Tell him to forget it—he's okay now, and it's no big deal.
  B. Put on one of his favorite tapes and try to distract him.
  C. Join him in putting down the other driver as a show of rapport.
  D. Tell him about a time something like this happened to you and how you felt as mad as he does now, but then you saw the other driver was on the way to the hospital emergency room.

(Continues)

7. You and your life partner have gotten into an argument that has escalated into a shouting match; you're both upset and, in the heat of anger, making personal attacks you don't really mean. What's the best thing to do?
   A. Take a 20-minute break and then continue the discussion.
   B. Just stop the argument—go silent, no matter what your partner says.
   C. Say you're sorry and ask your partner to apologize, too.
   D. Stop for a moment, collect your thoughts, then state your side of the case as precisely as you can.

8. You've been assigned to head a working team that is trying to come up with a creative solution to a nagging problem at work. What's the first thing you do?
   A. Draw up an agenda and allot time for discussion of each item so you make the best use of your time together.
   B. Have people take the time to get to know each other better.
   C. Begin by asking each person for ideas about how to solve the problem, while the ideas are fresh.
   D. Start out with a brainstorming session, encouraging everyone to say whatever comes to mind, no matter how wild.

9. Your 3-year-old son is extremely timid and has been hypersensitive about—and a bit fearful of—new places and people virtually since he was born. What do you do?
   A. Accept that he has a shy temperament and think of ways to shelter him from situations that would upset him.
   B. Take him to a child psychiatrist for help.
   C. Purposely expose him to lots of new people and places so he can get over his fear.
   D. Engineer an ongoing series of challenging but manageable experiences that will teach him he can handle new people and places.

10. For years you've been wanting to get back to learning to play a musical instrument you tried in childhood, and now, just for fun, you've finally gotten around to starting. You want to make the most effective use of your time. What do you do?

A. Hold yourself to a strict practice time each day.
B. Choose pieces that stretch your abilities a bit.
C. Practice only when you're really in the mood.
D. Pick pieces that are far beyond your ability, but that you can master with diligent effort.

Scoring

1. Anything but D—that answer reflects a lack of awareness of your habitual responses under stress.

   A = 20, B = 20, C = 20, D = 0

2. B is best. Emotionally intelligent parents use their children's moments of upset as opportunities to act as emotional coaches, helping their children understand what made them upset, what they are feeling, and alternatives the child can try.

   A = 0, B = 20, C = 0, D = 0

3. A. One mark of self-motivation is being able to formulate a plan for overcoming obstacles and frustrations and follow through on it.

   A = 20, B = 0, C = 0, D = 0

4. C. Optimism, a mark of emotional intelligence, leads people to see setbacks as challenges they can learn from, and to persist, trying out new approaches rather than giving up, blaming themselves, or getting demoralized.

   A = 0, B = 0, C = 20, D = 0

5. C. The most effective way to create an atmosphere that welcomes diversity is to make clear in public that the social norms of your organization do not tolerate such expressions. Instead of trying to change prejudices (a much harder task), keep people from acting on them.

   A = 0, B = 0, C = 20, D = 0

6. D. Data on rage and how to calm it show the effectiveness of distracting the angry person from the focus of their rage, empathizing with their feelings and perspective, and suggesting a less anger-provoking way of seeing the situation.

   A = 0, B = 5, C = 5, D = 20

7. A. Take a break of 20 minutes or more. It takes at least that long to clear the body of the physiological arousal

(Continues)

of anger—which distorts your perception and makes you more likely to launch damaging personal attacks. After cooling down, you'll be more likely to have a fruitful discussion.

A = 20, B = 0, C = 0, D = 0

8. B. Creative groups work at their peak when rapport, harmony, and comfort levels are highest—then people are freer to make their best contribution.

A = 0, B = 20, C = 0, D = 0

9. D. Children born with a timid temperament can often become more outgoing if their parents arrange an ongoing series of manageable challenges to their shyness.

A = 0, B = 0, C = 0, D = 20

10. B. By giving yourself moderate challenges, you are most likely to get into the state of flow, which is both pleasurable and where people learn and perform at their best.

A = 0, B = 20, C = 0, D = 0

The highest score is 200, and 100 is average.

repeat a phrase like "it's time to take a time out," or you can make a prior agreement with a relational partner that you will check every half hour to see if a time out is needed. You might want to list emotions in a journal so you can consult the list to remind yourself of the variety of emotion you might be experiencing. You can also monitor your physical changes to check for signals of emotion. As we noted in Table 7.2, emotion is often accompanied by physiological conditions such as a hot flush, a lump in the throat, and so on. And you can monitor your thoughts to see how they might relate to feelings.

Establishing that You Are Stating an Emotion

This step in the process provides a check to see that you are really in touch with emotion language. It isn't enough to simply say "I feel"; you must be sure that what follows really is an emotion. For instance, if you say "I feel like seeing a ball game," you are stating something you want to do, not an emotion you are experiencing. A better phrasing would be: "I feel restless because I have been working on this project all weekend and I'd like to get out and see a game."

Creating a Statement that Identifies Why You Are Feeling the Emotion

This step involves thinking about the antecedent conditions that are contextualizing your feelings. Ask yourself, "Why do I feel this way?" and "What led to this feeling?" Try to put the reasons into words. For example, statements such as the following form reasons for emotion:

- "I am angry because I studied hard and I got the same grade on the exam that I got when I didn't study."

- "I am feeling lonely. All my friends went to spend the weekend upstate and left me alone at home because I couldn't take time off from work."

- "I am feeling really happy, proud, and a little anxious. I finally got the job I wanted, and I worked especially hard to make a good impression at the interview. All the prep work I did paid off. But now I have to actually make good on everything I said I could do!"
- "I'm feeling guilty. I told my boyfriend I couldn't see him tonight because I had to study, but I really just felt like having a night to myself."

Going through this exercise should help you to clarify why you are experiencing a particular emotion or emotional mix. Further, it should point you in a direction to change something if you wish to. For instance, if you wish to reduce your guilt, tell your boyfriend that you need some time to yourself occasionally without having to give him a reason.

...at work

You have been working on an important project with a coworker, Angela. You become angry and upset because you believe that you are not being acknowledged for your contributions on the project. In fact, it seems like Angela is taking credit for work you did. You know you have done a good job and worked very hard, yet you're not getting the appropriate recognition. At the recent progress meeting with your supervisor, Angela wouldn't let you get a word in edgewise and you watched the supervisor nod approvingly when Angela described an idea you originated. Can you think of a way you could own your feelings and communicate them to Angela without causing an argument or being unprofessional?

...at your best friend's apartment

You and your best friend, Talbot, are at his apartment talking about a trip you will be taking this summer. You have been talking for a while when you notice that Talbot hasn't said anything for a long time—not even "hmmm" or "uh-huh." Talbot seems sad, and you aren't sure why. You like Talbot so much and you've had a long and rewarding friendship, but you feel a little resentful that you have to stop thinking about your wonderful, exciting trip plans to deal with Talbot's bad mood. It seems like something is always bothering him, and today you don't really want to get into it. You just want to feel happy. How do you respond in a way that honors Talbot's nonverbal communication as well as your own emotional reactions?

Analyze the Situation

After identifying your emotion, analyze the situation by asking yourself these questions:

1. *Do you wish to share your emotion with others?* As we mentioned previously, some emotional experiences are not ready for communication—that is, you may not completely understand the emotion yet or you may feel that you would quickly slide into conflict if you communicated the emotion. Or, you might decide that you are comfortable with the emotion and that you don't ever need to share it. For example, if you are looking through your high school yearbook and feel nostalgia for the time you spent there, you might enjoy your reminisces and not feel the need to talk about it with anyone. If you wake up early one morning and experience a beautiful sunrise, you may feel joy without needing to tell anyone about it.

2. *Is the time appropriate for sharing?* If you decide you want to communicate an emotion to someone else, an analysis of the situation helps you decide if the time is right. If your partner is under a great deal of stress at work, you might wait until the situation improves before talking

about your unhappiness at how little time you spend together. If you just found out you are pregnant with a wanted baby and your best friend has recently suffered a miscarriage, you also might decide to wait to share your joy.

3. *How should you approach the communication?* Analyzing the situation helps you think about how to share your emotion. If you are angry with your boss, you need to consider if and/or how to express your anger. Obviously, anger at a boss and anger at a partner provide entirely different situational constraints. Because the workplace climate is not conducive to emotional communication, you may decide not to tell your boss how you feel even though you would like to do so.

4. *Is there anything you can do to change the situation if needed?* Your analysis allows you to think about how and whether to change the situation. In the case of a workplace issue, you might consider instituting new norms at work, accepting the way things are, or looking for a new job.

Own Your Feelings

As we discussed in Chapter 4, **Owning** is the skill of verbally taking responsibility for your feelings. Owning is often accomplished by sending **I-messages**, which show that speakers understand that their feelings belong to them and aren't caused by someone else. I-messages take the following form:

"I feel _____ when you _____, and I would like _____."

For example, let's say that Vanessa is unhappy that her boyfriend, Charles, spends more time with his buddies than with her. Vanessa's I-message would be something like the following:

"I feel unhappy when you spend four nights a week with your friends, and I would like you to spend one of those nights with me."

I-messages differ from you-messages, in which I place the responsibility for my feelings on you. If Vanessa had sent a you-message to Charles, she might have said:

"You are so inconsiderate. All you do is hang out with your friends. I can't believe I am staying with you!"

You can see that Charles's reaction might be more positive to the I-message than to the you-message. Using I-messages does not guarantee that you will get what you ask for. Charles could still tell Vanessa that he wants to spend four nights with his friends. But I-messages help to ensure that Charles hears what Vanessa wants and that he doesn't get sidetracked into a defensive spiral where he argues with her characterization of him as inconsiderate. The I-message focuses on Vanessa's emotion, which is what she wants to talk about with Charles.

owning

Verbally taking responsibility for our own thoughts and feelings.

I-message

A message phrased to show we understand that our feelings belong to us and aren't caused by someone else.

interpersonal explorer

Before you finish reading this chapter, take a moment to review the theories and skills discussed. How do you think the theories discussed in this chapter can help you better understand interpersonal communication and emotion? In what ways can the skills discussed help you interact more effectively with other people in your life?

Theories that relate to emotion

- **Biological theory**
  Emotions are instinctual and universal because they're based in human biology
- **Social theory**
  Emotion is related to biology but it goes beyond that because social interactions and context teach us how to interpret and experience emotion

Practical skills for developing emotional communication skills

- Know your feelings
- Analyze the situation
- Own your feelings
- Reframe when needed
- Empathize

Explore your interpersonal choices

Are you ready to explore your interpersonal choices regarding emotions? Use your online Resource Center for *Understanding Interpersonal Communication* to access an interactive simulation that allows you to view the beginning of an

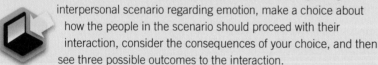

interpersonal scenario regarding emotion, make a choice about how the people in the scenario should proceed with their interaction, consider the consequences of your choice, and then see three possible outcomes to the interaction.

Reframe When Needed

Reframing refers to the ability to change the frame surrounding a situation to put it in a more productive light. When Jane Brody (2002) wrote about suggested methods for reducing hostile tendencies, she alluded to the skill of reframing. Brody quotes Dr. Norman Rosenthal, a psychiatrist in the Washington, DC, area who specializes in depression and anger. Rosenthal comments that a friend often grew angry when waiting in his car at long red lights. The friend's wife reframed for him by reminding him that "the red light doesn't care, so he might as well save his fury" (p. D7). Rosenthal suggests that it is easier for people to reframe their thinking about something than it is to change the world. He goes on to say that after you discover what makes you mad, you can reframe those irritants by changing the messages you give yourself. If you think of other people as rude, that frame may cause hostility. If you change the frame to respecting yourself for being polite, you will feel less anger and hostility.

Carol Tavris (2001) talks about a similar process when she recounts what anger management expert Ray Navaco advises clients who come to him for help in anger management. Navaco points out that "anger is fomented, maintained, and inflamed by the statements we make to ourselves and others when we are provoked—'who does he think he is to treat me like that?' 'What a vile and thoughtless woman she is!'" (p. 252). He teaches his clients to reframe and to substitute other statements, such as "Maybe he's having a tough day" and "She must be very unhappy if she would do such a thing."

Empathize

As we discussed in Chapter 6, empathy is the ability to put yourself in another's place so you are able to understand his or her point of view. Empathy is often accomplished through the skill of **active listening**, which calls for you to suspend your own responses for a while so you can concentrate on the other person. In active listening, you usually allow the other person a full hearing (no interruptions), and when it's your turn, you say something like, "You sound really troubled by your relationship with your dad. Tell me more about how you're feeling." This skill is valuable when you are the receiver of another person's emotional communication. For example, when Rob comes storming into his fraternity house, throwing his books on the table, and swearing about his problems with his girlfriend, Chloe, he needs someone to listen to him with empathy.

Often our response to hearing someone's emotional outburst is to attempt to solve his or her problem ("here's what you should say to her the next time you see her"), question the person ("how long has she been acting like this?"), tell a story about a similar problem that you have had ("hey, I know just how you feel, my ex-girlfriend did the same thing! That's why I dumped her") or evaluate the person's problem ("you know, all couples fight—it's not that big a deal"). Although some of those responses might prove useful later, empathizing is the best approach for early in the conversation because it keeps the focus on the person who is expressing the emotion and allows him or her to set the pace and the content of the conversation. In this way, that person can explore how he or she really feels while you lend a listening ear.

Although these skills take practice, knowing your feelings, recognizing your emotion, being able to identify reasons for your emotion, phrasing an emotion statement, analyzing the situation, owning, reframing, and empathizing all will contribute to your communication competence in emotional encounters.

For more about emotional competence and its role in a specific context—the workplace—read the article "Your Emotional Skills Can Make Or Break You," available through InfoTrac College Edition. Use your online Resource Center for *Understanding Interpersonal Communication* to access *InfoTrac College Edition Exercise 7.3: Emotional Skills at Work.*

reframe

To change something that has a negative connotation to something with a more positive connotation (e.g., a problem can become a concern, or a challenge can become an opportunity).

active listening

Suspending our own responses while listening so we can concentrate on what another person is saying.

Summary

Emotional language and emotional communication are inevitable in our daily interactions. *Emotion,* a complex term, is the critical internal structure that orients us to what matters in our lives, our feelings about ourselves and others. Emotion relates to the affective, or feeling tone, of our experiences.

Two systems of categorization allow us to classify specific emotions based on their attributes. One system uses positive-negative (valence) and active-passive dimensions and one classifies emotions according to their intensity. Although these classification schemes treat emotions as separate states, people often experience more than one emotion at once.

Western thought encourages dualistic thinking, which prompts us to see the mind and body as separate and emotion as separate from reasoning. However, such thinking is fallacious because emotion, reason, and physiology are interconnected. To add to the complexity of emotion, meta-emotion, or how people feel about expressing certain emotions, influences people's interactions.

The biological theory of emotion, based mainly on Darwin's ideas, states that emotions are related to instinct and are universal. This view places emphasis on observable emotional expressions, or "gestures" of emotion. On the other hand, the social theory of emotion, attributed to Hans Gerth and C. Wright Mills, states that the social situation, as well as biology, affects the experience of emotion. This view studies how the reactions of others to our gestures help us define our feelings.

People often use metaphors to talk about emotion, many of which make it seem as if emotional forces are beyond our control. Tools for emotional communication include facial expressions, vocal cues, gestures, and verbal cutes. Culture, gender, and context are three of the many factors that influence emotional communication. Emotional communication has a dark side and a bright side, which often overlap.

Becoming competent in emotional communication requires practicing the following techniques: knowing your feelings, analyzing the situation, owning your feelings, reframing when needed, and empathizing. Emotional communication is a complex activity that involves sensitivity, awareness, insight, and empathy. Just like any proficiency, emotional communication requires patience and persistence, but the rewards are worth the effort.

Understanding Interpersonal Communication Online

Now that you've read Chapter 7, use your online Resource Center for *Understanding Interpersonal Communication* for quick access to the electronic study resources that accompany this text. Your online Resource Center gives you access to the video of Regina and Allison's interaction on pages 215–216, the Ethics & Choice interactive activity on page 230, the Your Turn journal activity on page 241, the Communication Assessment Test on page 243, the Interpersonal Explorer activity on page 248, Info-Trac College Edition, and study aids including a digital glossary, review quizzes, and the chapter activities.

Terms for Review

active listening 249
activity 218
communicating
　　emotionally 225
dualism 218
emoticons 236
emotion 217

emotional communication
　　225
emotional contagion 225
emotional effects 226
emotional experience 225
empathy 245
feeling rules 235

I-messages 247
intensity 218
meta-emotion 229
owning 247
reframe 248
valence 218

Questions for Understanding

Comprehension Focus

1. Define emotion.

2. Compare and contrast the biological and social theories of emotion.

3. Distinguish among emotional experience, emotional communication, communicating emotionally, and emotional effects.

4. List three factors that influence emotional communication.

5. Define owning and provide an example.

Application Focus

1. CASE IN POINT Examine our opening story of Regina Chen and Allison Yang. What advice would you offer Regina? What should she say to Allison? What advice would you offer Allison? What should she say or do at this time? Does an understanding of emotional intelligence help you understand this case? Explain how it does or why it does not.

2. Discuss the relationship among thought, feeling, and the body. Do you see them as separate or intertwined? Use examples to support your opinion.

3. Provide your own definition of emotional communication. How does it differ from the definition presented in the chapter? Explain the reasons for those differences. Does emotional communication differ from emotion? Explain your answer.

4. Evaluate the theories of emotion that we presented in the chapter. Explain what you see as the strengths and weaknesses of each.

5. Discuss the research on culture as a factor that influences emotion and emotional communication. To what degree do you think that emotion is universal or transcends culture? Justify your answer with evidence and examples.

Interactive Activities and InfoTrac College Edition Exercises

Interactive Activities

InfoTrac College Edition Exercises

Chapter 8
Sharing Personal Information

chapter ✛ goals

Understand the complexity of self-disclosure

Identify the effects of individual differences, relational issues, culture, and gender and sex on self-disclosing

Describe the principles of self-disclosure

Present explanations for self-disclosing behavior

Explain the reasons for engaging and not engaging in self-disclosure

Utilize a variety of techniques to enhance your effectiveness as a discloser

CASEinPOINT
ROBERTA GILBERT AND PHILIP JERMAINE

Roberta Gilbert and Philip Jermaine had lived together for ten years, and both were happy with their relationship. They met when Roberta was 27 and Philip was 30, and they moved in together two years later. Before they bought their condo together, they'd spent a lot of time talking. Philip always said that one of his favorite things about Roberta was how easy it was to talk to her. They had told each other their likes and dislikes and confided about past relationships. They had discussed at length their views on marriage, and they agreed it was not for them.

However, in those discussions twelve years prior, Roberta hadn't been completely honest with Philip. She hadn't told him that she'd been married briefly when she was 19. The marriage was a hasty one, entered into on the spur of the moment, and Roberta honestly didn't know what she'd been thinking. It was almost like she and Carl just ran off and got married to have something to do on their date. Roberta's parents found out about the marriage and had it annulled almost immediately, to the relief of both Roberta and Carl. Now it had been so long since she'd seen Carl that, frankly, Roberta hardly even remembered she'd actually been married.

When she and Philip met, it didn't seem important to tell him about Carl. And after Philip spent so much time expressing his views on the evils of marriage—views she mainly agreed with—it would have been awkward to mention it. So, time went by and Roberta simply kept the information to herself. She reasoned that it didn't really make a difference whether she told Philip about this ancient history because she was totally honest with him about everything else.

However, Roberta's past was about to catch up with her. She had run into Carl at the grocery store! It was a shock to see him after so long. He said that he and his family had just moved into town. Because the town was so small, Roberta knew she had to tell Philip about their past relationship or he'd find out some other way. She was nervous, but she decided to tell him that night at dinner—she'd kept this secret long enough. She made a lovely candlelit dinner, and after they'd eaten she nervously mentioned that she'd seen an old

Use your online Resource Center for *Understanding Interpersonal Communication* to watch a video clip of Philip and Roberta's interaction.

> Access the resources for Chapter 8 and select "Roberta" to watch the video (it takes a minute for the video to load). As you watch the video, consider the reasons why Roberta chose not to self-disclose about her marriage. Do you think her reasons were good ones? > You can respond to this and other analysis questions, and then click "Done" to compare your answers with those provided by the authors.

friend at the store the day before. Philip looked mildly interested and, after a few false starts, she finally blurted out her story. There was a long pause. Finally, Philip cleared his throat and pushed away from the table.

Philip told Roberta that he wasn't upset that she'd had a brief marriage, but he couldn't understand why she hadn't told him before. Roberta had to admit she couldn't understand it herself. She swore she'd never keep anything like this from Philip again. Although he looked serious, he shrugged and told her he hoped there wouldn't be anything else like this to tell. He seemed to be making light of the situation, but privately he wondered if his and Roberta's relationship was as solid as he'd thought. He hoped they could get over this, and told Roberta he was glad she'd finally disclosed her secret.

S elf-disclosure is one of the most researched behaviors in the communication discipline. Most interpersonal communication scholars believe self-disclosure is a critically important communication skill because it helps relationships develop and contributes to our self concept. Ample evidence shows that greater disclosure is related to greater emotional involvement in a relationship (Finkenauer & Hazam, 2000) and that "disclosure is central to how people define what constitutes intimacy" (Lippert & Prager, 2001 p. 294).

In our opening scenario, Roberta and Philip's relationship may be in danger as a result of the long delay before Roberta's disclosure. Philip's sense of his intimate knowledge of Roberta is shaken. Further, Roberta's sense of herself is in question. Roberta sees herself as an honest person, and keeping this secret from Philip causes her to question herself. Yet both Philip and Roberta are glad to finally have this secret out in the open.

Researchers believe that self-disclosure and relationship development go hand-in-hand—and you probably think so, too. Most people can think of a time when a relationship became closer after one or both partners shared something personal. Because self-disclosure is integral to our interpersonal relationships, we need to examine this communication skill more closely. What does it really mean to self-disclose? Is it always a helpful behavior? What are the risks? What exactly are the boundaries between intimate information and information we're willing to make public? How can we become skillful self-disclosers? In this chapter we'll discuss this exciting, complex interpersonal communication behavior.

Definition of Self-Disclosure: Opening Up

Self-disclosure is personal information, shared intentionally, that another person would have trouble finding out without being told. Statements such as "I think I really like Dan," "I am sick of family gatherings," "I used to box professionally," or "I am concerned about our relationship—I'm having trouble trusting you like I used to" are all self-disclosures.

Implicit in this definition is the fact that self-disclosures are verbal behaviors. We do reveal information about ourselves nonverbally—for example, by dressing in certain clothes, wearing a wedding ring, or making facial expressions—but these types of revelations don't fit our definition of self-disclosure because they don't have the same intentionality as revelations told to a specific person. Nonverbal behaviors are more generally sent—for example, everyone we come in contact with sees what we wear. Our definition highlights several important features of self-disclosing, all discussed in this section: intentionality, choice, personal information, risk, and trust.

Intentionality and Choice

When you engage in self-disclosure, you choose to tell another person something about yourself. When Mike tells Elizabeth that he fears he isn't smart enough to make it in medical school, his disclosure is a conscious, voluntary decision to confide a vulnerability to a friend. Mike isn't coerced into telling Elizabeth his concerns; rather, he freely discloses them. Although disclosures sometimes slip out unintentionally (for example, when someone is drunk, overly tired, or otherwise impaired), these "slips" don't meet our definition for real self-disclosure.

We choose whether or not to tell something and we also choose how to tell it. For instance, Mike may tell Elizabeth about his fear of failing in medical school, but he may withhold the information that he did poorly on the GMAT (the entrance test for medical school). Mike is in control of how much he tells and, therefore, how vulnerable he allows himself to be in his relationship with Elizabeth.

As we choose whether and how much to self-disclose in our interpersonal relationships, we negotiate the boundaries between privacy and openness. Sandra Petronio (2000) observes that being both known by others and yet unknown "is essential to our communicative world" (p. xiii). Selectively self-disclosing helps us create the balance between what is private to ourselves, what is shared with intimates, what is disclosed to close friends, and what is known to many others.

self-disclosure

Evaluative and descriptive information about the self, shared intentionally, that another would have trouble finding out without being told.

Private Information and Risk

Self-disclosure involves information another would not be easily able to discover without being told; it must be private rather than public.

Public information consists of facts that we make parts of our public image—the parts of ourselves that we present to others. Usually, people strive to present socially approved characteristics as public information. Some researchers use the metaphor of the theatre to describe life, and they refer to public information as what is seen "on stage."

Private information reflects the self-concept, as we discussed in Chapter 2. Private information consists of the assessments—both good and bad—that we make about our selves. It also includes our personal values and our interests, fears, and concerns. In the "life as theatre" metaphor, private information is what is kept "backstage." When we're backstage, we can forget about some of the social niceties that are important for public information. The following dialogues illustrate the concepts of public and private conversation. The first conversation is between Gwen and her boss at Clarke Meat Packing Plant, Ms. Greene; the second is between Gwen and her best friend, Robin, who doesn't work at the plant.

Although it is tempting to think that we can know what this person might self-disclose based on what he looks like, the image he is trying to project via his use of nonverbal signals may differ quite dramatically from what he would disclose about himself in a personal conversation with a friend. Our nonverbal signals can reveal a lot about us, but real self-disclosure involves intentionality, choice, intimacy, risk, and trust.

Gwen:	Ms. Greene, I need to take a personal day a week from Friday.
Ms. Greene:	That's a problem, Gwen. Our new plant policy is that we don't allow personal days if they'll result in having to pay other workers overtime. As I look at the work flowchart, I see that there are only two workers scheduled for your shift a week from Friday. So, I'm afraid I'll have to deny your request.
Gwen:	I'm kind of surprised to hear that, Ms. Greene. When did that policy go into effect?
Ms. Greene:	It's been our policy for the past six months now, Gwen. Didn't your union rep inform you?

Gwen: Ah . . . no, ah, I don't think he did, but I may have missed the meeting—I can check with the rep. In the meantime, what do you suggest I do about my problem a week from Friday?

Ms. Greene: I suggest you come to work, Gwen. You know, if you don't like the conditions here, you can always look for another job.

Gwen: I like working here, Ms. Greene. I don't want another job.

In this dialogue, Gwen displays public information. She tries to show her supervisor that she is a cooperative, dedicated worker who enjoys working at the plant and who takes responsibility for her own problems (for example, she volunteers to talk to the union rep). In the next dialogue, Gwen is free to exhibit private information with her best friend.

Gwen: Oh, Robin, I'm so mad!! That witch, Greene, won't let me have a personal day. The entire plant is now being run just for the convenience of the bosses!

Robin: Hey, Gwen, slow down. What happened?

Gwen: I asked that jerk for a personal day a week from Friday, and she said no because it would mean she would have to pay someone else overtime. I hate my job. But Greene came out and told me if I didn't like it I could take a walk. I really wish I could—I should start looking for a new job, but I hate getting out and looking for work, and to be honest, I hate change, too. It would serve them right if I did leave and I didn't give any notice. I can't stand that place!

When displaying private information, Gwen is unconcerned about presenting herself as competent and responsible. Instead, she vents her emotions and reveals some of her less than positive self-assessments: she doesn't like change or job seeking. In short, she self-discloses.

Some researchers (Mathews, Derlega, & Morrow, 2006) have noted that past research on self-disclosure has left it to the researcher to define private information. These researchers wanted to know what people thought was personal, so they asked study participants what constituted highly personal information. They received answers ranging from self-concept to death and illness. See Table 8.1 on page 258 for a summary of their findings.

You can see from this discussion where risk comes into play. Self-disclosure involves sharing who we really are with another and letting ourselves be truly known by them. The scary part is that we may be rejected by the other person after we have exposed ourselves in this fashion. Risk may also be inherent in the situation. Some research (Theiss & Solomon, 2007) examines sexual self-disclosures. By this they don't mean telling another person about sex in general, but rather speaking to a partner before engaging in sex. They note that people rarely talk specifically about sex and when they do it's often

public information

Personal facts, usually socially approved characteristics, we make part of our public image.

private information

Assessments, both good and bad, that we make about ourselves, including our personal values and our interests, fears, and concerns.

Table 8.1   Highly personal topics for self-disclosure

Topic	Example
Self-concept	I may not have the drive to succeed in life.
Romantic relationships	When my boyfriend and I broke up, he wouldn't talk to me at all for a month. He ignored my emails and calls.
Sex	I'm a virgin, and I feel that makes me special.
Psychological problems	I've had to help my boyfriend with alcoholism.
Abuse	My father put his hands around my throat and pinned me to a wall.
Death/illness	My middle brother passed away right before my eyes.
Family relationships	My father left when I was seven and never looked back.
Moral issues	I hit a car on purpose.
Unplanned pregnancy	I recently became pregnant, and I'm not married.
Friendships	I hate my best friend's girlfriend.
Miscellaneous	I had to declare bankruptcy at the age of 24.

Adapted from Mathews et al., 2006 pp. 88–89.

indirect communication rather than a clear self-disclosure. They comment that it's important to take the risk to disclose at this time to avoid unwanted or unsafe sexual encounters.

REVISITING
CASE IN POINT

1. *How does Roberta's self-disclosure illustrate the quality of intentionality?*

2. *How does Roberta's self-disclosure illustrate the quality of risk?*

3. *How does Roberta's self-disclosure illustrate the quality of trust?*

You can answer these questions online under the resources for Chapter 8 at your online Resource Center for Understanding Interpersonal Communication.

Trust

Trust explains why we decide to take the plunge and reveal ourselves through self-disclosure. When we are in a relationship with a trusted other, we feel comfortable self-disclosing because we believe that our confidante can keep a secret, will continue to care for us, and won't get upset when we relate what we are thinking (Derlega, Metts, Petronio, & Margulis, 1993). Our perception of trust is a key factor in our decision to self-disclose, and most self-disclosures take place in the context of a trusting relationship.

For information about how to disclose private information about your health, use your online Resource Center for *Understanding Interpersonal Communication* to access *Interactive Activity 8.1: Disclosing Health Information.*

Self-Disclosure as a Subjective Process

As you've probably noticed, whether information is considered self-disclosure depends on subjective assessments made by the discloser. The degree of risk involved is a personal judgment; what one person considers to be risky might be information that someone else would find easy to tell. Taking this fact into consideration, let's make a distinction between *history* and *story*.

History consists of information that sounds personal to a listener but is relatively easy for a speaker to tell. Disclosures that are classified as history may be told easily because of the teller's temperament, changing times, or simply because the events happened a long time ago and have been told and retold. For instance, Nell was in a serious car accident when she was 19. The story of the accident and its aftermath is a dramatic one, but it doesn't feel risky to tell it because she has told it so many times that it has become routine. In another example, Melanie, who married Jeff in 1970, used to feel nervous about telling people that her husband had been married once before. By 1990, when she and Jeff had been married for 20 years and the divorce rate in the United States had reached almost 50 percent, Melanie stopped being concerned about that disclosure.

In contrast, **story**, or true self-disclosure, exists when the teller *feels* the risk he or she is taking in telling the information. A disclosure should be considered story (or authentic) even if it doesn't seem personal to the average listener. For instance, when Marie told her friend, Fernando, that she had never known a Mexican American person before, Fernando thought that she was simply making a factual observation. However, to Marie, that admission felt very risky. She was afraid that Fernando would think less of her and judge her as provincial because she was unfamiliar with people other than white Anglo-Saxons like herself. Marie was engaging in story even though Fernando heard it as history.

Another way to think about history and story relates to the topic of a disclosure. Some topics seem inherently more or less personal than others. For example, you could share a great deal of information about a topic like sports without seeming to become very personal ("I love the Green Bay Packers," "I think the Bears are the most improved team in the NFL," "I believe that professional athletes make too much money"). However, topics such as sex or money seem intrinsically more personal. Thus, disclosures are typed based on **topical intimacy**. However, a person can reveal an actual disclosure (that is, story) about what seems to be a low-intimacy topic. For instance, Jill might feel she's taking a risk to tell her feminist friends that she's a football fan. The reverse is also true; a person can reveal little personal information

history
Information that may sound personal to another person but that is relatively easy for us to tell.

story
Information we feel we are taking a risk telling another.

topical intimacy
The level of intimacy inherent in a topic.

about a high-intimacy topic. For example, when Mike says he wants to take a course in the sociology of sex, he may not think he's risking much. It all depends on the risk the teller feels while disclosing to a listener.

At this point in our discussion, you may be thinking of self-disclosure as an event in which one person tells another something of consequence. In fact, this is the way many researchers have talked about self-disclosure.

Ethics & Choice

Theo Henley was on his way to his third interview for a position he really wanted. After making it through the first and second interviews, Theo was feeling good about himself and thought he had a solid chance for an offer. At the previous interviews, he'd gotten along well with everyone and the more he learned about the job and the company, the better he felt. He thought that the job was a perfect fit for him.

However, despite his high hopes, he was worried. He faced the same old dilemma: Should he reveal anything about his disability, multiple sclerosis (MS), to the prospective employers? When he had been diagnosed seven years ago, it had seemed like a death sentence, but he'd learned to live with the disease. His situation was complicated by the fact that he had what his doctors called "invisible symptoms." Although he sometimes suffered because of the MS, no one knew he had it unless he told them. His worst symptom was excessive tiredness.

For the past three years, he'd been experiencing a remission, and his condition was much improved. However, he lived with the knowledge that the symptoms could return any time. The doctors knew little about this unpredictable disease.

Theo knew he could do the job. He was sure he could do it even if the symptoms returned, because he'd held down a job through the seven years of his illness. Occasionally he had called in sick because of the fatigue and disorientation brought on by the MS, but he didn't think he was absent more than anyone else. And he always got good performance reviews.

But he wasn't sure if it was right to keep this information from a prospective employer. Moreover, what if the MS returned and became even worse? If that happened, he would need to ask for some assistance at work. If he hadn't told the company before, he might be in a bad position if he needed help. In addition, he wanted to be honest. But he wasn't sure how this information would be received or if he needed to reveal this personal problem.

What do you think Theo should do? In answering this question, what ethical system of communication informs your decision (categorical imperative, utilitarianism, ethic of care, golden mean, significant choice)?

Go to your online Resource Center for *Understanding Interpersonal Communication* to access an interactive version of this scenario under the resources for Chapter 8. The interactive version of this scenario allows you to choose an appropriate response to this dilemma and then see what consequences your choice brings about. You can also compare your answers to the questions at the end of the scenario to those provided by the authors and, if requested, email your response to your instructor.

However, some people think that disclosures aren't discrete, finite events; rather, they are processes that occur on a continuum. Some research (Dindia, 1998) indicates that gay men saw self-disclosing their sexual identity as an ongoing process. Dindia quotes one of her participants as saying, "I . . . am in the process of coming out. . . . When you say, 'hey, I'm gay.' That's the beginning. Yeah, [first you come] out to yourself and then [you] slowly [come] out to other people as well" (p.87). Self-disclosures are unfinished business because there is always something more or someone else to tell.

Factors Affecting Disclosure

Although our definition of self-disclosure is fairly straightforward, the discussions of history and story, as well as considerations of self-disclosure as a process, show that it is not a simple concept or skill. A complete understanding of self-disclosure requires consideration of many factors, including individual differences, relational issues, cultural values, and gender and sex. We explore each below.

Individual Differences

People have different needs for openness. Whereas Karl has no problem telling his friends all about his personal feelings, Selena saves disclosures of that nature for her family and most intimate friends. Think about your own tendencies to share

Communication Assessment Test
Exploring Your Approach to Self-Disclosure

Directions: Complete the following sentences about your approach to self-disclosure. There are no right or wrong answers for this assessment, and there is no method of scoring. Rather, simply taking a moment to think about your approach to self-disclosure can help you make thoughtful choices about when and how you self-disclose in future interactions. You can take this test online. Go to your online Resource Center for *Understanding Interpersonal Communication* and look under the resources for Chapter 8.

1. Intimate communication to me means . . .
2. The hard thing about intimate communication is . . .
3. Sometimes I withdraw from intimate communication when . . .
4. When I disclose, I do so because . . .
5. One of the things I'd like people to know about me is . . .
6. When I try to talk about things that are important to me . . .
7. When I try to express intimate feelings . . .
8. If I were more open about expressing my feelings and opinions . . .
9. When people try to talk with me, sometimes I . . .
10. If I weren't concerned about the listener's response . . .
11. Sometimes I become blocked when . . .
12. One of the ways I sometimes make it difficult for people to disclose to me is . . .

Adapted from Michigan State University Counseling Center, 2003.

information with others in your life. Do you believe that some things are better left unsaid, or do you think friends and family should know everything about you?

Even people who have a high need to disclose don't wish to tell everyone everything. Although Deanna might tell her partner, Eric, about the fact that she was sexually abused by her stepfather, she may have no problem keeping that information secret from her friend Trish.

Relational Issues

Self-disclosures wax and wane over the life of a relationship. Telling each other every secret may be important early in the relationship, but in long-term friendships, marriages, or partnerships, self-disclosures account for a much smaller amount of communication time. "Getting to know you" is an important part of developing a new relationship, but as relationships endure and stabilize, the participants need to disclose less because they already know a great deal about one another (Knapp & Vangelisti, 2005).

Researchers suggest that some general patterns of self-disclosure may be related to the life of a relationship (see Figure 8.1). The first pattern pictured represents the general scenario we've described: People meet, get to know each other, begin to tell each other more and more personal information, and then decrease their disclosures as the relationship endures. This pattern shows a gradual increase in self-disclosing that parallels the growth of the relationship until the relationship stabilizes; at that point, self-disclosures decrease. One study (Huston, McHale, & Crouter, 1986) found that after one year of marriage, couples were less self-disclosing than they had been as newlyweds, yet they were still satisfied with their relationships.

The second pattern pictured in Figure 8.1 represents two people who know each other as casual friends for a long time before escalating the relationship with self-disclosures and increasing intimacy. The long-term relationship is characterized by low self-disclosures and then a spike up before a leveling off of openness. Let's look at an example. Steven, an emergency room nurse at a local hospital, has worked for four years on the same shift as Beth, an intern at the hospital. They have spoken to each other a lot about working conditions and emergency health care. Although Steven and Beth don't know each other well, they like each other and respect each other's medical skills and steadiness in an emergency. One night, Steven's father suffers a stroke and is brought into the emergency room. When his dad dies a few hours after being admitted, Steven finds comfort in sharing his feelings with Beth. This tragedy leads to increased disclosures between them. One year later, they refer to each other as best friends. This pattern shows that, as with the first pattern, Beth and Steven's disclosures will eventually decrease over time.

The third pattern, sometimes referred to as "clicking," shows a high incidence of self-disclosing almost immediately in the relationship. Researchers refer to these relationships as ones that just "click" from the start rather than needing a gradual build. For example, Ben and Marcus met twenty years ago as 12-year-olds at football camp. They immediately found each other easy to talk to and enjoyed being together. Now, two decades later, they still enjoy an openness and a deep friendship.

Researchers explain the clicking process by suggesting that people carry around relationship scripts in their heads, and when they find someone who fits the main elements of that script, they begin acting as though all the elements were there (Berg & Clark, 1986). In other words, let's say that Ben expects a friend to have the same interests he has, resemble him physically, be open and attractive, and have a good sense of humor. When he finds all those characteristics in Marcus, he quickly begins acting as though they have a developed friendship. If Marcus has a similar response, we should see the clicking pattern. Again, in this third pattern, we see a leveling off of self-disclosures over time.

In all three patterns in Figure 8.1, self-disclosures eventually level off—and, in many cases, they eventually decrease dramatically if relationships last a long time. However, when new issues arise, even longtime friends or couples

Figure 8.1 Three patterns of self-disclosure in relationships

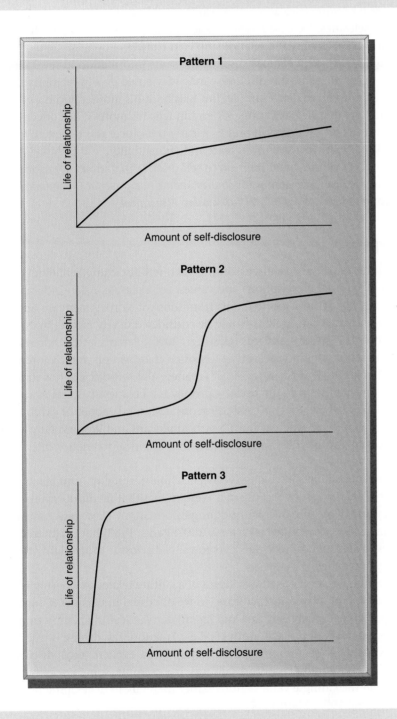

who have been together a long time self-disclose. Another time self-disclosures may increase is when people feel their relationship has fallen into a rut, and they wish to bring back some of its earlier excitement and intensity. Further, if self-disclosures decrease suddenly and radically between people, the decrease may signal that a relationship is in trouble.

Finally, although we may disclose the same information to several people, the way we frame our disclosure may vary based on our relationship with the person involved. For example, Jim tells both his mother and his good friend, Rose, that he has cancer. When Jim tells his mother, he concentrates on how hopeful his doctor is and how early the cancer was detected. When Jim tells Rose, he focuses on his fears and vulnerability.

To assess your own willingness to self-disclose in various situations, use your online Resource Center for *Understanding Interpersonal Communication* to access *Interactive Activity 8.2: Self-Disclosure Assessment.*

Culture

Like all the behaviors we discuss in this text, self-disclosing behavior is moderated by cultural prescriptions and values. For example, Asian Indians' sense of appropriate self-disclosure differs from those of North Americans and Western Europeans. Asian Indians would be considered overly private by North American or Western standards (Hastings, 2000). Parents and children in Pakistan self-disclose to each other less often than parents and children who are native to the United States. Most Japanese also self-disclose less than North Americans, primarily because privacy is a Japanese cultural value. Most Asians believe that successful persons do not talk about or exhibit feelings and emotions, whereas most North Americans and Western Europeans believe that a willingness to disclose feelings is critical to relationship development.

Some researchers have observed that scholars, students, and teachers focus on self-disclosure because of a Western bias that favors openness over privacy and disclosure over withholding information. These researchers (Bochner, 1982; Martin & Nakayama, 2007; Parks, 1982) have criticized the cultural biases that cause Westerners to value disclosure more highly than privacy and secrecy.

Further, the level of self-disclosure of a culture relates to whether it is a high-context or low-context culture. As we discussed in Chapter 3, high-context cultures (such as China and Japan) derive meaning mainly from activity and overall context, not verbal explanation; the reverse is true in low-context cultures (such as the United States). Thus, explicit verbal disclosures are unnecessary in high-context cultures. For example, some research confirms that the Chinese value actions rather than talk in developing relationships (Chen, 1995; Martin & Nakayama, 2007).

Considering the above, it should come as no surprise that North Americans are seen as more disclosive than Asians, yet it is important to recognize that within the United States, different ethnic groups vary in their frequency of disclosure (Klopf, 1998). For instance, European Americans are generally more disclosive than Latinos.

Gender and Sex

Many people believe that gender or sex is a major factor in self-disclosing behaviors. Yet the research is inconclusive on this topic. Some research suggests that in general, in the United States, women seem to self-disclose more than men, and they value self-disclosures more (Ivy & Backlund, 2000; Wood, 2000). This was confirmed in research (Maccoby, 1998) showing that when female friends talked, they usually related emotional disclosures. One study found that even at a young age (second graders), girls talked easily with one another and shared personal stories (Tannen, 1990). Other research shows that men do express closeness through talking, just not as much as women do (Canary & Dindia, 1998). And some researchers have noticed that when the goal in a situation is clear (for example, developing a relationship or impressing a partner who has high status), men can disclose as much or more than women (Derlega, Winstead, Wong, & Hunter, 1985; Shaffer & Ogden, 1986).

Yet an analysis of 205 studies examining sex differences in self-disclosure (Dindia & Allen, 1992) found that the differences between women and men were rather small. And, more recent research (Mathews, Derlega, & Morrow, 2006) found no sex differences in self-disclosures.

Biological sex might not be as important to differences in self-disclosure as other issues such as gender role or the composition of the couple. In terms of gender role, men who are **androgynous** (that is, they embody both masculine and feminine traits) hold the perspective that self-disclosure characterizes close relationships (Jones & Dembo, 1989). Androgynous men desire friends

androgynous

Having both masculine and feminine traits.

© Jason Harris

The common stereotype holds that women disclose a great deal about themselves and men disclose very little. However, research shows that the differences between men and women's self-disclosures are not that dramatic. For example, although men tend to establish close relationships by doing things together more than women tend to, men can disclose as much or more than women do, particularly in certain situations, such as when they are establishing a relationship.

who want to share themselves through talk, and they want to do the same. With reference to sex-composition, male-male pairs seem to disclose the least and female-female pairs the most (Burleson, Holmstrom, & Gilstrap, 2005).

Because the way in which gender or sex influences self-disclosing behavior is complex and uncertain, you might be tempted to fall back on stereotypes depicting disclosing women and silent men. However, most of the research doesn't support such a conclusion. The overall differences between women and men as self-disclosers are relatively small, and they are more likely to be differences of degree rather than kind (Dindia, 2000).

To read an interesting article about how the fear of self-disclosure prevents some people from seeking psychological help, use your online Resource Center for *Understanding Interpersonal Communication* to access *Interactive Activity 8.3: Fear of Self-Disclosure*. And to examine the relationship between what we expect will happen when we disclose personal information and what actually happens, access *InfoTrac College Edition Exercise 8.1: Expected versus Actual Responses* to read the article "Expected versus Actual Responses to Disclosure in Relationships of HIV-Positive African American Adolescent Females."

Principles of Self-Disclosure

From our discussion so far, you should have a picture of the self-disclosure process and how it is affected by factors we've mentioned, such as relational issues, culture, and gender and sex. To focus this picture further, we now examine four principles, or norms, of self-disclosure.

Your turn

Keep a record of self-disclosures you make and receive for the next two weeks. At the end of that time, see if you can discern a pattern in the disclosures. If you like, you can use your student workbook or your **Understanding Interpersonal Communication** Online Resources to complete this activity.

We Disclose a Great Deal in Few Interactions

This principle suggests that if we examine our total communication behavior, self-disclosures are somewhat rare. Some researchers estimate that only approximately 2 percent of our communication can be called self-disclosure (Dindia, Fitzpatrick, & Kenny, 1997; Pearce & Sharp, 1973; Rosenfeld, 2000). We generally spend a lot more time in small talk than in the relatively dramatic behavior of self-disclosure.

For instance, think about a typical day some of you may have. Maybe you get up at 7 a.m. and mumble a morning greeting to those you live with as you hurry to get ready for your day. You may grab a fast-food breakfast at a drive-through and then go to your part-time job. At work, you may have to give guidance to and take instructions from a variety of people. You might spend a little bit of time complaining to your coworkers that you are tired and have a great deal to do. You may make some phone calls and place orders, type up a report, and file some paperwork. For lunch, you meet a friend, and the two of you chat about the movie you saw together last week and engage in some trivial gossip about another friend who might be getting divorced. You leave lunch to hurry over to campus to take two classes. You don't speak much in class because you are busy taking notes during the lectures. After the classes, you head over to the library to check out a book. You ask the reference librarian for some help finding a source you need. You stop at the store on the way home to pick up the ingredients for a quick dinner. You run into a friend at the grocery and exchange a few words before hurrying home. When you get home, you turn on the television and watch a game show while you put dinner together. Over dinner the TV remains on, then you clean up the dishes and watch the news. You fall into bed by midnight.

In that scenario of a typical day, you probably have not self-disclosed at all, even though you did talk to many people. The kinds of interactions in the day described were routine, phatic, or instrumental and did not involve sharing much personal information. However, on another day, you might call a friend and spend an hour talking about a problem that has been bothering you. This generalized example about self-disclosure indicates that we disclose a large amount in a few interactions. Most of our interactions are short, routine, and relatively impersonal. Only a few of our interactions are truly self-disclosive. Yet, because of the emotional impact self-disclosure has on us and on our relationships, we (and researchers) pay it more attention than some of our other communication behaviors, which actually take up more of our time.

Self-Disclosures Occur between Two People in a Close Relationship

Although it is possible for us to tell personal information to small groups of people (or even to large groups, like on television talk shows), generally self-disclosure occurs when only two people are present. Further, how much and how frequently we self-disclose depends in great part on the nature of our relationship with another person. Some research suggests that people disclose the most in relationships that are close (for example, in marital, cohabiting or family relationships, and close friendships). In a study examining why people tell family secrets, the researchers found that people had to think their relationships were secure to feel comfortable enough to self-disclose (Vangelisti, Caughlin, & Timmerman, 2001).

However, a principle is only true *most* of the time, and there are some exceptions to this generalization. The main exception is called "the bus rider phenomenon" or "strangers on a train" (Thibaut & Kelley, 1959). This notion refers to self-disclosures made to strangers rather than to close friends or

© Image 100/Royalty-Free/Corbis

On an everyday basis, we tend not to disclose too much about ourselves to total strangers. However, when we're traveling for a long period of time, we may be willing to disclose quite a bit to someone we've just met. Have you ever disclosed personal information to a stranger while traveling? Did you disclose things you wouldn't have mentioned if you had struck up a conversation with the same person while standing in line to register for classes?

relatives. The phenomenon derives its name from the fact that such self-disclosures may often occur on public transportation like buses, planes, or trains where two people are confined together for a period of time with not much to do but talk to each other. In such cases, the relationship between the people is temporary and transient rather than close and ongoing. We're sure that many of you have heard a stranger's life story while traveling across the country on public transportation, or perhaps you have shared personal information with strangers in this context.

Self-Disclosures Are Reciprocal

The essence of this principle is **reciprocity**, or the tendency to respond in kind. Most research suggests that the self-disclosures of one member of a pair will be reciprocated by self-disclosures by the other. The **dyadic effect** describes the tendency for us to return another's self-disclosure with one that matches it in level of intimacy. For example, if Leila tells her friend Victoria that she was raped when she was 18 by a guy she was dating, Victoria's reciprocal disclosure would have to be about something equally serious and intimate. The norm of reciprocity suggests that Victoria would be unlikely to respond by simply telling Leila that at one time she dated a basketball player.

Reciprocity is sometimes explained by noting that it keeps people in the relationship on an equal footing. If two people have reciprocated disclosures, they have equalized the rewards and the risks of disclosing. In addition, researchers observe that disclosure reciprocity may be governed by global conversational norms such as the requirement that a response has to be relevant to the comment that preceded it (Grice, 1975). Thus, when Leila tells Victoria her story about date rape, Victoria responds with a story about how she narrowly escaped date rape herself. In doing so, Victoria matches Leila's intimacy level and keeps the conversation on the same topic.

However, conversations involving self-disclosures do not always contain immediate responses of reciprocal self-disclosures like the one we just described between Leila and Victoria. Victoria doesn't have to reciprocate immediately; she may simply listen with empathy (see Chapter 5) while Leila tells her story. Instead of telling about her own experience after hearing about Leila's, Victoria might express concern, or encourage Leila to tell her more about what happened, how she feels about it now, and so forth. Research suggests that expressing concern for the speaker is actually a better response (because it makes a more favorable impression on the discloser) than responding with a matching self-disclosure (Berg & Archer, 1980).

Does this mean that the norm of reciprocity is wrong? Not exactly, according to some research (Dindia , 2000). People in close relationships don't have to engage in immediate reciprocity but they should reciprocate within the conversation at some point. In other words, Leila would be unhappy about the conversation (and maybe her relationship with Victoria) if Victoria never revealed anything personal about herself. But Victoria's self-disclosures don't have to come immediately after Leila's to satisfy the norm of reciprocity.

When people are just getting to know one another, the need for immediate reciprocity is strong (Derlega, Metts, Petronio, & Margulis, 1993). As relationships develop and mature, this need is relaxed, and reciprocal disclosures may no longer need to occur within the same conversation. In these cases, the participants simply trust that disclosures will equalize over the course of their relationship. For example, Sarah might simply listen to her sister, Miranda, as she discloses that she is about to divorce her husband, without disclosing anything to Miranda at all. But Sarah has disclosed a lot to Miranda in the past and will continue to do so in the future as needed.

Self-Disclosures Occur Over Time

Disclosures generally happen incrementally over time. We usually tell a low-level self-disclosure to a relationship partner first and then increase the intimacy level of our disclosures as time goes by and our relationship with that person continues and deepens. In our example of Leila and Victoria this principle suggests that Leila would make her disclosure about date rape after she had already disclosed other, lower-level personal information about herself (for example, that she had flunked calculus and sometimes doubted that she belonged at the university). This principle illustrates how relationship development and self-disclosure are intertwined. Self-disclosures change the relationship, and the nature of the self-disclosures changes as the relationship matures or deteriorates.

This principle also shows us that time affects the meaning of disclosure. For example, the first time Rafe tells his partner a piece of personal information, it may be a sign of their relational growth. However, after they have been together for many years, that same information may be seen as a part of the overall pattern of their relationship. In another example, when Bethany tells her boyfriend early in their relationship that she's afraid to assert herself around authority figures he might respond with empathy and support. He might even think it's sweet that Bethany needs him to help her be assertive. But, if Bethany and her boyfriend stay together, the same disclosure 20 years later could be heard as an indication that Bethany refuses to grow up and take any responsibility for herself. In this case the disclosure would not be met with empathy and support. Therefore, the function and meaning of disclosures vary within the context of time.

Next, we turn our attention to ways to explain self-disclosures.

Explaining Self-Disclosure

People have suggested many ways to picture the process of self-disclosure so that we can understand it more clearly. We discuss two theories in this

reciprocity

The tendency to respond in kind to another's self-disclosure.

dyadic effect

The tendency for us to return another's self-disclosure with one that matches it in level of intimacy.

section: dialectics and social penetration. We also introduce a model of the self, the Johari Window, and illustrate how it can help us understand self-disclosure.

Dialectics Theory

Dialectics theory explains relational life as full of push-pull tensions resulting from the desire for polar opposites. In this chapter, we discuss the tension between wanting to be open with our relational partners and the opposing desire of wanting to maintain our privacy. In Chapter 10, we discuss some other tensions that dialectics theorists say people experience in relationships.

Before we discuss dialectics specifically, we need to talk about the polar oppositions of openness and privacy. In early research on self-disclosure, theorists asserted that self-disclosures created our sense of self and contained the essence of being human. Sidney Jourard (1971) is probably the researcher who most influenced our positive response to self-disclosure. He suggested that we must engage in self-disclosure to be psychologically and physically healthy. His position came to be known as the "ideology of intimacy" (Bochner, 1982; Parks, 1982) because he believed disclosing to create intimacy with another was the most important thing a person could do.

More recently, people have rejected this idea in favor of emphasizing the benefits of privacy and even deception. Some researchers now contend that concealing information can have positive effects on relationships. For example, Leda Cooks (2000) writes about discovering that the man who had raised her was not her birth father. Her mother told her this secret when Cooks was 30, revealing that no other members of the family, not even the man Cooks considered her father, knew the truth. Cooks was dumbfounded, but she eventually decided to keep the secret, believing that in doing so she would preserve her relationship with her custodial father and, more importantly, with her brother, to whom family meant everything.

Dialectics tries to integrate these opposing positions. It explains how we wish to have conflicting, seemingly incompatible things (in this case, being known and staying private) at the same time and how we try to deal with the tensions raised by this conflict. Dialectic thinking assumes that we all want to have *both* privacy *and* the comfort that comes from being known by others, although these two things seem like polar opposites. We feel conflict over our desire to both "let it all out" to a friend or relative and to keep it in to avoid the risks inherent in telling. According to dialectics, the real core of relational life consists of "communicators seeking a variety of important, yet apparently incompatible goals" (Rosenfeld, 2000, p. 5). Dialectics theory says that to reduce the tension of this process, we use several coping strategies: cyclic alternation, segmentation, selection, and integration (Baxter, 1988).

- **Cyclic alternation** helps communicators handle tension by featuring the oppositions at alternating times. For instance, if Eileen discloses a great deal with her mother when she is in high school and then

cyclic alternation

A strategy for dealing with dialectic tensions in a relationship that allows us to choose opposite poles of the dialectic at different times.

segmentation

A strategy for dealing with dialectic tensions in a relationship that allows us to isolate separate arenas, such as work and home, for using each pole in the opposition.

keeps much more information private from her mother when she goes to college, she is engaging in cyclic alternation. By sometimes being open and other times keeping silent, cyclic alternation allows Eileen to satisfy both goals.

- **Segmentation** allows people to isolate separate arenas for using privacy and openness. For example, if Mac Thomas works in a business with his father, Joe, they may not disclose to one another at work but do so when they are together in a family setting.

- **Selection** means that you choose one of the opposites and ignore your need for the other. For instance, Rosie might decide that disclosing to her friend, Tina, isn't working. Tina fails to be empathic and has occasionally told something Rosie told her in confidence to another friend. Rosie can use selection and simply stop disclosing to Tina altogether, making their relationship less open but less stressful.

- **Integration** can take one of the following three forms:

  - **Neutralizing** involves compromising between the two oppositions. For instance, if Traci and her sister Reva have been arguing because Reva feels Traci is leaving her out of her life and not telling her anything. Traci might decide to use neutralizing with Reva. Traci would then disclose a moderate amount to her—maybe telling Reva a little less than Reva wants to hear but a little more than she would normally tell her. Neutralizing copes with the tension by creating a happy medium.

  - **Disqualifying** allows people to cope with tensions by exempting certain issues from the general pattern. Emily might make some topics, like her love life, off limits for disclosure with her mom but otherwise engage in a lot of self-disclosure with her. This coping strategy creates **taboo topics**, or issues that are out of bounds for discussion. Most relationships contain topics that are not talked about by unspoken mutual consent. Many families avoid discussing sex and money. Even couples who engage in the most intimate of sexual behavior may not talk about sex to each

selection

A strategy for dealing with dialectic tensions in a relationship that allows us to choose one of the opposite poles of a dialectic and ignore our need for the other.

integration

A strategy for dealing with the dialectic tension in a relationship that allows us to synthesize the opposites. Integration can take three forms: neutralizing, disqualifying, and reframing.

neutralizing

A strategy for coping with dialectic tensions in a relationship that allows us to strike a compromise between the two opposing poles of a dialectic.

disqualifying

A strategy for coping with dialectic tensions in a relationship by exempting certain topics from discussion.

taboo topics

Issues that are out of bounds for discussion.

other. Another example of a taboo topic might be a family member's alcoholism.

- Reframing refers to rethinking the notion of opposition. In doing so, people redefine the dialectic. For instance, couples may say that they actually feel closer to each other if they don't tell each other everything. Reframing is illustrated in a couple's belief that if they keep some secrets, that makes what they do tell more significant.

Social Penetration

The **social penetration model** (Altman & Taylor, 1973) says that people, like onions, have many layers. A person's layers correspond to all the information about them ranging from the most obvious to the most personal. For example, when two strangers meet, some information—like sex, approximate height and weight, and hair color—is easily observable. This information makes up the outer layer. Other information—like gender (masculinity, femininity, androgyny), how a person feels about his or her height and weight, and whether his or her hair color is natural or dyed—is less accessible; conversation is necessary to "peel" these layers of the onion. Through interaction, people may choose to reveal these deeper layers of themselves to one another and, in so doing, perhaps deepen their relationship.

The social penetration model pictures all the topics of information about a person—such as their interests, likes, dislikes, fears, religious beliefs, and so forth—along the perimeter of an onion that has been sliced in half (see Figure 8.2). We can have a relationship with a casual friend where the only topics we discuss are at the surface layer of the onion. For example, Bette may know that her friend, Zach, is interested in communication, likes cats, doesn't like jazz, is afraid of snakes, loves to travel, has four brothers, and is a member of the Catholic church. Zach knows Bette loves to dance, is a business major, has a sister and two brothers, wants a dog, went to Spain a year ago, had an internship last semester, and can't carry a tune.

In this example, Betty and Zach's relationship has a fair degree of **breadth** (that is, they both know information about the other across several differ-

social penetration model

A model of self-disclosure and relational development that illustrates how sharing increasingly more personal information intensifies a relationship's intimacy level.

breadth

A dimension of self-disclosure that indicates the number of topics discussed within a relationship.

REVISITING
CASEINPOINT

1. *Before Roberta tells Philip about Carl, what strategy for coping with dialectic tension is she using?*

2. *After Roberta tells Philip about Carl, what strategy for coping with dialectic tension is she using?*

Y*ou can answer these questions online under Student Resources for Chapter 8 at the* Understanding Interpersonal Communication *website.*

Figure 8.2 The social penetration model

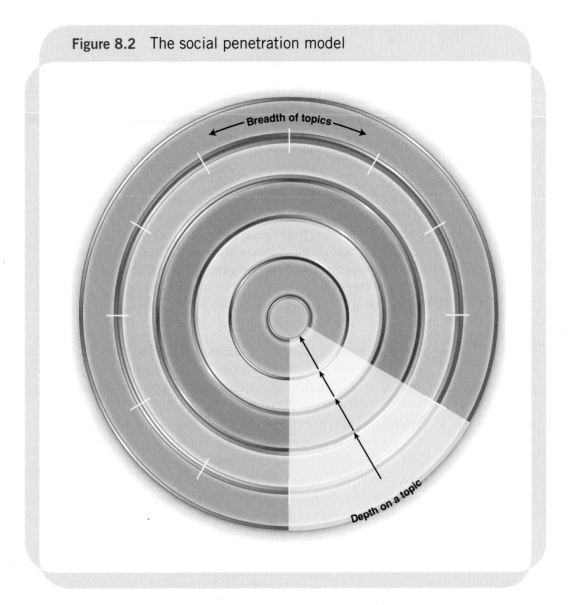

ent topics) but not much depth. **Depth** occurs when they tell each other how they feel about the topics—for example, that Zach's experiencing a crisis in his Catholic faith or that Bette is much closer to her youngest brother than anyone else in her family. Some relationships have a great deal of breadth without depth, and vice versa. Other relationships have a great deal of both; for example, an extremely close friend or partner would probably know a lot about us in a variety of areas. And yet other relationships involve not much of either, as when a distant relative knows only a few things about us not in much depth. The degree to which you self-disclose controls the social penetration described by the model. Using Figure 8.2 as an example, you could draw a separate diagram for each of your friends and relatives to determine how much depth and breadth you have in each relationship.

depth

A dimension of self-disclosure indicating how much detail we provide about a specific topic.

The Johari Window

The Johari Window is a model used to examine the self-disclosure process. Although "Johari" sounds like a term that comes from a mystical language, it is simply a combination of the first names of its creators, Joseph Luft and Harry Ingham (Luft, 1970). Luft and Ingham were interested in the self, and the model they created can help us understand more than just self-disclosure (for example, it can be used as a tool for self-awareness). For our purposes here, we examine how the window can be applied to the self-disclosure process.

The **Johari Window** provides a pictorial representation of how "known" you are to yourself and others. As Figure 8.3 illustrates, the model is a square with four panels. The entire, large square represents your self as a whole. It contains everything that there is to know about you. The square is divided by two axes: one representing what you know about yourself and one representing what you have revealed about yourself to others. The axes split the window into four panes: the open self, the hidden self, the blind self, and the unknown self.

- The **open self** includes all the information about you that you know and that you have shared with others through disclosures. Whenever you tell someone a piece of information about yourself (for example, your opinion or your concerns), the open self increases.

- The **hidden self** contains the information that you are aware of but that you have chosen not to disclose. When you decide that it is too soon to tell your friend that you feel like a bit of an outsider at school, that information remains in the hidden self.

- The **blind self** encompasses information that others know about you although you yourself are unaware of this information. For example, if you have a tendency to twist the rings on your fingers or chew gum loudly when you are nervous, others watching you know this, but you aren't conscious of your habit.

- The **unknown self** consists of the information that neither you nor others are aware of about you. Neither you nor any of your friends or family might know that you have a capacity for heroism. If you're never tested, that information might remain forever in the unknown self. Luft and Ingham believed that there is always something about each person that remains a mystery. So, there are always things about you to learn and discover.

In Figure 8.3, all the quadrants are the same size, but the Johari Window is a person-specific model, meaning that we need to draw a different window for each person with whom we interact. For instance, your Johari Window for you and your mother will differ from your Johari Window for you and your professor. Also, the sizes of the panes can change as your relationships evolve. For example, after you disclose something personal to a professor, in redraw-

Johari Window

A model used to understand the process of self-disclosure consisting of a square with four panels that provides a pictorial representation of how "known" we are to ourselves and others.

open self

In the Johari Window, the pane that includes all the information about us that we know and that we have shared with others through disclosures.

hidden self

In the Johari Window, the pane that includes the information about ourselves we are aware of but that we have chosen not to disclose.

blind self

In the Johari Window, the pane that includes information others know about us that we are unaware of.

unknown self

In the Johari Window, the pane that includes the information that neither we nor others are aware of about ourselves.

Figure 8.3   The Johari Window

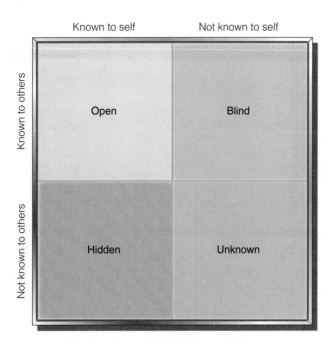

ing the window of your relationship with that professor, your open self panel will increase and your hidden self panel will decrease. See Figure 8.4 on page 276 for an illustration.

The Johari Window helps us understand self-disclosure in many ways. First, self-disclosures emanate from the parts of the self that are known to us: the hidden self and the open self. Second, self-disclosures regulate the relative sizes of the open and the hidden selves. As we choose to disclose, the open self becomes larger, and the hidden self becomes smaller; when we decide to withhold disclosures, we achieve the opposite result. Third, as others provide us with feedback, we learn more about ourselves, the blind self decreases, our ability to self-disclose (should we choose to do so) increases. Finally, as we have new experiences and learn more about ourselves, the unknown self decreases, and we have more available information that we may choose to disclose to others. To explore some uses of the Johari Window in professional contexts, use your online Resource Center for *Understanding Interpersonal Communication* to access *Interactive Activity 8.4: The Johari Window in a Professional Setting* and *InfoTrac College Edition Exercise 8.2: Pruning the Grapevine.*

Now that we understand more about self-disclosure, we will examine why people choose to self-disclose to their relational partners.

Figure 8.4 The Johari Window after self-disclosure

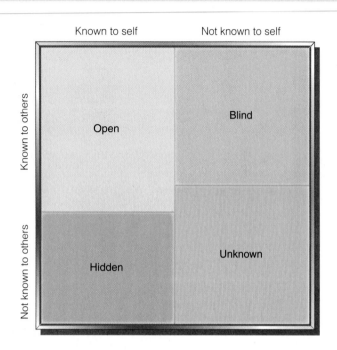

Reasons to Self-Disclose

Several specific motivations encourage people to take the risk and reveal themselves to another. Some of the reasons represent factors specific to an individual, whereas others relate to the relationship between people. Table 8.2 presents these motivations, and this section briefly discusses each of them.

To Experience Catharsis and Improve Psychological Health and Control

One reason psychologists are so interested in the concept of self-disclosure is probably because individuals experience **catharsis**, or a therapeutic release of tensions and negative emotion, through disclosing (Omarzu, 2000). In general, engaging in self-disclosure is seen as a method for helping individuals achieve psychological health. For example, some research suggests that although gay and lesbian adolescents find coming out to their parents difficult, doing so offers those adolescents many psychological benefits (Waldner & Magruder, 1999).

catharsis

A therapeutic release of tensions and negative emotion as a result of self-disclosing.

Table 8.2   Reasons to self-disclose

Individual Reasons	Relational Reasons
• To achieve catharsis (therapeutic release of tensions) and to maintain psychological health and control • To maintain physical health • To attain self-awareness	• To initiate a relationship • To maintain or enhance a relationship • To satisfy expectations for a close relationship • To achieve relational escalation (can be manipulative)

The adage "A trouble shared is a trouble halved" expresses the common wisdom that self-disclosing about troubles provides some relief from those troubles. In one study that tested that assumption, 243 Chinese workers in Hong Kong filled out questionnaires about occupational stress and disclosing

© AP/Wide World Photos

*The notion that self-disclosure can lead to catharsis and can improve psychological health is so captivating that we often see portrayals of therapists and their patients in movies and on television. Examples include **Good Will Hunting, Running with Scissors, Girl Interrupted, The Sixth Sense, The Sopranos,** and, of course, virtually any Woody Allen movie. In **The Sixth Sense,** we see a troubled young Cole famously reveal, "I see dead people." Interestingly, in this movie Cole's revelation brings about not only his own catharsis, but also that of his therapist Malcolm.*

to a best friend (Hamid, 2000). The researcher found that disclosing to a best friend did reduce the workers' perception of occupational stress. Sometimes the achievement of catharsis or a sense of control over an unpredictable situation can lead to inappropriate self-disclosures. Tamara Afifi and her colleagues (2007) investigated this type of disclosing behavior by examining parents who disclose information about their divorce to their children. The researchers found that parents who felt out of control and stressed tended to engage in more inappropriate disclosures. When parents felt that their partners had not treated them well in the divorce and that they weren't getting what they wanted, they tended to confide in their children even though they knew it wasn't healthy for them.

To Improve Physical Health

Evidence supports the belief that self-disclosure provides physical as well as psychological benefits for disclosers. In a 1959 article in the *Journal of Mental Hygiene,* Sidney Jourard stated that self-disclosure promotes physical health and that failure to disclose may cause ill health. This was a controversial position in 1959, and few others followed up on Jourard's thesis. Yet, it is a viable argument today because a great deal of evidence supports the relationship between self-disclosing and physical health (Tardy, 2000).

For example, a study of Holocaust survivors found that people who disclosed the most about their experiences showed better physical health than those who concealed more (Pennebaker, Barger, & Tiebout, 1989). Other researchers conducted a nine-year study of gay men with HIV positive status (Cole, Kemeny, Taylor, Visscher, & Fahey, 1996). They found that men who concealed their sexual identity and their health issues had more deterioration in their immune systems, a quicker onset of AIDS, and lived a shorter time with AIDS than did men who self-disclosed. In addition, a large body of research supports the contention that disclosing has a positive impact on blood pressure levels and resistance to cardiovascular disease (for example, see Tardy, 2000).

An episode of the old sitcom *Spin City* illustrated this benefit in a humorous fashion. When one character accidentally found out that two of his coworkers were having an affair, they told him he could not tell anyone else. He begged to be able to disclose this secret, but they refused permission. As he struggled to keep this information private, he broke out in hives. Throughout the show, his hives spread until he was completely covered. Then his nose began bleeding profusely. Unable to withstand all this physical trauma, he blurted out the secret to all the other coworkers and immediately his nose stopped bleeding and his hives completely disappeared!

To explore self-disclosure from the point of view of the medical professional rather than the patient, read the article "How Medical Students View Their Relationships with Patients," available through InfoTrac College Edition. Use your online Resource Center for *Understanding Interpersonal Communication* to access *InfoTrac College Edition Exercise 8.3: The Private and Public Selves of Medical Students.*

To Achieve Self-Awareness

Self-disclosures provide us with the means to become more self-aware. We are able to clarify our self-concepts by the feedback we receive from others when we disclose and by the process of hearing ourselves disclose. For example, when Kara discloses to her sister, Martha, that she feels stupid for not learning how to swim till she was an adult, Martha responds by praising Kara for having the courage to tackle a new skill later in life. Martha tells Kara that she is really proud of her and feels that she is setting a good example for their children that it's never too late to learn. Kara is pleased to hear her sister's comments. As she reflects on them, she realizes that persisting with swimming lessons was worthwhile, even though it was more difficult to learn at age 35 than it would have been at age 5. After talking to Martha and thinking about their conversation, Kara feels really good about herself.

In another example, when George discloses to his friend Julia that he is thinking about quitting his job and starting his own business, he surprises himself. Although he had been feeling discontented with work, until he hears himself tell Julia that he wants to start his own business, he hadn't really been sure of this. When he puts that thought into words for Julia, he begins to clarify his feelings for himself. This process is pictured in the Johari Window, which we described earlier; as we listen to ourselves disclose and receive feedback, we increase the side of the window that is known to us.

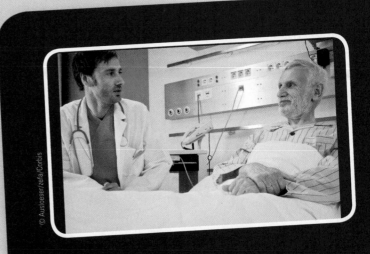

© Ausloeser/zefa/Corbis

IPC in the News

An article in *USA Today* discusses a study examining self-disclosures made by physicians during patient visits. The co-author of the study commented that he thought that self-disclosing to his patients would strengthen his connection with them. For instance, he would tell his older patients about his elderly mother, who was struggling with health issues. However, he found that when he disclosed this information, his patients became distracted, worried about his mother, and possibly even doubtful of his abilities as a doctor because he couldn't help his own parent. The study confirmed that self-disclosures from doctors to patients are inappropriate, noting that "empathy, understanding and compassion work better than self-disclosure" (p. 9D).

Rubin, R. (2007, June 26). Doctors often shift focus from their patients to themselves. *USA Today*, p. 9D.

To Initiate a Relationship

As we discussed previously, disclosers are prompted to tell private information as a way of developing a new relationship with someone who seems interesting. One study (Vittengl & Holt, 2000) supports the idea that self-disclosures help develop new relationships: "Self-disclosure within get-acquainted conversations is accompanied by liking or feelings of social

Self-disclosure is an integral part of initiating a relationship. When we want to get to know someone better, we often also want them to know us better, so we disclose information that we might not disclose to just a casual acquaintance.

attraction to conversational partners and by an increase in positive emotions" (p. 63). Here it is important to remember that "social attraction" includes friends, partners, coworkers, and so forth, not simply romantic and/or sexual attraction.

To illustrate these findings, let's examine the case of Anita and Zoe. Anita is a working single mother attending the local community college part time and holding down a part-time job as an administrative assistant at a law firm. Because she's so busy, she hasn't made many friends at school or work. One day when she is rushing to finish a project at the firm, she bumps into Zoe. Anita had met Zoe, who is also a single mother, during her orientation. Zoe works full time at the law firm and mentors new employees.

When they met, Anita had thought that it would be nice to get to know Zoe, but she just hadn't had the time. When they bump into each other, Anita is worrying about her son, Brad, who has been getting into fights at school. Zoe says "hi" in a friendly way and asks if Anita would like to have coffee later. Although Anita really doesn't have the time, she says yes and is surprised when, over coffee, she finds herself telling Zoe some of her concerns about Brad. Zoe listens with empathy and then responds that her son had some behavior problems when he was Brad's age, too, and that she, like Anita, had worried that her work schedule might have been partly to blame. Zoe mentions that she and her son had benefited from some counseling sessions with the school psychologist. When Zoe and Anita part, they both think they have begun a friendship.

To Maintain Existing Relationships

Existing relationships also benefit from self-disclosures. In an interesting study examining why people tell others about their dreams, researchers found that 100 percent of their participants attributed their disclosures to some type of relational goal (Ijams & Miller, 2000). People said they told a relational partner about a dream to enhance closeness, warmth, and trust. The authors quote one of their respondents, who explained why revealing dreams was important:

> "My brother and I have a good sibling relationship. We tell each other everything that goes on in our dreams. Each time we reveal something, the bond between us strengthens. It seems melodramatic, but there is a strong bond between us." (p. 141).

To Satisfy Expectations of What Constitutes a Good Relationship

As we mentioned earlier, the ideology of intimacy dictates that we should be completely open and self-disclosive with people in intimate relationships. If we fail to do so or if we consciously keep secrets from intimate others, we often believe that our relationships are flawed or not as good as we want them to be. Self-disclosing allows us to see our relationships in a positive light.

As an example, in the study referred to in the previous subsection (Ijams and Miller's, 2000), some study participants said they told a partner about their dream because the partner was already close to them, and the participants' expectation was that in a close relationship people tell each other everything, including their dreams. As one of their respondents stated: "'He knows everything about me. I love him and trust him and pretty much share everything with him'" (p. 141).

To Escalate a Relationship

As previously mentioned, self-disclosing provides a way to get to know someone and to allow that person to know you. This process escalates a relationship, often moving it from one stage to another. Casual acquaintances may become close friends after they spend some time telling each other personal information about themselves. For example, when Laurie tells her friend, Javier, that she used to suffer from bulimia and that she still worries every day that she might slip back into her old binge-and-purge habits, Javier feels honored that Laurie trusts him with this information. Her self-disclosure makes him feel closer to her and advances their relationship to a more intense level.

However, as we discussed elsewhere in the text, communication can be used for dark purposes as well as positive goals. Indeed, self-disclosures can be used to manipulate a relational partner. For example, a person can offer a self-disclosure that could be considered history (or inauthentic) to manipulate a relational partner, through the norm of reciprocity, into revealing something truly personal. In this manner, the relationship may escalate faster than it would have otherwise, which might be the devious objective of the first discloser. Or, one person may say "I love you" early in a relationship simply to advance the intimacy of the relationship.

Reasons Not to Self-Disclose

Although opening up to another person provides benefits, there are also compelling reasons to keep our secrets to ourselves. The dialectics model we discussed earlier argues that in any relationship, both desires are extremely important. We want to be open with our partners, but at the same time, we want to maintain our secrets. Although ethical questions arise when we keep something that is critically important from someone else, most of the time, maintaining privacy is ethical. We need to remember that it's our choice as to whether we disclose or not.

Some of the reasons people choose to be silent rather than to disclose are outlined in Table 8.3 and discussed in this section. As you read the examples, think about the ethical implications of choosing to keep silent.

To Avoid Hurt and Rejection

Perhaps the most common reason for keeping a secret is because we believe that the person we reveal it to may use the information to hurt us or may reject us when they know our inner selves. For example, Mick doesn't tell his friend, Marci, that he served time in a juvenile detention center for possession of drugs because he fears that she will be angry, respect him less, or bring it up in a taunting way in an argument. All of these negative outcomes are reasons for keeping a secret private.

If we share a really critical piece of information, even with a sympathetic friend, we have given this friend some potential power over us, and we can't

---

Table 8.3 Reasons to avoid self-disclosure

- To avoid hurt, rejection, or both
- To avoid conflict, protect a relationship, or both
- To keep one's image intact, maintain individuality, or both
- To reduce or forget about stress

be absolutely sure that our friend would never use this power against us or in a way that we would not like. When Audra confides in Allen that she thinks she's a lesbian, she figures he's a trustworthy confidante because he is a long-time friend who is gay himself. However, she doesn't realize Allen feels strongly that being homosexual is nothing to hide. Allen tells several mutual friends about Audra's disclosure. Although Audra doesn't believe that being a lesbian is shameful, she wasn't ready to tell their friends yet; she was still getting used to the idea herself. She was extremely hurt by what she saw as Allen's betrayal.

To Avoid Conflict and Protect a Relationship

Some secrecy may actually be helpful in a relationship. For example, Lois thinks she doesn't need to tell her friend, Raymond, that she voted Republican in the last election. Lois knows Raymond is a staunch Democrat and she believes the disclosure would cause a conflict that could harm their relationship.

As another example, Marsha does not like her brother's wife. When Marsha chooses not to tell this to her brother, Hal, she figures that her silence keeps the relationship between them more peaceful. Because Marsha knows that Hal is happy with his wife, it seems irrelevant to reveal that she isn't.

"You never tell me anything. Keep up the good work."

This secret does not affect their relationship much, because they live in different cities separated by thousands of miles, and Marsha and Hal keep in touch mainly by email and phone.

As discussed previously, culture influences people's views of self-disclosures and whether they help or harm a relationship. A study of Chinese business people (Hamid, 2000) found that disclosing to one's mother was negative for the relationship because it increased feelings of stress in both parties.

Finally, some research indicates that if you disclose to someone who responds in a negative fashion, you are likely to feel badly about the interaction, the other person, and about your relationship with the other person (Afifi & Guerreo, 2000; Roloff & Ifert, 2000). Some people may believe disclosing isn't worth that risk.

To Keep Your Image Intact and Maintain Individuality

Some people withhold self-disclosures because they're concerned that if they begin disclosing, they will lose control and be unable to stop. Further, these people fear that disclosures will bring with them unrestrained emotionality, perhaps causing them to cry uncontrollably. In a related vein, some people worry that self-disclosing will cause them to lose their sense of mystery and individuality. For instance, Caitlin may fear that if Nolan knows all about her, she won't seem interesting to him any longer. And Gary's fear is that if he tells his friend Lyle all about himself, Gary may become so much a part of this friendship that he'll disappear as a separate individual.

Further, if someone has established a particular role in a relationship, they may fear changing that role and their image. For example, Lucy and Rebecca have been friends for five years. In their relationship, Rebecca often turns to Lucy, who has been married for 15 years, for advice when she has problems with a boyfriend. When Lucy and her husband fight, she doesn't feel comfortable confiding in Rebecca because it seems to negate her identity as a happily married person who gives support but doesn't need to ask for it.

To Reduce Stress

In the previous section, we mentioned that people often engage in self-disclosures to reduce stress. Although this is frequently the case, some evidence indicates that self-disclosures can sometimes increase stress. For instance, Valerian Derlega and his colleagues (1993) give the following example:

> Bill, 20, and Mark, 21, are juniors at a state university. They are flying together to Florida for spring break. Bill is uncomfortable about flying, and he tells Mark about being nervous. Mark, in turn, describes an unpleasant experience when, on another flight, his plane had mechanical problems. As the plane takes off, neither of

them is feeling very good. Somehow, talking about their fears made
them feel worse rather than better. (p. 103)

Similarly, Anita Vangelisti and her colleagues (2001) observe that continuing
to think and talk about stressful issues can result in more stress. They note
that stress is reduced only when the disclosures begin to reflect a positive
outlook.

To explore the possible consequences of choosing not to reveal personal
information, read the article "The High Costs of Hidden Conditions," available through InfoTrac College Edition. Use your online Resource Center for
Understanding Interpersonal Communication to access *InfoTrac College Edition
Exercise 8.4: The Cost of Choosing Not to Disclose.*

Choices for Effective Disclosing

Although we may have good reasons for keeping silent at times, we need to
refine our self-disclosing skills for those times when we wish open up. In this
section, we outline important techniques for building our self-disclosing skills.

Use I-Statements

Owning, or the use of I-statements, which we've discussed in previous chapters, is the most basic verbal skill for self-disclosing. Saying "I think," "I feel,"
"I need," or "I believe" indicates that you accept that what you're saying is
your own perception, based on your own experiences, and affected by your
value system. When you self-disclose using owning, you take responsibility
for your feelings and experiences. In addition, your listener realizes that you
are speaking for yourself and not trying to make a generalization. Let's take a
look at an example of an owned self-disclosure. Edward tells Mike, "I don't
know if I will really be happy going to college in New York. It's so far away
from my family—I know I'll be homesick." This is different from Edward
stating, "It's important to stay near home for college. It's not good to put too
much distance between family members." When Edward uses the latter
phrasing, he doesn't own his feelings; instead, he presents them as a general
rule that all people should consider when deciding where to go to college.

Be Honest

Honesty in self-disclosure refers to being both clear and accurate. If you are too
ambiguous and unclear, your self-disclosures may not be "heard" as real disclosure. Yet, if you and your partner know each other very well, you may be able
to offer disclosures more indirectly (Petronio, 1991). For instance, if you know
your partner is struggling with several deadlines at work, you will be able to
hear a disclosure in your partner's sarcastic comment: "I had a great day at

.....at work

At work, self-disclosures can be difficult and may sometimes seem inappropriate. After all, self-disclosure is about sharing personal information, and the workplace is a public arena. But at times some type of self-disclosure is called for. For instance, let's say that your coworker Tanya asks your opinion about a report she needs to turn in next week. If you think that Tanya can improve the report significantly, you should use specific language to let her know the ways in which you feel it can be strengthened. You don't need to be unkind, but you do need to tell her exactly what you believe the report lacks. If you are not clear, Tanya may leave your conversation not knowing if she needs to change the report or not. Can you identify other instances where self-disclosure might be needed in the workplace?

... with your sister at a vacation hotel

It's spring break, and you and your sister, Ellen, have taken your first vacation together as adults. You're both in graduate school now and are discovering how much you enjoy each other's company. You've just come in from the pool and are sitting on the deck reminiscing about family vacations in the past. Ellen mentions a trip the family took to Florida when she was eight and you were ten. You feel a little chill because you've never told Ellen that you were the one who was responsible for her losing her prized stuffed dog on that trip. The family spent hours looking for Toto, and Ellen sobbed for a whole day when they finally gave up looking for it. You had seen it sitting on the restaurant bench when the family left after a lunch stop, but you were mad at Ellen at the time and didn't bother to let her know she was leaving it behind. Now you wonder—should you tell Ellen this story? Would she be furious or think it was funny? What factors of self-disclosure will influence your decision to tell or not?

work today. What a pleasure palace that job is!" Generally speaking however, you need to be clear and accurate in your disclosures. If you are dishonest or inaccurate while disclosing, you are defeating the purpose of self-disclosure.

Be Consistent with Your Verbal and Nonverbal Communication

Consistency means that your nonverbal communication should reinforce, not contradict, your verbal communication. For example, if Shannon tells Josie that she's really upset about her grades this semester, but she smiles while saying it, Josie may be confused about whether Shannon is upset or not.

Focus Your Nonverbal Communication

Try to focus your nonverbal communication on the issue at hand and provide nonverbal cues that add meaning rather than ones that distract from your message. For instance, if Mia continually taps her pencil against a table while telling her mother that she wants to quit school, her mother may be distracted by the gesture and have trouble concentrating on Mia's disclosure.

Be Sure Your Content Is Relevant

Relevancy to the context refers to an assessment of the appropriateness of the disclosure to the situation itself. For example, if Ron is at a company picnic, he may decide that it isn't the time or place to tell his boss that he is unhappy at work and wants more responsibility. In this chapter's opening Case in Point, Roberta tried to make a good context for her disclosure. She prepared a nice dinner to set the stage for telling Philip her secret.

Be Sure Your Topic Is Relevant

Relevancy to the topic means that you are able to weave your disclosure naturally into the conversation. When Jeff and Noel go out bowling together for the first time, they begin talking about their involvement in sports in the past. The situation and the topic seem to invite Jeff to tell Noel that he is insecure about his athletic abilities. If Jeff and Noel were at a restaurant talking about a movie they had both recently seen, the topic wouldn't have been so inviting for Jeff's disclosure.

Estimate the Risks and Benefits

To be competent in self-disclosure, you need to be able to estimate and balance its risks and benefits. As mentioned previously, there are compelling reasons to reveal and to withhold disclosures, many of which pertain to issues of self-identity. To be effective at self-disclosing, you need to practice judging when the benefits outweigh the risks, and vice versa.

Predict How Your Partner Will Respond

Your ability to decode messages of warmth, concern, and empathy on the part of the other person will help

interpersonal explorer

Before you finish reading this chapter, take a moment to review the theories and skills discussed. How do you think the theories discussed in this chapter can help you better understand interpersonal communication and self-disclosure? In what ways can the skills discussed help you interact more effectively with other people in your life?

Theories that relate to self-disclosure

- **Dialectics**
  Relationships are permeated with contradictory impulses like the impulse to share personal information with another and the impulse to keep the information to oneself
- **Social penetration theory**
  Getting to know someone is a process of penetrating the layers of information that make up a self. This proceeds through self-disclosures.

Practical skills for effective self-disclosure

- Use I-statements
- Be honest and clear
- Use consistent verbal and nonverbal communication
- Focus your nonverbal cues
- Be sure the context is relevant
- Be sure the topic is relevant
- Estimate the risks and benefits
- Predict how your partner will respond
- Match the disclosure to your relationship's level of intimacy
- Estimate the effect of the disclosure on your relationship

Explore your interpersonal choices

Are you ready to explore your interpersonal choices regarding self-disclosure? Use your online Resource Center for *Understanding Interpersonal Communication* to access an interactive simulation that allows you to view the beginning of an interpersonal scenario regarding self-disclosure, make a choice about how the people in the scenario should proceed with their interaction, consider the consequences of your choice, and then see three possible outcomes to the interaction.

you make judgments about when to tell and when to be silent. For instance, in this chapter's opening Case in Point, Roberta knew that Philip was a sympathetic listener. Therefore, although Roberta felt some fear about revealing such a serious disclosure, she felt that Philip was ready to hear her confession.

*"You just self-deprecated
yourself right out of a job."*

Be Sure the Amount and Type of Disclosure Are Appropriate

Although as we've said before there are a few exceptions to this rule, the amount and type of disclosure should match the perceived intimacy level of the relationship. Thus, on a first date, it may be unwise to tell all your insecurities and past indiscretions. Further, early in your relational life, you and your partner should share talk time. You don't want to dominate the conversation with long self-revelations. You should attempt to pace your disclosures so that they roughly match the developing intimacy of your relationship.

Estimate the Effect of the Disclosure on Your Relationship

Think about how the disclosure might affect the relationship. For example, Jake asks himself if telling Rochelle about his growing interest in her will actually cause the end of their friendship. Jane considers whether telling Marc about her trouble with commitment in the past will hurt or intensify their relationship. Of course, you can never know for sure what effect a disclosure will have, but making well-founded assessments of effects is an important skill to develop.

To read an interesting article that likens disclosure to a dance of veils and offers suggestions for making disclosure easier, check out "The Art of Self-Disclosure," available through InfoTrac College Edition. Use your online Resource Center for *Understanding Interpersonal Communication* to access *InfoTrac College Edition Exercise 8.5: Disclosure as a Dance of Veils*.

Summary

Self-disclosure is a complex, well-researched communication process. We define it as verbal communication that intentionally reveals personal information about our selves that our listener would be unlikely to discover without being told. This means that self-disclosing is a choice we make; we always have the option of not telling.

We generally choose to disclose in the context of a close, trusting relationship because self-disclosure is scary and implies risk. Not everyone self-discloses in the same way or at the same rate. Our disclosures are affected by individual differences, relational factors, cultural values, and gender and sex. We wish to emphasize that our knowledge of and attitude toward self-disclosure is heavily influenced by cultural norms; for example, in the United States, the culture favors openness over secrecy.

One norm of self-disclosures is that we disclose a great deal in a few interactions; only about 2 percent of our communication time is involved in this activity. Another principle is that self-disclosures occur between two people in a close relationship; however, exceptions to this rule include self-disclosing in public forums (such as on a TV talk show) or to a stranger while traveling ("the bus rider phenomenon"). Another guideline self-disclosures follow is that they are reciprocal; the dyadic effect describes the tendency for us to return another's self-disclosure with one that matches it in level of intimacy. Lastly, self-disclosures occur in the context of time—that is, self-disclosures get more intimate as a relationship progresses, and time affects the meaning of disclosure.

One way we can understand the process of self-disclosing is through the notion of social penetration. This theory pictures relational development as a gradual, incremental process facilitated by self-disclosures (like peeling back layers of an onion). We can also get a handle on self-disclosure from a dialectics perspective. This approach encourages us to see self-disclosure as a way to regulate our conflicting desires for privacy and openness in our relationships. Finally, the Johari Window provides information about self-disclosure by showing how the four panes of the window (the open self, the hidden self, the blind self, and the unknown self) shrink or expand as we disclose and get feedback.

People have both individual and relational reasons for disclosing to others. Reasons that provide primarily individual benefits include catharsis, psychological health, physical health, and self-awareness. Reasons involving relational life encompass developing a new relationship, maintaining a relationship, fulfilling the expectations for what should happen within a relationship, and exerting control over a relationship.

Reasons for not engaging in self-disclosure include avoiding hurt and rejection, avoiding conflict and protecting a relationship, keeping our image intact and maintaining our individuality, and thinking more about an issue. Dialectic thinking shows us that we are constantly doing a balancing act in our relationships related to providing and withholding information.

Understanding self-disclosure contributes to an understanding of interpersonal communication. To engage in skillful self-disclosure, you need to learn how to use I-statements, and you must be honest and consistent with your verbal and nonverbal communication. Remember to focus your nonverbal communication, and be sure your content and topic are relevant. Practice estimating the risks and benefits of self-disclosure and predicting how your partner will respond. Be sure the amount and type of disclosure are appropriate, and try to estimate the effect of the disclosure on your relationship.

Understanding Interpersonal Communication Online

Now that you've read Chapter 8, use your online Resource Center for *Understanding Interpersonal Communication* for quick access to the electronic study resources that accompany this text. Your online Resource Center gives you access to the video of Roberta and Philip's interaction on pages 253–254, the Ethics & Choice interactive activity on page 260, the Communication Assessment Test on page 261, the Your Turn journal activity on page 266, the Interpersonal Explorer activity on page 287, Info-Trac College Edition, and study aids including a digital glossary, review quizzes, and the chapter activities.

Terms for Review

androgynous 265	history 259	selection 271
blind self 274	integration 271	self-disclosure 255
breadth 272	Johari Window 274	social penetration model 272
catharsis 276	neutralizing 271	story 259
cyclic alternation 270	open self 274	taboo topics 271
depth 273	private information 256	topical intimacy 259
disqualifying 271	public information 256	unknown self 274
dyadic effect 268	reciprocity 268	
hidden self 274	segmentation 271	

Questions for Understanding

Comprehension Focus

1. Define self-disclosure and elaborate on each of the important elements in the definition.

2. Define public information and private information and give an example illustrating each.

3. Distinguish between history and story.

4. Describe the three patterns of self-disclosure.

5. List the four principles of self-disclosure.

Application Focus

1. CASE IN POINT Specifically, how does Roberta's disclosure fit our definition of self-disclosure? Use each of the attributes of the definition and show how Roberta's comments illustrate (or don't illustrate) the definition.

2. Do you agree with the criterion that self-disclosure has to be verbal? How important to the definition of self-disclosure is this assertion? Make a case for or against including nonverbal behaviors in the definition. Provide examples to strengthen your case.

3. What are some important cultural issues to consider when thinking about self-disclosure? Why do you think people in the United States, Western Europe, and other Western countries are so interested in a communication behavior that people may engage in for only 2 percent of their total communication time?

4. What are some of the factors that you think about before you tell someone something personal about yourself? How do your factors compare to the ones discussed in this chapter?

5. Which model of self-disclosure (social penetration, dialectics, or the Johari Window) do you think best explains the self-disclosure process? Defend your position and provide examples. How can the three models work together to help us understand the process?

Interactive Activities and InfoTrac College Edition Exercises

Interactive Activities

InfoTrac College Edition Exercises

Chapter 9
Communicating Conflict

chapter ✚ goals

Understand the complexities of conflict

Explain common myths about conflict

Detail communication patterns in conflict

Describe two theories of interpersonal conflict

Identify the relationship between power and conflict

Employ skills for communicating power and conflict that afford increased satisfaction in interpersonal interactions

CASEINPOINT

TAMARA WILEY AND JEFF HARRIS

Tamara Wiley glanced in the mirror before leaving her apartment and heading to her 8 a.m. class. She was having a bad hair day, so she had thrown on a scarf. Her quick check in the mirror told her the scarf covered most of the problem. After class she was supposed to meet her best friend, Jeff Harris, for coffee, but she was hoping he'd understand if she canceled because she was way behind on her physics assignment. On her way to class, she called and left Jeff a voice mail.

Meanwhile, Jeff was having a bad morning. He'd been late with a project at his part time job and his boss was not pleased. Jeff was really looking forward to seeing Tamara for coffee because she understood him and could cheer him out of his depression. When Jeff got to the coffee shop, he scanned the room for Tamara but didn't see her. He bought a latte for each of them and settled into an overstuffed chair to wait for her. When Tamara's latte got cold, Jeff started to get anxious. He called her apartment but there was no answer.

Jeff waited for another hour and finally left in disgust. Not only had he wasted a lot of time waiting, he missed talking to Tamara, so now he was feeling even worse than he had earlier. Later that evening when he finally reached her on the phone, he spoke rather harshly, asking her where the hell she'd been when she was supposed to meet him. Tamara was startled by his tone and replied rather coolly, "I left you a message that I had to do an assignment and couldn't make it to the coffee shop." Jeff became angrier, saying, "I didn't pick up my messages and you know I hate voice mail, Tamara. If you'd really wanted to let me know, you should have stopped by and just told me. I guess our relationship means more to me than it does to you!" Tamara raised her voice, too. "Hold on, Jeffrey," she said. "You are making a huge deal out of nothing. I just couldn't make it for coffee. Get over it and don't make something out of nothing." Jeff's voice grew cold: "Call me when you want to get together sometime—at your convenience, of course." Jeff slammed down the phone. Tamara was left holding the receiver, listening to the dial tone, and wondering what had just happened.

Use your online Resource Center for *Understanding Interpersonal Communication* to watch a video clip of Tamara and Jeff.

> Access the resources for Chapter 9 and select "Tamara" to watch the video (it takes a minute for the video to load). As you watch the video, consider how Tamara and Jeff could have handled their conflict more effectively. > You can respond to this and other analysis questions, and then click "Done" to compare your answers with those provided by the authors.

*E*ven though most people think conflict is unpleasant and even nasty (Turner & Shuter, 2004), it's impossible to be in a relationship without sometimes experiencing conflict. It's an unavoidable part of relational life. One researcher estimated that even couples in happy, stable relationships engage in conflict twice a week on average (Lloyd, 1987). Some relationships have many conflicts and others have fewer, but if you are involved in a close relationship, you're bound to eventually engage in conflict.

Conflicts are common in relationships because we're all unique individuals, and conflicts occur around differences between people. Not all differences cause conflict, however. Sometimes, people recognize differences between them that do not matter. For example, let's say that Patrice likes Ludacris and her cousin Melissa hates him. If Patrice and Melissa don't live together, don't go to concerts together, and don't talk about music when they see each other, this difference will probably not precipitate conflict.

Often, though, differences do cause friction. For instance, in our opening story, Jeff and Tamara perceive their differences on that particular day as a dilemma. Jeff really wants to talk to Tamara and is hurt and troubled when she doesn't seem to reciprocate. Tamara is angered and puzzled by Jeff's reaction to a missed meeting—a response that she feels is different from how she would behave if roles were reversed. In this scenario, we see that their differences challenge Jeff and Tamara, and conflict results.

When people first meet, they usually focus on their similarities, thus reducing opportunities for conflict. Part of the fun of getting to know someone is discovering things you have in common. However, later in the relationship, you may notice and discuss differences. For example, even though Jeff and Tamara have known each other for a while, this occasion was their first opportunity to see how they differ in their commitment to keeping appointments. Think back to the first time you met someone you later became good friends with or dated. Your early encounters with this person probably had fewer conflicts than your later interactions.

In some relationships, people notice differences relatively quickly because the nature of the relationship implies differing interests, concerns, and bases of power. For example, in a relationship between a worker, Carlos, and his boss, Manuel, the job titles indicate that despite the fact that they work for the same company, they'll have divergent perspectives. Manuel's job dictates that he's responsible for maximizing productivity and minimizing expense. This goal may run counter to Carlos's needs and desires. Further, the power relationship between the two is not symmetrical. Manuel has the power to punish or reward Carlos in ways that aren't reciprocal. These inherent differences make boss-worker friendships or romances tricky (although not impossible) to negotiate. Parent-child and teacher-student are other types of relationships where intrinsic differences between the roles played offer ripe arenas for difference and, thus, conflict. Some people suggest that relationships between people of different cultures and relationships between men

© Billy E. Barnes/PhotoEdit

Throughout our lives, the nature of many of our relationships implies differing interests, concerns, and bases of power. As such, conflict is inevitable. Learning how to handle conflict in a constructive way is one of the tricks to cultivating healthy interpersonal relationships.

and women maximize difference and provide opportunities for more conflicts than do relationships between more similar people.

In short, experiencing conflict in your relationships is inevitable. What is not preordained is how you and your partner deal with the normal conflicts of relational life. You have some control in this crucial arena and can implement skills that will influence how the conflict proceeds and affects your relationship. Before we learn how to manage conflict, we'll define the term and explain what constitutes interpersonal conflict.

Defining Conflict

We've all experienced conflict, but often it comes as a surprise, as it was for Tamara in our opening example. Like Tamara, we're left scratching our heads, wondering what happened. Knowing what conflict is all about won't stop you from experiencing discord, but it's the first step in helping you manage it better. Later in the chapter, we present specific ways to manage conflict.

Interpersonal conflict is commonly defined as "the interaction of interdependent people who perceive incompatible goals and interference from each other in achieving those goals" (Folger, Poole, & Stutman, 2001, p. 5). Several key parts of this definition, discussed in the following subsections, help us understand the meaning of conflict.

Interaction

Here, **interaction** means that conflicts are created and sustained through verbal and nonverbal communication (Canary, Cupach, & Serpe, 2001; Roloff,

interpersonal conflict

The interaction of interdependent people who perceive incompatible goals and interference from each other in achieving those goals.

interaction

A necessary condition for conflict, given that conflicts are created and sustained through verbal and nonverbal communication.

1987). Some conflicts involve yelling, crying, swearing, and screaming. Other conflicts consist of icy silences, cold shoulders, frowns, and withdrawal. However, regardless of the behaviors, remember that the definition specifies that conflict is interaction *between* people. In other words, if Cate talks to Jim like she always does, even though internally she's angry with him, they aren't in conflict by our definition. They enter into conflict only when she says or does something that shows how she feels.

Because this text is focused on explaining interpersonal communication, we emphasize the expression of conflict through verbal and nonverbal cues. However, this focus doesn't mean that we are not interested in the thoughts people have during conflicts. Our emphasis is on how thoughts influence talk; interaction is in the foreground, and cognition is in the background, but they work together, each affecting the other.

One study (Sillars, Roberts, Leonard, & Dun, 2000) examined the relationship between thoughts and communication behaviors in marital conflict. The researchers asked 118 married couples to discuss a current issue that caused conflict for them and then to watch videotapes of their discussion. The researchers noted that thought and talk go together. They said: "To appreciate the subtlety and complexity of communication in conflict, it is helpful to consider what people are thinking as they interact" (pp. 480–481).

The study found that in severe conflicts especially, husbands and wives tended to construct individual accounts that didn't agree with each other. Thus, as wives watched the tapes and recalled what they were thinking, they generated a very different picture from their husbands. The researchers comment that selective perception is a central dynamic in conflict interactions; people thought different things and attributed different motives to one another as they watched their tapes.

Interdependence

Interdependence means that the people involved in the conflict are in a relationship together and rely on one another. Parties must feel some degree of interdependence to experience conflict. If you have no relationship with a person, that person isn't important enough to you for conflict to exist. For example, let's say that Louise meets Justin at a party. Justin doesn't interest Louise much, and Louise finds herself disagreeing with his loudly stated political views. Louise decides to talk to someone else and politely excuses herself. On the other hand, if Louise and Justin are dating they may find their different political opinions lead to conflict.

Interdependence brings up one of the striking ironies of conflict. Although people's need for others is a basic, fundamental human desire, people rank conflicts with others one of the most critical stressors they experience. As one researcher observes, "it is ironic that the same relationships that people seek so eagerly are the source of many, perhaps most, of their greatest frustrations and unhappiness" (Kowalski, 2001, p. 297). Our connection to others provides us both pleasure and pain, both the joy of merger and the conflict surrounding differentiation.

interdependence

A necessary condition for conflict, given that people involved in conflict rely on each other, need each other, and are in a relationship with each other.

For example, when Marty thinks of his happiest moments, he usually thinks of the times he has spent with his best friend, Ray. However, Marty's unhappiest time was also associated with Ray. Ray had thought that Marty was flirting with Ray's girlfriend, and Ray had been furious, not speaking to Marty for a week, even when they were at basketball practice and classes together. Marty had felt a lot of pain because he'd thought that their friendship was over. Finally, Ray realized that Marty wasn't really guilty, and they were able to resume their friendship. Marty found it surprising that being around the same friend could sometimes be so much fun and other times feel like torture.

Interdependence is the main reason that conflict is a natural and inevitable part of life. The more we rely on another, the more potential there is for observing differences and being affected by them (Lulofs & Cahn, 2000).

Perception

Perception, as we discussed in Chapter 2, refers to the psychological process involved in sensing meaning. The definition of conflict states that for conflict to exist, the interdependent people have to *perceive* that they have incompatible goals. For example, Carmen wants to go on a family vacation to Florida. She misunderstands a statement that her husband, Dave, makes and jumps to the conclusion that he disagrees with the vacation destination. Even though Carmen and Dave really agree on where to take their vacation, if Carmen believes they disagree, they will come into conflict. This type of conflict persists until the parties come to understand that their goals really are similar.

Some researchers emphasize the importance of perception to the conflict process when they apply a competence model to interpersonal conflict. Competency suggests that people judge themselves and their conversational partners based on how well they communicate and how successful they are in reaching their conversational goals (Spitzberg & Cupach, 1984, 1989). When applying this model to conflict, one study (Canary et al., 2001) found that people's perceptions of competency during the conflict directly affected the relationship. For instance, if Josie and Melissa have an argument about cleaning the apartment, and each perceives that both of them are competent in their conflict, they will be more satisfied and happier with one another than they would be if they'd had the exact same conflict but thought they'd behaved less competently. Therefore, researchers argue that perception of communication competence is an extremely important dimension of interpersonal conflict.

Incompatible Goals

The definition of conflict specifies that friction results when people's goals differ (as in "I want to study, but Jorge wants me to go to a party with him") at the same time that they think others stand in the way of the achievement of personal goals (as in "I want to get promoted at work, but my supervisor wants me to stay in her department"). This feature of the definition implies that conflict is goal oriented—for instance, two cousins, Karla and Meredith, are roommates. One Sunday, Karla wants to go to the ocean and her cousin wants to stay home and have a barbeque. Because Karla's goal isn't compatible with what Meredith wants, they will engage in conflict (Lakey & Canary, 2001) if they are dependent on one another to accomplish their goals. For instance, if Karla needs Meredith to drive her to the ocean and Meredith needs Karla to start the barbeque, they are interdependent and have incompatible goals, which will likely cause conflict between them.

Your turn

Note and evaluate the times you engage in interpersonal conflict during a week. If you like, you can use your student workbook or your **Understanding Interpersonal Communication** Online Resources to complete this activity.

Types of Conflict

Now that we have defined conflict, we can further our understanding by learning about various types of conflict. Understanding these different types helps us gain a better sense of conflict communication.

Image Conflicts

Image conflicts concern self-presentation. For example, if Enid considers herself a competent adult, she may engage in conflict when her mother offers her suggestions about how to manage her career. Enid may feel that her mother isn't respecting her as an adult and, as such, is challenging Enid's image of herself. This type of conflict is especially difficult when two different images are in fact in play. For instance, if Enid's mother does still view Enid as a child, they do have two competing images. A similar problem can exist when a parent pushes a child to grow up faster than the child feels comfortable. In that case, the parent views the child as an adult, whereas the child may still see herself or himself as a child. Sometimes, image conflicts may masquerade as another type of conflict, but at the core of an image conflict is a disagreement about self-definition.

Content Conflicts

Content conflicts are often called "substantive" because they revolve around an issue. Interdependent people fight about myriad topics. Maeve calls her Internet provider to complain about the service, and the service provider tells her there is no evidence to support her complaint. Nanette likes a tree on her

image conflict

A conflict with another about one's sense of oneself.

content conflict

A conflict that revolves around an issue. Also called a substantive conflict.

SIPRESS

"Well, if it doesn't matter who's right and who's wrong, why don't I be right and you be wrong?"

property line, but her neighbor thinks its roots are responsible for cracking his driveway. Matt hates to bowl, and his best friend loves bowling. Ginna wants to spend some savings on a vacation, and her husband, Sean, thinks that would be a waste of money. Penny thinks that the data for her work group's presentation should be rechecked, and the other members of the group think they've been checked sufficiently. Marcus believes that even though he works part time, he should be respected as a member of the company and allowed a say in company policies; however, the full-time workers don't want the part-timers involved in those matters. Although all of these examples involve topics of disagreement, some of these content conflicts have undertones of the other types of conflicts within them. As we discuss the subsequent types, we'll point out this overlap.

Content conflicts can be subdivided (Johnson, 2002; Johnson, Becker, Wigley, Haigh, & Craig, 2007). Some content conflicts focus on **public issues**, or issues outside the relationship. Other content conflicts involve **personal issues** and relate more closely to the relationship. For instance, when Stan and Frank disagree about whether Bill Clinton was a great president, they are debating a public issue. When Stan complains that Frank has no time to hang out with him anymore because he is always spending time with his new girlfriend, they are tackling a private issue. Not surprisingly, research finds that people enjoy arguments about public issues more than conflicts about private issues.

public issue

An issue outside a relationship that can cause a content conflict.

personal issue

An issue related to a relationship that can cause a content conflict.

© David Young-Wolff/PhotoEdit

IPC *in the* News

Siblings engage in some measure of conflict throughout their lives, but according to a recent USA Today/ABC News/ Gallup Poll, 30 percent of siblings said that assisting aging parents significantly stressed their sibling relationships. Siblings have varied approaches to splitting up caregiving responsibilities for aging or ailing parents, and each can lead conflict to be manifest in different ways. For example, some siblings mentioned in the article resolved their conflict through a cooperative effort to care for a parent, while negotiations between other siblings deteriorated to caretaking arrangements where one sibling strains to care for a parent while the other sibling drops out of the situation altogether. The article indicates that for many siblings, the level of conflict present when caring for an aging parent mirrors the conflict siblings had when they all lived under the same roof. Conflict is learned and reinforced through the lifetime of a relationship, and practicing healthy conflict habits now could reduce stressful sibling conflict in later life.

Grossman, C. (2008, February 1). Navigating sibling relationships when caring for a parent can be difficult. *USA Today*.

value conflict

A conflict in which the content is specifically about a question of right and wrong.

Value Conflicts

Value conflicts are content conflicts in which the content is specifically a question of right and wrong. The neighbors who are arguing about the tree on their property line may be having a values conflict if they are discussing it in terms of ecosystems and environmental protection. When people disagree about war in Iraq, abortion, or capital punishment, they may be engaging in value conflicts because opinions on these topics largely depend on value judgments made by the participants. For example, arguments about capital punishment often hinge on the value placed on human life and the value placed on punishment and retribution.

Relational Conflicts

Relational conflicts focus on issues concerning the relationship between two people. For example, when Marge argues with Perry, telling him that the way he speaks to her makes her feel disrespected, they are engaging in relational conflict. Couples who argue about how much they should tell their in-laws and how much they should keep private also exemplify relational conflict. In a previous example, Ginna and Sean's fight about whether to spend savings on a vacation would be a relational conflict if it centers on how they make decisions in their relationship. The disagreement would be a values conflict if it underscores a difference in how the two value money.

To read short dialogues that illustrate four of the types of conflict, see Table 9.1. In addition, Figure 9.1 on page 302 presents a dialogue and a picture that show how these conflict types overlap. Even though the types cannot be completely separated, being able to identify what kind of conflict you're having is useful in helping you decide how to manage it.

Table 9.1 Types of conflict

Image conflict	
MARILYN:	Mom, why do you still treat me like a child although I am 22 years old?
MOM:	Marilyn, you are always going to be my little girl.
MARILYN:	That's ridiculous, Mom. You have to let me grow up.

Content conflict	
FRED:	Jeff, I don't think that New York has the largest population of any state in the United States. I am sure I read that it was California.
JEFF:	No, it's New York.
FRED:	Well, we can look it up.

Value conflict	
AMY:	Travis, I can't believe we're so close to getting married, and I am just finding out that you don't want to have kids! To me, that's what marriage is all about.
TRAVIS:	Are you kidding, Amy? I certainly don't believe that marriage is all about having kids. What about love, companionship, and fun? Aren't those the things that marriage is all about?

Relational conflict	
ANGELA:	Marlee, I know this sounds funny to bring up, but I am feeling kind of left out when you and I are together with Justine. You and I used to be best friends, and now it seems like you don't even want to be around me if you have the chance to hang out with Justine.
MARLEE:	That's not exactly true, Angela.
ANGELA:	It sure feels that way to me.
MARLEE:	Maybe I have been spending a lot of time with Justine, but that's just because we have the same major and are in a lot of classes together.

Serial Conflicts

Serial conflict differs from the other four types because it doesn't refer to the subject of the conflict. Instead, it refers to a time frame for the conflict. Up to this point, we've been talking about conflicts as discrete episodes, with specific starting points ("I'm so sick of you using up all the hot water every morning") and specific ending points ("OK, I'll take a quicker shower"). **Serial conflicts** are those that recur over time in people's everyday lives, without a resolution ("Last week you said you take a quicker shower, but you aren't doing that. It's the same thing over and over." "Well, you're always on my back! Leave me alone about the stupid shower."). Researchers (Bevan et al., 2007; Malis & Roloff, 2006) find that these serial conflicts tell us a lot about relational communication. In relationships with a long history (like dating, marriage or

relational conflict

A conflict that focuses on issues concerning the relationship between two people.

serial conflicts

Conflicts that recur over time in people's everyday lives, without a resolution.

Figure 9.1 Overlap in types of conflicts

Conflict Dialogue

Andre: "I am so happy George W. Bush won the 2004 election. He is strong where Kerry would have been weak on terrorism. And besides, he's a born-again Christian, so I know he has good values."

Michael: "Wow, Andre, I thought I knew you and now I am blown away that I knew you so little. Bush is a horrible person who supported the death penalty in Texas and got us into an immoral war. That's hardly good values! I am not sure I can be friends with someone who holds your views."

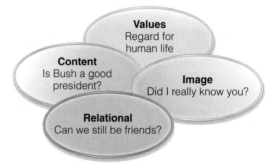

Values
Regard for human life

Content
Is Bush a good president?

Image
Did I really know you?

Relational
Can we still be friends?

REVISITING
CASE in POINT

1. *How would you type the conflict Tamara and Jeff had about the missed coffee date? Is it an image, content, value, relational, or serial conflict? Or is it some combination? Does it have elements of meta-conflict?*

2. *How does typing this conflict help in managing it?*

You can answer these questions *online under the resources for Chapter 9 at your online Resource Center for Under-standing Interpersonal Commu-nication.*

families) partners are likely to have unsettled issues that come up repeatedly whether they want them to or not.

Serial conflicts may also lead to **meta-conflicts**, which are conflicts about the way you conduct conflict! If Jennifer and Dominic argue about something repeatedly, they may also reflect on their conflict process. When Jennifer tells Dominic she hates it when he interrupts her and Dominic replies that he wouldn't do that if she'd get to the point, they are engaging in meta-conflict. Meta-conflicts can happen at any time but they are especially likely during serial conflict.

To read an interesting article about the different styles people use in communicating about conflict, use your online Resource Center for *Understanding Interpersonal Communication* to access *Interactive Activity 9.1: Conflict Styles*.

Myths about Conflict and Communication

As we've stated previously, conflict is a normal part of relational life, but many people find it unpleasant. As a result, people talk a great deal about conflict, which generates myths about it. We'll discuss the very common (but mistaken) beliefs that conflict is just miscommunication, all conflict can be resolved through good communication, and it is always best to talk through conflicts.

Many people believe that all conflict results from miscommunication or unclear communication. However, sometimes people communicate clearly to each other and, they disagree. For instance, if Jim wants to go to Harvard, and his parents tell him they do not want him to go to school so far away from home, Jim and his parents may continue to argue about this topic even though they know exactly what each other's positions are. The problem in this case is not that they haven't been clear; rather, they disagree about whose goal is more important and, possibly, who has the power in their relationship to make such a decision.

The corollary to the myth of miscommunication is the notion that all conflicts can be resolved through good communication. This myth tells us that if we master a certain set of skills for managing conflict, we can resolve all of our conflicts. Although we offer a set of skills later in this chapter, we recognize that some conflicts persist, and partners may have to agree to disagree. For example, no amount of good communication practices will convince Harry to vote Democratic even though his son, Michael, tries to persuade him that the Democrats advocate better policies than the Republicans do. Harry simply states that he has voted Republican his whole life and he is proud to continue to do so.

meta-conflict

A conflict about the way a conflict is conducted.

Communication Assessment Test

Argumentativeness Scale

Argumentativeness may be thought of as contributing to the negative aspects of conflict, but research by Dominic Infante and Andrew Rancer (1982) suggests that this is not always the case. They define argumentativeness as a willingness to argue for your point of view on significant issues. Infante and Rancer distinguish between argumentativeness and verbal aggressiveness, a more negative trait, by saying that whereas argumentativeness focuses on ideas, verbal aggressiveness focuses on winning an argument, even if it means verbally attacking the other person. You can take the following test online. Go to your online Resource Center for *Understanding Interpersonal Communication* and look under the resources for Chapter 9.

Directions:

This questionnaire contains statements about arguing about controversial issues. Indicate whether a statement describes you according to the following scale:

almost never true = 1   rarely true = 2   occasionally true = 3   often true = 4   almost always true = 5

_____ 1. While in an argument, I worry that the person I am arguing with will form a negative impression of me.

_____ 2. Arguing over controversial issues improves my intelligence.

_____ 3. I enjoy avoiding arguments.

_____ 4. I am energetic and enthusiastic when I argue.

_____ 5. After I finish an argument, I promise myself that I will not get into another.

_____ 6. Arguing with a person creates more problems for me than it solves.

_____ 7. I have a pleasant, good feeling when I win a point in an argument.

_____ 8. When I finish arguing with someone, I feel nervous and upset.

_____ 9. I enjoy a good argument over a controversial issue.

_____ 10. I get an unpleasant feeling when I realize I am about to get into an argument.

_____ 11. I enjoy defending my point of view on an issue.

_____ 12. I am happy when I keep an argument from happening.

_____ 13. I do not like to miss the opportunity to argue a controversial issue.

_____ 14. I prefer being with people who rarely disagree with me.

_____ 15. I consider an argument an exciting intellectual challenge.

_____ 16. I find myself unable to think of effective points during an argument.

_____ 17. I feel refreshed and satisfied after an argument on a controversial issue.

_____ 18. I have the ability to do well in an argument.

_____ 19. I try to avoid getting into arguments.

_____ 20. I feel excitement when I expect that a conversation I am in is leading to an argument.

Scoring

1. Add your scores for questions 2, 4, 7, 9, 11, 13, 15, 17, 18, and 20. These questions represent your willingness to engage in arguments.

2. Add 60 to this total.

3. Add your scores for questions 1, 3, 5, 6, 8, 10, 12, 14, 16, and 19. These questions represent your tendency to avoid arguments. Subtract this total from the total you obtained in the first two steps. This number represents your argumentativeness score.

(Continues)

Use the following guidelines for interpreting your score:

73–100 High argumentativeness
56–72 Moderate argumentativeness
20–55 Low argumentativeness

Remember, moderation is probably the most skillful position. Does the score you received seem to reflect how you operate in discussions of controversial issues? If your score is not in the moderate category, what do you think you can do to compensate for the problems you might face in conflict?

From D. A. Infante and A. S. Rancer, "A conceptualization and measure of argumentativeness," *Journal of Personality Assessment* 46: 72–80, 1982. Reprinted by permission.

Underlying these two myths is the idea that it's always best to talk about conflicts.

Relational partners often believe that they simply need to communicate more to reach a mutually satisfying solution to their conflicts. However, many scholars believe that this myth obscures the benefits of avoiding certain topics rather than talking about them in great detail (see for example, Baxter & Wilmot, 1985; Guerrero & Afifi, 1995; Petronio, 2002). Sometimes continuing to talk about a point of disagreement just exaggerates and prolongs the problem. Some arguments are not that important and if you ignore them, they really will go away. For instance, when Mel broke the rain gauge in their backyard, Tina was angry. However, because she realized that it was just a $10.00 item and that getting into a big discussion about it wouldn't be productive for their relationship, she didn't say anything.

Although we acknowledge that many people subscribe to these myths about conflict, they are not accurate. Not all conflicts are based on misunderstandings, are resolvable, or are best dealt with by talking. Remember that communication is an important part of managing interpersonal conflict, but conflict management isn't just about communicating well.

Factors Influencing Interpersonal Conflict

In this section, we briefly discuss two factors that affect conflict interaction: gender and sex, and culture. Although we review them separately, these variables most often act in concert to affect conflicts. For example, a German American man and a Chinese American woman who work together in a small software company may have a disagreement over how to invest their limited research and development budget. In this case, there are cultural forces and gendered messages interacting to influence their conflict. All conflicts take place between people who are gendered and who come from a specific cultural background.

Gender and Sex

As we discussed in Chapter 2, when we talk about gender, we are referring to gender socialization. Men and women are not inherently different in their orientations to conflict or in their conflict behaviors; rather, they have been taught a set of responsibilities and norms that affect their conflict interactions. Further, not all men or all women are socialized to the same degree (Bem, 1993). Thus, we see great variety in how women and men enact gendered social norms.

Because women are taught to be keepers of relational life and men are socialized to pay attention to public life (Sullivan & Turner, 1996), women often want to talk about relationship issues, and men do not. This imbalance may cause conflict within relationships. For example, when Moira tells Jack that she wants to talk about their relationship, Jack may perceive her statement as an indication that their relationship is in trouble and, as a result, try to avoid the problem. Moira may not have intended to imply that she wanted to discuss a specific problem; she just wanted to connect with Jack about the topic of their life together.

Some research suggests that women are more collaborative and men are more competitive in conflict interactions. However, recent studies call this generalization into question. A relatively recent study examining college students found that women were more likely than men to report that they used both cooperative and competitive conflict strategies (Rudawsky, Lundgren, & Grasha, 1999). Another study (Messman & Mikesell, 2000) found that women and men in romantic relationships did not differ in their use of competition as a conflict strategy.

One study (Shuter & Turner, 1997) found that European American women as a group were evaluated by African American women and by themselves as highly conflict avoidant. However, when the researchers asked individual women from both groups to talk about their own approaches to conflict, the responses did not differ significantly. The study concluded that people are affected by stereotypes when asked to talk about a group, but that they see themselves as not necessarily representative of the group to which they belong.

Some evidence does point to more enduring differences between women and men in conflict. For instance, Levenson and Gottman (1985) showed that men and women react differently to the stress of relational conflict. Whereas women seemed to be able to tolerate high levels of the physiological arousal found in conflict with a partner, men were more bothered by this arousal and sought to avoid it. In a more recent test of that conclusion, a study conducted in Belgium (Buysse, De Clercq, Verhofstadt, Heene, Roeyers, & Van Oost, 2000) found that men desired to avoid marital conflict more than women.

For more about gender and conflict, check out the study "Gender-Related Effects in Emotional Responding to Resolved and Unresolved Interpersonal Conflict," available through InfoTrac College Edition. Use your online

Resource Center for *Understanding Interpersonal Communication* to access
InfoTrac College Edition Exercise 9.1: Gender and Conflict.

Culture

As we have discussed many times throughout this text, we live in a world of increasing diversity. Differing cultural practices and norms may put us in conflict with one another. In the twenty-first century,

> direct contact with culturally different people in our neighbor-
> hoods, schools, and workplaces is an inescapable part of life. With
> immigrants and minority group members representing nearly 30%
> of the present workforce in the United States, an understanding of
> competent conflict management is especially critical in today's
> society. (Ting-Toomey & Oetzel, 2001, pp. 1–2)

All humans wish to be respected and shown approval, but the ways in which respect and approval are expressed often differ from culture to culture. Even the meaning of the word *conflict* may differ across cultures. For instance, for the French the term means warlike opposition. The negative connotations of conflict are extremely strong for the French. Further, for the Chinese, the

Ethics & Choice

When Daryl Mills left home to attend Metro College, she felt uncertain and afraid. Although everyone probably has some trepidation about leaving home and starting college, Daryl's fears were compounded by the fact that she had pink hair, two nose rings (as well as various other piercings), and several large tattoos. She hoped people at college would be more accepting of her than her classmates at Fairhurst High School had been. A lot of people in high school had whispered behind her back, and she could still feel the sting of hearing "freak" every time she passed by a group of kids.

She was hoping that there would be people like her at Metro, but after a few weeks there, Daryl was feeling nostalgic for high school. Metro College was five times as bad as Fairhurst High had been. At Fairhurst kids had whispered about her, but here they yelled right in her face. Daryl actually feared for her safety because the verbal abuse was so bad, and the threat of violence was clear. The teachers turned away when they saw the students menacing her, and Daryl felt she had nowhere to go for help. Finally, she decided to call home and talk to her mother.

Daryl told her mother there was no way she could continue at Metro—she was too scared. Just walking around campus put her in a panic, and she always had to be in "survival mode." Daryl's mother was sympathetic, but she counseled Daryl that she had to learn to get along with people who were more conservative in their dress and looks. Her mother told her, "You have to be tough and be able to withstand other people's disapproval if you choose to be different from the mainstream."

What do you see as the ethical implications of this story? What ethical responsibilities did Daryl, her mother, the students, teachers, and administrators at Metro College have? What do you think Daryl should do? In answering this question, what ethical system of communication informs your decision (categorical imperative, utilitarianism, ethic of care, golden mean, significant choice)?

Go to your online Resource Center for *Understanding Interpersonal Communication* to access an interactive version of this scenario under the resources for Chapter 9. The interactive version of this scenario allows you to choose an appropriate response to this dilemma and then see what consequences your choice brings about. You can also compare your answers to the questions at the end of the scenario to those provided by the authors and, if requested, email your response to your instructor.

meaning of the word *conflict* involves intense struggle and fighting. Not surprisingly, the Chinese do not like conflict, which they consider disruptive to the harmoniousness of interpersonal relationships.

Although those in the United States may not enjoy conflict either, they define the word more broadly than the French or the Chinese do, allowing for more possible responses to the interaction itself. The Spanish word for conflict doesn't have so many negative connotations, and many Hispanic cultures consider conflict an interesting exercise, allowing for dramatic flair that is enjoyable (Ting-Toomey & Oetzel, 2001).

Although the value of harmony still predominates in Chinese culture, conflict style differences exist within the culture. One study (Zhang, 2007) found that modern-day Chinese families seem to endorse conversation in conflict rather than simple conformity to preserve harmony. It may be the case that the Chinese are being influenced by Western values and losing some of their traditional approaches to conflict.

Culture affects our conduct of interpersonal conflict in myriad ways. A person whose primary orientation is toward individualism might conflict with a person whose primary orientation is toward collectivism because of their different values. An individualistic orientation leads to a concern with one's own image (self-face), whereas a collectivistic orientation leads to a concern for the other person's image (other-face). The individualist wishes to resolve a conflict so that the solution is equitable or fair. The collectivist wishes to resolve a conflict so that the solution benefits the community. The two people will have opposing communication behaviors (for example, competition vs. avoidance) during conflict, probably leading to an escalation of conflict and misunderstanding.

Some research examines conflict in interracial couples beginning with the premise that their racial differences will be the catalyst for more conflict than same race couples experience. Two studies (Troy, Lewis-Smith, & Laurenceau, 2006) found that this was not the case. In fact, partners in interracial relationships reported higher relational satisfaction than same race couples. There was no difference in the conflict patterns they reported.

To read an article about a study that compared the emotional responses of European American and Chinese American dating couples involved in interpersonal conflict, check out the study "Cultural Influences on Emotional Responding," available through InfoTrac College Edition. Use your online Resource Center for *Understanding Interpersonal Communication* to access *InfoTrac College Edition Exercise 9.2: Culture and Conflict.*

Communication Patterns in Conflict

Relational partners often notice that their communication behaviors form repeating patterns (Turk & Monahan, 1999). Although these patterns are sometimes negative and the participants wish to break out of them, they generally find it difficult to do so. Other times, the patterns are more productive. In this section, we review three negative and one positive conflict pattern.

Symmetrical Escalation

Symmetrical escalation exists when each partner chooses to increase the intensity of the conflict. When Mike yells at Sally and she yells back at him, they begin the symmetrical escalation pattern. If Mike then advances on Sally with a menacing look, she might slap his face. Each partner matches the other's escalating fight behaviors. Sometimes this pattern is called "fight-fight" (Knapp & Vangelisti, 2005).

Obviously, this pattern cannot go on indefinitely. Because the amount of escalation that is possible is limited and because the intensity in the conflict is negative, this pattern is a futile one for communicators.

Symmetrical Withdrawal

Symmetrical withdrawal means that when conflict occurs, neither partner is willing to confront the other. Thus, one person's move away is reciprocated by the other's move away. For example, if Jolene stops speaking to Marianne because she feels she did all the work for their joint presentation in Organizational Communication, and Marianne responds in kind, they both withdraw from their relationship. This pattern, like symmetrical escalation, spells the end of the relationship if it's carried to its logical conclusion. If both partners move away from each other when conflict happens, they will soon be so far apart that they will have difficulty reuniting.

symmetrical escalation
In a conflict, each party choosing to increase the intensity of the conflict.

symmetrical withdrawal
In a conflict, neither partner being willing to confront the other.

The pursuit-withdrawal and withdrawal-pursuit patterns are quite common, yet they are extremely unsatisfying for both participants in conflict—it can be maddening when one person wants to pursue a conflict and the other wants only to flee. Have you ever engaged in either of these patterns? If so, what was the outcome of the conflict, and did you feel good about it? If not, what could you have done to more effectively manage the conflict?

© Jason Harris

Pursuit-Withdrawal/Withdrawal-Pursuit

These patterns, unlike the previous two, are asymmetrical. This means that the behavior of one partner is complemented by the other's behavior rather than one partner mirroring the behavior of another. In the **pursuit-withdrawal** pattern, when one partner presses for a discussion about a source of conflict, the other partner withdraws. For example, Pam tells her son, Nicky, that they have to talk about his staying out so late on school nights, and Nicky disappears into his room and shuts the door. **Withdrawal-pursuit** is just the opposite. In this pattern, a partner's withdrawal prompts the other's pursuit. For example, when Anthony retreats to the attic to work on a project and Sissy runs up to the attic several times to try to get him to discuss buying a new car, they exhibit this pattern.

These patterns are extremely unsatisfying to the participants; they have the quality of a dog chasing its tail. Gregory Bateson (1972) referred to these types of conflicts as *schismogenesis:* both partners do what they wish the other would do for them, and both are rebuffed. Sissy wants Anthony to come talk to her about their conflict, so she pursues him. Anthony wants to avoid talking about it, so he withdraws. Anthony's withdrawal spurs Sissy to advance more, which in turn causes Anthony to withdraw further. Caughlin and Vangelisti (2000) noted that even though these patterns are so unsatisfying and are related to discord within relationships, they are extremely common in conflict behavior. The researchers suggest that personality characteristics such

pursuit-withdrawal

In a conflict, a pattern consisting of one party pressing for a discussion about a conflictual topic while the other party withdraws.

withdrawal-pursuit

In a conflict, a pattern in which one party withdraws, which prompts the other party to pursue.

as extroversion and introversion might be related to the use of this pattern; in general, the extroverts pursue, and the introverts withdraw.

Symmetrical Negotiation

Symmetrical negotiation is the one positive pattern we discuss. In this pattern, each partner mirrors the other's negotiating behaviors. They listen to each other and reflect back what they have heard. They offer suggestions for dealing with the conflict and are willing to talk as much or as little as necessary to come to a mutually satisfying resolution.

People in relationships don't use only one of these patterns exclusively to communicate. Even satisfied couples may use a negative pattern, but they are likely to break out of it and get back to discussing the problem in a more positive manner fairly quickly, using techniques we discuss at the end of the chapter. Now that we've reviewed negative and positive patterns of communicating during conflict, we'll turn our attention to negative and positive outcomes of conflict: the dark and bright sides to interpersonal conflict.

The Dark Side of Interpersonal Conflict

Conflict in relationships is often seen as dangerous and negative. And, indeed, when conflict is not well managed negative consequences can ensue. Here we discuss two: bullying and violence.

Bullying

Bullying is described as a particular form of conflict where the abuse is persistent and the person being bullied finds it very difficult to defend himself or herself (Hoel & Cooper, 2000). As a result bullying often takes place in situations in which there is a distinct power difference between partners. Such unequal power relationships occur often, but not exclusively, in schools (Smith-Sanders & Harter, 2007) or at work (Tracy, Alberts, & Rivera, 2007). By some estimates 15 percent of any given population in a school or workplace has been involved in bullying, either as the bully or the victim (http://www .bullyingawarenessweek.org). Others cite higher numbers, referencing schools stating that approximately 50 percent of all young people have been bullied at some point in their school career (http://www.girlshealth.gov/bullying/whatis.htm).

Communication behaviors characteristic of bullying include isolating or ignoring, nitpicking or excessively criticizing, humiliating, and even physically abusing someone (Tracy, Lutgen-Sandvik, & Alberts, 2006). Some research suggests that a big problem for those who are bullied at work involves convincing others to believe them. This research offers suggestions for getting others to listen to and believe accounts of bullying: speak rationally but express appropriate emotion. Tell a plausible story with consistent,

symmetrical negotiation

In a conflict, each party mirroring the other's negotiating behaviors.

bullying

A particular form of conflict in which the abuse is persistent and the person being bullied finds it very difficult to defend himself or herself.

relevant, specific details. Emphasize your own competence and show consideration for others' perspectives (Tracy, Alberts, & Rivera, 2007).

Violence and Aggression

Violence within interpersonal relationships is relatively common in the United States; "FBI statistics showed that 32% of the 3,419 women killed in the United States in 1998 died at the hands of a husband, a former husband, a boyfriend, or a former boyfriend" (Harvey & Weber, 2002, p. 145). Common couple violence, which includes minor acts of violence (like pushing and shoving) used when conflicts get out of hand, might affect as many as 50 percent of couples in the United States (Olson, 2002).

Violence and aggression may be seen as conflict going to extremes, occurring when one person imposes his or her will on someone else through verbal and nonverbal acts geared to hurt or cause suffering. Violence and aggression can be psychological (as when parents belittle their children) or physical (as when someone is hit or battered). These two types may often be seen together. Someone who's verbally aggressive may also be physically abusive (Roberto, Carlyle, & McClure, 2006). Because these two are related, teaching more constructive forms of conflict management to reduce verbal aggression could also reduce physical abuse (Wilson, Hayes, Bylund, Rack, & Herman, 2006).

In the communication discipline, most of the research on violence has focused on the family. Family violence ranges from child abuse, to spousal abuse, to sibling abuse, to incest. Some recent research examines how families can reconcile after violence (Cahn & Abigail, 2007). In this line of research, reconciliation doesn't mean excusing the violence or forgetting it happened, but instead focusing on forgiveness and moving forward.

While violence and aggression are significant social problems, we won't discuss them more extensively here. Interpersonal conflict can be managed without resorting to violence and aggression, and may even have positive outcomes. We now turn to those and discuss conflict's bright side.

The Bright Side of Interpersonal Conflict

Research on conflict metaphors (Buzzanell & Burrell, 1997; Turner & Shuter, 2004) indicates that when people think of comparisons for interpersonal conflict, they focus on the dark side and produce overwhelmingly negative comparisons (conflict is like war, hell, disease, or a natural disaster, for example). Yet, as previously discussed, relationships cannot exist without conflict. Further, there are many positives to engaging in conflict with a relational partner.

Managing conflict with sensitivity leads to positive evaluations of communication competence (Lakey & Canary, 2002). In addition, dealing productively with conflict in marriage promotes physical and mental health (Gottman, 1999). Other researchers have claimed the following benefits for conflict: getting feelings out in the open and increasing knowledge of one another, promoting feelings of confidence in relationships that survive conflicts, promoting genuine human contact, increasing the depth of a relationship, maximizing the chances of making a good decision, and shaking a relationship out of a rut. Although all conflict doesn't automatically produce positive outcomes for relationships, the possibility exists.

Further, it may be the case that it's not the presence of conflict *per se* that's an issue in marriage. For instance, if Ella and Larry fight five times a week while Grace and Steven argue 10 times a week, on average, it is still possible that Grace and Steven have a happy marriage. In fact, they could be happier than Ella and Larry. If during Grace and Steven's arguments they have a **positive interaction ratio** (i.e. they say more nice things to each other than negative things) they could be more satisfied in their relationship than Ella and Larry who fight less but have a **negative interaction ratio** (i.e. they're more negative than positive in their encounters).

This line of thinking began with psychologist John Gottman's work examining positive-to-negative ratios in marriage (i.e. Gottman & DeClaire, 2001). Gottman claims that five positives to one negative is the *magic ratio*, supporting this claim with substantial research data from couples in his Seattle lab. He and his colleagues predicted with 94 percent accuracy whether 700 newlywed couples would stay together or divorce based on whether they exhibited the magic ratio during conflict encounters.

Explaining Conflict

In this section, we review two theories that help us sort us out the complex phenomenon of conflict by diagramming its component parts. The four-part model (Satir, 1972) and the explanatory process model (Cupach & Canary, 2000) described below are useful in helping us think about the nature and the process of interpersonal conflict. This should help us be better communicators in conflict.

The Four-Part Model

This model depicts conflict as a circle divided into four sections that represent the critical parts of any conflict (see Figure 9.2 on page 314): you, me, the context, and the subject. *You* refers to one of the participants in the conflict and *me* refers to the other. *Context* comprises the emotional background surrounding the conflict—for example, whether it's the first conflict on this topic, whether the two participants are highly and equally invested in the conflict, whether the topic is extremely important to the relationship between the two parties, and so forth. *Subject* means what the parties are

positive interaction ratio

An interpersonal encounter in which the participants say more positive things to each other than negative things.

negative interaction ratio

An interpersonal encounter in which the participants say more negative things to each other than positive things.

Figure 9.2   The four-part conflict model

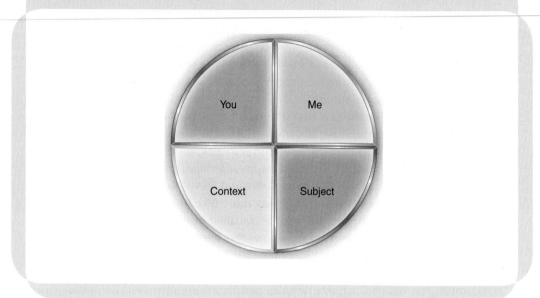

arguing about—for example, whether to move, whether to have children, whether to go to the basketball game or to the movies, whether abortion is wrong, whether the household chores are distributed fairly, and so forth.

Effective conflict management requires that each part be considered completely. All four parts are equally important, and if each part is not attended to, the conflict won't be managed successfully. The model assumes that the nature of conflict consists of the interdependence of all these parts; if one segment is ignored, the overall conflict cannot be completely resolved. As we've noted people generally fear or dislike conflict interaction. Perhaps because of this, they try to resolve conflicts as quickly as possible. However, if in our haste to conclude an argument, we ignore one or more of the four integral segments, ineffective conflict management results. Let's take a look at the consequences of ignoring or disqualifying each portion of the conflict.

When people disqualify the *me* in a conflict, they are being passive or ignoring their own needs in the situation. This passive response, which cancels out one's own position in a conflict, is called **placating**. For example, when George wants to compete with his coworker, Dina, for a promotion, but instead decides to tell her that he'll defer in her favor, George is placating. George doesn't have to fight Dina for the promotion; it is possible to opt out of competition with another for various reasons. For example, George might think that Dina is more qualified or might acknowledge that she has more seniority with the company than he does. Or it's possible that George is having problems at home, and he realizes that now isn't the right time to assume a more demanding position. However, if deferring to Dina is George's first response, exercised simply to avoid a conflict, the model tells us that's a mistake.

placating

Being passive or ignoring our own needs in a conflict.

When people disqualify the *you* in a conflict, they respond in an aggressive manner without acknowledging the needs of the other person in the conflict. This is **pouncing**. If George yells at Dina, telling her that she's a jerk for applying for a promotion that she knows he wants, he is pouncing. Anything that George might do to ignore Dina's side of the conflict and advance his own is considered pouncing, another ineffective strategy for conflict resolution. The *context* is the part of the model containing the emotional aspects of conflict. If someone disqualifies the context, they are **computing** or ignoring the conflict's emotional aspects and focusing only on the rational aspects. Conflicts touch emotions deeply and won't be effectively managed unless these emotions are addressed. For example, let's say that Dina is upset when she learns that George is also interested in the promotion. She raises her voice, pointing out that in a previous instance when she and George both competed for something at work, she'd stepped aside, so she feels that, in fairness, George needs to step aside now. If George responds by telling Dina not to yell and not to feel upset, he'd be shutting down an important aspect of their conflict. George and Dina have to confront the emotions involved in their conflict to resolve it.

If Dina comes into George's office to discuss her interest in the promotion, and George interrupts her to talk about a different topic, George would be disqualifying the *subject* of the conflict. This response is called **distracting** because it draws the parties' attention away from the subject of a conflict. People who laugh, cry, change the subject, or run out of the room when presented with a conflict engage in distracting responses.

In placating, pouncing, computing, and distracting, one portion of the conflict is ignored or disqualified. In so doing, the conflict interaction is rushed or skipped altogether. This accomplishes the immediate goal of minimizing the time that two people spend in conflict. However, in the long run, none of these responses will provide a long-term solution to the conflict. All four segments of the conflict circle are equally important, and if one is ignored, the conflict is not managed properly.

The Explanatory Process Model

The four-part model pictures each of the elements of a conflict as occurring simultaneously within a conflict interaction. In contrast, Cupach and Canary (2000) model conflict as a process that occurs in the following episodes: distal context, proximal context, conflict interaction, proximal outcomes, and distal outcomes. In this section, we discuss each of these episodes in turn. See Figure 9.3 on page 316 for an illustration of how the episodes fit together to make up the conflict process.

Conflict begins with a **distal context**, or the background that frames the specific conflict. The distal context sets the stage for conflict and contains the history between the two parties and the areas of disagreement they have discussed in the past. For example, when Ryan and Geoff become roommates, they have a history going back to the second grade. Geoff knows that Ryan is

pouncing

Responding in an aggressive manner without acknowledging the needs of another person in a conflict.

computing

Disqualifying the emotional aspects of a conflict (the context) and focusing on the rational aspects.

distracting

Disqualifying the subject of a conflict by distracting both people in the conflict with behaviors such as laughing, crying, or changing the subject.

distal context

The background that frames a specific conflict.

Figure 9.3   The explanatory process model

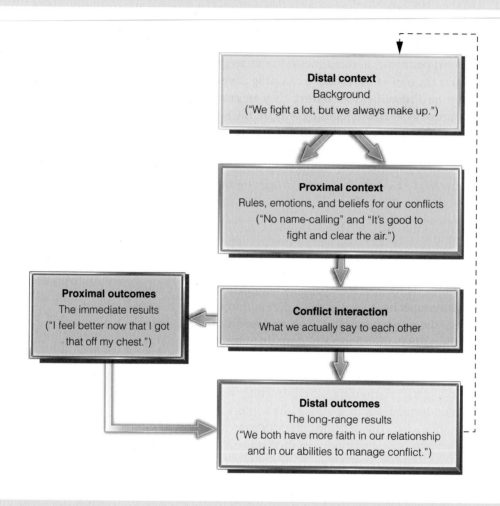

messier than he is and that Ryan doesn't care about his physical surroundings nearly as much. In addition, Geoff knows that Ryan is quieter and less inclined to enjoy conflict than he is. They had talked about how they would deal with these differences before moving in together.

The second episode in this model is the **proximal context**, which refers to the rules, emotions, and beliefs of the individuals involved in the conflict. If Ryan and Geoff set some rules about how to conduct conflict when it arises (e.g., no yelling, or no complaining behind the other's back) those rules will become part of the proximal context. Geoff's goal to keep the apartment clean and nice and Ryan's goal not to have to fuss about his living space also comprise the proximal context. Both the distal and the proximal contexts form the background for any overt conflict Geoff and Ryan may have.

proximal context

The rules, emotions, and beliefs of the individuals involved in a conflict.

The next episode is **conflict interaction**. This occurs when the differences between the partners become a problem and one or both people begin to address the issue. For instance, Geoff tells Ryan he has to start picking up the stuff he leaves lying out in the common spaces of the apartment, and Ryan responds. This episode includes what messages the two exchange and the patterns of their communication as they talk about the problem in their apartment.

The next episode is **proximal outcomes** or the immediate results after the conflict interaction. For instance, Ryan and Geoff might decide that they don't want to be roommates any longer because they can't come up with a plan to clean the apartment that satisfies them both. Or they might get sick of arguing about it and ignore the problem for a while until Geoff can't stand the mess anymore, and then the conflict begins again. Or they might decide that Ryan will pay for a cleaning person to come in once a month.

Finally, this model shows that conflicts are never completely over. The proximal outcomes affect the **distal outcomes** which include the residue of having engaged in the conflict and the feelings that both the participants have about their interaction. For instance, if they've decided that Ryan will hire a cleaning person, Geoff and Ryan might feel proud that they came up with a great idea that pleases them both—Geoff is glad that he gets to live in a clean apartment, and Ryan is relieved that he doesn't have to change life-long habits. Alternatively, Ryan could feel a little resentful about the solution. Even though he agreed to do it, he might feel that it's unfair that he has to pay a monthly fee beyond the rent just to keep Geoff happy.

In addition to the parties' responses to the solution, they both have feelings about the ways they interacted during the conflict. Geoff, for example, might congratulate himself for not losing his temper and confronting Ryan before building up too much resentment. Geoff might also feel grateful to Ryan for listening to his point of view and empathizing even though Ryan

conflict interaction

The point in the conflict process when the differences between two individuals become a problem and one or both people begin to address the issue.

proximal outcomes

The immediate results after a conflict interaction.

distal outcomes

The residue of having engaged in a conflict and the feelings that both the participants have about their interaction.

© Bonnie Kamin/PhotoEdit

The four-part model and the explanatory process model provide us with valuable information about how we can manage conflict effectively. Although it's not always easy to do during a conflict, practicing effective interpersonal skills, such as really listening to what another person has to say or sensitively addressing another person's emotion, can help us maintain good relationships over a lifetime.

REVISITING
CASEinPOINT

1. In the conflict between Tamara and Jeff, what is the proximal context?

2. In the conflict between Tamara and Jeff, what are the proximal outcomes?

You can answer these questions online under the resources for Chapter 9 at your online Resource Center for Understanding Interpersonal Communication.

can't see the point of thoroughly cleaning the apartment. For his part, Ryan might think he did a great job of listening and might feel happy that Geoff explained his position in such a way that it began to make sense to him. It is also possible that both men could feel a bit resentful about the way the conflict interaction unfolded. One or both of them might feel that he got pushed around by the other.

As Figure 9.3 illustrates, the distal outcomes feed into the distal context for the next conflict. For instance, if Geoff feels grateful to Ryan for his behavior during the conflict about cleaning the apartment, that will set the stage for how a later conflict—whether they should pitch in together to buy a flat-screen TV—unfolds. Geoff may be inclined to listen more carefully to Ryan's point of view in this conflict because he feels Ryan was so cooperative in their previous conflict. Thus, we see in this model how conflicts affect relationships and even define relational life.

The Relationship of Conflict to Power

Power can be defined as the ability to control the behavior of another. In conflict situations, power often influences the outcome as well as the process of the interaction. As we discussed in Chapter 1, power has relevance in all communication encounters; even simple conversations used to exchange demographic or superficial information may reflect power issues between the partners. Whether or not you agree that *all* communication rests on power differentials, it is true that conflict communication utilizes power in a variety of ways. The following sections discuss how people use power, sex differences in power, and the concept of empowerment.

power

In interpersonal relationships, the ability to control the behavior of another.

Using Power

Researchers (Folger, Poole, & Stutman, 2001) discuss four ways that people use power in conflict interactions: direct application, direct and virtual use, indirect application, and hidden use.

© Mark Richards/PhotoEdit

We often interact with people who have legitimate power over us, such as parents, teachers, and employers. When we experience conflict with authority figures like these, they are often able to exercise their power to take control of the conflict. However, at times, we may find that we don't respect an authority's power and may choose to create a conflict in an effort to establish a more even balance of power.

Direct application of power in a conflict situation involves using any resources at your disposal to compel the other to comply, regardless of their desires. When Marla spanks her 2-year-old son, Jerry, and sends him to his room, she is using direct application of power. Related to this mode, **direct and virtual use of power** involves communicating the *potential* use of direct application. The use of threats and promises are good illustrations of this way of using power. For example, when Dr. Moore says he will fail Lorna in his Introduction to Communication class unless she rewrites a paper to his satisfaction, he is exercising a threat. When Dr. Seltzer promises the students in his Communication Theory class that they will all receive A's if they complete all the written work on time, he is offering a promise. Threats and promises are two sides of the same coin.

The **indirect application of power** concerns employing power without making its employment explicit. For instance, if Gerard has heard his boss, Colleen, mention that she likes all office memos to be cc'ed to her, and he does that even though it's not an official office policy, Colleen has used indirect application of power. One example of the indirect application of power is the relational message. When people send **relational messages**, they define the relationship (and implicitly state that they have the power to do this). For instance, when Tim tells Sue how much he gave up so they could move to Ohio to be near her parents, he sends a message that in their relationship, Sue is indebted to him. Of course, partners may accept or contest the implicit message. If Sue agrees that Tim has done her an enormous favor at some cost to himself, she accepts his relationship definition and his power. If she argues with him that he really wanted to move, too, or that he didn't give up that much, they will conflict over the relationship definition.

direct application of power

In a conflict situation, the use of any resource at our disposal to compel another to comply, regardless of that person's desires.

direct and virtual use of power

Communicating the potential use of a direct application of power.

indirect application of power

Employing power without making its employment explicit.

relational message

A message that defines a relationship and implicitly states that the sender has the power to define the relationship.

Table 9.2   Using power

Method	Definition
Direct application	Using any means to get your way
Direct and virtual use	Using threats and promises
Indirect application	Using an implicit approach
Hidden use of power	Having the other follow your wishes without having to say anything

Most of the time we think of power as the ability to talk someone else into complying with what we want, but in the case of **hidden use of power** (also called "unobtrusive power"), we don't have to say a word. For example, if Sammy doesn't bring up a topic for discussion because he knows his friend, Dale, won't agree with him, Dale is exercising hidden power. And when Maria complies with her mother's wishes for a big, lavish wedding, although she and her fiancé really want a small, more conservative ceremony, Maria succumbs to her mother's hidden power. Maria doesn't even broach the subject; Maria lets her mother be in charge without argument even though she doesn't agree with her plans.

Throughout this discussion, we adopt a relational perspective on power. In other words, we see power, like conflict, as a process that is co-constructed by relational partners. Thus, although one partner may try to utilize direct application of power or any of the other power modes we have discussed, the power loop is not closed until the other partner responds. For instance, when Marla spanks her son, Jerry and sends him to his room, she checks in on him later to find that Jerry has thrown all his toys on the floor and ripped all the pages out of his books. Thus, the mother's direct application of power is not met with compliance; rather, it encounters resistance in the form of an exercise of direct power on Jerry's part.

See Table 9.2 for a summary of these ways of using power.

Sex Differences

hidden power

A type of power in which one person in a relationship suppresses or avoids decisions in the interest of one of the parties. Also called unobtrusive power.

Sex role stereotypes in the United States suggest that husbands have more power in decision making than their wives. But one study (Vogel, Murphy, Werner-Wilson, Cutrona, & Seeman, 2007) suggests that sex differences do not operate in stereotypical ways in marital decision making. In fact, wives exhibited more power in a decision-making exercise than their husbands did. Power was measured both by the verbal and nonverbal behaviors of the spouses and also by the results (i.e., who "gave in" to whom). The researchers found that wives talked more than their husbands and husbands accepted their wives' opinions and followed their lead in the study. In discussing the study, the lead author commented, "There's been research that suggests that's a marker of a healthy marriage—that men accept influence from their wives" (http://www.iastate.edu/~nscentral/news/2007/jun/wifepower.shtml).

Another study (Dunbar & Burgoon, 2005), examined the verbal and non-verbal indicators of power in married couples. This study found that men and women tended to mirror one another's communication of power. In other words, men and women were not significantly different in how they expressed power verbally and nonverbally; what one did—such as interrupt—the other did as well.

Empowerment

Another consideration concerning the relationship between power and conflict revolves around **empowerment**, or helping to actualize people's power. Stephen Littlejohn and Kathy Domenici (2001) note that some mediators refer to empowerment as "power balancing," or the efforts of a third party to equalize the power distribution so that the participants in the conflict can both listen and be heard. However, Littlejohn and Domenici find the term "power balancing" problematic:

> The problem is that the mediator, who is really an outsider, cannot know what sources of power parties might have available to them. It might look as though a man is out-powering a woman by dominating the conversation, but the woman may have a great deal of power in her silence. It may look as though a well-to-do business-person has more power than a blue-collar customer, but the customer may have connections and buying power that give him or her a great deal of power. It may look as though a parent has more power than a teen, but anyone who has raised teenagers might disagree. . . . Rather than judge who has the power, we want to empower both parties to do and say what needs to be done and said, to identify the problem in their own terms, to establish what a successful outcome would mean for them, and to create ideas for achieving that outcome. (pp. 78–79)

Whether you call the intricate power dynamics within our relationships power balancing or empowerment, managing conflict necessitates that each party is listened to and really heard.

Choices for Conflict Management

To manage conflict, you need to keep in mind several strategies. Remember that just because you have conflict in your interpersonal relationships does not mean that those relationships are destined to fail. Consider the following strategies for conflict management in your interactions with others.

empowerment

Helping to actualize our own or another person's power.

... at work

Reframing can make the difference between enjoying the workplace and dreading going to work. For instance, if your boss asks you to rewrite a few sections of a report you had thought was finished, you have several options. You could complain to your coworkers about how unreasonable the boss is. You could redo the work while privately steaming. You could refuse to work on the report again, telling the boss it doesn't need further revision. Or you could reframe by deciding to look at the boss's request as an opportunity to ensure that you have done the best work you could. Reframing in this manner could lead to the following conversation between you and your boss:

YOU: "I thought the report was complete, but I am happy to take another look at it, because it's always important to double-check."

BOSS: "Thanks, that will be great."

Can you identify other instances in which reframing might be used in the workplace?

... with a colleague in a coffee shop

You and Nolan are co-chairing the committee that is planning a fund-raising event for a candidate running for school board in your community. You are meeting at a local coffee shop to discuss plans. Nolan wants to invite his neighbor who sings and plays the guitar to perform a concert for the fund raiser. You are concerned—you don't think an amateur will be much of a draw, and you can imagine all the work it will take to set up a concert. You can also imagine how frustrated you'll be if you do all that work and don't end up raising much money for the candidate. You mention your reservations to Nolan, and he begins to yell that you never like his ideas and he can't work with someone who doesn't support him at all. You are surprised at Nolan's reaction, and you're not sure what prompted his outburst. What kinds of questions might you ask him that could be useful in this situation?

Lighten Up and Reframe

Lightening up refers to your ability to stay cool-headed when others get "hot." Techniques that can help you to do this include staying in the present and acknowledging that you have heard what your relational partner just said. Maintain eye contact and nod to show that you heard their contribution. You can say, "I understand you have a concern," or you can reframe by changing something that has a negative connotation to something with a more positive connotation. This is similar to what we discussed in Chapter 8 about dealing with dialectic tensions. Finally, lightening up might involve your asking permission to state your views: "May I tell you my perspective?" Keep your nonverbal communication genuine—avoid sarcasm.

Presume Good Will and Express Good Will

Go into each conflict interaction believing that you and your partner both want to come to a constructive resolution. Build rapport by focusing on the areas where you do agree. Reach out to your partner and expect that your partner will do the same for you. While you are engaging in conflict, tell your partner the things about him or her that you respect. Keep it real, but mix in praise with your complaints.

Ask Questions

Focus on the other. After you both have had a chance to speak, ask your partner if he or she has anything further to add. Reflect back what you have heard and ask if you got it correctly. Ask: "What would make this situation better?" "What would you like to see happen now?" "How can I understand your position better?" "What can you tell me that I seem to be misunderstanding?"

Listen

We detailed the role of listening in Chapter 5 and again highlight its importance here. A conflict is difficult to manage unless we spend time listening to the other person. Remember to practice all of the behaviors associated with effective listening, including looking at the other person, focusing on the words, and allowing the full story to unfold. In conflict situations, listening to another person is more than just hearing the words spoken; it's a way to show him or her that the conflict is important to resolve and that the relationship is valuable in your life.

Practice Cultural Sensitivity

Be mindful and tune into your own culture's norms and assumptions first before evaluating others (Ting-Toomey & Oetzel, 2001). Slow down your judgments of others; suspend your evaluations until you have had a chance to engage in an internal dialogue. Ask yourself questions such as: Am I respectful of the different cultural background of the other person? Am I using my own cultural lens to

understand what is being said? What types of strategies am I using to make sure that I don't inadvertently evaluate the person rather than the message? These are just a few of the questions to consider as you remember the cultural backgrounds of others.

To practice techniques that can help you deal with conflict effectively, use your online Resource Center for *Understanding Interpersonal Communication* to access *Interactive Activity 9.2: Techniques for Resolving Conflict*. To read a couple of articles that provides tips for managing conflict in relationships and in groups, check out "Relationships: How to Manage Conflict" and "Conflict Resolution—A Key Ingredient in Successful Teams," both available through InfoTrac College Edition. Access *InfoTrac College Edition Exercises 9.3: Managing Conflict in Relationships* and *9.4: Conflict in Groups*.

interpersonal explorer

Before you finish reading this chapter, take a moment to review the theories and skills discussed. How do you think the theories discussed in this chapter can help you better understand interpersonal communication and conflict? In what ways can the skills discussed help you interact more effectively with other people in your life?

Theories that relate to conflict

- **The four-part model**
  In conflict it's necessary to pay attention to four integral parts (you, me, emotions, and topic) to manage it effectively
- **The explanatory process model**
  Conflict follows a predictable course of several episodes. Each episode affects the next.

Practical skills for conflict management

- Lighten up and reframe
- Presume good will and express good will
- Ask questions
- Listen
- Practice cultural sensitivity

Explore your interpersonal choices

Are you ready to explore your interpersonal choices regarding conflict? Use your online Resource Center for *Understanding Interpersonal Communication* to access an ABC News video, "Sibling Rivalry," about how parents can help manage their children's interpersonal conflicts. Compare your answers to the questions at the end of the video with those provided by the authors.

Summary

Interpersonal conflict is a pervasive fact of relational life. Conflicts are interactions about important differences between interdependent people. These interactions can focus on image, content, values, and/or relational questions. Common myths that don't accurately describe interpersonal conflict are that conflict is always based on misunderstandings, resolvable, and best dealt with through more communication. Two factors that often influence conflict are gender and sex, and culture.

During conflicts, communication partners often repeat patterns of behavior, including symmetrical escalation, symmetrical withdrawal, withdrawal-pursuit or pursuit-withdrawal, and symmetrical negotiation. The only one of these patterns that is positive is symmetrical negotiation, in which each partner mirrors the other's negotiating behaviors.

Conflict has a dark side, and can result in bullying or violent behaviors. Yet it is also the case that engaging in conflict may result in positive outcomes for relational partners. Conflicts promote physical and mental health, get feelings out in the open, establish feelings of confidence in relationships, encourage genuine human contact, increase the depth of a relationship, maximize the chances of making a good decision, and shake a relationship out of a rut.

We can conceptualize conflict by using the four part model, which shows that conflict has four interdependent parts: you, me, context, and subject. Ignoring even one of these components results in ineffective conflict management. Another approach that is helpful in thinking about conflict is the explanatory process model, which explains conflict as a process with five episodes (distal context, proximal context, conflict interaction, proximal outcomes, and distal outcomes).

Power often influences the outcome as well as the process of conflict. Power may be used through direct application, direct and virtual use, indirect application, and hidden use. Sex difference research indicates that either women have more power than men in marriage or power is equal. Empowerment is a way to manage power positively encouraging good conflict outcomes.

To manage your conflicts, use the following strategies: lighten up and reframe, presume and express good will, ask questions, listen, and practice cultural sensitivity. Although no one can avoid conflict, these techniques should improve your satisfaction in conflict encounters. Effectively managed conflict will help you acquire necessary tools for satisfaction in your interpersonal interactions.

Understanding Interpersonal Communication Online

Now that you've read Chapter 9, use your online Resource Center for *Understanding Interpersonal Communication* for quick access to the electronic study resources that accompany this text. Your online Resource Center gives you access to the video of Tamara and Jeff on page 293, the Your Turn journal activity on page 298, the Communication Assessment Test on page 304, the Ethics & Choice interactive activity on page 308, the Interpersonal Explorer activity on page 323, InfoTrac College Edition, and study aids including a digital glossary, review quizzes, and the chapter activities.

Terms for Review

bullying 311
computing 315
conflict interaction 317

content conflict 298
direct and virtual use of
   power 319

direct application of power
   319
distal context 315

Questions for Understanding

Comprehension Focus

1. Define interpersonal conflict. Discuss each of the component parts of the definition.

2. List and describe five types of conflict.

3. Define empowerment and explain how it relates to conflict.

4. Describe the four-part model of conflict. What underlying assumption about conflict does the model reveal?

5. Describe the explanatory process model of conflict. What underlying assumption about conflict does the model reveal?

Application Focus

1. CASE IN POINT Is gender an issue in the case of Tamara and Jeff? If yes, explain how. If not, what other factors might be influencing their conflict? What skills might be useful in managing their conflict more productively? Rewrite the scenario so that both Jeff and Tamara can be more satisfied with their interaction.

2. Think about your general beliefs about conflict. Does your response reflect a belief in one or more of the myths we described? What factors form your concept of conflict?

3. Explain the relationship between power and conflict. Is it possible to have power differences without conflict? Is it possible to have conflict when there are no critical power differences? How do cultural differences affect your answers?

4. What does it mean to you to take a communication perspective on conflict? Do you agree that although you may typically respond to conflict in a certain way, your behavior is really most influenced by the interaction? Explain with examples.

5. Remember an instance when you think you took a productive approach to an interpersonal conflict. Describe what happened.

Interactive Activities and InfoTrac College Edition Exercises

Interactive Activities

InfoTrac College Edition Exercises

Chapter 10
Communicating in Close Relationships

chapter ➕ goals

Develop a definition of close relationships

Discuss the communication in friendships, romantic relationships, and families

Understand explanations for communication in close relationships

Demonstrate a variety of skills and techniques to enhance and maintain your communication in close relationships

CASEINPOINT

RANDY TANAKA AND HOPE REYNOLDS

Randy surveyed his work in Hope's house and was pleased with what he saw. He thought Hope would like the job he'd done, too. He smiled, remembering how nervous he'd been his first day working for her. He'd just started his own construction company. Hope seemed demanding, and Randy was afraid she'd be on his case a lot. He needn't have worried—the two of them hit it off right away. After he'd been working at her house a couple of weeks, they were talking like old friends.

Randy remembered the first time she'd offered him coffee, and they sat at the breakfast table and talked. He found himself telling her about his divorce from Laura, his new marriage to Beth, and his problems getting along with Beth's oldest son. Hope understood stepfamilies— her husband had been married before, and they shared custody of his three children from his previous marriage. Randy and Hope spent almost an hour chatting about the challenges and joys of step-parenting. Every day after that when Randy arrived Hope had the coffee on, and they spent some time talking. Hope was a great listener.

When Randy started working for Hope, he built some shelves for the living room, and then she'd found other jobs for him. Hope's husband traveled a great deal and didn't have time to do much around the house, so Hope found many chores for Randy. Her husband, Ned, joked about Randy being his biggest rival for Hope's affections. It was all in good fun; Randy and Hope shared a lot and enjoyed talking with each other, but both were devoted to their marriages. Finally, Randy tackled a kitchen remodel. Randy was excited about showing the kitchen to Hope, and her reaction didn't disappoint him—Hope was delighted with the results. Now, Randy had come to the end of the work. Hope's house was beautiful.

Both were so happy with how Randy's work had turned out, yet they each privately wondered if the end of the job would mean the end of their great friendship. They hoped their relationship wouldn't end because they'd become important friends to one another.

Use your online Resource Center for *Understanding Interpersonal Communication* to watch a video clip of Hope and Randy.

> Access the resources for Chapter 10 and select "Hope" to watch the video (it takes a minute for the video to load). As you watch the video, think about the fact that Hope and Randy would like to continue their friendship. > How could they best communicate this to each other? > You can respond to this and other analysis questions, and then click "Done" to compare your answers with those provided by the authors.

*O*ur close relationships mean a great deal to us. They help satisfy our need for connection. Abraham Maslow's (1968) famous hierarchy of needs (see Figure 10.1),
which ranks people's needs in order of importance, places social needs immediately after physical and safety needs. Satisfying social needs has been referred to as "the
human career" (Goldschmidt, 1990). A 1998 Gallup survey showed that 83 percent of people between the ages of 18 and 34 rated a close-knit family as their highest priority, and
64 percent of all those surveyed said that "relationships with loved ones are always on their
minds" (cited in Harvey & Weber, 2002, p. 4). Randy and Hope's story shows how social
needs pervade even business relationships.

Communication is central to relationships. One researcher observes, "to
maintain a relationship, partners must communicate with one another. Conversely, as long as people communicate, they have a relationship" (Dindia,
2003, p. 1). In our opening story, Randy and Hope developed their friendship
through their conversations. When they think about the future, they worry
because their daily interactions will soon end. They're afraid if they don't talk
every day their friendship will be jeopardized. In addition, the quality of a
relationship is judged by the quality of the communication within it. We think
of communication as both an indicator of our closeness with another person

Figure 10.1   Maslow's hierarchy of needs

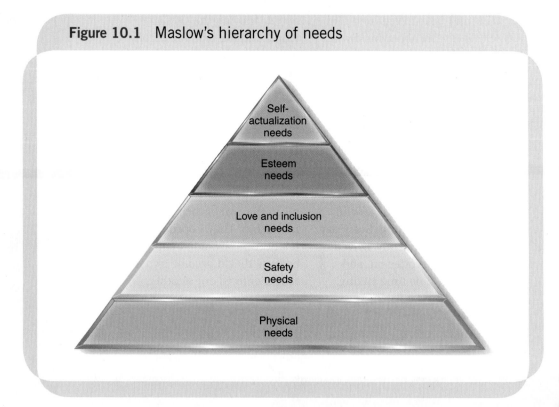

Communication Assessment Test
Relational Communication Scale

This test, adapted from work done by Judee Burgoon and Jerry Hale (1987), is meant to measure the eight themes that characterize communication in interpersonal relationships, which the researchers identified as the following:

- Immediacy (being involved in the conversation)
- Depth (caring what the other thinks)
- Trust (expressing that trust is desirable)
- Composure (acting in a calm manner)
- Formality (making the interaction formal)
- Dominance (talking more and deciding the topics discussed)
- Equality (treating the other person as an equal)
- Orientation (expressing a social or task orientation in the conversation)

Use the Relational Communication Scale (RCS) to determine how you and a selected partner rate in terms of each of these themes.

Directions: Think of a recent conversation you have had with a person who is in a close relationship with you. That person is the "they" in each item on the RCS. Focusing on this specific conversation, answer the following questions using the scale below. For example, if you strongly agree that the statement describes your impression of the conversation, rate it a 5; if you strongly disagree, rate it a 1; and so forth. Answer all the questions.

strongly disagree = 1   disagree = 2   undecided = 3   agree = 4   strongly agree = 5

You can take this test online. Go to your online Resource Center for *Understanding Interpersonal Communication* and look under the resources for Chapter 10.

_____ 1. They were intensely involved in the conversation.

_____ 2. They wanted to stick to the main purpose of the interaction.

_____ 3. They made me feel similar to them.

_____ 4. They attempted to persuade me.

_____ 5. They considered us equals.

_____ 6. They were sincere.

_____ 7. They felt very tense talking to me.

_____ 8. They made the interaction very formal.

_____ 9. They did not want a deeper relationship between us.

_____ 10. They wanted to cooperate with me.

_____ 11. They were more interested in social conversation than the task at hand.

_____ 12. They communicated coldness.

_____ 13. They acted like we were good friends.

_____ 14. They seemed to care that I liked them.

_____ 15. They were willing to listen to me.

_____ 16. They seemed nervous in my presence.

_____ 17. They wanted the conversation to be informal.

_____ 18. They had the upper hand in the conversation.

_____ 19. They were very work-oriented.

_____ 20. They acted bored by our conversation.

_____ 21. They tried to move the conversation to a deeper level.

_____ 22. They wanted me to trust them.

_____ 23. They were comfortable interacting with me.

_____ 24. They didn't attempt to influence me.

_____ 25. They were honest in communicating with me.

_____ 26. They seemed very relaxed talking with me.

_____ 27. They tried to control the conversation.

(Continues)

Scoring

Add all the numbers you gave as answers. However, for items 7, 9, 11, 12, 16, 17, 20, and 24, reverse your numbers; change 5 to 1, 4 to 2, 3 stays the same, 2 to 4, and 1 to 5. For example, if you gave yourself a 5 on item 7, add it in your total as a 1; if you gave yourself a 2, add it in your total as a 4. The higher your score, the more you were using all these themes of communication to structure your relationship in the conversation with the person you were thinking about.

Specific questions of the RCS relate to each theme. You can add your scores on each theme individually, as shown below (again using your reverse scores for items 7, 9, 11, 12, 16, 17, 20, and 24). Comparing your scores in each area will tell you which themes were most prevalent in the conversation.

- Immediacy (being involved in the conversation): 1, 9, 12, 20
- Depth (caring what the other thinks): 2, 13, 14, 21
- Trust (expressing that trust is desirable): 6, 15, 22, 25
- Composure (acting in a calm manner): 7, 16, 23, 26
- Formality (making the interaction formal): 2, 8, 17
- Dominance (talking more and deciding the topics discussed): 4, 18, 24, 27
- Equality (treating the other person as an equal): 5, 10
- Orientation (expressing a social or task orientation in the conversation): 2, 11, 19

Adapted from Burgoon & Hale, 1987.

("You're the only one I'd tell this to") and a means for developing this sense of closeness ("I feel so much closer to you now that we've talked about this").

Further, relationship type is reflected in and created by talk. For instance, Hope wouldn't talk to Randy in exactly the same way she speaks to her husband. She wouldn't be as familiar with Randy, she wouldn't discuss certain topics, and she'd probably be more polite and more careful of Randy's feelings than her husband's. Ironically, intimate partners tend to talk to each other with less consideration than they accord less intimate partners (Emmers-Sommer, 2003).

To take an online quiz that may help you better understand the nature of your own communication in your relationships, use your online Resource Center for *Understanding Interpersonal Communication* to access **Interactive Activity 10.1: Relationship Communication Quiz** under the resources for Chapter 10.

We have talked so far about the importance of close relationships and how they entwine with communication. We've been speaking as though everyone has the same understanding of a close relationship. Although we do have intuitive definitions for close relationships because they are such an important and ubiquitous part of our lives, we need to establish a common definition.

Understanding Close Relationships

One reason why it's difficult to define *close relationships* is that we experience many kinds of relationships in our lives. For instance, some relationships are role relationships (Guerrero, Andersen, & Afifi, 2007), meaning that the partners are interdependent while accomplishing a specific task. The server and customer at a restaurant have a role relationship. One key characteristic of role relationships is that the people in them are relatively interchangeable. That is, while you might like one server better than another, you can eat in a restaurant as long as someone is the server—anyone could fill the role and the relationship still exists. Role relationships may be fleeting and your interdependence on each other doesn't endure. When Jane wanted to buy a condo, she hired a realtor, Laura, who specialized in condo sales. Over the two months it took Jane to find the perfect place, she and Laura talked frequently. After Jane settled in, they no longer saw one another.

Close relationships, on the other hand, endure over time, consist of interdependent partners who satisfy each other's needs for connection and social inclusion, feel an emotional attachment to each other, are irreplaceable to one another, and enact unique communication patterns (Guerrero et al., 2007). Let's examine what research suggests those communication patterns are like (Hinde, 1995):

- **The content of the interactions:** What people talk about and do together. Robert and Nelson have a close relationship if they hang out together, engage in conversations beyond the superficial, and discuss a variety of topics.

- **The diversity of interactions:** The number of different experiences people share. Melanie and Lorraine are close if they go to the movies together, play together on the basketball team, study together, and spend time talking with one another about their futures and their jobs.

- **The qualities of the interactions:** How do the partners talk to one another? Most people agree that affectionate communication is extremely important in close relationships (Floyd & Morman, 2000). Affection can be expressed in a variety of ways—directly ("You are my best friend," "I love you") or indirectly (through giving support, compliments, or planning future activities together). As we discussed in Chapter 9, conflicts are also an inevitable part of relationships. People who speak affectionately to one another but also sometimes get into heated arguments probably have a close relationship.

- **The intimacy of the interactions:** How much do the partners self-disclose? Is their conversation characterized by a private language that identifies them as part of a unique, closed circle? What nonverbal behaviors do they exhibit? For example, Carla and Kevin share their problems with one another. They also call one another private nicknames based on elementary school experiences. Carla is "Tootsie" because Tootsie Rolls were her favorite candy, and Kevin is "Slurps" because he was famous for slurping his milk in the cafeteria. They always hug one another hello, and take walks together arm-in-

role relationships

A relationship in which the partners are interdependent while accomplishing a specific task, such as a server and a customer at a restaurant.

close relationships

A relationship that endures over time and that consists of interdependent partners who satisfy each other's needs for connection and social inclusion, feel an emotional attachment to each other, are irreplaceable to each other, and enact unique communication patterns.

arm. Such willingness to self-disclose, shared private language, and intimate nonverbal behavior all distinguish close relationships from more casual acquaintances.

- **The partners' perception of the interactions:** How do the partners see each other and the outside world? Kelly and Ray are in a close relationship because they see each other in a similar fashion and feel understood by each other. In addition, they share the same political beliefs and view the world similarly.

- **The commitment reflected in the interactions:** Does each partner feel the other is committed to the relationship? Diana and Cal have a close relationship because they speak openly about how devoted they are to one another.

- **The satisfaction expressed in the interactions:** How closely do the partners' interactions fit their ideal? Camille and Pat have a close relationship because they frequently say that they couldn't want a better friend than each other.

Although we've distinguished between role and close relationships, they can overlap. For instance, as an employee, John has a role relationship with his boss, Malcolm. But over time, they begin to talk about personal subjects, discover they have similar senses of humor, and come to feel that the other person could not simply be replaced with a new boss or a new employee. Their relationship has evolved into a close relationship.

We'll now elaborate our definition by examining the following perspectives for framing close relationships: cultural performances, cognitive constructs, or linguistic constructions. Then we'll discuss how culture and gender affect the definition.

Relationships as Cultural Performances

Close relationships are cultural performances (Baxter & Braithwaite, 2002) when they are defined by ongoing public and private exchanges. These exchanges include myriad communication practices such as private conversations, public rituals like weddings and commitment ceremonies, as well as public discourse by politicians and others indicating what marriages, families, and other relationships should be like and what values should define them. Thus, relationships are both defined by and enacted in the culture that surrounds them.

From this perspective, we would say that Brea and Tal have a close relationship because they do things that people in close relationships do. They had a wedding and publicly vowed that they were in a close relationship, labeled marriage. They go to parties together, own a home together, make budgets, take out loans, and have a joint checking account. In other words, they are performing a close relationship according to U.S. cultural and social rules.

Relationships as Cognitive Constructs

Some research examines the notion of *relationship scripts,* which are cognitive structures containing a pattern for the key events we expect in a relationship (Holmberg & MacKenzie, 2002). In the United States, we have both narrow scripts (what should happen on a first date) and broad scripts (how a friendship should progress). Relationship scripts serve several functions for people: They conserve brain energy, allowing us to process information about the relationship efficiently and rapidly; they help guide behavior, making it easier for us to know what to do in certain relational situations; and they enhance satisfaction when there's a match between script and experience.

We also frame close relationships as cognitive constructs when we define them as partners sharing mental images of the relationship (Wilmot, 1995). Mental images of relationships occur on two levels. At a basic level, people are simply aware of each other and the fact that they're in relationship with

© Bill Aron/PhotoEdit

Relationship scripts, such as what should happen in a dating relationship, are useful because they allow us to process information about a relationship quickly and efficiently, help us know how to behave in certain relational situations, and make us feel good when our scripts and our lived relationships match. What are some of your relationship scripts? Where do you think they came from? Do some of your scripts differ from those of the mainstream U.S. culture?

one another. The second level is more complex. On this level, several things happen in a specific order:

1. The communication between the partners becomes patterned, and they can imagine with some predictive accuracy what the other will say or do in different situations.

2. The partners perceive a past, present, and future together. They're able to bring the past forward into the present and future by holding a mental image of what the partner has done in the past and generalizing it to the present or the future ("When I brought her flowers before, she liked it, so she'll probably like it again."). This can be called "carrying the relationship with you" and it happens whenever people imagine what a relational partner's reaction to something might be.

3. People label their relationship ("this is my best friend," "this is my daughter," or "this is my girlfriend"). In the following section, we address the question of language and close relationships in more detail.

Relationships as Linguistic Constructions

Language influences our sense of close relationships. Giving a relationship a label (friendship, love, etc.) helps us feel "in relationship" to another. Yet, as we discussed in Chapter 6 when addressing lexical gaps, some relationships don't have convenient labels. What do you call your father's second wife, her children by her first marriage, your brother's former wife, or a person you're dating when both of you are in your 50s? What do children of gay parents call their two mothers or fathers? Some people think that it's difficult for men and women to be friends because the English language has so many terms for heterosexual love, romance, and sex, and few names for platonic friendship across the sexes. Language has not always kept pace with our relationships.

Another way that relationships exist in language is through figurative language, also discussed in Chapter 6. Figurative language—specifically, metaphors and similes—helps us understand relationships by comparing them to other phenomena (Lakoff & Johnson, 1980). In such linguistic comparisons, the qualities of the phenomenon to which a relationship is linked shed light on the qualities of the relationship itself (Burrell, Buzzanell, & McMillan, 1992; Foss, 1988; Turner & Shuter, 2004). For example, Dana understands her relationship with her mother better when she thinks of it as a Mama bear defending her cub.

In addition to offering a vocabulary for understanding our relationships, figurate language also *shapes* our understanding. It highlights some elements of the relationship while downplaying other elements. For example, the metaphor of relationship-as-dance features the coordination and enjoyment elements of a relationship while it downplays the conflicts and struggles. See Table 10.1 for a list of common relational metaphors.

Researchers argue that metaphors influence our thinking and communication (Owen, 1989). For instance, if Ben and Leslie picture their marriage as

Table 10.1 Common metaphors used to describe close relationships

Nature	Thunderstorm
	Volcano
	Sunny day
	Meadow with flowers
	Tree with deep roots
Machines	Well-oiled machine
	Leaky boat
	Merry-go-round
	Roller coaster
	Broken record
Food	Stew
	Gooey cake with ice cream
	TV dinner
	Milkshake
	Tossed salad
Clothing	Ripped sweater
	Comfortable old shoes
	Tie that's choking me
	Pair of pants with an elastic waist
	Party outfit

a "well-oiled machine," they may adopt communication behaviors that focus on efficiency ("keeping the wheels turning") and functioning ("we don't want a breakdown in communication") at the expense of emotional communication. If Melody and Kim picture their relationship as volcanic, their communication behaviors will probably highlight conflict and emotion ("if we don't talk about this, I'll just explode").

Spend two weeks collecting, and then evaluating, metaphors you hear in daily conversation referring to relationships. You can gather metaphors from television or other popular media as well as from conversations you participate in or overhear. If you like, you can use your student workbook or your **Understanding Interpersonal Communication** Online Resources to complete this activity.

Justin Lubin/© NBC/Courtesy Everett Collection

The stereotype that women are relational experts and men are relational idiots is common in the United States—check out most TV commercials. Yet, research shows that although women and men do differ in what they learn about relationships, ultimately what they want from relationships is quite similar. Interestingly, this similarity in relational goals is increasingly reflected in some of the relationships portrayed on popular television shows such as **ER** *and* **Californication**.

Relationships, Culture, and Gender

Two additional factors affect our definition of close relationships: culture and gender. As we discussed in Chapter 3, cultural norms, values, and expectations shape us in important ways. Thus, it should come as no surprise that culture plays a role in how we define close relationships. For example, traditional Hawaiian culture is fundamentally collectivistic, which affects how Hawaiians define family (or *'ohana*). For traditional Hawaiians *'ohana* is extended and expanded; it consists of the immediate family (people with blood and marital ties), those who have been adopted into the family (a common practice), and spiritual ancestors (Miura, 2000).

Hawaiian culture reflects values similar to the Latino(a) concept of *familism,* which focuses on an extended family that includes aunts, uncles, cousins, and dear friends. The African value of *collectivism* is also similar, but emphasizes the entire race or community, as reflected in the proverb "it takes a village to raise a child."

Some researchers speak of **relational culture** (Turner & West, 2006), observing that what defines a close relationship and influences what's appropriate to say and do within one has to do with the partners' shared understandings, roles, and rituals that are unique to their relationship. Elaine and Sophia define their friendship by doing things together like shopping, walking their dogs, and sitting and talking at the coffee shop. Jorge and Raul define their friendship by the fact that they grew up together. Each of these pairs of friends has created their own relational culture.

As we've discussed throughout this book, differences between men and women permeate our understanding of interpersonal communication. Close relationships provide another context in which gender differences (or perceived differences) have an impact. We take the perspective that differences between the sexes are learned—in other words, that cultural instructions guide girls to behave in ways that society has deemed feminine and teach boys to engage in what are considered masculine behaviors (McGeorge, 2001). Further, our notions of sex and gender are somewhat fluid, and they can change over time.

This perspective does not deny that sex and gender make a difference in our definitions of close relationships. In fact, recent research (Marano, 2004) indicates that biological differences between men and women, like responses to stress and propensity to depression, may affect how people think about close relationships. Some research (Reissman,1990) investigating reasons why people divorced found that men became dissatisfied with their marriages when their wives stopped doing certain things for them, like fixing dinner and greeting them at the door. Women's dissatisfaction came from a different source—they felt their marriages were headed for divorce when they and their husbands stopped talking to one another. Yet, both women and men attributed their dissatisfaction to the same overarching reason—they no longer felt cherished in the relationship. Thus, both sexes desired the feeling of being cherished, but men tended to feel that way when their wives did concrete favors for them, whereas women felt most cherished when they experienced good communication with their husbands.

REVISITING CASE IN POINT

1. How does Randy and Hope's relationship illustrate relational scripts?

2. What metaphor might Hope and Randy use for their relationship?

You can answer these questions online under the resources for Chapter 10 at your online Resource Center for Understanding Interpersonal Communication.

Some evidence exists that men and women possess a different relational awareness (Honeycutt, Cantrill, Kelly, & Lambkin, 1998). Men are more reticent in communicating and monitoring their relationships, and women are more tuned in to relational goals. However, this difference was slight, and it seems easily explained by social teaching, which categorizes women as relational experts.

Although women and men differ in what they have learned about, what they expect from, and what they experience within close relationships, popular writers like John Gray (who wrote *Men are from Mars, Women are from Venus* in 1992) have taken our cultural interest in sex differences to an extreme. They construct some differences where none really exist, overestimate the differences that do appear, and fail to talk about the cultural context framing these differences.

To read an interesting study about communication in same-sex versus other-sex relationships, particularly self-disclosure and emotional intimacy, check out the article "Close Emotional Relationships with Women versus Men," available through InfoTrac College Edition. Use your online Resource Center for *Understanding Interpersonal Communication* to access **InfoTrac College Edition Exercise 10.1: Who Are You Closer to Emotionally?** under the resources for Chapter 10.

Now that we have discussed several ways of defining close relationships, we turn our attention to communication in three specific types of close relationships: friendships, romantic relationships, and families.

To check out an interesting website that may help you learn more about your own close relationships, use your online Resource Center for *Understanding Interpersonal Communication* to access **Interactive Activity 10.2: Assessing Close Relationships.**

relational culture

The notion that relational partners collaborate and experience shared understandings, roles, and rituals that are unique to their relationship.

Types of Close Relationships

There are three primary types of close relationships: friendships, romantic relationships, and families.

Friendship

Unlike most family relationships, friendship is voluntary, There aren't any religious ceremonies to sanction friendships, or any legal bonds to make dissolving them difficult. This quality makes friendship a somewhat fragile close relationship. Friends may be sacrificed for family in the belief that family relationships are more primary. For instance, Maggie had to exclude her best friend, Leah, from her son's wedding rehearsal because only family members were invited. Friends may come and go based on situational factors. Randi found it hard to stay friends with Marlene after she got married and moved to California while Randi remained single in Chicago. She wanted to stay friends with Marlene, but the long distance and their different circumstances doomed the friendship.

Despite this fragility, friendship is a significant close relationship. Research indicates that friendships provide social support, companionship, and validation. African American men reported that they valued their friendships with women because of their positive qualities and the fact that they communicated strong emotional bonds within them (White, 2006). In a different study African American women said they depended on friendships with other African American women for opportunities to communicate a shared history and identity (Hughes & Heuman, 2006). Other research notes how daily conversation about routine activities like shopping, for instance, creates a deep sense of connection for friends, especially female friends (Braithwaite & Kellas, 2006; Metts, 2006).

Recently, some attention has been paid to the downsides of friendships. Psychologists have examined unhealthy friendships (Lerner, 2001; Parker, Low, Walker, & Gamm, 2005; Yager, 2002) characterized by jealousy, envy, anger, and a whole host of difficulties. There might be as many as twenty-one types of bad friendships, including those that lead you into antisocial or illegal activities (for example, when Sam convinces his friend, Craig, to steal a car with him), as well as those with people who insult, abuse, meddle, and lie.

Research has conceptualized friendship as either highly positive or toxic. But some researchers speculate that communication in friendship has both negative and positive potential (Rose, Carlson, & Waller, 2007). One study examining children's and adolescents' same-sex friendships, found that girls who engaged in what the researchers called *co-rumination,* or excessive discussion of personal problems, had simultaneous positive and negative outcomes. On the positive side, co-rumination increased the girls' feelings of closeness. However, it also increased the girls' depression and anxiety. Boys in the study did not experience depression and anxiety from co-rumination, but did develop increased feelings of closeness with their friend.

Sometimes positive outcomes in relationships are accomplished by communicating in traditionally frowned-upon ways. For instance, gossip may be seen as both aversive and bonding (Bergmann, 1993). Gossip is associated with relational ruin when it's negative and communicated to strangers, but acts as "social glue" when it's positive, communicated to friends, or both (Turner, Mazur, Wendel, & Winslow, 2003). Although gossip has a dark side, it may also be a way to establish intimacy. Sharing secrets together is a way to advance a relationship and to build cohesion and emotional ties (Rosnow, 2001).

The same claim has been made about swearing (Hughes & Heuman, 2006; Winters & Duck, 2001). If Rusty and Kim swear a lot around each other, they may be signaling that they have a friendship that defies social conventions. In general our society considers swearing an undesirable behavior. But when it performs this bonding function, swearing is a positive behavior for friendships.

Friendships, then, are close relationships in which communication plays an important role. Friends communicate social support, solidarity, and positive affect, as well as engage in other daily interactions that can intensify feelings of connection. But not all communication in friendship is positive; some communication behaviors may have both bad and good results. We now turn to communication in another important type of close relationship: the romantic relationship.

Romantic Relationships

A great deal of research interest centers on the romantic relationships of dating and marriage. These relationships are similar to friendships in that they are voluntary, but they differ because they involve sexual and romantic feelings and because they are not assumed to be as fragile as friendships.

Although we know that couples break up and divorce, romantic partners are supposed to exhibit commitment. Heterosexual romantic partners can demonstrate this commitment through the social, legal, or religious institution of marriage. Because same-sex marriage is not legal in most states, this option is not available to some gay and lesbian partners. Many of these couples display their intention to have a permanent relationship through a commitment ceremony.

As we discussed earlier, relational scripts influence communication in romantic relationships. Some research (e.g. Guerrero & Bachman, 2006; Knobloch, Miller, Bond, & Mannone, 2007; Levine, Aune, & Park, 2006) also suggests that individual differences affect how we communicate in romantic relationships. For example, one set of researchers found that an individual's love style—passionate, stable, playful, other-centered, logical, or obsessive—made a difference in three communication practices during three stages of a

© Colin Young-Wolff/PhotoEdit

IPC *in the* News

A recent article in the *Richmond Times-Dispatch* cautions daters of the Internet age not to skip through the age-old courtship steps that are meant to get couples off to the right start. Specifically, online meeting and dating moves quickly, and people can establish a false sense of intimacy early in relationships. Additionally, many dating sites encourage users to narrow their partner choices through specific sets of criteria, allowing people to "meet" only a limited number of people and eliminating the possibility of compatible but unexpected coupling. Although the articles mentions that online dating is still frowned upon by some, the relational experts cited in the article don't recommend ceasing the practice, just slowing it down. Says director of the Family Institute of Virginia Dr. Joan Winter, daters should consider meeting and courting online a precursor to a traditional meeting and courtship, not a replacement for going through the steps of courting in person.

Kapsidelis, K. (2008, January 27). Surfing for love. *Richmond Times-Dispatch.*

relationship: opening lines for picking up someone as a potential partner, intensification strategies for moving a relationship along to greater intimacy, and secret tests for checking on the state of a developing relationship. For example, if Pablo believes love is playful, he'll use cute, flippant pick up lines like "God must be a thief. He stole the stars from the skies and put them in your eyes" (Levine et al., p. 478) to initiate a relationship, sexual intimacy to intensify it, and indirect secret tests like joking and hinting to check the state of a romance. If Pablo is in a relationship with Adele, who has a logical love style, his pick up lines, intensification strategies, and secret tests may not be successful because Adele will have different communication preferences.

Other researchers (Guerrero & Bachman, 2006) found that how secure a person is affects how they communicate to maintain their romantic relationships. People who are more secure tend to use more positive or prosocial behaviors. For example, if Amina is a secure person who's not anxious about relationships, she'll be likely to try to maintain her relationship with Jerome by saying "I love you," touching Jerome affectionately, complimenting him, and being open in her conversations with him. A different group of researchers (Knobloch et al.) made a similar finding that married people who are uncertain about their marriages tend to interpret conversations pessimistically, whereas those who are more confident in their marriages draw more favorable conclusions.

One type of romantic relationship to receive research attention is the long distance dating relationship (LDDR), or a couple who continues to maintain a romantic relationship while separated geographically. While it would seem that being apart would strain LDDRs, some research has found that LDDRs are more stable than dating couples who are geographically close. This finding is explained by the fact that people in LDDRs engage in more romantic idealization of one another and their relationship ("he's the best boyfriend;" "we have a relationship that can stand anything") than couples who live near each other (Stafford & Merolla, 2007). This study also found that although LDDRs are more stable while the couple is apart, they often end when the couple becomes geographically close again.

Although the vast majority of research on romantic relationships has studied white heterosexual couples, some research focuses on gay and lesbian couples (Suter, Bergen, Dass, & Durham, 2006) and interracial couples (Thompson & Collier, 2006). Although many communication issues are the same across all romantic relationships, these relationships must also contend with issues of discrimination and identity. In both gay and interracial relationships, the partners are aware of social disapproval. In some instances, they are alienated from friends and families. They are required to consider social and historical forces concerning race and sexual identity in ways that other couples are not. Their communication behaviors reflect these concerns. Danica (a Black woman) tells her partner Brad (a White man) that they need to be vigilant when they're visiting his hometown because many of the people there are racist. Brad responds with some strategies they can use to combat any racist comments they might get on the visit.

Romantic relationships and the communication that occurs within them vary widely. Cultural scripts guide how people conduct conversations in romantic relationships, but, other factors influence communication in these relationships, too. These factors include individual differences like love style, and the degree of security or certainty about the relationship, as well as contextual considerations like geographic distance and social sanctions. We now address communication in families.

Families

Families are unique close relationships for many reasons. First, their ties can be voluntary or involuntary. Some families consist of people who come together of their own free will, such as married partners, communes, or *intentional families* who band together by choice rather than by blood relationships. But many family members have relationships with others they did not choose, such as parents, grandparents, aunts, uncles, siblings, and so forth.

Families are also distinctive because for many members the close relationship is life-long. Some research (Serewicz, Dickson, Morrison, & Poole, 2007) indicates that even though we expect children to leave the nest as they reach adulthood, continuity of relationships with family members is just as important as increasing autonomy. Finally, unlike friendship or dating relationships, family is a close relationship that receives social, cultural, and legal sanctions through, for example, marriage, adoption, and inheritance.

There is some controversy in the research (see for example, Galvin, 2006; Floyd, Mikkelson, & Judd, 2006) concerning how to define a family. Some researchers (e.g., Floyd et al.) advocate the definition of family as a "socially, legally, and genetically oriented relationship" (p. 37). Others (e.g., Galvin) argue for allowing functions like communication to define the family. In other words, if a group of people function like a family by sharing affection and resources, and refer to themselves as a family, then they are a family. We agree with the more inclusive, communication-based definition.

One communication practice that's been examined as unique to families is storytelling. **Family stories,** or those bits of lore about family members and activities that are told and retold, have been seen as a way for members to construct a sense of family identity and meaning (Kellas, 2005). Some researchers argue that families don't just tell stories, but that storytelling is a way of creating a family (Langellier & Peterson, 2006). When Marie brings her new friend, Danielle, home to meet her parents, the stories that are told to Danielle are a way to bring the family alive for her and to integrate Danielle into the family fold.

Family stories are often pleasurable and entertaining, but they can sometimes serve as cautionary tales about family members who went astray in some way. Phil recalls hearing the story about his great-Uncle Thomas who lost the family fortune by gambling. Phil always got the impression that the story was told repeatedly to warn his generation to keep working hard and avoid developing bad habits.

Another important family communication practice is the **ritual,** or a repeated patterned communication event in a family's life. Rituals can take three forms: *everyday interactions* (for example, the Gilbert family always says grace before eating dinner together), *traditions* (for instance, Rollie and Elizabeth mark their anniversary each year by eating dinner at McDonald's because they met when they both worked there together), and *celebrations* (for example, Meyer and Scott ask their children to each say one thing that they're thankful for every year at Thanksgiving dinner). Celebrations differ from traditions because they involve holidays that are shared throughout a culture as opposed to traditions, which are practices that evolve in a specific family.

We now turn our attention to ways researchers have tried to explain communication in close relationships.

Explaining Communication in Close Relationships

Given the importance of communication in close relationships, it's understandable that research provides many theories to explain it. In fact, trying to explain communication and our relationships is something everyone spends a lot of time doing. We're "naïve psychologists" (Heider, 1958) engaging in "implicit theory making." We often ask why relationships develop the way they do and why some communication helps relationship woes and other communication makes them worse. In this section, we review the basic tenets of four major theories advanced by researchers.

Systems Theory

Systems theory (von Bertalanffy, 1968) compares relationships to living systems (like cells or the body), which have six important properties:

family stories

Bits of lore about family members and activities that are told and retold as a way for family members to construct a sense of family identity and meaning.

ritual

A repeated patterned communication event in a family's life.

- Wholeness
- Interdependence
- Hierarchy
- Boundaries or openness
- Calibration or feedback
- Equifinality

Systems researchers find that understanding how each of these six properties operates allows them to understand how communication in relationships works. Let's consider each of the properties.

Wholeness means that you can't understand a system by taking it apart and understanding each of its parts in isolation from one another. Wholeness indicates that knowing Bert and Ernie separately is not the same as knowing about the relationship between Bert and Ernie. The relationship between people is like a third entity that extends beyond each of the people individually. If you think of a specific relationship that you are in, the concept of wholeness becomes quite clear. The way you act and communicate in that relationship is probably different from the way you act and communicate in other relationships. The other person's reactions, contributions, and perceptions of you make a difference in how you behave, and vice versa. Further, the way you perceive the relationship between the two of you matters. If you are longtime friends with someone, you don't have to explain things to them the same way you might to someone who is a newer friend of yours. Wholeness tells us that just because Karen knows Cara and Susie individually doesn't mean she knows them *in relationship* to each other.

Interdependence builds on the notion of wholeness by asserting that members of systems depend on each other and are affected by one another. If Kyle's sister is injured in a car accident, his life is affected because of his relationship with her. When you talk to the people in your close relationships, you monitor their behavior and respond to it—you are affected by their shifts in mood and tone, and your communication shifts accordingly.

Hierarchy states that these shifts and accommodations don't exist in a vacuum. Kyle's relationship with his sister is embedded in the larger system of his family (all of the members of which are interdependent), and his family is embedded in the larger system of his extended family, his neighborhood, his culture, and so forth. Lower-level systems are called **subsystems**, and higher-levels are called **suprasystems**. Kyle and his sister form a subsystem of his family. Kyle's neighborhood is a suprasystem around his family. (See Figure 10.2 on page 344.)

Boundaries or openness refers to the fact that hierarchy is formed by creating boundaries around each separate system (Kyle and his sister, the family as a whole, and so forth). However, human systems are inherently open, and information passes through these boundaries. (Therefore, some researchers call this element "openness," and some call it "boundaries.") For example, Marsha and Hal are best friends who have a very close relationship, and they

wholeness

A principle that states that we can't fully understand a system by simply picking it apart and understanding each of its parts in isolation from one another.

hierarchy

A principle that states that all relationships are embedded within larger systems.

subsystems

Lower-level systems of relationship, such as a sibling relationship within a family.

suprasystems

Higher-level systems of relationship, such as a neighborhood consisting of several families.

boundaries or openness

A systems principle referring to the fact that hierarchy is formed by creating boundaries around each separate system (e.g., a brother and sister, the family as a whole, and so forth). However, human systems are inherently open, which means that information passes through these boundaries. Therefore, some researchers call this principle "openness," and some call it "boundaries."

Figure 10.2   Hierarchy as a systems principle

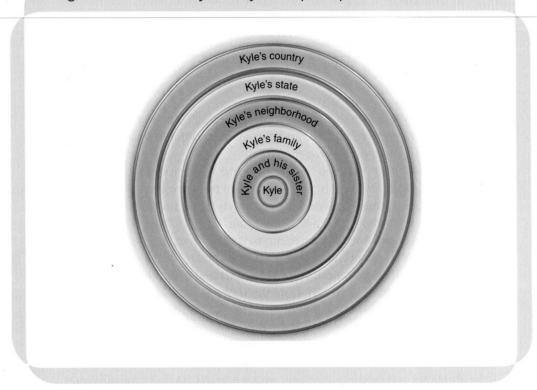

tell each other things that they don't tell their families. This closeness forms the boundary around their relationship. Yet if Marsha confides something to Hal that he finds disturbing, like that she is abusing drugs or feeling suicidal, Hal might ask members of his family or other friends for help. In so doing, Hal would expand the boundaries of their subsystem. Boundaries exist to keep information in the subsystem, but they also act to keep some information out of the subsystem. For instance, if Terry's mother doesn't like her boyfriend, Ron, Terry might work to keep that information away from the subsystem she and Ron create.

Calibration centers on how systems set their parameters, check on themselves, and self-correct. For example, Maggie and her grandmother have a close relationship, and the two of them form a subsystem of Maggie's extended family. When Maggie was 10, she and her grandmother calibrated their system by setting a weekly lunch date. As Maggie got older, she found it harder to meet her grandmother every Saturday for lunch because she wanted to do more activities with friends. She expressed this to her grandmother, and they **recalibrated** (or reset the rules of their system) by changing their lunch date to once a month. When systems experience such a change, it's a result of **positive feedback** (or feedback that's change producing). If they stay the same, the feedback is judged as **negative feedback** (or feedback that maintains the status quo).

---

calibration

The process of systems setting their parameters, checking on themselves, and self-correcting.

recalibrate

Adjust a relationship to accommodate changing needs of the parties.

positive feedback

Feedback that causes a system to recalibrate and change.

negative feedback

Feedback that causes a system to reject recalibration and stay the same.

Table 10.2 System properties and communication

Property	Communication outcome
Wholeness	The Thompson family is considered outgoing and funny. Ella Thompson is quiet and shy.
Interdependence	I can't talk to you when you act like that!
Hierarchy	Jake talks to his son, Marcus, about how his problems at work are making it hard for him to spend time with Marcus.
Boundaries or openness	Frieda tells a secret to her sister, Laya, and trusts her not to tell the rest of the family.
Calibration	Hap tells Miles they can't play basketball every Wednesday because he needs to spend more time with his son.
Equifinality	Laura and Roy are happily married, and they tell each other everything. Nadine and Bob are happily married, and they keep many things private and don't confide in each other as much.

Equifinality means the ability to achieve the same goals (or ends) by a variety of means. For instance, you may have some friends with whom you spend a lot of time and other friends with whom you spend less time. Some of your friends may be people you play tennis with, and others may be those you like to go to movies with. Each of these friendships may be close, but you become close (and maintain your closeness) in different ways.

Table 10.2 illustrates how each of the six properties of systems theory relates to communication behaviors. Systems theory doesn't explain all communication with our relational partners; it isn't specific enough to give us answers to questions like why some couples argue more than others or why some communication in friendships is more satisfying than others. However, it does give us an overall impression of how relationships work and how communication behaviors function within relationships.

Dialectics Theory

A different explanation for communication in close relationships comes from dialectics theory, which we discussed in Chapter 8. Dialectics focuses on the tensions relational partners feel as a result of desiring two opposing things at once. Dialectic thinking rejects "either–or" approaches in favor of "both–and." In Chapter 8 we talked about one specific tension or dialectic: openness

equifinality

The ability to achieve the same goals (or ends) by a variety of means.

How's this sound? "Man of steel seeks woman of Teflon for non-stick relationship. No women of silicone, please."

DAN PIRARO. BIZARRO.COM 8·24·04 Dist. by King Features

(disclosing) and protection (keeping silent). Now we'll discuss other tensions that people experience in close relationships.

Along with openness and protection, the most common tensions in relationships are autonomy and connection, and novelty and predictability. The contradiction between **autonomy and connection** centers on our desire to be independent or autonomous while simultaneously wanting to feel a connection with our partner. For example, this tension is apparent when Desiree wants to be with her own friends while also wanting to spend time with her boyfriend, Shane. The tension between **novelty and predictability** manifests in our simultaneous desires for excitement and stability. For example, Malcolm feels bored with the everyday routines he's established in his relationship with Tom, but he also feels comforted and reassured by them. It's scary to leave familiar routines, even when you might find them tedious. These three basic contradictions or dialectics are all seen as dynamic. This means that the interplay between the two opposites permeates the life of a relationship and is never fully resolved.

In addition to these, some other dialectics are found specifically in friendships (Rawlins, 1992). They include the following:

- Judgment and acceptance
- Affection and instrumentality
- Public and private
- Ideal and real

The tension between **judgment and acceptance** involves criticizing a friend as opposed to accepting them. People are often torn between offering (unwanted) advice and accepting a friend's behavior. For instance, if Maria has a friend, Josh, who is dating someone Maria thinks is wrong for him, or someone who is dishonest or untrustworthy, should she offer her opinion or simply accept Josh's choice? Most people want both things simultaneously; they want to be able to make and hear judgments, but they also want unconditional acceptance. The next dialectic, **affection and instrumentality**, poses a tension between framing your friendship with someone as an end in itself (affection) or seeing it as a means to another end (instrumentality). This dialectic

autonomy and connection dialectic

The tension between our desire to be independent or autonomous while simultaneously wanting to feel a connection with our partner.

novelty and predictability dialectic

Our simultaneous, opposing desires for excitement and stability in our relationships.

judgment and acceptance dialectic

Our desire to criticize a friend as opposed to accepting a friend for who he or she is.

affection and instrumentality dialectic

The tension between framing a friendship with someone as an end in itself (affection) or seeing it as a means to another end (instrumentality).

Table 10.3 Summary of dialectics

Most common relational dialectics

1. Autonomy and connection
2. Openness and protection
3. Novelty and predictability

Additional dialectics found in friendships

1. Judgment and acceptance
2. Affection and instrumentality
3. Public and private
4. Ideal and real

suggests that in close friendships, people want to both just enjoy their friends and get some help from them. For example, if Tony often gets a ride to work from his close friend, Michael, that friendship serves an instrumental function. But Tony values the friendship for affectionate reasons as well, such as the fun he and Michael have talking to each other on the way to work.

The two previous tensions are **internal dialectics** because they focus on how the partners communicate with one another. The next two are **external dialectics** because they have to do with how friends negotiate the more public aspects of their friendship. For instance, the dialectic between **public and private** specifically centers on how much of the friendship is demonstrated in public and what parts are kept private. Some emblems of friendship are fine for public consumption (like the fact that Kelly and Amy both like horror movies and always race to see the newest releases) while other things (like the silly nicknames they have for one another) might be kept between them. Some friendships, especially in adolescence, are kept more private. For instance, Terry, the football team captain at Metropolitan University, doesn't always share publicly that he's friends with Paul, a computer geek. In private, Terry and Paul get along well, but neither especially wants to publicize their friendship.

Finally, the dialectic between the **ideal and real** reveals the tension between an idealized vision of friendship and the real friends that one has. For example, we may carry images in our heads of how self-sacrificing, other-oriented, and altruistic friends should be. We get these mental images in large part from popular culture: television shows, buddy movies, books, and magazines that show examples of friendships. Although Georgia recognizes that these idealized images of friendship are fantasies, she can't help feeling some tension when her best friend, Alma, goes on a ski trip, even though Georgia can't make it. Georgia had hoped that Alma would refuse to go without her. (See Table 10.3 for a summary of the dialectics.)

internal dialectics

Tensions resulting from oppositions inherent in relational partners' communication with each other.

external dialectics

Tensions between oppositions that have to do with how relational partners negotiate the public aspects of their relationship.

public and private dialectic

The tension between how much of a friendship is demonstrated in public and what parts are kept private.

ideal and real dialectic

The tension between an idealized vision of friendship and the real friends one has.

REVISITING
CASEinPOINT

1. *How does Randy and Hope's relation-ship illustrate the autonomy-connection tension?*

2. *How does Randy and Hope's relation-ship illustrate the affection-instrumentality tension?*

You can answer these questions online under the resources for Chapter 10 at your online Resource Center for Under-standing Interpersonal Communication.

Like systems theory, the dialectics approach is rather general. Although it provides a framework for understanding how people struggle with oppo-sitions in relationships and helps us understand some communi-cation behavior as strategies for dealing with these tensions (see Chapter 8), it doesn't clearly predict which strategies people will use, nor does it tell us why some relationships are more stressed than others by these tensions. However, dialectics theory is a good starting place for revealing some of the under-currents that guide communica-tion in close relationships.

Social Exchange Theories

Social exchange theories come from a different line of thinking than the systems and dialectics approaches. Rather than providing a large framework for understanding communication in close relationships, social exchange theories are more specific and point us more directly toward testable predic-tions about it. Social exchange isn't just a single theory (Roloff, 1981); rather, several theories advance the same general assumptions of social exchange. We'll talk briefly about these assumptions and then profile one particular social exchange theory, John Thibaut and Harold Kelley's (1959) theory of interdependence.

Assumptions of Social Exchange

The heart of social exchange thinking lies in two concepts: costs and rewards. **Costs** are those things in relational life that people judge as negative. Exam-ples include having to do favors for friends, listen to Uncle Al's boring stories at family gatherings, or baby-sit for a bratty younger cousin. **Rewards** are those parts of being in a relationship that are pleasurable to people. Examples include having your spouse listen to your problems and offer empathy, shar-ing favorite activities with a friend, and laughing about private jokes with your brother. The social exchange perspective asserts that people are moti-vated to maximize their rewards while minimizing their costs (Molm, 2001). It assumes that all people do mental calculations about the costs and the rewards they experience in relationships, subtracting their costs from their rewards, and judging their relationships by the difference. The theories

costs

Those things in relational life that we judge as negative.

rewards

Those parts of being in a relationship that we find pleasurable.

assume that when costs exceed rewards, people will leave the relationship, if possible.

© Image 100/Royalty-Free/Corbis

Implicit in this discussion are three basic assumptions about human nature: people are motivated by rewards and wish to avoid punishments, people are rational, and people evaluate costs and rewards differently. For example, according to the first assumption, exchange theorists believe that Jennifer and Laurie each want to do things they find rewarding (like going to the movies together) and that neither want to do things that seem like punishment (Jennifer wouldn't want to do Laurie's laundry, for example). The next assumption clarifies the first by asserting that people are thinking rationally most of the time, enabling them to calculate accurately what the costs and rewards of any given relationship might be. People keep mental balance sheets about relational activities (for instance, "I had to spend two hours helping Dan with his economics homework, and he repaid me by buying my lunch yesterday").

Finally, according to the third assumption of social exchange theory, what is costly for one person might seem rewarding for another. For example, Matt finds baby-sitting for his cousin a drag. But Meg majored in early child-hood education and doesn't have a chance to spend time with children, so she welcomes the opportunity to baby-sit for her cousin. Further, both people in a relationship may see their costs and rewards differently. For instance, Hillary thinks that the fact that her parents don't like Pat is a huge cost to their relationship, but Pat isn't concerned about parental approval, so he ranks the cost much lower.

The social exchange theory assumes that we stay in relationships that provide us with more rewards than costs. What are some of the rewards and costs of your own close relationships? What rewards would cause you to stay in a relationship despite the costs? Conversely, what costs would cause you to leave a relationship despite the rewards?

Theory of Interdependence

Thibaut and Kelley's (1959) theory of interdependence builds on these assumptions of social exchange theory and adds an ingredient from systems theory—that is, the idea that relationships are interdependent. Whatever one person does in a relationship affects the other and their relationship as a whole. Further, this theory adds more explanation for why people stay or leave relationships. The general principle of social exchange says people stay in relationships in which rewards outweigh costs. However, we know that sometimes people stay in relationships that seem pretty bad, and some seem-ingly good relationships end.

The theory of interdependence contains some explanation for these situa-tions: comparison level, comparison level for alternatives, and relative power position. **Comparison level** is a person's expectations for a given relationship.

comparison level

A person's standard level for what types of costs and rewards should exist in a given relationship.

People learn from a variety of sources—like the media, their families, and their past experiences—what to expect from relationships. Your comparison level might tell you that friendship is a relationship in which you should expect to give and take in equal proportions, whereas love relationships require more giving than taking. The theory predicts that people will be satisfied in relationships where the actual relationship matches or exceeds their comparison level. When people are satisfied in a relationship, they are more likely to engage in relational maintenance behaviors (Stafford & Canary, 2006).

Comparison level for alternatives refers to comparing the costs and rewards of a current relationship to the possibility of doing better in a different relationship. For example, Melanie calculates that she has more costs than rewards in her relationship with her husband, Erik. However, she still might stay with Erik if she also calculates that her chances of doing better without him, either by finding a better relationship or being alone, are poor. Some researchers (for example, Walker, 1984) have used this theory to explain why women stay in abusive relationships.

Relative power position suggests that when people believe they have a higher power status than their partner's, they will engage in risky strategies without fearing the costs. This is especially the case in initiating relationships (Wildermuth, Vogl-Bauer, & Rivera, 2006). For example, if Rosemary thinks she's a "catch" and generally has success with men she wants to date, she may be motivated to make a slightly off-color joke to get Kyle's attention even though that's a strategy associated with high costs.

For more on social exchange theory, particularly how it relates to emotions and the emotional process, read the article "Bringing Emotions into Social Exchange Theory," available through InfoTrac College Edition. Use your online Resource Center for *Understanding Interpersonal Communication* to access *InfoTrac College Edition Exercise 10.2: Emotions and Social Exchange* under the resources for Chapter 10.

comparison level for alternatives

A comparison of the costs and rewards of a current relationship to the possibility of doing better in a different relationship.

relative power position

A situation in which a partner in a relationship believes he or she has a higher power status than the other partner, and so will engage in risky strategies without fearing the costs.

Stage Models: Step by Step

Each of the three theories we have just reviewed has a different premise about relationships: that they operate like systems, that they are fraught with tensions and contradictions, or that they are developed through self-interest. In contrast, stage models are concerned with how relationships develop and how communication changes as we deepen or weaken our relational ties with another. Perhaps the best known of the many stage models that describe relational life was originated by Mark Knapp (1978). Knapp actually built his model on social exchange theories; he argues that costs and rewards are the general motivating force for relational movement. However, his work differs from social exchange theories in that it further clarifies *how* the movement in relationships takes place and how communication characterizes relational growth and decay.

Table 10.4 Knapp's model of relationship development

Coming together

Stage	Sample communication
Initiating	"Hi, how are you?"
Experimenting	"Do you like water polo?"
Intensifying	"Let's take a vacation together this summer. We can play water polo!"
Integrating	"You are the best friend I could ever have!"
Bonding	"Let's wear our team shirts to the party. I want everyone to know we're on the same team!"

Coming apart

Stage	Sample communication
Differentiating	"I am surprised that you supported a Republican. I am a longtime Democrat."
Circumscribing	"Maybe we'd be better off if we didn't talk about politics."
Stagnating	"Wow, I could have predicted you'd say that!"
Avoiding	"I have too much homework to meet you for coffee."
Terminating	"I think we shouldn't hang out together anymore. It's just not fun now."

The model answers the following questions: "Are there regular and systematic patterns of communication that suggest stages on the road to a more intimate relationship? Are there similar patterns and stages that characterize the deterioration of relationships?" (Knapp & Vangelisti, 2000, p. 36). The model provides five stages of coming together and five stages of coming apart. See Table 10.4 for a summary of the model.

The model is useful for all kinds of relationships because it provides for relationships that end after only a couple of stages as well as relationships that do not move beyond an early stage (Knapp & Vangelisti, 2005). In addition, the model explains the movement of friendships as well as love relationships. As you read about the stages, try to imagine how they work in a variety of relationships.

Some people have criticized all stage models for presenting a linear picture of relationship development. These critics note that relational development doesn't happen neatly in stages and that the model doesn't clarify what happens when one partner moves to a new stage and the other doesn't. For example, one partner may want to terminate the relationship while the other resists. One study (Buchanan, O'Hair, & Becker, 2006) examines what strategies married partners tried to resist termination, including negativity, pointing out ways they're bonded, expressing commitment, and using violence in some way. All of these strategies proved unsuccessful—all of the respondents were divorced.

Stage models simplify a complicated process. Each stage may contain some behavior from other, earlier stages, and people sometimes slide back and forth between stages as they interact in their relationship. Thus, stage models give us a snapshot of the process of relationship development, but they don't tell the entire story. In the following sections, we briefly discuss each of the stages in the model.

Initiating

This stage is where a relationship begins. In the **initiating stage**, two people notice one another and indicate to each other that they are interested in making contact: "I notice you, and I think you're noticing me, too. Let's talk and see where it goes." Initiation depends on attraction, which can be seen as either short-term or long-term.

Short-term attraction, a judgment of relationship potential, propels us into the initiation stage. **Long-term attraction**, which makes you want to continue a relationship and move through the subsequent stages, sustains and maintains relationships. Sometimes the things that attract you to someone in the short term may be the things that turn you off in the long term. For example, Marge may have initially struck up a friendship with Anita because she saw Anita as outgoing and friendly. However, later in their relationship, Marge may come to resent how much Anita talks to others because it means less time for the two of them to interact.

Both types of attraction are based on several elements, such as physical attractiveness, charisma, physical closeness, similarity, complementary needs, positive outcomes, and reciprocation. People are attracted to others who fit their cultural ideal of attractiveness, but they are more likely to initiate relationships with others who tend to match their own level of attractiveness (Cash & Derlega, 1978; Hinsz, 1989; White, 1980). In other words, we feel more comfortable talking with people who are about as physically attractive as we see ourselves to be. We also like people who are confident and exude charisma. Furthermore, it's more likely that we'll be attracted to those who are in physical proximity to us than to those who are more distant, because it's more difficult to enter the initiating stage with someone who is far away.

We are also motivated to initiate conversations with those who share some of our own attributes, values, and opinions. A study investigating why people are attracted to one another, found that a "likes-attract" rule was much stronger than an "opposites-attract" rule for heterosexual couples in Western cultures (Buston & Emlen, 2003). Yet, too much similarity can be boring, so we may seek a partner with some attributes that complement ours as well. For example, if Chris is quiet and Glenn is talkative, they may want to initiate a conversation because they complement each other. Finally, we are attracted to others who seem attracted to us, or who reciprocate our inter-

initiating stage

The first stage in the coming together part of Knapp's model of relationship development, in which two people notice each other and indicate to each other that they are interested in making contact.

short-term attraction

A judgment of relationship potential that propels us into initiating a relationship.

long-term attraction

Judgment of a relationship that makes us want to continue a relationship after initiating it. This attraction sustains and maintains relationships.

est. For instance, when Renny smiles at Natalie at a party and she doesn't smile back, Renny probably won't go any further with the relationship.

Some of our relationships stay in the initiating stage. You may see the same person often in a place you frequent, such as a supermarket, bookstore, or coffee shop. Each time you see this person, you might exchange smiles and pleasantries. You may have short, ritualized conversations about the weather or other topics but never move on to any of the other stages in the model. Thus, you could have a long-term relationship that never moves out of initiating.

Experimenting

In the second stage, **experimenting**, people become acquainted by gathering information about one another. They engage in **small talk**—interactions that are relaxed, pleasant, uncritical, and casual. Through small talk, people learn about one another, reduce their uncertainties, find topics that they might wish to spend more time discussing, "test the waters" to see if they want to develop the relationship further, and maintain a sense of community.

Many of our relationships stay in the experimenting stage (Knapp & Vangelisti, 2005). We have many friends whom we know through small talk but not at a deeper level. If you see a friend in the coffee shop and go beyond "Hi, it sure is nice to see sunshine today" to small talk, you have deepened the relationship some, but you still have kept it at a low level of commitment. Further, even people in close relationships spend time in this stage, perhaps in an effort to understand their partner more, to pass the time, or to avoid uncomfortable feelings stirred up by a more intense conversation.

Intensifying

This stage begins to move the relationship to a closeness not seen in the previous stages. **Intensifying** refers to the deepening of intimacy in the relationship. During this stage, partners self-disclose, forms of address become more informal, and people may use nicknames or terms of endearment to address one another ("Hi, honey"). Relational partners begin to speak of a "we" or "us," as in "We like to go to the basketball games" or "It'll be nice for us to get a break from studying and go for a walk."

In this stage, people begin to develop their own language based on private symbols for past experiences or knowledge of each other's habits, desires, and beliefs. For instance, Missy and her mother still say "hmmm" to each other, because that's what Missy said when she was little to mean "I want more." And Neil says, "It's just like walking on a rocky path" when he wants Ana to do something because when they first became friends, he made Ana take a walk along a path scattered with rocks when Ana wanted to go the movies instead.

Further, this stage is marked by more direct statements of commitment— "I have never had a better friend than you," or "I am so happy being with you." Often these statements are met with reciprocal comments—"Me neither," or "Same here." In intensifying, the partners become more sophisticated nonverbally. They are able to read each other's nonverbal cues, may

experimenting stage

A stage in the coming together part of Knapp's model of relationship development in which two people become acquainted by gathering information about each other.

small talk

Conversational interactions that are relaxed, pleasant, uncritical, and casual.

intensifying stage

A stage in the coming together part of Knapp's model of relationship development in which the intimacy between the partners intensifies.

replace some verbalizations with a touch, and may mirror one another's non-verbal cues—how they stand, gesture, dress, and so forth may become more similar. One way Candi intensified her friendship with Tricia was to stop dressing like her old friends and to start wearing clothes and makeup that made her look like her new friend.

Integrating

In this fourth stage, the partners seem to coalesce. **Integrating** has also been called "coupling" (Davis, 1973) because it represents the two people forming a clear identity as a couple. This coupling is often acknowledged by the pair's social circles; they cultivate friends together, and are treated as a unit by their friends. They are invited to places together, and information shared with one is expected to be shared with the other.

Sometimes the partners designate common property. They may pick a song to be "our song," open a joint bank account, buy a dog, or move into an apartment together. In our case as authors of this book, coauthoring a series of books together has created a couple identity for us. We are often referred to together, and if people ask one of us to do something (such as make a presentation at a convention), they usually assume that the other will come along as well.

Bonding

The final stage in the coming together part of the model is **bonding**, which refers to a public commitment of the relationship. Bonding is easier in some types of relationships than in others. For heterosexual couples, the marriage ceremony is a traditional bonding ritual. Having a bonding ritual provides a certain social sanction for the relationship.

Other relationships don't have a well-recognized ritual to gain social sanction or public recognition. However, because bonding is important to many people, some have worked to create ceremonies. Examples include commitment ceremonies for gay and lesbian couples, naming ceremonies for new babies to welcome them to the family, and initiation ceremonies to welcome new "sisters" or "brothers" to sororities and fraternities.

integrating stage

A stage in the coming together part of Knapp's model of relationship development in which two partners form a clear identity as a couple.

bonding stage

The final stage in the coming together part of Knapp's model of relationship development, in which partners make a public commitment to their relationship.

Differentiating

The first stage in the coming apart section of the model, **differentiating** refers to beginning to notice ways in which the partners differ. In this stage, individuality is highlighted. This is unlike the coming together stages, which featured the partners' similarities. The most dramatic episodes of differentiating involve conflict, discussed in Chapter 9. However, people can differentiate without engaging in conflict. For example, the following seemingly inconsequential comment exemplifies differentiation: "Oh, you like that sweater? I never would have thought you'd wear sweaters with Christmas trees on them. I guess our taste in clothes is more different than I thought."

People switch from "we" to "I" in this stage and talk more about themselves as individuals than as part of a couple. According to the model, this stage is the beginning of the relationship's unraveling process. However, we know that relationships can oscillate between differentiation and some of the coming together stages, like intensifying. No two people can remain in a coming together stage such as intensifying, integrating, or bonding without experiencing some differentiating.

Circumscribing

The next stage, **circumscribing**, refers to restraining communication behaviors so fewer topics are raised (for fear of conflict) and more issues are out of bounds. The couple interacts less. This stage is characterized by silences and comments like "I don't want to talk about that anymore," "Let's not go there," and "It's none of your business." Again, relationships in all stages of the model may experience some taboo topics or behaviors that are typical of circumscribing. But when relationships enter circumscribing (in other words, if the biggest proportion of their communication is of this type), that is a sign of a decaying relationship. If measures aren't taken to repair the situation—sitting down and talking about why there's a problem, going to counseling, taking a vacation, or some other remedy—the model shows that people enter the next stage.

Stagnating

The third stage of coming apart, **stagnating**, consists of extending circumscribing so far that the couple no longer talks much. They express the feeling that there is no use to talk because they already know what the other will say. "There's no point in bringing this up—I know she won't like the idea" is a common theme during this stage. People feel "stuck," and their communication is draining, awkward, stylized, and unsatisfying.

Each partner may engage in **imagined conversations** (Honeycutt, 2003), where one partner plays the parts of both partners in a mental rehearsal of the negative communication that characterizes this stage. Me: "I want to go visit my parents." Me in Role of Partner: "Well, I'm too busy to go with you." Me: "You never want to do stuff with my family." Me in Role of Partner: "That may be true, but you certainly can't stand my family!" After this

differentiating stage
The first stage in the coming apart section of Knapp's model of relationship development, in which two people begin to notice ways in which they differ.

circumscribing stage
A stage in the coming apart section of Knapp's model of relationship development in which two people's communication behaviors are restrained so that fewer topics are raised (for fear of conflict), more issues are out of bounds, and they interact less.

stagnating stage
A stage in the coming apart section of Knapp's model of relationship development in which circumscribing is extended so far that a couple no longer talks much except in the most routinized ways.

imagined conversation
A conversation with oneself in which one partner plays the parts of both partners in a mental rehearsal.

rehearsal, people usually decide it's not worth the effort to engage in the conversation for real.

Avoiding

If a relationship stagnates for too long, the partners may decide that the relationship is unpleasant. As a result, they move to **avoiding**, a stage where partners try to stay out of the same physical environment. Partners make excuses for why they can't see one another ("Sorry, I have too much work to go out tonight;" "I'll be busy all week;" or "I've got to go home for the weekend"). They may vary their habits so that they do not run into their partner as they used to. For example, if people used to meet at a particular restaurant or a certain spot on campus, they change their routines and no longer stop by these places.

Sometimes it isn't possible to physically avoid a partner. If a couple is married and unable to afford two residences, or if siblings still live in their parents' home, it's difficult for the partners to be completely separate. In such cases, partners in the avoiding stage simply ignore one another or make a tacit agreement to segregate their living quarters as much as possible. For example, the married couple may sleep in separate rooms, and the siblings may come into the den at different times of day. When partners in the avoiding stage accidentally run into one another, they turn away without speaking.

Terminating

This stage comes after the relational partners have decided, either jointly or individually, to part permanently. **Terminating** refers to the process of ending a relationship. Some relationships enter terminating almost immediately: You meet someone at a party, go through initiating and experimenting, and then decide you don't want to see them anymore, so you move to terminating. Other relationships go through all or most of the stages before terminating. Some relationships endure in one stage or another and never go through terminating. And other relationships go through terminating and then begin again (people remarry and estranged friends reunite). Further, some relationships terminate in one form and then begin again in a redefined way. For

avoiding stage

A stage in the coming apart section of Knapp's model of relationship development in which two partners stay away from each other because they feel that being together is unpleasant.

terminating stage

The last stage in the coming apart section of Knapp's model of relationship development, in which a relationship is ending.

example, when Scott and Virginia get divorced, they end their relationship as married partners. However, because they have two children, they redefine their relationship and become friends.

Terminating a relationship can be simple ("We have to end this") or complicated (involving lots of discussion and even the intervention of third parties like counselors, mediators, and attorneys). It may happen suddenly or drag out over a long time. It can be accomplished with a lot of talk that reflects on the life of the relationship and the reasons for terminating it, or it can be accomplished with relatively little or no discussion.

For more about Knapp's relational stages model and information about strategies for terminating relationships, use your online Resource Center for *Understanding Interpersonal Communication* to access *Interactive Activity 10.3: Knapp's Relational Stages Model* under the resources for Chapter 10.

Choices in Communicating in Close Relationships

This section presents several ways to improve communication in close relationships. Because many factors affect relationship development, we are necessarily broad in offering these suggestions. As we have emphasized in this chapter, communicating with people in close relationships is our source of greatest pleasure and greatest grief.

Communication Skills for Beginning Relationships

Beginning a relationship requires a fair amount of skill, although you may not

Ethics & Choice

Connie and Paul Miller had been married for four years, and were very happy. They wanted children, but after trying unsuccessfully to conceive for almost a year, they were discouraged. They finally consulted a fertility expert, who told them the sad news that they'd never be able to conceive because Paul's sperm count was too low. However, the doctor did offer one intriguing possibility to the couple—a sperm donor. If they chose this option, Connie could carry the baby and give birth. They went home to think about it.

After they'd talked about it endlessly, they still weren't sure what to do. They decided to ask their family and friends what they thought of such a method of conception. They were a little afraid that they'd be seen as strange or freakish if they had a child using this technology. They knew that the procedure was common, but they didn't personally know anyone who had used a sperm donor, and the idea still seemed like science fiction to them.

At a family gathering one evening, Connie and Paul made seemingly offhand comments about how a friend was considering conception via sperm donor, and they were happy to find that no one seemed to consider the prospect too weird. The day after the family dinner, Paul got a call at work from his brother, Lucas. Lucas told Paul that he wondered if Paul and Connie were thinking about using a sperm donor to conceive. Paul was actually relieved that Lucas knew the truth, and by the end of their conversation, Lucas had volunteered to be the donor.

Connie and Paul accepted Lucas's offer gratefully, and soon Connie was carrying a child who was born healthy and perfect. The baby, whom they named Hannah, was a pure delight, and the Millers were completely happy. Yet, as Hannah got older, Connie began to wonder whether they should tell her that half of her genetic makeup was contributed by her uncle, not Paul. At first, they hadn't planned to tell her. Lucas hadn't asked them to do so, and he was very comfortable in his role as Hannah's uncle. Because Lucas and Paul were brothers, Hannah resembled her father, and there didn't seem to be any obvious reasons to make the disclosure.

However, lately Connie had been wondering if keeping a secret so big might cause some problems down the road for her family. She thought that Hannah had a right to know how she came into the world. Yet, Connie worried about how telling Hannah the truth might change the relationships among herself, Hannah, Paul, and Lucas, not to mention Paul's parents, who hadn't been told. Things seemed to be going so well, and Connie didn't want to disrupt her family's harmony.

(Continues)

think about developing these skills. Most people meet new people fairly frequently, and they don't consciously think about how they go about striking up conversations and cultivating new friends. One study (Douglas, 1987) examined the skills needed to initiate relationships; these techniques are described below.

Paul was very proud of his daughter, and Connie definitely didn't want to change how they regarded each other. Wrestling with this decision was keeping her up at night. What do you think Connie should do in this situation? How should she broach the subject with Paul, Lucas, and her in-laws? What are the implications of keeping family secrets? Do you agree that keeping secrets creates a toxic situation that erodes trust and ultimately damages relationships? Is it ethical to tell something that you know will hurt someone else, at least in the short run? In answering these questions, what ethical system of communication informs your decision (categorical imperative, utilitarianism, ethic of care, golden mean, significant choice)?

Go to your online Resource Center for *Understanding Interpersonal Communication* to access an interactive version of this scenario under the resources for Chapter 10. The interactive version of this scenario allows you to choose an appropriate response to this dilemma and then see what consequences your choice brings about. You can also compare your answers to the questions at the end of the scenario to those provided by the authors and, if requested, email your response to your instructor.

networking

In relational development, finding out information about a person from a third party.

offering

Putting ourselves in a good position for another to approach us in a social situation.

approaching

Providing nonverbal signals that indicate we'd like to initiate contact with another person, such as going up to a person or smiling in that person's direction.

Networking

Networking means finding out information about the person from a third party. Easing into a relationship with the help of a third person means that you're behaving efficiently and in a socially acceptable fashion.

Offering

Offering means putting yourself in a good position for another to approach you. If you sit near a person you'd like to get to know better, or walk along the same route that they do, you're putting proximity to work for you.

Approaching

Approaching means actually going up to a person or smiling in that person's direction to give a signal that you would like to initiate contact. Approaching allows the relationship to begin, with both parties involved in some interaction.

Sustaining

Sustaining means behaving in a way that keeps the initial conversation going. Asking appropriate questions is a way to employ sustaining.

Affinity Seeking

Affinity seeking means emphasizing the commonalities you think you share with the other person. Sometimes affinity seeking goes hand in hand with asking appropriate questions; you first ask questions to determine areas of common interest or experience, and then you comment on them. "Do you like reality shows?" "No kidding? I'm a big fan, too." According to research, people use a variety of affinity-seeking strategies to get others to like them (Bell & Daly, 1984) (see Table 10.5 for a summary of their strategies).

Table 10.5 Affinity-seeking strategies

1.	**Altruism**	Help the other person and offer to do things for him or her.
2.	**Assume control**	Take a leadership position.
3.	**Assume equality**	Don't show off. Treat the other as an equal.
4.	**Comfort**	Act at ease.
5.	**Concede control**	Allow the other to be in charge.
6.	**Conversational rules**	Follow the cultural norms for a conversation.
7.	**Dynamism**	Project excitement and enthusiasm.
8.	**Elicit disclosure**	Ask questions and encourage the other to talk.
9.	**Inclusion**	Include the other in activities and conversations.
10.	**Facilitate enjoyment**	Make time together enjoyable.
11.	**Closeness**	Indicate that the two of you have a close relationship.
12.	**Listening**	Lean in, listen intently, and respond appropriately.
13.	**Nonverbal immediacy**	Display good eye contact, appropriate touching, and so forth.
14.	**Openness**	Disclose appropriate personal information.
15.	**Optimism**	Display cheerfulness and positivity.
16.	**Personal autonomy**	Project independence.
17.	**Physical attraction**	Try to look good.
18.	**Present self as interesting**	Highlight past accomplishments and things of interest about self.
19.	**Reward association**	Offer favors and remind about past favors.
20.	**Confirmation**	Flatter the other.
21.	**Inclusion**	Spend time with the other.
22.	**Sensitivity**	Display empathy appropriately.
23.	**Similarities**	Point out things you have in common.
24.	**Supportiveness**	Be encouraging of the other and avoid criticism.
25.	**Trustworthiness**	Be dependable and sincere.

Adapted from Bell & Daly, 1984.

Communication Skills for Maintaining Relationships

Some people focus all their attention on beginning a relationship, thinking that after they have a friend, a boyfriend, or a girlfriend, they have achieved their goal. They fail to realize that close relationships need attention, and sometimes work, to keep them functioning. Recently people have recognized how much nurturing a close relationship requires and many popular books

sustaining

Behaving in a way that keeps an initial conversation going, such as asking questions.

affinity seeking

Emphasizing the commonalities we think we share with another person.

"We really need to talk about our relationship, so I've booked us on a TV show."

GREGORY

offer advice on enhancing relational quality (Egbert & Polk, 2006). Of course, close relationships aren't all work, or we wouldn't enjoy them so much. But if you ignore your closest relationships, they'll begin to falter and perhaps deteriorate. **Preventative maintenance** involves both partners paying attention to their relationship even when it's not experiencing trouble. Some relational maintenance behaviors include:

- offering assurances ("I am committed to our relationship")
- expressing openness ("Here's how I feel about our relationship")
- reflecting positivity ("You did such a great job on that!")
- sharing tasks ("If you'll clean the bathroom, I'll do the kitchen")
- including social networks ("Why don't you ask your sister to come to the movies with us?") (Canary & Stafford, 1992; Stafford, Dainton & Haas, 2000).

We will review in a bit more detail two related skills for preventative maintenance: expressing supportiveness and humor.

Supportiveness

A supportive communication climate, which encourages relational growth and maintenance, is conducive to maintaining relationships. However, supportive climates do not happen by chance; skillful communication is necessary to build this type of climate. The overall guidelines for developing supportive climates for communication (Gibb, 1961, 1964, 1970) are as follows:

- Make *descriptive* rather than evaluative comments ("You have interrupted me twice.")
- Speak in *provisional* ways rather than in a certain manner ("I'm not sure, but I think that's the case.")

---

preventative maintenance

Paying attention to our relationships even when they are not experiencing troubles.

relational transgressions

Negative behaviors in close relationships, such as betrayals, deceptions, and hurtful comments.

- Be more *spontaneous* than strategic ("Let's go on a picnic!")

- Strive for a *problem orientation* rather than a control orientation ("How can we solve this so we're both happy?")

- Provide *empathy* instead of neutrality to your partner ("I can tell that you're upset. Do you want to talk to me about it?")

- Establish *equality* between partners rather than superiority of one over the other ("What do you think? I really want to know your opinion.")

Using Humor

Humor also serves a preventative maintenance function. Joking and kidding are both indicators of enjoyment. Research supports the notion that humor promotes bonding and cohesion as well as stress management (Axmaker, 2002–2004). You can probably think of a time when you shared a joke with a friend or broke the tension with a humorous statement. Humor is a way of bringing people together (Young & Bippus, 2001). Bonding over something that's seen as amusing by both partners helps maintain relationships.

Communication Skills for Repairing Relationships

As we've discussed throughout this chapter, having close relationships is critically important to people. However, some communication in close relationships is unhealthy or toxic. In close relationships, people can betray, deceive, and say hurtful things to each other. Researchers call these negative behaviors **relational transgressions** (Bachman & Guerrero, 2006; Guerrero, Andersen & Afifi, 2007). When people in close relationships experience a relational transgression, they have to decide whether to repair or terminate the relationship. If they decide not to terminate the relationship, they must engage in the difficult task of **corrective maintenance**, or repair (Dindia, 1994). Remember that relational repair is the job of both partners. Repair skills are more difficult to implement than maintenance skills because repair involves correcting a problem,

...at work

At work, we may not feel that a supportive atmosphere is necessary or even possible. And, of course, there are boundaries in the workplace concerning pursuing personal relationships. Yet, it is possible to adapt some of the elements we've discussed for supportive climates to the workplace. For instance, empathy is a skill that may be useful on the job. If you and a coworker, Mel, are working together on a project, and Mel experiences a death in her family before the project is completed, you need to empathize. While your relationship with Mel might not be close, you will nonetheless need to acknowledge her personal issues before you can expect to be productive professionally. Can you identify other instances where a supportive climate can be helpful in the workplace?

...with your partner in your new house

You and your partner have just moved into your first new home together. You're excited—the house is beautiful and you're very much in love. You go into the kitchen and find that your partner has lit candles and set the card table up with flowers and two place settings. You are touched at your partner's thoughtfulness, and try to think of a reciprocal gesture to show how much you're looking forward to living in this home together. For some reason, you can't think of anything to say that seems meaningful enough. You can see your partner looking at you expectantly. What should you say or do to show your emotions? What skills of relational maintenance would come in handy for you now?

corrective maintenance

Repairing a relationship when it runs into trouble.

interpersonal explorer

Before you finish reading this chapter, take a moment to review the theories and skills discussed. How do you think the theories discussed in this chapter can help you better understand interpersonal communication and close relationships? In what ways can the skills discussed help you interact more effectively with other people in your life?

Theories that relate to relationships

- **Systems theory**
  Close relationships are like living systems that consist of interrelated and interdependent elements
- **Dialectics**
  Close relationships are characterized by contradictory impulses, like the impulse to bond with another and the impulse to maintain individuality
- **Social exchange theories**
  A group of theories stating that close relationships are governed by the partners' assessments of how costly or rewarding they are
- **Stage model**
  A close relationship follows five separate stages for coming together. Close relationships also follow five stages when they come apart. Each of the 10 stages is characterized by specific communication behaviors

Practical skills for beginning, maintaining, and repairing relationships

To begin
- Network
- Offer or make yourself approachable
- Approach others yourself
- Sustain the conversation
- Engage in affinity-seeking behaviors

To maintain
- Offer assurances of commitment
- Discuss relational feelings openly

- Be positive and offer compliments
- Share tasks fairly
- Include common friends and family members in activities
- Develop a supportive communication climate
- Use humor

To repair
- Metacommunicate
- Offer apologies and accounts

Explore your interpersonal choices

Are you ready to explore your interpersonal choices regarding relationships? Use your online Resource Center for *Understanding Interpersonal Communication* to access an ABC News video, "Romance at Work: Rules of Engagement," about how your communication with a romantic partner in the workplace is not always private, even when you want it to be. Compare your answers to the questions at the end of the video with those provided by the authors.

whereas maintenance is simply aimed at keeping things moving. We discuss two repair skills below: metacommunication and apology.

Metacommunication

Metacommunication means communicating about communication. If communication is the problem in the relationship, the partners need to address how to improve their communication. For example, if Mary tells her friend Mike that she doesn't like it when he raises his voice to her, she is engaging in metacommunication. Mike might respond that he raises his voice when he gets excited. Mary can then tell him that she interprets it as anger. After the two define the problem through metacommunication, they can work on figuring out how to repair the problem.

Apology

An **apology** is a simple statement like "I am really sorry." Sometimes apologies are accompanied by **accounts**, or explanations for the transgression. For example, Keisha and May had been really close friends all through high school. They had kept in touch after graduation, even through they had moved to opposite ends of the country. For several years, they exchanged Christmas cards, and they even saw each other from time to time. Each time they met, it was as if they had just been together. However, one year, Keisha sent May her usual Christmas card, and May

didn't respond. After a couple of years, Keisha stopped sending the cards, and the two ceased contact.

Three years later, May called and apologized. She told Keisha that problems she had been having with her family had demanded all her concentration. May just hadn't had the energy for keeping up any of her long-distance friendships. Keisha felt a lot better when she heard May's explanation, and the two were able to resume their friendship.

metacommunication

Communication about communication.

apology

A simple statement like "I am really sorry."

account

An explanation for a transgression that may accompany an apology.

Summary

In this chapter, we tackled a huge topic: communication in close relationships. According to Maslow's hierarchy of needs, establishing relationships is the third most important human need, behind only physical and safety needs. Researchers have been drawn to studying communication in the context of close relationships because the two have been shown to be inextricably intertwined and because close relationships are powerful forces for both good and ill in people's lives. As a result, we have a lot of information about communication in close relationships.

To organize the information, we distinguished between close relationships and role relationships, concluding that close relationships endure over time, consist of interdependent partners who satisfy each other's needs, feel an emotional attachment to each other, are irreplaceable to one another, and enact unique communication patterns. We examined close relationships from a cultural performance perspective as well as a cognitive and linguistic perspective. We noted the important role that language plays in establishing an understanding of what constitutes close relationships. Culture and gender and sex play a role in the definition as well because different cultures define relationships like family, for instance, differently. Furthermore,

whether you're male or female (masculine or feminine) will influence how you define and conduct close relationships.

Close relationships include friendships, romances, and family relationships. Communication in each type of close relationship is important and can intensify our satisfaction or dissatisfaction with the relationship.

Four frameworks (systems, dialectics, social exchange, and Knapp's model of relationship development) offer some explanation for how we communicate in close relationships. We discussed systems thinking, which allows us to see close relationships as highly interdependent, open, self-adjusting systems. We illustrated seven common relational dialectics—autonomy-connection, openness-protection, novelty-predictability, judgment-acceptance, affection-instrumentality, public-private, and real-ideal. We explored the central premise of social exchange: relationships are governed by self-interest or a desire to keep costs down and rewards high. Lastly, we considered the ten stages of coming together and coming apart in Mark Knapp's model.

Some guidelines for communicating in close relationships are helpful. In beginning relationships, you need to engage in networking, offering, approaching, sustaining, and affinity seeking. When maintaining relationships, you should offer assurances of commitment, discuss relational feelings openly, be positive and offer compliments, share tasks fairly, include friends and family members in activities, develop a supportive communication climate, and exhibit humor.

Metacommunication and apology are useful strategies for repairing relationships. As was the case throughout this book, all these skills provide suggestions, not prescriptions. Given the variety of close relationships and the factors that influence them, no one can come up with a single list of skills that will always be successful in every relationship across all cultures. Yet, we believe that the more we understand about communicating in close relationships, the more successful and life-enhancing our relationships will be.

Understanding Interpersonal Communication Online

Now that you've read Chapter 10, use your online Resource Center for *Understanding Interpersonal Communication* for quick access to the electronic study resources that accompany this text. Your online Resource Center gives you access to the video of Hope and Randy on page 327, the Communication Assessment Test on page 329, the Your Turn journal activity on page 335, the Ethics & Choice interactive activity on page 357, the Interpersonal Explorer activity on page 362, InfoTrac College Edition, and study aids including a digital glossary, review quizzes, and the chapter activities.

■ Terms for Review

account 362
affection and
    instrumentality
    dialectic 346
affinity seeking 358
apology 362
approaching 358
autonomy and connection
    dialectic 346
avoiding stage 356
bonding stage 354
boundaries or openness 343
calibration 344
circumscribing stage 355
close relationships 331
comparison level 349
comparison level for
    alternatives 350
corrective maintenance 361
costs 348
differentiating stage 355

equifinality 345
experimenting stage 353
external dialectic 347
family stories 342
hierarchy 343
ideal and real dialectic 347
imagined conversation 355
initiating stage 352
integrating stage 354
intensifying stage 353
internal dialectic 347
judgment and acceptance
    dialectic 346
long-term attraction 352
metacommunication 362
negative feedback 344
networking 358
novelty and predictability
    dialectic 346
offering 358
positive feedback 344

preventative
    maintenance 360
public and private
    dialectic 347
recalibrate 344
relational culture 336
relational transgressions 361
relative power position 350
rewards 348
ritual 342
role relationships 331
short-term attraction 352
small talk 353
stagnating stage 355
subsystems 343
suprasystems 343
sustaining 358
terminating stage 356
wholeness 343

Questions for Understanding

Comprehension Focus

1. Describe the difference between defining close relationships from a performance perspective and defining close relationships from a psychological perspective.

2. List the unique communication patterns thought to characterize a close relationship.

3. List the stages of coming together and coming apart. How does communication differ depending on the stage you are in?

4. List the main dialectics that researchers think characterize close relationships, including friendships.

5. What is the main metaphor that social exchange theory applies to communication in close relationships?

Application Focus

1. CASE IN POINT How can Hope and Randy stay friends after the reason that began their friendship has ended? What skills for relationship maintenance would it be useful for them to employ?

2. What do you think best explains communication in close relationships: dialectics, social exchange, systems, or Knapp's model of relationship development? Can you combine these to come up with a better explanation than any one theory on its own can offer? Explain your answer with communication examples.

3. In your experience, how do factors like gender affect communication in friendships? Be specific. Do you think it's possible to generalize about women's and men's communication in friendships? Explain.

4. Do you agree that friendships are more fragile than dating relationships? Explain your answer. Would your answer (or the question itself) be different if you looked at cultures other than the culture in the United States? Explain.

5. Describe the metaphor inherent in a stage model approach to explaining relationships. What information does it bring with it, and how does it guide us to perceive relational life? Why do people think of relationships as needing movement?

Interactive Activities and InfoTrac College Edition Exercises

Interactive Activities

InfoTrac College Edition Exercises

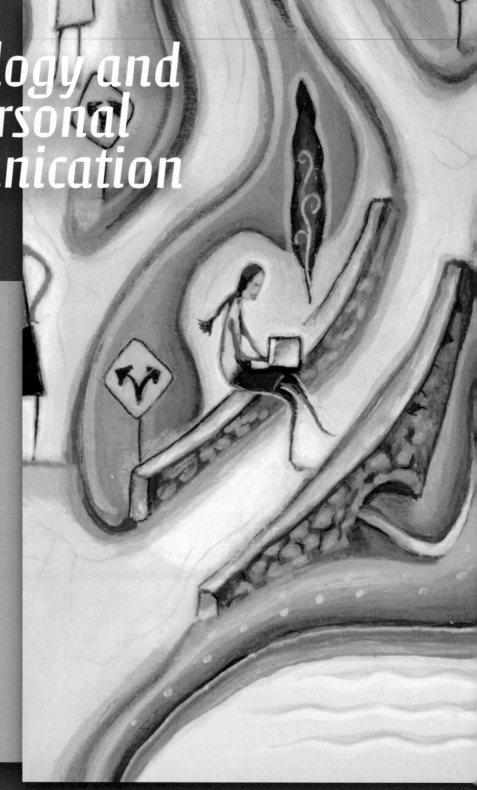

Chapter 11
Technology and Interpersonal Communication

chapter ➕ goals

Identify and explain characteristics of communication technology

Understand issues related to the presentation of self online

Articulate the dark and bright sides of CMC

Discuss the pervasiveness and importance of social networking

Explain how relationships function online

Utilize skills that help improve electronic discussions and relationships

CASEINPOINT
MATTHEW LEONE

M

atthew Leone had loved computers for as long as he could remember. When he was little, he'd had a Game Boy.

As he'd gotten older, his father had let him use his office computer so Matthew could download pictures of antique cars. Throughout college, Matthew not only emailed nearly everyone in his life, but also had a MySpace page where he uploaded pictures of such diverse events as his sister's wedding and his dog's birthday party. It was clear that Matthew loved computers, and as a cell phone junkie, iPod user, and DVD collector, he was also a lover of technology in general.

Matthew was graduating in the spring, so he spent the month of February working on his résumé and applying for jobs. He knew that his degree in economics and his 3.4 GPA would help him secure a good job, and he felt especially confident about his prospects after reading a glowing recommendation letter from one of his professors. Although Matthew's credentials were outstanding, he couldn't figure out why he wasn't being contacted for interviews. He sent his résumé and cover letter to all sorts of companies—large and small, public and private—but never scored even one interview.

He was confused and concerned, and it wasn't long before he emailed his best friend, Anna, to ask her what she thought.

Anna wrote that she was also surprised that Matthew hadn't been contacted for any interviews. As she rambled on in her email, she made one observation that stopped Matthew in his tracks. She told Matthew that she'd read a newspaper article about how "controversial" material on MySpace had prevented a man in Florida from getting a job. Apparently, the company the man had applied to had seen some damning pictures of him in a neo-Nazi jacket. Matthew immediately thought of the pictures he'd put on his website of his spring break vacation in Cancun, Mexico. He didn't finish reading the rest of Anna's email. He went immediately to his MySpace page and saw that, indeed, there were several provocative pictures of him drinking. In one picture taken in a bar, his friend Damien poured beer down Matthew's throat. Matthew sat motionless in front of his computer. Certainly, he thought, plenty of potential employers have been drunk and

Use your online
Resource Center
for *Understanding
Interpersonal
Communication*
to watch a video clip of
Matthew.

> Access the resources for Chapter 11 and select "Matthew" to watch the video (it takes a minute for the video to load). > As you watch the video, think about Matthew's situation. In what ways could he modify his online presence to make him look more attractive to potential employers? > You can respond to this and other analysis questions, and then click "Done" to compare your answers with those provided by the authors.

must know that these pictures were taken for fun. Still, he no longer wondered why he wasn't being called for interviews. Over his lifetime, Matthew Leone had loved technology. But now this technology was influencing his life in ways he had never imagined or considered.

W e have been using technology to communicate for more than 100 years. One technology, among many, seems to have ridden the technological wave for centuries now: the telephone. The invention of the telephone in 1875 allowed people to talk to a next-door neighbor or a distant cousin. It was a major invention at the time and today, the phone has undergone a transformation that even its inventor, Alexander Graham Bell, could never have imagined. Although "land lines" are a still a popular option for many households, it's likely that most people you know no longer have to untangle a telephone cord, use a rotary dial, or figure out if the phone is a "wall mount." Indeed, the telephone of yesteryear has largely been supplanted by the cell phone, which nearly 140 million people use daily in the United States (http://www.epa.gov/epaoswer/education/pdfs/life-cell .pdf). As Michael Bugeja (2004) notes, "cell phones remind us that we dwell in more than one place at most times, splitting consciousness in parks, cars, schools, restaurants, and malls" (p. B5).

Clearly, the phone—in all of its incarnations—has a rich past and continues to have a vibrant present and future. However, this chapter is about more than the phone. It is about all types of technology. Web feeds, virtual worlds, web conferencing, palm organizers, pagers, beepers, Zunes, instant messaging, and email, are, to name just a few, technological options available to us in our personal and professional lives. The effect that this technology has on our communication with others forms the basis of this chapter.

Just a few years ago, a chapter such as this was not found in an interpersonal communication textbook. But, we believe this topic merits serious consideration in our text now. We cannot ignore the influence that technology has on our conversations and relationships with others. What were once "ground rules" in meeting and conversing with others have changed.

To be sure, with the advent of content aggregation, our technological world will keep changing. **Content aggregation** has been called "information architecture" by some (http://www.usabilitysciences.com/services/field-studies-and-focus-groups/content-aggregation/). David King (www.daweed

content aggregation

The process of collecting online data from different and multiple sources to suit a particular need, such as populating a search engine or preparing digital slides for a presentation.

.blogspot.com) on his blog notes that content aggregation happens in two stages. First, someone writes text or records some audio or video clip and makes that available to the public. Secondly, someone else ends up subscribing to the content and then decides to absorb, study, scan, or delete the content and he or she aggregates (or collates) the content for a particular reason. In a sense, then, when you aggregate content, you are collecting data from different and multiple sources to suit your needs. In its broadest sense, content aggregation occurs when large search engines (e.g. Google, Yahoo!, etc.) aggregate content from other websites, which, interestingly, gives rise to complaints of copyright infringement. On a smaller scale, you might aggregate information from a video, website news stream, and podcast for a classroom presentation on diversity. The notion of content aggregation has been applied to advertising, computer technology, and marketing. As you read the chapter, you will soon see content aggregation as it applies to interpersonal communication.

It appears that many in the United States can't acquire technology fast enough. Our society seems to constantly crave the next level of innovation. We're ready to understand the next version of Windows, the newest Mac upgrade, or the latest video game software. Even toys for the youngest children, such as "Webkinz" (stuffed animals that serve as virtual pets) are linked with technology. We have also come to demand new technology that can be used in conjunction with our current technology. Responding to that need, Steven Jones (1998) comments that "technologies continue to converge" (p. xiv). **Convergence** is the integration of various technologies. We are living in a time where many technologies are morphing and interacting with other technologies. Think about voice-activated computers or cell phones that take pictures. Or, consider the evolution of the phone-fax-answering machine. More

convergence

The integration of various technologies, such as online radio or cell phones with cameras.

Photodisc/Getty Images

Since the advent of the personal computer and the mobile phone in the 1980s, the use of communication technology has exploded. Everywhere you look, someone is accessing email via a wireless connection, texting on a cell phone, or recording an appointment on a handheld organizer. What technologies do you use to communicate with your family, friends, and coworkers?

recently, the convergence of a digital camera, MP3 player, voice recorder, and camcorder resulted in a mobile phone. Finally, some of you may be familiar with PlayStation 2, which converges a CD player, DVD player, and the Internet.

As a society, we have grown accustomed to convergence. We tend to expect technologies to evolve so that they are more efficient and less cumbersome. Many people cannot afford a new technology when it first comes out, so they wait for prices to decrease. For example, when the plasma television came on the market in the 1990s, it cost more than $10,000. In recent years, the price has dropped by almost 80 percent. The lower the cost, the more affordable technology becomes. The more affordable, the more people will own it. And, the more people own it, the more they will tend to use it. And, as affordability occurs, people will use the technology and this same technology finds itself immersed in our conversations and interpersonal relationships.

Once people begin to use technology, that technology not only becomes part of our vocabulary (think of iPod or PlayStation, for instance), but also can affect the relationships we have with others and even our professional lives. In our opening story, Matthew Leone, who grew up with technology, now finds himself being negatively affected by the same technology he embraced so passionately. Although he never envisioned that a MySpace picture could influence his job prospects, technology has now given others the ability to view his (recent) past. Given that potentially millions of people post questionable words and images on social networking sites like MySpace, Matthew will likely not be the only person facing this difficult dilemma. We return to social networking sites later in this chapter.

Technology has the potential to affect who we are, what we do, and how we interact with others. For some, technology serves as a bonding mechanism. Consider the words of Alcestis Oberg (2003), who comments that families who use technology are more likely to remain close:

> My children and I all have moved together into cyberspace. It no longer matters anymore where we are physically. If home is where the heart is, then our hearts have moved into the invisible realm of mobile and wireless communications, and into the ethereal hometown called the Internet. There, we can be—and always will be—together. (p. 11A)

computer-mediated communication (CMC)

The use of various technologies to facilitate communication with others.

technological determinism

A theory that states that technology is irreversible, inevitable, and inescapable.

This chapter examines the role that technology plays in our interpersonal communication. Specifically, we focus on **computer-mediated communication (CMC)**, which refers to the use of various technologies to facilitate communication with others. A valuable theoretical framework to consider as you read this chapter is **technological determinism**, which suggests that technology is irreversible, inevitable, and inescapable (McLuhan & McLuhan, 1988). In other words, it's hard to ignore the impact that communication technologies have had upon us—and, according to technological determinists, we have no choice but to deal with that impact

As pervasive as technology is in our society, we need to remember that people have different technological fields of experience. We cannot operate

"Would you mind talking to me for a while? I forgot my cell phone."

under the assumption that everyone has the same background and technological access. Some of you grew up with a full awareness of, and expertise in, technology. You had at least one computer at home, you know how to set a VCR, you have a contract for a personal cell phone, you've created a blog, subscribed to a web feed, and are comfortable using almost any technology. For others of you, figuring out how to change the message on a telephone answering machine is a challenge. Because you and your classmates probably have various levels of experience and exposure to technology, we want to ensure that we all have the same foundation of knowledge in this area. Therefore, we begin with a discussion of the characteristics of communication technology.

Characteristics of Communication Technology

We need to understand the essential characteristics of technology so we are better prepared to make effective choices when using it. We consider three characteristics of technology: It is pervasive, paradoxical, and powerful.

When we state that technology is pervasive, we are saying that it is everywhere. We cannot escape or ignore technology in our lives. We wake with an alarm clock. We make telephone calls to our family. We fax reports at work. We take digital pictures on our vacations. We are beeped by our children, who ask what's for dinner. These same children sit down in front of the television to play video games. We text message our friends to ask them what time they want to meet. And some of us try to organize all of these activities on our BlackBerry or Sidekick.

Because technology is everywhere, we rely on it as a matter of course. Consider, for instance, how you would make it through the day without technology. Most of us would feel overwhelmed if we were deprived of the convenience that technology offers us. While some may lament the influence of technology on our lives, others embrace the fact that our lives are made easier because of technology. As communication and culture scholar Siva Vaidhyanathan (quoted by Neil Swidey, 2003), said, "It's the collapse of inconvenience. It turns out inconvenience was a really important part of our lives and we didn't realize it" (p. 11).

Technology is also paradoxical, meaning that it is conflicting, inconsistent, and ironic. To understand this concept, consider what communication theorist Marshall McLuhan (1964) called the **global village**. McLuhan coined this term to describe how communication technology ties the world into one political, economical, social, and cultural system. Although the phrase *global village* is almost a cliché these days, McLuhan is the one who, more than 40 years ago, expressed the idea that technology has the ability to bring people together. McLuhan stated that "the globe is no more than a village" (p. 5). The paradox is evident; the term *global* suggests an expansive view of the world, whereas the term *village* suggests a small community. The idea that technological devices, which mediate relationships in so many ways, can actually bring people together seems paradoxical.

When we say that technology is powerful, we mean that it influences people, events, and entire cultures. Technology can affect how people think, what

global village

The concept that communication technology ties the world into one political, economic, social, and cultural system.

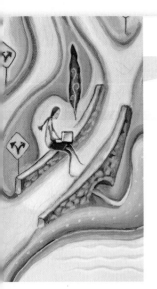

REVISITING
CASEinPOINT

1. Apply the relevancy of the phrase *global village* to Matthew Leone's situation.

2. Apply all three characteristics of communication technology to Matthew's experiences.

You can answer these questions online under the resources for Chapter 11 at your online Resource Center for Understanding Interpersonal Communication.

they think about, when they develop relationships, and how they process their emotions with others (Turkle, 2007). For instance, let's say that Jana is a student who decides to skip a group presentation. She emails some group members to let them know about an unplanned doctor's appointment. She sends a text message to other group members complaining about her lack of time to get things done. In this case, because Jana uses technology to inform her group members of her dilemmas and because technology does not allow for nonverbal communication to be present, it is likely that the group members will read her emails and text messages and reach different conclusions about her not being at the presentation. As we noted in Chapter 5, nonverbal communication influences meaning between and among people. In its absence, some may think Jana is lazy, others may view her as self-serving, and others may decide not to waste energy worrying about her motivations. Technology has the power to cause others to make judgments, even though the communicators are not face-to-face.

Thus far, we have addressed the overall importance of communication technology in our lives and identified its primary characteristics. We will now discuss technology's accessibility and various uses.

The Accessibility of Communication Technology

Accessibility refers to the availability of technology to everyone. Accessibility helps eliminate the technological gap that exists between people and between cultural communities. Some have called this gap the "digital divide" while others have called it a battle between the information "haves and have-nots." Some writers contend that there is no battle and that even the poorest of the poor have access to technology, specifically the Internet (Ghostman, 2007).

Of the approximately 6 billion people who populate the globe, more than 1 billion use the Internet (www.internetstats.com). Over 73 percent of people in the United States go online, according to the Pew Foundation (http://www.pewtrusts.org/news_room_ektid23772.aspx). Technology reporter Mike Wendland (2002) argues that if you live in a suburb, make lots of money, and are highly educated, you most likely have no problem understanding the Internet. If you dwell in a large city, have a low income, and possess a limited education, you're probably not connected to or benefiting from the Internet. Some racial and geographic differences concerning Internet use suggest a digital divide. The Pew Foundation's study of Internet use and race, for example, found that among the major racial groups, more than half of white people (58 percent) have used the Internet, as compared with 43 percent of African Americans, and 50 percent of Hispanics (http://www.pewtrusts.org/news_room_ektid23772.aspx). In studying rural and urban use of the Internet, Sandra Guy (2004) finds that "rural residents go online [for instance] for information and to seek support groups, sports leagues, and civic groups—communities they cannot find in their neighborhoods."

The Pew Foundation has discovered some trends in technology usage and grouped people into three categories: elite users, middle-of-the-road users, and those with few technological assets. Table 11.1 describes these groups and shows the pervasiveness of technology across the U.S. population.

Table 11.1 Groups of U.S. users of information and communication technology

	Group name	% of adult population	Their characteristics
Elite tech users (31% of American adults)	Omnivores	8%	They have the most information gadgets and services, which they use voraciously to participate in cyberspace, express themselves online, and do a range of Web 2.0 activities such as blogging or managing their own web pages.
	Connectors	7%	Between feature-packed cell phones and frequent online use, they connect to people and manage digital content using information and communication technologies (ICTs)—all with high levels of satisfaction about how ICTs let them work with community groups and pursue hobbies.
	Lackluster veterans	8%	They are frequent users of the Internet and less avid about cell phones. They are not thrilled with ICT-enabled connectivity.
	Productivity enhancers	8%	They have strongly positive views about how technology lets them keep up with others, do their jobs, and learn new things.
Middle-of-the-road tech users (20%)	Mobile centrics	10%	They fully embrace the functionality of their cell phones. They use the Internet, but not often, and like how ICTs connect them to others.
	Connected but hassled	10%	They have invested in a lot of technology, but they find the connectivity intrusive and information somewhat of a burden.
Few tech assets (49%)	Inexperienced experimenters	8%	They occasionally take advantage of interactivity, but if they had more experience, they might do more with ICTs.
	Light but satisfied	15%	They have some technology, but it does not play a central role in their daily lives. They are satisfied with what ICTs do for them.
	Indifferents	11%	Despite having either cell phones or online access, these users use ICTs intermittently and find connectivity annoying.
	Off the network	15%	Those with neither cell phones nor Internet connectivity tend to be older adults who are content with old media.

Adapted from Pew Internet & American Life Project (2007), *A Typology of Information and Communication Technology Users.*

The digital divide is evident with nearly all communication technology. And nowhere is the divide more apparent than in our telephone ownership and usage. Even telephones—one of the most ubiquitous of technologies—vary in their accessibility. The National Telecommunications and Information Administration (NTIA) (http://www.ntia.doc.gov/ntiahome/net2/falling .html), for example, notes that there is a significant divide among racial communities. The national survey showed that overall, households headed by white individuals have a higher telephone availability and usage (95 percent) than African American households (85.4 percent) and households headed by Hispanic individuals (84.6 percent). With respect to income, the NTIA notes that as the household income falls, so does telephone ownership. For instance, in households where income was between $5,000–9,999, over 15 percent of these homes did not have a telephone. In homes with less than $5,000 of income, that number soars to nearly 25 percent! And, be cautious in believing that these homes have a cell phone and not a land line; the fees, monthly costs of long-distance calls, among other expenses prohibit any phone accessibility for the very poor among us. Each of us, then, has to be thoughtful and sensitive in our assumptions about technology and the availability of technology.

For an alternate look at the current state of the digital divide in the United States, use your online Resource Center for *Understanding Interpersonal Communication* to access **Interactive Activity 11.1: What Digital Divide?** under the resources for Chapter 11.

What does accessibility to communication technology have to do with interpersonal communication? If everyone does not have an understanding of and access to the same technologies, problems with meaning will likely occur. It will be difficult for us to achieve meaning in our conversations if others cannot understand us when we talk about "video streaming," "mobile networking," or our "MP3 players." What many of you may take for granted (for example, a telephone call, a text message, an instant message, and so forth) may not be universally accepted or understood because of accessibility issues. Remember not to assume that a classmate has a certain technology available to them.

Accessibility to communication technology has many benefits for interpersonal communication: It increases safety, creates a sense of play, and improves psychological well-being between and among people. Making phone calls in case of emergencies seems instinctive to most of us. Playing chess on the computer or having a conversation with other dog owners in an online discussion group helps increase the element of play. We explore how technology can improve psychological well-being when we discuss the bright side of technology a bit later in this chapter.

To this point, we have been discussing the Internet as if each of us has the same understanding of it. To make sure we share a common understanding, let's talk about the background of the Internet as well as its dark and bright sides.

The Internet: Connecting Now

Imagine being on the streets of New York City. All the streets, from the major arteries to the small alleys, comprise a complex network. Now, imagine you are in the office of the city's Director of Streets and Sanitation looking at a lighted grid of every street in Manhattan. The grid encompasses the 22.4 square miles of the island.

This image should help you understand what the Internet is. The Internet has been called a "network of networks" because of its embedded connections and because it "has changed the way people work, learn, play, and communicate" (Barnes, 2003, p. 3). Although many people use the terms Internet and the World Wide Web ("the web") interchangeably, the distinction between the terms needs to be noted. The Internet connects computers together and the information that travels from one computer to another computer does so through various technological "languages." The web is just one of the ways that information is shared over the Internet. The web uses a language called *HTTP* to transmit data. In other words, the web is part of the Internet and is not synonymous with the Internet. In this chapter, we will focus primarily on the web. The Internet and the web promise to be an important presence in communication technology for years to come. We will begin by discussing how the web has changed since its inception. We will then discuss several cautionary tales and points of opportunity associated with the Internet.

Web 1.0 and Web 2.0

Web 1.0

The earliest incarnation of the World Wide Web, which was used primarily as a storehouse of online information and tools that could be accessed to achieve an end, such as finding a website, emailing a friend, or purchasing a product.

Web 2.0

The latest incarnation of the World Wide Web, which is increasingly used as a means of interactivity and personal expression; establishing online communities, sharing files, and blogging exemplify Web 2.0.

Scholars now refer to the web as it first appeared in the late 1970s as Web 1.0. **Web 1.0** provided a technological means to achieve an end. That is, recalling the linear model we discussed in Chapter 1, Web 1.0 enabled a user to accomplish an immediate goal (e.g., access a website, email a friend, etc.). The label Web 2.0 has been used to describe the web in the past several years, as it has become more expansive, more democratic, and more interactive. Blogger Paul Graham (www.paulgraham.com/web20.html) states that **Web 2.0** is "using the web the way it is meant to be used."

Former president of software giant *Oracle*, Ray Lane, believes Web 2.0 reflects development from "the bottom up" (http://www.businessweek.com/technology/content/jun2006/tc20060605_641388.htm). That is, an amateur can have as wide an audience as a professional. With Web 1.0, news was still largely controlled by major networks and news organizations. Web 2.0 offers a much broader range of perspectives through blogs, podcasts, and access to news sources worldwide. These changes have affected both the availability of news, as well as our perceptions of what is considered newsworthy.

According to Tim O'Reilly, one of the pioneers in thinking about Web 2.0, Yahoo!, Amazon.com, and eBay are all examples of Web 2.0. Each of these companies had its origins in Web 1.0, but were able to transition to

Table 11.2 Differences between Web 1.0 and Web 2.0

Web 1.0	Web 2.0
Britannica (Encyclopedia) Online	Wikipedia
Page views	Cost per click
Publishing	Participation
Personal websites	Blogging
Content management systems	Wikis
Evites	upcoming.org
Netscape	Google

Web 2.0 by incorporating "user engagement"—that is, each began to encourage interactivity. For instance, Amazon became more than a "bookseller" by engaging prospective customers with opportunities to review and, as O'Reilly notes, "invitations to participate in varied ways on virtually every page." Table 11.2 provides additional examples of differences that O'Reilly sees between Web 1.0 and Web 2.0. (http://www.oreilly.com/pub/a/oreilly/tim/news/2005/09/30/what-is-web-20.html).

The Dark Side of the Internet: Proceed with Caution

Communication technologies such as the Internet should be approached cautiously. Like nearly any technology, there is always the opportunity for something to go wrong. There are more than 108 million websites in the world (http://news.netcraft.com/archives/web_server_survey.html), with an average of 4–5 million sites added each month. The sheer volume makes it impossible to control web content. Anyone can put up a website, and no one has to verify its accuracy. In fact, as Verlyn Klinkenborg (2004) writes in the *New York Times*, "Make no mistake. The web is still a place where you find every kind of fraud, deceit, obscenity, and insanity—more of it than ever" (p. A24). In other words, a lot of stranger danger lurks on the Internet. Let's examine four significant issues to consider as you use the Internet: accountability, hate, flaming, and a sacrifice of privacy. (See Table 11.3 on page 378 for examples of each of these dangers.)

Little Accountability

It's easy to develop a web page. All you have to do is figure out a possible web address, find out if the domain name has been taken, and post the content

Table 11.3   The dark side of internet usage

Little accountability	*Example:* Chad decides to go online to a website that promotes itself as "the only website for single men who wish to meet accountants." After logging in, Chad meets a woman who claims to be an accountant for a large firm in the Midwest. After several email exchanges, he is favorably impressed and decides to give her his cell phone number. The problem is that Chad's online conversational partner is not an accountant; rather, she is an advertiser who wants to find out what sorts of hair care products he uses. The website was created by a large advertising company who specializes in men's cosmetics.
Fostering of hate	*Example:* Lena is assigned to examine various websites on "spiritual values" for her modern history class. When she types that phrase into a search engine, thousands of websites match that description. However, one website, called "Spiritual Values for the New Century," catches her attention. As appealing as that title sounds, Lena soon figures out that the website is filled with hate. The home page of the website states that "abortionists will burn in hell" if they don't "repent." Further, some links on the site allow Lena to read essays with such titles as "Why Abortionists Should Die," "What God said about the Abortion Doctors," and "Killing the Fetus Slowly." Lena soon discovers that the website promotes the execution of doctors who perform abortions.
Flaming	*Example:* David can't believe what he is reading. As a new parent, he had wanted to learn a bit more about temper tantrums. But, as his experience in a chat room on parenting is teaching him, people can be awfully vicious in their attacks. First, he reads the comments of one participant, who has no children, that every parent is a "selfish b**tard" and that "kids just boost egos!" A parent responds by telling the childless participant, "too bad your mom didn't fall down the steps carrying u!" David sits sadly by. He wants to jump in, but knows that he would probably just provoke even more incendiary remarks. He can't believe that people would discuss a topic such as parenting with such hostile and aggressive comments.
Sacrifice of privacy	*Example:* Cassandra loves her dad, but she is now disgusted with what she discovered about him. Using a special software package, Cassandra's dad discovered a way to find out what websites she surfs, what keyboard strokes she makes, and even passwords that she uses while online and using the family's computer. Cassandra is appalled that as a 14-year-old, she has nothing that is private. Years ago, she thought, a lot of parents found the key to a diary and tried to read the entries. Today, however, Cassandra finds the invasion of her privacy by her own parent more manipulative and intrusive.

on your site. There is no accountability for this information. Robert Danford (1999) writes,

> Users of the Web must approach the plethora of Web sites with the skills of a good consumer to see if the product offered is indeed what it purports to be, to see if the site will fulfill the user's need, to see which of the sites is available is the "best" in a given situation so that the user will be able to count on the information or services offered. (p. xiii)

hate speech

Extremely offensive language that is directed toward a particular group of people.

In other words, we shouldn't accept any information we find on the web at face value. We should always think critically about it. If we don't make ourselves accountable for determining a website's credibility, we have the potential to be misguided, misinformed, and manipulated.

For example, suppose Damian is interested in trying online dating. He has had little luck meeting interesting people in person and has heard success stories from his roommate, so Damian decides to go to the Internet. Although Damian may be inclined to start surfing the web for dating sites, he should first ask himself a few questions. What criterion is he using to locate a particular website? What evidence shows that the site he accesses is legitimate? Does the site have a sponsor? Will Damian have to pay fees, or does the site's revenue come from advertisements? What protections are in place to ensure his privacy? How do others looking for dates contact you? Is there a way of verifying the credentials of potential dates? What sorts of ads appear on the website? Are they sexually explicit or professional? Are there restrictions for downloading pictures or personal information? What is the site's record for successful matches?

Some progress has been made in helping people evaluate websites. For instance, software programs that provide Internet filters to weed out potentially objectionable sites are now available. But you must still take responsibility for assessing web content yourself. Doing anything less may result in communication consequences that you did not expect.

© Reuters/Corbis

Fostering Hate

Certainly, websites have the potential to positively affect your conversations and relationships with others. Yet, the dark side of communication technologies suggests that hate on the Internet is alive and proliferating. **Hate speech** can be defined as extremely offensive language that is directed toward a particular group of people. Although hate speech is protected by First Amendment rights, such extremist communication has the potential to negatively affect another's communication.

Websites that use hate speech have proliferated over the years. They cover the spectrum, focusing on everything from anti-abortion sites that promote the death of abortion providers to websites denying that the Holocaust occurred. The Internet has fueled intolerance, hatred, and incivility to the extent that some hate groups now have an immediate referent point in their antagonistic pursuits. Because offensive points of view are protected by First Amendment free-speech rights, hate speech on the Internet is probably here to stay. Websites that promote gay bashing, anti-Semitic views, the reinstitution of slavery, and so forth will continue. One way to combat this hatred is to visit sites that are dedicated to wiping out cultural hate. For

In the weeks following the terrorist attacks of September 11, 2001, many anti-Arab sites went up on the Internet, erroneously labeling some prominent Arab Americans as Islamic terrorists. The harmful effects of the misinformation spread by these sites illustrate the need for accountability on the Internet—not only were innocent people unfairly targeted, but many Internet providers spent time and money deleting these sites.

example, the Southern Poverty Law Center (www.splcenter.org) promotes the development of community coalitions to combat hate. And a relational step you can take to combat hate is to speak up to others to educate them about why their biases are misplaced.

Flaming

At times, relationships with others online can get tense. **Flaming** occurs when people exchange malicious, hostile, or insulting comments. Flamers using the Internet often suffer from some sort of social or psychological instability since many would not engage in this hostility in face-to-face interactions; the possibility for altercations and embarrassment are too strong. This lack of civility is like electronic road rage—it has the capacity to escalate. Janet Kornblum of *USA Today* (2007, July 31) notes that "the Internet has always had an anything-goes atmosphere where flame wars and harsh language are common" (p. 1A). Flaming may simply be an exercise of control over others or a bold attempt at aggression. Regardless of how long you may have known the flamer, flaming is best dealt with by disengaging and using more subtle ways of communicating. Avoiding capital letters, extreme punctuation (such as exclamation marks or ellipses), and accusatory language may help prevent further incivility. Consider the difference between the following two examples in a chat room of gay men:

Situation 1

Flamer:	U F*GS R GONNA BURN IN HELL!:)))))))
Participant 1:	UR the freakn @-hole!
Flamer:	STAY 2UNED. . .MORE>>ONS!!
Participant 2:	And we're afraid of what? A PIG ^ 0 ^ like you?
Flamer:	DIE F*GS!

Situation 2

Flamer:	U F*GS R GONNA BURN IN HELL!
Participant 1:	Get LOST!!!!!!
Flamer:	CAN'T TAKE IT? FEEL THE HEAT?
Participant 2:	Taking off Come back L8R.

Choosing disengagement and not becoming personally antagonistic, which is the strategy shown by Participant 2 in the second situation, should help you remove yourself from flaming and the flamer.

Consider how this interaction might have differed if it had happened in person instead of online. Some people find it easier to be uncivil in electronic than in face-to-face settings. Perhaps technological interactions provide a higher comfort level because a hateful person can be anonymous while cow-

flaming

Exchanging malicious, hostile, or insulting comments over the Internet.

ardly hiding behind a computer screen. Remember the wizard in *The Wizard of Oz?* He lost all of his composure, aggressiveness, and anger when the curtain was literally pulled open. Would cyberhate be limited if individuals were required to communicate in person?

Privacy Sacrificed

In Fall 2007, *Parade* magazine, one of the largest supplements in national newspapers, asked the following question on its cover: "Is Anything Private Anymore?" Clearly, with advances in communication technology, the answer to that question is a resounding "no." In the article, author Sean Flynn notes that "in today's world, maintaining a cocoon of privacy simply isn't practical" (p. 4). With people giving names, addresses, social security numbers, among other things, in order to get car loans, mortgage approvals, grocery store discounts, tollbooth easy lane passes, credit cards, and drivers licenses, we have to forfeit a great deal of private information.

The issuance of private information to others has resulted in an onslaught of privacy concerns, particularly pertaining to the Internet. Because we are citizens, consumers, and investors, according to one expert, our privacy has been sacrificed (Nehf, 2007). Our online activities with others are consequential, to be sure. When we choose to email others and disclose our personal thoughts or life experiences, for instance, as we noted in Chapter 8, we become more vulnerable. At one point or another in our lives, we have and will disclose something on the Internet. When we disclose on the Internet, we allow others a chance to frame our words in any manner they see fit. Unwittingly, we may be sacrificing our privacy further. In some cases, our personal emails have been intercepted and handed over to government investigators, client information has been sold to telemarketing companies, and credit records have been "misplaced" by unscrupulous lenders.

Some privacy experts (Tavani, 2000) suggest that search engines are able to "discover" personal information about you and for some, once they "google" their name, for instance, all of the information that they thought was private now is public. It is no wonder that some writers (e.g., Nehf, 2007) argue that despite privacy policies on various websites, most people do not take the time to read them nor do they "shop" for privacy among websites. It appears Janet Kornblum (2007, October 23) has it right when discussing the Internet, she states: "Privacy? That's so old-school" (p. 1D).

The Bright Side of the Internet: New Opportunities

Although the Internet certainly has its dark side, it also offers us unique opportunities. Generally speaking, we can communicate with people we might not have been able to communicate with otherwise. Further, such communication is quick and seamless, and even those with little technological know-how can quickly learn to communicate via the web. Let's look at

Table 11.4 The bright side of internet usage

Widen your social network	**Example:** As a newcomer to Chicago, Ramona isn't prepared to deal with the millions of people in the city. Her hometown has only 300 people, and although her previous job had taken her to the Windy City, she has never felt so alone in her life. Ramona isn't in the habit of going out; when she isn't at work, she usually stays home and watches television or emails her sister. However, one night Ramona decides to surf the Internet. She soon finds herself in a local chat room reading messages about one of her favorite topics, Hispanic history. She particularly likes reading about the history of mask making in Mexico. After several weeks in the chat room (during which she interacts with some of the other participants, sharing some of her thoughts on the topic), Ramona decides to meet several people from her chat room at a local museum that is featuring Aztecan masks. One person in particular catches Ramona's eye, they hit it off, and she soon thinks Chicago is one of the best cities in the world!
Enhance your educational accessibility	**Example:** Morgan stands in his dining room looking at pictures of his wife. She has been dead for nearly a year now, and he still finds himself crying all the time. He decides that he can either cry every day or make something out of the rest of his life. Not wanting to let his emotions control him, Morgan decides to do something he has been wanting to do for many years but had been reluctant to tackle because he was uncertain how to proceed—he decides to start his own handyman business. So, he goes to the Internet and types "starting a business" in his search engine. Morgan soon begins to learn about self-employment tax, state regulations, and other matters small business owners need to know. He trusts the government's Small Business Administration website and downloads all of the information he can digest in one sitting. Morgan is excited about finding an opportunity to learn about an area he had never thought he would understand.

two areas of Internet opportunities. First, the Internet has afforded us chances to widen our social network and second, it has enhanced our educational opportunities. (See Table 11.4 for examples of each of these benefits.)

Widening Your Social Network

With the Internet, and the web in particular, you can widen your social circles tremendously in a short period of time—something you can't do with face-to-face communication. Overall, computer-mediated communication (CMC) allows individuals to seek out information and to develop their relationships. Although we address social networks a bit later in this chapter, a few points merit attention.

First, in many ways, the Internet serves as a vehicle to secure information. Among the areas most sought out are chat rooms. Chat rooms are excellent venues to discover information about a particular subject—for example, the qualifications of political candidates, how to start a small business, or where to go on a cruise. In addition, information-seeking web users can facilitate online discussions with professionals who have credentials in a particular area. For example, let's say Marcie was recently diagnosed with diabetes and has no idea what the disease is all about. Marcie's first step will probably be to go to the Internet to find information using a search engine. After she discovers that there are literally hundreds of websites available on the topic, she has to decide which one to visit first. Inevitably, she will discover some chat rooms where physicians who specialize in the disease are able to answer her questions or respond to her concerns. However, keep in mind the important information about accountability that we discussed a bit earlier. Marcie should not be misled by those who are not qualified to offer suggestions in this area. Yet, along the way, Marcie is likely going to encounter a site where she and others with diabetes are able to communicate about their challenges and high-points.

In addition to getting relevant information, Barnes (2003) also noted that CMC can aid in the maintenance and expansion of our relationships, both romantic and professional. In fact, CMC is "redefining how people engage of relationships of all types" (Pauley & Emmers-Sommer, 2007, p. 411).

How can our relationships be maintained via electronic means? First, we live in a mobile society, with people transferring jobs or working across the miles; communication technology can bridge the geographic divide. Whether moving across town or across the country, migration usually requires adaptation to new surroundings and maintenance of existing relationships. Past friends and current family members, for example, will likely expect ongoing communication, and email can facilitate keeping in touch.

A second way in which our relationships are maintained via technology pertains to supporting others. In fact, some research indicates that entire communities are built and maintained online. For instance, Elena Larsen (2004) notes that faith communities in particular are flourishing and individuals are using the Internet to show their support for each other and each other's religious identity. Larsen concludes that "more than 90 percent of online congregations reported that their members email each other for fellowship purposes" (p. 47). Individuals can seek out others for prayer requests, spiritual assistance and advice, and even facilitate spiritual relationships that were previously nonexistent. With technology, individuals who were once strangers can become linked in ways unimagined prior to the Internet.

Enhancing Your Educational Accessibility

Earlier in this chapter, we talked about how the digital divide cuts across various racial groups. Another type of divide exists as well—a division between younger and older generations in terms of their Internet usage. Simply put, those who are younger (say, under the age of 60) tend to use the web (in particular) much more frequently than those who are older (say, those over 60 years old). Why is this the case? Karen Riggs (2004) believes that ageism may be at play. Many people—from employers to physicians—maintain stereotypes of older adults, including the belief that they are unable to adapt to new technology. Yet, Riggs argues that with some training and enough tenacity, older adults are able to rapidly and competently deal with any technological challenge.

Just because older adults may not go online as frequently as younger adults does not mean that this group remains technologically ignorant. Many will derive benefits from using technology. For example, when older adults do go online, research shows that they are less likely to report health-related problems and identify with stronger feelings of independence (Stark-Wroblewski, Edelbaum, & Ryan, 2007). Consider, for example, Jackson, a 55-year-old father of two, who decides to use the Internet to obtain information about employment discrimination. Or, Leo, a 70-year-old father of five, a diligent parent who browses the web for volunteer jobs. Cassandra, a 59-year-old single woman, goes online to find out about her recent diagnosis of ovarian cancer. And Rodney, a 65-year-old single man, seeks out potential mates on a website for single senior citizens. The new economy requires a host of technological experiences and expertise. People of all ages are an integral part of that technology.

Now that you better understand the characteristics of technology and the dark and bright sides of the web, we turn our attention to how people present themselves online and then to more specific forms of communication technology and how they affect interpersonal communication.

The Presentation of Self Online

In Chapter 2, we emphasized the role of the self in interpersonal communication. In this section, we describe the way individuals present themselves online. Sherry Turkle (1995) reminds us that people online develop a "cyber-self" and that in "virtual reality, we self-fashion and self-create" (p. 180). The following story reported by Alexandra Alter (2007, August 10) in the *Wall Street Journal* illustrates this point:

> On a scorching July afternoon, as the temperature creeps toward 118 degrees in a quiet suburb east of Phoenix, Rick Hoogestraat sits at his computer with the blinds drawn, smoking a cigarette. While his wife, Sue, watches television in the other room, Mr. Hoogestraat chats online with what appears on the screen to be a tall, slim redhead (p. W1).

Rick is part of a growing virtual world called Second Life, which, according to Alter, is a fantasyland in which a synthetic identity plays itself out in intriguing ways. Mr. Hoogestraat has become so entranced with Janet Spielman, the "redhead" with whom he has a "second life," that he has asked her to become his virtual wife. Alter writes that "The woman he's legally wed to is not amused" (p. W1).

This story underscores the growing presence of **avatars**, a digital fictional and fantasy representation of a user in a virtual world. Avatars have become dynamic interjections into people's relational lives. Alter (2007) quotes Edward Castronova, a telecommunications expert, who encapsulates the

avatar

A digital fictional and fantasy representation of a user in a virtual world.

Avatars allow you to communicate with others online in a visual and highly interactive way. These Second Life avatars have shrunk to the size of mice to interact with tiny aliens in a Second Life environment. Notice how idealized the human avatars are. The women are big-breasted supermodels and the man is a tall, stylish hunk. What do you think the real people who created these avatars are trying to communicate about themselves by creating such sexy online representations?

concern of many people in relationships with avatar-obsessed partners: "There's a fuzziness that's emerging between the virtual world and the real world" (p. W8).

We will begin with a brief examination of a few assumptions associated with the way identities are managed online, and then we sort out some of the identity markers available to those in electronic relationships. As you review this section of the chapter, keep in mind that much of it can be framed by **signaling theory**, which proposes that people have qualities that they wish to present to others. Your participation on an online site may be accompanied with technical expertise, particular language, and/or "bells and whistles." For instance, as Marcia places a personal ad on a dating website in order to attract a college-educated mate, she may use language that is clear and precise and have a personal biography of her accomplishments. Further, she may not want a great deal of flashy or twinkling icons, instead choosing to be more professional in her approach. In this way, Marcia is signaling her desire for a particular "type" of person. If she were looking for a "drinking buddy," Marcia would likely use a much different approach.

Assumptions of Online Presentations of the Self

Understanding a few assumptions of how individuals present themselves online will expand your thinking about the self and its relationship to technology. With each of the assumptions we describe, we draw comparisons to face-to-face (FtF) encounters.

signaling theory
A theory that proposes that people have qualities they wish to present to others.

PRNewsFoto/Rezzable Productions/Newscom

Assumption 1: The Computer Screen Can Deceive

When people are online, they often pretend to be someone or something they are not. Online dialogues can lead to deceitful presentations. Men can become women who want to talk to other women. Convicted felons can pose as young girls or boys interested in Miley Cyrus or Zac Efron. The unemployed can become corporate CEOs, and CEOs can present themselves as unemployed. . .or someone else.

For example, several years ago, John Mackey, the CEO of Whole Foods, disguised himself as another person and wrote anonymous attacks online against his company's biggest competitor. Under the name "Rahodeb" (an anagram based on his wife, Deborah's name), Mackey predicted bankruptcy for Wild Oats, and stated that its stock was overpriced. Eventually, Whole Foods received government permission to buy Wild Oats, but this episode remains a cloud over the company.

In face-to-face encounters, being deceitful to such an extent is usually much tougher. We can't lie about our biological sex, and we can't claim to be a tall and toned person when we are short and stocky. Our conversations with others are in the present; they are not delayed or responded to later, as are our online dialogues. If we ask a question, we expect a response. If we don't get a response, we may walk away from the encounter.

Bernadette Amarosa sat staring blankly at her computer screen. She had just done something she rarely did: She had lied. She hadn't meant to, she thought to herself, but she had gotten carried away with her online conversation with Michael and had typed in the lie before she thought it through.

As a divorced woman, Bernadette was not in the habit of going online to seek out a relationship. As a matter of fact, she laughed at her close friends—all of whom are married—when they encouraged her to visit some online dating websites. She thought that guys who placed personal ads online were rather desperate, and she certainly didn't want to date a desperate man! Yet, for some reason on this hot summer evening, Bernadette had decided to search for a website that specialized in dating. She had soon found herself entering some personal information, including her screen name ("Dot") and some other details, such as her dating preferences, including sex ("man"), age ("25–40"), profession ("be employed"), and location ("southeastern United States").

As she searched the personal ads, Bernadette was attracted to a profile of a man named Michael. She read his "stats" and felt something in common with him. She also thought that Michael, smiling with his baseball cap on backward in the picture, was cute. Bernadette finally worked up the nerve to email Michael. After a few minutes, he responded and said he was happy she connected. He said he had looked at her picture and profile and found her attractive.

(Continues)

Although chat rooms are in "real time," people can choose when they'd like to respond. Researchers have referred to the "real time" communication as **synchronous communication**, or communication between the sender and receiver taking place at the same time. If the sender and receiver do not have to synchronize before and after each communication exchange, they are engaged in **asynchronous communication**.

synchronous communication

Communication between a sender and a receiver that takes place at the same time, as in face-to-face communication.

asynchronous communication

Communication that doesn't require a sender and a receiver to have an exchange at the same time, as in online communication.

Assumption 2: Online Discussions Often Prompt Introspection

Imagine that Bob and Shelly email each other about what they thought of the midterm exam. Shelly tells Bob that she thought it was pretty easy, but Bob thought it was pretty tough. As Bob reads Shelly's email, he starts to think about why he and Shelly each had different perceptions. They had studied together, after all. Before responding to the email, Bob starts to think about the material he didn't understand. "Yeah," he thinks, "there was some stuff I just didn't get." Email, in this situation, inspired Bob to think about his own study habits, an introspective behavior that may not have occurred without his friend's prompting.

Not every email elicits this self-assessment. Yet, when we do email someone, we frequently engage in something similar to an internal dialogue. Think about when a supervisor emails an employee requesting a meeting as soon as possible but offers no specifics. Or, consider a time when a partner sends you an email wanting to break up, yet fails to explain why. These instances provoke us to reflect on both the message and our response to that message.

With FtF communication, this same introspection and self-dialogue is not as apparent. First, we often don't take the time to think about the words of another *while they are being stated.* Stopping to think about what another person was saying in the middle of a conversation would likely bring the conversation to a halt. We are not trained or conditioned to pause or stop conversations in this way. Instead, we typically mentally replay and analyze conversations once they are over. Most of our interpersonal encounters move rather freely from one point to another, with little reflection time.

Assumption 3: Online Discussions Promote Self-Orientation

In Chapter 3, we discussed individualism, which is a cultural orientation that favors the self over the group. When communicating online, we tend to value our way of doing things. Working on and with the computer is essentially a personal endeavor. We search out people, websites, and chat rooms in which we are interested. If others wish to contact us, we make a choice whether or not we want to respond to their overture. In electronic relationships, keep in mind that one or both individuals may either choose to reply or not to reply. Because we have no physical proximity, we are not compelled to interact. People communicate at their own convenience.

We typically must be collaborative in our conversations while FtF. Although we can choose to say nothing, our silence—as we learned in Chapter 7—can communicate a great deal. In addition, when we are speaking in person, there is give and take, questions require answers, and our answers usually result in further dialogue. People cannot avoid the ongoing and

Soon the two started emailing each other. Bernadette was not entirely truthful in her emails—for example, she didn't tell Michael that she was divorced and that she had two adult sons. Further, although she told Michael that she was in her 40s, she really was 53. As time went on, Bernadette grew more nervous about her deception. She thought she might have gotten herself in way too deep with her lies.

Bernadette faces a number of options in this technological predicament. She could tell Michael her real age and the fact that she has two children. Or, she could reveal part of this information to him. Or, she could choose to continue to conceal her true age and her children's existence. Are there other alternatives? What ethical issues are inherent in this circumstance? Reflecting on the five ethical system of communication we identified in Chapter 1 (categorical imperative, utilitarianism, ethic of care, golden mean, significant choice), explain your response with these frameworks in mind. Is one system more relevant than another? Explain.

Go to your online Resource Center for *Understanding Interpersonal Communication* to access an interactive version of this scenario under the resources for Chapter 11. The interactive version of this scenario allows you to choose an appropriate response to this dilemma and then see what consequences your choice brings about. You can also compare your answers to the questions at the end of the scenario to those provided by the authors and, if requested, email your response to your instructor.

transactional nature of communication in face-to-face conversations. And like FtF conversations, our conversations vis-à-vis CMC are transactional.

Assumption 4: Self-Disclosure Occurs Online

The process of revealing aspects of yourself to another is not confined to face-to-face conversations. Research shows that self-disclosure occurs online and that some people reveal quite a bit through electronic communication (Miura, 2007). Particularly with blogs, self-disclosure is at a premium. As we learned in Chapter 8, when people self-disclose, they are inclined to give people important pieces of information about themselves. Further, we know that self-disclosure tends to increase intimacy.

Some people feel comfortable disclosing online because they don't have to deal with immediate reactions of disgust, disappointment, or confusion. Individuals may find it easier to reveal emotionally laden information in a technological medium. The problem, according to Susan Barnes (2003), is that **postcyberdisclosure panic (PCDP)** can set in. PCDP is a situation in which someone discloses personal information in an email message or on a message board only to experience significant anxiety later because the discloser begins to think about the number of people who could have access to that message. For instance, if Fran emails a coworker about her past problems with alcohol, that information has the potential to be passed (even inadvertently) to others, both in and out of the workplace. Interestingly, people may reveal information about themselves online that they would never reveal while face to face, perhaps because the computer screen is an impersonal object that doesn't have the capacity to show emotion.

The self-disclosive conversations we have with people while FtF can be dramatically different from those we engage in via email. In face-to-face interactions, we have to contend with facial reactions. We are often asked to clar-

postcyberdisclosure panic (PCDP)

A situation in which we disclose personal information in an email message only to experience significant anxiety later because we begin to think about the number of people who could have access to that message.

ify our thoughts or disclosures, and we may find it difficult to simply leave. We can't "turn off" another person as easily as we can turn off our computer screen. Self-disclosure in person generally causes an immediate reaction, which is something we don't necessarily have to deal with while online. To read an interesting article that discusses self-disclosure on the Internet and how some people fared moving from online to face-to-face relationships, check out "Relationship Formation on the Internet: What's the Big Attraction?" available through InfoTrac College Edition. Use your online Resource Center for *Understanding Interpersonal Communication* to access *InfoTrac College Edition Exercise 11.1: Self-Disclosure Online* under the resources for Chapter 11. To read another article, "Can You See the Real Me?" which discusses the presentation of the true self online, access *InfoTrac College Edition Exercise 11.2: Can You See the Real Me—Online?*

Identity Markers on the Internet

On the Internet, individuals typically communicate who they are through identity markers. An **identity marker** is an electronic extension of who someone is. In other words, an identity marker is an expansion of the self. Two primary identity markers exist on the Internet: screen names and personal home pages.

Screen Names

As in face-to-face relationships, online relationships inevitably require introductions. Yet, unlike in interpersonal relationships, we can introduce ourselves online by using names that are odd, silly, fun, editorial, or outright offensive. These screen names are nicknames and often serve to communicate the uniqueness of the sender of a message. Many screen names function as a way for communicators to protect their identities from others until more familiarity and comfort develops.

People use a wide variety of screen names. Some are shaped by fiction (>madhatter< or >hobbit<), others by popular culture (>AmIdol< or >TRUMPthis<), and still others by a desire to reinforce personal values (>WARRingOUT<). Haya Bechar-Israeli (1996) observes that many people place a great deal of importance on their screen names and nicknames and that they invest a great deal of thought in their creation. According to Bechar-Israeli, "References to collective cultural, ethnic, and religious themes in nicknames might indicate that the individual belongs to a certain social group." (p. 12) Her research shows that rather than frequently changing their names, people tend to keep their names for a period of time, which underscores the fact that they commit themselves to a screen identity.

At first glance, screen names may seem unimportant in building an electronic discussion and relationship. However, unlike your name (which was probably given to you at birth), screen names are created by the individual and reflect some degree of creativity, a value that others may consider important when encountering people online. And despite the relative stability of

identity marker

An electronic extension that communicates a person's identity, such as a screen name or a personal home page.

screen names, people can change their names much more easily in virtual life than in real life. If you encounter someone who is verbally offensive online, you can leave a chat room, establish a different name, and reenter the chat room under an entirely different alias (remember our earlier story of the CEO of Whole Foods). Even wigs and cosmetic surgery can't achieve such a transformation so quickly! Finally, most of our given names at birth (for example, Joe, Luisa, Natalie) communicate little to others. On the other hand, screen names give others insight into people's interests or values. A screen name such as >STALKU< can tell others a lot. As we noted in our Chapter 6 discussion of email addresses, screen names that are appropriate for some aspects of our life may be inappropriate for others.

Your turn

Examine and evaluate different types of identity markers by surfing some chat rooms. If you like, you can use your student workbook or your **Understanding Interpersonal Communication** *Online Resources to complete this activity.*

Personal Home Pages

If an individual wants to communicate a great deal of personal information, a personal home page may be the first step. Personal home pages, sometimes called web pages, present a number of features that depict who the person is, such as information on personal hobbies and genealogy; photographs of the person and his or her family members, friends, pets, and home; and links to groups with advocacy causes or contacts.

Communicating one's identity via a personal home page is often enlightening to others. Personal websites can contain information that may be deliberate or accidental. First, as is the case with personal interactions, people may strategically present themselves in a certain way on their personal web pages. Digital photos, slick graphics, funky fonts, interesting links, and creative screen names may communicate a sense of organization, creativity, insight, and invitation. These sorts of intentional markers may be consciously presented on web pages so that others have a comprehensive understanding of who the person is and can find out a bit about his or her attitudes, beliefs, and values. The message is clear: "I'm a person you want to meet. I've got it together online. You can imagine how together I will have it when you meet me." However, some personal home page designers would do well to remember a corollary of Murphy's law: If nothing can go wrong, it will anyway! Someone may have the best intentions of communicating clarity and authenticity, but they go awry. Consider the following greeting on a personal home page: "Welcome to my home page. I hoop you get a kick out of reading the different stories me." Or, what about the web page that had inadvertently been linked to a pornographic website? And then there are personal home pages that have so much personal information on them that it feels like an episode of Dr. Phil. When people encounter spelling errors, accidental links to websites, and over-disclosing, they may skip over a home page rather than engage it. As in face-to-face encounters, although we mean well, the words (and pictures and links) sometimes come out wrong.

Screen names and home pages are just two ways that individuals communicate their identity on the Internet. By now, you should have a clear sense of how the Internet functions in online dating and how the self influences the process of electronic relationships. We now explore the interplay between communication technology and our interactions with others.

REVISITING
CASEɪɴPOINT

1. *Discuss what sorts of identity markers or other technology Matthew Leone might use in his communication with a potential employer during an interview.*

2. *What cautions would you provide to Matthew as he works toward eliminating his prior actions on the Internet?*

You can answer these questions online under the resources for Chapter 11 at your online Resource Center for Understanding Interpersonal Communication.

Communication Technology and Relational Maintenance

Communication between and among individuals is forever changed because of technology. People are now able to initiate, maintain, and terminate relationships through technological means. Years ago, to get a date with someone, you had to meet in a common place, such as a laundromat, church, grocery store, bar, or classroom. Today, if you're *wired* with the right *hardware*, a *mouse* will help you *google* a date on *cupid.com.* The effects of technology on our interpersonal relationships are unprecedented, unpredictable, and unstoppable. We begin this section by discussing the interplay between online and "traditional" relationships, and then discuss some online communication approaches. Finally, we look at social networking and the phenomenal rise of MySpace and Facebook.

Our interpersonal communication and our relationships with others are influenced by online technology. Indeed, communication technology is changing the way we look at relationships. In that spirit, we first explain the role that online relationships play in our lives, and then look at how people develop their virtual relationships into face-to-face relationships.

The Electronic and Face-to-Face Relationship

Researchers have examined the association between electronic and interpersonal communication (e.g., Pauley & Emmer-Sommers, 2007). This scholarship has helped to differentiate between online relationships and traditional relationships. Succinctly noting why online dating is a good idea, Judith Silverstein and Michael Lasky (2004) observe that "traditional dating is fundamentally random" (p. 10). What they mean is that during the dating stage, people tend to "stumble" onto others at a social gathering. You might find yourself in the right place at the right time and meet the right person. Or, you might not. Regardless, this way of meeting people involves a lot of luck.

However, developing an online relationship is not as random; online dating "reverses the standard rules of dating" (Shin, 2003, p. D2). Silverstein and Lasky (2004) note a number of advantages to meeting someone online:

- Many people online are available and seeking companionship.
- Before you exchange personal information, you have the power to secure a profile of the other person.
- You know something about how the other person thinks and writes.
- You know how to contact him or her.
- You have the chance to exchange email and talk on the phone without ever revealing your identity.
- You can do all of this for less than what it might cost for a typical first date, like dinner at a moderately priced restaurant.

In addition, many online dating services help match people who have similar qualities, interests, and relationship goals, increasing the chances that you will meet someone with whom you are compatible. Let's look at an example to explain how an online relationship might develop. After a breakup with his partner, Willy decides to post a personal ad and photograph with an online dating service. In a few days, he receives more than twenty inquiries from women all over the state. One woman in particular, Lena, is especially appealing to Willy. He emails Lena, she emails back, and he soon discovers that she shares one of his interests—she, too, is an amateur skier. After an ongoing exchange of email (in which they communicate their dating history, feelings about family, and other personal details), they swap phone numbers. Soon, they are talking every night. After several weeks of phone calls, Willy and Lena decide to set up a time to meet. Meeting strangers online and forming the sort of virtual relationship that Willy and Lena have formed is what Warren St. John (2001) calls "**hyperdating**," which is the development of an online relationship at "lightning speed" (p. D1).

At what point do we move from an online relationship to a face-to-face relationship? First, the all-important telephone call begins the process of moving from the computer screen to a live voice. The wise use of the phone is critical. As Silverstein and Lasky (2004) conclude, "The phone can hurt you or help you in online dating" (p. 237). As with all communication technology, the effectiveness and usefulness of the telephone can vary. Necessary cautions such as caller ID blocking and not disclosing personal details about one's self are essential. Ensuring that another person is not lying to you is also paramount. Remember, all communication has the potential to have a dark side.

hyperdating

The highly accelerated development of an online relationship.

The "Language" of Online Relationships

We observed in Chapter 6 that language is the primary way that people communicate with each other. We also concluded that the language of the Internet is unique. When we put that language in the context of interpersonal relationships, we have a recipe for an interesting electronic relationship. We capture some of this uniqueness here by exploring abbreviated language, graphic accents, and blogging.

Abbreviated Language

Because technology is often used while people are on the go, it makes sense to use **abbreviated language** for efficiency in online relationships. People commonly use abbreviations such as ASL (age/sex/location), AFK (away from keyboard), PAW (parents are watching), HAND (have a nice day), S^ (s'up—what's up?), A3 (anyplace, anytime, anywhere), SETE (smiling ear to ear), and one of our favorites, FMTYEWTK (far more than you ever wanted to know). One challenge with abbreviated language is that both the sender and the receiver have to understand the abbreviations. An additional challenge is that abbreviated language does not often lead to shared meaning. If you don't understand an acronym, will you ask its meaning? How do you go about getting clarification? Abbreviated language occurs quite a bit in text messages and its usage suggests the texter's familiarity with the person he's texting. If that familiarity is not there, this abbreviated wording may prevent meaning from being communicated.

Graphic Accents

Some writers talk about CMC as a "lean" medium for interaction. Users try to compensate for this spareness by using graphic accents. In Chapter 4, we mentioned that emoticons, such as smiley faces, are used to communicate emotions. An **articon** is a picture used in an electronic message; it can be downloaded from a website or created with keyboard characters. Researchers have discovered that using graphic icons can elaborate on the words being used. For example, Diane Witmer and Mary Lee Katzman (1997) discovered that emoticons and articons helped clarify for the reader the meaning of the written word. They also concluded that both men and women use graphic accents sparingly. Perhaps they feel that their words and abbreviations are sufficient. The use of emoticons and articons will become more frequent as computer graphic programs become more sophisticated and Internet users continue to download websites filled with faces, bodies, and objects depicting various emotions. In fact, on the horizon is an ever-growing list of artwork that, unlike most emoticons, does not require you to tilt your head, but rather allows you to look at the icon straight on:

(::[ ]::)	@(*0*)@	=^.^=
Band-Aid for comfort	koala for playfulness/cute	cat for frisky

These kinds of graphic accents show creativity and, when used by both communicators, allow for shared meaning. Although it may be easier for some to

abbreviated language

Shorthand used for efficient communication in online relationships.

articon

A graphic image used in an electronic message that can be downloaded from a website or compiled from keyboard characters. An articon may or may not be used to communicate emotion.

express their feelings via technological displays, eventually two people have to meet before they can facilitate an intimate bond.

Blogging

In our electronic relationships with others, we may also keep or read blogs. As many of you already know, a blog is a running commentary—a journal on the Internet—that usually includes personal thoughts and feelings about a particular topic or individual. Blogs detail everything, including information about family, work, and personal heartaches. Andrew Sullivan (2002) notes that blogs are "imbued with the temper of the writer." Blogging is a technological intrapersonal and interpersonal experience. It is intrapersonal in nature because the authors are communicating something about themselves every time they write something for others to read. Blogging is also an interpersonal experience because others may comment on what is written or may be directed to Internet links relevant to the conversation taking place.

Especially given Web 2.0, writing your thoughts and feelings for public consumption should be done cautiously. For example, blogging about work colleagues (also known as gossip!) can come back to haunt you (Armour, 2007). Imagine, for instance, blogging about a coworker's decision to elope or chatting about his mental illness. Further, as a result of search engines, remember that the original blog is often quickly placed on the Internet. Finally, keep in mind one fundamental tenet of this course: Communication is irreversible. Once you blog, that information is available and regret, remorse, or anxiety will not take back the words you post. Clearly, there are ethical considerations associated with such disclosures.

Social Networking: Beyond the Keyboard

No discussion on technology and interpersonal communication can be complete without some discussion of social networking. **Social networking**, in its broadest sense, refers to linking individuals and communities of people who share common interests, activities, and ideas. Most social networks allow users a vast array of means by which to electronically communicate with others: email, instant messaging, file sharing, blogs, and so forth. A person is able to place a personal profile online at a social networking site, "allow" others to post their comments, and subsequently, decide to develop an online relationship. Social networking allows users to connect from one profile to another, ultimately establishing a personal network. According to danah boyd and Nicole Ellison (2007), technology historians, what makes social networks unique is "not that they allow individuals to meet strangers, but that they enable users to articulate and make visible their social networks" (http://jcmc.indiana.edu/vol13/issue1/boyd.ellison.html).

The first social network appeared in 1997. Researchers boyd and Ellison (2007) note that from 1997–2003, 13 social network sites (SNSs) appeared, the most notable being Friendster. Because Friendster eventually became a fee-based site, its users began to post messages encouraging them to join a

social networking

Linking individuals and communities who share common interests, activities, and ideas through such online websites as Facebook or MySpace.

Communication Assessment Test
A Chat Self-Test

Internet users in chat rooms frequently create personal identities. To get a sense of whether you engage in identity management, answer the questions below. Make sure you respond spontaneously and select an honest reaction; try not to think too much about a question before answering it. Use the scale to respond to the statements. You can take this test online. Go to your online Resource Center for *Understanding Interpersonal Communication* and look under the resources for Chapter 11.

	YES	yes	?	no	NO

_____ 1. It's important for me to make sure people know my real name while I communicate with them online.

_____ 2. If chat room participants refuse to reveal their real names, they have something to hide.

_____ 3. I believe "cutesy" or "childish" screen names say a lot about a person.

_____ 4. When people start to make fun of others in a chat room, they are really creating a sense of play.

_____ 5. Using screen names creates an expressive connection.

_____ 6. Using emoticons or articons is an effective way to provide others some insight into who you are.

_____ 7. Chat rooms and other e-groups generally draw those who have nothing else to do with their time.

_____ 8. The typical person in a chat room tries to create a false identity of who he or she is.

_____ 9. All email in chat rooms should be archived and available to anyone.

_____ 10. There should be explicit rules of behavior for chat room participants.

Interpretation of Results

If you found yourself answering YES or NO to any of these questions, look at the individual statements. What guided your thinking for each? What online experiences have you had in chat rooms that would have influenced your responses? If you responded with a "?" to any of the statements, think about why you are not sure about your response. Does identity management play a role in your decisions? If so, in what capacity? Be sure to reflect on the importance of online identity in your response.

---

new free site: MySpace. It was then, according to boyd and Ellison, that MySpace "was able to grow rapidly by capitalizing on Friendster's alienation of its early adopters." A few years later in 2006, seeking to capture a niche in the college community, a site that required its users to have a college address was born. This site, Facebook, and MySpace soon became the two most popular SNSs on the Internet.

Over the past decade, social networking has proliferated. In fact, over 55 percent of all children who are 12–17 claim to have visited an SNS (Lenhart & Madden, 2007). A quick search will show that there are hundreds of millions of profiles contained on MySpace and Facebook with enormous opportunity for interpersonal commentary. In one month, in the United States alone, over 80 million people visited MySpace and Facebook, and the

Social and professional networking sites, like MySpace and LinkedIn, provide us with almost unlimited opportunities to connect with others. What types of interactions do you have on networking sites? Do your interactions on these sites differ in significant ways from the face-to-face interactions you have with people in your immediate social and professional circles?

© Colin Young-Wolff/PhotoEdit

two sites have an annual combined profit of about $300 million (Hamilton, 2007). We will now provide you with a brief introduction to each site.

I Need MySpace

Browsing, searching, inviting, filming, and mailing are just a few of the options available to users of the largest social networking site in the world: MySpace. By some estimates, there are over 115 million users of MySpace worldwide (Spencer, 2007) and its growth is approximately 50 percent per year. According to one expert, 5 percent of all global Internet traffic is on MySpace (Hicks, 2007). The site works like this: You join the site, create a profile with all sorts of options (e.g., favorite dog's name, most interesting place you've visited, favorite books and movies, etc.), and then invite your friends to join. You also "mine" the site to see if you already have friends on that site who become part of your "friend space," or your social network. When people choose what information to share in their profile, they communicate with their online social network—about themselves, their values, their beliefs, and their attitudes.

Let's Face(book) It

Founded by a Harvard University student, Facebook was originally available only to college students. Today, the site is open to everyone over the age of 13. It is ranked as the most popular site for the 18–24 age bracket; women are twice as likely as men to use it (Bulik, 2007). Facebook's 72 million users (Hamilton, 2007), like MySpace users, create a profile and establish an online network of friends. Facebook users can upload photos, write notes or develop a blog, get the latest news from other friends, post videos, and join a network in a particular region of the country or affiliated with a particular high school or college.

Once you've set up a profile in Facebook, there are several ways to interact with your online network. First, you can "poke" someone to say hello. A **poke** is an electronic invitation to another person to communicate with you. However, if he/she does not poke back, a user's face may be threatened, a topic we examined in Chapter 2. Mini-feeds are also available. Depending on your point of view, the feature is either a creepy invasion of privacy or an opportunity to "innocently stalk" someone (Prowse, 2006). **Mini-feeds** are streaming bulletins that announce almost all of the activities of your Facebook friends. For instance, a mini-feed might note: "1:10 p.m.-Sasha added the Dave Matthews Band to her Favorite Music" or "9:30 a.m.-Nicky deleted *Citizen Kane* from her Favorite Movies." These mini-feeds provide uninterrupted insights into your behaviors, which makes it challenging to be incremental in your self-disclosures. Finally, Facebook users can post and view comments on "the Wall." Andrew Hampp (2007) describes the Wall as follows: "Think of it as a yearbook you can sign 24/7. Friends can use it to recap the previous night's events ("OMG! I still have your keys from Amanda's party! LOL!"), schedule get-togethers ("Lunch with the crew on Saturday? Hit me up!"), or carry on entire conversations that would normally be conducted through phones, email or, at the very least, text messages" (p. 32). "Poking," mini-feeds, and "the Wall" represent new and unique ways of conducting interpersonal communication online.

As we noted, not all online discussions evolve into interpersonal relationships, and you should always err on the side of caution when communicating with others online, especially on such sites as MySpace and Facebook. Some people may be feigning interest in you and your profile, manipulating you to gain information, or simply having a good time at your expense. For a list of safety tips and warnings of potential dangers when meeting and communicating with potential friends or romantic partners online, use your online Resource Center for *Understanding Interpersonal Communication* to access *Interactive Activity 11.2: Safe Online Relationships* under the resources for Chapter 11. And for a good reminder that we are responsible for and can control our own safety on- and offline, access *InfoTrac College Edition Exercise 11.3: Finding Love Online the Safe Way* to check out the article "Finding Love Online—How to Be Safe and Secure," available through InfoTrac College Edition.

We close the chapter with specific skills to remember when communicating online.

Choices for Improving Online Communication Skills

Your ability to function effectively in social and professional settings depends a great deal on your ability to be competent with communication technology. As we have seen, individuals utilize technology to cultivate online relationships.

poke
On a social networking website, an electronic invitation to another person to communicate with you.

mini-feed
Streaming bulletins that announce the activities of a Facebook user's friends.

We close our discussion by exploring several skills to consider as both a sender and a receiver of electronic communication. We begin with the sender of electronic messages, move to the receiver, and then—following our transactional model of interpersonal communication, explained in Chapter 1—we expand our discussion to both sender and receiver.

Sender Skills for Electronic Messages

The following sender skills apply to the source of an electronic message. If you are an avid consumer of communication technology, you might try to identify additional skills that are not explained here.

Be Succinct When Necessary

You have probably written or received an email that goes on and on and on. This stream-of-consciousness writing is easy to do because the sender doesn't have to organize his or her thoughts before sending a message. For example, if you want to email another person about your likes and dislikes, your hobbies, and what you do in your spare time, your message could continue for several pages! Learn to abbreviate your thoughts. The longer the message, the more the receiver will be inclined to emphasize parts of your message that may not deserve such attention. Stay on point. Consider the following example:

> Hi. I'm really not all that excited about writing U. I waz nervous the first time we "talked" online. Of course, I realize that we weren't really talking, but it's strange anyway. So, HOW RU? I'm OK! So much 2 tell u. DAH! I should SU so U can talk!!!

The sender appears to be babbling aimlessly, which communicates some nervousness on the sender's part. The receiver may read far more into this stream-of-consciousness writing than the message warrants. Now, look at an alternate, more succinct opening:

> Hi. this online stuff is new to me, so help me out if i mess up. i hope you're OK. being online keeps me thinking. . . what am i gonna say next?

This is a much more concise way of opening up the dialogue and letting the receiver know that you're new to electronic discussions.

Write Literally

Regardless of whether communication is electronic or face to face, we must be precise in our wording to others. Using concrete and precise language avoids ambiguous and convoluted thoughts. Because a sender of an electronic message isn't privy to the recipient's facial reactions, body movements, and eye expressions, it is important to be as clear as possible when sending a message so that it is less likely to be misinterpreted.

Senders of email messages need to be especially careful in communicating feelings; an emoticon or articon isn't always sufficient. In fact, if you use one during a challenging discussion, the receiver might view it negatively. For example, sticking in a frowning face while talking about a family mem-

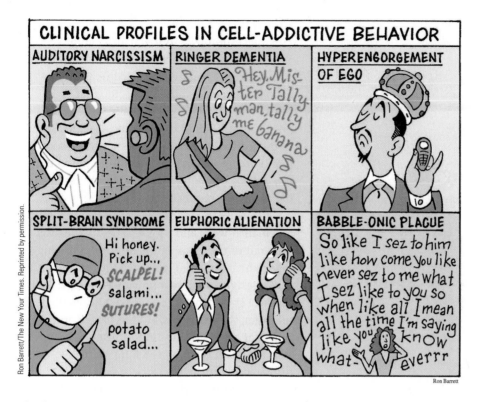

Ron Barrett/The New Your Times. Reprinted by permission.

Ron Barrett

ber's illness may be viewed by the receiver as flippant, which is probably a different message than what the sender intended.

Stay Polite

Although it's easy for us to suggest politeness, it's frequently difficult to practice. As in face-to-face conversations, when someone communicating online is passionate about a topic, he or she may blunder and be offensive. Keep in mind the permanency of the written word and the fact that communication is irreversible; after we write something mean or offensive, we can't take it back.

Let's look at an example. Breanna is mad that she didn't get the Friday night off from work that she requested, so when her boss emails her asking if she can work a double shift on Wednesday, Breanna sends the following message: "Sorry, can't do. I have to rest from being required to work Friday night!" Breanna's boss will surely perceive her message to be impolite. Now, consider an alternative response from Breanna: "I need to get back to you. Let me check it out, and I'll talk to you on Tuesday when I work." Courtesy and deference when communicating online are far more constructive than rudeness. Also, Breanna asks for a face-to-face conversation so that she can fully explain herself. Doing so will likely result in less misinterpretation than an email exchange would.

We are not suggesting that you simply roll with the punches all the time and avoid sticking up for yourself when matters become heated. At times, you do have to be direct in your email communication. Yet, we suggest that you temper your eagerness to make a point by recalling the power of words and their lasting effect upon both senders and receivers.

... on an online dating site

As you scroll through the personal ads on the dating website, you begin to wonder why you even placed an ad in the first place. Nearly all of those whom the website administrator identified as a "match" had ads that indicated that they were "in transition" with jobs, divorced, or "very willing." Disgusted with the options, you decide to utilize a different dating site and create a different personal ad to attract the sort of companion you seek. After receiving nearly a dozen replies to your ad, it's now time to respond to those who have taken the time to email you with their interests. What steps do you take as you construct messages to your senders? What cautions do you exercise as you send and receive electronic messages with potential partners?

Take a Deep Breath

This suggestion is both literal and figurative. When you inhale and release your breath, you reduce stress. Figuratively speaking, taking a deep break means thinking about what you want to write before you actually write it and press "Send." Reflect on your message. Reread it. In electronic discussions, we always recommend taking a deep breath before responding too quickly or taking action without first thinking about the ramifications.

Consider the following examples. Neil sent an email at work and forgot to delete the original draft of the email at the bottom of the message, which blasted a colleague for not responding quickly enough to a previous message. Marla, a student who received a poor grade on a midterm, wrote an email to the professor telling him that his questions didn't make sense and that the exam was way too long. And Tavo disclosed his entire life story in one email to a potential future partner online, unaware that his disclosure revealed that his ex-wife was the best friend of the woman he was dating! We can't urge you enough to take a deep breath before any online dialogue begins.

Receiver Skills for Electronic Messages

The receiver of information must also be savvy in the ways of online communication. Here, we explore receiver skills of online dialogues. As with the sender skills, think about additional receiver skills that may be needed.

Check In with the Sender

The receiver should always make sure that what he or she is responding to is what the sender intended. Checking in may be as simple as asking the sender to clarify. Or, a receiver may simply want to send out a brief **electronic trial balloon**, which is an overture that briefly responds to a sender's message. For example, when asked what she "does for fun" from someone responding to an online personal ad, Kia responds this way: "If U mean, what do I do in my spare time, I love animals. I volunteer at an animal shelter. What DID U mean?"

What Kia offered was an electronic trial balloon. She briefly responded to the question but then asked for more clarification. Checking in is an efficient form of communication because the receiver can avoid responding with unnecessary or irrelevant information. Checking in saves time and allows for clarity.

electronic trial balloon

An online overture that briefly responds to a sender's message in order to clarify the sender's intended message.

Show Empathy When Possible

When we discussed listening in Chapter 5, we addressed the need to be empathic. Empathy, as you recall, means to put yourself in another's position. In face-to-face conversations, empathy may take the form of hugging another when he's down and out or giving a "high-five" and shouting "yeah!" when a friend tells you she just got engaged. In our online discussions, we don't have the benefit of showing empathy in such ways. However, we can still show empathy for someone even though we aren't sharing the same physical space.

Being empathic online can take various forms. You might use articons (sparingly) to express how you feel about the situation in conjunction with words that show how you feel. For example, when Keith gets laid off from his job, Lee's written response should show some level of comfort: "We've all been there, buddy. You'll pull through this one (::():) I know you will." Lee's words accompanied by the symbol of comfort (a Band-Aid) provide some degree of empathy that Keith will likely appreciate.

Listen beyond the Words

Listening applies to electronic conversations as well as those we conduct in person. When you listen to others online, you need to read between the lines to figure out the intention, emotion, and intuition. Yet, we need to be careful since we may be attributing too much detail to words, and we may come to an inaccurate conclusion. That's why we need to check in with the sender, a skill we noted previously.

Listening beyond the words is difficult. Recall Chapter 5 where we stated that listening is easier said than done, particularly on topics about which we have strong beliefs or opinions. Further, during our online conversations, we may have more distractions than during our face-to-face interactions. For example, while online, you may choose to answer the door, make breakfast,

© Ahmad Al-Rubayal/AFP/Getty Images

New technologies allow us to communicate with loved ones more quickly and more efficiently than ever before. For example, parents can take pictures of their new baby with a digital camera and email them the same day to anyone in the family who has access to email—no photo developing or scanning required. And friends and family can easily email empathy and support to people in places where mail delivery is slow.

talk to a roommate, pay your bills, clean your bedroom, change a light bulb, or do a number of other things that you feel need attention. Of course, your online partner doesn't necessarily know you are doing anything else except communicating with him or her.

Sender and Receiver Skills for Electronic Messages

In Chapter 1, we introduced the transactional model of communication, which suggests that a sender and receiver simultaneously engage in the communication process. Like face-to-face interactions, online conversations are transactional in nature. Let's explore a few skills needed by both sender and receiver while online with each other.

Take Responsibility for Your Own Words

Many people tend to forget that they "own" the words they choose to use. That is, whether we are in front of a person or a computer screen, we need to take responsibility for what we say or write. When communicating with someone online, this language ownership becomes important when we consider that the written word has the power to be permanent; it's not available to only you for future use—it's available to virtually anyone!

We recommend that you adopt a mantra that places responsibility for what is written solely within yourself, regardless of whether you are a sender or a receiver. Consider an earlier skill we identified that encouraged you to reflect before writing anything. And if you write something you didn't mean to write, try to reframe the situation by placing your words in context. Try not to cast blame on another for the words you chose to use.

Build Your Dialogue

We can think of a face-to-face conversation as a play. The scene may need to be set up, the characters have to be notified about their parts, and the setting should be clear to the audience. In online relationships, a similar metaphor seems reasonable. Plays don't begin in the middle. You don't expect a cast member to know what happens next unless you give some sort of background. You present ideas and concerns as a process, not as an ultimatum.

Building a dialogue online ensures that topics and ideas are arranged in order of importance. Subordinate ideas should be given less attention than primary ideas. For instance, if Tess is concerned that her online conversation is taking a turn to the highly intimate with J. C., she might inform J. C. about her feelings first and then proceed to explain why she is concerned. Perhaps Tess feels that too much personal information is being shared early in the development of the electronic conversation. If so, she needs to clearly state her belief.

To read an article that discusses building a dialogue online by asking questions that can help you reduce your uncertainty of others, check out "Interrogative Strategies and Information Exchange in Computer-Mediated Communication," available through InfoTrac College Edition. Use your online Resource Center for *Understanding Interpersonal Communication* to access *InfoTrac College Edition Exercise 11.4: Reducing Uncertainty Online* under the resources for Chapter 11.

Recall the Challenge of Online Communication

Both senders and receivers of electronic messages must always remember that this type of communication is frequently ambiguous and fraught with misinterpretation. Even if you have extensive experience meeting people online, remember that others may not share your electronic expertise. Be careful when it comes to using abbreviations that are not universally understood. Think before stating too much too soon; others may be put off by your level of comfort.

Finally, don't assume that your words will be taken as you intended. Consider Carol, the mother of Laura, who is herself a mother of three children. As a 70-year old, Carol is a relative newcomer to email. Yet, early on, she learned that online conversations can be easily misconstrued. While communicating with her daughter, she indicated that she missed her grandchildren and wanted to see them by writing her daughter the following message:

> IT MUST BE NICE TO HAVE CHILDREN AROUND. I WISH I COULD SEE MY GRANDKIDS!

Her daughter responded:

> Why do you get mad every time you talk about my children? Just because you don't see them doesn't mean I'm somehow "protecting" them from you. CHILL OUT, mother. I'll make sure you see them next month.

The challenge of online communication is demonstrated in this online dialogue through the use of capital letters. Carol used capital letters because she simply forgot to

interpersonal explorer

Before you finish reading this chapter, take a moment to review the theories and skills discussed. How do you think the theories discussed in this chapter can help you better understand interpersonal communication and technology? In what ways can the skills discussed help you interact more effectively with other people in your life?

Theories that relate to electronic communication
- **Technological determinism**
  Technology is irreversible, inescapable, and inevitable
- **Signaling theory**
  Signals may vary in their reliability, but are ever-present in social networking

Practical skills for improving online communication

For senders
- Be succinct
- Write literally
- Stay polite
- Take a deep breath

For receivers
- Check in with the sender
- Show empathy
- Listen beyond the words

For senders and receivers
- Take responsibility for your own words
- Build your dialogue
- Recall the challenge of online communication

Explore your interpersonal choices
Are you ready to explore your interpersonal choices regarding technology and interpersonal communication? Use your online Resource Center for *Understanding Interpersonal Communication* to access an ABC News video, "Virtual Visitation," about how Webcam technology enables a separated father and daughter to communicate virtually over the internet. Compare your answers to the questions at the end of the video with those provided by the authors.

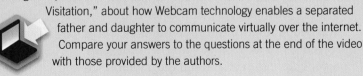

turn off the "Caps Lock" command on the keyboard. Laura, however, took the capitalized words as an intentional personal affront because using all capital letters in electronic communication is considered "shouting." Realizing the potential for confusion while online is essential for everyone in the communication process.

As we continuously note throughout this book, the communication process is transactional. Both the sender and receiver, then, become responsible for meaning making. In our electronic conversations with others, the transactional nature of communication becomes more critical because we don't have the privilege of a face-to-face interaction. Practicing the skills discussed in this section—whether as a sender or receiver—becomes paramount when we cultivate online interactions.

For a useful site that contains links to articles about netiquette (the rules of common courtesy for online communication) and a quiz you can take to help you better understand the do's and don'ts of communicating online, use your online resources for *Understanding Interpersonal Communication* to access *Interactive Activity 11.3: Netiquette Quiz* under the resources for Chapter 11.

Summary

We live in a time of unprecedented technological change. One new technology quickly replaces another and we talk about it, work with it, and engage it in ways never before seen in society. This technological evolution has also affected our interpersonal communication. The use of computer-mediated communication (CMC) is now commonplace among people of various races, ages, and cultures. With the advent of Web 2.0, in particular, CMC will be forever changed.

Technology plays an integral role in our communication with others. Because technology is pervasive, we rely on it. It is paradoxical that such a large, cumbersome entity as technology can draw people together—a concept encompassed by the idea of the *global village*. Another important characteristic of technology is that it is powerful; it influences people, events, and entire cultures. Lastly, the accessibility of technology varies depending on people's age, race, culture, and geographical setting—a phenomenon called the *digital divide*.

The Internet, a giant network of computers, has both a bright side and a dark side. Users should be wary of online sources until they are sure of those websites' accountability. Other websites might be filled with hate speech, or users might encounter flamers in a chat room. The anonymity of the web makes some users less civil than they would be in face-to-face interactions. The bright side of the Internet includes the opportunity to widen your social network; in fact, entire communities are developed and maintained online. You can also educate yourself by searching online via search engines for informational websites and chat rooms with professionals who give advice.

Keep in mind that people can lie or pretend to be someone else online. On the plus side, online discussions can prompt introspection and individualism. And by self-disclosing online, people can increase intimacy and avoid immediate reactions of disgust, disappointment, or confusion. However, be careful when you self-disclose online; if you send an electronic message and then decide you should not have disclosed something contained in the message (which could inadvertently be passed to someone else), you cannot retrieve it.

Identity markers are expressions of the self online. Screen names and personal home pages show individuality and give people insight into their originators. However, sometimes strange names or disorganized home pages give an unintended impression.

People are now able to initiate, maintain, and terminate conversations and relationships through technological means. People use abbreviated language and graphic accents to efficiently communicate, although these are open to misinterpretation. People can communicate using blogs (online journals), but they should use discretion when blogging about private matters. Further, social networking sites like MySpace and Facebook have created a new generation of computer users who, despite warnings and concerns from professionals, continue to put personal information out to the public.

Whereas traditional dating is random, involving good timing and luck, online dating is an inexpensive process that is not as arbitrary because many people are using the same venues for the same purpose. In addition, the user has control over the information divulged, can find out how the other thinks and writes, what the potential date looks like, and his or her likes and dislikes before deciding whether to meet face to face. Some people engage in hyperdating, or developing an online relationship quickly. Others find lifelong friends, not romantic partners, in online venues. Still other online relationships don't develop into interpersonal relationships.

To ably communicate online, senders and receivers need certain skills. Senders should be succinct, write clearly to avoid misinterpretation, stay polite, and reflect on their messages before sending them. Receivers should check about the sender's intent, show empathy when possible, and read between the lines. Both senders and receivers should take responsibility for their words, build their dialogue, and recall the challenge that online communication poses.

Communication technology continues to redefine how people meet and relate to one another. As technology evolves, it expands our relational horizons in unimagined directions. Despite the advances made in communication technology, as technology changes, new challenges await those who utilize it.

Understanding Interpersonal Communication Online

Now that you've read Chapter 11, use your online Resource Center for *Understanding Interpersonal Communication* for quick access to the electronic study resources that accompany this text. Your online Resource Center gives you access to the video of Matthew on page 380, the Ethics & Choice interactive activity on page 398, the Your Turn journal activity on page 402, the Communication Assessment Test on page 407, the Interpersonal Explorer activity on page 415, InfoTrac College Edition, and study aids including a digital glossary, review quizzes, and the chapter activities.

Terms for Review

abbreviated language 393	computer-mediated	electronic trial balloon 400
articon 393	communication	flaming 380
asynchronous	(CMC) 370	global village 372
communication 386	content aggregation 368	hate speech 378
avatar 384	convergence 369	hyperdating 392

Questions for Understanding

Comprehension Focus

1. Explain what convergence means and how it relates to interpersonal communication.

2. Discuss and differentiate among the characteristics of communication technology. Provide examples in your explanation.

3. Explore the implications of technological accessibility in the United States. Why is this topic particularly important in the twenty-first century?

4. Identify several dark and bright features of the Internet. Offer examples of each.

5. Describe each of the identify markers discussed in this chapter and provide examples of each in your response.

Application Focus

1. CASE IN POINT Review our opening vignette of Matthew Leone. Do you believe that Matthew's MySpace page will be a detriment to his job prospects or do you believe that most employers will simply "shrug it off" as an adolescent prank? What do you think of social networking sites that allow people like Matthew to place themselves in precarious circumstances? Should they be held accountable at all? Or, should individuals like Matthew know better?

2. Do you think that sites such as MySpace and Facebook are "filled with potential," "tech fads that will soon disappear," or something in between? Discuss your response in the context of the information presented in the chapter.

3. What additional markers, besides the ones discussed in this chapter, can you think of that serve to communicate another's identity online?

4. Defend or criticize the following statement: "When discussing interpersonal communication, the effects of technology cut both ways." What does the statement mean? What additional or substituted words would you place in the statement? Use examples to defend your view.

5. Explore future avenues of how technology and interpersonal interactions might intersect. In other words, what would you predict on the horizon with respect to communication technology and relationships? Provide examples.

Interactive Activities and InfoTrac College Edition Exercises

Interactive Activities

InfoTrac College Edition Exercises

Glossary

A

abbreviated language. Shorthand used for efficient communication in online relationships.

abstract. Not able to be seen, smelled, tasted, touched, or heard.

account. An explanation for a transgression that may accompany an apology.

acculturation. Occurs when a person learns, adapts to, and adopts the appropriate behaviors and rules of a host culture.

action-centered listening style. A listening style associated with listeners who want messages to be highly organized, concise, and error-free.

active listening. Suspending our own responses while listening so we can concentrate on what another person is saying.

activity. An attribute of emotion that refers to whether the emotion implies action or passivity.

affection and instrumentality dialectic. The tension between framing a friendship with someone as an end in itself (affection) or seeing it as a means to another end (instrumentality).

affinity seeking. Emphasizing the commonalities we think we share with another person.

ambushing. Listening carefully to a message and then using the information later to attack the sender.

American Sign Language (ASL). A visual rather than auditory form of communication that is composed of precise hand shapes and movements.

androgynous. Having both masculine and feminine traits.

apology. A simple statement like "I am really sorry."

approaching. Providing nonverbal signals that indicate we'd like to initiate contact with another person, such as going up to a person or smiling in that person's direction.

articon. A graphic image used in an electronic message that can be downloaded from a website or compiled from keyboard characters. An articon may or may not be used to communicate emotion. *See also* emoticon.

asynchronous communication. Communication that doesn't require a sender and a receiver to have an exchange at the same time, as in online communication.

attending and selecting. The first stage of the perception process, requiring us to use our visual, auditory, tactile, and olfactory senses to respond to stimuli in our interpersonal environment.

attribution theory. A theory that explains how we create explanations or attach meaning to another person's behavior or our own.

autonomy and connection dialectic. The tension between our desire to be independent or autonomous while simultaneously wanting to feel a connection with our partner.

avatar. A digital fictional and fantasy representation of a user in a virtual world.

avoiding stage. A stage in the coming apart section of Knapp's model of relationship development in which two partners stay away from each other because they feel that being together is unpleasant.

B

blind self. In the Johari Window, the pane that includes information others know about us that we are unaware of.

blog. An online journal that usually includes personal thoughts and feelings about a particular topic or individual.

bodily artifacts. Items we wear that are part of our physical appearance and that have the potential to communicate, such as clothing, religious symbols, military medals, body piercings, and tattoos.

body orientation. The extent to which we turn our legs, shoulders, and head toward (or away) from a communicator.

bonding stage. The final stage in the coming together part of Knapp's model of relationship development, in which partners make a public commitment to their relationship.

boundaries or openness. A systems principle referring to the fact that hierarchy is formed by creating boundaries around each separate system (e.g., a brother and sister, the family as a whole, and so forth). However, human systems are inherently open, which means that information passes through these boundaries. Therefore, some researchers call this principle "openness," and some call it "boundaries."

breadth. A dimension of self-disclosure that indicates the number of topics discussed within a relationship.

bright side of interpersonal communication. Altruistic, supportive, and affirming communication exchanges between people.

browser. A program that determines how documents are displayed on our computers, enabling us to view websites.

bullying. A particular form of conflict in which the abuse is persistent and the person being bullied finds it very difficult to defend himself or herself.

C

calibration. The process of systems setting their parameters, checking on themselves, and self-correcting.

categorical imperative. An ethical system, based on the work of philosopher Immanuel Kant, that advances the notion that individuals follow moral absolutes. The underlying tenet in this ethical system suggests that we should act as an example to others.

catharsis. A therapeutic release of tensions and negative emotion as a result of self-disclosing.

channel. A pathway through which a message is sent.

chat room. Live online dialogue with other people who share similar interests.

chronemics. The study of a person's use of time.

chunking. Placing pieces of information into manageable and retrievable sets.

circumscribing stage. A stage in the coming apart section of Knapp's model of relationship development in which two people's communication behaviors are restrained so that fewer topics are raised (for fear of conflict), more issues are out of bounds, and they interact less.

citing gestures. Gestures that acknowledge another's feedback in a conversation.

civil communication. The acceptance of another person as an equal partner in achieving meaning during communication.

close relationships. A relationship that endures over time and that consists of interdependent partners who satisfy each other's needs for connection and social inclusion, feel an emotional attachment to each other, are irreplaceable to each other, and enact unique communication patterns.

co-culture. A culture within a culture.

codability. The ease with which a language can express a thought.

code-switching. Shifting back and forth between languages in the same conversation.

collectivism. A cultural mindset that emphasizes the group and its norms, values, and beliefs over the self.

communicating emotionally. Communicating such that the emotion is not the content of the message but rather a property of it.

communication apprehension. A fear or an anxiety pertaining to the communication process. This fear or anxiety is the result of a legitimate life experience that usually negatively affects our communication with others.

communication competency. The ability to communicate with knowledge, skills, and thoughtfulness.

communication models. Visual, simplified representations of complex relationships in the communication process.

community. The common understandings among people who are committed to coexisting.

comparison level. A person's standard level for what types of costs and rewards should exist in a given relationship.

comparison level for alternatives. A comparison of the costs and rewards of a current relationship to the possibility of doing better in a different relationship.

computer-mediated communication (CMC). The use of various technologies to facilitate communication with others.

computing. Disqualifying the emotional aspects of a conflict (the context) and focusing on the rational aspects.

concrete. Able to be seen, smelled, tasted, touched, or heard.

confirmation. A response that acknowledges and supports another.

conflict interaction. The point in the conflict process when the differences between two individuals become a problem and one or both people begin to address the issue.

connotative meaning. The meaning of a verbal symbol that is derived from our personal and subjective experience with that symbol.

content aggregation. The process of collecting electronic data from different and multiple online sources to suit a particular need, such as populating a search engine or preparing digital slides for a presentation.

content conflict. A conflict that revolves around an issue. *Also called* a substantive conflict.

content-centered listening style. A listening style associated with listeners who focus on the facts and details of a message.

content level. The verbal and nonverbal information contained in a message that indicates the topic of the message.

context. The environment in which a message is sent. *See also* physical context, cultural context, social-emotional context, and historical context.

context orientation theory. The theory that meaning is derived from either the setting of the message or the words of a message and that cultures can vary in the extent to which message meaning is made explicit or implicit.

convergence. The integration of various technologies, such as online radio or cell phones with cameras.

conversational narcissism. Engaging in an extreme amount of self-focusing during a conversation, to the exclusion of another person.

corrective maintenance. Repairing a relationship when it runs into trouble.

costs. Those things in relational life that we judge as negative.

cultural context. The cultural environment in which communication occurs. In this type of context, messages are understood in relationship to the rules, roles, norms, and patterns of communication that are unique to particular cultures and co-cultures.

cultural empathy. The learned ability to accurately understand the experiences of people from diverse cultures and to convey that understanding responsively.

cultural imperialism. The process whereby individuals, companies, and/or the media impose their way of thinking and behaving upon another culture.

cultural relativity. The ability to avoid judging or condemning any practice in which any other culture engages.

cultural variability theory. A theory that describes the four value dimensions (individualism/collectivism, uncertainty avoidance, power distance, masculinity/femininity) that offer information regarding the value differences in a particular culture.

culture. The shared, personal, and learned life experiences of a group of individuals who have a common set of values, norms, and traditions.

culture clash. A conflict over cultural expectations and experiences.

cyclic alternation. A strategy for dealing with dialectic tensions in a relationship that allows us to choose opposite poles of the dialectic at different times.

D

dark side of interpersonal communication. Negative communica-

tion exchanges between people, such as manipulation, deceit, and verbal aggression.

decoding. The process of developing a thought based on hearing verbal symbols, observing nonverbal messages, or both.

defensive listening. Viewing innocent comments as personal attacks or hostile criticisms.

delivery gestures. Gestures that signal shared understanding between communicators in a conversation.

denotative meaning. The literal, conventional meaning of a verbal symbol that most people in a culture have agreed is the meaning of that symbol.

depth. A dimension of self-disclosure indicating how much detail we provide about a specific topic.

dialogue enhancers. Supporting statements, such as "I see" or "I'm listening," that indicate we are involved in a message.

differentiating stage. The first stage in the coming apart section of Knapp's model of relationship development, in which two people begin to notice ways in which they differ.

direct and virtual use of power. Communicating the potential use of a direct application of power.

direct application of power. In a conflict situation, the use of any resource at our disposal to compel another to comply, regardless of that person's desires.

disconfirmation. A response that fails to acknowledge and support another, leaving the person feeling ignored and disregarded.

disqualifying. A strategy for coping with dialectic tensions in a relationship by exempting certain topics from discussion.

distal context. The background that frames a specific conflict.

distal outcomes. The residue of having engaged in a conflict and

the feelings that both the participants have about their interaction.

distracting. Disqualifying the subject of a conflict by distracting both people in the conflict with behaviors such as laughing, crying, or changing the subject.

dualism. A way of thinking that constructs polar opposite categories to encompass the totality of a thing. Dualism prompts us to think about things in an "either-or" fashion.

dyadic effect. The tendency for us to return another's self-disclosure with one that matches it in level of intimacy.

E

electronic trial balloon. An online overture that briefly responds to a sender's message in order to clarify the sender's intended message.

emoticon. An icon that can be typed on a keyboard to express emotions; used to compensate for the lack of nonverbal cues in computer-mediated communication. *See also* articon.

emotion. The critical internal structure that orients us to and engages us with what matters in our lives: our feelings about ourselves and others. Emotion encompasses both the internal feelings of one person (for instance, anxiety or happiness) as well as feelings that can be experienced only in a relationship (for instance, jealousy or competitiveness).

emotional communication. Talking about an emotional experience.

emotional contagion. The process of transferring emotions from one person to another.

emotional effects. The ways in which an emotional experience impacts communication behavior.

emotional experience. The feeling of emotion.

empathy. The process of identifying with or attempting to experience the thoughts, beliefs, and actions of another.

empowerment. Helping to actualize our own or another person's power.

encoding. The process of putting thoughts and feelings into verbal symbols, nonverbal messages, or both.

enculturation. Occurs when a person—either consciously or unconsciously—learns to identify with a particular culture and a culture's thinking, way of relating, and worldview.

equifinality. The ability to achieve the same goals (or ends) by a variety of means.

equivocation. A type of ambiguity that involves choosing our words carefully to give a listener a false impression without actually lying.

ethic of care. An ethical system, based on the concepts of Carol Gilligan, that is concerned with the connections among people and the moral consequences of decisions.

ethics. The perceived rightness or wrongness of an action or behavior, determined in large part by society.

ethnocentrism. The process of judging another culture using the standards of our own culture.

euphemism. A milder or less direct word substituted for another word that is more blunt or negative.

expectancy violations theory. A theory that maintains that we expect other people to maintain a certain distance from us in their conversations with us.

experimenting stage. A stage in the coming together part of Knapp's model of relationship development in which two people become acquainted by gathering information about each other.

external dialectics. Tensions between oppositions that have to do with how relational partners negotiate the public aspects of their relationship.

F

face. The image of the self we choose to present to others in our interpersonal encounters.

fact. A piece of information that is verifiable by direct observation.

family stories. Bits of lore about family members and activities that are told and retold as a way for family members to construct a sense of family identity and meaning.

feedback. A verbal or nonverbal response to a message. *See also* internal feedback and external feedback.

feeling rules. The cultural norms used to create and react to emotional expressions.

feminine culture. A culture that emphasizes characteristics stereotypically associated with feminine people, such as sexual equality, nurturance, quality of life, supportiveness, affection, and a compassion for the less fortunate.

field of experience. The influence of a person's culture, past experiences, personal history, and heredity on the communication process.

flaming. Exchanging malicious, hostile, or insulting comments over the Internet.

framing theory. A theory that argues that when we compare two unlike things in a figure of speech, we are unconsciously influenced by the comparison.

four "Rs" of listening. The four components of the listening process: receiving, responding, recalling, and rating.

G

gap fillers. Listeners who think they can correctly guess the rest of the story a speaker is telling and don't need the speaker to continue.

gender. The learned behaviors a culture associates with being a male or female, known as masculinity or femininity.

gender role socialization. The process by which women and men learn the gender roles appropriate to their sex. This process affects the way the sexes perceive the world.

gender schema. A mental framework we use to process and categorize beliefs, ideas, and events as either masculine or feminine in order to understand and organize our world.

generic *he*. The use of the masculine pronoun *he* to function generically when the subject of the sentence is of unknown gender or includes both men and women.

global village. The concept that all societies, regardless of their size, are connected in some way. The term also can be used to describe how communication technology ties the world into one political, economic, social, and cultural system.

golden mean. An ethical system, articulated by Aristotle, that proposes a person's moral virtue stands between two vices, with the middle, or the mean, being the foundation for a rational society.

grammar. The rules that dictate the structure of language.

H

halo effect. Matching like qualities with each other to create an overall perception of someone or something.

haptics. The study of how we communicate through touch.

hate speech. Extremely offensive language that is directed toward a particular group of people.

hearing. The physical process of letting in audible stimuli without focusing on the stimuli.

hidden power. A type of power in which one person in a relationship suppresses or avoids decisions in the interest of one of the parties. *Also called* unobtrusive power.

hidden self. In the Johari Window, the pane that includes the information about ourselves we are aware of but that we have chosen not to disclose.

hierarchy. A principle that states that all relationships are embedded within larger systems.

high-context culture. A culture in which there is a high degree of similarity among members and in which the meaning of a message is drawn primarily from its context, such as one's surroundings, rather than from words.

historical context. A type of context in which messages are understood in relationship to previously sent messages.

history. Information that may sound personal to another person but that is relatively easy for us to tell.

hyperdating. The highly accelerated development of an online relationship.

I

ideal and real dialectic. The tension between an idealized vision of friendship and the real friends one has.

identity management theory. The theory that explains the manner in which you handle your "self" in various circumstances; includes competency, identity, and face.

identity marker. An electronic extension that communicates a person's identity, such as a screen name or a personal home page.

idiom. A word or a phrase that has an understood meaning within a culture but whose meaning is not derived by exact translation.

image conflict. A conflict with another about one's sense of oneself.

imagined conversation. A conversation with oneself in which one partner plays the parts of both partners in a mental rehearsal.

I-message. A message phrased to show we understand that our feelings belong to us and aren't caused by someone else.

implicit personality theory. The theory that we rely on a set of a few characteristics to draw inferences about others and use these inferences as the basis of our communication with them.

indexing. Avoiding generalizations by acknowledging the time frame in which we judge others and ourselves.

indirect application of power. Employing power without making its employment explicit.

individualism. A cultural mindset that emphasizes self-concept and personal achievement and that prefers competition over cooperation, the individual over the group, and the private over the public.

inference. A conclusion derived from a fact, but it does not reflect direct observation or experience.

in-group. A group to which a person feels he or she belongs.

initiating stage. The first stage in the coming together part of Knapp's model of relationship development, in which two people notice each other and indicate to each other that they are interested in making contact.

integrating stage. A stage in the coming together part of Knapp's model of relationship development in which two partners form a clear identity as a couple.

integration. A strategy for dealing with the dialectic tension in a relationship that allows us to synthesize the opposites. Integration can take three forms: neutralizing, disqualifying, and reframing.

intensifying stage. A stage in the coming together part of Knapp's model of relationship development in which the intimacy between the partners intensifies.

intensity. An attribute of emotion that refers to how strongly an emotion is felt.

interaction. A necessary condition for conflict, given that conflicts are created and sustained through verbal and nonverbal communication.

interaction adaptation theory. A theory that suggests individuals simultaneously adapt their communication behavior to the communication behavior of others.

interactional model of communication. A characterization of communication as a two-way process in which a message is sent from sender to receiver and from receiver to sender. In the interactional view, one can be both a sender and a receiver, but not both simultaneously.

intercultural communication. Communication between and among individuals and groups from different cultural backgrounds.

intercultural communication apprehension. A fear or anxiety pertaining to communication with people from different cultural backgrounds.

interdependence. A necessary condition for conflict, given that people involved in conflict rely on each other, need each other, and are in a relationship with each other.

internal dialectics. Tensions resulting from oppositions inherent in relational partners' communication with each other.

internal feedback. The feedback we give ourselves when we assess our own communication.

interpersonal communication. The process of message transaction between two people to create and sustain shared meaning.

interpersonal conflict. The interaction of interdependent people who perceive incompatible goals and interference from each other in achieving those goals.

interpreting. The third stage of the perception process, in which we assign meaning to what we perceive.

intimate distance. The distance that extends about eighteen inches around each of us that is normally reserved for people with whom we are close, such as close friends, romantic partners, and family members.

irreversibility. The fact that our communication with others cannot be "unsaid" or reversed.

J

Johari Window. A model used to understand the process of self-disclosure consisting of a square with four panels that provides a pictorial representation of how "known" we are to ourselves and others.

judgment and acceptance dialectic. Our desire to criticize a friend as opposed to accepting a friend for who he or she is.

K

kinesics. The study of a person's body movement and its effect on the communication process.

L

language. A system comprised of vocabulary and rules of grammar that allows us to engage in verbal communication.

lexical gaps. Experiences that are not named.

linear model of communication. A characterization of communication as a one-way process that transmits a message from a sender to a receiver.

linguistic determinism. A theory that argues that our language determines our ability to perceive and think about things. If we don't have a word for something in our language, this theory predicts we won't think about it or notice it.

linguistic relativity. A theory that states that language influences our thinking but doesn't determine it. Thus, if we don't have a word for something in our language, this

theory predicts it will be difficult, but not impossible, to think about it or notice it.

listening. The dynamic, transactional process of receiving, recalling, rating, and responding to stimuli, messages, or both.

listening gap. The time difference between our mental ability to interpret words and the speed at which they arrive at our brain.

listening style. A predominant and preferred approach to listening to the messages we hear.

long-term attraction. Judgment of a relationship that makes us want to continue a relationship after initiating it. This attraction sustains and maintains relationships.

low-context culture. A culture in which there is a high degree of difference among members and in which the meaning of a message must be explicitly related, usually in words.

M

man-linked words. Words that include the word *man* but that are supposed to operate generically to include women as well, such as *mankind*.

masculine culture. A culture that emphasizes characteristics stereotypically associated with masculine people, such as achievement, competitiveness, strength, and material success.

meaning. What communicators create together through the use of verbal and nonverbal messages.

message. Spoken, written, or unspoken information sent from a sender to a receiver.

message exchange. The transaction of verbal and nonverbal messages being sent simultaneously between two people.

message overload. The result when senders receive more messages than they can process.

metacommunication. Communication about communication.

meta-conflict. A conflict about the way a conflict is conducted.

meta-emotion. Emotion felt about experiencing another emotion.

mindful. Having the ability to engage our senses so that we are observant and aware of our surroundings.

mindless. Being unaware of the stimuli around us.

mini-feed. Streaming bulletins that announce the activities of a Facebook user's friends.

mixed message. The incompatibility that occurs when our nonverbal messages are not congruent with our verbal messages.

models of communication. Visual, simplified representations of complex relationships in the communication process.

multitasking. The simultaneous performance of two or more tasks.

muted group theory. Theory that explains what happens to people whose experiences are not well represented in verbal symbols and who have trouble articulating their thoughts and feelings verbally because their language doesn't give them an adequate vocabulary.

N

negative face. Our desire that others refrain from imposing their will on us, respect our individuality and our uniqueness, and avoid interfering with our actions or beliefs.

negative feedback. Feedback that causes a system to reject recalibration and stay the same.

negative halo. Occurs when we group negative qualities (e.g., unintelligent, rude, and temperamental) together.

negative interaction ratio. An interpersonal encounter in which the participants say more negative things to each other than positive things.

networking. In relational development, finding out information about a person from a third party.

neutralizing. A strategy for coping with dialectic tensions in a relationship that allows us to strike a compromise between the two opposing poles of a dialectic.

noise. Anything that interferes with accurate transmission or reception of a message. *See also* physical noise, physiological noise, psychological noise, and semantic noise.

nonjudgmental feedback. Feedback that describes another's behavior and then explains how that behavior made us feel.

nonverbal communication. All behaviors other than spoken words that communicate messages and create shared meaning between people.

novelty and predictability dialectic. Our simultaneous, opposing desires for excitement and stability in our relationships.

O

offering. Putting ourselves in a good position for another to approach us in a social situation.

openness and protection dialectic. Our desire for self-disclosures, which make us transparent to another, and our desire for withholding disclosures, which keeps us safe from another's disapproval.

open self. In the Johari Window, the pane that includes all the information about us that we know and that we have shared with others through disclosures.

opinion. A view, judgment, or appraisal based on our beliefs or values.

organizing. The second stage of the perception process, in which we place what are often a number of confusing pieces of information into an understandable, accessible, and orderly arrangement.

out-group. A group to which a person feels he or she does not belong.

outsourcing. A practice in which a nation sends work and workers to a different country because doing so is cost efficient.

owning. Verbally taking responsibility for our own thoughts and feelings.

P

paralanguage. The study of a person's voice. *Also called* vocalics.

paraphrasing. Restating the essence of a sender's message in our own words.

people-centered listening style. A listening style associated with concern for other people's feelings or emotions.

perception. The process of using our senses to understand and respond to stimuli. The perception process occurs in four stages: attending and selecting, organizing, interpreting, and retrieving.

personal distance. Ranging from eighteen inches to four feet, the space most people use during conversations.

personal issue. An issue related to a relationship that can cause a content conflict.

personal space. The distance we put between ourselves and others.

perspective-taking. Acknowledging the viewpoints of those with whom we interact.

phatic communication. Communication consisting of words and phrases that are used for interpersonal contact only and are not meant to be translated verbatim.

physical characteristics. Aspects of physical appearance, such as body size, skin color, hair color and style, facial hair, and facial features.

physical context. The tangible environment in which communication occurs.

physical environment. The setting in which our behavior takes place.

physical noise. Any stimuli outside of a sender or a receiver that interfere with the transmission or reception of a message. *Also called* external noise.

physiological noise. Biological influences on a sender or a receiver that interfere with the transmission or reception of a message.

placating. Being passive or ignoring our own needs in a conflict.

poke. On a social networking website, an electronic invitation to another person to communicate with you.

polarization. The tendency to use "either-or" language and speak of the world in extremes.

positive face. Our desire to be liked by significant others in our lives and have them confirm our beliefs, respect our abilities, and value what we value.

positive feedback. Feedback that causes a system to recalibrate and change.

positive halo. Occurs when we place positive qualities (e.g., warm, sensitive, and intelligent) together.

positive interaction ratio. An interpersonal encounter in which the participants say more positive things to each other than negative things.

postcyberdisclosure panic (PCDP). A situation in which we disclose personal information in an email message only to experience significant anxiety later because we begin to think about the number of people who could have access to that message.

pouncing. Responding in an aggressive manner without acknowledging the needs of another person in a conflict.

power. In interpersonal relationships, the ability to control the behavior of another.

power distance. How a culture perceives and distributes power.

preventative maintenance. Paying attention to our relationships even when they are not experiencing troubles.

private information. Assessments, both good and bad, that we make about ourselves, including our personal values and our interests, fears, and concerns.

process. When used to describe interpersonal communication, an ongoing, unending, vibrant activity that always changes.

process of abstraction. The ability to move up and down the ladder of abstraction from specific to general and vice versa.

proxemics. The study of how people use, manipulate, and identify their personal space.

proximal context. The rules, emotions, and beliefs of the individuals involved in a conflict.

proximal outcomes. The immediate results after a conflict interaction.

pseudolisten. To pretend to listen by nodding our heads, looking at the speaker, smiling at the appropriate times, or practicing other kinds of attention feigning.

psychological noise. Biases, prejudices, and feelings that interfere with the accurate transmission or reception of a message. *Also called* internal noise.

public and private dialectic. The tension between how much of a friendship is demonstrated in public and what parts are kept private.

public distance. Communication that occurs at a distance of twelve or more feet, allowing listeners to see a person while he or she is speaking.

public information. Personal facts, usually socially approved characteristics, we make part of our public image.

public issue. An issue outside a relationship that can cause a content conflict.

pursuit-withdrawal. In a conflict, a pattern consisting of one party pressing for a discussion about a conflictual topic while the other party withdraws.

R

rating. Evaluating or assessing a message.

recalibrate. Adjust a relationship to accommodate changing needs of the parties.

recalling. Understanding a message, storing it for future encounters, and remembering it later.

receiver. The intended target of a message.

receiving. The verbal and nonverbal acknowledgment of a message.

reciprocity. The tendency to respond in kind to another's self-disclosure.

referent. The thing a verbal symbol represents.

reframe. To change something that has a negative connotation to something with a more positive connotation (e.g., a problem can become a concern, or a challenge can become an opportunity).

reification. The tendency to respond to words or labels for things as though they were the things themselves.

relational conflict. A conflict that focuses on issues concerning the relationship between two people.

relational history. The prior relationship experiences two people share.

relational message. A message that defines a relationship and implicitly states that the sender has the power to define the relationship.

relational culture. The notion that relational partners collaborate and experience shared understandings, roles, and rituals that are unique to their relationship.

relational rules. Negotiable rules that indicate what two relational partners expect and allow when they talk to each other.

relational schema. A mental framework or memory structure that we rely on to understand experience and to guide our future behavior in relationships.

relational transgressions. Negative behaviors in close relationships, such as betrayals, deceptions, and hurtful comments.

relational uniqueness. The ways in which the particular relationship of two relational partners stands apart from other relationships they experience.

relational uppers. People who support and trust us as we improve our self-concept.

relationship level. The information contained in a message that indicates how the sender wants the receiver to interpret the message.

relative power position. A situation in which a partner in a relationship believes he or she has a higher power status than the other partner, and so will engage in risky strategies without fearing the costs.

responding. Providing observable feedback to a sender's message.

retrieving. The fourth and final stage of the perception process, in which we recall information stored in our memories.

rewards. Those parts of being in a relationship that we find pleasurable.

ritual. A repeated patterned communication event in a family's life.

role relationship. A relationship in which the partners are interdependent while accomplishing a specific task, such as a server and a customer at a restaurant.

rule. A prescribed guide that indicates what behavior is obligated, preferred, or prohibited in certain contexts.

S

Sapir-Whorf hypothesis. A theory that points to connections among culture, language, and thought. In its strong form, this theory is known as linguistic determinism, and in its weak form, it is known as linguistic relativity.

screen name. A nickname we use to introduce ourselves online.

second-guess. To question the assumptions underlying a message.

seeking gestures. Gestures that request agreement or clarification from a sender during a conversation.

segmentation. A strategy for dealing with dialectic tensions in a relationship that allows us to isolate separate arenas, such as work and home, for using each pole in the opposition.

selection. A strategy for dealing with dialectic tensions in a relationship that allows us to choose one of the opposite poles of a dialectic and ignore our need for the other.

selective listening. Responding to some parts of a message and rejecting others.

selective perception. Directing our attention to certain stimuli while ignoring other stimuli.

selective retention. Recalling information that agrees with our perceptions and selectively forgetting information that does not.

self-actualization. The process of gaining information about ourselves in an effort to tap our full potential, our spontaneity, and our talents, and to cultivate our strengths and eliminate our shortcomings.

self-awareness. Our understanding of who we are.

self-concept. A relatively stable set of perceptions we hold of ourselves.

self-disclosure. Evaluative and descriptive information about the self, shared intentionally, that another would have trouble finding out without being told.

self-esteem. An evaluation of who we perceive ourselves to be.

self-fulfilling prophecy. A prediction or expectation about our future behavior that is likely to come true because we believe it and thus act in ways that make it come true.

self-monitoring. Actively thinking about and controlling our public behaviors and actions.

semantic noise. Occurs when senders and receivers apply different meanings to the same message. Semantic noise may take the form of jargon, technical language, and other words and phrases that are familiar to the sender but that are not understood by the receiver.

semiotics. The study of signs and symbols in relation to their form and content.

sender. The source of a message.

serial conflict. Conflicts that recur over time in people's everyday lives, without a resolution.

sex. The biological make-up of an individual (male or female).

sexist language. Language that is demeaning to one sex.

short-term attraction. A judgment of relationship potential that propels us into initiating a relationship.

signaling theory. A theory that proposes that people have qualities they wish to present to others.

significant choice. An ethical system, conceptualized by Thomas Nilsen, underscoring the belief that communication is ethical to the extent that it maximizes our ability to exercise free choice. In this system, information should be given to others in a noncoercive way so that people can make free and informed decisions.

small talk. Conversational interactions that are relaxed, pleasant, uncritical, and casual.

social distance. Ranging from four to twelve feet, the spatial zone usually reserved for professional or formal interpersonal encounters.

social-emotional context. The relational and emotional environment in which communication occurs. In this type of context, messages are associated with the nature of a relationship.

social networking. Linking individuals and communities who share common interests, activities, and ideas through such online websites as Facebook or MySpace.

social penetration model. A model of self-disclosure and relational development that illustrates how sharing increasingly more personal information intensifies a relationship's intimacy level.

spam. Unsolicited junk mail on the Internet.

speech community. A group of people who share norms about how to speak, what words to use, and when, where, and why to speak.

stagnating stage. A stage in the coming apart section of Knapp's model of relationship development in which circumscribing is extended so far that a couple no longer talks much except in the most routinized ways.

static evaluation. The tendency to speak and respond to someone today the same way we did in the past, not recognizing that people and relationships change over time.

stereotyping. Categorizing individuals according to a fixed impression, whether positive or negative, of an entire group to which they belong.

story. Information we feel we are taking a risk telling another.

strategic ambiguity. Leaving out cues in a message on purpose to encourage multiple interpretations by others.

subsystems. Lower-level systems of relationship, such as a sibling relationship within a family.

suprasystems. Higher-level systems of relationship, such as a neighborhood consisting of several families.

sustaining. Behaving in a way that keeps an initial conversation going, such as asking questions.

symbolic interactionism theory. The theory that our understanding of ourselves and of the world is shaped by our interactions with those around us.

symbols. Arbitrary labels or representations (such as words) for feelings, concepts, objects, or events.

symmetrical escalation. In a conflict, each party choosing to increase the intensity of the conflict.

symmetrical negotiation. In a conflict, each party mirroring the other's negotiating behaviors.

symmetrical withdrawal. In a conflict, neither partner being willing to confront the other.

synchronous communication. Communication between a sender and a receiver that takes place at the same time, as in face-to-face communication.

T

taboo topics. Issues that are out of bounds for discussion.

talkaholic. A compulsive talker who hogs the conversational stage and monopolizes encounters.

technological determinism. A theory that states that technology is irreversible, inevitable, and inescapable.

terminating stage. The last stage in the coming apart section of Knapp's model of relationship development, in which a relationship is ending.

territoriality. Our sense of ownership of space that remains fixed.

territorial markers. Items or objects that humans use to mark their territories, such as a table in a coffee shop.

time-centered listening style. A listening style associated with listeners who want messages to be presented succinctly.

topical intimacy. The level of intimacy inherent in a topic.

transactional model of communication. A characterization of communication as the reciprocal sending and receiving of messages. In a transactional encounter, the sender and receiver do not simply send meaning from one to the other and then back again; rather, they build shared meaning through simultaneous sending and receiving.

turn gestures. Gestures that indicate that another person can speak or that are used to request to speak in a conversation.

turn-taking. In a conversation, nonverbal regulators that indicate who talks when and to whom.

two-culture theory. A theory that asserts that sex operates in the same way as culture in establishing different rules, norms, and language patterns for men and women.

U

uncertainty avoidance. A cultural mindset that indicates how tolerant (or intolerant) a culture is of uncertainty and change.

unknown self. In the Johari Window, the pane that includes the information that neither we nor others are aware of about ourselves.

utilitarianism. An ethical system, developed by John Stuart Mill, that suggests that what is ethical will bring the greatest good for the greatest number of people. In this system, consequences of moral actions, especially maximizing satisfaction and happiness, are important.

V

valence. An attribute of emotion that refers to whether the emotion reflects a positive or negative feeling.

value conflict. A conflict in which the content is specifically about a question of right and wrong.

verbal symbols. Words, or the vocabulary that make up a language.

vocal characterizers. Nonverbal behaviors such as crying, laughing, groaning, muttering, whispering, and whining.

vocal qualities. Nonverbal behaviors that include pitch, rate, volume, inflection, tempo, and pronunciation, as well as the use of vocal segregates and silence.

vocal distractors. The "ums" and "ers" used in conversation.

W

Web 1.0. The earliest incarnation of the World Wide Web, which was used primarily as a storehouse of online information and tools that could be accessed to achieve an end, such as finding a website, emailing a friend, or purchasing a product.

Web 2.0. The latest incarnation of the World Wide Web, which is increasingly used as a means of interactivity and personal expression; establishing online communities, sharing files, and blogging exemplify Web 2.0.

wholeness. A principle that states that we can't fully understand a system by simply picking it apart and understanding each of its parts in isolation from one another.

withdrawal-pursuit. In a conflict, a pattern in which one party withdraws, which prompts the other party to pursue.

working memory theory. A theory that states that we can pay attention to several stimuli and simultaneously store stimuli for future reference.

worldview. A unique personal frame for viewing life and life's events.

References

Acor, A. A. (2001). Employer's perceptions of persons with body art and an experimental test regarding eyebrow piercing (Doctoral dissertation, Marquette University, 2001). *Dissertation Abstracts International: Second B: The Sciences and Engineering, 61,* 3885.

Afifi, T. D., McManus, T., Hutchinson, S., & Baker, B. (2007). Inappropriate parental divorce disclosures, the factors that prompt them, and their impact on parents' and adolescents' well-being. *Communication Monographs, 74,* 78–102.

Afifi, W. A., & Guerrero, L. K. (2000). Motivations underlying topic avoidance in close relationships. In S. Petronio (Ed.), *Balancing the secrets of private disclosures* (pp. 165–179). Mahwah, NJ: Lawrence Erlbaum.

Alexander, J. E., & Tate, M. A. (1999). *Web wisdom: How to evaluate and create information quality on the web.* Mahwah, NJ: Lawrence Erlbaum.

Alter, A. (2007, August 10). Is this man cheating on his wife? *Wall Street Journal,* W7–W8.

Altman, I., & Taylor, D. (1973). *Social penetration: The development of interpersonal relationships.* New York: Holt, Rinehart & Winston.

American Cancer Society. (2001). *Talking with your doctor. Building a support network.* Retrieved February 10, 2005, from http://www.cancer.org/docroot/ESN/content/ESN_2_2x_Talking_with_your_doctor.asp?sitearea=ESN.

Andersen, J. (1996). *Communication theory: Epistemological foundations.* New York: Guilford.

Andersen, P. A. (1993). Cognitive schemata in personal relationships. In S. Duck (Ed.), *Individuals in relationships* (pp. 1–29). Newbury Park, CA: Sage.

Andersen, P. A. (2003). In different dimensions: Nonverbal communication and culture. In L. A. Samovar & R. E. Porter (Eds.), *Intercultural communication: A reader* (pp. 239–252). Belmont, CA: Wadsworth.

Anderson, R., & Ross, V. (2002). *Questions of communication: A practical introduction to theory.* New York: St. Martin's.

Are you suffering from data smog? (2003, August 21). *AskOxford.com.* Retrieved March 14, 2008, from http://www.askoxford.com/pressroom/archive/odelaunch/?view=uk.

Armour, S. (2007, September 10). Office gossip has never traveled faster, "thanks" to tech. *USA Today,* 1B.

Asante, M. K. (1998). *The Afrocentric idea.* Philadelphia: Temple University Press.

Aune, K. S., & Aune, R. K. (1996). Cultural differences in the self-reported experience and expression of emotions in relationships. *Journal of Cross-Cultural Psychology, 27,* 67–81.

"Axis of evil" remark sparks damaging backlash. (2002, February 19). *USA Today,* 16A.

Axmaker, L. (2002–2004). Is there humor in your relationships? Retrieved February 10, 2005, from http://vanderbiltowc.wellsource.com/dh/Content.asp?ID=690.

Babrow, A. S., Hines, S. C., & Kasch, C. R. (2000). Managing uncertainty in illness explanation: An application of problematic integration theory. In B. Whaley (Ed.), *Explaining illness: Research, theory, and strategies* (pp. 41–68). Mahwah, NJ: Lawrence Erlbaum.

Bachman, G. F., & Guerrero, L. K. (2006). Relational quality and communicative responses following hurtful events in dating relationships: An expectancy violations analysis. *Journal of Social and Personal Relationships, 23,* 943–963.

Ballard, D. I., & Seibold, D. R. (2000). Time orientation and temporal variation across work groups: Implications for group and organizational communication. *Western Journal of Communication, 64,* 218–242.

Baddeley, A. D., & Hitch, G. (1974). Working memory. In G.H. Bower (Ed.), *The psychology of learning and motivation: Advances in research and theory* (Vol. 8, pp. 47–89). New York: Academic Press.

Barker, L., & Watson, K. (2001). *Listen up: At home, at work, in relationships: How to harness the power of effective listening.* New York: St. Martin's.

Barnes, S. B. (2001). *Online connections: Internet interpersonal relationships.* Cresskill, NJ: Hampton.

Barnes, S. B. (2003). *Computer-mediated communication: Human-to-human communication across the Internet.* Boston: Allyn and Bacon.

Barnlund, D. C. (1970). A transactional model of communication. In K. K. Sereno & C. D. Mortensen (Eds.), *Foundations of communication theory* (pp. 83–102). New York: Harper and Row.

Basso, K. H. (1990). *Western Apache language and culture: Essays in linguistic anthropology.* Tucson, AZ: University of Arizona.

Bate, B., & Bowker, J. (1997). *Communication and the sexes* (2nd ed.). Prospect Heights, IL: Waveland.

Bates, B., & Cleese, J. (2001). The human face. London: BBC.

Bateson, G. (1972). *Steps to an ecology of mind.* New York: Ballantine Books.

Bavelas, J. B. (1994). Gestures as part of speech: Methodological implications. *Research on Language and Social Interaction, 27,* 201–222.

Baxter, L. A. (1987). Self-disclosure and relationship disengagement. In V. J. Derlega & J. H. Berg (Eds.), *Self-disclosure: Theory, research, and therapy* (pp. 155–174). New York: Plenum Press.

Baxter, L. A. (1988). A dialectical perspective on communication strategies in relationship development. In S. Duck (Ed.), *A handbook of personal relationships* (pp. 257–273). New York: Wiley.

Baxter, L. A., & Braithwaite, D. O. (2002). Performing marriage: Marriage renewal rituals as cultural performance. *Southern Communication Journal, 67,* 94–109.

Baxter, L. A., & Montgomery, B. M. (1996). *Relating: Dialogues and dialectics.* New York: Guilford.

Baxter, L. A., & Wilmot, W. (1985). Taboo topics in close relationships. *Journal of Social and Personal Relationships, 2,* 253–269.

Bechar-Israeli, H. (1996). From <Bonehead> to <CloNehEAd>: Nicknames, play and identity on the Internet relay chat. Retrieved October 21, 2007, from http://www.ascusc.org/jcmc/vol1/issue2/bechar.html.

Belkin, L. (2007, July 12). Let's talk. Let me outline the ways. *New York Times,* E2.

Bell, R. A., & Daly, J. A. (1984). The affinity-seeking function of communication. *Communication Monographs, 51,* 91–115.

Bem, S. (1993). *The lenses of gender: Transforming the debate on sexual inequality.* New Haven, CT: Yale University.

Benjamin, B., & Werner, R. (2004). Touch in the Western world. *Massage Therapy Journal, 43,* 28–32.

Bentley, S. C. (2000). Listening in the 21st century. *International Journal of Listening, 14,* 129–142.

Berg, J. H., & Archer, R. L. (1980). Disclosure or concern: A second look at liking for the norm-breaker. *Journal of Personality, 48,* 245–257.

Berg, J. H., & Clark, M. S. (1986). Differences in social exchange between intimate and other relationships: Gradually evolving or quickly apparent? In V. J. Derlega & B. A. Winstead (Eds.), *Friendship and social interaction* (pp. 101–128). New York: Springer-Verlag.

Bergmann, J. R. (1993). *Discreet indiscretions: The social organization of gossip.* New York: Aldine de Gruyter.

Berkman, L. F., Leo-Summers, C., & Horowitz, R. I. (1992). Emotional support and survival after myocardial infarction: A prospective population-based study of the elderly. *Annals of Internal Medicine, 117,* 1003–1009.

Bernstein, F. A. (2004, March 7). On campus, rethinking biology 101. *New York Times,* 9-1, 9-6.

Bevan, J. L., Tidgewell, K. D., Bagley, K. C., Cusanelli, L., Hartstern, M., Holbeck, D., & Hale, J. L. (2007). Serial argumentation goals and their relationships to perceived resolvability and choice of conflict tactics. *Communication Quarterly, 55,* 61–77.

Bharat, K., & Broder, A. (1998). *Measuring the web.* http://research.compaq.com/SRC/whatsnew/sem.html.

Blumer, H. (1969). *Symbolic interactionism: Perspective and method.* Englewood Cliffs, NJ: Prentice Hall.

Bochner, A. P. (1982). On the efficacy of openness in close relationships. In M. Burgoon (Ed.), *Communication yearbook 5* (pp. 109–124). New Brunswick, NJ: Transaction Books.

Bodine, A. (1990). Androcentrism in prescriptive grammar: Singular "they," sex-indefinite "he," and "he or she." In D. Cameron (Ed.), *The feminist critique of language* (pp. 166–186). London: Routledge.

"Body art and tattoos in the workplace." Retrieved October 27, 2007, from http://www.foxnews.com/story/0,2933,223178,00.html.

Booth, R., & Yung, M. (1996). *Romancing the net.* Rocklin, CA: Prima Publishing.

Booth-Butterfield, M., & Booth-Butterfield, S. (1998). *Emotionality and affective orientation.* In J. C. McCroskey, J. A. Daly, M. M. Martin, & M. J. Beatty (Eds.), *Communication and personality: Trait perspectives* (pp. 171–190). Cresskill, NJ: Hampton.

Bostrom, R. N. (1990). *Listening behavior: Measurement and application.* New York: Guilford.

Bostrom, R. N., & Waldhart, E. S. (1988). Memory models in the measurement of listening. *Communication Education, 37,* 1–12.

Bowdle, B. F., & Gentner, D. (2005). The career of metaphor. *Psychological Review, 112,* 193–216.

boyd, d., & Ellison, N. (2007). Social network sites: Definition, history, and scholarship. *Journal of Computer-Mediated Communication, 13* (http://jcmc.indiana.edu/vol13/issue1).

Bradford, L. (1993). *A cross-cultural study of strategic embarrassment in adolescent socialization.* (Doctoral dissertation, Arizona State University, 1993). *Dissertation Abstracts International. A: The humanities and social sciences, 29,* 2003.

Bradford, L., & Petronio, S. (1998). Strategic embarrassment: The culprit of emotion. In P. A. Andersen & L. K. Guerrero (Eds.), *The handbook of communication and emotion* (pp. 99–121). San Diego, CA: Academic Press.

Braithwaite, D., & Kellas, J. K. (2006). Shopping for and with friends: Everyday communication at the shopping mall. In J. T. Wood & S. Duck (Eds.), *Composing relationships: Communication in everyday life* (pp. 86–95). Belmont, CA: Wadsworth.

British girl baffles teacher with SMS essay. (2003, March 2). *Yahoo News.* http://story.news.yahoo.com/news?tmpl=story2&u=/nm/20030303/wr_mn/odd_britain_texting_dc.

Brody, J. E. (2002, May 28). Why angry people can't control the short fuse. *New York Times,* D7.

Brownell, J. (2002). *Listening: Attitudes, principles, and skills* (2nd ed.). Boston: Allyn and Bacon.

Bryner, J. (2007, April 11). Hip e-mail addresses bad for resumes. Retrieved August 13, 2007, from http://www.msnbc.msn.com/id/18057158.

Buber, M. (1970). *I and thou* (W. Kaufmann, Trans.). New York: Scribner.

Buchanan, M. C., O'Hair, H. D., & Becker, J. A. H. (2006). Strategic communication during marital relationship dissolution: Disengagement resistance strategies. *Communication Research Reports, 23,* 139–147.

Bugeja, M. (2004, July 30). Unshaken hands on the digital street. *Chronicle of Higher Education,* B5.

Bulik, B. (2007, October 4). *Apple, Target, Facebook* tops for college students. *Advertising Age,* 31.

Burgoon, J. K., Buller, D. B., & Woodall, W. G. (1996). *Nonverbal communication: The unspoken dialogue.* New York: McGraw-Hill.

Burgoon, J. K., & Hale, J. L. (1987). Validation and measurement of the fundamental themes of relational communication. *Communication Monographs, 54,* 19–41.

Burgoon, J. K., & Hoobler, G. D. (2002). Nonverbal signals. In M. L. Knapp & J. A. Daly (Eds.), *Handbook of interpersonal communication* (pp. 240–299). Thousand Oaks, CA: Sage.

Burgoon, J. K., Stern, L. A., & Dillman, L. (1995). *Interpersonal adaptation: Dyadic interaction patterns.* New York: Cambridge University Press.

Burleson, B. R. (2003). Emotional support skills. In J. O. Greene & B. R. Burleson (Eds.), *Handbook of communication and social interaction skills* (pp. 551–594). Mahwah, NJ: Lawrence Erlbaum.

Burleson, B. R., Holmstrom, A. J., & Gilstrap, C. M. (2005). "Guys can't say *that* to guys": Four experiments assessing the normative motivation account for deficiencies in the emotional support provided by men. *Communication Monographs, 72,* 468–501.

Burleson, B. R., & Planalp, S. (2000). Producing emotion(al) messages. *Communication Theory, 10,* 221–250.

Burrell, N. A., Buzzanell, P. M., & McMillan, J. J. (1992). Feminine tensions in conflict situations as revealed by metaphoric analyses. *Management Communication Quarterly, 6,* 115–149.

Buston, P. M., & Emlen, S. T. (2003). Cognitive processes underlying human mate choice: The relationship between self-perception and mate preference in Western society. *Proceedings of the National Academy of Sciences, 100,* 8805–8810.

Buysse, A., De Clercq, A., Verhofstadt, L., Heene, E., Roeyers, H., & Van Oost, P. (2000). Dealing with relational conflict: A picture in milliseconds. *Journal of Social and Personal Relationships, 17,* 574–597.

Buzzanell, P. M., & Burrell, N. A. (1997). Family and workplace conflict: Examining metaphorical conflict schemas and expressions across context and sex. *Human Communication Research, 24,* 109–146.

Buzzanell, P. M., Sterk, H., & Turner, L. H. (2004). Introduction: Challenging common sense. In P. M. Buzzanell, H. Sterk, & L. H. Turner (Eds.), *Gender in applied communication contexts* (pp. xiii–xxii). Thousand Oaks, CA: Sage.

Buzzanell, P. M., & Turner, L. H. (2003). Emotion work revealed by job loss discourse: Backgrounding-foregrounding of feelings, construction of normalcy, and (re)instituting of traditional masculinities. *Journal of Applied Communication Research, 31,* 27–57.

Cahn, D., & Abigail, R. (2007). *Conflict management through communication.* Boston: Allyn & Bacon.

Calloway-Thomas, C., Cooper, P. J., & Blake, C. (1999). *Intercultural communication: Roots and routes.* Boston: Allyn and Bacon.

Canary, D. J., Cupach, W. R., & Serpe, R. T. (2001). A competence-based approach to examining interpersonal conflict: Test of a longitudinal model. *Communication Research, 28,* 79–104.

Canary, D. J., & Dindia, K. (Eds.). (1998). *Sex differences and similarities in communication.* Mahwah, NJ: Lawrence Erlbaum.

Canary, D. J., & Hause, K. S. (1993). Is there any reason to research sex differences in communication? *Communication Quarterly, 41,* 129–144.

Canary, D. J., & Stafford, L. (1992). Relational maintenance strategies and equity in marriage. *Communication Monographs, 59,* 243–267.

Capaldi, N. (2004). *John Stuart Mill: A biography.* Cambridge, England: Cambridge University Press.

Carbaugh, D. (1999). "Just listen": "Listen" and landscape among the Blackfeet. *Western Journal of Communication, 63,* 250–270.

Career Solutions Training Group. (2000). *Quick skills: Listening.* Mason, OH: Thomson South-Western.

Carrasquillo, H. (1997). Puerto Rican families in America. In M. K. DeGenova (Ed.), *Families in cultural context: Strengths and challenges in diversity* (pp. 155–172). Mountain View, CA: Mayfield.

Cash, T. F., & Derlega, V. J. (1978). The matching hypothesis: Physical attractiveness among same-sexed friends. *Personality and Social Psychology Bulletin, 4,* 240–243.

Caughlin, J. P., & Vangelisti, A. L. (2000). An individual difference explanation of why married couples engage in the demand/withdraw pattern of conflict. *Journal of Social and Personal Relationships, 17,* 523–551.

Chang, H. N. (1999). Multiculturalism benefits society. In M. E. Williams (Ed.), *Culture wars: Opposing viewpoints* (pp. 140–147). San Diego, CA: Greenhaven.

Chen, G.-M. (1995). Differences in self-disclosure patterns among Americans versus Chinese: A comparative study. *Journal of Cross-Cultural Psychology, 26,* 84–91.

Chen, G.-M., & Starosta, W. J. (1998). *Foundations of intercultural communication.* Boston: Allyn and Bacon.

Chen, G.-M., & Starosta, W.J. (2006). Intercultural awareness. In L. A. Samovar, R. E. Porter, & E. McDaniel (Eds.), *Intercultural communication: A reader* (pp. 357–365). Belmont, CA: Wadsworth.

Chen, L. (2004). How we know what we know about Americans: Chinese sojourners account for their experiences. In A. Gonzalez, M. Houston, & V. Chen (Eds.), *Our voices: Essays in culture, ethnicity, and communication* (pp. 266–273). Los Angeles: Roxbury.

Chopra, R. (2001). Retrieving the father: Gender studies, "father love" and the discourse of mothering. *Women's Studies International Forum, 24,* 445–455.

ClickZ Stats staff. (2004, September 10). *Population explosion!* Retrieved October 23, 2007 from http://www.clickz.com/stats/sectors/geographics/article.php/151151.

Cline, R. J., & McKenzie, N. J. (1996). HIV/AIDS, women, and threads of discrimination: A tapestry of disenfranchisement. In E. B. Ray (Ed.), *Communication and disenfranchisement: Social health issues and implications* (pp. 365–386). Mahwah, NJ: Lawrence Erlbaum.

Coates, J., & Cameron, D. (Eds.). (1989). *Women and their speech communities.* New York: Longman.

Cole, S. W., Kemeny, M. E., Taylor, S. E., Visscher, B. R., & Fahey, J. L. (1996). Accelerated course of human immunodeficiency virus infection in gay men who conceal their homosexual identity. *Psychosomatic Medicine, 58,* 219–231.

Cooks, L. (2000). Family secrets and the lie of identity. In S. Petronio (Ed.), *Balancing the secrets of private disclosures* (pp. 197–211). Mahwah, NJ: Lawrence Erlbaum.

Coplin, W. (2004). *10 things employers want you to learn in college.* Berkeley, CA: Ten Speed Press.

Corballis, M. C. (2002). *From hand to mouth: The origins of language.* Princeton, NJ: Princeton University.

Coupland, N., & Nussbaum, J. F. (Eds.). (1993). *Discourse and lifespan identity.* Newbury Park, CA: Sage.

Coyne, J. C., Rohrbaugh, M. J., Shoham, V., Cranford, J. A., Nicklas, J. M., & Sonnega, J. (2001). Prognostic importance of marital quality for survival of congestive heart failure. *American Journal of Cardiology, 88,* 526–529.

Craig, R. T. (2003). Discursive origins of a communication discipline. Paper presented at the annual meeting of the National Communication Association, Miami, FL.

Cramer, D. (1998). *Close relationships: The study of love and friendship.* London: Arnold.

Crane, D. R., Allgood, S. M., Larson, J. H., & Griffin, W. (1990). Assessing marital quality with distressed and nondistressed couples: A comparison and equivalency table for three frequently used measures. *Journal of Marriage and the Family, 52,* 87–93.

Cupach, W. R., & Canary, D. G. (2000). *Competence in interpersonal conflict.* Prospect Heights, IL: Waveland Press.

Cupach, W. R., & Metts, S. M. (1994). *Facework.* Thousand Oaks, CA: Sage.

Cupach, W. R., & Spitzberg, B. H. (2004). *The dark side of relationship pursuit: From attraction to obsession and stalking.* Mahwah, NJ: Lawrence Erlbaum.

Cupach, W. R., & Spitzberg, B. H. (Eds.). (1994). *The dark side of interpersonal communication.* Mahwah, NJ: Lawrence Erlbaum.

Daly, J. A., McCroskey, J. C., Ayres, J., Hopf, T., & Ayers, D. M. (Eds.) (2007), *Avoiding communication: Shyness, reticence, and communication apprehension* (3rd ed.). Creskill, NJ: Hampton Press.

Darling, A., & Dannels, D. P. (2003). Practicing engineers talk about the importance of talk: A report on the role of oral communication in the workplace. *Communication Education, 52,* 1–16.

Darrand, T. C., & Shupe, A. (1983). *Metaphors of social control.* New York: Edwin Mellen Press.

Davis, M. S. (1973). *Intimate relations.* New York: Free Press.

de Sousa, R. (1987). *The rationality of emotion.* Cambridge, MA: MIT Press.

Deetz, S. A. (1992). *Democracy in an age of corporate colonization: Developments in communication and the politics of everyday life.* Albany: SUNY Press.

DeFrancisco, V. P., & Palczewski, C. H. (2007). *Communicating gender diversity.* Thousand Oaks, CA: Sage.

Derlega, V. J., Metts, S., Petronio, S., & Margulis, S. T. (1993). *Self-disclosure.* Newbury Park, CA: Sage.

Derlega, V. J., Winstead, B. A., Wong, P. T. P., & Hunter, S. (1985). Gender effects in an initial encounter: A case where men exceed women in disclosure. *Journal of Social and Personal Relationships, 2,* 25–44.

Dickson, F. C., & Walker, K. L. (2001). The expression of emotion in later-life married men. *Qualitative Research Reports in Communication, 2,* 66–71.

Diggs, R. C., & Clark, K. D. (2002). It's a struggle but worth it: Identifying and managing identities in an interracial friendship. *Communication Quarterly, 50,* 368–390.

Dillard, J. P. (1990). Primary and secondary goals in interpersonal influence. In M. J. Cody & M. L. McLaughlin (Eds.), *The psychology of tactical communication* (pp. 70–90). Clevedon, England: Multilingual Matters.

Dindia, K. (1994). A multiphasic view of relationship maintenance strategies. In D. J. Canary & L. Stafford (Eds.), *Communication and relational maintenance* (pp. 91–110). San Diego, CA: Academic Press.

Dindia, K. (1998). "Going into and coming out of the closet": The dialectics of stigma disclosure. In B. M. Montgomery & L. A. Baxter (Eds.), *Dialectical approaches to studying personal relationships* (pp. 83–108). Mahwah, NJ: Lawrence Erlbaum.

Dindia, K. (2000). Sex differences in self-disclosure, reciprocity of self-disclosure, and self-disclosure and liking: Three meta-analyses reviewed. In S. Petronio (Ed.), *Balancing the secrets of private disclosures* (pp. 21–35). Mahwah, NJ: Lawrence Erlbaum.

Dindia, K. (2003). Definitions and perspectives on relational maintenance communication. In D. J. Canary & M. Dainton (Eds.), *Maintaining relationships through communication: Relational, contextual, and cultural variations* (pp. 1–28). Mahwah, NJ: Lawrence Erlbaum.

Dindia, K., & Allen, M. (1992). Sex-differences in self-disclosure: A meta-analysis. *Psychological Bulletin, 112,* 106–124.

Dindia, K., Fitzpatrick, M. A., & Kenny, D. A. (1997). Self-disclosure in spouse and stranger dyads: A social relations analysis. *Human Communication Research, 23,* 388–412.

Do you know? (2002, February). *Allure,* 28.

Docan-Morgan, T., & Docan, C. A. (2007). Internet infidelity: Double standards and the differing views of women and men. *Communication Quarterly, 55,* 317–342.

Domenici, K., & Littlejohn, S. W. (2006). *Facework: Bridging theory and practice.* Thousand Oaks, CA: Sage.

Donaghue, E. (2007, July 25). Communication now part of the cure. *USA Today,* D1.

Douglas, W. (1987). Affinity-testing in initial interaction. *Journal of Social and Personal Relationships, 4,* 3–16.

Dow, B., & Wood, J. T. (Eds.) (2006). *The SAGE handbook of gender and communication.* Thousand Oaks, CA: Sage.

DuBrin, A.J. (2007). *Human relations: Interpersonal job-oriented skills.* New York: Prentice-Hall.

Duck, S., & Wood, J. T. (1995). For better, for worse, for richer, for poorer: The rough and smooth of relationships. In S. Duck & J. T. Wood (Eds.), *Confronting relationship challenges* (pp. 1–21). Thousand Oaks, CA: Sage.

Duck, S. (2007). *Human relationships.* Thousand Oaks, CA: Sage.

Dunbar, N. E., & Burgoon, J. K. (2005). Perceptions of power and interactional dominance in interpersonal relationships. *Journal of Social and Personal Relationships, 22,* 207–233.

Dunbar, R. (1998). *Grooming, gossip, and the evolution of language.* Cambridge, MA: Harvard University Press.

Egbert, N., & Polk, D. (2006). Speaking the language of relational maintenance: A validity test of Chapman's (1992) five love languages. *Communication Research Reports, 23,* 19–26.

Eisenberg, E. M. (1984). Ambiguity as strategy in organizational communication. *Communication Monographs, 51,* 227–242.

Emmers-Sommer, T. M. (2003). When partners falter: Repair after a transgression. In D. J. Canary & M. Dainton (Eds.), *Maintaining relationships through communication: Relational, contextual, and cultural variations* (pp. 185–205). Mahwah, NJ: Lawrence Erlbaum.

Englehardt, E. E. (2001). *Ethical issues in interpersonal communication.* Fort Worth, TX: Harcourt.

Erard, M. (2004, January 3). Just like, er, words, not, um, throwaways. *New York Times,* B7.

Ethnocentrism scale (n.d.). http://www.jamescmccroskey.com/measures/ ethnocentrism_scale.htm.

Eugenides, J. (2002). *Middlesex.* New York: Farrar, Straus, and Giroux.

Fehr, B., & Russell, J. A. (1984). Concept of emotion viewed from a prototype perspective. *Journal of Experimental Psychology, 113,* 464–486.

Fels, A. (2002, May 21). Mending of hearts and minds. *New York Times,* D5.

Field, T. (1999). American adolescents touch each other less and are more aggressive toward their peers as compared with French adolescents. *Adolescence, 34,* 753–759.

Filley, A. C. (1975). *Interpersonal conflict resolution.* Glenview, IL: Scott, Foresman.

Finkenauer, C., & Hazam, H. (2000). Disclosure and secrecy in marriage: Do both contribute to marital satisfaction? *Journal of Social and Personal Relationships, 17,* 245–263.

Fleishman, J., Sherbourne, C., & Crystal, S. (2000). Coping, conflictual social interactions, social support, and mood among HIV-infected persons. *American Journal of Community Psychology, 28,* 421–453.

Floyd, K., Mikkelson, A. C., Judd, J. (2006). Defining the family through relationships. In L.H. Turner & R. West (Eds.), *The family communication sourcebook* (pp. 21–39). Thousand Oaks, CA: Sage.

Floyd, K., & Morman, M. T. (2000). Reacting to the verbal expression of affection in same-sex interaction. *Southern Journal of Communication, 65,* 287–299.

Floyd, K., & Parks, M. (1995). Manifesting closeness in the interactions of peers: A look at siblings and friends. *Communication Reports, 8,* 69–76.

Flynn, S. (2007). Is anything private anymore? *Parade Magazine,* 406.

Folger, J. P., Poole, M. S., & Stutman, R. K. (2001). *Working through conflict: Strategies for relationships, groups, and organizations.* New York: Longman.

Forbes, G. B. (2001). College students with tattoos and piercings: Motives, family experiences, personality factors, and perception by others. *Psychological Reports, 89,* 774–786.

Forgas, J. P. (2002). How to make the right impression. In J. A. DeVito (Ed.), *The interpersonal communication reader* (pp. 28–33). Boston: Allyn and Bacon.

Foss, S. K. (1988). *Rhetorical criticism: Exploration and practice.* Prospect Heights, IL: Waveland.

French, J. R. P., Jr., & Raven, B. (1968). The bases of social power. In D. Cartwright & A. Zander (Eds.), *Group dynamics: Research and theory* (pp. 259–269). New York: Harper and Row.

Frymier, A. B., & Nadler, M. K. (2007). *Persuasion: Integrating theory, research, and practice.* Dubuque, IA: Kendall-Hunt.

Fulghum, R. (1989). *All I really need to know I learned in kindergarten.* New York: Ivy.

Galvin, K. M. (2004). International and transracial adoption: A communication research agenda. *Journal of Family Communication, 3,* 237–253.

Galvin, K. M. (2006). Diversity's impact on defining the family: Discourse-dependence and identity. In L.H. Turner & R. West (Eds.), *The family communication sourcebook* (pp. 3–19). Thousand Oaks, CA: Sage.

Galvin, K. M., & Wilkinson, C. A. (2006). The communication process: impersonal and interpersonal. In K. M. Galvin & P. J. Cooper (Eds.), *Making connections: Readings in relational communication* (pp. 4–10). Los Angeles, CA: Roxbury.

Gao, G., & Ting-Toomey, S. (1998). *Communicating effectively with the Chinese.* Thousand Oaks, CA: Sage.

Gastil, J. (1990). Generic pronouns and sexist language: The oxymoronic character of masculine generics. *Sex Roles, 23,* 629–641.

Georgia considers banning "evolution." (2004, January 30). *CNN.com.* Retrieved March 14, 2007, from http://www.cnn.com/2004/EDUCATION/01/30/striking .evolution.ap/.

Gerth, H., & Mills, C. W. (1964). *Character and social structure: The psychology of social institutions.* New York: Harcourt, Brace & World.

Getz, M. A. (2002). *Improvement in physical health and social relationships among very elderly women in a rural county after participation in arthritis courses.* Retrieved March 14, 2007, from http://ruralwomenshealth.psu.edu/sposter_mgetz.html.

Gibb, J. (1961). Defensive communication. *Journal of Communication, 11,* 141–148.

Gibb, J. (1964). Climate for trust formation. In L. Bradford, J. Gibb, & K. Benne (Eds.), *T-group theory and laboratory method* (pp. 279–309). New York: Wiley.

Gibb, J. (1970). Sensitivity training as a medium for personal growth and improved interpersonal relationships. *Interpersonal Development, 1,* 6–31.

Giles, H., & Le Poire, B. A. (2006). The ubiquity and social meaningfulness of nonverbal communication: An introduction. In V. Manusov & M. Patterson (Eds.), *Handbook of nonverbal behavior* (pp. xv–xxvii). Thousand Oaks, CA: Sage.

Gilligan, C. (1982). *In a different voice: Psychological theory and women's development.* Cambridge, MA: Harvard University Press.

Goffman, E. (1959). *The presentation of self in everyday life.* New York: Anchor.

Goldschmidt, W. (1990). *The human career: The self in the symbolic world.* Cambridge, England: Blackwell Publishers.

Goldsmith, D. J., & Fulfs, P. A. (1999). "You just don't have the evidence": An analysis of claims and evidence. In M. E. Roloff (Ed.), *Communication yearbook 22* (pp. 1–49). Thousand Oaks, CA: Sage.

Goleman, D. (1995). *Emotional intelligence: Why it can matter more than IQ.* New York: Bantam Books.

Goleman, D. (n.d.). *Emotional intelligence test.* Retrieved March 15, 2007, from http://www.utne.com/interact/test_iq.html.

Goleman, D. (2006). *Social intelligence: The new science of human relationships.* New York: Bantam.

Goode, E. (2002). Therapists redraw line of self-disclosure. *New York Times,* D5, D7.

Gosselin, P., Kirouac, G., & Dore, F. Y. (1995). Components and recognition of facial expression in the communication of emotion by actors. *Journal of Personality and Social Psychology, 68,* 83–96.

Gottman, J. M. (2004, March 25). *Fresh Air* interview [radio show].

Gottman, J. M. (1994). *Why marriages succeed or fail.* New York: Simon and Schuster.

Gottman, J. M. (1999). *The marriage clinic: A scientifically based marital therapy.* New York: W. W. Norton and Company.

Gottman, J. M., & DeClaire, J. (2001). *The relationship cure.* New York: Three Rivers Press.

Gottman, J. M., Katz, L. F., & Hooven, C. (1997). *Metaemotion: How families communicate emotionally.* Mahwah, NJ: Lawrence Erlbaum.

Graham, E. E. (2003). Dialectic contradictions in postmarital relationships. *Journal of Family Communication, 4,* 193–214.

Graham, E. E. (1997). Turning points and commitments in post-divorce relations. *Communication Monographs, 64,* 350–368.

Graham, P. (2005, November). *Web 2.0.* Retrieved February 5, 2008, from http://www.paulgraham.com/web20.html.

Grau, J., & Grau, C. (2003). New communication demands of the 21st century. *Listening Professional, 2,* 3–19.

Gray, J. (1992). *Men are from Mars, women are from Venus: A practical guide to improving communication and getting what you want in your relationships.* New York: HarperCollins.

Grice, H. P. (1975). Logic and conversation. In P. Cole & J. L. Morgan (Eds.), *Syntax and semantics: Vol. 3. Speech acts* (pp. 41–58). New York: Seminar.

Griffin, C. L. (2006). *An invitation to public speaking.* Belmont, CA: Wadsworth.

Gudykunst, W. B., & Kim, Y. Y. (1997). *Communicating with strangers: An approach to intercultural communication.* New York: McGraw-Hill.

Gudykunst, W. B., Ting-Toomey, S., Sudweeks, S., & Stewart, L. P. (1995). *Building bridges: Interpersonal skills for a changing world.* Boston: Houghton Mifflin.

Gueguen, N., & De Gail, M. (2003). The effect of smiling on helping behavior: Smiling and good Samaritan behavior. *Communication Reports, 16,* 133–140.

Guerrero, L. K., & Afifi, W. A. (1995). What parents don't know: Topic avoidance in parent-child relationships. In T. J. Socha & G. H. Stamp (Eds.), *Parents, children, and communication: Frontiers of theory and research* (pp. 219–245). Mahwah, NJ: Lawrence Erlbaum.

Guerrero, L. K., Andersen, P. A., Afifi, W. A. (2007). *Close encounters: Communication in relationships.* Los Angeles, CA: Sage.

Guerrero, L. K., Andersen, P. A., & Trost, M. R. (1998). Communication and emotion: Basic concepts and approaches. In P. A. Andersen & L. K. Guerrero (Eds.), *Handbook of communication and emotion: Research, theory, applications, and contexts* (pp. 3–27). San Diego, CA: Academic Press.

Guerrero, L. K., & Backhman, G. F. (2006). Associations among relational maintenance behaviors, attachment-style categories, and attachment dimensions. *Communication Studies, 57,* 341–361.

Guy, S. (2004, Feb 18). "Digital divide" continues to split urban, rural dwellers. Retrieved February 10, 2005, from http://www.suntimes.com.

Hall, B. J. (2005). *Among cultures: The challenge of communication.* Fort Worth, TX: Harcourt.

Hall, E. T. (1959). *The silent language.* New York: Doubleday.

Hall, E. T., & Hall, M. R. (1990). *Understanding cultural differences.* Yarmouth, ME: Intercultural Press.

Hall, J. A., Carter, J. D., & Horgan, T. G. (2000). Gender differences in nonverbal communication of emotion. In A. H. Fischer (Ed.), *Gender and emotion: Social psychological perspectives* (pp. 97–117). Cambridge, England: Cambridge University Press.

Hamacheck, D. E. (1992). *Encounters with the self.* Fort Worth, TX: Harcourt.

Hamid, P. N. (2000). Self-disclosure and occupational stress in Chinese professionals. *Psychological Reports, 87,* 1075–1082.

Hamilton, A. (2007, December 3). Is Facebook overrated? *Time,* 46–51.

Hamilton, W. L. (2004, July 5). For Bantu refugees, hard-won American dreams. *New York Times,* A1, A14.

Hammond, A. (2001, March /April). *Digitally empowered development.* Retrieved March 13, 2008, from http://www.digitaldividend.org/pdf/0201ar04.pdf.

Hampp, A. (2007, July 9). Your guide to the *Facebook* lingo. *Advertising Age,* 22.

Harris, T. M. (2004). "I know it was the blood": Defining the biracial self in a Euro-American society. In A. Gonzalez, M. Houston, & V. Chen (Eds.), *Our voices: Essays in culture, ethnicity, and communication* (pp. 203–209). Los Angeles: Roxbury.

Harvey, J. H., & Weber, A. L. (2002). *Odyssey of the heart: Close relationships in the 21st century.* Mahwah, NJ: Lawrence Erlbaum.

Hashem, M. (2004). The power of Wastah in Lebanese speech. In A. Gonzalez, M. Houston, & V. Chen (Eds.), *Our voices: Essays in culture, ethnicity, and communication* (4th ed.) (pp. 169–173). Los Angeles, CA: Roxbury.

Hastings, S. O. (2000). "Egocasting" in the avoidance of disclosure: An intercultural perspective. In S. Petronio (Ed.), *Balancing the secrets of private disclosures* (pp. 235–248). Mahwah, NJ: Lawrence Erlbaum.

Hatfield, E. (1984). The dangers of intimacy. In V. J. Derlega (Ed.), *Communication, intimacy, and close relationships* (pp. 207–220). New York: Academic Press.

Hayakawa, S. I. (1990). *Language in thought and action.* San Diego, CA: Harcourt Brace.

Hayavadana, R. C. (1996). *Indian caste system.* Delhi, India: AES.

Hecht, M. L., Collier, M. J., & Ribeau, S. A. (1993). *African American communication: Ethnic identity and cultural interpretation.* Newbury Park, CA: Sage.

Heider, F. (1958). *The psychology of interpersonal relations.* New York: Wiley.

Heisterkamp, B., & Alberts, J. K. (2000). Control and desire: An analysis of teasing and joking interactions among gay couples. *Communication Studies, 51,* 388-404.

Hickson, M., Stacks, D. W., & Moore, N.-J. (2004). *Nonverbal communication: Studies and applications.* Los Angeles, Roxbury.

Hinde, R. A. (1995). A suggested structure for a science of relationships. *Personal Relationships, 2,* 1–15.

Hinsz, V. B. (1989). Facial resemblance in engaged and married couples. *Journal of Social and Personal Relationships, 6,* 223–229.

Hochschild, A. R. (1983). *The managed heart: Commercialization of human feeling.* Berkeley: University of California Press.

Hof, R. (2006, June 5). A VC's view of web 2.0. *Business Week.* Retrieved February 5, 2008, from http://www.businessweek.com/technology/content/jun2006/tc20060605_641388.htm.

Hoffman, C. (2003, May 14). At Brandeis, unlikely partners in peace. *New York Times,* A22.

Hofstede, G. (1980). *Culture's consequences.* Beverly Hills, CA: Sage.

Hofstede, G. (1984). The cultural relativity of the quality of life concept. *Academy of Management Review, 9,* 389–398.

Hofstede, G. (1991). *Cultures and organizations: Software of the mind.* New York: McGraw-Hill.

Hofstede, G. (2001). *Culture's consequence: Comparing values, behaviors, institutions, and organizations across nations.* Thousand Oaks, CA: Sage.

Hoijer, H. (1994). The Sapir-Whorf hypothesis. In L. A. Samovar & R. E. Porter (Eds.), *Intercultural communication: A reader.* Belmont, CA: Wadsworth.

Holmberg, D., & MacKenzie, S. (2002). So far, so good: Scripts for romantic relationship development as predictors of relational well-being. *Journal of Social and Personal Relationships, 19,* 777–796.

Honeycutt, J. M. (2003). *Imagined interactions.* Cresskill, NJ: Hampton Press.

Honeycutt, J. M., Cantrill, J. G., Kelly, P., & Lambkin, D. (1998). How do I love thee? Let me consider my options: Cognition, verbal strategies, and the escalation of intimacy. *Human Communication Research, 25,* 39–63.

Horton, D., & Wohl, R. (1956). Mass communication and parasocial interaction: Observation on intimacy at a distance. *Psychiatry, 19,* 215–229.

Houston, M. (2004). When Black women talk with White women: Why dialogues are difficult. In A. Gonzalez, M. Houston, & V. Chen (Eds.), *Our voices: Essays in culture, ethnicity, and communication* (4th ed.) (pp. 133–139). Los Angeles: Roxbury.

Hughes, P. C., & Heuman, A. N. (2006). The communication of solidarity in friendships among African American women. *Qualitative Research Reports in Communication, 7,* 33–41.

Hunter, M. (2000, December). Getting in touch with your emotions. *Phoenix Newspaper*. Retrieved March 14, 2008, from http://www.phoenixrecovery.org/backissues/00december-article.html.

Huston, T. L., McHale, S. M., & Crouter, A. C. (1986). When the honeymoon's over: Changes in the marriage relationship over the first year. In R. Gilmour & S. Duck (Eds.), *The emerging science of personal relationships* (pp. 109–132). Hillsdale, NJ: Lawrence Erlbaum.

Iezzoni, L. I., & O'Day, B. (2006). *More than ramps: A guide to improving health care quality and access for people with disabilities*. New York: Oxford.

Ijams, K., & Miller, L. D. (2000). Perceptions of dream-disclosure: An exploratory study. *Communication Studies, 51*, 135–148.

Imahori, T. T. (2006). On becoming "American." In M. W. Lusting & J. Koester (Eds.), *AmongUS: Essays on identity, belonging, and intercultural competence* (pp. 258–269). Boston, MA: Pearson Education.

Infante, D. A., & Rancer, A. S. (1982). A conceptualization and measure of argumentativeness. *Journal of Personality Assessment, 46*, 72–80.

Imhof, M. (2003). The social construction of the listener: Listening behavior across situations, perceived listener status, and cultures. *Communication Research Reports, 20*, 357–366.

In the news. (1999, October 1). *Commercial Appeal* [an E.W. Scripps newspaper], A-1.

International Telework Association and Council. (2004). *Advancing work from anywhere*. Retrieved March 28, 2008, from http://www.telecommute.org/resources.

Internet statistics. (n.d.) Retrieved January 2, 2008, from http://www.internetstats.com.

Ishii-Kuntz, M. (1997). Japanese American families. In M. K. DeGenova (Ed.), *Families in cultural context: Strengths and challenges in diversity* (pp. 109–130). Mountain View, CA: Mayfield.

Ivy, D. K., & Backlund, P. (2000). *Exploring genderspeak*. New York: McGraw-Hill.

Ivy, D. K., Bullis-Moore, L., Norvell, K., Backlund, P., & Javidi, M. (1995). The lawyer, the babysitter, and the student: Inclusive language usage and instruction. *Women and Language, 18*, 13–21.

Jackson, R. L. (2002). Cultural contracts theory: Toward an understanding of identity negotiation. *Communication Quarterly, 50*, 359–367.

Jamison, S. L. (2003, December 12). Clicking on the links to friendship. *New York Times*, C13.

Jandt, F. E. (2006). *An introduction to intercultural communication: Identities in a global community*. Thousand Oaks, CA: Sage.

Jensen, J. V. (1997). *Ethical issues in the communication process*. Mahwah, NJ: Lawrence Erlbaum.

Johanneson, R. L. (2000). *Ethics in human communication*. Prospect Heights, IL: Waveland.

Johnson, A. J. (2002). Beliefs about arguing: A comparison of public issue and personal issue arguments. *Communication Reports, 15*, 99–111.

Johnson, A. J., Becker, J. A. H., Wigley, S., Haigh, M. M., & Craig, E. A. (2007). Reported argumentativeness and verbal aggressiveness levels: The influence of type of argument. *Communication Studies, 58*, 189–205.

Johnson, F. L. (1996). Friendships among women: Closeness in dialogue. In J. T. Wood (Ed.), *Gendered relationships* (pp. 79–94). Mountain View, CA: Mayfield.

Johnson, F. L. (2000). *Speaking culturally: Language diversity in the United States*. Thousand Oaks, CA: Sage.

Johnston, M. K., Weaver, J. B., Watson, K. W., & Barker, L. B. (2000). Listening styles: Biological or psychological differences? *International Journal of Listening, 14*, 32–46.

Johnson, M. P. (1995). Patriarchal terrorism and common couple violence: Two forms of violence against women. *Journal of Marriage and the Family, 57*, 283–294.

Joinson, A. N. (2001). Knowing me, knowing you: Reciprocal self-disclosure in Internet-based surveys. *Cyberpsychology and Behaviour, 4*, 587–591.

Jonas, M. (2007, August 5). The downside of diversity. *Boston Globe*, D2, D4.

Jones, D. (2004, January 9). Women trump the men in first episode. *USA Today*, 3B.

Jones, D. C. (2001). Social comparison and body image: Attractiveness comparisons to models and peers among adolescent girls and boys. *Sex Roles, 45*, 645–664.

Jones, G. P., & Dembo, M. H. (1989). Age and sex role differences in intimate friendships during childhood and adolescence. *Merrill-Palmer Quarterly of Behavior and Development, 35*, 445–462.

Jones, S. E., & Yarbrough, A. E. (1985). A naturalistic study of the meanings of touch. *Communication Monographs, 52*, 19–56.

Jones, S. G. (1998). Introduction. In S. G. Jones (Ed.), *Cybersociety 2.0* (pp. xi–xvii). Thousand Oaks, CA: Sage.

Jones, S. M., & Wirtz, J. G. (2007). "Sad monkey see, monkey do": Nonverbal matching in emotional support encounters. *Communication Studies, 58*, 71–86.

Jourard, S. M. (1959). Healthy personality and self-disclosure. *Journal of Mental Hygiene, 43*, 499–507.

Jourard, S. M. (1971). *The transparent self*. New York: Van Nostrand-Reinhold.

Kakutani, M. (2001, October 20). Fear: The new virus of a connected era. *New York Times*, 13.

Keeley, M. P. (2007). "Turning toward death together:" The functions of messages during final conversations in close relationships. *Journal of Social and Personal Relationships, 24*, 225–253.

Kellas, J. K. (2005). Family ties: Communicating identity through jointly told family stories. *Communication Monographs, 72*, 365–389.

King, D. (2005, March 3). Content aggregation. *Dave's blog*. Retrieved February 5, 2008, from http://daweed.blogspot.com/search?q=content+aggregation.

Kirtley, M. D., & Honeycutt, J. (1996). Listening styles and their correspondence with second-guessing. *Communication Research Reports, 13*, 1–9.

Kitzinger, C. (2000). How to resist an idiom. *Research on Language and Social Interaction, 33*, 121–154.

Klinkenborg, V. (2004, February 27). Behind the rise of Google lies the rise in Internet credibility. *New York Times*, A24.

Klopf, D. W. (1998). *Intercultural encounters: The fundamentals of intercultural communication*. Englewood, CO: Morton Publishing.

Knapp, M. L. (1978). *Social intercourse: From greeting to goodbye*. Boston: Allyn and Bacon.

Knapp, M. L., & Hall, J. A. (2002). *Nonverbal communication in human interaction*. Belmont, CA: Wadsworth.

Knapp, M. L., & Vangelisti, A. L. (2000). *Interpersonal communication and human relationships* (4th ed.). Boston: Allyn and Bacon.

Knapp, M. L., & Vangelisti, A. L. (2005). *Interpersonal communication and human relationships* (5th ed.). Boston: Allyn and Bacon.

Knobloch, L. K., Miller, L. E., Bond, B. J., Mannone, S. E. (2007). Relational uncertainty and message processing in marriage. *Communication Monographs, 74*, 154–180.

Knott, J. (2006). *Handbook of inclusive education for educators, administrators, and planners: Within walls, without boundaries*. Thousand Oaks, CA: Sage.

Koch, E. J. (2002). Relational schemas, self-esteem, and the processing of social stimuli. *Self & Identity, 1*, 272–279.

Kornblum, J. (2003, February 10). Online dating: No longer in the "geeky" domain. *USA Today*, 6D.

Kornblum, J. (2007, July 31). Rudeness, threats make the web a cruel world. *USA Today*, 1D–2D.

Kornblum, J. (2007, October 23). Privacy? That's old-school. *USA Today*, 1D–2D.

Korzybski, A. (1958). *Science and sanity: An introduction to non-Aristotelian systems and general semantics* Lakeville, CT: International Non-Aristotelian Library Publishing Company.

Kovecses, Z. (2000). *Metaphor and emotion: Language, culture, and body in human feeling*. Cambridge, England: Cambridge University Press.

Kowalski, R. M. (2001). The aversive side of social interaction revisited. In R. M. Kowalski (Ed.), *Behaving badly: Aversive behaviors in interpersonal relationships* (pp. 297–309). Washington, DC: American Psychological Association.

Kramarae, C. (1981). *Women and men speaking*. Rowley, MA: Newbury House.

Kroeber, A. L., & Kluckhohn, C. (1993). *Culture: A critical review of concepts and definitions*. New York: Vintage.

Kuehn, M. (2001). *Kant: A biography*. New York: Cambridge University Press.

Labov, W. (1972). *Sociolinguistic patterns*. Philadelphia: University of Pennsylvania Press.

Lakey, S. G., & Canary, D. J. (2001, July). The role of interpersonal goals in conflict tactic choice. Paper presented at the annual joint meeting of the International Network of Personal Relationships/International Society for the Study of Personal Relationships, Prescott, AZ.

Lakey, S. G., & Canary, D. J. (2002). Actor goal achievement and sensitivity to partner as critical factors in understanding interpersonal communication competence and conflict strategies. *Communication Monographs, 69*, 217–235.

Lakoff, G. (2003, August, 1). Framing the Dems. *The American Prospect*. Retrieved August 10, 2007, from http://www.prospect.org/cs/articles?article=framing_the_dems.

Lakoff, G., & Johnson, M. (1980). *Metaphors we live by*. Chicago: University of Chicago Press.

Lakoff, R. (1975). *Language and women's place*. New York: Harper and Row.

Langellier, K. M., & Peterson, E. E. (2006). Narrative performance theory: Telling stories, doing family. In D. O. Braithwaite & L. A. Baxter (Eds.), *Engaging theories in family communication* (pp. 99–114). Thousand Oaks, CA: Sage.

Langer, E. (1989). *Mindfulness*. Reading, MA: Addison-Wesley.

Larsen, E. (2004). Deeper understanding, deeper ties: Taking faith online. In P. N. Howard & S. Jones (Eds.), *Society online: The Internet in context* (pp. 43–56). Thousand Oaks, CA: Sage.

Lazarus, R. S. (1991). *Emotion and adaptation.* New York: Oxford University Press.

Leggitt, J. S., & Gibbs, R. W. (2000). Emotional reactions to verbal irony. *Discourse Processes, 29,* 1–24.

Lenhart, A., & Madden, M. (2007, April 18). Teens, privacy, & online social networks. *Pew Internet and American Life Project Report.* Retrieved February 5, 2008, from http://www.pewinternet.org/pdfs/PIP_Teens_Privacy_SNS_Report_Final.pdf

Lerner, H. (2001). *The dance of connection.* New York: Harper-Collins.

Levenson, R. W., & Gottman, J. M. (1985). Physiological and affective predictors of change in relationship satisfaction. *Journal of Personality and Social Psychology, 45,* 587–597.

Levine, T. R., Aune, K. S., & Park, H. S. (2006). Love styles and communication in relationships: Partner preferences, initiation, and intensification. *Communication Quarterly, 54,* 465–486.

Levinson, D. (1996–2004). It's only words. *Gay and Lesbian Issues.* Retrieved March 14, 2008, from http://www.rslevinson.com/gaylesissues/features/main/gl970822.htm.

Lewis, R. D. (1999). *When cultures collide: Managing successfully across cultures.* London: Nicholas Brealey.

Liesse, J. Getting to know the millenials. *Advertising Age, 78,* A1, A2, A4, A6.

Linguistic Society of America (1997, January). *LSA resolution on the Oakland "Ebonics" issue.* Retrieved March 15, 2008 from http://www.linguistlist.org/topics/ebonics/lsa-ebonics.html.

Lippert, T., & Prager, K. J. (2001). Daily experiences of intimacy: A study of couples. *Personal Relationships, 8,* 283–298.

Lippman, W. (1922). *Public opinion.* New York: Macmillan.

Littlejohn, S. W., & Domenici, K. (2001). *Engaging communication in conflict.* Thousand Oaks, CA: Sage.

Lloyd, S. A. (1987). Conflict in premarital relationships: Differential perceptions of males and females. *Family Relations, 36,* 290–294.

Loftus, E. F., & Palmer, J. C. (1974). Reconstruction of automobile destruction: An example of the interaction between language and memory. *Journal of Verbal Learning and Verbal Behavior, 13,* 585–589.

Luft, J. (1970). *Group process: An introduction to group dynamics.* Palo Alto, CA: Mayfield.

Lulofs, R. S., & Cahn, D. D. (2000). *Conflict: From theory to action* (2nd ed.). Boston: Allyn and Bacon.

Lustig, M. W., & Koester, J. (1999). *Intercultural competence: Interpersonal communication across cultures.* New York: Longman.

Lustig, M. W., & Koester, J. (2000). The nature of cultural identity. In M. W. Lustig & J. Koester (Eds.), *AmongUS: Essays on identity, belonging, and intercultural competence* (pp. 3–8). New York: Addison-Wesley.

Maccoby, E. (1998). *The two sexes: Growing up apart, coming together.* Cambridge, MA: Harvard University Press.

Mackay, H. (2001). *Listening is the hardest of the "easy" tasks.* Retrieved March 15, 2008, from http://www.listen.org/pages/mackay.

Malis, R. S., & Roloff, M. E. (2006). Features of serial arguing and coping strategies: Links with stress and well-being. In B. A. Le Poire & R. M. Dailey (Eds.), *Applied interpersonal communication matters: Family, health, and community relations* (pp. 39–66). New York: Peter Lang.

Maltz, D. J., & Borker, R. A. (1982). A cultural approach to male-female miscommunication. In J. J. Gumpertz (Ed.), *Language and social identity* (pp. 196–216). Cambridge, England: Cambridge University Press.

Marano, H. E. (2004). The new sex scorecard. *Psychology Today.* Retrieved March 15, 2008, from http://cms.psychologytoday.com/articles.

Martin, J., & Nakayama, T. (2007). *Experiencing intercultural communication: An introduction.* New York: McGraw-Hill.

Martin, J. N., & Nakayama, T. K. (2008). *Intercultural communication in contexts* (4th ed.). New York: McGraw-Hill.

Martinez, R. (2000, July 16). The next chapter: America's next great revolution in race relations is already underway. *New York Times Magazine,* 11–12.

Martyna, W. (1978). What does "he" mean? Use of the generic masculine. *Journal of Communication, 28,* 131–138.

Marwell, G., & Schmitt, D. R. (1967). Dimensions of compliance-gaining behavior: An empirical analysis. *Sociometry, 30,* 350–364.

Marwell, G., & Schmitt, D. R. (1990). An introduction. In J. P. Dillard (Ed.), *Seeking compliance: The production of interpersonal influence messages* (pp. 3–5). Scottsdale, AZ: Gorsuch Scarisbrick.

Maslow, A. H. (1954/1970). *Motivation and personality.* New York: Harper and Row.

Maslow, A. H. (1968). *Toward a psychology of being.* New York: Van Nostrand Reinhold.

Mathews, A., Derlega, V. J., & Morrow, J. (2006). What is highly personal information and how is it related to self-disclosure decision-making? The perspective of college students. *Communication Research Reports, 23,* 85–92.

Matsumoto, D. (2006). Culture and nonverbal behavior. In V. L. Manusov & M. Wadsworth (Eds.), *The SAGE handbook of nonverbal communication* (pp. 219–236). Thousand Oaks, CA: Sage.

McCroskey, J. C., & Richmond, V. P. (1995). Correlates of compulsive communication: Quantitative and qualitative characteristics. *Communication Quarterly, 43,* 39–52.

McDaniel, E. R. (2006). Japanese nonverbal communication: A reflection on cultural themes. In L. A. Samovar, R. E. Porter, & E. McDaniel (Eds.), *Intercultural communication: A reader* (pp. 266–274). Belmont, CA: Wadsworth.

McFedries, P. (2004). *Word spy: The word lover's guide to modern culture.* New York: Broadway Books.

McGeorge, C. (2001). Mars and Venus: Unequal planets. *Journal of Marital and Family Therapy, 27,* 55–68.

McGlone, M. S., Beck, G., & Pfiester, A. (2006). Contamination and camouflage in euphemisms. *Communication Monographs, 73,* 261–282.

McGowan, W. (2001). *Coloring the news: How crusading for diversity has corrupted American journalism.* San Francisco: Encounter.

McIlwain, C. D. (2002). Death in Black and White: A study of family differences in the performance of death rituals. *Qualitative Research Reports in Communication, 3,* 1–6.

McLuhan, M. (1964). *Understanding media: The extensions of man.* New York: McGraw-Hill.

McLuhan, M., & McLuhan, E. (1988). *Laws of media: The new science.* Toronto, Canada: Toronto Press.

McQuail, D., & Windahl, S. (1993). *Communication models.* New York: Longman.

Mead, G. H. (1934). *Mind, self and society: From the standpoint of a social behaviorist.* Chicago: University of Chicago Press.

Medved, C. E., & Kirby, E. L. (2005). Family CEOs: A feminist analysis of corporate mothering discourses. *Management Communication Quarterly, 18,* 435–418.

Meer, J. (1985, September). The light touch. *Psychology Today,* 60–67.

Mehrabian, A. (1981). *Silent messages: Implicit communication of emotions and attitudes* (2nd ed.). Belmont, CA: Wadsworth.

Mehrabian, A., & Ferris, S. R. (1967). Inference of attitudes from nonverbal communication in two channels. *Journal of Consulting Psychology, 21,* 248–252.

Mental Health Net (n.d.). *Methods for Developing Skills.* Retrieved March 28, 2008, from http://mentalhelp.net/psyhelp/chap13.

Merriam-Webster Online Dictionary. (2004). Retrieved March 15, 2008, from http://www.m-w.com/cgi-bin/dictionary.

Messman, S. J., & Mikesell, R. L. (2000). Competition and interpersonal conflict in dating relationships. *Communication Reports, 13,* 21–34.

Metts, S. (2006). Hanging out and doing lunch: Enacting friendship closeness. In J. T. Wood & S. Duck (Eds.), *Composing relationships: Communication in everyday life* (pp. 76–85). Belmont, CA: Wadsworth.

Metzger, D. (1995). *The lost cause of rhetoric: The relation of rhetoric and geometry in Aristotle and Lacan.* Carbondale, IL: Southern Illinois University.

Meyers, S. A., & Berscheid, E. (1997). The language of love: The difference a preposition makes. *Personality and Social Psychology Bulletin, 23,* 347–362.

Michigan State University Counseling Center (2003). *Improving communication skills: Suggestions for improving communication skills in relationships.* Retrieved March 15, 2008, from http://www.couns.msu.edu/self-help/suggest.htm.

Migration Policy Institute (2007). *Annual immigration to the United States: The real numbers.* Washington, D.C.: Migration Policy Institute.

Miller, G. R., & Parks, M. R. (1982). Communication in dissolving relationships. In S. Duck (Ed.), *Personal relationships 4: Dissolving personal relationships* (pp. 127–154). New York: Academic Press.

Miller, G. R., & Steinberg, M. (1975). *Between people: A new analysis of interpersonal communication.* Chicago: Science Research Associates.

Miller, J. B., Plant, E. A., & Hanke, E. (1993). Girls' and boys' views of body type. In C. Berryman-Fink, D. Ballard-Reisch, L. H. Newman (Eds.), *Communication and sex-role socialization* (pp. 49–58). New York: Garland.

Miller, K. I. (2007). Compassionate communication in the workplace: Exploring processes of noticing, connecting, and responding. *Journal of Applied Communication Research, 35,* 223–245.

Mills, S. (2003). Caught between sexism, anti-sexism and "political correctness": Feminist women's negotiations with naming practices. *Discourse and Society, 14,* 87–110.

Miura, S. Y. (2000). The mediation of conflict in the traditional Hawaiian family: A collectivistic approach. *Qualitative Research Reports in Communication, 1,* 19–25.

Miura, A., & Yamashita, K. (2007). Psychological and social influences on blog writing: An online survey of blog authors in Japan. *Journal of Computer-Mediated Communication, 12* (http://jcmc.indiana.edu/vol12/issue1).

Molloy, J. T. (1978). *Dress for success.* New York: Warner.

Molm, L. D. (2001). Theories of social exchange and exchange networks. In G. Ritzer & B. Smart (Eds.), *Handbook of social theory* (pp. 260–272). London: Sage.

Morrison, T., Conaway, W. A., & Borden, G. A. (1994). *Kiss, bow, or shake hands.* Holbrook, MA: Adams Media.

Morton, J. B., & Trehub, S. E. (2001). Children's understandings of emotions in speech. *Child Development, 72,* 834–843.

Moyers, B. (1993). *Healing and the mind.* New York: Doubleday.

Mulac, A., Bradac, J. J., & Gibbons, P. (2001). Empirical support for the gender-as-culture hypothesis: An intercultural analysis of male/female language differences. *Human Communication Research, 27,* 121–152.

Mulac, A., Incontro, C. R., & James, M. R. (1985). Comparison of the gender-linked language effect and sex role stereotypes. *Journal of Personality and Social Psychology, 49,* 1098–1109.

Murphy, D. E. (2002, May 26). Letting go: Beyond justice: The eternal struggle to forgive. *New York Times,* C1–C3.

Myers, S. A., & Bryant, L. E. (2002). Perceived understanding, interaction involvement, and college student outcomes. *Communication Research Reports, 19,* 146–155.

Nakayama, T. K., & Martin, J. N. (1999). Introduction: Whiteness as the communication of social identity. In T. K. Nakayama & J. N. Martin (Eds.), *Whiteness: The communication of social identity* (pp. vi–xiv). Thousand Oaks, CA: Sage.

National Association of Colleges and Employers (2002). *Do employers and colleges see eye to eye? College student development and assessment.* Retrieved March 15, 2008, from http://www.naceweb.com.

National Communication Association (n.d.) *How Americans communicate* [poll conducted by Roper Starch Worldwide in the summer of 1998]. Retrieved March 15, 2008, from http://www.natcom.org/research/Poll/how_americans_communicate .htm.

National Council on Economic Education. (2000–2004). *A case study: United States international trade in goods and services—July 2002.* Retrieved March 15, 2008, from http://www.econedlink.org.

National Telecommunications and Information Administration. (n.d.). *Falling through the net II: New data on the digital divide.* Retrieved February 1, 2008, from http://www.ntia.doc.gov/ntiahome/net2/falling.html.

National Telecommunications and Information Administration (1999). *Falling through the net: Defining the digital divide.* Retrieved March 15, 2008, from http:// www.ntia.doc.gov/ntiahome/fttn99/contents.html.

National Telecommunications and Information Administration (2002). *A nation online: How Americans are expanding their use of the Internet.* Retrieved March 15, 2008, from http://www.ntia.doc.gov/ntiahome/dn/.

Neff, G., & Stark, D. (2004). Permanently beta: Responsive organization in the Internet era. In P. Howard & S. Jones (Eds.), *Society online: The Internet in context* (pp. 173–188). Thousand Oaks, CA: Sage.

Nehf, J. B. (2007). Shopping for privacy on the net. *Journal of Consumer Affairs, 41,* 351–365.

Netcraft. (2007, November 23). *November 2007 web server survey.* Retrieved February 7, 2008, from http://news.netcraft.com/archives/2007/11/23/november_2007_web_ server_survey.html.

Nettle, D., & Romaine, S. (2000). *Vanishing voices: The extinction of the world's languages.* Oxford, England: Oxford University Press.

Nichols, R. (1948). Factors in listening comprehension. *Speech Monographs, 15,* 154–163.

Nilsen, T. (1966). *Ethics of speech communication.* Indianapolis, IN: Bobbs-Merrill.

Noll, A. M. (1997). *Highway of dreams.* Mahwah, NJ: Lawrence Erlbaum.

Nunberg, G. (2003, May 29). *Fresh Air* interview [radio show].

Oatley, K., & Duncan, E. (1992). Incidents of emotion in daily life. In K. T. Strongman (Ed.), *International review of studies on emotion* (Vol. 2, pp. 249–293). Chichester, England: Wiley.

Oberg, A. C. (2003, August 26). New umbilical cords tie young adults to parents. *USA Today,* 11A.

Ogden, C. K., & Richards, I. A. (1923). *The meaning of meaning.* London: Kegan, Paul, Trench, Trubner.

Okimoto, J. D., & Stegall, P. J. (1987). *Boomerang kids: How to live with adult children who return home.* New York: Pocket.

Olson, L. N. (2002). Compliance gaining strategies of individuals experiencing "common couple violence." *Qualitative Research Reports in Communication, 3,* 7–14.

Olson, L. N. (2003). "From lace teddies to flannel PJ's": An analysis of males' experience and expressions of love. *Qualitative Research Reports in Communication, 4,* 38–44.

Omarzu, J. (2000). A disclosure decision model: Determining how and when individuals will self-disclose. *Personality and Social Psychology Review, 4,* 174–185.

Orbe, M. P. (1998). *Constructing co-cultural theory: An explication of culture, power, and communication.* Thousand Oaks, CA: Sage.

O'Reilly Media. (2005, September 30). *What is web 2.0?* Retrieved February 5, 2008, from http://www.oreillynet.com/pub/a/oreilly/tim/news/2005/09/30/what-is-web-20.html.

Orrego, V. O., Smith, S. W., Mitchell, M. M., Johnson, A. J., Yun, K. A., & Greenberg, B. (2000). Disclosure and privacy issues on television talk shows. In S. Petronio (Ed.), *Balancing the secrets of private disclosures* (pp. 249–259). Mahwah, NJ: Lawrence Erlbaum.

Ortony, A., Clore, G. L., & Foss, M. (1987). The referential structure of the affective lexicon. *Cognitive Science, 11,* 361–384.

Owen, W. F. (1989). Image metaphors of women and men in personal relationships. *Women's Studies in Communication, 12,* 37–57.

Pais, S. (1997). Asian Indian families in America. In M. K. DeGenova (Ed.), *Families in cultural context: Strengths and challenges in diversity* (pp. 173–190). Mountain View, CA: Mayfield.

Palmer, K. S. (2002, October 10). Cultures clash in workplaces. *USA Today,* 13A.

Pan, Y. (2000). *Politeness in Chinese face-to-face interaction.* Stamford, CT: Ablex.

Parker, J. G., Low, C. M., Walker, A. R., & Gamm, B. K. (2005). Friendship jealousy in young adolescents: Individual differences and links to sex, self-esteem, aggression and social adjustment. *Developmental Psychology, 41,* 235–250.

Parks, M. R. (1982). Ideology in interpersonal communication: Off the couch and into the world. In M. Burgoon (Ed.), *Communication yearbook 6* (pp. 79–107). Newbury Park, CA: Sage.

Parks, M. R., & Floyd, K. (1996). Meanings for closeness and intimacy in friendship. *Journal of Social and Personal Relationships, 13,* 85–107.

Pearce, W. B., & Sharp, S. M. (1973). Self-disclosing communication. *Journal of Communication, 23,* 409–425.

Pauley, P. M., & Emmers-Sommer, T. M. (2007). The impact of internet technologies on primary and secondary romantic relationship development. *Communication Studies, 58,* 411–427.

Pearson, J. C. (1992). *Lasting love: What keeps couples together.* Dubuque, IA: Wm. C. Brown.

Pearson, J. C., West, R., & Turner, L. H. (1995). *Gender and communication.* Madison, WI: Brown and Benchmark.

Peel, K. (1997). *The family manager's everyday survival guide.* New York: Ballantine Books.

Pennebaker, J. W., Barger, S. D., & Tiebout, J. (1989). Trauma and health among Holocaust survivors. *Psychosomatic Medicine, 51,* 577–589.

Petronio, S. (1991). Communication boundary management: A theoretical model of managing disclosures of private information between marital couples. *Communication Theory, 1,* 311–335.

Petronio, S. (2000). Preface. In S. Petronio (Ed.), *Balancing the secrets of private disclosures* (pp. xiii–xvi). Mahwah, NJ: Lawrence Erlbaum.

Petronio, S. (2002). *Boundaries of privacy: Dialectics of disclosure.* Albany, NY: SUNY Press.

Pew Charitable Trusts. (2006, April 3). *73 percent of Americans go online.* Retrieved December 1, 2007, from http://www.pewtrusts.org/news_room_ektid23772.aspx.

Pew Internet and American Life Project. (2004). *Internet use by region in the United States.* Retrieved March 15, 2008, from http://www.pewinternet.org/pdfs/PIP_ Regional_Report_Aug_2003.pdf.6.

Pfeiffer, R. S., & Forsberg, R. L. (2005). *Ethics on the job: Cases and strategies.* Belmont, CA: Wadsworth.

Pfeiffer, S. (2007, July 23). You can't read minds, but . . . . *Boston Globe,* E1, E4.

Pipher, M. (2003, March/April). In praise of hometowns: Staying home in the global village. *UU World, XVII,* 39–41.

Planalp, S. (1998). Communicating emotion in everyday life: Cues, channels, and processes. In P. A. Andersen & L. K. Guerrero (Eds.), *Handbook of communication and emotion: Research, theory, applications, and contexts* (pp. 30–48). San Diego, CA: Academic Press.

Planalp, S. (1999). *Communicating emotion: Social, moral, and cultural processes.* Cambridge, England: Cambridge University Press.

Planalp, S., DeFrancisco, V., & Rutherford, D. (1996). Varieties of cues to emotion in naturally occurring situations. *Cognition and Emotion, 10,* 137–153.

Planalp, S., & Fitness, J. (1999). Thinking/feeling about social and personal relationships. *Journal of Social and Personal Relationships, 16,* 731–750.

Plutchik, R. (1984). Emotions: A general psychoevolutionary theory. In K. R. Scherer & P. Ekman (Eds.), *Approaches to emotion* (pp. 197–219). Hillsdale, NJ: Lawrence Erlbaum.

Poole, M., & Walther, J. (Eds.) (2002). *Communication: Ubiquitous, complex, consequential.* Washington, D.C.: National Communication Association.

Priest, P. J. (1995). *Public intimacies: Talk show participants and tell-all T.V.* Cresskill, NJ: Hampton Press.

Primitive Baptist Web Station (n.d.). *Common emoticons and acronyms.* http://www.pb.org/emotican.html.

Prowse, R. (2006, September 11). New *Facebook* mini-feed deemed creepy, invasion of privacy by some users. *East Tennessean*, 1.

Pullum, G. K. (1991). *The great Eskimo vocabulary hoax and other irreverent essays on the study of language.* Chicago: University of Chicago Press.

Purdy, M. (2004). *Listen up, move up.* Retrieved March 15, 2008, from http://www.featuredreports.monster.com.

Ramirez, Jr., A., & Zhang, S. (2007). When online meets offline: The effect of modality switching on relational communication. *Communication Monographs, 74,* 287–310.

Ravitch, D. (2003). *The language police: How pressure groups restrict what students learn.* New York: Alfred A. Knopf.

Rawlins, W. K. (1992). *Friendship matters: Communication, dialectics, and the life course.* New York: Aldine de Gruyter.

Reissman, C. (1990). *Divorce talk: Women and men make sense of personal relationships.* New Brunswick, NJ: Rutgers University Press.

Ribeau, S. A., Baldwin, J. R., & Hecht, M. L. (2000). An African American communication perspective. In L. A. Samovar & R. E. Porter (Eds.), *Intercultural communication: A reader* (pp. 128–135). Belmont, CA: Wadsworth.

Richmond, V. P., & McCroskey, J. C. (1998). *Communication: Apprehension, avoidance, and effectiveness.* Needham Heights, MA: Allyn & Bacon.

Riggs, K. E. (2004). *Granny at work: Aging and technology on the job in America.* New York: Routledge.

Ritts, V., Patterson, M. L., & Tubbs, M. E. (1992). Expectations, impressions, and judgments of physically attractive students: A review. *Review of Educational Research, 64,* 413–426.

Roberto, A. J., Carlyle, K. E., & McClure, L. (2006). Communication and corporal punishment: The relationship between parents' use of verbal and physical aggression. *Communication Research Reports, 23,* 27–33.

Roethlisberger, F. L., & Dickson, W. (1939). *Management and the worker.* New York: Wiley.

Roloff, M. E. (1981). *Interpersonal communication: The social exchange approach.* Beverly Hills, CA: Sage.

Roloff, M. E. (1987). Communication and conflict. In C. R. Berger & S. H. Chaffee (Eds.), *Handbook of communication science* (pp. 484–534). Newbury Park, CA: Sage.

Roloff, M. E., & Ifert, D. E. (2000). Conflict management through avoidance: Withholding complaints, suppressing arguments, and declaring topics taboo. In S. Petronio (Ed.), *Balancing the secrets of private disclosures* (pp. 151–163), Mahwah, NJ: Lawrence Erlbaum.

Rose, A., & Asher, S. (2000). Children's friendships. In C. Hendrick & S. Hendrick (Eds.), *Close relationships: A sourcebook* (pp. 47–57). Thousand Oaks, CA: Sage.

Rose, A. J., Carlson, W., & Waller, E. M. (2007). Prospective associations of co-rumination with friendship and emotional adjustment: Considering the socioemotional trade-offs of co-rumination. *Developmental Psychology, 43,* 1019–1031.

Rosenfeld, L. B. (2000). Overview of the ways privacy, secrecy, and disclosure are balanced in today's society. In S. Petronio (Ed.), *Balancing the secrets of private disclosures* (pp. 3–17). Mahwah, NJ: Lawrence Erlbaum.

Rosnow, R. L. (2001). Rumor and gossip in interpersonal interaction and beyond: A social exchange perspective. In R. M. Kowalski (Ed.), *Behaving badly: Aversive behaviors in interpersonal relationships* (pp. 203–232). Washington, DC: American Psychological Association.

Rough Guide (2007, August). *Harper's,* 22–23.

Rourke, L., Anderson, T., Garrison, D. R., & Archer, W. (2001). Assessing social presence in asynchronous text-based computer conferencing. *Journal of Distance Education, 14,* 50–71.

Rubin, R. B., Palmgreen, P., & Sypher, H. E. (Eds.). (1994). *Communication research measures: A sourcebook.* New York: Guilford Press.

Rudawsky, D. J., Lundgren, D. C., & Grasha, A. F. (1999). Competitive and collaborative responses to negative feedback. *International Journal of Conflict Management, 10,* 172–190.

Russell, J. A. (1978). Evidence of convergent validity of the dimensions of affect. *Journal of Personality and Social Psychology, 36,* 1152–1168.

Russell, J. A. (1980). A circumplex model of affect. *Journal of Personality and Social Psychology, 39,* 1161–1178.

Russell, J. A. (1983). Pancultural aspects of the human conceptual organization of emotions. *Journal of Personality and Social Psychology, 45,* 1281–1288.

Sadka, D. (2004). *The Dewey color system.* New York: Three Rivers Press.

Sahlstein, E. M. (2006). Making plans: Praxis strategies for negotiating uncertainty-certainty in long-distance relationships. *Western Journal of Communication, 70,* 147–165.

Samovar, L. A., & Porter, R. E. (2004). *Communication between cultures.* Belmont, CA: Wadsworth.

Sargent, S. L., Weaver, J. B., III, & Kiewitz, C. (1997). Correlates between communication apprehension and listening style preferences. *Communication Research Reports, 14,* 74–78.

Satir, V. (1972). *Peoplemaking.* Palo Alto, CA: Science & Behavior Books.

Schramm, W. L. (1954). *The process and effects of mass communication.* Urbana, IL: University of Illinois.

Schrodt, P., Ledbetter, A. M., Ohrt, J. K. (2007). Parental confirmation and affection as mediators of family communication patterns and children's mental well-being. *Journal of Family Communication, 7,* 23–46.

Seay, E. (2004, February 11). Lost city, lost languages. *Princeton Alumni Weekly, 17,* 43.

Segrin, C. (1998). Interpersonal communication problems associated with depression and loneliness. In P. A. Andersen & L. K. Guerrero (Eds.), *Handbook of communication and emotion: Research, theory, applications, and contexts* (pp. 215–242). San Diego, CA: Academic Press.

Seiter, J. S., & Bruschke, J. (2007). Deception and emotion: The effects of motivation, relationship type, and sex on expected feelings of guilt and shame following acts of deception in United States and Chinese samples. *Communication Studies, 58,* 1–16.

Sender, K. (2006). Queens for a day: *Queer Eye for the Straight Guy* and the neoliberal project. *Critical Studies in Media Communication, 23,* 131–151.

Sentence completion (2004). *TakeSAT.com.* Retrieved March 15, 2008, from http://www.takesat.com/sentence.php.

Serewicz, M. C., & Petronio, S. (2007). Communication privacy management theory. In B. Whaley & W. Samter (Eds.), *Explaining communication: Contemporary theories and exemplars.* Mahwah, NJ: Lawrence Erlbaum Associates.

Serewicz, M. C. M., Dickson, F. C., Morrison, J. H. T. A., Poole, L. L. (2007). Family privacy orientation, relational maintenance, and family satisfaction in young adults' family relationships. *Journal of Family Communication, 7,* 123–142.

Shaffer, D. R., & Ogden, J. K. (1986). On sex differences in self-disclosure during the acquaintance process: The role of anticipated future interaction. *Journal of Personality and Social Psychology, 51,* 92–101.

Shannon, C. E., & Weaver, W. (1949). *The mathematical theory of communication.* Urbana, IL: University of Illinois.

Shannon, C. E., & Weaver, W. (1999). *The mathematical theory of communication* (50th ed.). Urbana, IL: University of Illinois.

Shaver, P. R., Schwartz, J., Kirson, D., & O'Connor, C. (1987). Emotion knowledge: Further explorations of a prototype approach. *Journal of Personality and Social Psychology, 17,* 69–79.

Shields, S. A. (2000). Thinking about gender, thinking about theory: Gender and emotional experience. In A. H. Fischer (Ed.), *Gender and emotion: Social psychological perspectives* (pp. 3–23). Cambridge, England: Cambridge University Press.

Shields, S. A., & Crowley, J. C. (1996). Appropriating questionnaires and rating scales for a feminist psychology: A multimethod approach to gender and emotion. In S. Wilkinson (Ed.), *Feminist social psychologies* (pp. 218–232). Philadelphia, PA: Open University Press.

Shimanoff, S. B. (1980). *Communication rules: Theory and research.* Beverly Hills, CA: Sage.

Shimanoff, S. B. (1985). Expressing emotions in words: Verbal patterns of interactions. *Journal of Communication, 35,* 16–31.

Shimanoff, S. B. (1987). Types of emotional disclosures and request compliance between spouses. *Communication Monographs, 54,* 85–100.

Shin, L. (2003, May 9). Ah, sweet mystery of e-mail. *New York Times,* D2.

Shlain, L. (1998). *The alphabet versus the goddess: The conflict between word and image.* New York: Penguin/Arkana.

Shuter, R., & Turner, L. H. (1997). African American and European American women in the workplace: Perceptions of conflict communication. *Management Communication Quarterly, 11,* 74–96.

Sillars, A. L., Roberts, L., Leonard, K. E., & Dun, T. (2000). Cognition during marital conflict: The relationship of thought and talk. *Journal of Social and Personal Relationships, 17,* 479–502.

Silva-Corvalán, C. (1994). *Language contact and change: Spanish in Los Angeles.* New York: Oxford University Press.

Silverstein, J., & Lasky, M. (2004). *Online dating for dummies.* Indianapolis, IN: Wiley.

Simonton, B. (2005). *Leading people to be highly motivated and committed.* Sun City Center, Florida: Simonton Associates.

Simpson, L. (2003). Get around resistance and win over the other side. *Harvard Management Communication Letter,* 3–5.

Smitherman, G. (2000). *Black talk: Words and phrases from the hood to the amen corner.* Boston: Houghton Mifflin.

Smith-Sanders, A. K., & Harter, L. M. (2007). Democracy, dialogue, and education: An exploration of conflict resolution at Jefferson Junior High School. *Southern Communication Journal, 72,* 109–126.

Snorton, R. (2004). *New poll shows at least 5% of America's high school students identify as gay or lesbian.* Retrieved July 18, 2007, from http://www.glsen.org/cgi-bin/iowa/all/library/record/1724.html.

Snyder, M. (1979). Self-monitoring processes. In L. Berkowitz (Ed.), *Advances in experimental social psychology* (pp. 86–131). New York: Academic Press.

Soliz, J., Lin, M.-C., Anderson, K., & Harwood, J. (2006). Friends and allies: Communication in grandparent-grandchild relationships. In K. Floyd & M. Morman (Eds.), *Widening the family circle: New research on family communication.* (pp. 63–79). Newbury Park, CA: Sage.

Sopory, P. (2006). Metaphor and attitude accessibility. *Southern Communication Journal, 71,* 251–272.

Southern Poverty Law Center. (2004). *About the center: Advocates for justice and equality.* Retrieved March 28, 2008, from http://www.splcenter.org/center/about.jsp2004.

Spencer, T. (1994). Transforming relationships through ordinary talk. In S. Duck (Ed.), *Understanding relationship processes 4: Dynamics of relationships* (pp. 58–85). Thousand Oaks, CA: Sage.

Spiegel, D., & Kimerling, R. (2001). Group psychotherapy for women with breast cancer: Relationships among social support, emotional expression, and survival. In C. D. Ryff & B. H. Singer (Eds.), *Emotion, social relationships, and health* (pp. 97–123). Oxford, England: Oxford University Press.

Spitzberg, B. H., & Cupach, W. R. (1984). *Interpersonal communication competence.* Beverly Hills, CA: Sage.

Spitzberg, B. H., & Cupach, W. R. (1989). *Handbook of interpersonal communication research.* New York: Springer-Verlag.

Spitzberg, B. H., & Cupach, W. R. (Eds.) (1998). *The dark side of close relationships.* Mahwah, NJ: Lawrence Erlbaum.

Spooner, T., & Rainie, L. (2000). *African Americans and the Internet.* The Pew Internet and American Life Project: Washington, DC.

Stafford, L., & Canary, D. J. (2006). Equity and interdependence as predictors of relational maintenance strategies. *Journal of Family Communication, 6,* 227–254.

Stafford, L., Dainton, M., & Haas, S. (2000). Measuring routine and strategic relational maintenance: Scale revision, sex versus gender roles, and the prediction of relational characteristics, *Communication Monographs, 67,* 306–323.

Stafford, L., & Merolla, A. J. (2007). Idealization, reunions, and stability in long-distance dating relationships. *Journal of Social and Personal Relationships, 24,* 37–54.

Stark-Wroblewski, K., Edelbaum, J. K., & Ryan, J. J. (2007). Senior citizens who use email. *Educational Gerontology: An International Journal, 33*(4), 293–307.

Stearns, P. N. (1994). *American cool: Constructing a twentieth-century emotional style.* New York: New York University Press.

Sternberg, R. J., & Whitney, C. (2002). How to think clearly about relationships. In J. A. DeVito (Ed.), *The interpersonal communication reader* (pp. 152–161). Boston: Allyn & Bacon.

St. John, W. (2001, April 21). Young, single and dating at hyperspeed. *New York Times,* D1, D2.

St. John, W. (2002, August 24). Sorrow so sweet: A guilty pleasure in another's woe. *New York Times,* B7, B9.

Stone, D., Patton, B., & Heen, S. (2002). How to understand another person's understanding. In J. A. DeVito (Ed.), *The interpersonal communication reader* (pp. 34–39). Boston: Allyn & Bacon.

Stringer, J. L., & Hopper, R. (1998). Generic *he* in conversation? *Quarterly Journal of Speech, 84,* 209–221.

Sullivan, A. (2002, May). *The blogging revolution.* Retrieved March 15, 2008, from http://wired.com/wired.archive.

Sullivan, P. A., & Turner, L. H. (1996). *From the margins to the center: Contemporary women and political communication.* Westport, CT: Praeger.

Support4Hope. (2004). *Support4Hope chats.* Retrieved December 13, 2007, from http://support4hope.com/testimonial.htm.

Suter, E. A., Bergen, K. M., Dass, K. L., & Durham, W. T. (2006). Lesbian couples' management of public-private dialectical contradictions. *Journal of Social and Personal Relationships, 23,* 349–365.

Sweeney, N. (2004, March 7). Cyber cool: Teens' witty screen names don't always seem so at college time. *Milwaukee Journal Sentinel,* B1–B2.

Swidey, N. (2003, February 2). A nation of voyeurs. *Boston Globe Magazine,* 10–13, 21–25.

Tamosaitis, N. (1995). *Net.sex.* Emeryville, CA: Ziff-Davis Press.

Tannen, D. (1990). *You just don't understand: Women and men in conversation.* New York: William Morrow.

Tannen, D. (1995). *Gender and discourse.* Oxford, England: Oxford University Press.

Tardy, C. H. (2000). Self-disclosure and health: Revisiting Sidney Jourard's hypothesis. In S. Petronio (Ed.), *Balancing the secrets of private disclosures* (pp. 111–122). Mahwah, NJ: Lawrence Erlbaum.

Tavris, C. (2001). Anger defused. In K. Scott & M. Warren (Eds.), *Perspectives on marriage: A reader* (pp. 243–253). New York: Oxford University Press.

Taylor, D. A., & Altman, I. (1987). Communication in interpersonal relationships: Social penetration processes. In M. E. Roloff & G. R. Miller (Eds.), *Interpersonal processes: New directions in communication research* (pp. 257–277). Newbury Park: Sage.

Tedeschi, B. (2002, February 4). E-commerce report. *New York Times,* C6.

Theiss, J. A., & Solomon, D. H. (2007). Communication and the emotional, cognitive, and relational consequences of first sexual encounters between partners. *Communication Quarterly, 55,* 179–206.

Thibaut, J., & Kelley, H. (1959). *The social psychology of groups.* New York: Wiley.

Thomas, R. W., & Seibold, D. W. (1996). Communicating with alcoholics: A strategic influence approach to personal intervention. In E. B. Ray (Ed.), *Communication and disenfranchisement: Social health issues and implications* (pp. 405–432). Mahwah, NJ: Lawrence Erlbaum.

Thompson, J., & Collier, M. J. (2006). Toward contingent understandings of intersecting identifications among selected U.S. interracial couples: Integrating interpretive and critical views. *Communication Quarterly, 54,* 487–507

Thompson, T. L. (1996). Allowing dignity: Communication with the dying. In E. B. Ray (Ed.), *Communication and disenfranchisement: Social health issues and implications* (pp. 387–404). Mahwah, NJ: Lawrence Erlbaum.

Thurlow, C., Lengel, L., & Tomic, A. (2004). *Computer-mediated communication.* Thousand Oaks, CA: Sage.

Tidwell, L. C., & Walther, J. B. (2002). Computer-mediated communication effects on disclosure, impressions, and interpersonal evaluations: Getting to know one another a bit at a time. *Human Communication Research, 28,* 317–348.

Ting-Toomey, S. (1999). *Communicating across cultures.* New York: Guilford.

Ting-Toomey, S., & Chung, L. C. (2005). *Understanding intercultural communication.* Los Angeles, CA: Roxbury.

Ting-Toomey, S., & Oetzel, J. G. (2001). *Managing intercultural conflict effectively.* Thousand Oaks, CA: Sage.

Toppo, G. (2002, December 10). Teens grasp sign language. *USA Today,* 9D.

Tracy, S. J. (2005). Locking up emotion: Moving beyond dissonance for understanding emotion labor discomfort. *Communication Monographs, 72,* 261–283.

Tracy, S. J., Alberts, J. K., Rivera, K. D. (2007, January 31). How to bust the office bully. Report # 0701, The Project for Wellness and Work-Life, The Hugh Downs School of Human Communication.

Tracy, S. J., Lutgen-Sandvik, P., & Alberts, J. K. (2006). Nightmares, demons and slaves: Exploring the painful metaphors of workplace bullying. *Management Communication Quarterly, 20,* 148–185.

Treichler, P. A., & Kramarae, C. (1983). Women's talk in the ivory tower. *Communication Quarterly, 31,* 118–132.

Trenholm, S. (1986). *Human communication theory.* Englewood Cliffs, NJ: Prentice Hall.

Trenholm, S., & Jensen, A. (2003). *Interpersonal communication.* New York: Oxford University Press.

Troy, A. B., Lewis-Smith, J., Laurenceau, J-P. (2006). Interracial and intraracial romantic relationships: The search for differences in satisfaction, conflict, and attachment style. *Journal of Social and Personal Relationship, 23,* 65–80.

Turk, D. R., & Monahan, J. L. (1999). "Here I go again": an examination of repetitive behaviors during interpersonal conflicts. *Southern Communication Journal, 64,* 232–244.

Turkle, S. (1995). *Life on the screen: Identity in the age of the Internet.* New York: Simon and Schuster.

Turkle, S. (2007). *Evocative objects: Things we think with.* Cambridge, MA: MIT Press.

Turner, L. H., Dindia, K., & Pearson, J. C. (1995). An investigation of female/male verbal behaviors in same-sex and mixed-sex conversations. *Communication Reports, 8,* 86–96.

Turner, L. H., & Shuter, R. (2004). African American and European American women's visions of workplace conflict: A metaphorical analysis. *Howard Journal of Communications, 15,* 169–183.

Turner, L. H., & West, R. (2006). *Perspectives on family communication.* New York: McGraw-Hill.

Turner, M. M., Mazur, M. A., Wendel, N., & Winslow, R. (2003). Relational ruin or social glue? The joint effect of relationship type and gossip valence on liking, trust, and expertise. *Communication Monographs, 70,* 129–141.

Tutu, D. (1999). *No future without forgiveness.* New York: Image/Doubleday.

Ullrich, P. M., & Lutgendorf, S. K. (2002). Journaling about stressful events: Effects of cognitive processing and emotional expression. *Annals of Behavioral Medicine, 24,* 244–250.

U.S. Census Bureau. (2000). *Fact sheet.* Retrieved December 22, 2006, from http://www.factfinder.census/gov.

U.S. Census Bureau. (2004, July 1). [Map of United States diversity.] *USA Today,* 7A.

U.S. Census Bureau. (2006). *More than 300 counties now "majority-minority."* Retrieved October 27, 2007 from http://www.census.gov/PressRelease/www/releases/archives/population/010482.html.

U.S. Census Bureau. (2007). *Top ten countries with which the U.S. trades.* Retrieved October 27, 2007, from http://www.census.gov/foreign-trade/top/dst/current/balance.html.

U.S. Environmental Protection Agency. (2004, August). *The life cycle of a cell phone.* Retrieved February 4, 2008, from http://www.epa.gov.epaoswer/education/pdfs/life-cell.pdf.

Unified communications business case. Retrieved October 27, 2007, from http://unibears.berkeley.edu/uc-business-case.html.

Usability Sciences. (2007). *Content aggregation.* Retrieved February 5, 2008, from http://www.usabilitysciences.com/services/field-studies-and-focus-groups/content-aggregation.

VanGelder, L. (1990). The strange case of the electronic lover. In G. Gumpert & S. L. Fish (Eds.), *Talking to strangers: Mediated therapeutic communication* (pp. 128–142). Norwood, NJ: Ablex.

Vangelisti, A. L., Caughlin, J. P., & Timmerman, L. (2001). Criteria for revealing family secrets. *Communication Monographs, 68,* 1–27.

Vangelisti, A. L., Knapp, M., & Daly, J. (1990). Conversational narcissism. *Communication Monographs, 57,* 251–274.

Vangelisti, A. L., & Young, S. L. (2000). When words hurt: The effects of perceived intentionality on interpersonal relationships. *Journal of Social and Personal Relationships, 17,* 395–425.

Vedantam, S. (2002, September 9). Psychiatrists back new class of illness. *Milwaukee Journal Sentinel,* 1G–2G.

Victor, D. A. (1992). *International business communication.* New York: HarperCollins.

Villareal, C. (2007). Cultural relativity: My world, your world, our world. *ETC: A Review of General Semantics, 64,* 230–234.

Vittengl, J. R., & Holt, C. S. (2000). Getting acquainted: The relationship of self-disclosure and social attraction to positive affect. *Journal of Social and Personal Relationships, 17,* 53–66.

Vogel, D. L., Murphy, M. J., Werner-Wilson, R. J., Cutrona, C. E., & Seeman, J. (2007). Sex differences in the use of demand and withdraw behavior in marriage: Examining the social structure hypothesis. *Journal of Counseling Psychology, 54,* 165–177.

von Bertalanffy, L. (1968). *General system theory.* New York: George Braziller.

Wade, N. (2003, July 15). Early voices: The leap to language. *New York Times,* D1, D4.

Waldner, L. K., & Magruder, B. (1999). Coming out to parents: Perceptions of family relations, perceived resources, and identity expression as predictors of identity disclosure for gay and lesbian adolescents. *Journal of Homosexuality, 37,* 83–100.

Waldron, V. R., & Kelley, D. L. (2005). Forgiving communication as a response to relational transgressions. *Journal of Social and Personal Relationships, 22,* 723–742.

Walker, L. (1984). *The battered woman syndrome.* New York: Springer.

Walther, J. B. (1994). Anticipated ongoing interaction versus channel effects on relational communication in computer-mediated interaction. *Human Communication Research, 20,* 473–501.

Walther, J. B., & Bazarova, N. (2007). Misattribution in virtual groups. *Human Communication Research, 33,* 1–26.

Walther, J. B., Gay, G, & Hancock, J. T. (2005). How do communication and technology researchers study the Internet? *Journal of Communication, 55,* 632–657.

Walther, J. B., & Parks, M. R. (2002). Cues filtered out, cues filtered in: Computer-mediated communication and relationships. In M. L. Knapp & J. A. Daly (Eds.), *Handbook of interpersonal communication* (3rd ed., pp. 529–563). Thousand Oaks, CA: Sage.

Warren, E. (2004, January 6). Grandma? No, please call her Moogie. *Chicago Tribune,* pp. 5-1, 5-6.

Watson, K. W., & Barker, L. L. (1995). *Winning by listening around.* Tega Cay, SC: SPECTRA Incorporated.

Watson, K. W., Lazarus, C. J., & Thomas, T. (1999). First year medical students' listener preferences: A longitudinal study. *International Journal of Listening, 13,* 1–11.

Watzlawick, P., Beavin, J., & Jackson, D. D. (1967). *Pragmatics of human communication.* New York: Norton.

Weinraub, B. (2004, March, 22). Love fest for soap opera fans, in two languages. *New York Times,* B1, B8.

Wendland, M. (2002, October 21). Poll: Rich people, suburbanites likelier to use Net. Retrieved March 15, 2008, from http://www.freepress.com/newslibrary.

White, A. (2006). "You've got a friend": African American men's cross-sex feminist friendships and their influence on perceptions of masculinity and women. *Journal of Social and Personal Relationships, 23,* 523–542.

White, G. L. (1980). Physical attractiveness and courtship progress. *Journal of Personality and Social Psychology, 39,* 660–668.

Whorf, B. (1956). *Language, thought, and reality.* Cambridge, MA: MIT Press.

Wildermuth, S. M., & Vogl-Bauer, S. (2007). We met on the net: Exploring the perceptions of online romantic relationship participants. *Southern Communication Journal, 72(3),* 211–227.

Wildermuth, S. M., Vogl-Bauer, S., & Rivera, J. (2006). Practically perfect in every way: Communication strategies of ideal relational partners. *Communication Studies, 57,* 239–257.

Williams, A. (2007, July 29). (-: Just between you and me ;-). *New York Times,* D1, D9.

Wilmot, W. W. (1995). *Relational communication.* New York: McGraw-Hill.

Wilmot, W. (2006). The relational perspective. In K. M. Galvin & P. J. Cooper (Eds.), *Making connections: Readings in relational communication* (pp. 11–19). Los Angeles, CA: Roxbury.

Wilson, S. R., Hayes, J., Bylund, C., Rack, J. J., Herman, A. P. (2006). Mothers' trait verbal aggressiveness and child abuse potential. *Journal of Family Communication, 6,* 279–296.

Winters, A. M., & Duck, S. (2001). You ****!: Swearing as an aversive and a relational activity. In R. M. Kowalski (Ed.), *Behaving badly: Aversive behaviors in interpersonal relationships* (pp. 59–77). Washington, DC: American Psychological Association.

Witmer, D. F. & Katzman, M. L. (1997). *On-line smiles: Does gender make a difference in the use of graphic accents?* Retrieved December 22, 2007, from http://www.ascusc.org/jcmc/vol2/issue4/witmer1.html.

Wolf, A. (2000). Emotional expression online: Gender differences in emoticon use. *Cyberpsychology and Behavior, 3,* 827–833.

Wolvin, A. D., & Coakley, C. G. (1996). *Listening.* Madison, WI: Brown and Benchmark.

Wolvin, A. D., & Coakley, C. G. (2000). Listening education in the 21st century. *International Journal of Listening, 14,* 143–152.

Wood, D. B. (2004, April 6). A not-so-mobile society. Retrieved March 15, 2008, from http://www.csmonitor.com/2004/0406/p01s03-ussc.html.

Wood, J. T. (1998). *But I thought you meant . . . misunderstandings in human communication.* Mountain View, CA: Mayfield.

Wood, J. T. (2002). A critical essay on John Gray's Mars and Venus portrayals of men and women. *Southern Communication Journal, 67,* 201–210.

Wood, J. T. (2005). *Gendered lives: Communication, gender, and culture* (6th ed.). Belmont, CA: Wadsworth.

Wrench, J. S., Corrigan, M. W., McCroskey, J. C., & Punyanunt-Carter N. M. (2006). Religious fundamentalism and intercultural communication: The relationships among ethnocentrism, intercultural communication apprehension, religious fundamentalism, homonegativity, and tolerance for religious disagreements. *Journal of Intercultural Communication Research, 35,* 23–44.

Wyer, R. S., & Adaval, R. (2003), "Message reception skills in social communication," in J. O. Greene & B. R. Burleson (Eds.), *Handbook of communication and social interaction skills* (pp. 291–355). Mahwah, NJ: Lawrence Erlbaum.

Yager, J. (2002). *When friendship hurts.* New York: Simon and Schuster.

Young, S. L., & Bippus, A. M. (2001). Does it make a difference if they hurt you in a funny way? Humorously and nonhumorously phrased hurtful messages in personal relationships. *Communication Quarterly, 49,* 35–52.

Zhang, Q. (2007). Family communication patterns and conflict styles in Chinese parent-child relationships. *Communication Quarterly, 55,* 113–128.

Index